NCERT
EXEMPLAR
Problems-Solutions

Mathematics

Detailed Explanation to all Objective
& Subjective Problems

Swati Mareja • Priyanka Sharma

ARIHANT
PRAKASHAN, MEERUT

ARIHANT
PRAKASHAN, MEERUT

🌢 Administrative & Production Offices

Corporate Office: 'Ramchhaya' 4577/15, Agarwal Road, Darya Ganj, New Delhi -110002
Tele: 011- 47630600, 43518550; Fax: 011- 23280316

Head Office: Kalindi, TP Nagar, Meerut (UP) - 250002
Tele: 0121-2401479, 2512970, 4004199; Fax: 0121-2401648
All disputes subject to Meerut (UP) jurisdiction only.

🌢 Sales & Support Offices
Agra, Ahmedabad, Bengaluru, Bhubaneswar, Bareilly, Chennai, Delhi, Guwahati, Haldwani Hyderabad, Jaipur, Jalandhar, Jhansi, Kolkata, Kota, Lucknow, Meerut, Nagpur & Pune

🌢 ISBN 978-93-5251-153-2

🌢 Price : ₹ 250

PRINTED & BOUND BY
ARIHANT PUBLICATIONS (I) LTD. (PRESS UNIT)

For further information about the products from Arihant
log on to www.arihantbooks.com or email to info@arihantbooks.com

PREFACE

The Department of Education in Science & Mathematics (DESM) & National Council of Educational Research & Training (NCERT) developed Exemplar Problems in Science and Mathematics for Upper Primary Stage, Secondary and Senior Secondary Classes with the objective to provide the students a large number of quality problems in various forms and format viz. Multiple Choice Questions, Short Answer Questions, Long Answer Questions etc., with varying levels of difficulty.

The problems given in Exemplar books are not meant to some merely as question bank for examination but are Primarily meant to improve the quality of teaching/ learning process in schools and finally will impart the problem solving skills in students and it is a widely at acknowledged fact that in this century analytical thinking, problem solving ability, creativity and speculative ability will be key skills for success.

This book **NCERT Exemplar Problems-Solutions Mathematics VII** contains Explanatory & Accurate Solutions to all the questions given in NCERT Exemplar Mathematics book.

For the overall benefit of the students we have made unique this book in such a way that it presents not only hints and solutions but also detailed and authentic explanations. Through these detailed explanations, students can learn the concepts which will enhance their thinking and learning abilities.

For the completion of this book, we would like to thank Mr. Prince Mittal (Project Coordinator, Arihant Prakashan) who helped us at project management level.

With the hope that this book will be of great help to the students, we wish great success to our readers.

Authors

CONTENTS

1

Integers

Multiple Choice Questions (MCQs)

Q. 1 When the integers 10, 0, 5, − 5, − 7 are arranged in descending or ascending order, then find out which of the following integers always remains in the middle of the arrangement.

    (a) 0   (b) 5   (c) − 7   (d) − 5

Sol. *(a)* To arrange these integers in ascending or descending order, first we locate these points on number line.

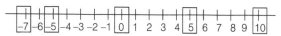

As we know, if a point or number lies on the right side to the other number, then the number is greater. Then,

Ascending order → −7, − 5, 0, 5, 10
Middle term = 0
Descending order → 10, 5, 0, − 5, − 7
Middle term = 0
Hence, zero always remains in the middle of the arrangement.

Q. 2 By observing the number line, state which of the following statements is not true?

    (a) *B* is greater than − 10   (b) *A* is greater than 0

    (c) *B* is greater than *A*   (d) *B* is smaller than 0

Sol. *(c)* As we know that, if a point or number lies on the right side to the other number, then the number is greater.

Here, *B* is greater than − 10 but smaller than 0 and *A* is greater than 0 but smaller than 10. Also, *B* is smaller than *A*.

Q. 3 By observing the above number line, state which of the following statements is true?

(a) B is 2   (b) A is − 4   (c) B is − 13   (d) B is − 4

Sol. (*d*)   Since, B lies at the left side of 0, so it will be negative and it is at 4th place.

So, B = − 4

Similarly, A lies at the right side of 0, so it will be positive and it is at 7th place.

So, A = 7. Hence, the value of A = 7 and value of B = − 4.

Q. 4 Next three consecutive numbers in the pattern 11, 8, 5, 2, __, __, __ are

(a) 0, − 3, − 6   (b) −1, − 5, − 8   (c) − 2, − 5, − 8   (d) − 1, − 4, − 7

Sol. (*d*)   By observing the series, difference between two consecutive numbers is 3,

i.e. $11 - 8 = 3$

$8 - 5 = 3$

$5 - 2 = 3$

So, next number will be

$2 - 3 = -1$

Similarly, next two numbers are

$-1 - 3 = -4$

$-4 - 3 = -7$

Q. 5 The next number in the pattern − 62 , − 37, − 12 is _____.

(a) 25   (b) 13   (c) 0   (d) − 13

Sol. (*b*)   By observing the series, difference between two consecutive numbers is 25,

i.e. $-37 - (-62) = -37 + 62 = 25$

$-12 - (-37) = -12 + 37 = 25$

So, next number will be

$-12 + 25 = 13$

Q. 6 Which of the following statements is not true?

(a) When two positive integers are added, we always get a positive integer.

(b) When two negative integers are added, we always get a negative integer.

(c) When a positive integer and a negative integer are added, we always get a negative integer.

(d) Additive inverse of an integer 2 is (− 2) and additive inverse of (− 2) is 2.

Sol. (*c*)   (a) True, when two positive integers are added, the resultant number is also a positive integer.

(b) True, while adding integers, if both the numbers have same sign, the resultant number also get that sign.

(c) False, while adding the integers of different signs, the resultant number get the sign of greater number.

(d) True, additive inverse of an integer is the same integer value, with opposite sign.

Q. 7 On the following number line value, 'zero' is shown by the point

  (a) X (b) Y (c) Z (d) W

Sol. *(c)* All the points are equally spaced.

One division = 5 units

So,
$$X = -15 + 5 = -10$$
$$Y = -10 + 5 = -5$$
$$Z = -5 + 5 = 0$$

Hence, zero is shown by the point Z.

Q. 8 If $\otimes$, $\bigcirc$, $\oslash$ and $\bullet$ represent some integers on number line, then descending order of these numbers is

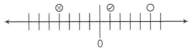

  (a) $\bullet, \otimes, \oslash, \bigcirc$ (b) $\otimes, \bullet, \oslash, \bigcirc$ (c) $\bigcirc, \oslash, \otimes, \bullet$ (d) $\bigcirc, \bullet, \otimes, \oslash$

Sol. *(c)* Descending order in number line, is from right to left.

Accordingly,

$\bigcirc$ comes first $\oslash$ comes second

$\otimes$ comes third $\bullet$ comes fourth

Hence, descending order is $\bigcirc, \oslash, \otimes, \bullet$.

Q. 9 On the number line, the value of $(-3) \times 3$ lies on right hand side of

  (a) -10 (b) -4 (c) 0 (d) 9

Sol. *(a)* $(-3) \times 3$ equals to -9.

On the number line, it is shown as

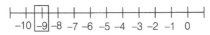

So, as we can see -9 lies on the right hand side of -10.

Q. 10 The value of $5 \div (-1)$ does not lie between

  (a) 0 and -10 (b) 0 and 10   (c) -4 and -15 (d) -6 and 6

Sol. *(b)* $5 \div (-1)$ equals to -5.

On the number line, it is placed as

Now, as we can see, -5 lies between (0 and -10), (-4 and -15) and (-6 and 6). But it does not lie between 0 and 10.

Q. 11 Water level in a well was 20 m below ground level. During rainy season, rainwater collected in different water tanks was drained into the well and the water level rises 5 m above the previous level. The wall of the well is 1 m 20 cm high and a pulley afixed at a height of 80 cm. Raghu wants to draw water from the well. The minimum length of the rope, that he can use is

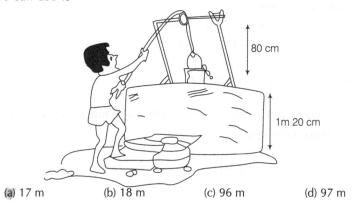

(a) 17 m   (b) 18 m   (c) 96 m   (d) 97 m

Sol. *(a)*   Details given in the question, can be described in the figure shown below

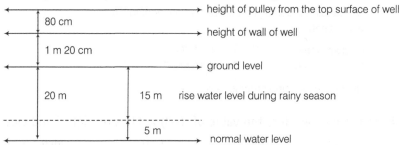

From the above figure, it is clear that,

Minimum length of the rope required to draw the water during the rainy season

= Distance between pulley and wall of well + Height of wall of well + Distance between water level during rainy season and ground level

= 80 cm + 1 m 20 cm + 15 m

$= (0.8 + 1.2 + 15) \, m \left[\because 1 \, cm = \dfrac{1}{100} \, m \Rightarrow 80 \, cm = \dfrac{80}{100} \, m = 0.80 \, m \text{ and } 1 \, m \, 20 \, cm = 1.20 \, m \right]$

= 17 m

Q. 12 $(-11) \times 7$ is not equal to

(a) $11 \times (-7)$ (b) $-(11 \times 7)$ (c) $(-11) \times (-7)$ (d) $7 \times (-11)$

Sol. *(c)* $(-11) \times 7 = (-77)$ (we know, in multiplication, if sign of both numbers are different, then the sign of the resultant is negative and if sign of both numbers are same, then the sign of the resultant is positive.)

Option (a), $11 \times (-7) = -77$

Option (b), $-(11 \times 7) = -77$

Option (c), $(-11) \times (-7) = 77$

Option (d), $7 \times (-11) = -77$

Q. 13 $(-10) \times (-5) + (-7)$ is equal to

    (a) -57 (b) 57   (c) -43 (d) 43

Sol. *(d)* $(-10) \times (-5) + (-7) = \{(-10) \times (-5)\} + (-7) = 50 + (-7) = 50 - 7 = 43$

Q. 14 Which of the following is not the additive inverse of a?

    (a) $-(-a)$ (b) $a \times (-1)$ (c) $-a$ (d) $a \div (-1)$

Sol. *(a)* Additive inverse of a is $(-a)$.

        [∵ additive inverse of an integer is the same integer value, with opposite sign]

        So,

        Option (a), $-(-a) = a$

        Option (b), $a \times (-1) = -a$

        Option (c), $-a$

        Option (d), $a \div (-1) = -a$

Q. 15 Which of the following is the multiplicative identity for an integer a?

    (a) a (b) 1   (c) 0   (d) -1

Sol. *(b)* Multiplicative identity for an integer a is 1.

        [∵ a multiplicative identity is that identity in which any number is multiplied by that identity, it gives out the same number.]

Q. 16 $[(-8) \times (-3)] \times (-4)$ is not equal to

    (a) $(-8) \times [(-3) \times (-4)]$ (b) $[(-8) \times (-4)] \times (-3)$

    (c) $[(-3) \times (-8)] \times (-4)$ (d) $(-8) \times (-3) - (-8) \times (-4)$

Sol. *(d)* $[(-8) \times (-3)] \times (-4) = [(-3) \times (-8)] \times (-4)$

                [∵ as multiplication is commutative, i.e. $a \times b = b \times a$]

        $= (-3) \times [(-8) \times (-4)]$ [∵ as multiplication is associative, i.e.

                                    $a \times (b \times c) = (a \times b) \times c$]

        $= [(-8) \times (-4)] \times (-3)$

        $= (-8) \times [(-4) \times (-3)]$

        $= (-8) \times [(-3) \times (-4)]$

    Hence, $[-(8) \times (-3)] \times (-4)$ is not equal to $(-8) \times (-3) - (-8) \times (-4)$.

Q. 17 $(-25) \times [6 + 4]$ is not same as

    (a) $(-25) \times 10$ (b) $(-25) \times 6 + (-25) \times 4$

    (c) $-25 \times 6 \times 4$ (d) -250

Sol. *(c)* $(-25) \times [6 + 4] = (-25) \times 10$

    Also, $(-25) \times [6 + 4] = -25 \times 6 + (-25) \times 4$

                [using distributive property, i.e. $a \times (b + c) = a \times b + a \times c$]

        $= -150 - 100 = -250$

    Hence, $(-25) \times (6 + 4)$ is not same as $-25 \times 6 \times 4$.

Q. 18 -35×107 is not same as

(a) $-35 \times (100 + 7)$ (b) $(-35) \times 7 + (-35) \times 100$

(c) $-35 \times 7 + 100$ (d) $(-30 - 5) \times 107$

Sol. (c) $-35 \times 107 = -35 \times (100+7) = (-35) \times 100 + (-35) \times 7$ [using distributive property, i.e. $a \times (b + c) = a \times b + a \times c$]

$= (-35) \times 7 + (-35) \times 100$ [as addition is commutative, i.e. $a + b = b + a$]

Also, $-35 \times 107 = (-30 - 5) \times 107$ [$\because (-30 - 5) = (-35)$]

Hence, -35×107 is not same as $-35 \times 7 + 100$.

Q. 19 $(-43) \times (-99) + 43$ is equal to

(a) 4300   (b) -4300 (c) 4257   (d) -4214

Sol. (a) $(-43) \times (-99) + 43 = (-1)(43) \times (-99) + 43$

$= 43 \{-(-99) + 1\}$ [taking 43 as common]

$= 43 (99 + 1) = 43 \times 100 = 4300$

Q. 20 $(-16) \div 4$ is not same as

(a) $(-4) \div 16$ (b) $-(16 \div 4)$ (c) $16 \div (-4)$ (d) -4

Sol. (a) $(-16) \div 4 = -(16 \div 4) = 16 \div (-4) = \dfrac{16}{-4} = -4$

But division is not commutative, hence

$$-16 \div 4 \neq (-4) \div 16.$$

Q. 21 Which of the following does not represent an integer?

(a) $0 \div (-7)$ (b) $20 \div (-4)$ (c) $(-9) \div 3$ (d) $(-12) \div 5$

Sol. (d)   An integer is a whole number (not a fractional number) that can be positive, negative or zero. So,

(a) $\dfrac{0}{-7} = 0$ (b) $\dfrac{20}{-4} = -5$

(c) $\dfrac{-9}{3} = -3$ (d) $\dfrac{-12}{5}$ (not an integer)

Q. 22 Which of the following is different from the others?

(a) $20 + (-25)$ (b) $(-37) - (-32)$

(c) $(-5) \times (-1)$ (d) $45 \div (-9)$

Sol. (c)   Option (a), $20 + (-25) = 20 - 25 = -5$

Option (b), $(-37) - (-32) = -37 + 32 = -5$

Option (c), $(-5) \times (-1) = 5$

Option (d), $(45) \div (-9) = \dfrac{45}{-9} = -5$

Q. 23 Which of the following shows the maximum rise in temperature?

(a) $23°$ to $32°$ (b) $-10°$ to $1°$

(c) $-18°$ to $-11°$ (d) $-5°$ to $5°$

Sol. *(b)* Rise in temperature,

(a) $32° - 23° = 9°$

(b) $1° - (-10)° = 1° + 10° = 11°$ (maximum)

(c) $-11° - (-18)° = -11° + 18° = 7°$

(d) $5° - (-5°) = 5° + 5° = 10°$

Q. 24 If a and b are two integers, then which of the following may not be an integer?

(a) $a + b$ (b) $a - b$ (c) $a \times b$ (d) $a \div b$

Sol. *(d)* Addition, subtraction and multiplication of two or more integers is always an integer. But, division of integers may or may not be an integer.

e.g. $2 \div 3 = \dfrac{2}{3}$ (not an integer)

$3 \div 3 = 1$ (integer)

Q. 25 For a non-zero integer a, which of the following is not defined?

(a) $a \div 0$ (b) $0 \div a$ (c) $a \div 1$ (d) $1 \div a$

Sol. *(a)* Division of any number by zero is not defined.

$a \div 0 =$ not defined

In questions 26 to 30, encircle the odd one of the following:

Q. 26   (a) $(-3, 3)$ (b) $(-5, 5)$ (c) $(-6, 1)$ (d) $(-8, 8)$

Sol. *(c)* By observation, we can say that both the values are same in options (a), (b) and (d). So, odd one is option (c).

Q. 27   (a) $(-1, -2)$ (b) $(-5, 2)$ (c) $(-4, 1)$ (d) $(-9, 7)$

Sol. *(d)* By observation, we can say that the sum of both values are same in options (a), (b) and (c). So, odd one is option (d).

Q. 28   (a) $(-9) \times 5 \times 6 \times (-3)$ (b) $9 \times (-5) \times 6 \times (-3)$

(c) $(-9) \times (-5) \times (-6) \times 3$ (d) $9 \times (-5) \times (-6) \times 3$

Sol. *(c)* (a) $(-9) \times 5 \times 6 \times (-3) = (-45) \times (-18) = 810$

(b) $9 \times (-5) \times 6 \times (-3) = (-45) \times (-18) = 810$

(c) $(-9) \times (-5) \times (-6) \times 3 = 45 \times (-18) = -810$

(d) $9 \times (-5) \times (-6) \times 3 = (-45) \times (-18) = 810$

So, odd one is option (c).

Q. 29   (a) $(-100) \div 5$ (b) $(-81) \div 9$

(c) $(-75) \div 5$ (d) $(-32) \div 9$

Sol. *(d)*   (a) $\dfrac{-100}{5} = -20$ (b) $\dfrac{-81}{9} = -9$

(c) $\dfrac{-75}{5} = -15$ (d) $\dfrac{-32}{9}$

Here, option (a), (b) and (c) are the negative integers, but option (d) is not the negative integer. So, odd one is option (d).

Q. 30 (a) $(-1) \times (-1)$ (b) $(-1) \times (-1) \times (-1)$

     (c) $(-1) \times (-1) \times (-1) \times (-1)$ (d) $(-1) \times (-1) \times (-1) \times (-1) \times (-1) \times (-1)$

Sol. *(b)*   (a) $(-1) \times (-1) = 1$

         (b) $(-1) \times (-1) \times (-1) = -1$

         (c) $(-1) \times (-1) \times (-1) \times (-1) = 1$

         (d) $(-1) \times (-1) \times (-1) \times (-1) \times (-1) \times (-1) = 1$

         Hence, value of options (a), (c), (d) are same but value of option (b) is different.

Fill in the Blanks

In questions 31 to 71, fill in the blanks to make the statements true.

Q. 31 $(-a) + b = b +$ additive inverse of ___A___ .

Sol.   Additive inverse is the negation of a number.

         As we know, addition is commutative for integers, i.e. $-a + b = b + (-a)$

         Now '$-a$' is the additive inverse of a. So, **a** will be the answer.

Q. 32 ___-0___ $\div (-10) = 0$

Sol.   Division of 0 by any number, results as zero. So, the answer is 0.

Q. 33 $(-157) \times (-19) + 157 =$ ___3140___ .

Sol. $(-157) \times (-19) + 157 = (-1) \times (157) \times (-19) + 157$

                 $= 157 \{-(-19) + 1\}$ [taking 157 as common]

                 $= 157 \{19 + 1\} = 157 \times 20 = 3140$

Q. 34 $[(-8) +$ ___(-3)___ $] +$ ___8___ $=$ ___(-8)___ $+ [(-3) +$ ___8___ $] = -3$

Sol. $[(-8) + (-3)] + 8 = (-8) + [(-3) + 8]$

                          [$\because$ addition is associative, i.e. $a + (b + c) = (a + b) + c$]

            $= -8 + 5 = -3$

Q. 35 On the following number line, $(-4) \times 3$ is represented by the point ___D___ .

Sol. $(-4) \times 3 = (-12)$

         On the number line, each division has equal spacing of 2 units.

         So, $A = -20 + 2 = -18$

                       $B = -18 + 2 = -16$

                       $C = -16 + 2 = -14$

                       $D = -14 + 2 = -12$

         Hence, $(-4) \times 3$ is represented by the point **D**.

Integers

Q. 36 If x, y and z are integers, then $(x + \underline{y}) + z = \underline{x} + (y + \underline{z})$

Sol. Addition is associative for integers, i.e. $(a + b) + c = a + (b + c)$
$\Rightarrow \quad (x + y) + z = x + (y + z)$

Q. 37 $(-43) + \underline{0} = (-43)$

Sol. Zero (0) is an additive identity for integers, i.e. $a + 0 = 0 + a = a$ for any integer a.
So, $(-43) + 0 = -43$

Q. 38 $(-8) + (-8) + (-8) = \underline{-24} \times (-8)$

Sol. Let x be the missing number.
Then, $\qquad -8 - 8 - 8 = x \times (-8)$
$\Rightarrow \qquad -24 = x \times (-8) \qquad\qquad [\because -8-8-8 = -24]$
$\Rightarrow \qquad \dfrac{-24}{-8} = x$
$\Rightarrow \qquad x = 3$
Hence, $(-8) + (-8) + (-8) = 3 \times (-8)$

Q. 39 $11 \times (-5) = -(\underline{11} \times \underline{5}) = \underline{-55}$

Sol. We can write the equation as,
$11 \times (-5) = -(11 \times 5) = -55$

Q. 40 $(-9) \times 20 = \underline{180}$

Sol. $(-9) \times 20 = -180 \qquad [\because$ in multiplication of integers, if both the numbers have different signs, then the result is a negative number]

Q. 41 $(-23) \times (42) = (-42) \times \underline{23}$

Sol. $(-23) \times (42) = (-1) \times (23) \times (42) = (-1) \times (42) \times (23)$
$\qquad\qquad [\because$ multiplication is commutative, i.e. $a \times b = b \times a]$
$= (-42) \times (23)$

Q. 42 While multiplying a positive integer and a negative integer, we multiply them as _whole_ numbers and put a _negative_ sign before the product.

Sol. When multiplying a positive integer and a negative integer, we multiply them as **whole** numbers and put a **negative** sign before the product.

Q. 43 If we multiply _even_ number of negative integers, then the resulting integer is positive.

Sol. If we multiply **even** numbers of negative integers, then the resulting integer is positive.

Q. 44 If we multiply six negative integers and six positive integers, then the resulting integer is positive

Sol. If we multiply six negative integers and six positive integers, then the resulting integer is **positive**, because even numbers of negative integers, in multiplication becomes positive.

Q. 45 If we multiply five positive integers and one negative integer, then the resulting integer is negative

Sol. If we multiply 5 positive integers and one negative integer, then the resulting integer is **negative**.

Q. 46 1 is the multiplicative identity for integers.

Sol. 1 is the multiplicative identity for integers, i.e. $a \times 1 = 1 \times a = a$ for any integer a.

Q. 47 We get additive inverse of an integer a, when we multiply it by (−1)

Sol. Additive inverse of an integer is the same integer value, with opposite sign. So, we get additive inverse of integer a, when we multiply it by (− **1**).

Q. 48 $(- 25) \times (- 2) = 50$

Sol. Two negative integers make the resultant integer, positive.
$$(- 25) \times (- 2) = \mathbf{50}$$

Q. 49 $(- 5) \times (- 6) \times (- 7) = -210$

Sol. Odd negative integers make the resultant integer, negative.
$$(- 5) \times (- 6) \times (- 7) = 30 \times (- 7) = - \mathbf{210}$$

Q. 50 $3 \times (- 1) \times (- 15) = 45$

Sol. Two negative integers and one positive integer make the resultant integer, positive.
$$3 \times (-1) \times (-15) = (-3) \times (- 15) = \mathbf{45}$$

Q. 51 $[12 \times (- 7)] \times 5 = 12 \times [(- 7) \times 5]$

Sol. Multiplication is associative for integers, i.e.
$$(a \times b) \times c = a \times (b \times c)$$
So, $[12 \times (- 7)] \times 5 = \mathbf{12} \times [(- 7) \times \mathbf{5}]$

Q. 52 $23 \times (- 99) = 23 \times (- 100 + 1) = 23 \times 100 + 23 \times 1$

Sol. We can write the equation as,
$$23 \times (- 99) = \mathbf{23} \times (- 100 + 1) = 23 \times (- \mathbf{100}) + 23 \times \mathbf{1}$$
$$[\because \text{integers show distributive property of multiplication}$$
$$\text{over addition, i.e. } a \times (b + c) = a \times b + a \times c]$$

Q. 53 $35 \times (- 1) = - 35$

Sol. $35 \times (- 1) = - 35$ $\qquad \left[\because \left(\dfrac{-35}{-1}\right) = 35\right]$

Q. 54 $\underline{-47} \times (-1) = 47$

Sol. $(-47) \times (-1) = 47$

$$\left[\because \frac{47}{-1} = (-47) \right]$$

Q. 55 $88 \times \underline{-1} = -88$

Sol. $88 \times (-1) = -88$

$$\left[\because \frac{-88}{88} = (-1) \right]$$

Q. 56 $\underline{-1} \times (-93) = 93$

Sol. $(-1) \times (-93) = 93$

$$\left[\because \frac{93}{-93} = (-1) \right]$$

Q. 57 $(-40) \times \underline{-2} = 80$

Sol. $(-40) \times (-2) = 80$

$$\left[\because \frac{80}{-40} = (-2) \right]$$

Q. 58 $\underline{40} \times (-23) = -920$

Sol. $(40) \times (-23) = -920$

$$\left[\because \left(\frac{-920}{-23} \right) = 40 \right]$$

Q. 59 When we divide a negative integer by a positive integer, we divide them as whole numbers and put a ___ sign before quotient.

Sol. When we divide a negative integer by a positive integer or a positive integer by a negative integer, we divide them as whole numbers and put a **negative** sign before quotient.

Q. 60 When (-16) is divided by ___ the quotient is 4.

Sol. When (-16) is divided by **negative integer**, i.e. -4 the quotient is 4 as both signs are cancelled out.

Q. 61 Division is the inverse operation of ___ multiplication

Sol. Division is the inverse operation of **multiplication**.

Q. 62 $65 \div (-13) = \underline{-5}$

Sol. $65 \div (-13) = 65 \times \dfrac{1}{(-13)}$

$$= -5$$

[∵ division is inverse of multiplication]

Q. 63 $(-100) \div (-10) = \underline{10}$

Sol. $(-100) \div (-10) = (-100) \times \dfrac{1}{(-10)}$

$$= 10$$

[∵ division is inverse of multiplication]

Q. 64 $(-225) \div 5 = \underline{45}$

Sol. $(-225) \div 5 = -225 \times \dfrac{1}{5}$ [∵ division is inverse of multiplication]

$$= -45$$

Q. 65 $\underline{83} \div (-1) = (-83)$

Sol. $83 \div (-1) = -83$ $\left[\because \dfrac{-83}{-1} = 83\right]$

Q. 66 $\underline{-75} \div (-1) = 75$

Sol. $-75 \div (-1) = 75$ $\left[\because \dfrac{75}{-1} = (-75)\right]$

Q. 67 $51 \div \underline{(-1)} = (-51)$

Sol. $51 \div (-1) = (-51)$ $\left[\because \dfrac{51}{-51} = (-1)\right]$

Q. 68 $113 \div \underline{(-113)} = (-1)$

Sol. $113 \div (-113) = (-1)$ $\left[\because \dfrac{113}{-1} = (-113)\right]$

Q. 69 $-95 \div \underline{(-1)} = 95$

Sol. $-95 \div (-1) = 95$ $\left[\because \dfrac{-95}{95} = (-1)\right]$

Q. 70 $(-69) \div 69 = \underline{(-1)}$

Sol. $(-69) \div 69 = (-1)$

Q. 71 $(-28) \div (-28) = \underline{1}$

Sol. $(-28) \div (-28) = 1$

True / False

In questions 72 to 108, state whether the statements are True or False.

Q. 72 $5 - (-8)$ is same as $5 + 8$. T

Sol. *True*

$$5 - (-8) = 5 + 8$$

Q. 73 $(-9) + (-11)$ is greater than $(-9) - (-11)$. F

Sol. *False*

$(-9) + (-11) = -9 - 11 = -20$

and $(-9) - (-11) = -9 + 11 = 2$

So, $(-9) - (-11)$ is greater than $(-9) + (-11)$.

Q. 74 Sum of two negative integers always gives a number smaller than both the integers.

Sol. *True*

e.g. Taking two negative integers, i.e. (-5) and (-3).
$$(-5) + (-3) = -5 - 3 = -8$$
$$= -8 < -5 \text{ and } -8 < -3$$

Q. 75 Difference of two negative integers cannot be a positive integer.

Sol. *False*

e.g. Taking two negative integers, i.e. -4 and -5.
$$\Rightarrow \qquad -4 - (-5) = -4 + 5 = 1 \qquad \text{[positive integer]}$$

Q. 76 We can write a pair of integers, whose sum is not an integer.

Sol. *False*

Because, sum of two integers, is always be an integer.

Q. 77 Integers are closed under subtraction.

Sol. *True*

Because, if we subtract two integers we get another integer.

Q. 78 $(-23) + 47$ is same as $47 + (-23)$.

Sol. *True*

Because, addition is commutative, i.e. $a + b = b + a$
$$\Rightarrow \qquad (-23) + 47 = 47 + (-23)$$

Q. 79 When we change the order of integers their sum remains the same.

Sol. *True*

Because, sum of two integers is commutative, i.e. $a + b = b + a$ for two integers a and b.

Q. 80 When we change the order of integers, their difference remains the same.

Sol. *False*

Subtraction of two integers is not commutative, i.e. $a - b \neq b - a$ for two integers a and b.

Q. 81 Going 500 m towards East first and then 200 m back, is same as going 200 m towards West first and then going 500 m back.

Sol. *True*

Case I Going 500 m towards East first, i.e. point A to B and then 200 m back, i.e. B to C.

As per the above figure shown, final position is C, i.e. 300 m in East.

Case II Going 200 m towards West first, i.e. point A to B and then 500 m back, i.e. point B to C

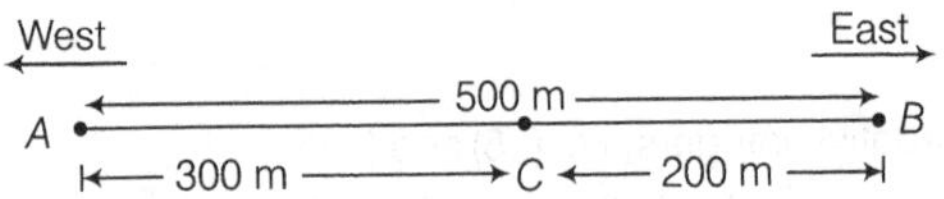

As per the above figure shown, final position is C, i.e. 300 m in East.

Q. 82 $(-5) \times (33) = 5 \times (-33)$

Sol. *True*

$$\therefore \quad LHS = (-5) \times 33 = (-165)$$

and $RHS = 5 \times (-33) = (-165)$

Hence, $LHS = RHS$

Q. 83 $(-19) \times (-11) = 19 \times 11$

Sol. *True*

Product of two negative integers is a positive integer, i.e. $(-a) \times (-b) = a \times b$ where, a and b are positive integers.

$$\Rightarrow \quad LHS = (-19) \times (-11) = 209$$

$$RHS = 19 \times 11 = 209$$

Hence, $LHS = RHS$

Q. 84 $(-20) \times (5 - 3) = (-20) \times (-2)$

Sol. *False*

$$\because \quad LHS = (-20) \times (5 - 3) = (-20) \times 2 = (-40)$$

$$RHS = (-20) \times (-2) = 40$$

Hence, $LHS \neq RHS$

Q. 85 $4 \times (-5) = (-10) \times (-2)$

Sol. *False*

$$\because \quad LHS = 4 \times (-5) = -20$$

$$RHS = (-10) \times (-2) = 20$$

Hence, $LHS \neq RHS$

Q. 86 $(-1) \times (-2) \times (-3) = 1 \times 2 \times 3$

Sol. *False*

$$\because \quad LHS = (-1) \times (-2) \times (-3) = (-6)$$

$$RHS = 1 \times 2 \times 3 = 6$$

Hence, $LHS \neq RHS$

Q. 87 $(-3) \times 3 = (-12) - (-3)$ T

Sol. *True*

   ∵ LHS $= (-3) \times 3 = (-9)$
      RHS $= (-12) - (-3) = (-12) + 3 = (-9)$
   Hence, LHS = RHS

Q. 88 Product of two negative integers is a negative integer. F

Sol. *False*

   Product of two negative integers is a positive integer, i.e. $(-a) \times (-b) = ab$
   where, a and b are two positive integers.

Q. 89 Product of three negative integers is a negative integer. T

Sol. *True*

   Product of three negative integers is a negative integer, i.e.
   $(-a) \times (-b) \times (-c) = (-abc)$
   where, a, b and c are three positive integers.

Q. 90 Product of a negative integer and a positive integer is a positive integer. F

Sol. *False*

   Product of a negative integer and a positive integer is a negative integer,
   i.e. $a \times (-b) = -ab$
   where, a and b are two positive integers.

Q. 91 When we multiply two integers their product is always greater than both F
the integers.

Sol. *False*

   e.g. Let two integers are (-5) and 2.
   So, $(-5) \times 2 = -10$
   ⇒ $(-10) < (-5)$ and $(-10) < 2$.

Q. 92 Integers are closed under multiplication. T

Sol. *True*

   If we multiply two integers, we get an integer.

Q. 93 $(-237) \times 0$ is same as $0 \times (-39)$. T

Sol. *True*

   When we multiply a number with 0, we always get 0.
   ⇒ $(-237) \times 0 = 0$

Q. 94 Multiplication is not commutative for integers. F

Sol. *False*

   Multiplication is commutative for integers, i.e. $a \times b = b \times a$
   for any two integers a and b.

Q. 95 (−1) is not a multiplicative identity of integers.

Sol. *True*

1 is multiplicative identity for integers, i.e. $a \times 1 = 1 \times a = a$ for any integer a.

Q. 96 99 × 101 can be written as (100 − 1) × (100 + 1).

Sol. *True*

∵ $99 \times 101 = 9999$

and $(100 − 1) \times (100 + 1) = 100 \times (100 + 1) − 1 \times (100 + 1)$
$$= 100 \times 100 + 1 \times 100 − 1 \times 100 − 1 \times 1 \text{ [using distributive property]}$$
$$= 10000 + 100 − 100 − 1 = 9999$$

Q. 97 If a, b and c are integers and $b \neq 0$, then $a \times (b − c) = a \times b − a \times c$

Sol. *True*

Multiplication can be distributive over subtraction.

i.e. $a \times (b − c) = a \times b − a \times c$

Q. 98 $(a + b) \times c = a \times c + a \times b$

Sol. *False*

Integers show distributive property of multiplication over addition.
i.e. $a \times (b + c) = a \times b + a \times c$, where a, b and c are integers.

Q. 99 $a \times b = b \times a$

Sol. *True*

Multiplication is commutative for integers, i.e. $a \times b = b \times a$
where, a and b are integers.

Q. 100 $a \div b = b \div a$

Sol. *False*

Division is not commutative for integers, i.e. $a \div b \neq b \div a$
where, a and b are integers.

Q. 101 $a − b = b − a$

Sol. *False*

Subtraction is not commutative for integers, i.e. $a − b \neq b − a$
where, a and b are integers.

Q. 102 $a \div (− b) = − (a \div b)$

Sol. *True*

Division of a negative integer and a positive integer is always a negative integer

i.e. $\dfrac{a}{−b} = \dfrac{−b}{a} = − \left(\dfrac{a}{b}\right)$ where, a and b are integers.

Q. 103 $a \div (-1) = -a$

Sol. *True*

$a \div (-1) = \dfrac{a}{(-1)} = -a$ [as division of a negative and positive integer is always negative]

Q. 104 Multiplication fact $(-8) \times (-10) = 80$ is same as division fact $80 \div (-8) = (-10)$.

Sol. *True*

Multiplication fact	Division fact
$(-8) \times (-10) = 80$	$80 \div (-8) = (-10)$
LHS $= (-1) \times 8 \times (-1) \times 10$	LHS $= 80 \div (-8) = \dfrac{80}{-8}$
$= (-1)(-1) \times 8 \times 10$	
$= 1 \times 80 = 80 = $ RHS	$= (-10) = $ RHS

Q. 105 Integers are closed under division.

Sol. *False*

Because, when we divide two integers, we may or may not get an integer.

e.g. $\dfrac{2}{1} = 2$ (integer) and $\dfrac{2}{3}$ (not an integer).

Q. 106 $[(-32) \div 8] \div 2 = -32 \div [8 \div 2]$

Sol. *False*

∵   LHS $= [(-32) \div 8] \div 2 = \left[\dfrac{-32}{8}\right] \div 2 = -4 \div 2 = -2$

and RHS $= (-32) \div [8 \div 2] = (-32) \div \left[\dfrac{8}{2}\right] = (-32) \div 4 = \dfrac{(-32)}{4} = -8$

Hence, LHS $\neq$ RHS

Q. 107 The sum of an integer and its additive inverse is zero (0).

Sol. *True*

Additive inverse is the number, that when added to a given number yields zero.

Q. 108 The successor of $0 \times (-25)$ is $1 \times (-25)$.

Sol. *False*

We know that, successor means adding 1 to the given number.

Here, given number is $0 \times (-25) = 0$

[on multiplying by 0 to any number the result is zero]

Hence, the successor of $0 = 0 + 1 = 1$ but $1 \neq 1 \times (-25)$.

Q. 109 Observe the following patterns and fill in the blanks to make the statements true:

(a) $-5 \times 4 = -20$

$-5 \times 3 = -15 = -20 - (-5)$

$-5 \times 2 = \underline{-10} = -15 - (-5)$

$-5 \times 1 = \underline{-5} = \underline{(-10)} - \underline{(-5)}$

$-5 \times 0 = 0 = \underline{(-5)} - \underline{(-5)}$

$-5 \times (-1) = 5 = \underline{0} - \underline{(-5)}$

$-5 \times (-2) = \underline{10} = \underline{5} - \underline{(-5)}$

(b) $7 \times 4 = 28$

$7 \times 3 = \underline{21} = 28 - 7$

$7 \times 2 = \underline{14} = \underline{21} - 7$

$7 \times 1 = 7 = \underline{14} - 7$

$7 \times 0 = \underline{0} = \underline{7} - \underline{7}$

$7 \times (-1) = \underline{-7} = \underline{0} - \underline{-7}$

$7 \times (-2) = \underline{(-14)} = \underline{(-7)} - \underline{7}$

$7 \times (-3) \underline{(-21)} = \underline{(-14)} - 7$

Sol. (a) By observing the pattern, we find that Ist column is constant, i.e. -5, IInd column is decreasing by 1, IIIrd column is increasing by 5, IVth column is also increasing by 5 and Vth column is constant, i.e. -5. So, accordingly,

I	II	III	IV	V

$-5 \times 4 = -20$

$-5 \times 3 = -15 = (-20) - (-5)$

$-5 \times 2 = -10 = (-15) - (-5)$

$-5 \times 1 = -5 = (-10) - (-5)$

$-5 \times 0 = 0 = (-5) - (-5)$

$-5 \times (-1) = 5 = 0 - (-5)$

$-5 \times (-2) = 10 = 5 - (-5)$

(b) By observing the pattern, we find that Ist column is constant, i.e. 7, IInd column is decreasing by 1, IIIrd column is decreasing by 7, IVth column is also decreasing by 7 and Vth column is constant, i.e. $+7$. So, accordingly,

I	II	III	IV	V

$7 \times 4 = 28$

$7 \times 3 = 21 = 28 - 7$

$7 \times 2 = 14 = 21 - 7$

$7 \times 1 = 7 = 14 - 7$

$7 \times 0 = 0 = 7 - 7$

$7 \times (-1) = (-7) = 0 - 7$

$7 \times (-2) = (-14) = (-7) - 7$

$7 \times (-3) = (-21) = (-14) - 7$

Q. 110 Science Application An atom consists of charged particles called electrons and protons. Each proton has a charge of +1 and each electron has a charge of −1. Remember number of electrons is equal to number of protons, while answering these questions:

  (a) What is the charge on an atom?

  (b) What will be the charge on an atom, if it loses an electron?

  (c) What will be the charge on an atom, if it gains an electron?

Sol. (a) Let a be the number of electrons in an atom.

Number of protons in the atom, will also be equal to a. Since, an atom has equal number of protons and electrons.

∴ Charge on one electron = (−1)

∴ Total charge in a electrons = $a \times (-1) = -a$

∴ Charge on one proton = (+1)

∴ Total charge in a protons = $a \times (+1) = +a$

Hence, total charge on the atom = Charge of electrons + Charge of protons
$$= -a + a = 0$$

(b) If an atom loses an electron, it will have (a − 1) electrons and a protons.

∴ Charge in one electron = (−1)

∵ Charge in (a−1) electrons = $(a - 1) \times (-1) = -(a - 1) = (1 - a)$

∴ Charge in one proton = (+1)

∵ Charge in a protons = $(+1) \times a = (+a)$

Hence, total charge on the atom = Charge of electrons + Charge of protons
$$= 1 - a + a = +1$$

(c) If an atom gains an electron, it will have (a + 1) electrons and a protons

∴ Charge in one electron = −1

Charge in (a + 1) electrons = $-1 \times (a + 1) = -(a + 1)$

∴ Charge in one proton = (+1)

Charge in a protons = $(+1) \times a = (+a)$

Hence, total charge on the atom = Charge of electrons + Charge of protons
$$= a - (a + 1) = (-1)$$

Q. 111 An atom changes to a charged particle called ion, if it loses or gains electrons. The charge on an ion is the charge on electrons plus charge on protons. Now, write the missing information in the table given below:

Name of ion	Proton charge	Electron charge	Ion charge
(a) Hydroxide ion	+9	−10	−1
(b) Sodium ion	+11	−10	+1
(c) Aluminium ion	+13	−10	+3
(d) Oxide ion	+8	−10	−2

Sol. (a) For Hydroxide ion,

Proton charge + Electron charge = Ion charge

Electron charge = Ion charge − Proton charge

Electron charge = $-1 - 9 = -10$

Hence, the electron charge in a Hydroxide ion is −10.

(b) For Sodium ion,
Electron charge = Ion charge – Proton charge = + 1 – 11 = – 10
Hence, the electron charge in a Sodium ion is –10.

(c) For Aluminium ion,
Ion charge = Proton charge + Electron charge
Ion charge = 13 – 10 = 3
Hence, the ion charge in an Aluminium ion is 3.

(d) For Oxide ion,
Ion charge = Proton charge + Electron charge
Ion charge = 8 – 10 = – 2
Hence, the ion charge in an Oxide ion is –2.

Q. 112 Social Studies Application remembering that 1 AD came immediately after 1 BC, while solving following problems take 1 BC as −1 and 1 AD as +1.

    (a) The Greeco-Roman era, when Greece and Rome ruled Egypt, started in the year 330 BC and ended in the year 395 AD. How long did this era last?   725 year

    (b) Bhaskaracharya was born in the year 1114 AD and died in the year 1185 AD. What was his age when he died? 71 year old

    (c) Turks ruled Egypt in the year 1517 AD and Queen Nefertis ruled Egypt about 2900 years, before the Turks ruled. In what year did she rule? 1383 BC Daught

    (d) Greek Mathematician Archimedes lived between 287 BC and 212 BC and Aristotle lived between 380 BC and 322 BC. Who lived during an earlier period?

Sol.   (a) Total duration of the era = End year – Start year

$$= (395 \text{ AD}) - (330 \text{ BC})$$
$$= + 395 - (- 330)$$
$$= 395 + 330 = 725 \text{ yr}$$

Hence, total duration of this era was 725 yr.

(b) Age, when Bhaskaracharya died = Year in which he died – Year in which he born

$$= (1185 \text{ AD}) - (1114 \text{ AD})$$
$$= (+ 1185) - (+ 1114)$$
$$= 1185 - 1114 = 71 \text{ yr}$$

Hence, Bhaskaracharya was died in the age of 71 yr.

(c) Year in which Queen Nefertis ruled = Year in which Turks ruled – 2900 yr

$$= (1517 \text{ AD}) - 2900$$
$$= (+ 1517) - 2900$$
$$= - 1383 = 1383 \text{ BC}$$

Hence, Queen Nefertis ruled in the year 1383 BC.

(d) Aristotle lived in an earlier period, as 380 BC and 322 BC is earlier than 287 BC and 212 BC.

Q. 113 The table shows the lowest recorded temperatures for each continent. Write the continents in order from the lowest recorded temperature to the highest recorded temperature.

The Lowest Recorded Temperatures	
Continent	**Temperature** (in Fahrenheit)
Africa	$-11°$
Antarctica	$-129°$
Asia	$-90°$
Australia	$-9°$
Europe	$-67°$
North America	$-81°$
South America	$-27°$

Sol. Lowest to heights (ascending order) in a negative number, the number that has greater value of actually smaller and *vice-versa*.

So, accordingly, we arrange them in ascending order

Antarctica $<$ Asia $<$ North America $<$ Europe $<$ South America $<$ Africa $<$ Australia
$(-129°)$ $(-90°)$ $(-81°)$ $(-67°)$ $(-27°)$ $(-11°)$ $(-9°)$

Q. 114 Write a pair of integers whose product is -12 and there lies seven integers between them (excluding the given integers). $-6 \times 2 = -12$

Sol. For a pair of integers, whose product is -12 and there lies seven integers between them, Two solutions are possible, i.e. $(-6$ and $2)$ and $(-2$ and $6)$.

$\Rightarrow -6 \times 2 = -12, \ -2 \times 6 = -12$

Ist Pair Let first integer $= -6$ and second integer $= 2$

$\Rightarrow (-6) \times 2 = (-12)$ and 7 integers are lying between them.

IInd Pair Let first integer $= -2$ and second integer $= 6$

$\Rightarrow (-2) \times 6 = -12$ and 7 integers are lying between them.

Q. 115 From given integers in Column I, match an integer of Column II, so that their product lies between -19 and -6.

Column I	Column II
-5	1
6	-1
-7	3
8	-2

Dought

Sol. $-5 \times 3 = (-15)$ which lies between -19 and -6.

$6 \times (-2) = (-12)$ which lies between -19 and -6.

$-7 \times 1 = (-7)$ which lies between -19 and -6.

$8 \times (-1) = (-8)$ which lies between -19 and -6.

Q. 116 Write a pair of integers, whose product is -36 and whose difference is 15.

Sol. For a pair of integers, whose product is -36 and difference is 15, one possible solution is $(-3, 12)$.

So, first integer $= -3$ and second integer $= 12$

Their product $= (-3) \times 12 = -(3 \times 12) = -36$

and the difference between these two integers is $12 - (-3) = 15$.

Q. 117 Match the following:

	Column I		Column II
(a)	$a \times 1$	(i)	Additive inverse of a
(b)	1	(ii)	Additive identity
(c)	$(-a) \div (-b)$	(iii)	Multiplicative identity
(d)	$a \times (-1)$	(iv)	$a \div (-b)$
(e)	$a \times 0$	(v)	$a \div b$
(f)	$(-a) \div b$	(vi)	a
(g)	0	(vii)	$-a$
(h)	$a \div (-a)$	(viii)	0
(i)	$-a$	(ix)	-1

Sol. (a) → (vi)

$\quad a \times 1 = a$

(b) → (iii)

$\quad$ 1 is multiplicative identity.

(c) → (v)

$\quad -a \div (-b) = a \div b$ [both signs are cancelled with each other]

(d) → (vii)

$\quad a \times (-1) = -a$

(e) → (viii)

$\quad a \times 0 = 0$ [any value, when multiplies with 0 becomes zero]

(f) → (iv)

$\quad (-a) \div b = a \div (-b)$

(g) → (ii)

$\quad$ 0 is an additive identity.

(h) → (ix)

$\quad a \div (-a) = \dfrac{a}{-a} = -1$

(i) → (i)

$\quad -a$ is additive inverse of a.

Q. 118 You have ₹ 500 in your saving account at the beginning of the month. The record below, shows all of your transactions during the month. How much money is in your account after these transactions?

Cheque no.	Date	Transaction description	Payment	Deposit
384102	4/9	Jal Board	₹ 120	₹ 200
275146	12/9	Deposit		
384103	22/9	LIC India	₹ 240	₹ 150
801351	29/9	Deposit		

How much money is in your account after these transactions?

Sol. According to the question,
Already available amount = ₹ 500
On 4/9 with cheque number 384102 withdraw ₹ 120.
Also, with cheque number 275146 on 12/9 deposited amount was ₹ 200.
In the same way, on 22/9 with cheque number 384103, ₹ 240 paid to LIC of India, also.
On 29/9 with cheque number 801351, deposited amount was ₹ 150.
Thus, net amount available in bank account will be
= Already saved amount + Deposited amount – Debited amount (paid amount)
= 500 + 200 + 150 – 120 – 240
= 850 + (– 360) = ₹ 490

Q. 119 (a) Write a positive integer and a negative integer whose sum is a negative integer.

$-10 + 8 = -2$

Sol. A number of solutions can be possible.
e.g. Let first integer = 4 and second integer = (–6)
Sum = 4 + (– 6) = – 2   [negative integer]

(b) Write a positive integer and a negative integer whose sum is a positive integer.

$+10 + 8 = 18$

Sol. A number of solutions can be possible.
e.g. Let first integer = 8 and second integer = – 2
Sum = 8 + (– 2) = 6   [positive integer]

(c) Write a positive integer and a negative integer whose difference is a negative integer.

$-10 + (-8) = -2$

Sol. A number of solutions can be possible.
e.g. Let first integer = (– 7) and second integer = 2
Difference = (– 7 – 2) = (– 9)   [negative integer]

(d) Write a positive integer and a negative integer whose difference is a positive integer.

$+10 + (-8) = 2$

Sol. A number of solutions can be possible.
e.g. Let first integer = 4 and second integer = (– 3)
Difference = 4 – (– 3) = 7   [positive integer]

(e) Write two integers, which are smaller than − 5 but their difference is − 5.

Sol.   For two integers, which are smaller than − 5 but their difference is − 5.

Let first integer = − 11 and second integer = (− 6)   [∵ −11 < (−5) and −6 < (−5)]

Difference = − 11 − (− 6) = − 11 + 6 = (− 5)

(f) Write two integers which are greater than − 10 but their sum is smaller than − 10.

Sol.   For two integers which are greater than −10 but their sum is smaller than −10.

Let first integer = − 4 and second integer = − 7   [∵ −4 > (−10) and −7 > − 10]

Sum = − 4 + (− 7) = − 11 < − 10

(g) Write two integers which are greater than − 4 but their difference is smaller than − 4.

Sol.   For two integers which are greater than − 4 but their difference is smaller than − 4.

Let first integer = (− 1) and second integer = 4   [∵ −1 > − 4 and 4 > − 4]

Difference = − 1 − 4 = − 5 < (− 4)

(h) Write two integers which are smaller than − 6 but their difference is greater than − 6.

Sol.   For two integers which are smaller than − 6 but their difference is greater than − 6.

e.g. Let first integer = (− 8) and second integer = (− 9)   [∵ − 8 < − 6 and − 9 < − 6]

Difference = − 8 − (− 9) = −8 + 9 = 1 > (− 6)

(i) Write two negative integers whose difference is 7.

Sol.   A number of solutions can be possible.

e.g. Let first integer = (− 3) and second integer = (− 10)

Difference = − 3 − (− 10) = 7

(j) Write two integers, such that one is smaller than − 11 and other is greater than − 11 but their difference is − 11.

Sol.   For two integers, such that one is smaller than − 11 and other is greater than − 11.

Let first integer = − 20 and second integer = − 9   [∵ −20 < − 11 and −9 > − 11]

Difference = − 20 − (− 9) = (− 11)

(k) Write two integers whose product is smaller than both the integers.

Sol.   A number of solutions can be possible.

e.g. Let first integer = − 3 and second integer = 5

Product = − 3 × 5 = − 15   [∵ −15 < − 3 and −15 < 5]

(l) Write two integers, whose product is greater than both the integers.

Sol.   A number of solutions can be possible.

e.g. Let first integer = 4 and second integer = 6

Product = 6 × 4 = 24   [∵ 24 > 6 and 24 > 4]

Q. 120 What's the error? Ramu evaluated the expression $-7 - (-3)$ and came up with the answer -10. What did Ramu do wrong?

Sol. Ramu went wrong in solving $-(-3)$ and took it as -3 only.

Correct answer $= -7 - (-3) = -7 + 3 = -4$

Q. 121 What's the error? Reeta evaluated $-4 + d$ for $d = -6$ and gave an answer of 2. What might Reeta have done wrong?

Sol. Reeta went wrong in solving $+(-6)$ and took it as $+6$.

Correct answer $= -4 + d = -4 + (-6) = -4 - 6 = -10$

Q. 122 The table given below, shows the elevations relative to sea level of four locations. Taking sea level as zero (0), answer the following questions.

Location	Elevation (in m)
A	-180
B	1600
C	-55
D	3200

(a) Which location is closest to sea level?

(b) Which location is farthest from sea level?

(c) Arrange the locations from the least to the greatest elevation.

Sol. (a) From the adjacent figure, we can clearly see that C is closest to sea level.

(b) D is farthest from sea level.

(c) Locations from the least to the greatest elevation will be in the order A, C, B and D.

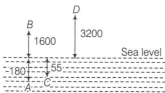

Q. 123 You are at an elevation 380 m above sea level as you start a motor ride. During the ride, your elevation changes by the following metres 540 m, -268 m, 116 m, -152 m, 490 m, -844 m, 94 m. What is your elevation relative to the sea level at the end of the ride?

Sol. As per the given information, initial position of motor was 380 m.

During the ride, change in elevation was 540 m, -268 m, 116 m, -152 m, 490 m, -844 m and 94 m.

Net change in position $= 540 + (-268) + (116) + (-152) + (490) + (-844) + 94 = -24$ m

Initial position was 380 m. So, at the end of the ride the position would be

$$= 380 + (-24) = 356 \text{ m}$$

Q. 124 Evaluate the following, using distributive property.

    (i) -39×99 (ii) $(-85) \times 43 + 43 \times (-15)$

    (iii) $53 \times (-9) - (-109) \times 53$ (iv) $68 \times (-17) + (-68) \times 3$

Sol.   (i) $-39 \times 99 = (-40 + 1) \times (100 - 1)$

                   $= -40 \times (100 - 1) + 1 \times (100 - 1)$

        Now, using distributive property,

         $= (-40 \times 100) + (-1 \times -40) + (1 \times 100) + (1 \times -1)$ $[\because a \times (b + c) = a \times b + a \times c]$

         $= -4000 + 40 + 100 - 1 = -3861$

   (ii) $(-85) \times 43 + 43 \times (-15)$

        Taking 43 as common

         $= 43 \times (-85 - 15)$ $[\because a \times b + a \times c = a \times (b + c)]$

         $= 43 \times (-100) = -4300$

   (iii) $53 \times (-9) - (-109) \times 53$

        Taking 53 as common,

         $= 53 \times [-9 - (-109)]$

         $= 53 \times (-9 + 109) = 53 \times 100 = 5300$ $[\because a \times b + a \times c = a \times (b + c)]$

   (iv) $68 \times (-17) + (-68) \times 3$

         $= 68 \times (-17) - 68 \times 3$

        Taking 68 as common,

         $= 68 \times (-17 - 3)$ $\left[\begin{array}{l} \because a \times b + a \times c = a \times (b + c) \\ \text{i.e. using distributive property} \end{array}\right]$

         $= 68 \times (-20)$

         $= -1360$

Q. 125 If '$*$' is an operation have, such that for integers a and b. We have

    $a * b = a \times b + (a \times a + b \times b)$, then find

    (i) $(-3) * (-5)$ (ii) $(-6) * 2$

Sol.   (i) We have, $a * b = a \times b + (a \times a + b \times b)$

        Now, put $a = (-3)$ and $b = (-5)$

         $(-3) * (-5) = (-3) \times (-5) + [(-3) \times (-3) + (-5) \times (-5)]$

              $= 15 + (9 + 25) = 15 + 34 = 49$

   (ii) Now, put $a = -6$ and $b = 2$

         $(-6) * 2 = (-6 \times 2) + \{(-6) \times (-6) + 2 \times 2\}$

           $= -6 \times 2 + (36 + 4) = -12 + 40 = 28$

Q. 126 If Δ is an operation, such that for integers a and b. We have

    $a \Delta b = a \times b - 2 \times a \times b + b \times b(-a) \times b + b \times b$, then find

    (i) $4 \Delta (-3)$ (ii) $(-7) \Delta (-1)$

    Also, show that $4 \Delta (-3) \neq (-3) \Delta 4$ and $(-7) \Delta (-1) \neq (-1) \Delta (-7)$

Sol.   (i) We have, $a \Delta b = a \times b - 2 \times a \times b + b \times (b) (-a) \times b + b \times b$

        Now, put $a = 4$ and $b = (-3)$

         $4 \Delta (-3) = 4 \times (-3) - 2 \times 4 (-3) + (-3) \times (-3) \times (-4) \times (-3) + (-3) \times (-3)$

           $= -12 - 2 \times (-12) + (9)(12) + 9 = -12 + 24 + 108 + 9$

           $= 129$

Now, put $a = -3$ and $b = 4$

$\Rightarrow \quad (-3)\Delta 4 = (-3) \times 4 - 2 \times (-3) \times (4) + 4 \times 4\{-(-3)\} \times 4 + 4 \times 4$

$= (-12) + 24 + 16(3) \times 4 + 16$

$= (-12) + 24 + 192 + 16$

$= 220$

Clearly, $4\Delta(-3) \neq (-3)\Delta 4$

(ii) Now, put $a = (-7)$ and $b = (-1)$

$\Rightarrow (-7)\Delta(-1) = (-7) \times (-1) - 2 \times (-7) \times (-1) + (-1) \times (-1)\{-(-7)\} \times (-1) + (-1) \times (-1)$

$= 7 - 14 + 1 \times 7 \times (-1) + 1$

$= 7 - 14 - 7 + 1 \Rightarrow -13$

Now, put $a = (-1)$ and $b = (-7)$

$\Rightarrow (-1)\Delta(-7) = (-1) \times (-7) - 2 \times (-1) \times (-7) + (-7) \times (-7)\{-(-1)\} \times (-7) + (-7) \times (-7)$

$= 7 - 14 + 49(1) \times (-7) + 49$

$= 7 - 14 - 343 + 49$

$= -301$

Clearly, $(-7)\Delta(-1) \neq (-1)\Delta(-7)$

Q. 127 Below u, v, w and x represent different integers, where $u = (-4)$ and $x \neq 1$. By using following equations, find each of the values
$u \times v = u$, $x \times w = w$ and $u + x = w$

(a) v (b) w (c) x

Explain your reason, using the properties of integers.

Sol. We have, three equations

$$u \times v = u \qquad \qquad \qquad \qquad \qquad \qquad \text{...(i)}$$
$$x \times w = w \qquad \qquad \qquad \qquad \qquad \qquad \text{...(ii)}$$
$$u + x = w \qquad \qquad \qquad \qquad \qquad \qquad \text{...(iii)}$$

and $\qquad\qquad u = -4$

(a) By putting the value of u in Eq. (i), we get

$$(-4) \times v = (-4)$$

$\Rightarrow \qquad\qquad v = \dfrac{(-4)}{(-4)} \Rightarrow v = 1$

(b) From Eq. (ii),

$$x \times w = w \Rightarrow x = \frac{w}{w} \Rightarrow x = 1$$

But, $\qquad\qquad\qquad\qquad\qquad x \neq 1$

Hence, $x \times w = w$, (ii) is possible, when $w = 0 \, (x \neq 1)$.

(c) From Eq. (iii), $u + x = w$

Put $\quad u = -4$ and $w = 0$, we get

$\Rightarrow \qquad\qquad -4 + x = 0 \Rightarrow x = 4$

$\therefore \qquad v = 1$, $x = 4$ and $w = 0$

Q. 128 Height of a place A is 1800 m above sea level. Another place B is 700 m below sea level. What is the difference between the levels of these two places?

Sol. As per the given information, we can draw the diagram,

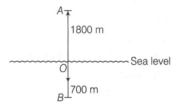

Let O be the point of level of sea.

Difference between these two points, A and B

= Height between sea level and point A+Height between point B and sea level

$= AO+OB=1800+700 = 2500$ m

Q. 129 The given table shows the freezing points in °F of different gases at sea level. Convert each of these into °C to the nearest integral value using the relation and complete the table, $C = \dfrac{5}{9}(F - 32)$

Gas	Freezing point at sea level (°F)	Freezing point at sea level (°C)
Hydrogen	−435	
Krypton	−251	
Oxygen	−369	
Helium	−458	
Argon	−309	

Sol. We have, $C = \dfrac{5}{9}(F - 32)$

For Hydrogen, put $F = (-435)$

$\Rightarrow \qquad C = \dfrac{5}{9}(-435-32) = \dfrac{5}{9} \times (-467) = -259.44$

$\Rightarrow \qquad C = -259.44$

For Krypton, put $F = (-251)$

$\Rightarrow \qquad C = \dfrac{5}{9}(-251-32) = \dfrac{5}{9} \times (-283) = -157.22$

$\Rightarrow \qquad C = -157.22$

For Oxygen, put $F = (-369)$

$\qquad C = \dfrac{5}{9}(-369-32) = \dfrac{5}{9} \times (-401)$

$\Rightarrow \qquad C = -222.7$

$\Rightarrow \qquad C = -223$

For Helium, put $F = (-458)$

$$C = \frac{5}{9}(-458 - 32) = \frac{5}{9} \times (-490) = -272.22$$

$$C = -272.22$$

For Argon, put $F = (-309)$

$$C = \frac{5}{9}(-309 - 32) = \frac{5}{9}(-341) = -189.44$$

$\Rightarrow$ $\qquad C = -189.44$

Q. 130 Sana and Fatima participated in an apple race. The race was conducted in 6 parts. In the first part, Sana won by 10 seconds. In the second part, she lost by 1 min, then won by 20 seconds in the third part and lost by 25 seconds in the fourth part, she lost by 37 seconds in the fifth part and won by 12 seconds in the last part. Who won the race finally?

Sol. Let difference in time denoted by positive, when Sana wins the race and negative, when Sana loses the race.

Total difference in time taken by Sana in all the six parts

$$= 10 - 60 + 20 - 25 - 37 + 12 = -80 \text{ s} \qquad [\because 1 \text{ min} = 60 \text{ s}]$$

Hence, Fatima won the race by 80 s.

Q. 131 A green grocer had a profit of ₹47 on Monday, a loss of ₹12 on Tuesday and loss of ₹8 on Wednesday. Find his net profit or loss in 3 days.

Sol. As per the given information,

Profit on Monday = ₹47 and loss on Tuesday = ₹12

and loss on Wednesday = ₹8

$\therefore$ Net profit = Total profit – Total loss

Now, total profit = ₹47 and total loss = $12 + 8 = ₹20$

$\therefore$ Net profit = $47 - 20 = ₹27$

Q. 132 In a test, +3 marks are given for every correct answer and −1 mark are given for every incorrect answer. Sona attempted all the questions and scored +20 marks, though she got 10 correct answers.

(i) How many incorrect answers has she attempted?

(ii) How many questions were given in the test?

Sol. Let x be the correct answers and y be the incorrect answers, given by Sona.

It is given that, if she gives 10 correct answers and her score is 20. Since, for every correct answer, +3 is given and for every incorrect answer, −1 is given.

Hence,

(i) $3 \times$ (Correct answer) + $(-1) \times$ (Incorrect answer) = Total score

$\Rightarrow \qquad 3 \times 10 + (-1) \times y = 20$

$\Rightarrow \qquad 30 - y = 20$

$\Rightarrow \qquad 30 - 20 = y$

$\Rightarrow \qquad y = 10$

(ii) Total number of questions = Correct answer + Incorrect answer

$$= x + y = 10 + 10 = 20$$

Q. 133 In a true-false test containing 50 questions, a student is to be awarded 2 marks for every correct answer and −2 for every incorrect answer and 0 for not supplying any answer. If Yash scored 94 marks in a test, what are the possibilities of his marking correct or wrong answer?

Sol. Since, Yash scored 94 marks.

So, minimum correct answer = $\dfrac{\text{Total marks}}{\text{Marks for 1 correct answer}} = \dfrac{94}{2} = 47$

Hence, there are two possibilities:

(i) 47 correct answers and 3 unattempted.

(ii) 48 correct answers, 1 unattempted and 1 wrong answer.

Q. 134 A multistory building has 25 floors above the ground level each of height 5 m. It also has 3 floors in the basement each of height 5m. A lift in building moves at a rate of 1m/s. If a man starts from 50m above the ground, how long will it take him to reach at 2nd floor of basement?

Sol. Man covers the distance above the ground = 50 m

and man covers the distance below the ground = 2 × 5 = 10 m

[∵ distance between two floors = 5 m]

Thus, total distance = 50 m + 10 m = 60 m

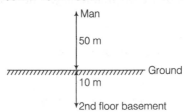

∵ Speed of the lift = 1m/s   [given]

Hence, time taken to reach second floor of basement = $\dfrac{\text{Distance}}{\text{Speed}} = \dfrac{60\,\text{m}}{1\,\text{m/s}} = 60$ s or 1min

Q. 135 Taking today as zero on the number line, if the day before yesterday is 17 January, what is the date 3 days after tomorrow?

Sol.

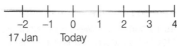

If we take today as zero, then two days before today is 17 January. Hence, 3 days after tomorrow will be at 4th place from zero on the number line.

So, required date will be (17+6) January =23 January

Q. 136 The highest point measured above sea level is the summit of Mt. Everest, which is 8848 m above sea level and the lowest point is challenger deep at the bottom of Mariana Trench which is 10911 m below sea level. What is the vertical distance between these two points?

Sol. As per the given information, we can draw the diagram,

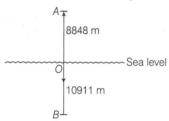

Let A be the point above the sea level and B be the point below the sea level.

∴ Vertical distance between points A and B = Distance between point A and sea level + Distance between point B and sea level

$$= AO + OB = 8848 + 10911 = 19759 \text{ m}$$

2

Fractions and Decimals

Multiple Choice Questions (MCQs)

Q. 1 $\frac{2}{5} \times 5\frac{1}{5}$ is equal to

(a) $\frac{26}{25}$

(b) $\frac{52}{25}$

(c) $\frac{2}{5}$

(d) 6

Sol. *(b)* Given, $\frac{2}{5} \times 5\frac{1}{5}$

$\because$
$$5\frac{1}{5} = \frac{(5 \times 5) + 1}{5}$$
$$= \frac{25 + 1}{5} = \frac{26}{5}$$

$\therefore$
$$\frac{2}{5} \times 5\frac{1}{5} = \frac{2}{5} \times \frac{26}{5} = \frac{52}{25}$$

Q. 2 $3\frac{3}{4} \div \frac{3}{4}$ is equal to

(a) 3

(b) 4

(c) 5

(d) $\frac{45}{16}$

Sol. *(c)* Given, $3\frac{3}{4} \div \frac{3}{4}$

$\because$
$$3\frac{3}{4} = \frac{(3 \times 4) + 3}{4} = \frac{12 + 3}{4} = \frac{15}{4}$$

$\therefore$
$$3\frac{3}{4} \div \frac{3}{4} = \frac{15}{4} \times \frac{4}{3} = 5$$

$$\left[\because \text{ reciprocal of } \frac{3}{4} = \frac{4}{3} \right]$$

Q. 3 A ribbon of length $5\frac{1}{4}$ m is cut into small pieces each of length $\frac{3}{4}$ m. Number of pieces will be

    (a) 5   (b) 6   (c) 7   (d) 8

Sol. *(c)* Number of pieces

$$= \frac{\text{Total length of ribbon}}{\text{Length of one piece}} = \frac{\left(5\frac{1}{4}\right)}{\left(\frac{3}{4}\right)}$$

$$= \left(\frac{(5 \times 4) + 1}{\frac{4}{\frac{3}{4}}}\right) = \frac{\left(\frac{21}{4}\right)}{\left(\frac{3}{4}\right)}$$

$$= \frac{21}{4} \times \frac{4}{3} \qquad\qquad \left[\because \text{ reciprocal of } \frac{3}{4} = \frac{4}{3}\right]$$

$$= 7$$

Q. 4 The ascending arrangement of $\frac{2}{3}, \frac{6}{7}, \frac{13}{21}$ is

    (a) $\frac{6}{7}, \frac{2}{3}, \frac{13}{21}$ (b) $\frac{13}{21}, \frac{2}{3}, \frac{6}{7}$ (c) $\frac{6}{7}, \frac{13}{21}, \frac{2}{3}$ (d) $\frac{2}{3}, \frac{6}{7}, \frac{13}{21}$

Sol. *(b)* Given, $\frac{2}{3}, \frac{6}{7}, \frac{13}{21}$

LCM of (3, 7, 21) = 21

$$\therefore \qquad \frac{2}{3} = \frac{2}{3} \times \frac{7}{7} = \frac{14}{21},$$

$$\frac{6}{7} = \frac{6}{7} \times \frac{3}{3} = \frac{18}{21}$$

and $\qquad \frac{13}{21} = \frac{13}{21}$

Now, compare $\frac{14}{21}, \frac{18}{21}$ and $\frac{13}{21}$.

So, $\qquad \frac{13}{21} < \frac{14}{21} < \frac{18}{21}$

Hence, $\frac{13}{21} < \frac{2}{3} < \frac{6}{7}$ (ascending order)

Note *With same denominators, fraction with larger numerator is greater.*

Q. 5 Reciprocal of the fraction $\frac{2}{3}$ is

    (a) 2   (b) 3   (c) $\frac{2}{3}$ (d) $\frac{3}{2}$

Sol. *(d)* The reciprocal of a non-zero fraction is obtained by interchanging its numerator and denominator.

Hence, the reciprocal of $\frac{2}{3}$ is $\frac{3}{2}$.

Q. 6 The product of $\dfrac{11}{13}$ and 4 is

(a) $3\dfrac{5}{13}$

(b) $5\dfrac{3}{13}$

(c) $13\dfrac{3}{5}$

(d) $13\dfrac{5}{3}$

Sol. (*a*) We have, $\dfrac{11}{13} \times 4$

$\therefore \dfrac{11}{13} \times 4 = \dfrac{44}{13} = 3\dfrac{5}{13}$

Hence, the product of $\dfrac{11}{13}$ and 4 is $3\dfrac{5}{13}$.

Q. 7 The product of 3 and $4\dfrac{2}{5}$ is

(a) $17\dfrac{2}{5}$

(b) $\dfrac{24}{5}$

(c) $13\dfrac{1}{5}$

(d) $5\dfrac{1}{13}$

Sol. (*c*) Given, $3 \times 4\dfrac{2}{5}$

$\because \qquad 4\dfrac{2}{5} = \dfrac{(4 \times 5) + 2}{5} = \dfrac{22}{5}$

$\therefore \qquad 3 \times 4\dfrac{2}{5} = 3 \times \dfrac{22}{5} = \dfrac{66}{5} = 13\dfrac{1}{5}$

Hence, the product of 3 and $4\dfrac{2}{5}$ is $13\dfrac{1}{5}$.

Q. 8 Pictorial representation of $3 \times \dfrac{2}{3}$ is

(a)
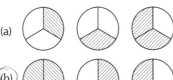

(b)

(c)
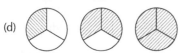

(d)

Sol. (*b*) $3 \times \dfrac{2}{3}$ means 3 times the two-third part of anything.

$\therefore$ Option (b) is correct.

Q. 9 $\dfrac{1}{5} \div \dfrac{4}{5}$ is equal to

(a) $\dfrac{4}{5}$ (b) $\dfrac{1}{5}$ (c) $\dfrac{5}{4}$ (d) $\dfrac{1}{4}$

Sol. *(d)* Given, $\dfrac{1}{5} \div \dfrac{4}{5} = \dfrac{1}{5} \times \dfrac{5}{4}$ $\left[\because \text{reciprocal of } \dfrac{4}{5} = \dfrac{5}{4} \right]$

$$= \dfrac{1}{4}$$

Q. 10 The product of 0.03×0.9 is

(a) 2.7   (b) 0.27   (c) 0.027   (d) 0.0027

Sol. *(c)* Given, 0.03×0.9

Here, $3 \times 9 = 27$

$\because$ Sum of the decimal places to the right of the decimal point is 0.03 and 0.9 is 3.

So, $0.03 \times 0.9 = 0.027$

Q. 11 $\dfrac{5}{7} \div 6$

(a) $\dfrac{30}{7}$ (b) $\dfrac{5}{42}$ (c) $\dfrac{30}{42}$ (d) $\dfrac{6}{7}$

Sol. *(b)* Given, $\dfrac{5}{7} \div 6 = \dfrac{5}{7} \times \dfrac{1}{6}$ $\left[\because \text{reciprocal of 6 or } \dfrac{6}{1} = \dfrac{1}{6} \right]$

$$= \dfrac{5}{42}$$

Q. 12 $5\dfrac{1}{6} \div \dfrac{9}{2}$ is equal to

(a) $\dfrac{31}{6}$ (b) $\dfrac{1}{27}$ (c) $5\dfrac{1}{27}$ (d) $\dfrac{31}{27}$

Sol. *(d)* Given, $5\dfrac{1}{6} \div \dfrac{9}{2}$

$\because 5\dfrac{1}{6} = \dfrac{(5 \times 6) + 1}{6} = \dfrac{30 + 1}{6} = \dfrac{31}{6}$

$\therefore 5\dfrac{1}{6} \div \dfrac{9}{2} = \dfrac{31}{6} \times \dfrac{2}{9} = \dfrac{31}{27}$ $\left[\because \text{reciprocal of } \dfrac{9}{2} = \dfrac{2}{9} \right]$

Q. 13 Which of the following represents $\dfrac{1}{3}$ of $\dfrac{1}{6}$?

(a) $\dfrac{1}{3} + \dfrac{1}{6}$ (b) $\dfrac{1}{3} - \dfrac{1}{6}$

(c) $\dfrac{1}{3} \times \dfrac{1}{6}$ (d) $\dfrac{1}{3} \div \dfrac{1}{6}$

Sol. *(c)* We have, $\dfrac{1}{3}$ of $\dfrac{1}{6} = \dfrac{1}{3} \times \dfrac{1}{6}$

Note *'of' represents multiplication (×).*

Q. 14 $\dfrac{3}{7}$ of $\dfrac{2}{5}$ is equal to

(a) $\dfrac{5}{12}$　　　　(b) $\dfrac{5}{35}$　　　　(c) $\dfrac{1}{35}$　　　　(d) $\dfrac{6}{35}$

Sol. (d) Given, $\dfrac{3}{7}$ of $\dfrac{2}{5} = \dfrac{3}{7} \times \dfrac{2}{5} = \dfrac{6}{35}$

Q. 15 One packet of biscuits requires $2\dfrac{1}{2}$ cups of flour and $1\dfrac{2}{3}$ cups of sugar. Estimated total quantity of both ingredients used in 10 such packets of biscuits will be

(a) less than 30 cups　　　　　　(b) between 30 cups and 40 cups
(c) between 40 cups and 50 cups　　(d) above 50 cups

Sol. (c) Total quantity of both ingredients in one packet of biscuits

$$= \text{Quantity of flour} + \text{Quantity of sugar}$$
$$= 2\dfrac{1}{2}\text{ cups} + 1\dfrac{2}{3}\text{ cups}$$
$$= \dfrac{(2 \times 2) + 1}{2} + \dfrac{(1 \times 3) + 2}{3}$$
$$= \dfrac{4+1}{2} + \dfrac{3+2}{3}$$
$$= \dfrac{5}{2} + \dfrac{5}{3}$$
$$= \dfrac{5 \times 3 + 2 \times 5}{6} \qquad [\because \text{LCM of 2 and 3} = 6]$$
$$= \dfrac{15+10}{6}$$
$$= \dfrac{25}{6}$$

∴ Total quantity of both ingredients used in 10 packets

$$= 10 \times \text{Total quantity of ingredients in one packet}$$
$$= 10 \times \dfrac{25}{6} = \dfrac{250}{6}$$

Since, $\dfrac{250}{6}$ lies between 40 and 50.

Q. 16 The product of 7 and $6\dfrac{3}{4}$ is

(a) $42\dfrac{1}{4}$　　　　(b) $47\dfrac{1}{4}$　　　　(c) $42\dfrac{3}{4}$　　　　(d) $47\dfrac{3}{4}$

Sol. (b) Given, $7 \times 6\dfrac{3}{4}$

$$\because \qquad 6\dfrac{3}{4} = \dfrac{(6 \times 4) + 3}{4} = \dfrac{24+3}{4} = \dfrac{27}{4}$$
$$\therefore \qquad 7 \times 6\dfrac{3}{4} = 7 \times \dfrac{27}{4} = \dfrac{189}{4} = 47\dfrac{1}{4}$$

Hence, the product of 7 and $6\dfrac{3}{4}$ is $47\dfrac{1}{4}$.

Q. 17 On dividing 7 by $\frac{2}{5}$, the result is

(a) $\frac{14}{2}$ (b) $\frac{35}{4}$ (c) $\frac{14}{5}$ (d) $\frac{35}{2}$

Sol. *(d)* Given, $7 \div \frac{2}{5} = 7 \times \frac{5}{2}$ $\left[\because \text{reciprocal of } \frac{2}{5} = \frac{5}{2}\right]$

$$= \frac{35}{2}$$

Hence, on dividing 7 by $\frac{2}{5}$, we get $\frac{35}{2}$.

Q. 18 $2\frac{2}{3} \div 5$ is equal to

(a) $\frac{8}{15}$ (b) $\frac{40}{3}$ (c) $\frac{40}{5}$ (d) $\frac{8}{3}$

Sol. *(a)* Given, $2\frac{2}{3} \div 5 = \frac{(2 \times 3) + 2}{3} \div 5 = \frac{6 + 2}{3} \div 5$

$$= \frac{8}{3} \times \frac{1}{5} \qquad \left[\because \text{reciprocal of } 5 = \frac{1}{5}\right]$$

$$= \frac{8}{15}$$

Hence, $2\frac{2}{3} \div 5$ is equal to $\frac{8}{15}$.

Q. 19 $\frac{4}{5}$ of 5 kg apples were used on Monday. The next day $\frac{1}{3}$ of what was left was used. Weight (in kg) of apples left now is

(a) $\frac{2}{7}$ (b) $\frac{1}{14}$ (c) $\frac{2}{3}$ (d) $\frac{4}{21}$

Sol. *(c)* Apples used on Monday $= \frac{4}{5}$ of $5 = \frac{4}{5} \times 5$

$$= 4\,\text{kg}$$

Remaining apples $= 5 - 4$

$$= 1\,\text{kg}$$

Apples used next day $= \frac{1}{3}$ of remaining apples

$$= \frac{1}{3} \times 1\,\text{kg} = \frac{1}{3}\,\text{kg}$$

So, weight of apples left now

$$= \text{Total apples} - \text{Apples used on Monday}$$

$$- \text{Apples used next day}$$

$$= \left(5 - 4 - \frac{1}{3}\right)$$

$$= \frac{15 - 12 - 1}{3} \qquad \text{[taking LCM]}$$

$$= \frac{2}{3}\,\text{kg}$$

Q. 20 The picture

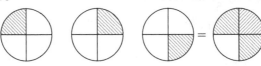

interprets

(a) $\dfrac{1}{4} \div 3$ (b) $3 \times \dfrac{1}{4}$ (c) $\dfrac{3}{4} \times 3$ (d) $3 \div \dfrac{1}{4}$

Sol. *(b)*

This interprets $\dfrac{1}{4}$ th part of a circle.

$\therefore$

  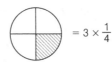

Hence, the whole picture represents $3 \times \dfrac{1}{4}$ i.e. $\dfrac{3}{4}$ th part

Fill in the Blanks

In questions 21 to 44, fill in the blanks to make the statements true.

Q. 21 Rani ate $\dfrac{2}{7}$ part of a cake while her brother Ravi ate $\dfrac{4}{5}$ of the remaining. Part of the cake left is _____.

Sol. Given, Rani ate $\dfrac{2}{7}$ part of the cake, then

Remaining part $= 1 - \dfrac{2}{7} = \dfrac{7-2}{7} = \dfrac{5}{7}$

Her brother ate $\dfrac{4}{5}$ of $\dfrac{5}{7} = \dfrac{4}{5} \times \dfrac{5}{7} = \dfrac{4}{7}$

So, remaining part of the cake $= \dfrac{5}{7} - \dfrac{4}{7} = \dfrac{5-4}{7} = \dfrac{1}{7}$

Hence, part of the cake left is $\dfrac{1}{7}$.

Q. 22 The reciprocal of $\dfrac{3}{7}$ is _____.

Sol. The reciprocal of $\dfrac{3}{7}$ is $\dfrac{7}{3}$.

> **Note** *The reciprocal of a non-zero fraction is obtained by interchanging its numerator and denominator.*

Q. 23 $\frac{2}{3}$ of 27 is __18__ .

Sol. Given, $\frac{2}{3}$ of $27 = \frac{2}{3} \times 27 = 18$

Hence, $\frac{2}{3}$ of 27 is **18.**

Q. 24 $\frac{4}{5}$ of 45 is __36__ .

Sol. Given, $\frac{4}{5}$ of $45 = \frac{4}{5} \times 45 = 4 \times 9$

$$= 36$$

Hence, $\frac{4}{5}$ of 45 is **36.**

Q. 25 $4 \times 6\frac{1}{3}$ is equal to __$25\frac{1}{3}$__ .

Sol. Given, $4 \times 6\frac{1}{3} = 4 \times \frac{(6 \times 3) + 1}{3} = 4 \times \frac{19}{3} = \frac{76}{3} = 25\frac{1}{3}$

Hence, $4 \times 6\frac{1}{3} = \mathbf{25\frac{1}{3}}$

Q. 26 $\frac{1}{2}$ of $4\frac{2}{7}$ is __$\frac{15}{7}$__ .

Sol. Given, $\frac{1}{2}$ of $4\frac{2}{7} = \frac{1}{2} \times \frac{(4 \times 7) + 2}{7}$

$$= \frac{1}{2} \times \frac{30}{7} = \frac{30}{14}$$

$$= \frac{15}{7}$$

Hence, $\frac{1}{2}$ of $4\frac{2}{7}$ is $\mathbf{\frac{15}{7}}$.

Q. 27 $\frac{1}{9}$ of $\frac{6}{5}$ is __$\frac{2}{15}$__ .

Sol. Given, $\frac{1}{9}$ of $\frac{6}{5} = \frac{1}{9} \times \frac{6}{5} = \frac{2}{15}$

Hence, $\frac{1}{9}$ of $\frac{6}{5}$ is $\mathbf{\frac{2}{15}}$.

Q. 28 The lowest form of the product $2\frac{3}{7} \times \frac{7}{9}$ is __$1\frac{8}{9}$__ .

Sol. Given, $2\frac{3}{7} \times \frac{7}{9} = \frac{(2 \times 7) + 3}{7} \times \frac{7}{9} = \frac{17}{7} \times \frac{7}{9} = \frac{17}{9}$

$$= 1\frac{8}{9}$$

Hence, the lowest form of the product $2\frac{3}{7} \times \frac{7}{9}$ is $\mathbf{\frac{17}{9}}$ or $\mathbf{1\frac{8}{9}}$.

Q. 29 $\dfrac{4}{5} \div 4$ is equal to _____ $\dfrac{1}{5}$.

Sol. Given, $\dfrac{4}{5} \div 4 = \dfrac{4}{5} \times \dfrac{1}{4} = \dfrac{1}{5}$ $\left[\because \text{reciprocal of } 4 = \dfrac{1}{4} \right]$

Hence, $\dfrac{4}{5} \div 4$ is equal to $\dfrac{1}{5}$.

Q. 30 $\dfrac{2}{5}$ of 25 is _____ 10 .

Sol. Given, $\dfrac{2}{5}$ of $25 = \dfrac{2}{5} \times 25 = 2 \times 5$

$= 10$

Hence, $\dfrac{2}{5}$ of 25 is **10**.

Q. 31 $\dfrac{1}{5} \div \dfrac{5}{6} = \dfrac{1}{5}$ ✗ $\dfrac{6}{5}$

Sol. Given, $\dfrac{1}{5} \div \dfrac{6}{5}$

$\therefore \dfrac{1}{5} \div \dfrac{5}{6} = \dfrac{1}{5} \times \dfrac{6}{5}$ $\left[\because \text{reciprocal of } \dfrac{5}{6} = \dfrac{6}{5} \right]$

Q. 32 $3.2 \times 10 =$ _____ 32 .

Sol. Given, $3.2 \times 10 = \dfrac{32}{10} \times 10 = 32$

Hence, $3.2 \times 10 = $ **32**

Q. 33 $25.4 \times 1000 =$ _____ 25400 .

Sol. Given, $25.4 \times 1000 = \dfrac{254}{10} \times 1000$

$= 25400$

Hence, $25.4 \times 1000 = $ **25400**

Q. 34 $93.5 \times 100 =$ _____ 9350 .

Sol. Given, $93.5 \times 100 = \dfrac{935}{10} \times 100$

$= 9350$

Hence, $93.5 \times 10 = $ **9350**

Q. 35 $4.7 \div 10 =$ _____ 0.47 .

Sol. Given, $4.7 \div 10 = \dfrac{47}{10} \times \dfrac{1}{10}$ $\left[\because \text{reciprocal of } 10 = \dfrac{1}{10} \right]$

$= \dfrac{47}{100} = 0.47$

Hence, $4.7 \div 10 = $ **0.47**

Q. 36 $4.7 \div 100 = \underline{0.047}$.

Sol. Given, $4.7 \div 100 = \dfrac{47}{10} \times \dfrac{1}{100}$ $\qquad\qquad\qquad \left[\because \text{reciprocal of } 100 = \dfrac{1}{100} \right]$

$$= \dfrac{47}{1000}$$

$$= 0.047$$

Hence, $4.7 \div 100 = \mathbf{0.047}$

Q. 37 $4.7 \div 1000 = \underline{0.0047}$.

Sol. Given, $4.7 \div 1000 = \dfrac{47}{10} \times \dfrac{1}{1000}$ $\qquad\qquad \left[\because \text{reciprocal of } 1000 = \dfrac{1}{1000} \right]$

$$= \dfrac{47}{10000}$$

$$= 0.0047$$

Hence, $4.7 \div 1000 = \mathbf{0.0047}$

Q. 38 The product of two proper fractions is _less_ than each of the fractions that are multiplied.

Sol. The product of two proper fractions is **less** than each of the fractions that are multiplied.

e.g. $\qquad \dfrac{1}{2} \times \dfrac{1}{3} = \dfrac{1}{6}$

$\therefore \qquad \dfrac{1}{6} < \dfrac{1}{2}$ and $\dfrac{1}{6} < \dfrac{1}{3}$

Q. 39 While dividing a fraction by another fraction, we _multiply_ the first fraction by the _reciprocal_ of the other fraction.

Sol. While dividing a fraction by another fraction, we **multiply** the first fraction by the **reciprocal** of the other fraction.

e.g. $4 \div \dfrac{1}{2} = 4 \times 2 = 8$ $\qquad\qquad\qquad \left[\because \text{reciprocal of } \dfrac{1}{2} = 2 \right]$

Q. 40 $8.4 \div \underline{\quad 4 \quad} = 2.1$

Sol. Let x be the missing number, then

$$8.4 \div x = 2.1$$

$\Rightarrow \qquad 8.4 \times \dfrac{1}{x} = 2.1$ $\qquad\qquad\qquad \left[\because \text{reciprocal of } x = \dfrac{1}{x} \right]$

$\Rightarrow \qquad 8.4 = 2.1\, x$ $\qquad\qquad\qquad\qquad$ [by cross-multiplication]

$\Rightarrow \qquad x = \dfrac{8.4}{2.1}$

$\Rightarrow x = \dfrac{84}{21} \times \dfrac{10}{10} = 4$

$\Rightarrow \qquad x = 4$

Hence, $8.4 \div 4 = 2.1$

Q. 41 $52.7 \div \underline{100} = 0.527$

Sol. Let x be the missing number, then $52.7 \div x = 0.527$

$$\Rightarrow \quad \frac{527}{10} \times \frac{1}{x} = \frac{527}{1000}$$

$\left[\because \text{reciprocal of } x = \frac{1}{x} \right]$

$$\Rightarrow \quad \frac{527}{10} \times \frac{1000}{527} = x$$

$$\Rightarrow \quad x = 100$$

Hence, $52.7 \div 100 = 0.527$

Q. 42 $0.5 \underline{\times} 0.7 = 0.35$

Sol. $\because \quad 0.5 = \frac{5}{10}$

and $0.7 = \frac{7}{10}$

$\therefore 0.5 \times 0.7 = \frac{5}{10} \times \frac{7}{10} = \frac{35}{100} = 0.35$

Hence, $0.5 \times 0.7 = 0.35$

Q. 43 $2 \underline{\times} \frac{5}{3} = \frac{10}{3}$

Sol. Since, on multiplying 2 by $\frac{5}{3}$, we get $\frac{10}{3}$.

Hence, $2 \times \frac{5}{3} = \frac{10}{3}$

Q. 44 $2.001 \div 0.003 = \underline{667}$

Sol. Given, $2.001 \div 0.003$

$\because \quad 2.001 = \frac{2001}{1000}$

and $\quad 0.003 = \frac{3}{1000}$

$\therefore \quad 2.001 \div 0.003 = \frac{2001}{1000} \div \frac{3}{1000} = \frac{2001}{1000} \times \frac{1000}{3}$

$\left[\because \text{reciprocal of } \frac{3}{1000} = \frac{1000}{3} \right]$

$= 667$

Hence, $2.001 \div 0.003 = 667$

True/False

In questions 45 to 54, state whether the statements are True or False.

Q. 45 The reciprocal of a proper fraction is a proper fraction.

Sol. *False*

The reciprocal of a proper fraction is always an improper fraction.

e.g. $\frac{5}{6} \longrightarrow$ Proper fraction

Its reciprocal is $\frac{6}{5}$, i.e. improper fraction.

Q. 46 The reciprocal of an improper fraction is an improper fraction. F

Sol. *False*

The reciprocal of an improper fraction is a proper fraction.

e.g. $\dfrac{7}{6} \longrightarrow$ Improper fraction

Its reciprocal is $\dfrac{6}{7}$, i.e. proper fraction.

Q. 47 Product of two fractions $= \dfrac{\text{Product of their denominators}}{\text{Product of their numerators}}$ F

Sol. *False*

Two fractions are multiplied by multiplying their numerators and denominators separately and writing the product as,

Product of two fractions $= \dfrac{\text{Product of their numerators}}{\text{Product of their denominators}}$

Q. 48 The product of two improper fractions are less than both the fractions. F

Sol. *False*

The product of two improper fractions are greater than both the fractions.

e.g. $\dfrac{3}{2} \times \dfrac{7}{4} = \dfrac{21}{8}$

Hence, $\dfrac{21}{8}$ is greater than both $\dfrac{3}{2}$ and $\dfrac{7}{4}$.

Q. 49 A reciprocal of a fraction, is obtained by inverting it upside down. T

Sol. *True*

Let $\dfrac{a}{b}$ be the fraction. Then, for obtaining its reciprocal, numerator and denominator are interchanged.

$\therefore$ Reciprocal of $\dfrac{a}{b} = \dfrac{b}{a}$

Q. 50 To multiply a decimal number by 1000, we move the decimal point in the number to the right by three places. T

Sol. *True*

e.g. $2.732 \times 1000 = 2732$ (moving the decimal to right by three places)

Q. 51 To divide a decimal number by 100, we move the decimal point in the number to the left by two places. T

Sol. *True*

e.g. $\dfrac{273.2}{100} = 2.732$ (moving decimal point to the left by two places)

Q. 52 1 is the only number which is its own reciprocal. T

Sol. *True*

For obtaining the reciprocal of a number, we simply interchange the numerator and denominator.

Hence, reciprocal of 1 will be $\frac{1}{1}$, i.e. 1.

Q. 53 $\frac{2}{3}$ of 8 is same as $\frac{2}{3} \div 8$. F

Sol. *False*

$$\frac{2}{3} \text{ of } 8 = \frac{2}{3} \times 8 = \frac{16}{3}$$

$$\frac{2}{3} \div 8 = \frac{2}{3} \times \frac{1}{8} = \frac{2}{24}$$

$$\therefore \quad \frac{2}{3} \text{ of } 8 \neq \frac{2}{3} \div 8$$

Hence, $\frac{2}{3}$ of 8 is not same as $\frac{2}{3} \div 8$.

Q. 54 The reciprocal of $\frac{4}{7}$ is $\frac{4}{7}$. F

Sol. *False*

Reciprocal of $\frac{4}{7}$ is $\frac{7}{4}$.

Q. 55 If 5 is added to both the numerator and the denominator of the fraction $\frac{5}{9}$, will the value of the fraction be changed? If so, will the value increase or decrease?

Sol. Given fraction = $\frac{5}{9}$

Now, adding 5 to numerator and denominator = $\frac{5+5}{9+5} = \frac{10}{14} = \frac{5}{7}$

Obviously, $\frac{5}{7} > \frac{5}{9}$

So, the value will increase.

Q. 56 What happens to the value of a fraction, if the denominator of the fraction is decreased while numerator is kept unchanged?

Sol. When the numerator is kept unchanged and the denominator of the fraction is decreased, the value of fraction would increase.

e.g. Fraction = $\frac{2}{3}$

New fraction = $\frac{2}{2}$

Obviously $\frac{2}{2} > \frac{2}{3}$ [$\because 1 > 0.66$]

Q. 57 Which letter comes $\frac{2}{5}$ of the way among A and J?

Sol. D

From A to J, there are 10 letters.

So, letter at $\frac{2}{5}$ place = $\left(\frac{2}{5} \times 10\right)$th letter = 4th letter = D

Q. 58 If $\frac{2}{3}$ of a number is 10, then what is 1.75 times of that number?

Sol. Let the number be x.

According to the question, $\frac{2}{3}$ of $x = 10$ $\Rightarrow$ $\frac{2}{3} \times x = 10$

On multiplying both sides by $\frac{3}{2}$, we get

$$\frac{2}{3} \times x \times \frac{3}{2} = 10 \times \frac{3}{2} \quad \Rightarrow \quad x = 5 \times 3 \quad \Rightarrow \quad x = 15$$

1.75 times of 15 = 1.75 of 15 = 1.75 × 15 = $\frac{175}{100} \times 15 = \frac{2625}{100} = 26.25$

Q. 59 In a class of 40 students, $\frac{1}{5}$ of the total number of students like to eat rice only, $\frac{2}{5}$ of the total number of students like to eat chapati only and the remaining students like to eat both. What fraction of the total number of students like to eat both?

Sol. Total number of students = 40   [given]

Students who eat rice only = $\frac{1}{5}$ of total students = $\frac{1}{5} \times 40 = 8$

Students who eat chapati only = $\frac{2}{5}$ of total students

$$= \frac{2}{5} \times 40 = 16$$

∴ Students who eat both chapati and rice

= Total number of students − (Students who eat rice only
+ Students who eat chapati only)

= 40 − (8 + 16)

= 40 − 24 = 16

∴ Fraction of students who eat both chapati and rice

$$= \frac{\text{Number of students eat both chapati and rice}}{\text{Total number of students}}$$

$$= \frac{16}{40}$$

$$= \frac{2}{5}$$

Q. 60 Renu completed $\frac{2}{3}$ part of her home work in 2 hours. How much part of her home work had she completed in $1\frac{1}{4}$ hours?

Sol. The part of the work finished by Renu in 2 h $= \frac{2}{3}$

So, the part of the work finished by Renu in 1 h $= \frac{2}{3} \times \frac{1}{2} = \frac{1}{3}$

∴ The part of the work finished by Renu in $1\frac{1}{4}$ h $= \frac{1}{3} \times 1\frac{1}{4}$

$$= \frac{1}{3} \times \frac{(1 \times 4) + 1}{4}$$

$$= \frac{1}{3} \times \frac{5}{4} = \frac{5}{12} \text{ part}$$

Hence, $\frac{5}{12}$ part of Renu's home work is completed by her in $1\frac{1}{4}$ h.

Q. 61 Reemu read $\frac{1}{5}$ th pages of a book. If she reads further 40 pages, she would have read $\frac{7}{10}$ th pages of the book. How many pages are left to be read?

Sol. Let total pages of the book be x.

According to the question, $\frac{1}{5}x + 40 = \frac{7}{10}x$

$\Rightarrow$ $\qquad 40 = \frac{7}{10}x - \frac{1}{5}x = \frac{7x - 2x}{10}$

$\Rightarrow$ $\qquad 40 = \frac{5x}{10}$

$\Rightarrow$ $\qquad x = \frac{400}{5} = 80$

∴ Total pages of a book = 80

Hence, pages left to be read = Total pages of a book $- \left(\frac{7}{10}x \right)$

$$= 80 - \frac{7}{10} \times 80$$

$$= 80 - 56 = 24 \text{ pages}$$

Q. 62 Write the number in the box $\square$, such that $\frac{3}{7} \times \square = \frac{15}{98}$.

Sol. Let the missing number be x.

Then, $\qquad \frac{3}{7} \times x = \frac{15}{98}$

$\Rightarrow$ $\qquad x = \frac{15}{98} \div \frac{3}{7} = \frac{15}{98} \times \frac{7}{3}$ $\qquad \left[\because \text{reciprocal of } \frac{3}{7} = \frac{7}{3} \right]$

$$x = \frac{5}{14}$$

Hence, $\qquad \frac{3}{7} \times \boxed{\frac{5}{14}} = \frac{15}{98}$

Q. 63 Will the quotient $7\frac{1}{6} \div 3\frac{2}{3}$ be a fraction greater than 1.5 or less than 1.5? Explain.

Sol. Yes,

Given, $7\frac{1}{6} \div 3\frac{2}{3} = \frac{(7 \times 6) + 1}{6} \div \frac{(3 \times 3) + 2}{3}$

$= \frac{42 + 1}{6} \div \frac{9 + 2}{3} = \frac{43}{6} \div \frac{11}{3}$

$= \frac{43}{6} \times \frac{3}{11}$ $\left[\because \text{reciprocal of } \frac{11}{3} = \frac{3}{11}\right]$

$= \frac{43}{22} = 1.95$

Obviously, $1.95 > 1.5$

Hence, $7\frac{1}{6} \div 3\frac{2}{3} > 1.5$

Q. 64 Describe two methods to compare $\frac{13}{17}$ and 0.82. Which do you think is easier and why?

Sol.   **Method I** Convert both into decimals

$$\frac{13}{17} = 0.76$$

$\therefore$ $0.76 < 0.82$

Hence, $\frac{13}{17} < 0.82$

Method II Convert both into fractions

$$0.82 = \frac{82}{100} = \frac{41}{50}$$

Now, compare $\frac{13}{17}$ and $\frac{41}{50}$.

To compare these fractions, we have to make the denominator same,

$\therefore$ $\frac{13}{17} = \frac{13}{17} \times \frac{50}{50} = \frac{650}{850}$

$\frac{41}{50} = \frac{41}{50} \times \frac{17}{17} = \frac{697}{850}$

$\therefore$ $\frac{697}{850} > \frac{650}{850}$

Hence, $\frac{13}{17} < 0.82$

Conclusion Method II is easier.

Q. 65 Health: The directions for a pain reliever recommend that an adult of 60 kg and overtake 4 tablets every 4 hours as needed, and an adult who weighs between 40 kg and 50 kg take only $2\frac{1}{2}$ tablets every 4 hours as needed. Each tablet weighs $\frac{4}{25}$ gram.

(a) If a 72 kg adult takes 4 tablets, how many grams of pain reliever is he or she receiving?

(b) How many grams of pain reliever is recommended dose for an adult weighing 46 kg?

Sol. (a) Given, 72 kg adult takes 4 tablets and each tablet weighs $\dfrac{4}{25}$ g.

∴ Total weight of pain reliever, he/she is receiving

$$= 4 \times \frac{4}{25} \, g = \frac{16}{25} \, g$$

(b) Given, Adult weighing 46 kg takes $2\dfrac{1}{2}$ tablets and each tablet weighs $\dfrac{4}{25}$ g.

∴ Total weight of pain reliever, he/she is receiving

$$= \left(\frac{4}{25} \times 2\frac{1}{2} \right) g = \left[\frac{4}{25} \times \frac{(2 \times 2) + 1}{2} \right] g$$

$$= \left(\frac{4}{25} \times \frac{5}{2} \right) g$$

$$= \frac{2}{5} \, g$$

Q. 66 Animals: The label on a bottle of pet vitamins lists dosage guidelines. What dosage would you give to each of these animals?

(a) a 18 kg adult dog   (b) a 6 kg cat

(c) a 18 kg pregnant dog

• **Do Good Pet Vitamins**

• Adult dogs:

$\dfrac{1}{2}$ tsp (tea spoon full) per 9 kg body weight

• Puppies, pregnant dogs, or nursing dogs:

$\dfrac{1}{2}$ tsp per 4.5 kg body weight

• Cats:

$\dfrac{1}{4}$ tsp per 1 kg body weight

Sol. (a) Dosage prescribed for a adult dog is $\dfrac{1}{2}$ tsp per 9 kg body weight.

$$\therefore \text{ For a 18 kg adult dog, dosage} = \frac{\left(\dfrac{1}{2}\right)}{9} \times 18 = \frac{1}{2 \times 9} \times 18$$

$$= \frac{1}{18} \times 18 = 1 \text{ tsp}$$

(b) Dosage prescribed for a cat is $\dfrac{1}{4}$ tsp per 1 kg body weight.

$$\therefore \text{ For a 6 kg cat, dosage} = \frac{\left(\dfrac{1}{4}\right)}{1} \times 6 = \frac{1}{4} \times 6 \text{ tsp}$$

$$= \frac{6}{4} = \frac{3}{2} \text{ tsp}$$

$$= 1\frac{1}{2} \text{ tsp}$$

(c) Dosage prescribed for pregnant dog is $\dfrac{1}{2}$ tsp per 4.5 kg body weight.

$$\therefore \text{For a 18 kg pregnant dog, dosage} = \frac{\left(\dfrac{1}{2}\right)}{4.5} \times 18$$

$$= \frac{1}{2 \times 4.5} \times 18 = \frac{1}{9} \times 18$$

$$= \frac{18}{9} \text{ tsp} = 2 \text{ tsp}$$

Q. 67 How many $\dfrac{1}{16}$ kg boxes of chocolates can be made with $1\dfrac{1}{2}$ kg chocolates?

Sol. Total chocolates $= 1\dfrac{1}{2}$ kg $= \dfrac{(1 \times 2) + 1}{2} = \dfrac{3}{2}$ kg

$\therefore$ Number of boxes of chocolates of $\dfrac{1}{16} = \dfrac{\text{Total chocolates}}{\text{Weight of 1 box}} = \left(\dfrac{3}{2} \div \dfrac{1}{16}\right)$

$$= \frac{3}{2} \times 16 \qquad\qquad [\because \text{reciprocal of } \tfrac{1}{16} = 16]$$

$$= 3 \times 8$$

$$= 24$$

Q. 68 Anvi is making bookmarker like the one shown in the given figure. How many bookmarker can she make from a 15 m long ribbon?

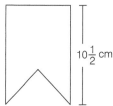

$10\frac{1}{2}$ cm

Sol. Height of one bookmarker $= 10\dfrac{1}{2}$ cm

$$= \frac{(10 \times 2) + 1}{2} = \frac{21}{2} \text{ cm}$$

Length of ribbon $= 15$ m $= 1500$ cm

∴ Number of bookmarkers $= \dfrac{\text{Length of ribbon}}{\text{Height of one bookmarker}}$ \hfill $[\because 1\text{m} = 100 \text{ cm}]$

$$= \frac{1500}{\dfrac{21}{2}}$$

$$= \frac{1500}{21} \times 2$$

$$= 142.85 \approx 142$$

Hence, 142 bookmarkers can be made from a 15 m long ribbon.

Q. 69 A rule for finding the approximate length of diagonal of a square is to multiply the length of a side of the square by 1.414.

Find the length of the diagonal when:

(a) the length of a side of the square is 8.3 cm.

(b) the length of a side of the square is exactly 7.875 cm.

Sol. (a) Side of square $= 8.3$ cm

∴ Length of diagonal $=$ Length of side of the square $\times$ 1.414

$$= 8.3 \times 1.414$$

$$= 11.7362$$

$$= 11.74 \text{ cm (approx.)}$$

(b) Side of square $= 7.875$ cm

∴ Length of diagonal $=$ Length of side of the square $\times$ 1.414

$$= 7.875 \times 1.414$$

$$= 11.13525$$

$$= 11.14 \text{ cm (approx.)}$$

Q. 70 The largest square that can be drawn in a circle has a side whose length is 0.707 times the diameter of the circle. By this rule, find the length of the side of such a square, when the diameter of the circle is

(a) 14.35 cm   (b) 8.63 cm

Sol. Given,

Side of square $= 0.707 \times$ Diameter of circle

(a) We have,

Diameter of circle $= 14.35$ cm

∴ Side of square $= 0.707 \times 14.35$

$$= 10.15 \text{ cm}$$

(b) We have,

Diameter of circle $= 8.63$ cm

∴ Side of square $= 0.707 \times 8.63$

$$= 6.10 \text{ cm}$$

Q. 71 To find the distance around a circular disc, multiply the diameter of the disc by 3.14.

What is the distance around the disc, when
(a) the diameter is 18.7cm?
(b) the radius is 6.45cm?

Sol. Given,

Distance around a circular disc = Diameter of disc × 3.14

(a) Diameter of disc = 18.7 cm

Distance around a circular disc = 18.7 × 3.14

= 58.718 cm

(b) Radius of disc = 6.45 cm

Diameter of disc = 2× Radius of disc = 2 × 6.45 = 12.9 cm

Distance around a circular disc = 12.9 × 3.14

= 40.506 cm

Q. 72 What is the cost of 27.5 m of cloth at ₹ 53.50 per metre?

Sol. By unitary method,

Cost of 1 m of cloth = ₹ 53.50

Cost of 27.5 m of cloth = ₹ (53.50 × 27.5)

$$= ₹ \left(\frac{5350}{100} \times \frac{275}{10} \right) = ₹ \left(\frac{1471250}{1000} \right)$$

= ₹ 1471.25

Q. 73 In a hurdle race, Nidhi is over hurdle B and $\frac{2}{6}$ of the way through the race, as shown in the given figure.

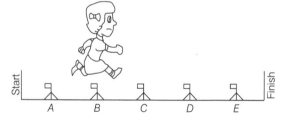

Then, answer the following:

(a) Where will Nidhi be, when she is $\frac{4}{6}$ of the way through the race?

(b) Where will Nidhi be, when she is $\frac{5}{6}$ of the way through the race?

(c) Give two fractions to tell what part of the race Nidhi has finished, when she is over hurdle C.

Sol. Since, if Nidhi is at B, then $\frac{2}{6}$ of the way is completed.

$\therefore$ If she is at A, she will cover $= \dfrac{\left(\frac{2}{6}\right)}{2} \times 1 = \dfrac{2}{6 \times 2}$

$= \dfrac{1}{6}$ way

(a) When she is $\frac{4}{6}$ of the way, she will be at $\dfrac{\left(\frac{4}{6}\right)}{\left(\frac{1}{6}\right)}$ position

$= \left(\dfrac{4}{6} \times \dfrac{6}{1}\right)$ $\left[\because \text{reciprocal of } \dfrac{1}{6} = 6\right]$

$= 4\text{th position}$

$= D$

(b) When she is $\frac{5}{6}$ of the way, she will be at $\dfrac{\left(\frac{5}{6}\right)}{\left(\frac{1}{6}\right)}$ position

$= \dfrac{5}{6} \times \dfrac{6}{1} = 5\text{th position}$

$= E$

(c) When she is over hurdle C, she has completed half race. Hence, she will be at $\frac{3}{6}$ way

$= \dfrac{3}{6} = \dfrac{1}{2}$ way

Q. 74 Diameter of Earth is 12756000 m. In 1996, a new planet was discovered, whose diameter is $\dfrac{5}{86}$ of the diameter of Earth. Find the diameter of this planet in km.

Sol. Given, diameter of Earth $= 12756000\,\text{m} = \dfrac{12756000}{1000} = 12756\,\text{km}$

According to the question,

Diameter of new planet $= \dfrac{5}{86}$ of diameter of Earth

$= \dfrac{5}{86} \times 12756 = \dfrac{63780}{86}$

$= 741.62\,\text{km}$

Q. 75 What is the product of $\dfrac{5}{129}$ and its reciprocal?

Sol. $\because$ Reciprocal of $\dfrac{5}{129} = \dfrac{129}{5}$

$\therefore$ Product of $\dfrac{5}{129}$ and its reciprocal

$= \dfrac{5}{129} \times \dfrac{129}{5} = 1$

Note *Product of any number and its reciprocal is always 1.*

Q. 76 Simplify: $\dfrac{2\dfrac{1}{2}+\dfrac{1}{5}}{2\dfrac{1}{2}\div\dfrac{1}{5}}$

Sol. Given, $\dfrac{2\dfrac{1}{2}+\dfrac{1}{5}}{2\dfrac{1}{2}\div\dfrac{1}{5}} = \dfrac{\dfrac{(2\times2)+1}{2}+\dfrac{1}{5}}{\dfrac{(2\times2)+1}{2}\div\dfrac{1}{5}}$

$= \dfrac{\dfrac{5}{2}+\dfrac{1}{5}}{\dfrac{5}{2}\div\dfrac{1}{5}} = \dfrac{\dfrac{25+2}{10}}{\dfrac{5}{2}\times 5}$ $\left[\because \text{reciprocal of } \dfrac{1}{5}=5\right]$

$= \dfrac{\dfrac{27}{10}}{\dfrac{25}{2}} = \dfrac{27}{10}\times\dfrac{2}{25}$ $\left[\because \text{reciprocal of } \dfrac{25}{2}=\dfrac{2}{25}\right]$

$= \dfrac{27}{125}$

Q. 77 Simplify: $\dfrac{\dfrac{1}{4}+\dfrac{1}{5}}{1-\dfrac{3}{8}\times\dfrac{3}{5}}$

Sol. Given, $\dfrac{\dfrac{1}{4}+\dfrac{1}{5}}{1-\dfrac{3}{8}\times\dfrac{3}{5}} = \dfrac{\dfrac{5+4}{20}}{1-\dfrac{9}{40}}$

$= \dfrac{\dfrac{9}{20}}{\dfrac{40-9}{40}}$

$= \dfrac{\dfrac{9}{20}}{\dfrac{31}{40}} = \dfrac{9}{20}\times\dfrac{40}{31}$ $\left[\because \text{reciprocal of } \dfrac{31}{40}=\dfrac{40}{31}\right]$

$= \dfrac{18}{31}$

Q. 78 Divide $\dfrac{3}{10}$ by $\left(\dfrac{1}{4}\text{ of }\dfrac{3}{5}\right)$.

Sol. Given, $\dfrac{3}{10}\div\left(\dfrac{1}{4}\text{ of }\dfrac{3}{5}\right) = \dfrac{3}{10}\div\left(\dfrac{1}{4}\times\dfrac{3}{5}\right)$

$= \dfrac{3}{10}\div\left(\dfrac{3}{20}\right)$

$= \dfrac{3}{10}\times\dfrac{20}{3}$ $\left[\because \text{reciprocal of } \dfrac{3}{20}=\dfrac{20}{3}\right]$

$= 2$

Q. 79 $\frac{1}{8}$ of a number equals $\frac{2}{5} \div \frac{1}{20}$. What is the number?

Sol. Let the number be x.

Then, $\frac{1}{8}$ of a number $= \frac{2}{5} \div \frac{1}{20}$ [given]

$\Rightarrow$ $\frac{1}{8} \times x = \frac{2}{5} \times 20$ $\left[\because \text{reciprocal of } \frac{1}{20} = 20 \right]$

$\Rightarrow$ $\frac{x}{8} = 8$

$\Rightarrow$ $x = 8 \times 8$

$\Rightarrow$ $x = 64$

Hence, the number is 64.

Q. 80 Heena's father paid an electric bill of ₹ 385.70 out of a ₹ 500 note. How much change should he have received?

Sol. Given, total rupees = ₹ 500

and money paid = ₹ 385.70

∴ Change he received = ₹ (500 − 385.70) = ₹ 114.30

Q. 81 The normal body temperature is 98.6°F. When Savitri was ill, her temperature rose to 103.1°F. How many degrees above normal was that?

Sol. Given, normal body temperature = 98.6° F

and temperature rise to = 103.1° F

∴ Rise in temperature = (103.1 − 98.6)° F

= 4.5° F

Q. 82 Meteorology One measure of average global temperature shows how each year varies from a base measure. The table shows results for several years.

Year	1958	1964	1965	1978	2002
Difference from base	0.10°C	−0.17°C	−0.10°C	$\left(\frac{1}{50}\right)^{\circ}$ C	0.54°C

See the table and answer the following:

(a) Order the five years from coldest to warmest.

(b) In 1946, the average temperature varied by −0.03°C from the base measure. Between which two years should 1946 fall, when the years are ordered from coldest to warmest?

Sol. In year 1978, temperature is $\left(\frac{1}{50}\right)^{\circ}$ C = 0.02°C

(a) By observing coldest to warmest order is ascending order.

∴ − 0.17°C < − 0.10°C < 0.02°C < 0.10°C < 0.54°C

Order of years is

1964 < 1965 < 1978 < 1958 < 2002

(b) In 1946, temperature is – 0.03°C.

We know that, – 0.03°C lies between – 0.10°C and $\left(\dfrac{1}{50}\right)^{\circ}$ C or 0.02° C

∴ – 0.10°C < – 0.03° C < 0.02° C

Hence, the coldest to warmest order including 1946 is

1964 < 1965 < 1946 < 1978 < 1958 < 2002.

Science Application

Q. 83 In her Science class, Jyoti learned that the atomic weight of Helium is 4.0030; of Hydrogen is 1.0080; and of Oxygen is 16.0000. Find the difference between the atomic weights of:

(a) Oxygen and Hydrogen
(b) Oxygen and Helium
(c) Helium and Hydrogen.

Sol. Given, atomic weight of Helium = 4.0030, Hydrogen = 1.0080

and Oxygen = 16.0000

(a) Difference between atomic weights of Oxygen and Hydrogen

$$\begin{array}{r} 16.0000 \\ -\ 01.0080 \\ \hline 14.9920 \end{array}$$

(b) Difference between atomic weights of Oxygen and Helium

$$\begin{array}{r} 16.0000 \\ -\ 04.0030 \\ \hline 11.9970 \end{array}$$

(c) Difference between atomic weights of Helium and Hydrogen

$$\begin{array}{r} 4.0030 \\ -\ 1.0080 \\ \hline 2.9950 \end{array}$$

Q. 84 Measurement made in Science lab must be as accurate as possible. Ravi measured the length of an iron rod and said, it was 19.34 cm long; Kamal said 19.25 cm; and Tabish said 19.27 cm. The correct length was 19.33 cm. How much of error was made by each of the boys?

Sol. The actual length of an iron rod = 19.33 cm

Measured Ravi = 19.34 cm

Error = Measured value – Actual value

= (19.34 – 19.33) cm = 0.01 cm

Kamal measured = 19.25 cm

Error = (19.25 – 19.33) cm = – 0.08 cm

Tabish measured = 19.27 cm

Error = (19.27 – 19.33) cm = – 0.06 cm

Q. 85 When 0.02964 is divided by 0.004, what will be the quotient?

Sol. Given, $0.02964 \div 0.004 = \dfrac{\dfrac{2964}{100000}}{\div} \dfrac{\dfrac{4}{1000}}{}$

$$= \dfrac{2964}{100000} \times \dfrac{1000}{4} \qquad \left[\because \text{reciprocal of } \dfrac{4}{1000} = \dfrac{1000}{4}\right]$$

$$= \dfrac{741}{100} = 7.41$$

Q. 86 What number divided by 520 gives the same quotient as 85 divided by 0.625?

Sol. Let the number be x.

According to the question, $\dfrac{x}{520} = \dfrac{85}{0.625}$

$\Rightarrow \qquad\qquad x = \dfrac{85 \times 520 \times 1000}{625} = \dfrac{44200000}{625}$ [by corss-multiplication]

$\Rightarrow \qquad\qquad x = 70720$

Hence, the number is 70720.

Q. 87 A floor is 4.5 m long and 3.6 m wide. A 6 cm square tile costs ₹ 23.25. What will be the cost to cover the floor with these tiles?

Sol. Length of floor = 4.5 m and width of floor = 3.6 m

Area of floor = Length × Breadth = 4.5×3.6 m^2 [∵ width = breadth = 3.6 m]

Side of square tile = 6 cm = $\dfrac{6}{100}$ = 0.06 m

Area of one tile = (Side)^2 = 0.06×0.06 m^2

Number of tiles = $\dfrac{\text{Area of floor}}{\text{Area of one tile}} = \dfrac{4.5 \times 3.6}{0.06 \times 0.06} = 4500$

∵ Cost of 1 tile = ₹ 23.25

∴ Cost of 4500 tiles = ₹ 23.25 × 4500 = ₹ 104625

Hence, ₹ 104625 are required to cover the floor with tiles.

Q. 88 Sunita and Rehana want to make dresses for their dolls. Sunita has $\dfrac{3}{4}$ m of cloth and she gave $\dfrac{1}{3}$ of it to Rehana. How much did Rehana have?

Sol. Given, Sunita has $\dfrac{3}{4}$ m of cloth.

∴ She gave cloth to Rehana = $\dfrac{1}{3}$ of $\dfrac{3}{4} = \dfrac{1}{3} \times \dfrac{3}{4}$

$$= \dfrac{1}{4} \text{ m}$$

Hence, Rehana has $\dfrac{1}{4}$ m of cloth.

Q. 89 A flower garden is 22.50 m long. Sheela wants to make a border along one side using bricks that are 0.25 m long. How many bricks will be needed?

Sol. Length of flower garden = 22.50 m

Length one of brick = 0.25 m

Number of bricks used in one side

$$= \frac{\text{Length of flower garden}}{\text{Length of a brick}} = \frac{22.50}{0.25} = \frac{2250}{25} = 90$$

Hence, 90 bricks will be needed.

Q. 90 How much cloth will be used in making 6 shirts, if each required $2\frac{1}{4}$ m of cloth, allowing $\frac{1}{8}$ m for waste in cutting and finishing in each shirt?

Sol. Cloth required in making one shirt

$$= \left(2\frac{1}{4} + \frac{1}{8}\right) = \frac{(2 \times 4) + 1}{4} + \frac{1}{8}$$

$$= \frac{9}{4} + \frac{1}{8} = \frac{18 + 1}{8} \qquad [\because \text{LCM of 4 and 8} = 8]$$

$$= \frac{19}{8} \text{ m}$$

∴ Total cloth required in making such 6 shirts = 6 × Cloth required in one shirt

$$= 6 \times \frac{19}{8} = \frac{114}{8} = \frac{57}{4} = 14\frac{1}{4} \text{ m}$$

Hence, $14\frac{1}{4}$ m cloth will be used in making 6 shirts.

Q. 91 A picture hall has seats for 820 persons. At a recent film show, one usher guessed it was $\frac{3}{4}$ full, another that it was $\frac{2}{3}$ full. The ticket office reported 648 sales. Which usher (first or second) made the better guess?

Sol. Given, picture hall has seats = 820

One usher guessed, picture hall was $\frac{3}{4}$ full.

∴ $\frac{3}{4}$ of 820 = $\frac{3}{4} \times 820 = \frac{3 \times 820}{4} = \frac{2460}{4} = 615$

Another usher guessed, picture hall was $\frac{2}{3}$ full.

∴ $\frac{2}{3}$ of 820 = $\frac{2}{3} \times 820 = \frac{2 \times 820}{3} = \frac{1640}{3} = 546.66$

Since, 648 tickets are sold that is near to 615.

So, first usher guess was better.

Note *In many situations, we solve our problems by approximation or guessing.*

Q. 92 For the celebrating children's day, students of Class VII bought sweets for ₹740.25 and cold drink for ₹70. If 35 students contributed equally what amount was contributed by each student?

Sol. Cost of sweets = ₹ 740.25

Cost of cold drink = ₹ 70

Total cost = ₹ (740.25 + 70) = ₹ 810.25

Given that, 35 students are contributing equally.

∴ Amount contributed by each student

$$= ₹\frac{810.25}{35} = ₹\frac{81025}{35 \times 100} = ₹\frac{2315}{100}$$

$$= ₹23.15$$

Hence, each student contributed ₹ 23.15.

Q. 93 The time taken by Rohan in five different races to run a distance of 500 m was 3.20 minutes, 3.37 minutes, 3.29 minutes, 3.17 minutes and 3.32 minutes. Find the average time taken by him in the races.

Sol. Total time taken by Rohan in five races

$$= (3.20 + 3.37 + 3.29 + 3.17 + 3.32)$$

$$= 16.35 \text{ min}$$

∴ Average time taken by Rohan

$$= \frac{\text{Total time taken}}{\text{Total number of observations}} = \frac{\text{Total time taken}}{5} = \frac{16.35}{5} = \frac{1635}{5 \times 100} = \frac{327}{100} = 3.27 \text{ min}$$

Q. 94 A public sewer line is being installed along $80\frac{1}{4}$ m of road. The supervisor says that the labourers will be able to complete 7.5 m in one day. How long will the project take to complete?

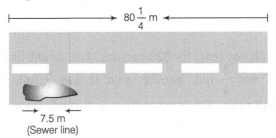

$80\frac{1}{4}$ m

7.5 m
(Sewer line)

Sol. Total sewer line to be installed $= 80\frac{1}{4}$ m $= \frac{(80 \times 4) + 1}{4} = \frac{321}{4}$ m

In one day labourers can complete = 7.5 m

∴ Number of days to complete the project

$$= \frac{\text{Total sewer line to be installed}}{\text{One day work}} = \frac{\left(\frac{321}{4}\right)}{7.5}$$

$$= \frac{321}{4 \times 7.5} = \frac{312}{30}$$

$$= 10.4 \text{ days} \approx 11 \text{ days}.$$

∴ Hence, the number of days to complete the project will be 11 days.

Q. 95 The weight of an object on Moon is $\dfrac{1}{6}$ its weight on Earth. If an object weighs $5\dfrac{3}{5}$ kg on Earth, how much would it weigh on the Moon?

Sol. Weight of an object on the Moon is $\dfrac{1}{6}$ of its weight on Earth.

Object weighs on Earth $= 5\dfrac{3}{5}$ kg $= \dfrac{(5\times5)+3}{5} = \dfrac{28}{5}$ kg

Weight on Moon $= \dfrac{1}{6}$ of $\dfrac{28}{5}$ kg

$\qquad = \dfrac{1}{6}\times\dfrac{28}{5} = \dfrac{28}{30} = \dfrac{14}{15} = 0.93$ kg

Hence, the weigh of an object on the Moon is 0.93 kg.

Q. 96 In a survey, 200 students were asked what influenced them most to buy their latest CD. The results are shown in the circle graph.

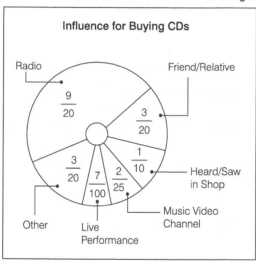

(a) How many students said radio influenced them most?

(b) How many students were influenced by radio than by a music video channel?

(c) How many said a friend or relative influenced them or they heard the CD in a shop?

Sol (a) Fraction of radio (in figure) $= \dfrac{9}{20}$

Total number of students $= 200$

$\therefore$ Number of students influenced by radio the most $\dfrac{9}{20}$ of 200 $= \dfrac{9}{20}\times200$

$\qquad\qquad\qquad\qquad\qquad\qquad\qquad\qquad = 90$

(b) We have to find,

(Students influenced by radio) − (Students influenced by music video channel)

$$= \text{(Fraction of radio} \times \text{Total number of students)}$$
$$- \text{(Fraction of music video channel} \times \text{Total number of students)}$$
$$= \frac{9}{20} \text{ of } 200 - \frac{2}{25} \text{ of } 200$$
$$= \frac{9}{20} \times 200 - \frac{2}{25} \times 200$$
$$= 90 - 16$$
$$= 74$$

Hence, 74 more students were influenced by radio than by a music video channel.

(c) We have to find,

(Students who influenced by a friend or relative) + (Students who influenced by hearing song in shop)

$$= \frac{3}{20} \text{ of } 200 + \frac{1}{10} \text{ of } 200$$
$$= \frac{3}{20} \times 200 + \frac{1}{10} \times 200$$
$$= 30 + 20 = 50$$

Q. 97 In the morning, a milkman filled $5\frac{1}{2}$ L of milk in his can. He sold to Renu, Kamla and Renuka $\frac{3}{4}$ L each; to Shadma he sold $\frac{7}{8}$ L; and to Jassi he gave $1\frac{1}{2}$ L. How much milk is left in the can?

Sol. Given, milk in can $= 5\frac{1}{2}$ L

$$= \frac{(5 \times 2)+1}{2} = \frac{10+1}{2} = \frac{11}{2} \text{ L}$$

If $\frac{3}{4}$ L sold to Renu, Kamla and Renuka.

Then, total milk sold $= \frac{3}{4} + \frac{3}{4} + \frac{3}{4} = \frac{3+3+3}{4} = \frac{9}{4}$ L

Milk sold to Shadma $= \frac{7}{8}$ L

Milk sold to Jassi $= 1\frac{1}{2}$ L $= \frac{(1 \times 2)+1}{2} = \frac{3}{2}$ L

Total milk sold $= \frac{9}{4} + \frac{7}{8} + \frac{3}{2} = \frac{18+7+12}{8} = \frac{37}{2}$ L

∴ Total milk left in can $= \frac{11}{2} - \left(\frac{37}{8}\right) = \frac{44-37}{8} = \frac{7}{8}$ L   [∵ LCM of 2 and 8 = 8]

Hence, $\frac{7}{8}$ L milk is left in the can.

Q. 98 Anuradha can do a piece of work in 6hours. What part of the work can she do in 1hour, in 5hours and in 6hours?

Sol. It is given that, Anuradha can do a piece of work in 6 h.

In other words,

In 6 h, Anuradha can do = Complete the work

In 1 h, Anuradha can do $= \dfrac{1}{6}$ part of work

In 5 h, Anuradha can do $= \dfrac{1}{6} \times 5 = \dfrac{5}{6}$ part of work

Q. 99 What portion of a 'saree' can Rehana paint in 1 hour, if it requires 5hours to paint the whole saree? In $4\dfrac{3}{5}$ hours? In $3\dfrac{1}{2}$ hours?

Sol. In 5 h, Rehana paints = Whole saree

In 1 h, she paints $= \dfrac{1}{5}$ part of saree

In $4\dfrac{3}{5}$ h, she paints $= \dfrac{1}{5} \times 4\dfrac{3}{5} = \dfrac{1}{5} \times \dfrac{(5 \times 4) + 3}{5} = \dfrac{1}{5} \times \dfrac{23}{5}$

$= \dfrac{23}{25}$ part of saree

In $3\dfrac{1}{2}$ h, she paints $= \dfrac{1}{5} \times 3\dfrac{1}{2} = \dfrac{1}{5} \times \dfrac{(3\times2)+1}{2}$

$= \dfrac{1}{5} \times \dfrac{7}{2} = \dfrac{7}{10}$ part of saree

Q. 100 Rama has $6\dfrac{1}{4}$ kg of cotton wool for making pillows. If one pillow takes $1\dfrac{1}{4}$ kg, how many pillows can she make?

Sol. Given, Rama has $6\dfrac{1}{4}$ kg of cotton for making pillows

i.e. $6\dfrac{1}{4}$ kg $= \dfrac{(6 \times 4) + 1}{4} = \dfrac{24 + 1}{4} = \dfrac{25}{4}$ kg

where, one pillow can be made from $1\dfrac{1}{4}$ kg

i.e. $1\dfrac{1}{4}$ kg $= \dfrac{(1 \times 4) + 1}{4} = \dfrac{4 + 1}{4} = \dfrac{5}{4}$ kg

∴ Number of pillows $= \dfrac{\text{Total quantity of cotton available}}{\text{Cotton used in one pillow}}$

$= \dfrac{\left(\dfrac{25}{4}\right)}{\left(\dfrac{5}{4}\right)} = \dfrac{25}{4} \times \dfrac{4}{5} = \dfrac{25}{5} = 5$ [∵ division is reverse of the multiplication]

Hence, Rama can make 5 pillows.

Q. 101 It takes $2\frac{1}{3}$ m of cloth to make a shirt. How many shirts can Radhika make from a piece of cloth $9\frac{1}{3}$ m long?

Sol. Given, Radhika takes $2\frac{1}{3}$ m of cloth to make a shirt

i.e. $2\frac{1}{3}$ m $= \frac{(2 \times 3)+1}{3} = \frac{6+1}{3} = \frac{7}{3}$ m

If Radhika has $9\frac{1}{3}$ m long cloth

i.e $9\frac{1}{3}$ m $= \frac{(9 \times 3)+1}{3} = \frac{27+1}{3} = \frac{28}{3}$ m

Then, number of shirts that can be made $= \dfrac{\text{Available cloth}}{\text{Required cloth to make one shirt}}$

$= \dfrac{28/3}{7/3} = \dfrac{28}{3} \times \dfrac{3}{7}$ [∵ division is reverse of the multiplication]

$= \dfrac{28}{7} = 4$

Hence, Radhika can make 4 shirts from available piece of cloth.

Q. 102 Ravi can walk $3\frac{1}{3}$ km in one hour. How long will it take him to walk to his office which is 10 km from his home?

Sol. Given, Ravi can walk $3\frac{1}{3}$ km in 1 h.

∴ Ravi's speed $= 3\frac{1}{3}$ km/h $= \dfrac{(3 \times 3)+1}{3}$ $\left[\because \text{speed} = \dfrac{\text{distance}}{\text{time}} \right]$

$= \dfrac{9+1}{3} = \dfrac{10}{3}$ km/h

∵ Distance between Ravi and his office $= 10$ km

∴   Time $= \dfrac{\text{Distance between Ravi and his office}}{\text{Ravi's speed in 1 h}}$

$= \dfrac{10}{\frac{10}{3}} = \dfrac{10}{1} \times \dfrac{3}{10}$ [∵ division is reverse of the multiplication]

$= \dfrac{30}{10} = 3$ h

Hence, Ravi reaches his office in 3 h.

Q. 103 Raj travels 360 km on three-fifth of his petrol tank. How far would he travel at the same rate with a full tank of petrol?

Sol. Given, Raj travels 360 km on three-fifth of his petrol tank.

∴ Total distance travelled = Reciprocal of $\frac{3}{5} \times 360$ km

$= \dfrac{5}{3} \times 360 = 5 \times 120 = 600$ km

Hence, total distance travelled by Raj from the available petrol tank is 600 km.

Q. 104 Kajol has ₹ 75. This is $\dfrac{3}{8}$ of the amount she earned. How much did she earn?

Sol. Given, Kajol has rupees ₹ 75.

According to the question, $75 = \dfrac{3}{8}$ of amount earned

$\Rightarrow$ $75 = \dfrac{3}{8} \times$ amount earned

$\therefore$ Amount earned $= \dfrac{75}{3} \times 8 = ₹200$

Q. 105 It takes 17 full specific type of trees to make one tonne of paper. If there are 221 such trees in a forest, then

    (i) what fraction of forest will be used to make

        (a) 5 tonne of paper?

        (b) 10 tonne of paper?

    (ii) To save $\dfrac{7}{13}$ part of the forest, how much of paper we have to made?

Sol. (i) (a) 1 tonne of paper require = 17 trees

$\therefore$ 5 tonne of paper require $= 17 \times 5$ trees = 85 trees

Now, there are 221 trees in the forest.

So, 85 trees covers $= \dfrac{85}{221}$ fraction of forest

$= \dfrac{5}{13}$ fraction of forest

(b) Similarly,

10 tonne of paper require $= 17 \times 10$ trees $= 170$ trees

So, 170 trees covers $= \dfrac{170}{221}$ fraction of forest

$= \dfrac{10}{13}$ fraction of forest

(ii) $\dfrac{7}{13}$ part of forest $= \dfrac{7}{13} \times 221$ trees $= 119$ trees

$\therefore$ Number of tonnes of paper which can be made by 119 trees $= \dfrac{119}{17} = 7$

Q. 106 Simplify and write the result in decimal form:

$$\left(1 \div \dfrac{2}{9}\right) + \left(1 \div 3\dfrac{1}{5}\right) + \left(1 \div 2\dfrac{2}{3}\right)$$

Sol. Given, $\left(1 \div \dfrac{2}{9}\right) + \left(1 \div 3\dfrac{1}{5}\right) + \left(1 \div 2\dfrac{2}{3}\right)$

$= \left(1 \div \dfrac{2}{9}\right) + \left(1 \div \dfrac{(5 \times 3)+1}{5}\right) + \left(1 \div \dfrac{(2 \times 3)+2}{3}\right)$

$$= \left(1 \times \frac{9}{2}\right) + \left(1 \div \frac{16}{5}\right) + \left(1 \div \frac{8}{3}\right) = \left(1 \times \frac{9}{2}\right) + \left(1 \times \frac{5}{16}\right) + \left(1 \times \frac{3}{8}\right)$$

$$= \frac{9}{2} + \frac{5}{16} + \frac{3}{8}$$

$$= \frac{72 + 5 + 6}{16} \qquad\qquad \text{[taking LCM]}$$

$$= \frac{83}{16}$$

$$= 5.1875$$

Q. 107 Some pictures (a) to (f) are given below. Tell which of them show:

(1) $2 \times \frac{1}{4}$ (2) $2 \times \frac{3}{7}$ (3) $2 \times \frac{1}{3}$

(4) $\frac{1}{4} \times 4$ (5) $3 \times \frac{2}{9}$ (6) $\frac{1}{4} \times 3$

(a)
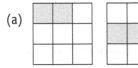
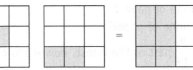

(b)

(c)

(d)

(e)
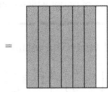

(f)

Fractions and Decimals

Sol. (1) → (d)

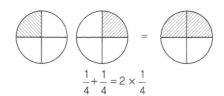

$$\frac{1}{4}+\frac{1}{4}=2\times\frac{1}{4}$$

(2) → (f)

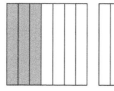

$$\frac{3}{7}+\frac{3}{7}=2\times\frac{3}{7}$$

(3) → (c)

$$\frac{1}{3}+\frac{1}{3}=2\times\frac{1}{3}$$

(4) → (b)

$$\frac{1}{4}+\frac{1}{4}+\frac{1}{4}+\frac{1}{4}=4\times\frac{1}{4}$$

(5) → (a)

$$\frac{2}{9}+\frac{2}{9}+\frac{2}{9}=3\times\frac{2}{9}$$

(6) → (e)

$$\frac{1}{4}+\frac{1}{4}+\frac{1}{4}=3\times\frac{1}{4}$$

Q. 108 Evaluate: $(0.3) \times (0.3) - (0.2) \times (0.2)$

Sol. Given, $(0.3) \times (0.3) - (0.2) \times (0.2)$

$\because\ 0.3 = \dfrac{3}{10}$ and $0.2 = \dfrac{2}{10}$

$\therefore\ \left(\dfrac{3}{10} \times \dfrac{3}{10}\right) - \left(\dfrac{2}{10} \times \dfrac{2}{10}\right) = \dfrac{9}{100} - \dfrac{4}{100}$

$\qquad\qquad\qquad\qquad = \dfrac{9-4}{100} = \dfrac{5}{100}$ [taking LCM]

$\qquad\qquad\qquad\qquad = 0.05$

Q. 109 Evaluate: $\dfrac{0.6}{0.3} + \dfrac{0.16}{0.4}$

Sol. Given, $\dfrac{0.6}{0.3} + \dfrac{0.16}{0.4}$

$\because\ 0.6 = \dfrac{6}{10}$ and $0.3 = \dfrac{3}{10},\ 0.16 = \dfrac{16}{100}$ and $0.4 = \dfrac{4}{10}$

$\therefore\ \dfrac{0.6}{0.3} + \dfrac{0.16}{0.4} = \dfrac{\frac{6}{10}}{\frac{3}{10}} + \dfrac{\frac{16}{100}}{\frac{4}{10}} = \left(\dfrac{6}{10} \times \dfrac{10}{3}\right) + \left(\dfrac{16}{100} \times \dfrac{10}{4}\right)$ [∵ division is reverse of the multiplication]

$\qquad\qquad = \dfrac{60}{30} + \dfrac{160}{400} = \dfrac{6}{3} + \dfrac{16}{40} = \dfrac{2}{1} + \dfrac{4}{10} = \dfrac{20+4}{10}$ [∵ LCM of 1 and 10 = 10]

$\qquad\qquad = \dfrac{24}{10} = \dfrac{12}{5} = 2.4$

Q. 110 Find the value of $\dfrac{(0.2 \times 0.14) + (0.5 \times 0.91)}{(0.1 \times 0.2)}$.

Sol. Given, $\dfrac{(0.2 \times 0.14) + (0.5 \times 0.91)}{(0.1 \times 0.2)}$

$\because\ 0.2 = \dfrac{2}{10},\ 0.14 = \dfrac{14}{100}$ and $0.5 = \dfrac{5}{10}$

$0.91 = \dfrac{91}{100},\ 0.1 = \dfrac{1}{10}$ and $0.2 = \dfrac{2}{10}$

$\therefore \dfrac{(0.2 \times 0.14) + (0.5 \times 0.91)}{(0.1 \times 0.2)} = \dfrac{\left(\dfrac{2}{10} \times \dfrac{14}{100}\right) + \left(\dfrac{5}{10} \times \dfrac{91}{100}\right)}{\left(\dfrac{1}{10} \times \dfrac{2}{10}\right)} = \dfrac{\dfrac{2 \times 14}{1000} + \dfrac{5 \times 91}{1000}}{\dfrac{1 \times 2}{100}}$

$\qquad\qquad = \dfrac{\dfrac{28}{1000} + \dfrac{455}{1000}}{\dfrac{2}{100}}$

$\qquad\qquad = \dfrac{\dfrac{28+455}{1000}}{\dfrac{2}{100}} = \dfrac{\dfrac{483}{1000}}{\dfrac{2}{100}} = \dfrac{483}{1000} \times \dfrac{100}{2}$ [∵ division is reverse of the multiplication]

$\qquad\qquad = \dfrac{483}{10 \times 2} = \dfrac{241.5}{10} = 24.15$

Q. 111 A square and an equilateral triangle have a side in common. If side of triangle is $\dfrac{4}{3}$ cm long, find the perimeter of figure formed (see the figure).

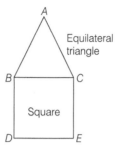

Sol. As square and equilateral triangle both have a common side, i.e. *BC*.

So, all the sides of square and triangle will be equal and of measure $\dfrac{4}{3}$ cm.

∴ Perimeter of the figure = *AB*+ *BD*+ *DE*+ *EC* + *AC*

$$= 5\times AB \qquad\qquad \text{[since, all the lengths are equal]}$$
$$= 5\times\dfrac{4}{3}$$
$$= \dfrac{20}{3}\ cm$$

Q. 112 Rita has bought a carpet of size $4\,m\times 6\dfrac{2}{3}$ m. But her room size is $3\dfrac{1}{3}m\times 5\dfrac{1}{3}$ m. What fraction of area should be cut-off to fit wall-wall carpet into the room?

Sol. Given, carpet size = $4\ m\times 6\dfrac{2}{3}\ m = 4\times\dfrac{(6\times 3)+2}{3}$

$$= 4\times\dfrac{(18+2)}{3} = 4\times\dfrac{20}{3}$$
$$= \dfrac{4}{1}\times\dfrac{20}{3} = \dfrac{80}{3} = \dfrac{80}{3}\ m^2$$

∵ Room size $= 3\dfrac{1}{3}\ m\times 5\dfrac{1}{3}\ m$

$$= \dfrac{(3\times 3)+1}{3}\times\dfrac{(5\times 3)+1}{3} = \dfrac{(9+1)}{3}\times\dfrac{(15+1)}{3}$$
$$= \dfrac{10}{3}\times\dfrac{16}{3} = \dfrac{160}{9}\ m^2$$

∴ Difference between the area of carpet and room sizes = Size of the carpet

– Size of the room

$$= \dfrac{80}{3} - \dfrac{160}{9} = \dfrac{240-160}{9} = \dfrac{80}{9}m^2 \qquad [\because \text{LCM of 3 and 9 = 9}]$$

In fraction,

$$\frac{\text{Area that will be cut - off}}{\text{Original area}} = \frac{\left(\dfrac{80}{9}\right)}{\left(\dfrac{80}{3}\right)} = \frac{80}{9} \times \frac{3}{80} = \frac{1}{3}$$

Hence, $\dfrac{1}{3}$ of area should be cut-off.

Q. 113 Family photograph has length $14\dfrac{2}{5}$ cm and breadth $10\dfrac{2}{5}$ cm. It has border of uniform width $2\dfrac{3}{5}$ cm. Find the area of framed photograph.

Sol. Length of family photograph $=14\dfrac{2}{5}$ cm

$$= \frac{(14 \times 5) + 2}{5} = \frac{72}{5} \text{ cm}$$

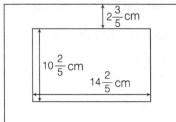

Breadth of family photograph $=10\dfrac{2}{5}$ cm

$$= \frac{(10 \times 5) + 2}{5} = \frac{52}{5} \text{ cm}$$

New length including border (from both sides)

$$= \frac{72}{5} + \left(2\frac{3}{5} \times 2\right) = \frac{72}{5} + \left(\frac{13}{5} \times 2\right)$$

$$= \frac{72}{5} + \frac{26}{5} = \frac{72 + 26}{5} = \frac{98}{5} \text{ cm}$$

New width including border (from both sides)

$$= \frac{52}{5} + \left(2\frac{3}{5} \times 2\right) = \frac{52}{5} + \frac{26}{5} = \frac{52 + 26}{5}$$

$$= \frac{78}{5} \text{ cm}$$

$\therefore$ Area of framed photograph = Length $\times$ Breadth $= \dfrac{98}{5} \times \dfrac{78}{5} = \dfrac{7644}{25}$

$$= 305\frac{19}{25} \text{ cm}^2$$

Hence, the area of framed photograph is $305\dfrac{19}{25}$ cm^2.

Q. 114 Cost of a burger is ₹ $20\frac{3}{4}$ and of macpuff is ₹ $15\frac{1}{2}$. Find the cost of 4 burgers and 14 macpuffs.

Sol. Cost of 1 burger = ₹ $20\frac{3}{4}$ = ₹ $\frac{(20 \times 4) + 3}{4}$ = ₹ $\frac{83}{4}$

∴ Cost of 4 burgers = ₹ $4 \times \frac{83}{4}$ = ₹ 83

Cost of 1 macpuffs = ₹ $15\frac{1}{2}$ = ₹ $\frac{31}{2}$

Cost of 14 macpuffs = ₹ $14 \times \frac{31}{2}$ = ₹ 217

∴ Total cost of 4 burgers and 14 macpuffs = ₹ (83 + 217)
$$= ₹\ 300$$

Q. 115 A hill, $101\frac{1}{3}$ m in height, has $\frac{1}{4}$th of its height under water. What is the height of the hill visible above the water?

Sol. Given, height of the hill = $101\frac{1}{3}$ m = $\frac{(101 \times 3) + 1}{3}$

$$= \frac{303 + 1}{3} = \frac{304}{3}\ m$$

∵ Height of the hill under water = $\frac{1}{4}$ of the height of the hill

$$= \frac{1}{4} \times \frac{304}{3}$$

$$= \frac{76}{3}\ m$$

∴ Height of the hill above the water

= Height of the hill − Height of the hill under water

$$= \frac{304}{3} - \frac{76}{3} = \frac{228}{3} = 76\ cm$$

Hence, height of the hill above the water is 76 cm.

Alternate Method

Fraction of height of the hill above water = $1 - \frac{1}{4} = \frac{4-1}{4} = \frac{3}{4}$

So, $\frac{3}{4}$ of the height of the hill is visible.

∴ Height of the hill above the water = $\frac{3}{4} \times$ Height of the hill

$$= \frac{3}{4} \times 101\frac{1}{3}$$

$$= \frac{3}{4} \times \frac{(101 \times 3) + 1}{3}$$

$$= \frac{3}{4} \times \frac{304}{3} = 76\ m$$

Q. 116 Sports: Reaction time measures, how quickly a runner reacts to the starter pistol? In the 100 m dash at the 2004 Olympic Games, Lauryn Williams had a reaction time of 0.214 second. Her total race time, including reaction time, was 11.03 seconds. How long did it take her to run the actual distance?

Sol.　Time taken to run the actual distance = Total race time – Reaction time

$$= (11.03 - 0.214)\,s$$
$$= 10.816\,s$$

Q. 117 State whether the answer is greater than 1 or less than 1. Put a '√' mark in appropriate box.

Questions	Greater than 1	Less than 1
$\dfrac{2}{3} \div \dfrac{1}{2}$		
$\dfrac{2}{3} \div \dfrac{2}{1}$		
$6 \div \dfrac{1}{4}$		
$\dfrac{1}{5} \div \dfrac{1}{2}$		
$4\dfrac{1}{3} \div 3\dfrac{1}{2}$		
$\dfrac{2}{3} \times 8\dfrac{1}{2}$		

Sol.　(i) $\dfrac{2}{3} \div \dfrac{1}{2} = \dfrac{2}{3} \times \dfrac{2}{1} = \dfrac{4}{3} = 1.33\,(>1)$　　(ii) $\dfrac{2}{3} \div \dfrac{2}{1} = \dfrac{2}{3} \times \dfrac{1}{2} = \dfrac{1}{3} = 0.33\,(<1)$

(iii) $6 \div \dfrac{1}{4} = 6 \times \dfrac{4}{1} = 24\,(>1)$　　(iv) $\dfrac{1}{5} \div \dfrac{1}{2} = \dfrac{1}{5} \times \dfrac{2}{1} = \dfrac{2}{5} = 0.4\,(<1)$

(v) $4\dfrac{1}{3} \div 3\dfrac{1}{2} = \dfrac{13}{3} \div \dfrac{7}{2} = \dfrac{13}{3} \times \dfrac{2}{7} = \dfrac{26}{21} = 1.24\,(>1)$

(vi) $\dfrac{2}{3} \times 8\dfrac{1}{2} = \dfrac{2}{3} \times \dfrac{17}{2} = \dfrac{17}{3} = 5.67\,(>1)$

Questions	Greater than 1	Less than 1
$\dfrac{2}{3} \div \dfrac{1}{2}$	√	
$\dfrac{2}{3} \div \dfrac{2}{1}$		√
$6 \div \dfrac{1}{4}$	√	
$\dfrac{1}{5} \div \dfrac{1}{2}$		√
$4\dfrac{1}{3} \div 3\dfrac{1}{2}$	√	
$\dfrac{2}{3} \times 8\dfrac{1}{2}$	√	

Q. 118 There are four containers that are arranged in the ascending order of their heights. If the height of the smallest container given in figure is expressed as $\dfrac{7}{25}x = 10.5$ cm. Then, find the height of the largest container.

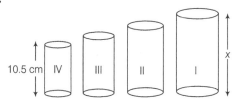

Sol. From the above figure, it is given that height of the smallest cylinder is 10.5 cm.

It is also given that, height of smallest cylinder in terms of x is $\dfrac{7}{25}x$, where x is height of largest cylinder.

Then,
$$\dfrac{7}{25}x = 10.5$$

$\Rightarrow$
$$x = \dfrac{10.5}{1} \times \dfrac{25}{7} = \dfrac{10.5 \times 25}{7} = \dfrac{262.5}{7} = 37.5 \text{ cm}$$

Hence, height of the container is 37.5 cm.

In questions 119 to 122, replace '?' with appropriate fraction.

Q. 119

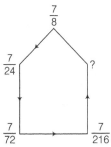

Sol. Given sequence is $\dfrac{7}{8}, \dfrac{7}{24}, \dfrac{7}{72}, \dfrac{7}{216}, ?$.

We observe that each fraction is divided by 3 to get next fraction.

So,
$$? = \dfrac{7}{216} \div 3 = \dfrac{7}{216} \times \dfrac{1}{3} = \dfrac{7}{648}$$

Q. 120

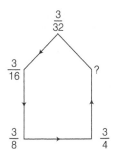

Sol. Given sequence is $\dfrac{3}{32}, \dfrac{3}{16}, \dfrac{3}{8}, \dfrac{3}{4}, ?$.

We observe that, each fraction is multiplied by 2 to get next fraction.

So, $? = \dfrac{3}{4} \times 2 = \dfrac{3}{2}$

Q. 121

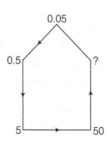

Sol. Given sequence is 0.05, 0.5, 5, 50, ?.

We observe that, each number is multiplied by 10 to get next number.

$\therefore ? = 50 \times 10 = 500$

Q. 122

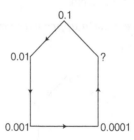

Sol. Given sequence is 0.1, 0.01, 0.001, 0.0001, ?.

We observe that, each number is divided by 10 to get next number.

$\therefore ? = \dfrac{0.0001}{10} = 0.00001$

What is the error in each of questions 123 to 125?

Q. 123 A student compared $-\dfrac{1}{4}$ and -0.3. He changed $-\dfrac{1}{4}$ to the decimal -0.25 and wrote, "Since, 0.3 is greater than 0.25, -0.3 is greater than -0.25." What was the student's error?

Sol. If the numbers are negative, then the numbers whose absolute value is greater, will be smaller. Hence, -0.25 is greater than -0.3.

So, the student made the error that $(-0.3) > -(0.25)$

Q. 124 A student multiplied two mixed fractions in the following manner:
$2\frac{4}{7}\times3\frac{1}{4}=6\frac{1}{7}$. What error the student has done?

Sol. For multiplying two mixed fractions, first convert them into improper fraction.

So, $2\frac{4}{7}\times3\frac{1}{4}=\frac{2\times7+4}{7}\times\frac{3\times4+1}{4}$

$=\frac{18}{7}\times\frac{13}{4}=\frac{234}{28}$

$=\frac{117}{14}=8\frac{5}{14}$

Q. 125 In the pattern $\frac{1}{3}+\frac{1}{4}+\frac{1}{5}+\ldots$, which fraction makes the sum greater than 1 (first time)? Explain.

Sol. $\frac{1}{3}+\frac{1}{4}+\frac{1}{5}=\frac{20+15+12}{60}=\frac{47}{60}<1$ [∵ numerator < denominator]

According to the pattern, next number will be $\frac{1}{6}$.

∴ $\frac{1}{3}+\frac{1}{4}+\frac{1}{5}+\frac{1}{6}=\frac{40+30+24+20}{120}$

$=\frac{114}{120}<1$ [∵ numerator < denominator]

Now, according to the pattern, next number after $\frac{1}{6}$ is $\frac{1}{7}$.

∴ $\frac{1}{3}+\frac{1}{4}+\frac{1}{5}+\frac{1}{6}+\frac{1}{7}$

$=\frac{280+210+168+140+120}{840}$

$=\frac{918}{840}>1$ [∵ numerator > denominator]

Hence, $\frac{1}{7}$ makes the sum greater than 1 (first time).

3

Data Handling

Multiple Choice Questions (MCQs)

Q. 1 Let x, y and z be three observations. The mean of these observations is

(a) $\dfrac{x \times y \times z}{3}$
(b) $\dfrac{x + y + z}{3}$
(c) $\dfrac{x - y - z}{3}$
(d) $\dfrac{x \times y + z}{3}$

Sol. *(b)* Here, x, y and z be three observations.

We know that, $\text{Mean} = \dfrac{\text{Sum of observations}}{\text{Number of observations}}$

$$= \dfrac{x + y + z}{3}$$

Q. 2 The number of trees in different parks of a city are 33, 38, 48, 33, 34, 34, 33 and 24. The mode of this data is

(a) 24
(b) 34
(c) 33
(d) 48

Sol. *(c)* We have, 33, 38, 48, 33, 34, 34, 33 and 24.
On arranging the data in ascending order, we get
24, 33, 33, 33, 34, 34, 38 and 48.
Here, 33 occurs more frequently, i.e. 3 times.
∴ Mode of data = 33

Note *Mode is the observation that occurs most frequently in the data.*

Q. 3 Which measures of central tendency get affected, if the extreme observations on both the ends of a data arranged in descending order are removed?

(a) Mean and mode
(b) Mean and median
(c) Mode and median
(d) Mean, median and mode

Sol. *(a)* **Mean** Mean is defined as follows:

$$\text{Mean} = \dfrac{\text{Sum of all the observations}}{\text{Number of observations}}$$

So, if we remove the extreme values that both sum and total number of observations will change. Hence, mean will also change.

Mode is that observation which occurs the most. So, if extreme value of those values which occurs mostly than mode can affect it they are removed.

Median is the mid value. So, if extreme values are removed than the mid value remains same. Hence, median will not change.

Q. 4 The range of the data 21, 6, 17, 18, 12, 8, 4, 13 is

(a) 17   (b) 12   (c) 8   (d) 15

Sol. (a)   Here,

Highest observation = 21

Lowest observation = 4

Range = Highest observation − Lowest observation

= 21 − 4 = 17

Q. 5 The median of the data 3, 4, 5, 6, 7, 3, 4 is

(a) 5   (b) 3   (c) 4   (d) 6

Sol. (c)   We know that, median is the middle most observation.

For finding the median of the data firstly, we arrange the data in ascending order.

i.e. Ascending order is 3, 3, 4, 4, 5, 6, 7.

$$n = 7 \text{ (odd)}$$

$$\therefore \text{ Median} = \text{Value of } \left(\frac{n+1}{2}\right) \text{th observation} = \text{Value of } \left(\frac{7+1}{2}\right) \text{th observation}$$

$$= \text{4th observation} = 4$$

Q. 6 Out of 5 brands of chocolates in a shop, a boy has to purchase the brand which is most liked by children. What measure of central tendency would be most appropriate, if the data is provided to him?

(a) Mean   (b) Mode   (c) Median   (d) Any of the three

Sol. (b)   Mode is the most appropriate central tendency because it is the observation that occurs most frequently.

Here, by the measurement of mode, we can find out the chocolates which is most liked by children.

Q. 7 There are 2 aces in each of the given set of cards placed face down. From which set are you certain to pick the two aces in the first go?

(a)   (b)

(c)   (d)

Sol. (c)   From third set, we are certain to pick the two aces in the first go because it has only 2 cards and it is given that every set has 2 aces.

Q. 8 In the previous question, what is the probability of picking up an ace from set (d)?

(a) $\dfrac{1}{6}$ (b) $\dfrac{2}{6}$ (c) $\dfrac{3}{6}$ (d) $\dfrac{4}{6}$

Sol. *(b)*   Probability $= \dfrac{\text{Number of possible outcomes}}{\text{Total number of outcomes}}$

Total number of cards in set (d) = 6

Number of possible outcomes = 2   [∵ 2 aces in every set, given]

So, probability $= \dfrac{2}{6}$

Q. 9 The difference between the highest and the lowest observations in a data is its

(a) frequency   (b) width   (c) range   (d) mode

Sol. *(c)*   The difference between the highest and the lowest observations in a data is its range.

Q. 10 In a school, only 2 out of 5 students can participate in a quiz. What is the chance that a student picked at random makes it to the competition?

(a) 20%   (b) 40%   (c) 50%   (d) 30%

Sol. *(b)*   Total number of outcomes = Total number of students = 5

Number of possible outcomes = Students participating in a quiz = 2

∴ Probability $= \dfrac{\text{Number of possible outcomes}}{\text{Total number of outcomes}} = \dfrac{2}{5}$

To find percentage, we have to multiply it by hundred $= \dfrac{2}{5} \times 100 = 40\%$

Q. 11 Some integers are marked on a board. What is the range of these integers?

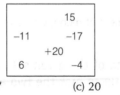

(a) 31   (b) 37   (c) 20   (d) 3

Sol. *(b)*   Here, highest observation = + 20 and lowest observation = –17

As we know,

Range = Highest observation – Lowest observation = + 20 – (– 17) = 20 + 17 = 37

Q. 12 On tossing a coin, the outcome is

(a) only head   (b) only tail

(c) neither head nor tail   (d) either head or tail

Sol. *(d)*   When we toss a coin, two outcomes are possible, i.e. head or tail.

Q. 13 The mean of three numbers is 40. All the three numbers are different natural numbers. If lowest is 19, what could be highest possible number of remaining two numbers?

    (a) 81   (b) 40   (c) 100   (d) 71

Sol. *(a)*   Mean of three numbers = 40 and lowest number = 19   [given]

Let the three observations be 19, x and y, respectively.

$$\therefore \qquad \text{Mean} = \frac{\text{Sum of all observations}}{\text{Total number of observations}}$$

$$\Rightarrow \qquad 40 = \frac{19 + x + y}{3} \qquad [\because \text{mean} = 40, \text{given}]$$

$$\Rightarrow \qquad 3 \times 40 = 19 + x + y$$

$$\Rightarrow \qquad 120 = 19 + x + y$$

$$\Rightarrow \qquad x + y = 120 - 19$$

$$\Rightarrow \qquad x + y = 101 \qquad \qquad \dots \text{(i)}$$

Since, 19 is the lowest observation.

Hence, for highest possible value of remaining two numbers, one must be 20.

Let $x = 20$

From Eq. (i), we get

$$20 + y = 101$$

$$\Rightarrow \qquad y = 101 - 20$$

$$\Rightarrow \qquad y = 81$$

Q. 14 Khilona earned scores of 97, 73 and 88 respectively in her first three examinations. If she scored 80 in the fourth examination, then her average score will be

    (a) increased by 1
    (b) increased by 1.5
    (c) decreased by 1
    (d) decreased by 1.5

Sol. *(d)*   Average score $= \dfrac{\text{Sum of scores in all exams}}{\text{Total number of exams}}$

$\therefore$ Average score in first three examinations $= \dfrac{97 + 73 + 88}{3} = \dfrac{258}{3} = 86$

Also, average score in four examinations $= \dfrac{97 + 73 + 88 + 80}{4} = \dfrac{338}{4} = 84.5$

Hence, average score is decreased by $(86 - 84.5) = 1.5$

Q. 15 Which measure of central tendency best represents the data of the most popular politician after a debate?

    (a) Mean   (b) Median
    (c) Mode   (d) None of these

Sol. *(c)*   Mode is the most frequent observation in a data. So, the measure of central tendency best represents the data of most popular politician after a debate.

Q. 16 Which of the following has the same mean, median and mode?

(a) 6, 2, 5, 4, 3, 4, 1   (b) 4, 2, 2, 1, 3, 2, 3

(c) 2, 3, 7, 3, 8, 3, 2   (d) 4, 3, 4, 3, 4, 6, 4

Sol. *(d)*   We have to find out measure of central tendencies in the four given data.

For option (a)

Data (in ascending order) → 1, 2, 3, 4, 4, 5, 6

Here, $n = 7$ (odd)

Median = Value of $\left(\dfrac{n+1}{2}\right)$ th observation = Value of $\left(\dfrac{8}{2}\right)$ th observation = 4

Mean = $\dfrac{\text{Sum of observations}}{n} = \dfrac{1+2+3+4+4+5+6}{7} = \dfrac{25}{7} = 3.57$

Mode = Most frequent observation = 4

Hence,

Mean ≠ Median = Mode

For option (b)

Data (in ascending order) → 1, 2, 2, 2, 3, 3, 4

Here, $n = 7$ (odd)

Median = Value of $\left(\dfrac{n+1}{2}\right)$ th observation = Value of $\left(\dfrac{7+1}{2}\right)$ th observation = 2

Mean = $\dfrac{\text{Sum of observations}}{n} = \dfrac{1+2+2+2+3+3+4}{7} = \dfrac{17}{7} = 2.428$

Mode = Most frequent observation = 2

Hence,

Mean ≠ Median = Mode

For option (c)

Data (in ascending order) → 2, 2, 3, 3, 3, 7, 8

Here, $n = 7$ (odd)

Median = Value of $\left(\dfrac{n+1}{2}\right)$ th observation = Value of $\left(\dfrac{7+1}{2}\right)$ th observation = 3

Mode = Most frequent data = 3

Mean = $\dfrac{\text{Sum of observations}}{n} = \dfrac{2+2+3+3+3+7+8}{7} = \dfrac{28}{7} = 4$

Hence,

Mean ≠ Median = Mode

For option (d)

Data (in ascending order) → 3, 3, 4, 4, 4, 4, 6

Here, $n = 7$ (odd)

Median = Value of $\left(\dfrac{n+1}{2}\right)$ th observation = Value of $\left(\dfrac{7+1}{2}\right)$ th observation = 4

Mode = Most frequent data = 4

Mean = $\dfrac{\text{Sum of observations}}{n} = \dfrac{3+3+4+4+4+4+6}{7} = \dfrac{28}{7} = 4$

Hence,

Mean = Mode = Median

Fill in the Blanks

In questions 17 to 31, fill in the blanks to make the statements true.

Q. 17 The difference between the highest and the lowest observations of a data is called _____.

Sol.   The difference between the highest and the lowest observations of a data is called **range**.

Q. 18 The mean of a data is defined as _____.

Sol.   Mean $= \dfrac{\text{Sum of all observations}}{\text{Number of observations}}$

Q. 19 In a set of observations, the observation that occurs the most often is called _____.

Sol.   **Mode** is the most often occurring observation in a set of data.

Q. 20 In a given data, arranged in ascending or descending order, the middle most observation is called _____.

Sol.   **Median** is the value of middle most observation of a given data, which arranged in ascending or descending order.

Q. 21 Mean, median and mode are the measures of _____.

Sol.   Mean, median and mode are the measures of **central tendency**.

Q. 22 The probability of an event which is certain to happen is _____.

Sol.   The probability of an event which is certain to happen is **1**. In other words, probability of a sure event is 1.

Q. 23 The probability of an event which is impossible to happen is _____.

Sol.   Probability of an impossible event is **0**. As impossible events are those which cannot happen.

Q. 24 When a die is thrown, the probability of getting a number less than 7, is

_____.

Sol.   When we throw a die, 6 outcomes are possible, i.e. 1, 2, 3, 4, 5, 6.
Total outcomes = 6
Possible outcomes less than 7 = 6   [∵ all the outcomes are less than 7]
∵ Probability $= \dfrac{\text{Possible outcomes}}{\text{Total outcomes}} = \dfrac{6}{6} = 1$

Q. 25 In throwing a die, the number of possible outcomes is _____.

Sol.   When we throw a die, **6** outcomes are possible. They are 1, 2, 3, 4, 5 and 6.

Q. 26 _____ can be used to compare two collections of data.

Sol.   **A double bar graph** can be used to compare two collections of data.

Q. 27 The representation of data with bars of uniform width is called _____.

Sol. The representation of data with bars of uniform width is called **bar graph**.

Q. 28 If the arithmetic mean of 8, 4, x, 6, 2, 7 is 5, then the value of x is _____.

Sol. We know that,

$$\text{Mean} = \frac{\text{Sum of all observations}}{\text{Total number of observations}}$$

$$\Rightarrow \quad 5 = \frac{8 + 4 + x + 6 + 2 + 7}{6} \qquad [\because \text{mean} = 5, \text{given}]$$

$$\Rightarrow \quad 30 = 27 + x$$
$$\Rightarrow \quad 30 - 27 = x$$
$$\Rightarrow \quad 3 = x$$
$$\therefore \quad x = 3$$

Hence, the value of x is **3**.

Q. 29 The median of any data lies between the _____ and _____ observations.

Sol. The median of any data lies between the **minimum** and **maximum** observations.

Q. 30 Median is one of the observations in the data, if number of observations is _____.

Sol. If number of observations (n) is **odd**, then median is one of the observations in the data.

Note Case I If n = odd,

$$Median = Value\ of\ \left(\frac{n+1}{2}\right)th\ observation$$

Case-II If n = even,

$$Median = \frac{Value\ of\ \left(\frac{n}{2}\right)th\ observation + Value\ of\ \left(\frac{n}{2}+1\right)th\ observation}{2}$$

Q. 31 Rohit collected the data regarding weights of students of his class and prepared the following table:

Weight (in kg)	44-47	48-51	52-55	56-59
Number of students	3	5	25	7

A student is to be selected randomly from his class for some competition. The probability of selection of the student is highest whose weight is in the interval _____.

Sol. We know that,

$$\text{Probability} = \frac{\text{Number of favourable outcomes}}{\text{Total number of possible outcomes}}$$

$\therefore$ To make the probability highest, we have to take the interval where number of students, i.e. possible outcomes are highest.

Here, probability is highest whose weight is in the interval **52-55**.

True / False

In questions 32 to 49, state whether the statements are True or False.

Q. 32 If a die is thrown, the probability of getting a number greater than 6 is 1.

Sol. *False*

As we know, a die has six numbers on it, i.e. 1 to 6. So, it is impossible to get a number greater than 6. Hence, if a die is thrown, the probability of getting a number greater than 6 is 0.

Q. 33 When a coin is tossed, there are 2 possible outcomes.

Sol. *True*

If a coin is tossed, then
Maximum outcomes = 2, i.e. head or tail.

Q. 34 If the extreme observations of both the ends of a data arranged in ascending order are removed, the median gets affected.

Sol. *False*

If the extreme observations on both the ends of a data arranged in ascending order are removed, then the mean and mode gets affected but median remains same.

Q. 35 The measures of central tendency may not lie between the maximum and minimum values of data.

Sol. *False*

The measures of central tendency lie between the maximum and minimum values of the data.

Q. 36 It is impossible to get a sum of 14 of the numbers on both die, when a pair of dice is thrown together.

Sol. *True*

When a die is thrown, maximum possible outcomes are 6, i.e. 1, 2, 3, 4, 5, 6.
So, when a pair of dice is thrown together, maximum sum will be 12, if and only if both dice get 6 together. So, that pair will be (6, 6) and the sum is 12.
∴ It is impossible to get a sum of 14 on both dice, when a pair of dice is thrown together.

Q. 37 The probability of the spinning arrow stopping in the shaded region in the given figure is $\frac{1}{2}$.

Sol. *True*

Favourable outcomes = Number of shaded regions = 2
Total number of possible outcomes = Total number of regions = 4
∴ Probability = $\dfrac{\text{Favourable outcomes}}{\text{Total number of possible outcomes}} = \dfrac{2}{4} = \dfrac{1}{2}$

Q. 38 A coin is tossed 15 times and the outcomes are recorded as follows:

H T T H T H H H H T T H T H T T

The chance of occurrence of a head is 50%.

Sol. *False*

Number of times in which head occurs = 7

Total number of times, the coin is tossed = 15

∴ Probability of getting a head = $\dfrac{7}{15}$

Q. 39 Mean, median and mode may be the same for some data.

Sol. *True*

Mean, median and mode can be the same for some data.

See Q. No. 16.

Q. 40 The probability of getting an ace out of a deck of cards is greater than 1.

Sol. *False*

Probability of an event can never be greater than 1. It always remains from 0 and 1 for any event.

$$0 \le P(E) \le 1$$

∴ Maximum probability can be 1.

Q. 41 Mean of the data is always from the given data.

Sol. *False*

It is not compulsory that mean of the data is always from the given data. It may or may not be the observation from given data.

Q. 42 Median of the data may or may not be from the given data.

Sol. *True*

e.g.

(i) 2, 4, 6, 8, 10

Here, $n = 5$ (odd)

Median = Value of $\left(\dfrac{n+1}{2}\right)$th observation = Value of $\left(\dfrac{5+1}{2}\right)$th observation

= Value of 3rd observation = 6

(ii) 4, 6, 8, 8, 12, 14, 15, 16

Here, $n = 8$ (even)

Median = $\dfrac{\text{Value of } \left(\dfrac{n}{2}\right)\text{th observation + Value of } \left(\dfrac{n}{2}+1\right)\text{th observation}}{2}$

$= \dfrac{\text{Value of 4th observation + Value of 5th observation}}{2} = \dfrac{8+12}{2} = \dfrac{20}{2} = 10$

Q. 43 Mode of the data is always from the given data.

Sol. *True*

Mode of the data is always from the given data as it is the most frequent observation in the data.

Q. 44 Mean of the observations can be lesser than each of the observations.

Sol. *False*

Mean is the average value of all the observations. Some of the observations are less than it and some of observations are more than it.

Q. 45 Mean can never be a fraction.

Sol. *False*

e.g. Mean between $\dfrac{1}{4}$ and $\dfrac{1}{6}$ = $\dfrac{\text{Sum of } \dfrac{1}{4} \text{ and } \dfrac{1}{6}}{n}$ = $\dfrac{\dfrac{1}{4} + \dfrac{1}{6}}{2}$ [$\because n$ (number of terms) = 2]

$$= \dfrac{\dfrac{6+4}{24}}{2} = \dfrac{10}{24} \times \dfrac{1}{2} = \dfrac{5}{24}$$

Q. 46 Range of the data is always from the data.

Sol. *False*

It is not necessary as range is the difference of highest observation and lowest observation.

Q. 47 The data 12, 13, 14, 15, 16 has every observation as mode.

Sol. *True*

Given data is 12, 13, 14, 15, 16.

Here, each observation has same frequency, so every observation is a mode.

Q. 48 The range of the data 2, −5, 4, 3, 7, 6 would change, if 2 was subtracted from each value in the data.

Sol. *False*

Range before subtraction by 2 = Highest observation − Lowest observation

$$= 7 - (-5) = 7 + 5 = 12$$

Data after subtract by 2

$$= 2 - 2, -5 - 2, 4 - 2, 3 - 2, 7 - 2, 6 - 2, \text{ i.e. } 0, -7, 2, 1, 5, 4$$

Range = Highest observation − Lowest observation = $5 - (-7) = 5 + 7 = 12$

So, the range is same.

Q. 49 The range of the data 3, 7, 1, −2, 2, 6, −3, −5 would change, if 8 was added to each value in the data.

Sol. *False*

Because, range before adding 8 = Maximum observation − Minimum observation

$$= 7 - (-5) = 7 + 5 = 12$$

Data after adding 8

$$= 3 + 8, 7 + 8, 1 + 8, -2 + 8, 2 + 8, 6 + 8, -3 + 8, -5 + 8, \text{ i.e. } 11, 15, 9, 6, 10, 14, 5, 3$$

So, the range is same. Range = Maximum observation − Minimum observation = $15 - 3 = 12$

Q. 50 Calculate the mean, median and mode of the following data:

5, 10, 10, 12, 13

Are these three equal?

Sol.   Given data is 5, 10, 10, 12, 13.

Sum of all observations = $5 + 10 + 10 + 12 + 13 = 50$

Number of observations = 5

$$\text{Mean} = \frac{\text{Sum of all observations}}{\text{Total observations}} = \frac{50}{5} = 10$$

Here, $n = 5$ (odd)

So, median = value of $\left(\frac{n+1}{2}\right)$ th observation

= value of $\left(\frac{5+1}{2}\right)$ th observation = value of 3 rd observation = 10

Mode = Most frequent data = 10

Hence,

Mean = Median = Mode

Yes,

Mean, median and mode are equal.

Q. 51 Find the mean of the first ten even natural numbers.

Sol.   First ten even natural numbers = 2, 4, 6, 8, 10, 12, 14, 16, 18, 20.

Sum of all observations = $2 + 4 + 6 + 8 + 10 + 12 + 14 + 16 + 18 + 20 = 110$

Number of observations = 10

$$\text{Mean} = \frac{\text{Sum of all observations}}{\text{Number of observations}}$$

$$\therefore \qquad \text{Mean} = \frac{110}{10} = 11$$

Q. 52 A data constitutes of heights (in cm) of 50 children. What do you understand by mode for the data?

Sol.   Since, mode is the observation that occurs most frequently in a set of observation.

Q. 53 A car seller collects the following data of cars sold in his shop:

Colour of car	Number of cars sold
Red	15
Black	20
White	17
Silver	12
Others	9

(a) Which colour of the car is most liked?

(b) Which measure of central tendency was used in (a)?

Sol.   (a) Red colour of the car liked by people = 15

Black colour of the car liked by people = 20

White colour of the car liked by people = 17

Silver colour of the car liked by people = 12

Other colour of the car liked by people = 9

Hence, black colour of the car is the most liked.

(b) Mode concept used in (a).

Q. 54 The marks in a subject for 12 students are as follows:

31, 37, 35, 38, 42, 23, 17, 18, 35, 25, 35, 29.

For the given data, find the

(a) Range   (b) Mean

(c) Median   (d) Mode

Sol. Given data is 31, 37, 35, 38, 42, 23, 17, 18, 35, 25, 35, 29.

Rearranging the given data in ascending order,

17, 18, 23, 25, 29, 31, 35, 35, 35, 37, 38, 42

(a) Range = Highest observation – Lowest observation = 42 – 17 = 25

(b) Mean = $\dfrac{\text{Sum of all observations}}{\text{Total number of observations}}$

$= \dfrac{17 + 18 + 23 + 25 + 29 + 31 + 35 + 35 + 35 + 37 + 38 + 42}{12}$

$= \dfrac{365}{12} = 30.41$

(c) Here, $n = 12$ (even)

Median $= \dfrac{\text{Value of } \left(\frac{n}{2}\right)\text{th observation} + \text{Value of } \left(\frac{n}{2}+1\right)\text{th observation}}{2}$

$= \dfrac{\text{Value of 6th observation} + \text{Value of 7th observation}}{2}$

$= \dfrac{31 + 35}{2} = \dfrac{66}{2} = 33$

(d) Mode = Most frequent observation = 35

Q. 55 The following are weights (in kg) of 12 persons:

70, 62, 54, 57, 62, 84, 75, 59, 62, 65, 78, 60

(a) Find the mean of the weights of the people.

(b) How many people weight above the mean weight?

(c) Find the range of the given data.

Sol. (a) The weights of 12 persons are 70, 62, 54, 57, 62, 84, 75, 59, 62, 65, 78 and 60.

Sum of weights of 12 people

$= 70 + 62 + 54 + 57 + 62 + 84 + 75 + 59 + 62 + 65 + 78 + 60 = 788$

Number of observations (persons) = 12

$\therefore$ Mean $= \dfrac{\text{Sum of all observations (weight of 12 persons)}}{\text{Number of observations}} = \dfrac{788}{12} = 65.66$

(b) Weights above 65.66 are 70, 84, 75 and 78, i.e. 4 persons.

(c) Range = Maximum observation – Minimum observation = 84 – 54 = 30

Q. 56 Following cards are put facing down:

A	E	I	O	U

What is the change of drawing out

(a) a vowel?

(b) a card marked U?

(c) A or I?

(d) a consonant?

Sol. (a) We can clearly see that all the 5 letters are vowels, i.e. A, E, I, O, U. Hence, it is certain to draw a vowel, i.e. probability of drawing a vowel is 1.

(b) Probability $= \dfrac{\text{Number of cards marked } U}{\text{Total number of cards}} = \dfrac{1}{5}$

(c) Probability $= \dfrac{\text{Number of cards marked } A \text{ or } I}{\text{Total number of cards}} = \dfrac{2}{5}$

(d) Probability $= \dfrac{\text{Number of cards marked with a consonant}}{\text{Total number of cards}} = \dfrac{0}{5} = 0$

Hence, it is impossible to draw a consonant.

Q. 57 For the given data below, calculate the mean of its median and mode.

$$6, 2, 5, 4, 3, 4, 4, 2, 3$$

Sol. Given, data in ascending order is 2, 2, 3, 3, 4, 4, 4, 5, 6

Hence, $n = 9$ (odd)

Median = Value of $\left(\dfrac{n+1}{2}\right)$ th observation $= \left(\dfrac{9+1}{2}\right)$ th observation = 5th observation = 4

Mode = Most frequent observation = 4

Mean is the central value.

$\therefore$
$$\text{Mean} = \dfrac{1}{2}[3 \times \text{Median} - \text{Mode}]$$
$$= \dfrac{1}{2}[3 \times 4 - 4] = \dfrac{1}{2}[12 - 4]$$
$$= \dfrac{1}{2} \times 8 = 4$$

Q. 58 Find the median of the given data, if the mean is 4.5.

$$5, 7, 7, 8, x, 5, 4, 3, 1, 2$$

Sol. Given, mean = 4.5

We know that, $\text{Mean} = \dfrac{\text{Sum of all observations}}{\text{Total number of observations}}$

$\Rightarrow \qquad 4.5 = \dfrac{5+7+7+8+x+5+4+3+1+2}{10}$

$\Rightarrow \qquad 4.5 \times 10 = 42 + x \Rightarrow 45 - 42 = x$

$\therefore \qquad x = 3$

Now, arrange the data in ascending order

$$1, 2, 3, 3, 4, 5, 5, 7, 7, 8.$$

Here, $n = 10$ (even)

$\text{Median} = \dfrac{\text{Value of } \left(\dfrac{n}{2}\right)\text{th observation} + \text{Value of }\left(\dfrac{n}{2}+1\right)\text{th observation}}{2}$

$= \dfrac{\text{Value of 5th observation} + \text{Value of 6th observation}}{2} = \dfrac{4+5}{2} = \dfrac{9}{2} = 4.5$

Q. 59 What is the probability of the sun setting tomorrow?

Sol.   Setting of the sun is a sure event. Hence, its probability is 1.

Q. 60 When a spinner with three colours given in figure is rotated, which colour has more chance to show up with arrow than the others?

Sol.   From the figure, area covered by the yellow colour is maximum out of the given three colours. Hence, chances of yellow colour to show up with arrow will be more.

Q. 61 What is the probability that a student chosen at random out of 3 girls and 4 boys is a boy?

Sol.   Given, total children = 7 = 4 boys and 3 girls.
So, favourable outcomes for a day = 4
Total number of possible outcomes = 7
$$\therefore \text{Probability} = \frac{\text{Favourable outcomes}}{\text{Total number of possible outcomes}} = \frac{4}{7}$$

Q. 62 The letters written on paper slips of the word MEDIAN and put in a bag. If one slip is drawn randomly, what is the probability that it bears the letter D?

Sol.   In the word 'MEDIAN', there is only one D.
So, favourable outcomes = number of letter D = 1
Total number of possible outcomes = 6
$$\therefore \text{Probability} = \frac{\text{Favourable outcomes}}{\text{Total number of possible outomes}} = \frac{1}{6}$$

Q. 63 Classify, the following events as certain to happen, impossible to happen, may or may not happen.
   (a) Getting a number less than 1 on throwing a die.
   (b) Getting head when a coin is tossed.
   (c) A team winning the match.
   (d) Christmas will be on 25 December.
   (e) Today moon will not revolve around the earth.
   (f) A ball thrown up in the air will fall down after sometime.

Sol. (a) Getting a number less than 1 on throwing a die is **impossible**, as a die does not have a number less than 1 on it.

(b) Getting head, when a coin is tossed **may** or **may not happen** as a coin has head and tail on its two faces. So, we might get a head or a tail on tossing it.

(c) A team **may or may not** win a match.

(d) Christmas is **certain to happen** on 25th December.

(e) It is **impossible** that moon will not revolve around the earth.

(f) It is **certain to happen** that a ball thrown up in the air will fall down after sometime due to gravity.

Q. 64 A die was thrown 15 times and the outcomes recorded were
5, 3, 4, 1, 2, 6, 4, 2, 2, 3, 1, 5, 6, 1, 2.
Find the mean, median and mode of the data.

Sol. Given data is 5, 3, 4, 1, 2, 6, 4, 2, 2, 3, 1, 5, 6, 1, 2

Arranging the data in ascending order, we have
1, 1, 1, 2, 2, 2, 2, 3, 3, 4, 4, 5, 5, 6, 6.

$$\text{Mean} = \frac{\text{Sum of all observations}}{\text{Total number of observations}}$$

$$= \frac{1+1+1+2+2+2+2+3+3+4+4+5+5+6+6}{15} = \frac{47}{15} = 3.13$$

Mode = Most frequent data = 2

Here, $n = 15$ (odd)

$$\text{Median} = \text{Value of } \left(\frac{n+1}{2}\right) \text{th observation} = \text{Value of } \left(\frac{15+1}{2}\right) \text{th observation}$$

$$= \text{Value of 8th observation} = 3$$

Q. 65 Find the mean of first six multiples of 4.

Sol. First six multiples of 4 are 4, 8, 12, 16, 20, 24.

$$\text{Mean} = \frac{\text{Sum of all observations}}{\text{Total number of observations}}$$

$$= \frac{4+8+12+16+20+24}{6} = \frac{84}{6}$$

$$= 14$$

Hence, the mean of first six multiples of 4 is 14.

Q. 66 Find the median of first nine even natural numbers.

Sol. First nine even natural numbers are
2, 4, 6, 8, 10, 12, 14, 16, 18.

Here, $n = 9$ (odd)

$$\therefore \text{Median} = \text{Value of } \left(\frac{n+1}{2}\right) \text{th observation} = \text{Value of } \left(\frac{9+1}{2}\right) \text{th observation}$$

$$= \text{Value of 5th observation} = 10$$

Hence, the median of first nine even natural numbers is 10.

Q. 67 The mean of three numbers is 10. The mean of other four numbers is 12. Find the mean of all the numbers.

Sol. Mean of three numbers $= \dfrac{\text{Sum of three numbers}}{3}$

$\Rightarrow \qquad 10 = \dfrac{\text{Sum of three numbers}}{3}$ $[\because \text{mean of three numbers} = 10, \text{given}]$

Hence, sum of three numbers $= 30$

Mean of other four numbers $= \dfrac{\text{Sum of other four numbers}}{4}$

$\Rightarrow \qquad 12 = \dfrac{\text{Sum of other four numbers}}{4}$ $[\because \text{mean of other four numbers} = 12, \text{given}]$

Hence, sum of other four numbers $= 48$

$\therefore$ Mean of all the numbers $= \dfrac{\text{Sum of all the numbers}}{\text{Total numbers}}$

$= \dfrac{[\text{Sum of first three numbers} + \text{Sum of other four numbers}]}{7}$

$= \dfrac{30 + 48}{7} = \dfrac{78}{7} = 11.14$

Hence, mean of all the numbers is 11.14.

Q. 68 Find the mode of the given data.

$$10,\ 8,\ 4,\ 7,\ 8,\ 11,\ 15,\ 8,\ 4,\ 2,\ 3,\ 6,\ 8$$

Sol. We know that, mode is the most frequent observation in the data.

$\therefore$ Mode $= 8$

Q. 69 Given below are heights of 15 boys of a class measured in centimetres:

128, 144, 146, 143, 136, 142, 138, 129, 140, 152, 144, 140, 150, 142, 154.

Find

    (a) the height of the tallest boy   (b) the height of the shortest boy

    (c) the range of the given data   (d) the median height of the boys

Sol. Given, height (data) of 15 boys of a class are

128, 144, 146, 143, 136, 142, 138, 129, 140, 152, 144, 140, 150, 142, 154.

Arranging the given data in ascending order, we have

128, 129, 136, 138, 140, 140, 142, 142, 143, 144, 144, 146, 150, 152, 154

(a) By observing the data, height of the tallest boy $= 154$ cm

(b) By observing the data, height of the shortest boy $= 128$ cm

(c) Here, highest observation $= 154$ and lowest observation $= 128$

   $\therefore$ Range $=$ Highest observation $-$ Lowest observation $= 154 - 128 = 26$ cm

(d) Here, $n = 15$ (odd)

   $\therefore$ Median $=$ Value of $\left(\dfrac{n+1}{2}\right)$th observation $=$ Value of $\left(\dfrac{15+1}{2}\right)$th observation

      $=$ Value of 8 th observation

      $= 142$ cm

Q. 70 Observe the data and answer the questions that follow:

16, 15, 16, 16, 8, 15, 17

(a) Which data value can be put in the data so that the mode remains the same?

(b) Atleast how many and which value(s) must be put into change the mode to 15?

(c) What is the least number of data values that must be put into change the mode to 17? Name them.

Sol. Given data; 16, 15, 16, 16, 8, 15, 17

Arranging the given data in ascending order, we have

8, 15, 15, 16, 16, 16, 17

(a) As per the given data, 16 is the mode of data, since it has highest frequency, i.e. 3.

Now, if 15 is added to the given data, mode will get changed to 15 and 16, whereas if any other number, i.e. 8, 16 or 17 is added, mode will remain same.

(b) Atleast two 15's should be added to change the mode to 15. On adding two 15's the frequency of 15 will be maximum, i.e. 4.

(c) We will have to add atleast three 17's to change the mode to 17. On adding three 17's, the frequency of 17 will be maximum, i.e. 4.

Q. 71 Age (in years) of 6 children of two groups are recorded as below:

Age (in years)	
Group A	**Group B**
7	7
7	9
9	11
8	12
10	12
10	12

(a) Find the mode and range for each group.

(b) Find the range and mode, if the two groups are combined together.

Sol. From the given table, age of children in group $A = 7$ yr, 7 yr, 9 yr, 8 yr, 10 yr, 10 yr

Age of children in group $B = 7$ yr, 9 yr, 11 yr, 12 yr, 12 yr, 12 yr

(a) Mode in group $A = 7$ yr and 10 yr. [∵ 7 yr and 10 yr occurs most frequent, i.e. 2 times]

Range in group A = Maximum value − Minimum value = 10 − 7 = 3

Mode in group $B = 12$ yr   [∵ 12 yr is the most frequent, i.e. 3]

Range in group B = Maximum value − Minimum value = 12 − 7 = 5

(b) If both groups are combined together 7, 7, 7, 9, 9, 11, 8, 12, 10, 12, 10, 12.

Mode = 7 and 12   [∵ 7 and 12 occurs most frequent, i.e. 3 times]

∴ Range = Maximum value − Minimum value = 12 − 7 = 5

Q. 72 Observe the given bar graph carefully and answer the questions that follow.

XYZ Automobiles Ltd.

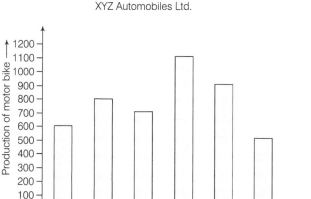

(a) What information does the bar graph depict?

(b) How many motor bikes were produced in the first three months?

(c) Calculate the increase in production in May over the production in January.

(d) In which month the production was minimum and what was it?

(e) Calculate the average (mean production of bikes in 6 months).

Sol. (a) The given bar graph shows the production of motor bikes by XYZ automobiles Ltd. during January to June.

(b) Total number of motor bikes produced in first three months = Motor bikes produced in January + Motor bikes produced in February + Motor bikes produced in March

$$= 600 + 800 + 700$$
$$= 2100$$

(c) Increase in production in May over the production in January

$$= \text{Production in May} - \text{Production in January} = 900 - 600 = 300$$

(d) By observing the graph, we can say that the production was minimum in the month of June, i.e. 500.

(e) Average production $= \dfrac{\text{Total production}}{\text{Number of months}}$

$$= \frac{600 + 800 + 700 + 1100 + 900 + 500}{6}$$

$$= \frac{4600}{6} = 767 \text{ bikes (approx.)}$$

Q. 73 The bar graph given below shows the marks of students of a class in a particular subject:

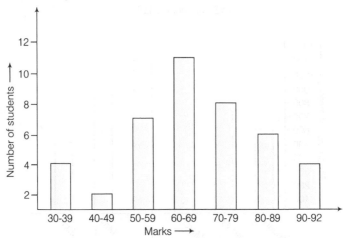

Study the bar graph and answer the following questions:

(a) If 40 is the pass marks, then how many students have failed?

(b) How many students got marks from 50 to 69?

(c) How many students scored 90 marks and above?

(d) If students who scored marks above 80 are given merits, then how many merit holders are three?

(e) What is the strength of the class?

Sol.   (a) If 40 is the pass marks, then students who got marks less than 40 will be failed.

∴ Number of students who failed = 4

(b) Number of students who got marks from 50 to 69

= Number of students who got marks from 50 to 59
+ Number of students who got marks from 60 to 69

= 7 + 11 = 18

(c) Number of students scored 90 marks and above

= Number of students who scored marks 90 to 92

= 4

(d) Number of students who scored marks above 80

= Number of students who score 80 to 89
+ Number of students who score 90 to 92

= 6 + 4 = 10

Since, students who scored marks above 80 are given merits.

∴ Number of students who are merit holders = 10

(e) Strength of the class = Total number of students who scored different marks

= 4 + 2 + 7 + 11 + 8 + 6 + 4

= 42

Q. 74 Study the bar graph given below and answer the questions that follow:

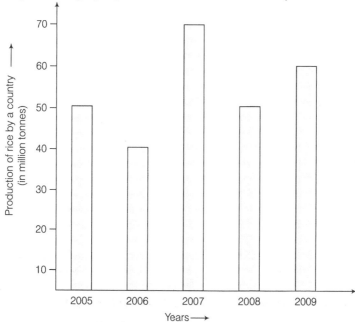

(a) What information does the above bar graph represent?

(b) In which year was production the least?

(c) After which year was the maximum rise in the production?

(d) Find the average production of rice during the 5 years.

(e) Find difference of rice production between years 2006 and 2008.

Sol. After studying the bar graph, we have

Production of rice in 2005 = 50 million tonne

Production of rice in 2006 = 40 million tonne

Production of rice in 2007 = 70 million tonne

Production of rice in 2008 = 50 million tonne

Production of rice in 2009 = 60 million tonne

(a) The bar graph shows the production of rice in million tonne by a country during years 2005 to 2009.

(b) The production of rice was the least in 2006, i.e. 40 million tonne.

(c) The maximum production of rice was in 2007. The production rose after 2006.

(d) For average production,

Sum of productions = 50 + 40 + 70 + 50 + 60 = 270

$$\text{Average production} = \frac{\text{Sum of observations}}{\text{Number of observations}}$$

$$\text{Average production} = \frac{270}{5} = 54 \text{ million tonne}$$

(e) Production in 2006 = 40 million tonne and production in 2008 = 50 million tonne

Difference = 50 – 40 = 10 million tonne.

Q. 75 Study the bar graph given below and answer the questions that follow:

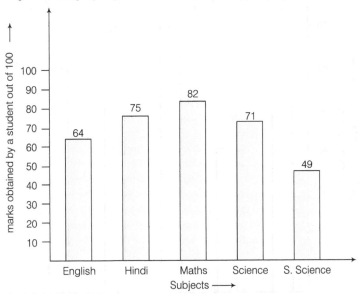

(a) What information is depicted from the bar graph?

(b) In which subject is the student very good?

(c) Calculate the average marks of the student.

(d) If 75 and above marks denote a distinction, then name the subjects in which the student got distinction.

(e) Calculate the percentage of marks the student got out of 500.

Sol. (a) The given bar graph shows marks obtained by a student in different subjects out of 100.

(b) Subject in which student is very good, Maths as he scored highest marks, i.e. 82.

(c) Average marks = $\dfrac{\text{Sum of all marks obtained in various subjects}}{\text{Total subjects}}$

$= \dfrac{64 + 75 + 82 + 71 + 49}{5}$

$= \dfrac{341}{5}$

$= 68.2\%$

(d) In Hindi and Maths, student got 75 and 82 marks, respectively. Since, the marks equal to 75 or above denote a distinction. Hence, student got distinction in Hindi and Maths.

(e) Percentage marks = $\dfrac{\text{Total marks scored}}{\text{Total marks}} \times 100\%$

$= \dfrac{341}{500} \times 100\%$

$= 68.2\%$

Q. 76 The bar graph given below represents the circulation of newspapers (dailies) in a town in six languages (the figures are approximated to hundreds).

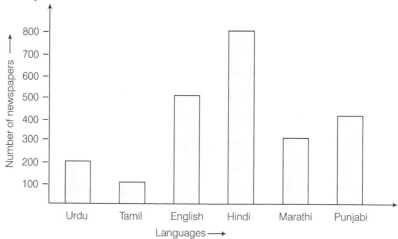

Study the bar graph and answer the following questions:

(a) Find the total number of newspapers read in Hindi, Punjabi, Urdu, Marathi and Tamil.

(b) Find the excess number of newspapers read in Hindi than those in English.

(c) Name the language in which the least number of newspapers are read.

(d) Write the total circulation of newspaper in the town.

Sol. Number of newspapers in Urdu = 200
Number of newspapers in Tamil = 100
Number of newspapers in English = 500
Number of newspapers in Hindi = 800
Number of newspapers in Marathi = 300
Number of newspapers in Punjabi = 400

(a) Total number of newspapers read in Hindi, Punjabi, Urdu, Marathi and Tamil
    = 800 + 400 + 200 + 300 + 100
    = 1800

(b) Excess number of newspapers read in Hindi than those in English
    = Number of newspapers read in Hindi – Number of newspapers read in English
    = 800 – 500 = 300

(c) Out of all the newspapers, least number of newspapers in Tamil, i.e. 100 newspapers are read.

(d) Total circulation of newspapers in the town
    = Number of newspapers in six different languages
    = 200 + 100 + 500 + 800 + 300 + 400
    = 2300

Q. 77 Study the double bar graphs given below and answer the following questions:

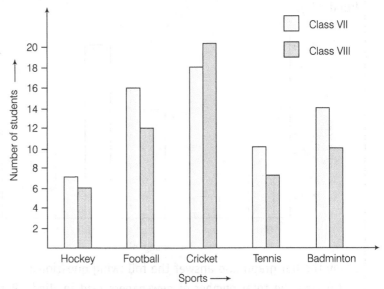

(a) Which sport is liked the most by class VIII students?

(b) How many students of class VII like Hockey and Tennis in all?

(c) How many students are there in class VII?

(d) For which sport is the number of students of class VII less than that of class VIII?

(e) For how many sports students of class VIII are less than class VII?

(f) Find the ratio of students who like Badminton in class VII to students who like Tennis in class VIII.

Sol. (a) By observing the graph, we can say that the height of the bar corresponding to cricket for class VIII student is largest. Hence, cricket is liked the most by class VIII students.

(b) Height of bar corresponding to hockey and tennis for class VII are 7 and 10 respectively. So, total students of class VII who like hockey and tennis = 7 + 10 = 17

(c) Total number of students in class VII = Sum of heights of all the bars for class VII

$$= 7 + 16 + 18 + 10 + 14 = 65$$

(d) The sport for which number of students of class VII is less than that of class VIII will be that for which height of bar is less.

By observing the graph in case of cricket height of bar is less for class VII as compared to class VIII.

(e) We can clearly see from the double bar graph for Hockey, Football, Tennis and Badminton, the number of students are less for class VIII as compared to class VII.

(f) Number of students who like badminton in class VII = 14

and number of students who like tennis in class VIII = 7

∴ Required ratio = 14 : 7 = 2 : 1

Q. 78 Study the double bar graph shown below and answer the questions that follow:

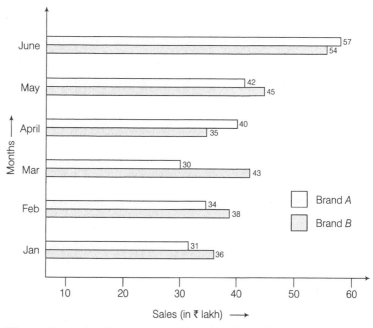

Sales (in ₹ lakh) ⟶

(a) What information is represented by the above double bar graph?

(b) In which month sales of brand *A* decreased as compared to the previous month?

(c) What is the difference in sales of both the brands for the month of June?

(d) Find the average sales of brand *B* for the six months.

(e) List all months for which the sales of brand *B* was less than that of brand *A*.

(f) Find the ratio of sales of brand *A* as compared to brand *B* for the month of January.

Sol. (a) The above double bar graph compares the sale of brands *A* and *B* during the months of January to June.

(b) We can clearly see from the double bar graph that sales for brand *A* reduced in the month of March compared to that of February.

(c) Sales of brand *A* in June = ₹ 57 lakh and sales of brand *B* in June = ₹ 54 lakh

Difference in sales = 57 − 54 = ₹ 3 lakh

(d) Average sales of brand *B*

$= \dfrac{\text{Total sales of brand } B \text{ in six months from January to June}}{6}$

$= \dfrac{36 + 38 + 43 + 35 + 45 + 54}{6} = \dfrac{251}{6} = ₹ \, 41.83 \text{ lakh}$

(e) We can clearly see from the double bar graph that sales of brand B is less than sales of brand A in the month of April and June.

(f) Sales of brand A in January = 31 and sales of brand B in January = 36

∴ Required ratio = $\dfrac{31}{36}$ or 31 : 36

Q. 79 Study the double bar graph shown given below and answer the question that follow:

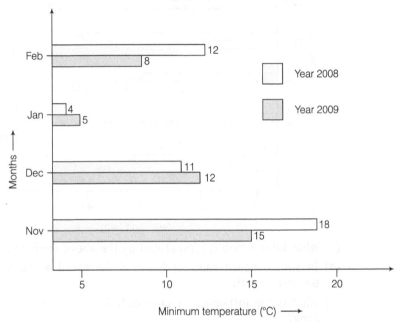

Minimum temperature (°C) ⟶

(a) What information is compared in the above given double bar graph?

(b) Calculate the ratio of minimum temperatures in the year 2008 to the year 2009 for the month of November.

(c) For how many months was the minimum temperature in the year 2008 greater than that of year 2009? Name those months.

(d) Find the average minimum temperature for the year 2008 for the four months.

(e) In which month is the variation in the two temperatures maximum?

Sol. (a) The above double bar graph compares the minimum temperature during the month November to February for the years 2008 and 2009.

(b) Minimum temperature of November in year 2008 = 18°C

Minimum temperature of November in year 2009 = 15°C

∴ Required ratio = $\dfrac{18}{15}$ = 18 : 15 = 6 : 5

(c) We can clearly see from the double bar graph that the minimum temperature in the year 2008 greater than that of the year 2009 for the month of February and November.

(d) Average minimum temperature for year 2008

$$= \frac{\text{Total temperature for year 2008 in four months}}{4}$$

$$= \frac{18 + 11 + 4 + 12}{4}$$

$$= \frac{45}{4}$$

$$= 11.25$$

(e) Difference of temperature for different months can be shown by following table:

Month	Difference of temperature
November	$18 - 15 = 3$
December	$12 - 11 = 1$
January	$5 - 4 = 1$
February	$12 - 8 = 4$

From the above table, it is clear that for the month of February variation in two temperatures is maximum.

Q. 80 The following table shows the average intake of nutrients in calories by rural and urban groups in a particular year. Using a suitable scale for the given data, draw a double bar graph to compare the data.

Foodstuff	Rural	Urban
Pulses	35	49
Leafy vegetables	14	21
Other vegetables	51	89
Fruits	35	66
Milk	70	250
Fish and flesh foods	10	22
Fats and oils	9	35
Sugar/Jaggery	19	31

Sol. Steps to construct the bar graphs are as follows:

Step I Firstly, we draw two lines perpendicular to each other on a graph paper and call them horizontal and vertical axes.

Step II Along the horizontal axis, we mark the foodstuff and along the vertical axis, we mark the intake of nutrients (calories).

Step III We choose a suitable scale to determine the heights of bars. Here, we choose the scale as 1 small division to represent 20.

Step IV First, we draw the bars for rural and then bars of urban for different foodstuff.

Bars for rural and urban are shaded separately and the shading is shown at the top right corner of the graph paper.

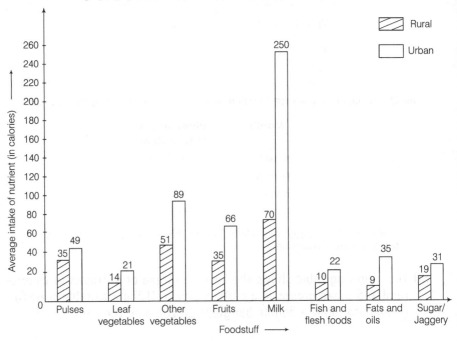

Q. 81 Study the double bar graph and answer the questions that follow:

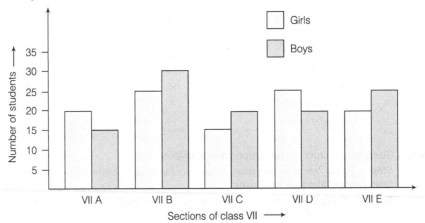

(a) What information does the double bar graph represent?

(b) Find the total number of boys in all sections of class VII.

(c) In which sections, number of girls is greater than number of boys?

(d) In which section, the number of boys is the maximum?

(e) In which section, the number of girls is the least?

Sol.   (a) The above graphs shows the number of students (boys and girls) in different sections of class VII.

(b) It is clear from the graph, total number of boys in all sections of class VII = Sum of heights of all the bars corresponding to boys in different sections = 15 + 30 + 20 + 20 + 25 = 110

(c) It is clear from the graph that in sections VII A and VII D, the number of girls are greater than the number of boys.

(d) From the graph, it is clear that in section VII B, number of boys is maximum.

(e) From the graph, it is clear that in section VII C, number of girls is minimum.

Q. 82 In a public library, the following observations were recorded by the librarian in a particular week.

Days	Mon	Tue	Wed	Thur	Fri	Sat
Newspaper readers	400	600	350	550	500	350
Magazine readers	150	100	200	300	250	200

(a) Draw a double bar graph choosing a appropriate scale.

(b) On which day, the number of readers in the library was maximum?

(c) What is the mean number of magazine readers?

Sol. (a) Steps to construct the bar graphs are as follows:

Step I We draw two lines perpendicular to each other on a graph paper and call them horizontal and vertical axes.

Step II Along the horizontal axis, we mark the days and along the vertical axis, we mark the readers.

Step III We choose a suitable scale to determine the heights of bars. Here, we choose the scale as 1 small division to represent 50.

Step IV First, we draw the bars for newspaper readers and then bars for magazine readers for different days.

Bars for newspapers and magazine readers are shaded separately and the shading is shown in the top right corner of the graph paper.

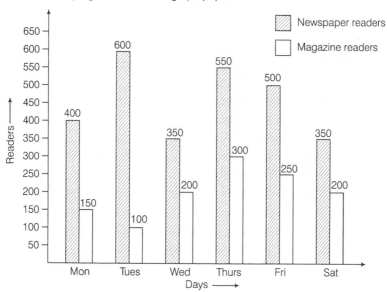

(b) Total number of both readers on different days are

Day	Readers
Mon	$400 + 150 = 550$
Tue	$600 + 100 = 700$
Wed	$350 + 200 = 550$
Thur	$550 + 300 = 850$
Fri	$500 + 250 = 750$
Sat	$350 + 200 = 550$

Hence, it is clear that the number of readers was maximum on Thursday.

(c) Mean of readers $= \dfrac{\text{Sum of all the magazine readers on six days}}{6}$

$= \dfrac{150 + 100 + 200 + 300 + 250 + 200}{6}$

$= \dfrac{1200}{6} = 200$

Q. 83 Observe the following data:

Government School, Chandpur

Daily attendance		Date: 15. 04. 2009
Class	Total students	Number of students present on that day
VI	90	81
VII	82	76
VIII	95	91
IX	70	65
X	63	62

(a) Draw a double bar graph choosing an appropriate scale. What do you infer from the bar graph?

(b) Which class has the maximum number of students?

(c) In which class, the difference of total students and number of students present is minimum?

(d) Find the ratio of number of students present to the total number of students of class IX.

(e) What percentage of class VI students were absent?

Sol. (a) A double bar graph is shown below:

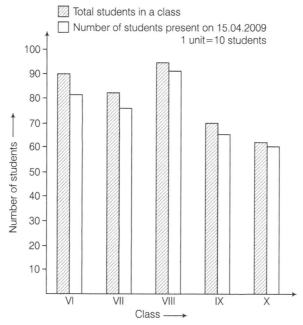

We infer from the bar graph that maximum number of students were absent in class VI on 15.04.2009, whereas minimum number of students were absent in class X.

(b) Clearly, class VIII has maximum number of students, i.e. 95.

(c) The difference of total number of students and number of students present is minimum for class X i.e. 63 − 62 = 1

(d) Number of students present in class IX = 65

Total number of students in class IX = 70

Hence, required ratio $= \dfrac{65}{70} = \dfrac{13}{14}$ or 13 : 14

(e) Total number of students in class VI = 90

Number of students present in class VI = 81

Number of absent students = 90 − 81 = 9

$\therefore$ Percentage of absent students of class VI $= \left(\dfrac{\text{Number of absent students}}{\text{Total number of students}} \times 100\right)\%$

$= \left(\dfrac{9}{90} \times 100\right)\% = 10\%$

Q. 84 Observe the given data:

Days of the week	Mon	Tues	Wed	Thurs	Fri	Sat
Number of mobile phone sets sold	50	45	30	55	27	60

(a) Draw a bar graph to represent the above given information.

(b) On which day of the week was the sales maximum?

(c) Find the total sales during the week.

(d) Find the ratio of the minimum sale to the maximum sale.

(e) Calculate the average sale during the week.

(f) On how many days of the week was the sale above the average sales?

Sol. (a) In order to construct a bar graph representing the above data, we follow the following steps:

Step I Take a graph paper and draw two mutually perpendicular lines OX and OY. Call OX as the horizontal axis and OY as the vertical axis.

Step II Along OX, mark days and along OY, mark number of mobile phone sets sold.

Step III Along OX, choose the uniform (equal) width of the bars and the uniform gap between them, according to the space available for the graph.

Step IV Choose a suitable scale to determine the heights of the bars, according to the availability of space. Here, we choose 1 small division to represent 5 mobile sets.

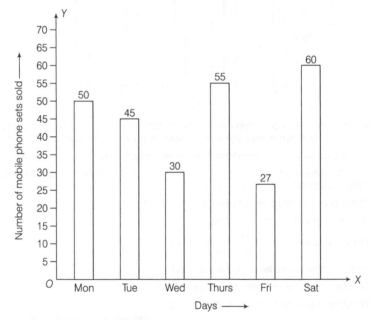

(b) It is clear from graph that on Saturday the sales was maximum.

(c) Total sale during the week = Sum of all the sales on each day

$$= 50 + 45 + 30 + 55 + 27 + 60 = 267$$

(d) Minimum sale on Friday = 27

Maximum sale on Saturday = 60

∴   Required ratio = 27 : 60 = 9 : 20

(e) Average sale = $\dfrac{\text{Total sale}}{6}$

$= \dfrac{267}{6}$

$= 44.5$

(f) On Monday, Tuesday, Thursday and Saturday, i.e. 4 days the sale was above the average sale.

Q. 85 Below is a list of 10 tallest buildings in India.

This list ranks buildings in India that stand atleast 150 m (492 ft.) tall, based and standard height measurement. This includes spires and architectural details but does not include antenna marks. Following data in given as per the available information till 2009. Since, new buildings are always under construction, go online to check new taller buildings.

Use the information given in the table about skyscrapers to answer the following questions:

Name	City	Height	Floors	Year
Planet	Mumbai	181 m	51	2009
UB Tower	Bengaluru	184 m	20	2006
Ashok Towers	Mumbai	193 m	49	2009
The Imperial I	Mumbai	249 m	60	2009
The Imperial II	Mumbai	249 m	60	2009
RNA Mirage	Mumbai	180 m	40	2009
Oberoi Woods Tower I	Mumbai	170 m	40	2009
Oberoi Woods Tower II	Mumbai	170 m	40	2009
Oberoi Woods Tower III	Mumbai	170 m	40	2009
MVRDC	Mumbai	156 m	35	2002

(a) Find the height of each storey of the three tallest buildings and write them in the following table:

Building	Height	Number of storeys	Height of each storey

(b) The average height of one storey for the buildings given in (a) is _____ .

(c) Which city in this list has the largest percentage of skyscrapers?

(d) What is the range of data?

(e) Find the median of the data.

(f) Draw a bar graph for given data.

Sol. (a) Clearly, Imperial I, Imperial II and Ashok Towers are three tallest buildings.

Building	Height	Number of storeys	Height of each storey
Imperial I	249 m	60	$249 / 60 = 4.15$
Imperial II	249 m	60	$249 / 60 = 4.15$
Ashok Towers	193 m	49	$193 / 49 = 3.94$

(b) Average height of each storey of the buildings given in (a)

$$= \frac{[\text{Sum of heights of each storey of three tallest buildings}]}{3} = \frac{4.15 + 4.15 + 3.94}{3}$$

$$= \frac{12.24}{3} = 4.08$$

(c) We can clearly see from the data, Mumbai has maximum number of skyscrapers from the list given. It has 9 skyscrapers out of the list of 10 buildings given.

$\therefore$ Required percentage $= \dfrac{9}{10} \times 100 = 90\%$

(d) Range of data = Maximum height – Minimum height = 249 – 156 = 93

(e) Arranging the data in ascending order, we get 156, 170, 170, 170, 180, 181, 184, 193, 249, 249. Since, there are ten observations, median will be the mean of 5th and 6th observations.

$n = 10$ (even)

$\therefore$ Median $= \dfrac{\dfrac{n}{2}\text{th observation} + \left(\dfrac{n}{2}+1\right)\text{th observation}}{2}$

$= \dfrac{\left(\dfrac{10}{2}\right)\text{th observation} + \left(\dfrac{10}{2}+1\right)\text{th observation}}{2} = \dfrac{\text{5th observation} + \text{6th observation}}{2}$

$= \dfrac{180 + 181}{2} = 180.5$

(f) A bar graph is as shown below:

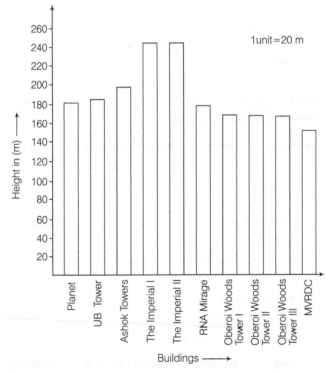

Q. **86** The marks out of 100 obtained by Kunal and Soni in the half yearly examination are given below:

Subjects	English	Hindi	Maths	Science	S. Science	Sanskrit
Kunal	72	81	92	96	64	85
Soni	86	89	90	82	75	82

(a) Draw a double bar graph by choosing appropriate scale.

(b) Calculate the total percentage of marks obtained by Soni.

(c) Calculate the total percentage of marks obtained by Kunal.

(d) Compare the percentages of marks obtained by Kunal and Soni.

(e) In how many subjects did Soni get more marks than Kunal? Which are those subjects?

(f) Who got more marks in S. Science and what was the difference of marks?

(g) In which subject the difference of marks was maximum and by how much?

Sol. (a) Steps to construct the bar graphs are as follows :

Step I We draw two lines perpendicular to each other on a graph paper and call them horizontal and vertical axes.

Step II Along the horizontal axis, *OX* mark the subjects and along vertical axis, *OY* mark the marks obtained.

Step III We choose a suitable scale to determine the heights of bars. Here, we choose the scale as 1 small division to represent 5 marks.

Step IV First, we draw the bars for Kunal and then bars for Soni for different years.

Bars for Kunal and Soni shaded separately and the shading is shown in the top right corner of the graph paper.

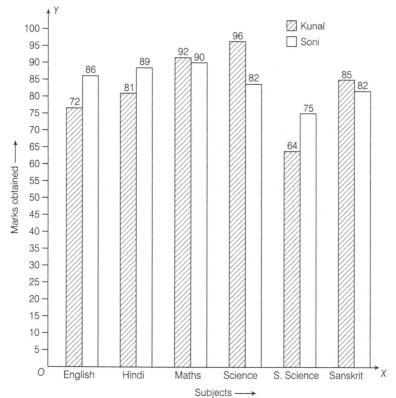

(b) Total percentage of marks obtained by Soni

$$= \left(\frac{\text{Total marks obtained by Soni in six subjects}}{600} \times 100 \right)\%$$

$$= \left(\frac{86 + 89 + 90 + 82 + 75 + 82}{600} \times 100 \right)\% = \left(\frac{504}{600} \times 100 \right)\% = 84\%$$

(c) Total percentage of marks obtained by Kunal

$$= \left(\frac{\text{Total marks obtained by Kunal in six subjects}}{600} \times 100 \right)\%$$

$$= \left(\frac{72 + 81 + 92 + 96 + 64 + 85}{600} \times 100 \right)\% = \left(\frac{490}{600} \times 100 \right)\% = 81.6\%$$

(d) Ratio of percentage marks obtained by Kunal and Soni = 81.6 : 84 = 34 : 35

(e) In English, Hindi and S.Science, Soni get more marks than Kunal.

(f) Marks obtained by Kunal and Soni is S. Science are 64 and 75, respectively. Therefore, Soni got more marks than Kunal by 11 marks.

(g) In English and Science, the difference of marks was maximum = (504 – 490), i.e.14 marks.

Q. 87 The students of class VII have to choose one club from Music, Dance, Yoga, Dramatics, Fine arts and Electronics clubs. The data given below shows the choices made by girls and boys of the class. Study the table and answer the questions that follow:

Clubs	Music	Dance	Yoga	Dramatics	Fine Arts	Electronics
Girls	15	24	10	19	27	21
Boys	12	16	8	17	11	30

(a) Draw a double bar graph using appropriate scale to depict the above data.

(b) How many students are there in class VII?

(c) Which is the most preferred club by boys?

(d) Which is the least preferred club by girls?

(e) For which club the difference between boys and girls is the least?

(f) For which club is the difference between boys and girls the maximum?

Sol. (a) Steps to construct the bar graph are as follows :

Step I We draw two lines perpendicular to each other on a graph paper and call them horizontal and vertical axes.

Step II Along the horizontal axis, OX mark the clubs and along the vertical axis, OY mark the number of boys and girls.

Step III We choose a suitable scale to determine the heights of bars. Here, we choose the scale as 1 small division to represent 2.

Step IV First, we draw the bars for girls and then bars for boys for different years. Bars for girls and boys are shaded separately and the shading is shown in the top right corner of the graph paper.

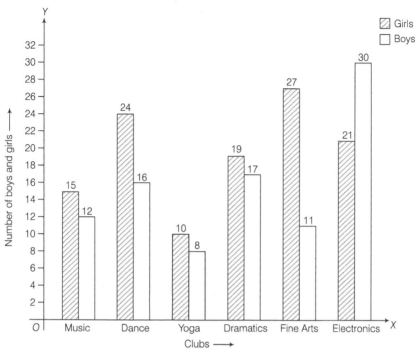

(b) Total students in class VII

= 15 + 12 + 24 + 16 + 10 + 8 + 19 + 17 + 27 + 11 + 21 + 30 = 210

(c) From the given data, we can say that most preferred club by boys is Electronics.

(d) From the given data, we can say that least preferred club by girls is Yoga.

(e) It is clear from the given data in Yoga and Dramatics, the difference between boys and girls is the least, i.e. (19 –17) = 2

(f) It is clear from the given data in Fine Arts the difference between boys and girls is maximum, i.e. (27 – 11) = 16

Q. 88 The data given below shows the production of motor bikes in a factory for some months of two consecutive years.

Months	Feb	May	Aug	Oct	Dec
2008	2700	3200	6000	5000	4200
2007	2800	4500	4800	4800	5200

Study the table given above and answer the following questions:

(a) Draw a double bar graph using appropriate scale to depict the above information and compare them.

(b) In which year was the total output the maximum?

(c) Find the mean production for the year 2007.

(d) For which month was the difference between the production for the two years the maximum?

(e) In which month for the year 2008, the production was the maximum?

(f) In which month for the year 2007, the production was the least?

Sol.   (a) Steps to construct the bar graphs are as follows:

Step I We draw two lines perpendicular to each other on a graph paper and call them horizontal and vertical axes.

Step II Along the horizontal axis, OX mark the months and along the vertical axis, OY mark the production of motor bikes.

Step III We choose a suitable scale to determine the heights of bars. Here, we choose the scale as 1 big division to represent 400.

Step IV First, we draw the bars for Year 2008 and then bars for Year 2007 for different months.

Bars for year 2008 and year 2007 months are shaded separately and the shading is shown in the top right corner of the graph paper.

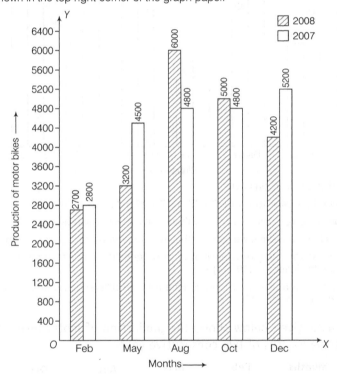

(b) Total output in year 2008 = 2700 + 3200 + 6000 + 5000 + 4200 = 21100

Total output in year 2007 = 2800 + 4500 + 4800 + 4800 + 5200 = 22100

∴ Total output in year 2007 is more than year 2008.

(c) Mean production for the year 2007 = $\dfrac{\text{Total production in year 2007 for 5 months}}{5}$

$$= \dfrac{22100}{5} = 4420$$

(d) It is clear from the given data in May the difference between the production for the two years in maximum, i.e. 1300.

(e) In August the production was maximum, i.e. 6000 as compared to other months of year 2008.

(f) In February the production was minimum, i.e. 2800 as compared to other months of year 2007.

Q. 89 The table below compares the population (in hundreds) of 4 towns over two years:

Towns	A	B	C	D
2007	2900	6400	8300	4600
2009	3200	7500	9200	6300

Study the table and answer the following questions:

    (a) Draw a double bar graph using appropriate scale to depict the above information.

    (b) In which town was the population growth maximum?

    (c) In which town was the population growth least?

Sol.   (a) Steps to construct the bar graph are as follows :

    Step I We draw two lines perpendicular to each other on a graph paper and call them horizontal and vertical axes.

    Step II Along the horizontal axis, OX mark the towns and along the vertical axis, OY mark the population.

    Step III We choose a suitable scale to determine the heights of bars. Here, we choose the scale as 1 small division to represent 500.

    Step IV First, we draw the bars for year 2007 and then bars for year 2009 for different towns.

    Bars for year 2007 and 2009 are shaded separately and the shading is shown in the top right corner of the graph paper.

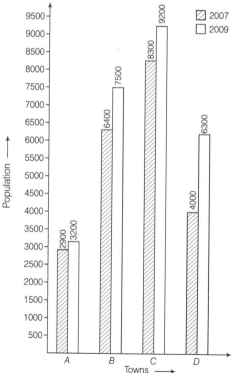

    (b) It is clear from the graph, the population growth of town D was maximum.

    (c) It is clear from the graph, the population growth of town A was minimum.

Q. 90 The table below gives the data of tourists visiting 5 hill stations over two consecutive years. Study the table and answer questions that follow:

Hill stations	Nainital	Shimla	Manali	Mussoorie	Kullu
2008	4000	5200	3700	5800	3500
2009	4800	4500	4200	6200	4600

(a) Draw a double bar graph to depict the above information using appropriate scale.

(b) Which hill station was visited by the maximum number of tourists in 2008?

(c) Which hill station was visited by least number of tourists in 2009?

(d) In which hill stations was there increase in number of tourists in 2009?

Sol.   (a) Steps to construct the bar graph as follows:

Step I We draw two lines perpendicular to each other on a graph paper and call them horizontal and vertical axes.

Step II Along the horizontal axis, *OX* mark the hill stations and along the vertical axis, *OY* mark the tourist visitors.

Step III We choose a suitable scale to determine the heights of bars. Here, we choose the scale as 1 small division to represent 400 tourists.

Step IV First, we draw the bars for year 2008 and then bars for year 2009 for different hill stations.

Bars for years 2008 and 2009 are shaded separately and the shading is shown in the top right corner of the graph paper.

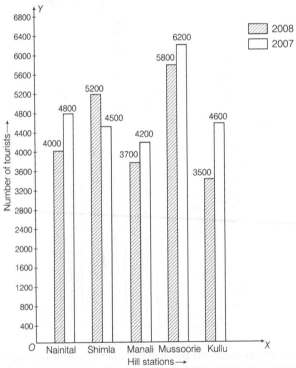

(b) It is clear from the given data that in year 2008 tourists visit Mussoorie the most maximum.

(c) It is clear from the given data that in year 2009 tourists visit Manali the least.

(d) From the graph, we can say that in 2009, there is increase in tourist visitors in the places; Manali, Nainital, Mussoorie and Kullu.

Q. 91 The table below gives the flavours of ice-cream liked by children (boys and girls) of a society.

Flavours	Vanilla	Chocolate	Strawberry	Mango	Butterscotch
Boys	4	9	3	8	13
Girls	8	12	7	9	10

Study the table and answer the following questions:

(a) Draw a double bar graph using appropriate scale to represent the above information.

(b) Which flavour is liked the most by the boys?

(c) How many girls are there in all?

(d) How many children liked chocolate flavour of ice-cream?

(e) Find the ratio of children who liked strawberry flavour to vanilla flavour of ice-cream.

Sol. (a) Bar graph of the given data is:

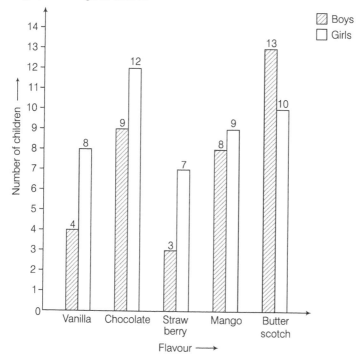

(b) On observing the bar graph, we can say that boys like butterscotch the most because the bar for butterscotch in case of boys is of highest length, i.e. 13.

(c) Total number of girls = Sum of heights of bars corresponding to girls

$$= 8 + 12 + 7 + 9 + 10 = 46$$

(d) Number of children who like chocolate flavour = Sum of heights of bars for both boys and girls corresponding to chocolate = 9 + 12 = 21

(e) Total number of children who like strawberry = 3 + 7 = 10

Total number of children who like vanilla = 4 + 8 = 12

∴ Ratio of children who like strawberry flavour to vanilla flavour of ice-cream

$$= 10 : 12 = 5 : 6$$

4

Simple Equations

Multiple Choice Questions (MCQs)

Q. 1 The solution of the equation $ax + b = 0$

(a) $\dfrac{a}{b}$ (b) $-b$ (c) $-\dfrac{b}{a}$ (d) $\dfrac{b}{a}$

Sol. *(c)*   Given equation is $ax + b = 0$

$\Rightarrow$ $ax = -b$ [transposing b to RHS]

$\Rightarrow$ $x = -\dfrac{b}{a}$ [on dividing both sides by a]

Q. 2 If a and b are positive integers, then the solution of the equation $ax = b$ will always be a

(a) positive number   (b) negative number

(c) 1   (d) 0

Sol. *(a)*   Given equation is $ax = b$

On dividing the equation by a, we get

$$x = \frac{b}{a}$$

Now, if a and b are positive integers, then the solution of the equation is also positive number as division of two positive integers is also a positive number.

Q. 3 Which of the following is not allowed in a given equation?

(a) Adding the same number to both sides of the equation.

(b) Subtracting the same number from both sides of the equation.

(c) Multiplying both sides of the equation by the same non-zero number.

(d) Dividing both sides of the equation by the same number.

Sol. *(d)*   Dividing both sides of the equation by the same non-zero number is allowed in a given equation, division of any number by zero is not allowed as set division of number by zero is not defined.

Note *If we add same number to both sides of the equation while adding, subtracting, then there will be no change in the given equation.*

Q. 4 The solution of which of the following equations is neither a positive fraction nor an integer?

(a) $2x + 6 = 0$

(b) $3x - 5 = 0$

(c) $5x - 8 = x + 4$

(d) $4x + 7 = x + 2$

Sol. *(d)*   Let us solve the equations:

(a) Given equation is $2x + 6 = 0$

$\Rightarrow$ $\qquad\qquad 2x = -6$ [transposing 6 to RHS]

$\Rightarrow$ $\qquad\qquad x = -\dfrac{6}{2}$ [dividing both sides by 2]

$\Rightarrow$ $\qquad\qquad x = -3$ (integer)

(b) Given equation is $3x - 5 = 0$

$\Rightarrow$ $\qquad\qquad 3x = 5$ [transposing 5 to RHS]

$\Rightarrow$ $\qquad\qquad k = \dfrac{5}{3}$ (fraction) [dividing both sides by 3]

(c) Given equation is $5x - 8 = x + 4$

$\Rightarrow$ $\qquad\qquad 5x = x + 4 + 8$ [transposing 8 to RHS]

$\Rightarrow$ $\qquad\qquad 5x = x + 12$

$\Rightarrow$ $\qquad\qquad 5x - x = 12$ [transposing x to LHS]

$\Rightarrow$ $\qquad\qquad 4x = 12$

$\Rightarrow$ $\qquad\qquad x = 3$ (integer) [dividing both sides by 4]

(d) Given equation is $4x + 7 = x + 2$

$\Rightarrow$ $\qquad\qquad 4x + 7 - x = 2$ [transposing x to LHS]

$\Rightarrow$ $\qquad\qquad 3x = 2 - 7$ [transposing 7 to RHS]

$\Rightarrow$ $\qquad\qquad 3x = -5$

$\Rightarrow$ $\qquad\qquad x = -\dfrac{5}{3}$ [dividing both sides by 3]

which is neither a positive fraction nor an integer.

Q. 5 The equation which can not be solved in integers is

(a) $5y - 3 = -18$

(b) $3x - 9 = 0$

(c) $3z + 8 = 3 + z$

(d) $9y + 8 = 4y - 7$

Sol. *(c)*   Let us solve the equations:

(a) Given equation is $5y - 3 = -18$

$\Rightarrow$ $\qquad\qquad 5y = -18 + 3$ [transposing 3 to RHS]

$\Rightarrow$ $\qquad\qquad 5y = -15$

$\Rightarrow$ $\qquad\qquad y = -3$ (integer) [dividing both sides by 5]

(b) Given equation is $3x - 9 = 0$

$\Rightarrow$ $\qquad\qquad 3x = 9$ [transposing 9 to RHS]

$\Rightarrow$ $\qquad\qquad x = 3$ (integer) [dividing both sides by 3]

(c) Given equation is $3z + 8 = 3 + z$

On transposing z and 8 to LHS and RHS respectively, we get

$\Rightarrow$ $\qquad\qquad 3z - z = 3 - 8$

$\Rightarrow$ $\qquad\qquad 2z = -5$

$\qquad\qquad z = -\dfrac{5}{2}$ [dividing both sides by 2]

which is neither a positive fraction nor an integer.

(d) Given equation is $9y + 8 = 4y - 7$

On transposing $4y$ and 8 to LHS and RHS respectively, we get

$\Rightarrow$ $\qquad\qquad 9y - 4y = -7 - 8$

$\qquad\qquad\qquad\qquad 5y = -15$

$\Rightarrow$ $\qquad\qquad \dfrac{5y}{5} = -\dfrac{15}{5}$ $\qquad\qquad$ [dividing both sides by 5]

$\Rightarrow$ $\qquad\qquad y = -3 \,(\text{integer})$

Q. 6 If $7x + 4 = 25$, then x is equal to

(a) $\dfrac{29}{7}$ $\qquad$ (b) $\dfrac{100}{7}$ $\qquad$ (c) 2 $\qquad$ (d) 3

Sol. *(d)* Given equation is $7x + 4 = 25$

$\Rightarrow$ $\qquad\qquad\qquad 7x = 25 - 4$ $\qquad\qquad$ [transposing 4 to RHS]

$\Rightarrow$ $\qquad\qquad\qquad 7x = 21$

On dividing the above equation by 7, we get

$\qquad\qquad\qquad\qquad x = 3$

Hence, the solution of the given equation is 3.

Q. 7 The solution of the equation $3x + 7 = -20$ is

(a) $\dfrac{17}{7}$ $\qquad$ (b) -9 $\qquad$ (c) 9 $\qquad$ (d) $\dfrac{13}{3}$

Sol. *(b)* Given equation is $\quad 3x + 7 = -20$

$\Rightarrow$ $\qquad\qquad\qquad 3x = -20 - 7$ $\qquad\qquad$ [transposing 7 to RHS]

$\Rightarrow$ $\qquad\qquad\qquad 3x = -27$

On dividing the above equation by 3, we get

$\qquad\qquad\qquad\qquad x = -9$

Hence, the solution of the given equation is -9.

Q. 8 The value of y for which the expressions $(y - 15)$ and $(2y + 1)$ become equal is

(a) 0 $\qquad$ (b) 16 $\qquad$ (c) 8 $\qquad$ (d) -16

Sol. *(d)* It is given that both the expressions are equal. So, the equation is

$\Rightarrow$ $\qquad\qquad y - 15 = 2y + 1$

$\Rightarrow$ $\qquad\qquad y - 2y = 1 + 15$ $\qquad$ [transposing $2y$ to LHS and (-15) to RHS]

$\qquad\qquad\qquad -y = 16$

Multiplying both sides by (-1), we get

$\qquad\qquad\qquad y = -16$

Q. 9 If $k + 7 = 16$, then the value of $8k - 72$ is

(a) 0 $\qquad\qquad\qquad\qquad$ (b) 1

(c) 112 $\qquad\qquad\qquad\quad$ (d) 56

Sol. *(a)* Given equation is $k + 7 = 16$

On transposing 7 to RHS, we get
$$k = 16 - 7 = 9$$
Put the value of k in the equation $(8k - 72)$, we get
$$8(9) - 72 = 72 - 72 = 0$$

Q. 10 If $43m = 0.086$, then the value of m is

(a) 0.002　　(b) 0.02　　(c) 0.2　　(d) 2

Sol. *(a)* Given equation is $43m = 0.086$

On dividing the given equation by 43, we get
$$m = \frac{0.086}{43}$$
If we remove the decimal, we get 1000 in denominator
$$m = \frac{86}{43} \times \frac{1}{1000} = \frac{2}{1000} = 0.002$$

Q. 11 x exceeds 3 by 7, can be represented as

(a) $x + 3 = 2$　　(b) $x + 7 = 3$　　(c) $x - 3 = 7$　　(d) $x - 7 = 3$

Sol. *(c)* The given statement means x is 7 more than 3.

So, the equation is $x - 7 = 3$

We can also write it as $x - 3 = 7$.

Q. 12 The equation having 5 as a solution is

(a) $4x + 1 = 2$　　(b) $3 - x = 8$

(c) $x - 5 = 3$　　(d) $3 + x = 8$

Sol. *(d)* Let us solve the equations:

(a) Given equation is $4x + 1 = 2$
$$\Rightarrow \quad 4x = 2 - 1 \;\Rightarrow\; 4x = 1 \;\Rightarrow\; x = \frac{1}{4}$$
(b) Given equation is $3 - x = 8$
$$\Rightarrow \quad -x = 8 - 3 \;\Rightarrow\; -x = 5 \;\Rightarrow\; x = -5$$
(c) Given equation is $x - 5 = 3$
$$\Rightarrow \quad x = 3 + 5 \;\Rightarrow\; x = 8$$
(d) Given equation is $3 + x = 8$
$$\Rightarrow \quad x = 8 - 3 \;\Rightarrow\; x = 5$$

Q. 13 The equation having -3 as solution is

(a) $x + 3 = 1$　　(b) $8 + 2x = 3$

(c) $10 + 3x = 1$　　(d) $2x + 1 = 3$

Sol. *(c)* Let us solve the equations:

(a) Given equation is $x + 3 = 1$
$$\Rightarrow \qquad x = 1 - 3$$
$$\Rightarrow \qquad x = -2$$

(b) Given equation is $8 + 2x = 3$

$\Rightarrow \qquad\qquad 2x = 3 - 8$

$\Rightarrow \qquad\qquad 2x = -5$

$\Rightarrow \qquad\qquad x = -\dfrac{5}{2}$

(c) Given equation is $10 + 3x = 1$

$\Rightarrow \qquad\qquad 3x = 1 - 10$

$\Rightarrow \qquad\qquad 3x = -9$

$\Rightarrow \qquad\qquad x = -3$

Now, we don't have to solve next equation as we get the answer.

Q. 14 Which of the following equations can be formed starting with $x = 0$?

(a) $2x + 1 = -1$ \qquad (b) $\dfrac{x}{2} + 5 = 7$ \qquad (c) $3x - 1 = -1$ \qquad (d) $3x - 1 = 1$

Sol. *(c)* We have, $x = 0$

On multiplying both the sides by 3, we get

$$3 \times x = 3 \times 0$$

$\Rightarrow \qquad\qquad 3x = 0$

On adding (-1) both the sides, we get

$$3x + (-1) = 0 + (-1)$$

$\Rightarrow \qquad\qquad 3x - 1 = -1$

Q. 15 Which of the following equations cannot be formed using the equation $x = 7$?

(a) $2x + 1 = 15$ \qquad (b) $7x - 1 = 50$ \qquad (c) $x - 3 = 4$ \qquad (d) $\dfrac{x}{7} - 1 = 0$

Sol. *(b)* We have, $x = 7$

On multiplying both the sides by 7, we get

$$7 \times x = 7 \times 7 \Rightarrow 7x = 49$$

On adding (-1) both the sides, we get

$$7x + (-1) = 49 + (-1)$$

$\Rightarrow \qquad\qquad 7x - 1 = 49 - 1$

$\Rightarrow \qquad\qquad 7x - 1 = 48$

Q. 16 If $\dfrac{x}{2} = 3$, then the value of $3x + 2$ is

(a) 20 \qquad (b) 11 \qquad (c) $\dfrac{13}{2}$ \qquad (d) 8

Sol. *(a)* Given, $\dfrac{x}{2} = 3$

On multiplying both sides by 2, we get $\dfrac{x}{2} \times 2 = 3 \times 2$

$\Rightarrow \qquad\qquad x = 3 \times 2 = 6$

Put $x = 6$ in the equation $3x + 2$, we get

$$3(6) + 2 = 18 + 2 = 20$$

Q. 17 Which of the following numbers satisfy the equation $-6 + x = -12$?

    (a) 2   (b) 6   (c) -6 (d) -2

Sol. *(c)*   Let us put the values given in the options in equation $-6 + x = -12$

    (a) Put $x = 2$

$$\Rightarrow \qquad -6 + 2 = -12$$
$$\Rightarrow \qquad -4 = -12$$
$$\therefore \qquad \text{LHS} \neq \text{RHS}$$

    (b) Put $x = 6$

$$\Rightarrow \qquad -6 + (6) = -12$$
$$\Rightarrow \qquad 0 = -12$$
$$\therefore \qquad \text{LHS} \neq \text{RHS}$$

    (c) Put $x = -6$

$$\Rightarrow \qquad -6 + (-6) = -12$$
$$\Rightarrow \qquad -6 - 6 = -12$$
$$\Rightarrow \qquad -12 = -12$$
$$\therefore \qquad \text{LHS} = \text{RHS (satisfied)}$$

    Now, there is no need to check the next option.

    Hence, $x = -6$ satisfies the given equation.

Q. 18 Shifting one term from one side of an equation to another side with a change of sign is known as

    (a) commutativity   (b) transposition
    (c) distributivity   (d) associativity

Sol. *(b)*   Transposition means shifting one term from one side of an equation to another side with a change of sign.

Fill in the Blanks

In questions 19 to 48, fill in the blanks to make the statements true.

Q. 19 The sum of two numbers is 60 and their difference is 30.

    (a) If smaller number is x, the other number is _____.
    (b) The difference of numbers in term of x is _____ .
    (c) The equation formed is _____ .
    (d) The solution of the equation is _____ .
    (e) The numbers are _____ and _____ .

Sol.   Given, the sum of two numbers is 60 and difference is 30.

    (a) If the smaller number is x, then the other number is **$(60 - x)$**, since the sum of both numbers is 60.

    (b) Given, one number $= x$ [from (a)]

    Then, other number $= (60 - x)$

    $\therefore$ Difference $= (60 - x) - x = \mathbf{60 - 2x}$

(c) We are given that difference between two numbers is 30.

So, the equation formed is $60 - 2x = 30$

$\Rightarrow \qquad\qquad -2x = 30 - 60$ \hfill [transposing 60 to RHS]

$\Rightarrow \qquad\qquad -2x = -30$

$\Rightarrow \qquad\qquad 2x = 30$ \hfill [multiplying both sides by (– 1)]

(d) Let us solve the equation for x,

$$2x = 30$$

On dividing the above equation by 2, we get

$$\frac{2x}{2} = \frac{30}{2}$$

$\Rightarrow \qquad\qquad x = 15$

Hence, the solution of the equation is **15**.

(e) The numbers are x and $(60 - x)$.

Now, put the value of x, we get

First number = **15**

Second number = $60 - 15 = $ **45**

Q. 20 Sum of two numbers is 81. One is twice the other.

(a) If smaller number is x, the other number is _____.

(b) The equation formed is _____.

(c) The solution of the equation is _____.

(d) The numbers are _____ and _____.

Sol. (a) We are given that one number is twice the other.

If smaller number is x, then the other number is **2x**.

(b) We are given that sum of two numbers is 81. So, the equation will be

$$x + 2x = 81$$

(c) Now, solve the equation for x,

$\Rightarrow \qquad\qquad x + 2x = 81$

$\Rightarrow \qquad\qquad 3x = 81$

$\Rightarrow \qquad\qquad \dfrac{3x}{3} = \dfrac{81}{3}$ \hfill [dividing both sides by 3]

$\qquad\qquad x = 27$

Hence, the solution of the equation is **27**.

(d) The two numbers are $x = $ **27** and $2x = 2 \times 27 = $ **54**.

Q. 21 In a test, Abha gets twice the marks as that of Palak. Two times Abha's marks and three times Palak's marks make 280.

(a) If Palak gets x marks, Abha gets _____ marks.

(b) The equation formed is _____.

(c) The solution of the equation is _____.

(d) Marks obtained by Abha are _____.

Sol. (a) If Palak gets x marks, then Abha gets twice the marks as that of Palak, i.e. **2x**.

(b) Two times of Abha's marks $= 2(2x) = 4x$ and three times the Palak marks $= 3(x) = 3x$.

Now, two times Abha's marks and three times Palak's marks make 280.

So, the equation formed is **4x + 3x = 280**.

(c) Solve the equation for x,

$$\Rightarrow \qquad 4x + 3x = 280$$
$$\Rightarrow \qquad 7x = 280$$
$$\Rightarrow \qquad \frac{7x}{7} = \frac{280}{7} \qquad \text{[dividing both sides by 7]}$$
$$x = 40$$

Hence, the solution of the equation is **40**.

(d) Marks obtained by Abha are $2x$, i.e. $2 \times 40 = $ **80**.

Q. 22 The length of a rectangle is two times its breadth. Its perimeter is 60cm.

(a) If the breadth of rectangle is x cm, the length of the rectangle is_____.

(b) Perimeter in terms of x is_____.

(c) The equation formed is _____.

(d) The solution of the equation is _____.

Sol. (a) It is given that the length of the rectangle is two times its breadth.

$\therefore$ Length = **2x cm**

(b) Perimeter of rectangle $= 2$ (Length + Breadth) $= $ **2 (2x + x)**

(c) As we are given that perimeter of rectangle is 60 cm.

So, the equation formed is $2(2x + x) = 60$

$$\Rightarrow \qquad 2(3x) = 60$$
$$\Rightarrow \qquad 6x = 60$$

(d) On dividing the equation by 6, we get

$$\frac{6x}{6} = \frac{60}{6}$$
$$\Rightarrow \qquad x = 10$$

Hence, the solution of the equation is **10**.

Q. 23 In a bag, there are ₹5 and ₹2 coins. If they are equal in number and their worth is ₹ 70, then

(a) The worth of x coins of ₹ 5 each_____.

(b) The worth of x coins of ₹ 2 each_____.

(c) The equation formed is _____.

(d) There are _____ ₹5 coins and _____ ₹2 coins.

Sol. Let number of coins of ₹ 5 $= x$

Then, number of coins of ₹ 2 $= x$

(a) Number of coins of ₹ 5 $= x$

So, the worth of ₹ 5 of x coins $= ₹ 5 \times x = ₹$ **5x**

(b) Similarly, the worth of ₹ 2 of x coins $= ₹$ **2x**

(c) It is given that, combined value/worth of ₹ 5 and ₹ 2 coins is ₹ 70.

So, the equation formed is

Worth of ₹ 5 coins + Worth of ₹ 2 coins = ₹ 70

$\Rightarrow$ $\qquad$ **5x + 2x = 70**

(d) Solve the equation for x,

$$5x + 2x = 70$$
$\Rightarrow$ $\qquad$ $7x = 70$
$\Rightarrow$ $\qquad$ $x = 10$ $\qquad$ [dividing both sides by 7]

Hence, there are **10**, ₹ 5 coins and **10**, ₹ 2 coins.

Q. 24 In a Mathematics quiz, 30 prizes consisting of 1st and 2nd prizes only are to be given. 1st and 2nd prizes are worth ₹ 2000 and ₹ 1000, respectively. If the total prize money is ₹ 52000, then show that

(a) If 1st prizes are x in number the number of 2nd prizes are _____.

(b) The total value of prizes in terms of x are _____.

(c) The equation formed is _____.

(d) The solution of the equation is _____.

(e) The number of 1st prizes are _____ and the number of 2nd prizes are _____.

Sol. Given, number of prizes = 30

Total prize money = ₹ 52000, 1st and 2nd prizes are worth ₹ 2000 and ₹ 1000, respectively.

(a) It 1st prizes are x in number, the number of 2nd prizes are **(30 − x)**, because total number of prizes are 30.

(b) Total value of prizes in terms of x are **2000x + 1000 (30 − x)**.

(c) The equation formed is 1000x + 30000 = 52000

From (b), $2000x + 1000(30 - x) = 52000$
$\Rightarrow$ $\qquad$ $2000x + 30000 - 1000x = 54000$
$\Rightarrow$ $\qquad$ **1000x + 30000 = 52000**

(d) The solution of the equation is **22**.

From (c), $1000x + 30000 = 52000$
$\Rightarrow$ $\qquad$ $1000x = 52000 - 30000 = 22000$
$\Rightarrow$ $\qquad$ $x = \dfrac{22000}{1000} = 22$

(e) The number of 1st prizes are **22** and the number of 2nd prizes are **8**.

From (b), $2000x + 1000(30 - x) = 52000$
$$2x + (30 - x) = 52 \qquad \text{[dividing both sides by 1000]}$$
$$x + 30 = 52$$
$\Rightarrow$ $\qquad$ $x = 52 - 30 = 22$
$\therefore$ $\qquad$ Number of 2nd prizes = 30 − 22 = 8

Q. 25 If $z + 3 = 5$, then $z = $ _____.

Sol. Solve the given equation for z,

$$z + 3 = 5$$
$$\Rightarrow \qquad z = 5 - 3 \qquad \text{[transposing 3 to RHS]}$$
$$\Rightarrow \qquad z = 2$$

Q. 26 _____ is the solution of the equation $3x - 2 = 7$.

Sol. Solve the given equation for x,

$$3x - 2 = 7$$
$$\Rightarrow \qquad 3x = 7 + 2 \qquad \text{[transposing } (-2) \text{ to RHS]}$$
$$\Rightarrow \qquad 3x = 9$$
$$\Rightarrow \qquad \frac{3x}{3} = \frac{9}{3} \qquad \text{[dividing both sides by 3]}$$
$$\Rightarrow \qquad x = 3$$

Q. 27 _____ is the solution of $3x + 10 = 7$.

Sol. Solve the given equation for x,

$$\Rightarrow \qquad 3x + 10 = 7$$
$$\Rightarrow \qquad 3x = 7 - 10 \qquad \text{[transposing 10 to RHS]}$$
$$\Rightarrow \qquad 3x = -3$$
$$\Rightarrow \qquad \frac{3x}{3} = \frac{-3}{3} \qquad \text{[dividing both sides by 3]}$$
$$x = -1$$

Q. 28 If $2x + 3 = 5$, then value of $3x + 2$ is.

Sol. Solve the given equation for x,

$$2x + 3 = 5$$
$$\Rightarrow \qquad 2x = 5 - 3 \qquad \text{[transposing 3 to RHS]}$$
$$\Rightarrow \qquad \frac{2x}{2} = \frac{2}{2} \qquad \text{[dividing both sides by 2]}$$
$$\Rightarrow \qquad x = 1$$

Put the value of x in $(3x + 2)$, we get
$$3(1) + 2 = 3 + 2 = 5$$

Q. 29 In integers, $4x - 1 = 8$ has _____ solution.

Sol. Solve the given equation for x,

$$4x - 1 = 8$$
$$\Rightarrow \qquad 4x = 8 + 1 \qquad \text{[transposing } (-1) \text{ to RHS]}$$
$$\Rightarrow \qquad 4x = 9$$
$$\Rightarrow \qquad \frac{4x}{4} = \frac{9}{4} \qquad \text{[dividing both sides by 4]}$$
$$\Rightarrow \qquad x = \frac{9}{4}$$

Since, the solution of the equation is not an integer, hence the equation has **no** solution.

Q. 30 In natural numbers, $4x + 5 = -7$ has _____ solution.

Sol. Solve the equation for x, $\qquad 4x + 5 = -7$

$\Rightarrow \qquad\qquad\qquad\qquad 4x = -7 - 5$ [transposing 5 to RHS]

$\Rightarrow \qquad\qquad\qquad\qquad 4x = -12$

$\Rightarrow \qquad\qquad\qquad\qquad x = -3$ [dividing both sides by 3]

Since, the value of x is not natural number, hence the equation has **no** solution in natural numbers.

Q. 31 In natural numbers, $x - 5 = -5$ has _____ solution.

Sol. Solve the given equation for x.

$\qquad\qquad\qquad\qquad x - 5 = -5$

$\Rightarrow \qquad\qquad\qquad\qquad x = -5 + 5$ [transposing (– 5) to RHS]

$\Rightarrow \qquad\qquad\qquad\qquad x = 0$

Since, natural numbers do not contain zero, hence the equation has **no** solution.

Q. 32 In whole numbers, $x + 8 = 12 - 4$ has _____ solution.

Sol. Solve the given equation for x,

$\qquad\qquad\qquad\qquad x + 8 = 12 - 4$

$\Rightarrow \qquad\qquad\qquad\qquad x + 8 = 8$

$\Rightarrow \qquad\qquad\qquad\qquad x = 8 - 8$ [transposing 8 to RHS]

$\Rightarrow \qquad\qquad\qquad\qquad x = 0$

Since, zero is in the range of whole numbers, hence the equation has **one** solution.

Q. 33 If 5 is addes to three times a number, it becomes the same as 7 is subtracted from four times the same number. This fact can be represented as _____.

Sol. Let the number be x.

Now, 5 is added to 3 times the number $5 + 3x$.

It is same as 7 is subtracted from 4 times the number, i.e. $4x - 7$.

So, the equation formed is **$5 + 3x = 4x - 7$**.

Q. 34 $x + 7 = 10$ has the solution _____ .

Sol. Solve the given equation for x,

$\qquad\qquad\qquad\qquad x + 7 = 10$

$\Rightarrow \qquad\qquad\qquad\qquad x = 10 - 7$ [transposing 7 to RHS]

$\Rightarrow \qquad\qquad\qquad\qquad x = 3$

Q. 35 $x - 0 =$ _____ when $3x = 12$.

Sol. Given that, $3x = 12$

$\Rightarrow \qquad\qquad\qquad\qquad \dfrac{3x}{3} = \dfrac{12}{3}$ [dividing both sides by 3]

$\Rightarrow \qquad\qquad\qquad\qquad x = 4$

$\therefore \qquad\qquad\qquad\qquad x - 0 = 4 - 0 = \mathbf{4}$

Q. 36 $x - 1 =$ _____, when $2x = 2$

Sol. Given that, $2x = 2$

⇒ $\dfrac{2x}{2} = \dfrac{2}{2}$ [dividing both sides by 2]

⇒ $x = 1$

∴ $x - 1 = 1 - 1 = 0$

Q. 37 $x -$ _____ $= 15$; when $\dfrac{x}{2} = 6$

Sol. Given that, $\dfrac{x}{2} = 6$

⇒ $x = 12$ [multiplying both sides by 2]

∴ $12 - (-3) = 15$

Hence, $x - (-3) = 15$

Q. 38 The solution of the equation $x + 15 = 19$ is.

Sol. Solve the equation for x,

⇒ $x + 15 = 19$

⇒ $x = 19 - 15$ [transposing 15 to RHS]

                                                      $x = 4$

Hence, the solution of the given equation is **4**.

Q. 39 Finding the value of a variable in a linear equation that _____ the equation is called a _____ of the equation.

Sol. Finding the value of a variable in a linear equation that **satisfies** the equation is called a **root** of the equation.

Q. 40 Any term of an equation may be transposed from one side of the equation to the other side of the equation by changing the _____ of the term.

Sol. Any term of an equation may be transposed from one side of the equation to the other side of the equation by changing the **sign** of the term.

Q. 41 If $\dfrac{9}{5}x = \dfrac{18}{5}$, then $x =$ _____ .

Sol. Given that, $\dfrac{9}{5}x = \dfrac{18}{5}$

On dividing both sides by $\dfrac{9}{5}$, we get

$$\dfrac{9}{5}x \div \dfrac{9}{5} = \dfrac{18}{5} \div \dfrac{9}{5}$$

⇒ $x = \dfrac{18}{5} \times \dfrac{5}{9} = 2$

Q. 42 If $3 - x = -4$, then $x = $ _____ .

Sol. Given that,

$$3 - x = -4$$
$$\Rightarrow \quad -x = -4 - 3 \qquad \text{[transposing 3 to RHS]}$$
$$\Rightarrow \quad -x = -7$$
$$\Rightarrow \quad x = 7 \qquad \text{[multiplying both sides by } (-1)\text{]}$$

Q. 43 If $x - \dfrac{1}{2} = -\dfrac{1}{2}$, then $x = $ _____ .

Sol. Given that,

$$x - \frac{1}{2} = -\frac{1}{2}$$
$$\Rightarrow \quad x = \frac{1}{2} - \frac{1}{2} \qquad \text{[transposing } (-\tfrac{1}{2}) \text{ to RHS]}$$
$$\Rightarrow \quad x = 0$$

Q. 44 If $\dfrac{1}{6} - x = -\dfrac{1}{6}$, then $x = $ _____ .

Sol. Given that,

$$\frac{1}{6} - x = \frac{1}{6}$$
$$\Rightarrow \quad -x = \frac{1}{6} - \frac{1}{6} \qquad \text{[transposing } \tfrac{1}{6} \text{ to RHS]}$$
$$\Rightarrow \quad -x = 0$$
$$\Rightarrow \quad x = 0 \qquad \text{[multiplying both sides by } (-1)\text{]}$$

Q. 45 If 10 less than a number is 65, then the number is _____ .

Sol. Let the number be x.
Then, the equation will be $x - 10 = 65$
Now, solving the equation for x,

$$x = 65 + 10 \qquad \text{[transposing } (-10) \text{ to RHS]}$$
$$\Rightarrow \quad x = 75$$

Hence, the number is **75**.

Q. 46 If a number is increased by 20, it becomes 45. Then, the number is

_____ .

Sol. Let the number be x.
If it is increased by 20, it becomes $(x + 20)$.
So, the equation formed is

$$x + 20 = 45$$
$$\Rightarrow \quad x = 45 - 20 \qquad \text{[transposing 20 to RHS]}$$
$$\Rightarrow \quad x = 25$$

Hence, the number is **25**.

Q. 47 If 84 exceeds another number by 12, then the other number is _____ .

Sol. Let the number be x.

If 84 exceeds the number by 12, then the equation formed is

$\Rightarrow$ $84 - x = 12$

$\Rightarrow$ $-x = 12 - 84$ [transposing 84 to RHS]

$\Rightarrow$ $-x = -72$

                                         $x = 72$ [multiplying both sides by (− 1)]

Hence, the number is **72**.

Q. 48 If $x - \dfrac{7}{8} = \dfrac{7}{8}$, then $x =$ _____.

Sol.   Given equation is $x - \dfrac{7}{8} = \dfrac{7}{8}$

$$x = \frac{7}{8} + \frac{7}{8}$$ $\left[\text{transposing}\left(-\dfrac{7}{8}\right)\text{to RHS}\right]$

$$x = \frac{7 + 7}{8}$$ [taking LCM]

$$x = \frac{14}{8} = \frac{7}{4}$$

True/ False

In questions 49 to 55, state whether the statements are True or False.

Q. 49 5 is the solution of the equation $3x + 2 = 17$.

Sol.   *True*

Solve the equation for x, $3x + 2 = 17$

$\Rightarrow$ $3x = 17 - 2$ [transposing 2 to RHS]

$\Rightarrow$ $\dfrac{3x}{3} = \dfrac{15}{3}$ [dividing both sides by 3]

$\Rightarrow$ $x = 5$

Q. 50 $\dfrac{9}{5}$ is the solution of the equation $4x - 1 = 8$.

Sol.   *False*

Solve the equation for x,

$\Rightarrow$ $4x - 1 = 8$

$\Rightarrow$ $4x = 8 + 1$ [transposing (− 1) to RHS]

$\Rightarrow$ $4x = 9$

                                        $x = \dfrac{9}{4}$ [dividing both sides by 4]

Q. 51 $4x - 5 = 7$ does not have an integer as its solution.

Sol. *False*

Given equation is $\qquad 4x - 5 = 7$

$\Rightarrow \qquad\qquad\qquad 4x = 7 + 5 \qquad$ [transposing (– 5) to RHS]

$\Rightarrow \qquad\qquad\qquad 4x = 12$

On dividing both sides by 4, we get

$$x = 3 \,(\text{integer})$$

Q. 52 One-third of a number added to itself gives 10, can be represented as $\dfrac{x}{3} + 10 = x$.

Sol. *False*

Let the number be x.

Then, the equation formed is $\dfrac{x}{3} + x = 10$.

Q. 53 $\dfrac{3}{2}$ is the solution of the equation $8x - 5 = 7$.

Sol. *True*

Solve the equation for x,

$\Rightarrow \qquad\qquad\qquad 8x - 5 = 7$

$\Rightarrow \qquad\qquad\qquad 8x = 7 + 5 \qquad$ [transposing (– 5) to RHS]

$\Rightarrow \qquad\qquad\qquad 8x = 12$

$\Rightarrow \qquad\qquad\qquad \dfrac{8x}{8} = \dfrac{12}{8} \qquad$ [dividing both sides by 8]

$$x = \dfrac{3}{2}$$

Q. 54 If $4x - 7 = 11$, then $x = 4$.

Sol. *False*

Solve the equation for x,

$\Rightarrow \qquad\qquad\qquad 4x - 7 = 11$

$\Rightarrow \qquad\qquad\qquad 4x = 11 + 7 \qquad$ [transposing (– 7) to RHS]

$\Rightarrow \qquad\qquad\qquad 4x = 18$

$\Rightarrow \qquad\qquad\qquad \dfrac{4x}{4} = \dfrac{18}{4} \qquad$ [dividing both sides by 4]

$$x = \dfrac{9}{2}$$

Q. 55 If 9 is the solution of variable x in the equation $\dfrac{5x-7}{2} = y$, then the value of y is 28.

Sol. *False*

Given that, $x = 9$

Put the value of x in the equation, we get

$$\dfrac{5(9)-7}{2} = y$$

$\Rightarrow$ $$\dfrac{45-7}{2} = y$$

$\Rightarrow$ $$\dfrac{38}{2} = y$$

$\Rightarrow$ $$y = 19$$

Q. 56 Match each of the entries in Column I with the appropriate entries in Column II.

Column I		Column II	
(i)	$x + 5 = 9$	(a)	$-\dfrac{5}{3}$
(ii)	$x - 7 = 4$	(b)	$\dfrac{5}{3}$
(iii)	$\dfrac{x}{12} = -5$	(c)	4
(iv)	$5x = 30$	(d)	6
(v)	The value of y which satisfies $3y = 5$	(e)	11
(vi)	If $p = 2$, then the value of $\dfrac{1}{3}(1-3p)$	(f)	-60
		(g)	3

Sol. (i) →(c) Given equation is $x + 5 = 9$

$\Rightarrow$ $x = 9 - 5$ [transposing 5 to RHS]

$\Rightarrow$ $x = 4$

(ii) →(e) Given equation is $x - 7 = 4$

$\Rightarrow$ $x = 4 + 7$ [transposing (− 7) to RHS]

$\Rightarrow$ $x = 11$

(iii) →(f) Given equation is $\dfrac{x}{12} = -5$

$\Rightarrow 12 \times \dfrac{x}{12} = -5 \times 12$ [multiplying both sides by 12]

$\Rightarrow$ $x = -60$

(iv) →(d) Given equation is $5x = 30$

$\Rightarrow$ $\dfrac{5x}{5} = \dfrac{30}{5}$ [dividing both sides by 5]

$\Rightarrow$ $x = 6$

(v) →(b) Given equation is $3y = 5$

$\Rightarrow \quad \dfrac{3y}{3} = \dfrac{5}{3}$ [dividing both sides by 3]

$\Rightarrow \quad y = \dfrac{5}{3}$

(vi) →(a) Given, $p = 2$

Put the value of p in the equation $= \dfrac{1}{3} \times (1 - 3p)$, we get

$$= \dfrac{1}{3}(1 - 3 \times 2) = \dfrac{1}{3} \times (1 - 6)$$

$$= \dfrac{1}{3} \times (-5)$$

$$= -\dfrac{5}{3}$$

In questions from 57 to 67, express each of the given statements as an equation.

Q. 57 13 subtracted from twice of a number gives 3.

Sol. Let the number be x.

13 is subtracted from twice of a number i.e. $2x - 13$ and it results 3.

So, the equation formed is $2x - 13 = 3$

Q. 58 One-fifth of a number is 5 less than that number.

Sol. Let the number be x.

Then, $\dfrac{1}{5}$th of the number $= \dfrac{x}{5}$

Now, $\dfrac{x}{5}$ is 5 less than x.

So, the equation formed is $\dfrac{x}{5} = x - 5$.

Q. 59 A number is 7 more than one-third of itself.

Sol. Let the number be x.

Then, $\dfrac{1}{3}$rd of number $= \dfrac{x}{3}$

So, the equation formed is $x = 7 + \dfrac{x}{3}$.

Q. 60 Six times a number is 10 more than the number.

Sol. Let the number be x.

Then, 6 times of a number $= 6x$

So, the equation formed is $6x = 10 + x$.

Q. 61 If 10 is subtracted from half of a number, the result is 4.

Sol.   Let the number be x.

Then, 10 is subtracted from $\dfrac{x}{2}$ i.e. $\dfrac{x}{2} - 10$ and its results 4.

So, the equation formed is $\dfrac{x}{2} - 10 = 4$.

Q. 62 Subtracting 5 from p, the result is 2.

Sol.   Subtract 5 from p i.e. $p - 5$ and its results 2.

Hence, the equation formed is $p - 5 = 2$.

Q. 63 Five times a number increased by 7 is 27.

Sol.   Let the number be x. Then, five times of number be $5x$.

Since, it is increased by 7 i.e. $5x + 7$ and it gives result 27.

Hence, the equation formed is $5x + 7 = 27$

Q. 64 Mohan is 3 years older than Sohan. The sum of their ages is 43 years.

Sol.   Let age of Sohan be x yr. Then, the age of Mohan is $(x + 3)$ yr.

$\therefore$ Sum of their ages = 43

So, the equation formed is $x + (x + 3) = 43$

Q. 65 If 1 is subtracted from a number and the difference is multiplied by $\dfrac{1}{2}$, the result is 7.

Sol.   Let the number be x.

Then, 1 is subtracted from a number and the difference is multiplied by $\dfrac{1}{2}$ i.e $\dfrac{1}{2}(x - 1)$

It gives result 7.

So, the equation formed is $\dfrac{1}{2}(x - 1) = 7$

Q. 66 A number divided by 2 and then increased by 5 is 9.

Sol.   Let the number be x.

Then, x is divided by 2 and increased by 5, i.e. $\dfrac{x}{2} + 5$ and gives result 9.

So, the equation formed is $\dfrac{x}{2} + 5 = 9$

Q. 67 The sum of twice a number and 4 is 18.

Sol.   Let the number be x.

Then, sum of twice of a number and 4 gives result 18.

Hence, $2x + 4 = 18$ is the equation.

Q. 68 The age of Sohan Lal is four times that of his son Amit. If the difference of their ages is 27 years, find the age of Amit.

Sol. Let x yr be the age of Amit.

Then, age of Sohan Lal = $4x$ yr

According to the question,

$$4x - x = 27 \Rightarrow 3x = 27 \Rightarrow x = \frac{27}{3} = 9$$

Hence, the age of Amit is 9 yr.

Q. 69 A number exceeds the other number by 12. If their sum is 72, find the numbers.

Sol. Let x be a number, then another number will be $x + 12$.

According to the question, $x + x + 12 = 72$

$\Rightarrow$ $2x = 72 - 12$ [transposing 12 to RHS]

$\Rightarrow$ $2x = 60$

$\Rightarrow$ $x = 30$ [dividing both sides by 2]

Hence, the numbers are 30 and $(30 + 12)$ i.e. 30 and 42.

Q. 70 Seven times a number is 12 less than thirteen times the same number. Find the number.

Sol. Let the number be x.

Then, seven times of this number = $7x$ and thirteen times of this number = $13x$.
According to the question,

$\Rightarrow$ $13x - 7x = 12$

$\Rightarrow$ $6x = 12$

$\Rightarrow$ $x = 2$ [dividing both sides by 6]

Hence, the required number is 2.

Q. 71 The interest received by Karim is ₹ 30 more than that of Ramesh. If the total interest received by them is ₹ 70, find the interest received by Ramesh.

Sol. Let the interest received by Karim be ₹x, then interest received by Ramesh will be ₹ $(x - 30)$. So, the interest received by both will be ₹ $(x + x - 30)$.

According to the question, $x + x - 30 = 70$

$\Rightarrow$ $2x = 70 + 30$ [transposing $(- 30)$ to RHS]

$\Rightarrow$ $2x = 100$

$\Rightarrow$ $x = ₹ 50$ [dividing both sides by 2]

So, the interest received by Ramesh = ₹ $(x - 30) = ₹ (50 - 30) = ₹ 20$

Q. 72 Subramaniam and Naidu donate some money in a Relief Fund. The amount paid by Naidu is ₹ 125 more than that of Subramaniam. If the total money paid by them is ₹ 975, find the amount of money donated by Subramaniam.

Sol. Let ₹ x be the amount donated in a Relief fund by Subramaniam. Then, the amount donated by Naidu will be ₹ $(x + 125)$.

According to the question,

$$x + x + 125 = 975$$
$$\Rightarrow \qquad 2x = 975 - 125 \qquad \text{[transposing 125 to RHS]}$$
$$\Rightarrow \qquad 2x = 850$$
$$\Rightarrow \qquad x = ₹\ 425 \qquad \text{[dividing both sides by 2]}$$

Hence, the amount of money donated by Subramaniam is ₹ 425.

Q. 73 In a school, the number of girls is 50 more than the number of boys. The total number of students is 1070. Find the number of girls.

Sol. Let x be the number of boys in the school. Then, the number of girls in the school will be $x + 50$.

According to the question,

$$x + (x + 50) = 1070$$
$$\Rightarrow \qquad 2x + 50 = 1070$$
$$\Rightarrow \qquad 2x = 1070 - 50 \qquad \text{[transposing 50 to RHS]}$$
$$\Rightarrow \qquad 2x = 1020$$
$$\Rightarrow \qquad x = 510 \qquad \text{[dividing both sides by 2]}$$

So, the number of boys in the school $= 510$

∴ Number of girls in the school $= 510 + 50 = 560$

Q. 74 Two times a number increased by 5 equals 9. Find the number.

Sol. Let the number be x.

It is given that two times this number increased by 5 equals 9.

$$\therefore \qquad 2x + 5 = 9$$
$$\Rightarrow \qquad 2x = 9 - 5$$
$$\Rightarrow \qquad 2x = 4$$
$$\Rightarrow \qquad x = 2 \qquad \text{[dividing both sides by 2]}$$

Hence, the required number is 2.

Q. 75 9 added to twice a number gives 13. Find the number.

Sol. Let the required number be x.

It is given that 9 added to twice this number gives 13.

$$\therefore \qquad 2x + 9 = 13$$
$$\Rightarrow \qquad 2x = 13 - 9 \qquad \text{[transposing 9 to RHS]}$$

$$\Rightarrow \qquad\qquad 2x = 4$$

$$\Rightarrow \qquad\qquad \frac{2x}{2} = \frac{4}{2} \qquad\qquad \text{[dividing both sides by 2]}$$

$$\Rightarrow \qquad\qquad x = 2$$

Hence, the required number is 2.

Q. 76 1 subtracted from one-third of a number gives 1. Find the number.

Sol. Let the number be x. Then, one-third of the number $= \frac{1}{3}x$.

According to the question,

$$\frac{1}{3}x - 1 = 1$$

$$\Rightarrow \qquad\qquad \frac{1}{3}x = 1 + 1 \qquad\qquad \text{[transposing } (-1) \text{ to RHS]}$$

$$\Rightarrow \qquad\qquad \frac{1}{3}x = 2$$

$$\Rightarrow \qquad\qquad x = 3 \times 2 \qquad\qquad \text{[multiplying both sides by 3]}$$

$$\Rightarrow \qquad\qquad x = 6$$

Hence, the required number is 6.

Q. 77 After 25 years, Rama will be 5 times as old as he is now. Find his present age.

Sol. Let Rama's present age be x yr.
Then, Rama's age after 25 yr $= (x + 25)$ yr
It is given that after 25 yr, Rama's age will be 5 times his present age.
Therefore, the equation is

$$x + 25 = 5x$$

$$\Rightarrow \qquad\qquad 25 = 5x - x \qquad\qquad \text{[transposing } x \text{ to RHS]}$$

$$\Rightarrow \qquad\qquad 25 = 4x$$

$$\Rightarrow \qquad\qquad \frac{25}{4} = \frac{4x}{4} \qquad\qquad \text{[dividing both sides by 4]}$$

$$\Rightarrow \qquad\qquad 6\frac{1}{4} = x$$

Hence, the present age of Rama is $6\frac{1}{4}$ yr.

Q. 78 After 25 years, Manoj will be 5 times as old as he is now. Find his present age.

Sol. Let the present age of Manoj be x yr.
Then, Manoj's age after 20 yr $= (x + 20)$ yr
It is given that after 20 yr, Manoj's age will be 5 times his present age.
Therefore, the equation is

$$x + 20 = 5x$$

$$\Rightarrow \qquad\qquad 20 = 5x - x \qquad\qquad \text{[transposing } x \text{ to RHS]}$$

$\Rightarrow$ $\qquad\qquad\qquad$ $\dfrac{20}{4} = \dfrac{4x}{4}$ $\qquad\qquad$ [dividing both sides by 4]

$\Rightarrow$ $\qquad\qquad\qquad$ $5 = x$

Hence, the present age of Manoj is 5 yr.

Q. 79 My younger sister's age today is 3 times what it will be 3 years from now minus 3 times what her age was 3 years ago. Find her present age.

Sol. Let the age of my younger sister be x yr.

Then, her age after 3 yr = $(x + 3)$ yr

Also, her age 3 yr ago = $(x - 3)$ yr

It is given that her present age is 3 times her age after 3 yr minus 3 times her age 3 yr ago.

Therefore, we obtain the following equation

$\qquad\qquad\qquad$ $x = 3(x + 3) - 3(x - 3)$

$\Rightarrow$ $\qquad\qquad\qquad$ $x = 3x + 9 - 3x + 9$ $\qquad$ [using the distributive property]

$\Rightarrow$ $\qquad\qquad\qquad$ $x = 18$ yr

Hence, her present age is 18 yr.

Q. 80 If 45 is added to half a number, the result is triple the number. Find the number.

Sol. Let x be the number. Then, half of the number is $\dfrac{x}{2}$.

According to the question,

$\qquad\qquad$ $\dfrac{x}{2} + 45 = 3x$ $\quad \Rightarrow \quad$ $\dfrac{x + 90}{2} = 3x$

$\Rightarrow$ $\qquad\qquad$ $x + 90 = 6x$ $\quad \Rightarrow \quad$ $x = \dfrac{90}{5} = 18$

Hence, the number is 18.

Q. 81 In a family, the consumption of wheat is 4 times that of rice. The total consumption of the two cereals is 80 kg. Find the quantities of rice and wheat consumed in the family.

Sol. As per the given information in the question, total consumption of the two cereals = 80 kg

Let x be the consumption of rice.

Then, consumption of wheat = $4x$

According to the question,

$\qquad\qquad\qquad$ $x + 4x = 80$

$\Rightarrow$ $\qquad\qquad\qquad$ $5x = 80$

$\Rightarrow$ $\qquad\qquad\qquad$ $x = \dfrac{80}{5} = 16$ kg

$\therefore$ Consumption of wheat = $4x = 4 \times 16 = 64$ kg

Hence, the consumption of rice and wheat are 16 kg and 64 kg, respectively.

Q. 82 In a bag, the number of one rupee coins is three times the number of two rupees coins. If the worth of he coins is ₹ 120, find the number of 1 rupee coins.

Sol. Let the number of two rupee coins be y. Then, the number of one rupee coins is $3y$.

Total money by two rupee coins $= 2 \times y = 2y$

Total money by one rupee coin $= 1 \times 3y = 3y$

Total worth of coins $= ₹ 120$

So, the equation formed is

$$2y + 3y = 120 \qquad \text{[given]}$$
$$\Rightarrow \qquad 5y = 120$$
$$\frac{5y}{5} = \frac{120}{5} \qquad \text{[dividing both sides by 5]}$$
$$\Rightarrow \qquad y = 24$$

∴ Number of two rupee coins $= y = 24$ and number of one rupee coins $= 3y = 3 \times 24 = 72$

Q. 83 Anamika thought of a number. She multiplied it by 2, added 5 to the product and obtained 17 as the result. What is the number she has thought of?

Sol. Let x be the number thought by Anamika.

If she multiplied it be 2, then the number will be $2x$.

Also, added 5 to it and obtained 17 as the result.

$$\therefore \qquad 2x + 5 = 17$$
$$\Rightarrow \qquad 2x = 17 - 5 \qquad \text{[transposing 5 to RHS]}$$
$$\Rightarrow \qquad x = \frac{12}{2} = 6$$

Hence, the number 6 is thought by Anamika.

Q. 84 One of the two numbers is twice the other. The sum of the numbers is 12. Find the numbers.

Sol. Le x be the one of the number. Then, other number is twice the first one $= 2x$

According to the question,

$$x + 2x = 12$$
$$\Rightarrow \qquad 3x = 12$$
$$\Rightarrow \qquad \frac{3x}{3} = \frac{12}{3} \qquad \text{[dividing both sides by 3]}$$
$$\Rightarrow \qquad x = 4$$

Hence, the numbers are $x = 4$ and $2x = 2 \times 4 = 8$.

Q. 85 The sum of three consecutive integers is 5 more than the smallest of the integers. Find the integers.

Sol. Let one number be x. Then, the next two consecutive numbers will be $x + 1$ and $x + 2$.

∴ Sum of these three numbers $= x + (x + 1) + (x + 2) = 3x + 3$

According to the question, $3x + 3 = x + 5$

$\Rightarrow$ $3x - x = 5 - 3$ [transposing x to LHS and 3 to RHS]

$\Rightarrow$ $2x = 2$

$\Rightarrow$ $\dfrac{2x}{2} = \dfrac{2}{2}$ [dividing both sides by 2]

$\Rightarrow$ $x = 1$

$\therefore$ Hence, the numbers are 1, 1+ 1, 1+ 2 i.e, 1, 2, 3.

Q. 86 A number when divided by 6 gives the quotient 6. What is the number?

Sol. Let the required number be x. Then, x divided by $6 = \dfrac{x}{6}$.

It is given that when is x is divided by 6, gives the quotient as 6.

So, we obtain the following equation

$$\dfrac{x}{6} = 6$$

$\Rightarrow$ $\dfrac{x}{6} \times 6 = 6 \times 6$ [multiplying both sides by 6]

$\Rightarrow$ $x = 36$

Hence, the required number is 36.

Q. 87 The perimeter of a rectangle is 40 m. The length of the rectangle is 4 m less than 5 times its breadth. Find the length of the rectangle.

Sol. As per the given information in the question, the perimeter of a rectangle is 40 m.

[$\because$ perimeter of rectangle = 2 (length + breadth)]

Let x be the breadth of the rectangle.

Then, length of the rectangle = $5x - 4$

According to the question, $2x + 2(5x - 4) = 40$

$\Rightarrow$ $2x + 10x - 8 = 40$

$\Rightarrow$ $12x = 48$

$\Rightarrow$ $x = 4$

Hence, length of the rectangle = $5x - 4 = (5 \times 4) - 4 = 20 - 4 = 16\,\text{m}$.

Q. 88 Each of the 2 equal sides of an isosceles triangle is twice as large as the third side. If the perimeter of the triangle is 30 cm, find the length of each side of the triangle.

Sol. Let third side of an isosceles triangle be x. Then, two other equal sides are twice.

So, the both equal sides are $2x$ and $2x$.

We know that, perimeter of a triangle is sum of all sides of the triangle.

According to the question,

$$x + 2x + 2x = 30 \quad \Rightarrow \quad 5x = 30$$

On dividing both sides by 5, we get

$$\dfrac{5x}{5} = \dfrac{30}{5} \quad \Rightarrow \quad x = 6\,\text{cm}$$

$\therefore$ Third side = $x = 6$ cm

So, the other equal sides are $2x = 2 \times 6 = 12$ cm and $2x = 2 \times 6 = 12$ cm.

Q. 89 The sum of two consecutive multiples of 2 is 18. Find the numbers.

Sol. Let the two consecutive multiples of 2 be $2x$ and $2x + 2$.

According to the question,

$$2x + 2x + 2 = 18$$
$$\Rightarrow \qquad 4x + 2 = 18$$
$$\Rightarrow \qquad 4x = 18 - 2 \qquad \text{[transposing 2 to RHS]}$$
$$\Rightarrow \qquad 4x = 16$$
$$\Rightarrow \qquad \frac{4x}{4} = \frac{16}{4} \qquad \text{[dividing both sides by 4]}$$
$$\Rightarrow \qquad x = 4$$

Hence, the required numbers are $2x = 2 \times 4 = 8$ and $2x + 2 = 2 \times 4 + 2 = 10$.

Q. 90 Two complementary angles differ by 20°. Find the angles.

Sol. Let one of the angle be x, then other will be $x - 20$.

According to the question,

$$x + (x - 20) = 90° \qquad [\because \text{sum of complementary angles is } 90°]$$
$$\Rightarrow \qquad x + x - 20 = 90°$$
$$\Rightarrow \qquad 2x - 20 = 90°$$
$$\Rightarrow \qquad 2x = 90 + 20 \qquad \text{[transposing} (-20) \text{ to RHS]}$$
$$\Rightarrow \qquad 2x = 110°$$
$$\Rightarrow \qquad \frac{2x}{2} = \frac{110°}{2} \qquad \text{[dividing both sides by 2]}$$
$$\Rightarrow \qquad x = 55°$$

Hence, the required angles are 55° and $(55 - 20)°$ i.e. 55° and 35°.

Q. 91 150 has been divided into two parts such that twice the first part is equal to the second part. Find the parts.

Sol. Let one part be x, then other part will be $2x$ as second part is twice the first part.

Since, 150 has been divided into above two parts.

According to the question,

$$x + 2x = 150$$
$$\Rightarrow \qquad 3x = 150$$
$$\Rightarrow \qquad \frac{3x}{3} = \frac{150}{3} \qquad \text{[dividing both sides by 3]}$$
$$\Rightarrow \qquad x = 50$$

Hence, the first part is 50 and the second part is $2 \times 50 = 100$.

Q. 92 In a class of 60 students, the number of girls is one third the number of boys. Find the number of girls and boys in the class.

Sol. As per the given information in the question, the total number of students in the class = 60.

Let x be the number of boys in the class.

Then, the number of girls in the class $= \dfrac{x}{3}$

According to the question,

$$x + \frac{x}{3} = 60$$

$$\Rightarrow \quad \frac{3x + x}{3} = 60$$

$$\frac{4x}{3} = 60$$

$$\Rightarrow \quad 4x = 60 \times 3$$

$$\Rightarrow \quad 4x = 180$$

$$\Rightarrow \quad x = \frac{180}{4} = 45$$

Hence, the number of boys in the class is 45 and the number of girls in the class is $\frac{45}{3}$ i.e. 15.

Q. 93 Two-third of a number is greater than one-third of the number by 3. Find the number.

Sol. Let the number be x.

Then, two-third of this number $= \frac{2}{3}x$ and one-third of this number $= \frac{1}{3}x$.

According to the question,

$$\frac{2}{3}x = \frac{1}{3}x + 3$$

$$\Rightarrow \quad \frac{2}{3}x - \frac{1}{3}x = 3$$

$$\Rightarrow \quad \frac{2x - x}{3} = 3 \qquad \text{[taking LCM on LHS]}$$

$$\Rightarrow \quad \frac{x}{3} = 3$$

$$\Rightarrow \quad \frac{x}{3} \times 3 = 3 \times 3 \qquad \text{[multiplying both sides by 3]}$$

$$\Rightarrow \quad x = 9$$

Hence, the required number is 9.

Q. 94 A number is as much greater than 27 as it is less than 73. Find the number.

Sol. Let the number be x. If we subtract 27 from x i.e. $(x - 27)$ and subtract x from 73 i.e. $(73 - x)$, we get the same result. Therefore, we get the following equation

$$x - 27 = 73 - x$$

$$\Rightarrow \quad x + x = 73 + 27$$

$$\text{[transposing}(-27)\text{ to RHS and }(-x)\text{ to LHS]}$$

$$\Rightarrow \quad 2x = 100$$

$$\Rightarrow \quad \frac{2x}{2} = \frac{100}{2} \qquad \text{[dividing both sides by 2]}$$

$$\Rightarrow \quad x = 50$$

Hence, the required number is 50.

Q. 95 A man travelled two fifth of his journey by train, one third by bus. One-fourth by car and the remaining 3 km on foot. What is the length of his total journey?

Sol. Let his total journey length be x.

∴ Then, travelled by train $= \dfrac{2}{5}x$,

Travelled by bus $= \dfrac{1}{3}x$ and travelled by car $= \dfrac{1}{4}x$

∴ Total journey travelled by train, bus and car $= \dfrac{2}{5}x + \dfrac{1}{3}x + \dfrac{1}{4}x$

$$= \dfrac{12 \times 2x + 20 \times x + 15 \times x}{60}$$

$$[\because \text{LCM of 5, 3 and } 4 = 60]$$

$$= \dfrac{24x + 20x + 15x}{60} = \dfrac{59x}{60}$$

∴ Remaining journey $= \dfrac{x}{1} - \dfrac{59x}{60} = \dfrac{60x - 59x}{60} = \dfrac{x}{60}$

According to the question, remaining journey is 3 km.

∴ $$\dfrac{x}{60} = 3$$

⇒ $$x = 3 \times 60 = 180 \text{ km} \quad [\text{by cross-multiplication}]$$

Hence, the length of his total journey is 180 km.

Q. 96 Twice a number added to half of itself equals 24. Find the number.

Sol. Let the number be x. Then, twice of this number $= 2x$ and half of this number $= \dfrac{1}{2}x$.

According to the question, $2x + \dfrac{1}{2}x = 24$

Multiplying both sides by 2, we get $4x + x = 48$

⇒ $$5x = 48$$

$$\dfrac{5x}{5} = \dfrac{48}{5} \quad [\text{dividing both sides by 5}]$$

⇒ $$x = 9.6$$

Hence, the required number is 9.6.

Q. 97 Thrice a number decreased by 5 exceeds twice the number by 1. Find the number.

Sol. Let the number be x. Then, thrice of this number $= 3x$ and twice of this number $= 2x$.
If we decrease thrice of x by 5, we get $(3x - 5)$.
According to the question,

$$(3x - 5) - (2x) = 1$$

⇒ $$3x - 5 - 2x = 1$$

⇒ $$x - 5 = 1$$

⇒ $$x = 1 + 5 \quad [\text{transposing } (-5) \text{ to RHS}]$$

⇒ $$x = 6$$

Hence, the required number is 6.

Q. 98 A girl is 28 years younger than her father. The sum of their ages is 50 years. Find the ages of the girl and her father.

Sol. Let x be the age of the girl.

Then, age of her father $= (x + 28)$ yr

According to the question,

$\therefore$ $x + (x + 28) = 50$

$\Rightarrow$ $2x + 28 = 50$

$\Rightarrow$ $2x = 50 - 28$

$\Rightarrow$ $2x = 22$

$\Rightarrow$ $x = \dfrac{22}{2} = 11$ yr

Hence, the age of the girl is 11 yr and age of her father's age is $(11 + 28)$, i.e. 39 yr.

Q. 99 The length of a rectangle is two times its width. The perimeter of the rectangle is 180 cm. Find the dimensions of the rectangle.

Sol. Let x be the width of the rectangle. Then, length of the rectangle will be $2x$.

$\because$ Perimeter of a rectangle $= 2$ [Length + Width]   [$\because$ width=breadth]

According to the question,

                   $2(x + 2x) = 180$

$\Rightarrow$ $2(3x) = 180$

$\Rightarrow$ $6x = 180$

                   $x = \dfrac{180}{6} = 30$ cm

Hence, width of the rectangle is 30 cm and length of the rectangle is 2×30, i.e. 60 cm.

Q. 100 Look at this riddle?

If she answers the riddle correctly how ever will she pay for the pencils ?

Sol. Let, the cost of one pencil be ₹ x.

Now, cost of such 7 pencils will be ₹ $7x$ and of 5 pencils will be ₹ $5x$.

It is given that cost of 7 pencils is ₹ 6 more than cost of 5 pencils. Therefore, we get the following equation

                   $7x - 5x = 6$

$\Rightarrow$ $2x = 6$

$\Rightarrow$ $\dfrac{2x}{2} = \dfrac{6}{2}$ [dividing both sides by 2]

$\Rightarrow$ $x = 3$

Since, cost of one pencil is ₹ 3.

So, the cost of 10 pencils = $3 \times 10 = $ ₹ 30

Thus, she have to pay ₹ 30 for 10 pencils.

Q. 101 In a certain examination, a total of 3768 students secured first division in the years 2006 and 2007. The number of first division in 2007 exceeded those in 2006 by 34. How many students got first division in 2006?

Sol. Let the number of students who got first division in year 2006 be x. Since, the number of first division in year 2007 exceeded those in year 2006 by 34, therefore the number of students who got first division in year 2007 will be $(x + 34)$.

It is given that total number of students who got first division in years 2006 and 2007 is 3768.

According to the question, $x + (x + 34) = 3768$

$\Rightarrow$ $2x + 34 = 3768$

$\Rightarrow$ $2x = 3768 - 34$ [transposing 34 to RHS]

$\Rightarrow$ $2x = 3734$

$\Rightarrow$ $\dfrac{2x}{x} = \dfrac{3734}{2}$ [dividing both sides by 2]

$\Rightarrow$ $x = 1867$

Hence, 1867 students got first division in year 2006.

Q. 102 Radha got ₹ 17480 as her monthly salary and overtime. Her salary exceeds the overtime by ₹ 10000. What is her monthly salary?

Sol. Radha's monthly salary and over-time = ₹ 17480 [given]

Let ₹ x be the her monthly salary.

Then, overtime = ₹ $(x - 10000)$

$\therefore$ $17480 - x = x - 10000$

$\Rightarrow$ $2x = 27480$

$\Rightarrow$ $x = 13740$

Hence, her monthly salary is ₹ 13740.

Q. 103 If one side of a square is represented by $18x - 20$ and the adjacent side is represented by $42 - 13x$, find the length of the side of the square.

Sol. Given, one side of a square is $18x - 20$ and adjacent side is $42 - 13x$.

We know that, all the sides of a square are always equal.

$\therefore$ $18x - 20 = 42 - 13x$

$\Rightarrow$ $18x + 13x = 42 + 20$

$\Rightarrow$ $31x = 62 \Rightarrow x = \dfrac{62}{31} = 2$ units

Hence, side of the square is $(18 \times 2) - 20 = 36 - 20 = 16$ units.

Q. 104 Follow the directions and correct the given incorrect equation, written in Roman numerals:

   (a) Remove two of these matchsticks to make a valid equation :

$$IX - VI = V$$

   (b) Move one matchstick to make the equation valid. Find two different solutions.

$$VI + IV = XI$$

Sol.   (a) Given, $IX - VI = V$

According to the question, we have to remove two matchsticks to make a valid equation.

Hence, $X - V = V$ [in numerical system]

$\Rightarrow$ $10 - 5 = 5$

   (b) Given $VI + IV = XI$

According to the question, we have to move one mathchstick to make a valid equation.

   (i) $VI + IV = X$

$\Rightarrow$ $6 + 4 = 10$ [in numerical system]

   (ii) $VI - V = XI$

$\Rightarrow$ $6 + 5 = 11$ [in numerical system]

Q. 105 What does a duck do when it flies upside down? The answer to this riddle is hidden in the equation given below :

If $i + 69 = 70$, then $i = $? If $8u = 6u + 8$, then $u = $?

If $4a = -5a + 45$, then $a = $? If $4q + 5 = 17$, then $q = $?

If $-5t - 60 = -70$, then $t = $? If $\dfrac{1}{4}s + 98 = 100$, then $s = $?

If $\dfrac{5}{3}p + 9 = 24$, then $p = $?

If $3c = c + 12$, then $c = $?

If $3(k + 1) = 24$, then $k = $?

For riddle answer : substitute the number for the letter it equals

$$\underline{}\quad\underline{}\Big/\underline{}\quad\underline{}\quad\underline{}\quad\underline{}\quad\underline{}\quad\underline{}\Big/\underline{}\quad\underline{}$$
$$\;1\quad\;2\;\Big/\;3\quad\;4\quad\;5\quad\;6\quad\;7\quad\;8\;\Big/\;4\quad\;9$$

Sol.   We have, $i + 69 = 70$

$\Rightarrow$ $i = 70 - 69$ [transposing 69 to RHS]

$\Rightarrow$ $i = 1$

   and $8u = 6u + 8$

$\Rightarrow$ $8u - 6u = 8$ [transposing $6u$ to LHS]

$\Rightarrow$ $2u = 8$

$$\Rightarrow \qquad \frac{2u}{2} = \frac{8}{2} \qquad \text{[dividing both sides by 2]}$$

$$\Rightarrow \qquad u = 4$$

We have, $\qquad 4a = -5a + 45$

$$\Rightarrow \qquad 4a + 5a = 45 \qquad \text{[transposing (–5a) to LHS]}$$

$$\Rightarrow \qquad 9a = 45$$

$$\Rightarrow \qquad \frac{9a}{9} = \frac{45}{9} \qquad \text{[dividing both sides by 9]}$$

$$\Rightarrow \qquad a = 5$$

and $\qquad 4q + 5 = 17$

$$\Rightarrow \qquad 4q = 17 - 5 \qquad \text{[transposing 5 to RHS]}$$

$$\Rightarrow \qquad 4q = 12$$

$$\Rightarrow \qquad \frac{4q}{4} = \frac{12}{4} \qquad \text{[dividing both sides by 4]}$$

$$\Rightarrow \qquad q = 3$$

We have, $\qquad -5t - 60 = -70$

$$\Rightarrow \qquad -5t = -70 + 60 \qquad \text{[transposing (–60) to RHS]}$$

$$\Rightarrow \qquad -5t = -10$$

$$\Rightarrow \qquad \frac{-5t}{-5} = \frac{-10}{-5} \qquad \text{[dividing both sides by (–5)]}$$

$$\Rightarrow \qquad t = 2$$

and $\qquad \frac{1}{4}s + 98 = 100$

$$\Rightarrow \qquad \frac{1}{4}s = 100 - 98 \qquad \text{[transposing 98 to RHS]}$$

$$\Rightarrow \qquad \frac{1}{4}s = 2$$

$$\Rightarrow \qquad \frac{4}{4}s = 4 \times 2 \qquad \text{[multiplying both sides by 4]}$$

$$\Rightarrow \qquad s = 8$$

We have, $\qquad \frac{5}{3}p + 9 = 24$

$$\Rightarrow \qquad \frac{5}{3}p = 24 - 9 \qquad \text{[transposing 9 to RHS]}$$

$$\Rightarrow \qquad \frac{5}{3}p = 15$$

$$\Rightarrow \qquad \frac{3}{5} \times \frac{5}{3}p = \frac{3}{5} \times 15 \qquad \text{[multiplying both sides by } \frac{3}{5}\text{]}$$

$$\Rightarrow \qquad p = 9$$

We have, $\qquad 3c = c + 12$

$$\Rightarrow \qquad 3c - c = 12 \qquad \text{[transposing c to LHS]}$$

$$\Rightarrow \qquad 2c = 12$$

$$\Rightarrow \qquad \frac{2c}{2} = \frac{12}{2} \qquad \text{[dividing both sides by 2]}$$

$$\Rightarrow \qquad c = 6$$

We have, $3(k + 1) = 24$

$\Rightarrow$ $\dfrac{3(k + 1)}{3} = \dfrac{24}{3}$ [dividing both sides by 3]

$\Rightarrow$ $k + 1 = 8$

$\Rightarrow$ $k = 8 - 1$ [transposing 1 to RHS]

$\Rightarrow$ $k = 7$

By substituting the number for the letter it equals, we get

$$\dfrac{i}{1}\dfrac{t}{2} / \dfrac{q}{3}\dfrac{u}{4}\dfrac{a}{5}\dfrac{c}{6}\dfrac{k}{7}\dfrac{s}{8} / \dfrac{u}{4}\dfrac{p}{9}$$

Q. 106 The three scales below are perfectly balanced, if $\bullet = 3$. What are the values of $\triangle$ and *?

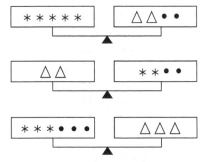

Sol. Let the value of $\triangle$ and * be x and y, respectively and it is given that $\bullet = 3$.

From (a), $y + y + y + y + y = x + x + 3 + 3$

$\Rightarrow$ $5y = 2x + 6$

$\Rightarrow$ $5y - 2x = 6$

$\Rightarrow$ $2x - 5y = -6$ ...(i)

From (b), $x + x = y + y + 3 + 3$

$\Rightarrow$ $2x = 2y + 6$

$\Rightarrow$ $2x - 2y = 6$

$\Rightarrow$ $x - y = 3$ [dividing both sides by 2]...(ii)

From (c), $y + y + y + 3 + 3 + 3 = x + x + x$

$\Rightarrow$ $3y + 9 = 3x$

$\Rightarrow$ $3x - 3y = 9$

$\Rightarrow$ $x - y = 3$ [dividing both sides by 3]...(iii)

From Eq. (iii), $x - y = 3 \Rightarrow x = y + 3$

On putting $x = y + 3$ in Eq. (i), we get

$$2(y + 3) - 5y = -6$$

$\Rightarrow$ $2y + 6 - 5y = -6$

$$-3y + 6 = -6$$

$\Rightarrow$ $-3y = -6 - 6 = -12$

$$y = \dfrac{12}{3} = 4$$

On putting $y = 4$ in Eq. (ii), we get $x - y = 3$

$\Rightarrow$ $x - 4 = 3$

$\Rightarrow$ $x = 3 + 4 = 7$

$\Rightarrow$ $x = 7$

$\therefore$ Value of $\Delta = x = 7$ and value of $* = y = 4$.

Q. 107 The given figure represents a weighing balance. The weights of some objects in the balance are given. Find the weight of each square and the circle.

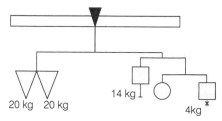

20 kg   20 kg   14 kg   4kg

Sol. From the given figure,

              20 kg = Weight of square + 14 kg

$\Rightarrow$ 20 kg − 14 kg = Weight of square   [transposing 14 to LHS]

$\Rightarrow$ Weight of square = 6 kg

Also,   20 kg = Weight of circle + Weight of square + 4 kg

$\Rightarrow$ 20 kg = Weight of circle + 6 kg + 4 kg

$\Rightarrow$ 20 kg = Weight of circle + 10 kg

$\Rightarrow$ 20 kg − 10 kg = Weight of circle   [transposing 10 to LHS]

$\therefore$ Weight of circle = 10 kg

5

Lines and Angles

Multiple Choice Questions (MCQs)

Q. 1 The angles between North and West and South and East are

    (a) complementary   (b) supplementary

    (c) both are acute   (d) both are obtuse

Sol. *(b)*

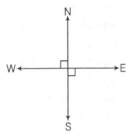

From the above figure, it is clear that the angle between North and West is 90° and South and East is 90°.

∴ Sum of these two angles = 90° + 90° = 180°

Hence, the two angles are supplementary, as their sum is 180°.

Q. 2 Angles between South and West and South and East are

    (a) vertically opposite angles   (b) complementary angles

    (c) making a linear pair   (d) adjacent but not supplementary

Sol. *(c)*

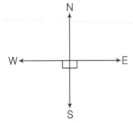

From the above figure, we can say that angle between South and West is 90° and angle between South and East is 90°. So, their sum is 180°.

Hence, both angles make a linear pair.

Q. 3 In the given figure, PQ is a mirror, AB is the incident ray and BC is the reflected ray. If $\angle ABC = 46°$, then $\angle ABP$ is equal to

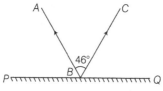

   (a) 44°   (b) 67°
   (c) 13°   (d) 62°

Sol. (b) We know that, the angle of incidence is always equal to the angle of reflection.
$$\angle ABP = \angle CBQ$$
i.e. $a = b$

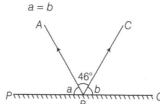

Now, sum of all the angles on a straight line is 180°. $[\because \angle ABC = 46°, \text{given}]$
$\therefore$ $a + 46° + b = 180°$
$\Rightarrow$ $2a = 180° - 46°$ $[\because a = b]$
$\Rightarrow$ $2a = 134°$
$\Rightarrow$ $a = \dfrac{134°}{2} = 67°$
$\therefore$ $\angle ABP = 67°$

Q. 4 If the complement of an angle is 79°, then the angle will be of
        (a) 1°   (b) 11°
        (c) 79°   (d) 101°

Sol. (b) Let the angle be $x°$. Then, the complement of x will be $(90 - x)°$.
Given, complement of $x°$ is 79°.
$\therefore$ $(90 - x)° = 79°$
$\Rightarrow$ $x° = 90° - 79° = 11°$
Therefore, the required angle is 11°.
Note *Sum of the complementary angles is* 90°.

Q. 5 Angles, which are both supplementary and vertically opposite are
        (a) 95°, 85°   (b) 90°, 90°
        (c) 100°, 80°   (d) 45°, 45°

Sol. (b) Two angles are said to be supplementary, if their sum is 180°. Also, if two angles are vertically opposite, then they are equal.
Therefore, angles given in option (b) are supplementary as well as vertically opposite.

Q. 6 The angle which makes a linear pair with an angle of 61°, is of

(a) 29°   (b) 61°
(c) 122°   (d) 119°

Sol. *(d)*   Let the required angle be $x°$. It is given that $x°$ makes a linear pair with 61°.

∴ $x + 61° = 180°$ [∵ sum of angles forming linear pair is 180°]

⇒ $x = 180° - 61° = 119°$

Q. 7 The angles x and $90° - x$ are

(a) supplementary   (b) complementary
(c) vertically opposite   (d) making a linear pair

Sol. *(b)*   Sum of the given angles $= x + 90° - x = 90°$

Since, the sum of given two angles is 90°.

Hence, they are complementary to each other.

Q. 8 The angles $x - 10°$ and $190° - x$ are

(a) interior angles on the same side of the transversal
(b) making a linear pair
(c) complementary
(d) supplementary

Sol. *(d)*   Sum of the given angles $= (x - 10°) + (190° - x) = x - 10° + 190° - x$

$= (x - x) + (190° - 10°) = 0 + 180° = 180°$

Since, the sum of given angles is 180°, Hence, they are supplementary.

Q. 9 In the given figure, the value of x is

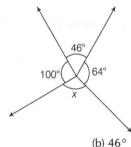

(a) 110°   (b) 46°
(c) 64°   (d) 150°

Sol. *(d)*   We know that, the sum of all angles around a point is 360°.

∴ $100° + 46° + 64° + x = 360°$

⇒ $210° + x = 360°$

⇒ $x = 360° - 210°$

⇒ $x = 150°$

Q. 10 In the given figure, if $AB \parallel CD$, $\angle APQ = 50°$ and $\angle PRD = 130°$, then $\angle QPR$ is

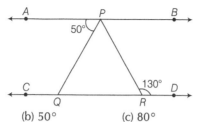

(a) 130°   (b) 50°   (c) 80°   (d) 30°

Sol. (c)   Since, AB and CD are parallel and PR is a transversal.

∴ $\angle BPR + \angle PRD = 180°$ [∵ sum of consecutive interior angles is 180°]

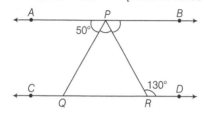

$\Rightarrow$ $\angle BPR + 130° = 180°$ [∵ $\angle PRD = 130°$]

$\Rightarrow$ $\angle BPR = 180° - 130°$

$\Rightarrow$ $\angle BPR = 50°$

Also, $\angle APQ + \angle QPR + \angle BPR = 180°$

   [∵ sum of all the angles on a straight line is 180°]

$\Rightarrow$ $50° + \angle QPR + 50° = 180°$

$\Rightarrow$ $\angle QPR + 100° = 180°$

$\Rightarrow$ $\angle QPR = 180° - 100°$

∴ $\angle QPR = 80°$

Q. 11 In the given figure, lines l and m intersect each other at a point. Which of the following is false?

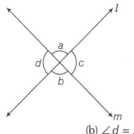

(a) $\angle a = \angle b$ (b) $\angle d = \angle c$

(c) $\angle a + \angle d = 180°$ (d) $\angle a = \angle d$

Sol. (d)   From the given Figure it is clear that, $\angle a = \angle b$ and $\angle c = \angle d$

   [vertically opposite angles]

Also, $\angle a + \angle d = 180°$

and $\angle b + \angle c = 180°$ [linear pair]

Q. 12 If angle P and angle Q are supplementary and the measure of angle P is 60°, then the measure of angle Q is

    (a) 120°   (b) 60°   (c) 30°   (d) 20°

Sol. *(a)*   It is given that, angles P and Q are supplementary. Hence, the sum of P and Q will be 180°.

$\therefore$ $\angle P + \angle Q = 180°$

$\Rightarrow$ $60° + \angle Q = 180°$ $[\because \angle P = 60°, \text{given}]$

$\Rightarrow$ $\angle Q = 180° - 60°$

$\Rightarrow$ $\angle Q = 120°$

Q. 13 In the given figure, POR is a line. The value of a is

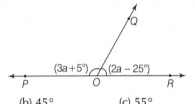

    (a) 40°   (b) 45°   (c) 55°   (d) 60

Sol. *(a)*   Since, POR is a line. So, the sum of angles forming linear pair is 180°.

$\therefore$ $\angle POQ + \angle ROQ = 180°$

$\Rightarrow$ $(3a + 5)° + (2a - 25°) = 180°$

$\Rightarrow$ $3a + 5° + 2a - 25° = 180°$

$\Rightarrow$ $5a - 20° = 180°$

$\Rightarrow$ $5a = 180° + 20°$

$\Rightarrow$ $5a = 200°$

$\Rightarrow$ $a = \dfrac{200°}{5}$

$\Rightarrow$ $a = 40°$

Hence, the value of a is 40°.

Q. 14 In the given figure, POQ is a line. If $x = 30°$, then $\angle QOR$ is

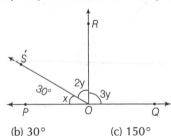

    (a) 90°   (b) 30°   (c) 150°   (d) 60°

Sol. *(a)*   It is given that, POQ is a line. Since, sum of all the angles on a straight line is 180°.

Therefore, $x + 2y + 3y = 180°$

$\Rightarrow$ $x + 5y = 180°$ $[\because x = 30°, \text{given}]$

$\Rightarrow$ $30° + 5y = 180°$

$\Rightarrow$ $5y = 180° - 30°$

$\Rightarrow$ $5y = 150°$

$$\Rightarrow \qquad\qquad y = \frac{150°}{5}$$

$$\Rightarrow \qquad\qquad y = 30°$$

$$\therefore \qquad\qquad \angle QOR = 3y = 3 \times 30° = 90°$$

Q. 15 The measure of an angle which is four times its supplement, is

(a) 36°   (b) 144°   (c) 16°   (d) 64°

Sol. (b)   Let the required angle be x. Then, its supplement will be $(180° - x)$.

It is given that, the angle is four times its supplement.

Therefore, $\qquad\qquad x = 4(180° - x)$

$$\Rightarrow \qquad\qquad x = 4 \times 180° - 4x$$

$$\Rightarrow \qquad\qquad x + 4x = 720°$$

$$\Rightarrow \qquad\qquad 5x = 720°$$

$$\Rightarrow \qquad\qquad x = \frac{720°}{5}$$

$$\Rightarrow \qquad\qquad x = 144°$$

Hence, the required angle is 144°.

Q. 16 In the given figure, the value of y is

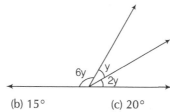

(a) 30°   (b) 15°   (c) 20°   (d) 22.5°

Sol. (c)   Since, sum of all the angles on a straight line is 180°.

Therefore, $\qquad\qquad 6y + y + 2y = 180°$

$$\Rightarrow \qquad\qquad 9y = 180°$$

$$\Rightarrow \qquad\qquad y = \frac{180°}{9}$$

$$\therefore \qquad\qquad y = 20°$$

Q. 17 In the given figure, $PA \parallel BC \parallel DT$ and $AB \parallel DC$. Then, the values of a and b are respectively

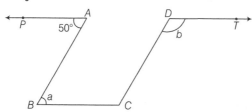

(a) 60°, 120°   (b) 50°, 130°
(c) 70°, 110°   (d) 80°, 100°

Sol. *(b)*   It is given that, $PA \parallel BC$ and AB is transversal.

$\therefore \qquad\qquad\qquad \angle PAB = \angle ABC$ [alternate interior angles]

$\Rightarrow \qquad\qquad\qquad 50° = a$

Also, $AB \parallel DC$ and BC is transversal.

$\therefore \qquad\qquad \angle ABC + \angle DCB = 180°$ [consecutive interior angles]

$\Rightarrow \qquad\qquad a + \angle DCB = 180°$

$\Rightarrow \qquad\qquad\qquad \angle DCB = 180° - a$

$\Rightarrow \qquad\qquad\qquad \angle DCB = 180° - 50°$ $[\because a = 50°]$

$\Rightarrow \qquad\qquad\qquad \angle DCB = 130°$

Also, $BC \parallel DT$ and DC is transversal.

$\therefore \qquad\qquad\qquad \angle CDT = \angle DCB$ [alternate interior angles]

$\Rightarrow \qquad\qquad\qquad b = 130°$ $[\because \angle DCB = 130°]$

Q. 18 The difference of two complementary angles is 30°. Then, the angles are

(a) 60°, 30°   (b) 70°, 40°
(c) 20°, 50°   (d) 105°, 75°

Sol. *(a)*   Let one of the angle be x. Since, the difference between the two angles is 30°, then the other angle will be $(x - 30°)$.

Also, the two angles are complementary, so their sum is equal to 90°.

$\therefore \qquad\qquad x + (x - 30°) = 90°$

$\Rightarrow \qquad\qquad x + x - 30° = 90°$

$\Rightarrow \qquad\qquad\qquad 2x = 90° + 30°$

$\Rightarrow \qquad\qquad\qquad 2x = 120°$

$\Rightarrow \qquad\qquad\qquad x = \dfrac{120°}{2}$

$\Rightarrow \qquad\qquad\qquad x = 60°$

$\therefore$ Required angles are 60° and $(60° - 30°)$, i.e. 60° and 30°.

Q. 19 In the given figure, $PQ \parallel SR$ and $SP \parallel RQ$. Then, angles a and b are respectively

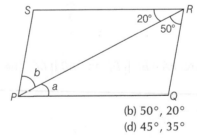

(a) 20°, 50°   (b) 50°, 20°
(c) 30°, 50°   (d) 45°, 35°

Sol. *(a)*   Given, $PQ \parallel SR$ and PR is transversal.

$\therefore \qquad\qquad\qquad \angle QPR = \angle SRP$ [alternate interior angles]

$\Rightarrow \qquad\qquad\qquad a = 20°$

Also, $SP \parallel RQ$ and PR is transversal.

$\therefore \qquad\qquad\qquad \angle SPR = \angle QRP$ [alternate interior angles]

$\Rightarrow \qquad\qquad\qquad b = 50°$

Q. 20 In the given figure, a and b are

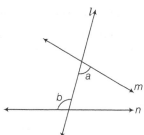

(a) alternate exterior angles   (b) corresponding angles
(c) alternate interior angles   (d) vertically opposite angles

Sol. *(c)*   In the given figure, a and b are alternate interior angles as both lie on opposite sides of transverse line.

Q. 21 If two supplementary angles are in the ratio 1 : 2, then bigger angle is

(a) $120°$ (b) $125°$ (c) $110°$ (d) $90°$

Sol. *(a)*   It is given that the angles are in the ratio of 1 : 2. Let the angles will be x and $2x$.
Also, the two angles are supplementary, i.e. their sum is equal to $180°$.

$$\therefore \qquad x + 2x = 180°$$
$$\Rightarrow \qquad 3x = 180°$$
$$\Rightarrow \qquad x = \frac{180°}{3}$$
$$\Rightarrow \qquad x = 60°$$

Hence, the required angles are $60°$ and $2 \times 60°$, i.e. $60°$ and $120°$.
$\therefore$ Bigger of the two angles is $120°$.

Q. 22 In the given figure, $\angle ROS$ is a right angle and $\angle POR$ and $\angle QOS$ are in the ratio 1 : 5. Then, $\angle QOS$ measures

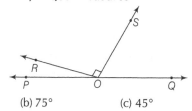

(a) $150°$ (b) $75°$ (c) $45°$ (d) $60°$

Sol. *(b)*   Since, $\angle POR$ and $\angle QOS$ are in the ratio 1 : 5. Let angles will be x and $5x$, respectively.
We know that, the sum of angles forming linear pair is $180°$.

$$\therefore \qquad \angle POR + \angle ROS + \angle QOS = 180°$$
$$\Rightarrow \qquad x + 90° + 5x = 180°$$
$$\Rightarrow \qquad 6x = 180° - 90°$$
$$\Rightarrow \qquad 6x = 90° \quad \Rightarrow \quad x = \frac{90°}{6}$$
$$\Rightarrow \qquad x = 15°$$
$$\therefore \qquad \angle QOS = 5x = 5 \times 15°$$
$$\Rightarrow \qquad \angle QOS = 75°$$

Q. 23 Statements (I) and (II) are as given below:

   I: If two lines intersect, then the vertically opposite angles are equal.

   II: If a transversal intersects two other lines, then the sum of two interior angles on the same side of the transversal is 180°.

   Then,

   (a) both (I) and (II) are true   (b) (I) is true and (II) is false
   (c) (I) is false and (II) is true   (d) both (I) and (II) are false

Sol. *(b)* **Statement I**

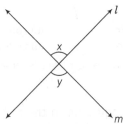

If lines l and m intersect each other, then x and y are known as vertically opposite angles. The vertically opposite angles so formed are equal.

∴ $x = y$

Statement II

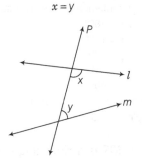

If two lines l and m are intersected by a transversal P, then the sum of two interior angles will be 180°, only if l and m are parallel.

Q. 24 For the given figure, statements p and q are given below:

   p : a and b are forming a linear pair.

   q : a and b are forming a pair of adjacent angles.

   Then,

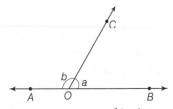

   (a) both p and q are true   (b) p is true and q is false
   (c) p is false and q is true   (d) both p and q are false

Sol. *(a)* Two angles are called adjacent angles, if they have a common vertex and a common arm but no common interior points. A linear pair is a pair of adjacent angles whose non-common sides are opposite rays.

∴ a and b are pair of adjacent angles and form a linear pair.

Q. 25 In the given figure, $\angle AOC$ and $\angle BOC$ form a pair of

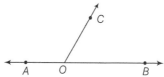

(a) vertically opposite angles
(b) complementary angles
(c) alternate interior angles
(d) supplementary angles

Sol. *(d)* Since, $\angle AOC$ and $\angle BOC$ are on the same line *AOB* and forming linear pair.

∴ $\qquad\qquad \angle AOC + \angle BOC = 180°$

Hence, $\angle AOC$ and $\angle BOC$ are supplementary angles.

Q. 26 In the given figure, the value of a is

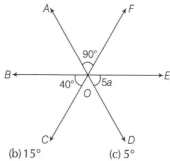

(a) 20°   (b) 15°   (c) 5°   (d) 10°

Sol. *(d)* From the given figure, we can say that

$\qquad\qquad \angle BOC = \angle EOF \qquad$ [vertically opposite angles]

⇒ $\qquad\qquad 40° = \angle EOF$

Since, sum of all the angles on a straight line is 180°.

∴ $\qquad\qquad \angle AOF + \angle FOE + \angle EOD = 180°$

⇒ $\qquad\qquad 90° + 40° + 5a = 180°$

⇒ $\qquad\qquad 130° + 5a = 180° \Rightarrow 5a = 180° - 130°$

⇒ $\qquad\qquad 5a = 50°$

⇒ $\qquad\qquad a = \dfrac{50°}{5} = 10°$

Q. 27 In the given figure, if $QP \| SR$, the value of a is

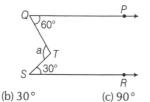

(a) 40°   (b) 30°   (c) 90°   (d) 80°

Sol. (*c*)   Draw a line *l* parallel to *QP*.

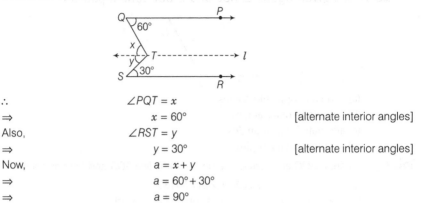

∴   ∠PQT = x

⇒   x = 60°   [alternate interior angles]

Also,   ∠RST = y

⇒   y = 30°   [alternate interior angles]

Now,   a = x + y

⇒   a = 60° + 30°

⇒   a = 90°

Q. 28 In which of the following figures, *a* and *b* are forming a pair of adjacent angles?

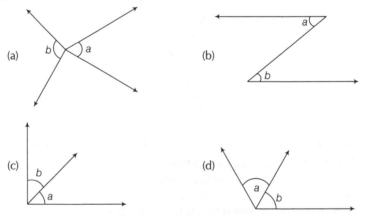

Sol. (*d*)   Two angles are called adjacent angles, if they have a common vertex and a common arm but no common interior points.

∴ In option (d), *a* and *b* form a pair of adjacent angles.

Q. 29 In a pair of adjacent angles, (i) vertex is always common, (ii) one arm is always common, and (iii) uncommon arms are always opposite rays.

Then,

(a) all (i), (ii) and (iii) are true   (b) (iii) is false

(c) (i) is false but (ii) and (iii) are true   (d) (ii) is false

Sol. (*b*)   Two angles are called adjacent angles, if they have a common vertex and a common arm but no common interior points. It is not necessary that uncommon arms must be always opposite rays.

Q. 30 In the given figure, lines PQ and ST intersect at O. If $\angle POR = 90°$ and $x:y = 3:2$, then z is equal to

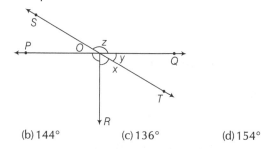

(a) 126°   (b) 144°   (c) 136°   (d) 154°

Sol. **(b)** Since, $\angle POR$, $\angle ROT$ and $\angle TOQ$ lies on a straight line POQ, then their sum is equal to 180°.

$$\therefore \qquad \angle POR + \angle ROT + \angle TOQ = 180°$$
$$\Rightarrow \qquad 90° + x + y = 180°$$
$$\Rightarrow \qquad x + y = 180° - 90°$$
$$\Rightarrow \qquad x + y = 90° \qquad\qquad \text{...(i)}$$

Also, $\qquad\qquad x:y = 3:2 \qquad\qquad$ [given]

Let $\qquad\qquad x = 3a \text{ and } y = 2a$

$$\therefore \qquad\qquad 3a + 2a = 90° \qquad\qquad \text{[from Eq. (i)]}$$
$$\Rightarrow \qquad\qquad 5a = 90°$$
$$\Rightarrow \qquad\qquad a = \frac{90°}{5} \quad = 18°$$

Now, $x = 3a = 3 \times 18° = 54°$ and $y = 2a = 2 \times 18° = 36°$

Since, y and z forms a linear pair.

$$\therefore \qquad\qquad y + z = 180°$$
$$\Rightarrow \qquad\qquad 36° + z = 180° \Rightarrow z = 180° - 36° \qquad [\because y = 36°]$$
$$\Rightarrow \qquad\qquad z = 144°$$

Q. 31 In the given figure, POQ is a line, then a is equal to

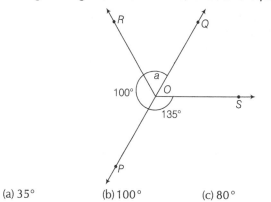

(a) 35°   (b) 100°   (c) 80°   (d) 135°

Sol. *(c)*   Since, *POQ* is a line.

Here, ∠*POR* and ∠*QOR* form a linear pair.

$$∴ \qquad\qquad ∠POR + ∠QOR = 180°$$ [∵ sum of the linear pair is 180°]

$$⇒ \qquad\qquad 100° + a = 180°$$

$$⇒ \qquad\qquad a = 180° - 100° = 80°$$

Q. 32 Vertically opposite angles are always

(a) supplementary   (b) complementary

(c) adjacent   (d) equal

Sol. *(d)*   When two lines intersect, then vertically opposite angles so formed are equal.

Q. 33 In the given figure, $a = 40°$. The value of b is

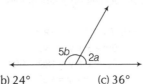

(a) 20°   (b) 24°   (c) 36°   (d) 120°

Sol. *(a)*   From the given figure it is clear that,

$$2a + 5b = 180°$$ [linear pair]

$$⇒ \qquad 2 × 40° + 5b = 180°$$ [∵ a = 40°]

$$⇒ \qquad 80° + 5b = 180°$$

$$⇒ \qquad 5b = 180° - 80°$$

$$⇒ \qquad 5b = 100°$$

$$⇒ \qquad b = \frac{100°}{5}$$

$$∴ \qquad b = 20°$$

Q. 34 If an angle is 60° less than two times of its supplement, then the greater angle is

(a) 100°   (b) 80°   (c) 60°   (d) 120°

Sol. *(a)*   Let the angle be x, then its supplement will be $(180° - x)$.

It is given that, the angle 60° less than 2 times of its supplement.

Then, $\qquad\qquad 2(180° - x) - x = 60°$

$$⇒ \qquad\qquad 360° - 2x - x = 60°$$

$$⇒ \qquad\qquad 360°\ \ 3x = 60°$$

$$⇒ \qquad\qquad 360° - 60° = 3x$$

$$⇒ \qquad\qquad 300° = 3x$$

$$⇒ \qquad\qquad x = \frac{300°}{3}$$

$$⇒ \qquad\qquad x = 100°$$

If $x = 100°$, then other angle $= 180° - x = 180° - 100° = 80°$

So, the greater angle is 100°.

Q. 35 In the given figure, $PQ \parallel RS$. If $\angle 1 = (2a+b)^\circ$ and $\angle 6 = (3a-b)^\circ$, then the measure of $\angle 2$ in terms of b is

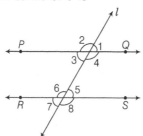

(a) $(2+b)^\circ$ (b) $(3-b)^\circ$
(c) $(108-b)^\circ$ (d) $(180-b)^\circ$

Sol. (c) From the given figure, $\angle 1 = \angle 5$ [corresponding angles]

$\Rightarrow$ $\angle 5 = (2a+b)^\circ$ $[\because \angle 1 = (2a+b)^\circ, \text{ given}]$

Also, $\angle 5 + \angle 6 = 180^\circ$ [linear pair]

$\Rightarrow$ $(2a+b)^\circ + (3a-b)^\circ = 180^\circ$ $[\because \angle 6 = (3a-b)^\circ, \text{ given}]$

$\Rightarrow$ $(2a+3a) + (b-b) = 180^\circ$

$\Rightarrow$ $5a = 180^\circ$

$\Rightarrow$ $a = \dfrac{180^\circ}{5}$

$\Rightarrow$ $a = 36^\circ$

Now, $\angle 1 + \angle 2 = 180^\circ$ [linear pair]

$\Rightarrow$ $\angle 2 = 180^\circ - \angle 1$

$\Rightarrow$ $\angle 2 = 180^\circ - (2a+b)^\circ$ $[\because \angle 1 = (2a+b)^\circ, \text{ given}]$

$\Rightarrow$ $\angle 2 = 180^\circ - 2a - b$

$\Rightarrow$ $\angle 2 = 180^\circ - 2 \times 36^\circ - b$ $[\because a = 36^\circ]$

$\Rightarrow$ $\angle 2 = 180^\circ - 72^\circ - b$

$\Rightarrow$ $\angle 2 = (108-b)^\circ$

Q. 36 In the given figure, $PQ \parallel RS$ and $a:b = 3:2$. Then, f is equal to

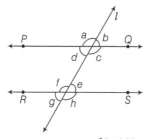

(a) 36° (b) 108°
(c) 72° (d) 144°

Sol. (b)   We have, $a:b = 3:2$

Let $a = 3x$ and $b = 2x$

Since, a and b form a linear pair.

$\therefore$ $a+b = 180°$

$\Rightarrow$ $3x+2x = 180°$

$\Rightarrow$ $5x = 180°$ [∵ sum of linear pair of angles is 180°]

$\Rightarrow$ $x = \dfrac{180°}{5}$

$\Rightarrow$ $x = 36°$

$\therefore$ $a = 3x \Rightarrow a = 3\times36° = 108°$

Now, $f = a$ [corresponding angles]

$\Rightarrow$ $f = 108°$

Q. 37 In the given figure, line l intersects two parallel lines PQ and RS. Then, which one of the following is not true?

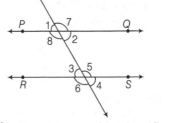

(a) $\angle 1 = \angle 3$ (b) $\angle 2 = \angle 4$ (c) $\angle 6 = \angle 7$ (d) $\angle 4 = \angle 8$

Sol. (d)   From the given figure, $PQ \parallel RS$ and l is transversal. Therefore,

$\angle 1 = \angle 3$ [corresponding angles]

$\angle 2 = \angle 4$ [corresponding angles] ... (i)

Also, $\angle 5 = \angle 6$ [vertically opposite angles] ...(ii)

and $\angle 5 = \angle 7$ [corresponding angles] ...(iii)

$\Rightarrow$ $\angle 6 = \angle 7$ [from Eqs. (ii) and (iii)]

Also, $\angle 2 + \angle 8 = 180°$ [linear pair]

$\Rightarrow$ $\angle 4 + \angle 8 = 180°$ [$\angle 2 = \angle 4$]

Q. 38 In the above figure (Q. No. 37), which one of the following is not true?

(a) $\angle 1 + \angle 5 = 180°$ (b) $\angle 2 + \angle 5 = 180°$

(c) $\angle 3 + \angle 8 = 180°$ (d) $\angle 2 + \angle 3 = 180°$

Sol. (d)   From the above figure, $\angle 2$ and $\angle 3$ are alternate interior angles.

Hence, $\angle 2 = \angle 3$

Q. 39 In the given figure (Q.No. 37), which of the following is true?

(a) $\angle 1 = \angle 5$ (b) $\angle 4 = \angle 8$ (c) $\angle 5 = \angle 8$ (d) $\angle 3 = \angle 7$

Sol. (c)   From the above figure, $\angle 5$ and $\angle 8$ are alternate interior angles.

Hence, $\angle 5 = \angle 8$

Q. 40 In the given figure, $PQ \parallel ST$. Then, the value of $x + y$ is

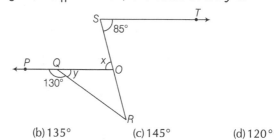

(a) 125°   (b) 135°   (c) 145°   (d) 120°

Sol. *(b)* Since, $PQ \parallel ST$, then PO will also parallel to ST.

Now, $PO \parallel ST$ and OS is transversal.
Therefore,

	$x = 85°$	[alternate interior angles]
Now,	$y + 130° = 180°$	[linear pair]
$\Rightarrow$	$y = 180° - 130°$	
$\Rightarrow$	$y = 50°$	
$\therefore$	$x + y = 85° + 50° = 135°$	

Q. 41 In the given figure, if $PQ \parallel RS$ and $QR \parallel TS$, then the value of a is

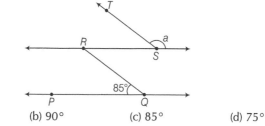

(a) 95°   (b) 90°   (c) 85°   (d) 75°

Sol. *(a)* Since, $PQ \parallel RS$ and QR is transversal.

$\therefore$	$\angle PQR = \angle SRQ$	[alternate interior angles]
$\Rightarrow$	$\angle SRQ = 85°$	
Also, $ST \parallel QR$ and RS is transversal.		
$\therefore$	$\angle SRQ = \angle RST$	[alternate interior angles]
$\Rightarrow$	$\angle RST = 85°$	
Now,	$\angle RST + a = 180°$	[linear pair]
$\Rightarrow$	$a = 180° - \angle RST$	
$\Rightarrow$	$a = 180° - 85°$	
$\Rightarrow$	$a = 95°$	[$\because \angle RST = 85°$]

Fill in the Blanks

In questions 42 to 56, fill in the blanks to make the statements true.

Q. 42 If sum of measures of two angles is 90°, then the angles are ____.
Sol. Complementary
The sum of two complementary angles is 90°.

Q. 43 If the sum of measures of two angles is 180°, then they are _____.
Sol. Supplementary
The sum of two supplementary angles is 180°.

Q. 44 A transversal intersects two or more than two lines at _____ points.
Sol. Distinct
A transversal intersects two or more than two lines at distinct points.

In question 45 to 48, if a transversal intersects two parallel lines, then

Q. 45 sum of interior angles on the same side of a transversal is _____.
Sol. 180°
Sum of interior angles on the same side of a transversal is 180°.

In the above figure, $x + y = 180°$.

Q. 46 Alternate interior angles have one common _____ .
Sol. Arm
Two alternate interior angles have one common arm.

Q. 47 Corresponding angles are on the _____ side of the transversal.
Sol. Same
Two corresponding angles are on the same side of the transversal.

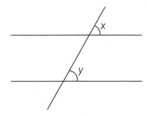

Q. 48 Alternate interior angles are on the _____ side of the transversal.

Sol. Opposite

Two alternate interior angles are on the opposite side of the transversal.

Q. 49 Two lines in a plane which do not meet at a point anywhere, are called _____ lines.

Sol. Parallel

If two lines are parallel, then they will never meet each other.

Q. 50 Two angles forming a _____ pair are supplementary.

Sol. Linear

If two angles form a linear pair, then their sum will be 180°. Hence, they are supplementary.

Q. 51 The supplement of an acute angle is always _____ angle.

Sol. Obtuse

If angle is acute angle, then its supplement will be an obtuse angle. As, if we subtract an angle which is less than 90° from 180°, then result will be an angle greater than 90°.

Q. 52 The supplement of a right angle is always _____ angle.

Sol. Right

Let x be the supplement of the right angle.

Then, $\qquad x + 90° = 180° \Rightarrow x = 180° - 90° = 90°$

Q. 53 The supplement of an obtuse angle is always _____ angle.

Sol. Acute

The supplement of an obtuse angle is always an acute angle. As, if we subtract an obtuse angle from 180°, then result will be an acute angle, i.e. 90°.

Q. 54 In a pair of complementary angles, each angle cannot be more than _____.

Sol. 90°

Two angles are said to be complementary angles, if their sum is 90°. Hence, if two angles are complementary, then each angle cannot be more than 90°.

Q. 55 An angle is 45°. Its complementary angle will be _____.

Sol. 45°

Let x be the required angle.

Then, $x + 45° = 90° \Rightarrow x = 90° - 45° = 45°$

Q. 56 An angle which is half of its supplement is of _____.

Sol. 60°

Let the required angle be x. Then, its supplement will be $(180° - x)$.

It is given that x is the half of it supplement i.e. $(180° - x)$.

Therefore, $x = \dfrac{1}{2}(180° - x)$

$\Rightarrow$ $2x = 180° - x$

$\Rightarrow$ $2x + x = 180°$

$\Rightarrow$ $3x = 180°$

$\Rightarrow$ $x = \dfrac{180°}{3}$

$\Rightarrow$ $x = 60°$

True/False

In questions 57 to 71, state whether the statements are True or False.

Q. 57 Two right angles are complementary to each other.

Sol. *False*

Measure of right angle is 90°. So, the sum of two right angles = 90° + 90° = 180°. Complementary angles are those whose sum is equal to 90°.

Hence, two right angles are never be complementary.

Q. 58 One obtuse angle and one acute angle can make a pair of complementary angles.

Sol. *False*

Since, sum of two complementary angles is 90°, so sum of one obtuse and one acute angles cannot make a pair of complementary angles as obtuse angle is greater than 90°.

Q. 59 Two supplementary angles are always obtuse angles.

Sol. *False*

If two angles are supplementary angles, then it is not necessary that they are always obtuse angles.

e.g. 60° and 120° are supplementary angles but both are not obtuse.

Q. 60 Two right angles are always supplementary to each other.

Sol. *True*

Measure of a right angle is 90°. Then, sum of two right angles will be $(90° + 90°) = 180°$. So, two right angles are always supplementary to each other.

Q. 61 One obtuse angle and one acute angle can make a pair of supplementary angles.

Sol. *True*

One obtuse angle and one acute angle can make a pair of supplementary angles.

e.g. 60° and 120° are supplementary angles. So, one is 60° i.e. acute angle and other is 120°, i.e. obtuse angle.

Q. 62 Both angles of a pair of supplementary angles can never be acute angles.

Sol. *True*

Acute angles are those which are less than 90°.

∴ Both angles of a pair of supplementary angles can never be acute.

Q. 63 Two supplementary angles always form a linear pair.

Sol. *False*

Linear pair is always in a straight line.

Q. 64 Two angles making a linear pair are always supplementary.

Sol. *True*

Because linear pair is always in a straight line and straight line makes 180° angle.

Q. 65 Two angles making a linear pair are always adjacent angles.

Sol. *True*

e.g.

From the above figure, ∠1 and ∠2 form a linear pair and are adjacent angles.

Q. 66 Vertically opposite angles form a linear pair.

Sol. *False*

Two angles making a linear pair are always adjacent angles.

Q. 67 Interior angles on the same side of a transversal with two distinct parallel lines are complementary angles.

Sol. *False*

Interior angles on the same side of a transversal with two distinct parallel lines are supplementary angles.

Q. 68 Vertically opposite angles are either both acute angles or both obtuse angles.

Sol. *True*

Vertically opposite angles are equal. So, if one angle is acute, then other angle will be acute and if one angle is obtuse, then the other will be obtuse.

Q. 69 A linear pair may have two acute angles.

Sol.   *False*

A linear pair either have both right angles or one acute and one obtuse angle, because angles forming linear pair is 180°.

Q. 70 An angle is more than 45°. Its complementary angle must be less than 45°.

Sol.   *True*

e.g. Let one angle = 50°

∴ The other angle = 90 − 50° = 40° < 45°

Q. 71 Two adjacent angles always form a linear pair.

Sol.   *False*

Two adjacent angles do not always form a linear pair, but the angles forming linear pair are always adjacent angles.

Q. 72 Write down each pair of adjacent angles shown in the following figures.

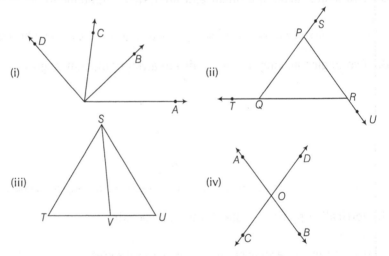

Sol.   Two angles are called adjacent angles, if they have a common vertex and a common arm but no common interior points.

Hence, following are adjacent angles:

(i) (a) ∠AOB, ∠BOC   (b) ∠AOB, ∠BOD
     (c) ∠BOC, ∠COD   (d) ∠AOC, ∠COD

(ii) (a) ∠PQR, ∠PQT   (b) ∠SPR, ∠RPQ
     (c) ∠PRQ, ∠QRU

(iii) (a) ∠TSV, ∠VSU   (b) ∠SVU, ∠SVT

(iv) (a) ∠AOC, ∠AOD   (b) ∠AOD, ∠BOD
     (c) ∠BOD, ∠BOC   (d) ∠BOC, ∠AOC

Q. 73 In each of the following figures, write, if any, (i) each pair of vertically opposite angles, and (ii) each linear pair.

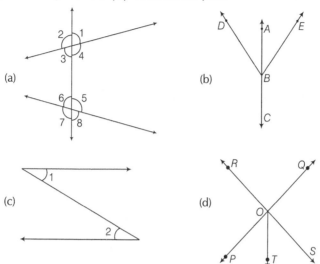

(a)

(b)

(c)

(d)

Sol. Vertically opposite angles are the angles, opposite to each other when two lines cross. A linear pair is a pair of adjacent angles whose non-common sides are opposite rays. Following are vertically opposite angles and linear pair in the above figure:

Figure	Vertically opposite angles	Linear pair
(a)	$\angle 1, \angle 3$; $\angle 2, \angle 4$; $\angle 5, \angle 7$; $\angle 6, \angle 8$	$\angle 1, \angle 2$; $\angle 1, \angle 4$; $\angle 4, \angle 3$; $\angle 3, \angle 2$; $\angle 5, \angle 8$; $\angle 8, \angle 7$; $\angle 7, \angle 6$; $\angle 6, \angle 5$
(b)	Nil	$\angle ABD, \angle DBC$; $\angle ABE, \angle EBC$.
(c)	Nil	Nil
(d)	$\angle ROQ, \angle POS$; $\angle ROP, \angle QOS$	$\angle ROP, \angle POS$; $\angle ROT, \angle TOS$; $\angle QOS, \angle SOP$; $\angle QOT, \angle TOP$; $\angle ROQ, \angle QOS$; $\angle ROQ, \angle ROP$.

Q. 74 Name the pairs of supplementary angles in the following figures:

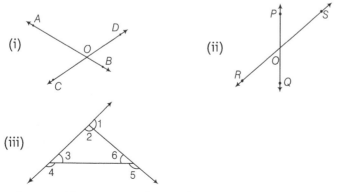

(i)

(ii)

(iii)

Sol. When the sum of the measures of two angles is 180°, the angles are called supplementary angles. Linear pair angles are supplementary angles as their sum is 180°.

Following are the pairs of supplementary angles in the above figures:

Figure	Pair of supplementary angles
(i)	∠AOD, ∠AOC; ∠AOC, ∠BOC; ∠BOC, ∠BOD; ∠AOD, ∠BOD
(ii)	∠POS, ∠SOQ; ∠POR, ∠QOR
(iii)	∠1, ∠2; ∠5, ∠6; ∠3, ∠4

Q. 75 In the given figure, PQ || RS, TR || QU and ∠PTR = 42°. Find ∠QUR.

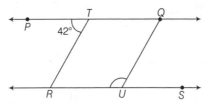

Sol. Since, PQ and RS are parallel and TR is transversal.

Therefore,

$$\angle PTR = \angle TRU \qquad \text{[alternate interior angles]}$$

⇒   ∠TRU = 42°

Now, TR is parallel to QU and RS is transversal.

Therefore,   ∠TRU + ∠RUQ = 180°   [consecutive interior angles]

⇒   42° + ∠RUQ = 180°

⇒   ∠RUQ = 180° − 42°   = 138°

Q. 76 The drawings below (figure), show angles formed by the goalposts at different positions of a football player. The greater the angle, the better chance the player has of scoring a goal. e.g. The player has a better chance of scoring a goal from position A than from position B.

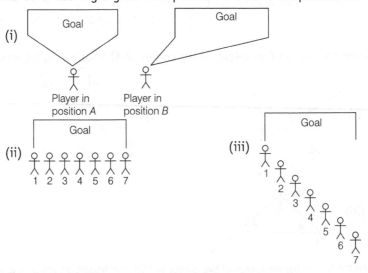

In parts (a) and (b) given below, it may help to trace the diagrams and draw and measure angles.

   (a) Seven football players are practicing their kicks. They are lined up in a straight line infront of the goalpost [figure (ii)]. Which player has the best (the greatest) kicking angle?

   (b) Now the players are lined up as shown in figure (iii). Which player has the best kicking angle?

   (c) Estimate atleast two situations, such that the angles formed by different positions of two players are complement to each other.

Sol. (a)

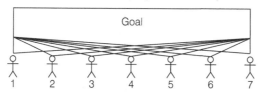

Since, angle made by 4 is greatest. Hence, he has the best kicking angle.

(b)

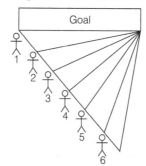

From the above figure, we can say that player 4 has the best kicking angle, as it is greatest.

(c) Since, the angles are complementary. Hence, two situations are 45°, 45° and 30°, 60°.

Q. 77 The sum of two vertically opposite angles is 166°. Find each of the angles.

Sol. When two lines intersect, then vertically opposite angles so formed are equal.

Let x be the measure of each vertically opposite angles.

Then, $\qquad\qquad\qquad x + x = 166°$

$\Rightarrow \qquad\qquad\qquad 2x = 166°$

$\Rightarrow \qquad\qquad\qquad x = \dfrac{166°}{2} = 83°$

So, the measure of each angle is 83°.

Q. 78 In the given figure, $l \parallel m \parallel n$. $\angle QPS = 35°$ and $\angle QRT = 55°$. Find $\angle PQR$.

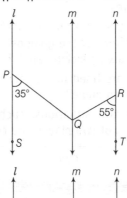

Sol.

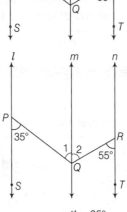

From the above figure, $\angle 1 = 35°$ [alternate angles]
                                          $\angle 2 = 55°$ [alternate angles]
∴ $\angle PQR = \angle 1 + \angle 2 = 35° + 55° = 90°$

Q. 79 In the given figure, P, Q and R are collinear points and $TQ \perp PR$.

Name:

   (a) pair of complementary angles.
   (b) two pairs of supplementary angles.
   (c) four pairs of adjacent angles.

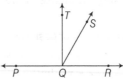

Sol.   (a) Complementary angles are those whose sum is 90°.

∴ $\angle TQS$ and $\angle SQR$ are pair of complementary angles, as their sum is 90°.

   (b) Supplementary angles are those whose sum is 180°.

∴ $\angle SQR$, $\angle SQP$; $\angle TQR$, $\angle TQP$ are pair so supplementary angles.

   (c) Two angles are called adjacent angles, if they have a common vertex and a common arm but no common interior points.

∴ $\angle SQR$, $\angle SQT$; $\angle TQR$, $\angle TQP$; $\angle SQT$, $\angle TQP$; $\angle PQS$, $\angle SQR$ are pairs of adjacent angles.

Q. 80 In the given figure, $OR \perp OP$.

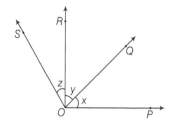

(i) Name all the pairs of adjacent angles.

(ii) Name all the pairs of complementary angles.

Sol. By definition of adjacent angles and complementary angles, we can say that following pairs are adjacent angles and complementary angles.

Adjacent angles: $\angle x$, $\angle y$; $\angle x + \angle y$, $\angle z$; $\angle y$, $\angle z$; $\angle x$, $\angle y + \angle z$.

Complementary angles: $\angle x$, $\angle y$.

Q. 81 If two angles have a common vertex and their arms form opposite rays (figure). Then,

(a) how many angles are formed?

(b) how many types of angles are formed?

(c) write all the pairs of vertically opposite angles.

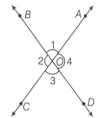

Sol. (a) Total 13 angles are formed, namely $\angle AOB$, $\angle BOC$, $\angle COD$, $\angle DOA$, $\angle AOC$, $\angle BOD$, $\angle DOB$, $\angle AOD$, $\angle BOA$, $\angle COB$, $\angle DOC$, $\angle AOA$.

(b) Following types of angles are formed:

(i) Linear pair

(ii) Supplementary

(iii) Vertically opposite

(iv) Adjacent

(c) Following are the pair of vertically opposite angles:

$\angle 1$, $\angle 3$; $\angle 2$, $\angle 4$.

Q. 82 In the given figure, are the following pairs of angles adjacent? Justify your answer.

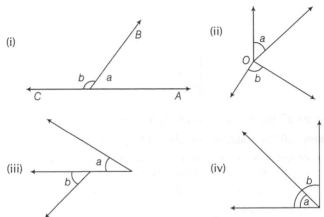

Sol.   Two angles are called adjacent angles, if they have a common vertex and a common arm but no common interior points. Hence, *a* and *b* form a pair of adjacent angle only in (i).

Q. 83 In the given figure, write all the pairs of supplementary angles.

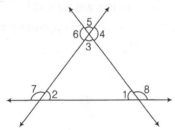

Sol.   Supplementary angles are those angles whose sum is 180°. Hence, following are the pairs of supplementary angles:

(i) ∠1, ∠8   (ii) ∠2, ∠7

(iii) ∠3, ∠4   (iv) ∠4, ∠5

(v) ∠5, ∠6   (vi) ∠6, ∠3

Q. 84 What is the type of other angle of a linear pair, if

      (a) one of its angle is acute?

      (b) one of its angles is obtuse?

      (c) one of its angles is right?

Sol.   Sum of angles of linear pair is 180°.

    (a) If one angle is acute angle, then other angle will be obtuse. As, if we subtract an acute angle from 180°, we get an angle which is greater than 90°.

    (b) If one angle is obtuse angle, then other angle will be acute. As, if we subtract an obtuse angle from 180°, we get an angle which is less than 90°.

    (c) If one angle is right angle, then other angle will also be right angle. As, if we subtract 90° from 180°, we get 90°.

Q. 85 Can two acute angles form a pair of supplementary angles? Give reason in support of your answer.

Sol. Acute angles are those angles which are less than 90°. If we add two angles which are less than 90°, we get the result less than 180°. e.g. If we add 60° and 70°, we get 60° + 70° = 130° < 180°.

Hence, two acute angles cannot form a pair of supplementary angles.

Q. 86 Two lines *AB* and *CD* intersect at 0 (see the figure). Write all the pairs of adjacent angles by taking angles 1, 2, 3 and 4 only.

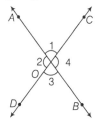

Sol. Two angles are called adjacent angles, if they have a common vertex and a common arm, but no common interior points.

Hence, following are the pairs of adjacent angles taking 1, 2, 3, 4 angles only,

i.e. ∠1, ∠2 ; ∠2, ∠3; ∠3, ∠4; ∠4, ∠1.

Q. 87 If the complement of an angle is 62°, then find its supplement.

Sol. Let the angle be $x°$. We know that, sum of two complementary angles is 90°.

∴ $x + 62° = 90° \Rightarrow x = 90° - 62° = 28°$

Supplement of any angle is (180° – angle).

∴ Supplement of $x = 180° - 28° = 152°$

Q. 88 A road crosses a railway line at an angle of 30° as shown in the figure. Find the values of *a*, *b* and *c*.

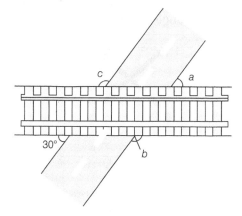

Sol. Lines l and m are parallel, P is transversal and $x = 30°$.
Therefore,

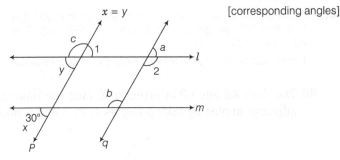

$$x = y \qquad \text{[corresponding angles]}$$

$\Rightarrow$	$y = 30°$	
Now,	$c + y = 180°$	[linear pair]
$\Rightarrow$	$c + 30° = 180°$	
$\Rightarrow$	$c = 180° - 30°$	
$\Rightarrow$	$c = 150°$	
Now,	$\angle 1 + c = 180°$	[linear pair]
$\Rightarrow$	$\angle 1 + 150° = 180°$	
$\Rightarrow$	$\angle 1 = 180° - 150° = 30°$	
$\therefore$	$\angle 1 = a$	[corresponding angles]
$\Rightarrow$	$a = 30°$	
Also,	$\angle 2 + a = 180°$	[linear pair]
$\Rightarrow$	$\angle 2 + 30° = 180°$	
$\Rightarrow$	$\angle 2 = 180° - 30° = 150°$	
Again,	$\angle 2 = b$	[alternate interior angles]
$\Rightarrow$	$b = 150°$	

Hence, $a = 30°$, $b = 150°$ and $c = 150°$

Q. 89 The legs of a stool make an angle of 35° with the floor, as shown in the given figure. Find the angles x and y.

Sol.

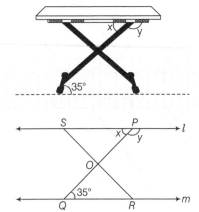

Since, l m are parallel lines and PQ is transversal.

∴ $\qquad\qquad x = \angle PQR$ $\qquad$ [alternate interior angles]

⇒ $\qquad\qquad x = 35°$ $\qquad$ [∵ $\angle PQR = 35°$]

Again, $\qquad\qquad x + y = 180°$ $\qquad$ [linear pair]

⇒ $\qquad\qquad 35° + y = 180°$

⇒ $\qquad\qquad y = 180° - 35° = 145°$

Q. 90 Iron rods a, b, c, d, e and f are making a design in a bridge as shown in the given figure, in which $a\|b$, $c\|d$ and $e\|f$. Find the marked angles between

(i) b and c $\qquad\qquad$ (ii) d and e

(iii) d and f $\qquad\qquad$ (iv) c and f

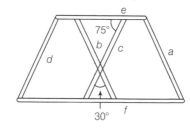

Sol.

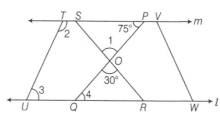

Since, l, m are two parallel lines and PQ, RS and TU are transversal.

Then, $\qquad\qquad \angle 4 = \angle QPS$ $\qquad$ [alternate interior angles]

⇒ $\qquad\qquad \angle 4 = 75°$ $\qquad$ [∵ $\angle QPS = 75°$]

Again, $\qquad\qquad \angle 1 = \angle QOR$ $\qquad$ [vertically opposite angles]

⇒ $\qquad\qquad \angle 1 = 30°$ $\qquad$ [∵ $\angle QOR = 30°$]

Also, PQ and TU are parallel and m and l are transversal.

Therefore, $\qquad \angle 2 + \angle QPT = 180°$ $\qquad$ [consecutive interior angles]

⇒ $\qquad\qquad \angle 2 = 180° - 75°$ $\qquad$ [∵ $\angle QPT = 75°$, given]

⇒ $\qquad\qquad \angle 2 = 105°$

Also, $\qquad\qquad \angle 2 + \angle 3 = 180°$

⇒ $\qquad\qquad 105° + \angle 3 = 180°$

⇒ $\qquad\qquad \angle 3 = 180° - 105°$

⇒ $\qquad\qquad \angle 3 = 75°$

Hence,

(i) 30° $\qquad\qquad$ (ii) 105°

(iii) 75° $\qquad\qquad$ (iv) 75°

Q. 91 Amisha makes a star with the help of line segments a, b, c, d, e and f, in which $a \| d$, $b \| e$ and $c \| f$. Chhaya marks an angle as 120° as shown in the given figure and Amisha to find the $\angle x$, $\angle y$ and $\angle z$. Help Amisha in finding the angles.

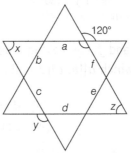

Sol.   From the given figure, we have

	$\angle a = 120°$	[vertically opposite angles]
Now,	$\angle x + \angle a = 180°$	[consecutive interior angles]
$\Rightarrow$	$\angle x + 120° = 180°$	
$\Rightarrow$	$\angle x = 180° - 120° = 60°$	

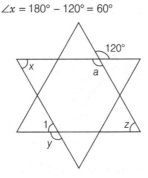

Again,	$\angle x = \angle 1$	[alternate interior angles]
$\Rightarrow$	$60° = \angle 1$	
Also,	$\angle 1 + \angle y = 180° \Rightarrow 60° + \angle y = 180°$	[linear pair]
$\Rightarrow$	$\angle y = 180° - 60° = 120°$	
Also,	$\angle z + \angle a = 180°$	[consecutive interior angles]
$\Rightarrow$	$\angle z + 120° = 180°$	
$\Rightarrow$	$\angle z = 180° - 120° = 60°$	

Q. 92 In the given figure, $AB \| CD$, $AF \| ED$, $\angle AFC = 68°$ and $\angle FED = 42°$. Find $\angle EFD$.

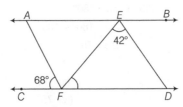

Sol. *AF* and *ED* are parallel and *EF* is transversal.

Then, $\angle AFE = \angle FED$ [alternate interior angles]

$\Rightarrow$ $\angle AFE = 42°$ [$\because \angle FED = 42°$]

Now, $\angle AFC + \angle AFE + \angle EFD = 180°$

[$\because$ sum of all the angles on a straight line is 180°]

$\Rightarrow$ $68° + 42° + \angle EFD = 180°$

$\Rightarrow$ $110° + \angle EFD = 180°$

$\Rightarrow$ $\angle EFD = 180° - 110° = 70°$

Q. 93 In the given figure, *OB* is perpendicular to *OA* and $\angle BOC = 49°$. Find $\angle AOD$.

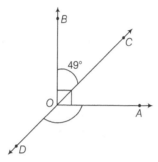

Sol. From the given figure, we have

$\angle DOB + \angle BOC = 180°$ [linear pair]

$\Rightarrow$ $\angle DOB + 49° = 180°$ [$\because \angle BOC = 49°$]

$\Rightarrow$ $\angle DOB = 180° - 49° = 131°$

Now, $\angle DOB + \angle BOA + \angle AOB = 360°$

[$\because$ sum of all the angles around a point is 360°]

$\Rightarrow$ $131° + 90° + \angle AOD = 360°$ [$\because \angle DOB = 131°, \angle BOA = 90°$]

$\Rightarrow$ $221° + \angle AOD = 360°$

$\Rightarrow$ $\angle AOD = 360° - 221° = 139°$

Q. 94 Three lines *AB*, *CD* and *EF* intersect each other at *O*. If $\angle AOE = 30°$ and $\angle DOB = 40°$ (see the figure) find $\angle COF$.

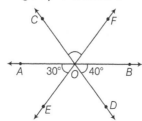

Sol.   From the given figure, we have

$$\angle AOE + \angle EOD + \angle DOB = 180°$$

[∵ sum of all the angles on a straight line is 180°]

⇒ $30° + \angle EOD + 40° = 180°$

⇒ $\angle EOD = 180° - 70°$

⇒ $\angle EOD = 110°$

Again, $\angle EOD = \angle COF$ [vertically opposite angles]

⇒ $\angle COF = 110°$

Q. 95 Measures (in degrees) of two complementary angles are two consecutive even integers. Find the angles.

Sol.   Let the two consecutive angles be x and $x + 2$. Since, both angles are complementary. So, their sum will be 90°.

∴ $x + (x + 2) = 90°$

⇒ $x + x + 2 = 90°$

⇒ $2x = 90° - 2$

⇒ $2x = 88°$

⇒ $x = 44°$

Therefore, the angles are 44° and 44° + 2 = 46°.

Q. 96 If a transversal intersects two parallel lines and the difference of two interior angles on the same side of a transversal is 20°, find the angles.

Sol.   Let the two interior angles on the same side of transversal are x and y.

Given, their difference is 20°.

∴ $x - y = 20°$ ⇒ $y = x - 20°$ ...(i)

Since, l and m are parallel and P is transversal.

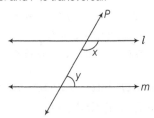

Then, $x + y = 180°$ [∵ sum of an interior angles is 180°]

∴ $x + x - 20° = 180°$ [from Eq. (i)]

⇒ $2x = 180° + 20°$

⇒ $2x = 200°$

⇒ $x = \dfrac{200°}{2} = 100°$

Now, $y = x - 20°$

∴ $y = 100° - 20° = 80°$

Therefore, the angles are 100° and 80°, respectively

Q. 97 Two angles are making a linear pair. If one of them is one-third of the other, then find the angles.

Sol. Let one angle be x. It is given that other angle is one-third of first.

So, other angle will be $\frac{1}{3}x$.

Again, given that both the angles are making a linear pair.
So, their sum will be 180°.

$\therefore$ $\qquad x + \frac{1}{3}x = 180°$

$\Rightarrow$ $\qquad \frac{3x + x}{3} = 180°$ [taking LCM of 1 and 3 on LHS]

$\Rightarrow$ $\qquad \frac{4x}{3} = 180°$

$\Rightarrow$ $\qquad x = \frac{180° \times 3}{4}$

$\Rightarrow$ $\qquad x = 135°$

Hence, the angles are 135° and $\frac{1}{3} \times 135°$, i.e. 135° and 45°.

Q. 98 Measures (in degrees) of two supplementary angles are consecutive odd integers. Find the angles.

Sol. Let two consecutive odd integers x, $x + 2$. It is given that both are supplementary angles. So, their sum will be 180°.

$\therefore$ $\qquad x + (x + 2) = 180°$

$\Rightarrow$ $\qquad 2x = 180° - 2$

$\Rightarrow$ $\qquad 2x = 178° = \frac{178°}{2}$

$\Rightarrow$ $\qquad x = 89°$

Hence, the two angles are 89° and 91°.

Q. 99 In the given figure, $AE \| GF \| BD$, $AB \| CG \| DF$ and $\angle CHE = 120°$. Find $\angle ABC$ and $\angle CDE$.

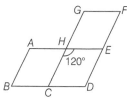

Sol. Since, $BD \| AE$ and CG is transversal.

Therefore, $\qquad \angle BCH = \angle EHC$ [alternate interior angles]

$\Rightarrow$ $\qquad \angle BCH = 120°$

Again, $CG \| DF$ and BD is transversal.

Therefore, $\qquad \angle BCH = \angle CDE$ [corresponding angles]

$\Rightarrow$ $\qquad \angle CDE = 120°$

Also, $AB \| CG$ and BC is transversal.

Therefore, $\qquad \angle ABC + \angle BCH = 180°$ [consecutive angles]

$\Rightarrow$ $\qquad \angle ABC = 180° - 120°$

$\Rightarrow$ $\qquad \angle ABC = 60°$

Q. 100 In the given figure, find the value of $\angle BOC$, if points A, O and B are collinear.

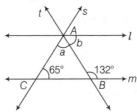

Sol. Since, A, O and B are collinear. Then, AOB will be a straight line and sum of all the angles on a straight line is $180°$.

$\therefore$ $\angle AOD + \angle DOC + \angle COB = 180°$

$\Rightarrow$ $(x - 10)° + (4x - 25)° + (x + 5)° = 180°$

$\Rightarrow$ $x - 10° + 4x - 25° + x + 5 = 180°$

$\Rightarrow$ $6x - 30° = 180°$

$\Rightarrow$ $6x = 180° + 30°$

$\Rightarrow$ $6x = 210° \Rightarrow x = 35°$

Now, $\angle BOC = (x + 5)°$

     $= (35 + 5)° = 40°$

Q. 101 In the given figure, if $l \parallel m$, find the values of a and b.

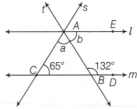

Sol. Since, l, m are parallel lines and t is transversal.

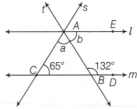

Therefore, $\angle EAB + \angle DBA = 180°$ [consecutive interior angles]

$\Rightarrow$ $b + 132° = 180°$

$\Rightarrow$ $b = 180° - 132°$

$\Rightarrow$ $b = 48°$

Again, l, m are parallel lines and s is transversal.

Therefore, $\angle EAC + \angle BCA = 180°$ [consecutive interior angles]

$\Rightarrow$ $a + b + 65° = 180°$

$\Rightarrow$ $a + 48° + 65° = 180°$ [$\because b = 48°$]

$\Rightarrow$ $a = 180° - 48° - 65°$

$\Rightarrow$ $a = 67°$

Q. 102 In the given figure, $l \parallel m$ and a line t intersects these lines at P and Q, respectively. Find the sum $2a + b$.

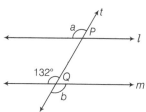

Sol.

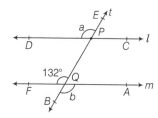

From the above figure, we can say that

$$\angle AQB = \angle FQP \qquad \text{[vertically opposite angles]}$$

$$\Rightarrow \qquad b = 132°$$

Since, l, m are parallel lines and t is transversal.

Therefore,

$$\angle EPD = \angle PQF \qquad \text{[corresponding angles]}$$

$$\Rightarrow \qquad a = 132°$$

Now, $\quad 2a + b = 2 \times 132° + 132° = 264° + 132° = 396°$

Q. 103 In the given figure, $QP \parallel RS$. Find the values of a and b.

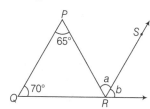

Sol. Since, $QP \parallel RS$ and PR is transversal.

Therefore,

$$\angle QPR = \angle SRP \qquad \text{[alternate interior angles]}$$

$$\Rightarrow \qquad 65° = a \quad \Rightarrow \quad a = 65°$$

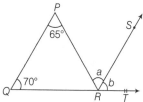

Also,

$$\angle SRT = \angle PQR \qquad \text{[corresponding angles]}$$

$$\Rightarrow \qquad b = 70°$$

Q. 104 In the given figure, $PQ \parallel RT$. Find the value of $a + b$.

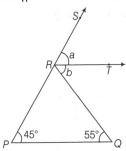

Sol. Since, $PQ \parallel RT$ and RQ is transversal.

Therefore, $\angle TRQ = \angle RQP$ [alternate interior angles]

$\Rightarrow$ $b = 55°$

Also, $\angle SRT = \angle SPQ$ [corresponding angles]

$\Rightarrow$ $a = 45°$

$\therefore$ $a + b = 45° + 55° = 100°$

Q. 105 In the given figure, PQ, RS and UT are parallel lines.

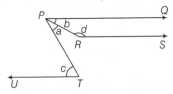

(i) If $c = 57°$ and $a = \dfrac{c}{3}$, find the value of d.

(ii) If $c = 75°$ and $a = \dfrac{2}{5}c$, find b.

Sol. (i) Since, $PQ \parallel UT$ and PT is transversal.

Therefore, $\angle QPT = \angle UTP$ [alternate interior angles]

$\Rightarrow$ $a + b = c$

$\Rightarrow$ $\dfrac{c}{3} + b = c$ $\left[\because a = \dfrac{c}{3}, \text{given} \right]$

$\Rightarrow$ $b = c - \dfrac{c}{3}$

$\Rightarrow$ $b = \dfrac{3c - c}{3}$

$\Rightarrow$ $b = \dfrac{2c}{3} = \dfrac{2}{3} \times 57°$ [$\because c = 57°$, given]

$\therefore$ $b = 38°$

Again, $PQ \parallel RS$ and PR is transversal.

Therefore, $\angle QPR + \angle PRS = 180°$ [consecutive interior angles]

$\Rightarrow$ $b + d = 180°$

$\Rightarrow$ $d = 180° - b$

$\Rightarrow$ $d = 180 - 38°$ [$\because b = 38°$]

$\Rightarrow$ $d = 142°$

(ii) Since, $PQ\,||\,UT$ and PT is transversal.

Therefore,	$\angle QPT = \angle UTP$	[alternate interior angles]
$\Rightarrow$	$a + b = c$	
$\Rightarrow$	$b = c - a$	
$\Rightarrow$	$b = c - \dfrac{2}{5}c$	$\left[\because a = \dfrac{2}{5}c, \text{given}\right]$
$\Rightarrow$	$b = \dfrac{5c - 2c}{5}$	
$\Rightarrow$	$b = \dfrac{3c}{5}$	
$\Rightarrow$	$b = \dfrac{3 \times 75^\circ}{5}$	$[\because c = 75^\circ, \text{given}]$
$\Rightarrow$	$b = 45^\circ$	

Q. 106 In the given figure, $AB\,||\,CD$. Find the reflex $\angle EFG$.

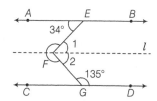

Sol. Construct a line l parallel to AB, passing through F. l is parallel to both AB and CD.

Then,	$\angle 1 = 34^\circ$	[alternate angles]
and	$\angle 2 + 135^\circ = 180^\circ$	[consecutive angles]
$\Rightarrow$	$\angle 2 = 180^\circ - 135^\circ$	
$\Rightarrow$	$\angle 2 = 45^\circ$	
$\therefore$	$\angle EFG = \angle 1 + \angle 2$	
$\Rightarrow$	$\angle EFG = 34^\circ + 45^\circ$	
$\Rightarrow$	$\angle EFG = 79^\circ$	
$\therefore$	Reflex of $\angle EFG = 360^\circ - \angle EFG$	
	$= 360^\circ - 79^\circ$	$[\because \angle EFG = 79^\circ]$
	$= 281^\circ$	

Q. 107 In the given figure, two parallel lines l and m are cut by two transversals n and p. Find the values of x and y.

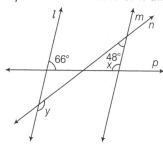

Sol. Since, lines l and m are parallel and p is transversal.

Therefore, $x + 66° = 180°$ [consecutive angles]

$\Rightarrow$ $x = 180° - 66°$

$\Rightarrow$ $x = 114°$

Again, lines l, m are parallel and n is transversal.

Therefore, $y + 48° = 180°$ [consecutive angles]

$\Rightarrow$ $y = 180° - 48°$

$\Rightarrow$ $y = 132°$

Q. 108 In the given figure, l, m and n are parallel lines, and the lines p and q are also parallel. Find the values of a, b and c.

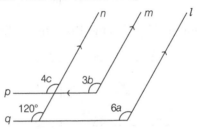

Sol. Since, lines l, n are parallel and q is transversal.

Therefore, $6a = 120°$ [corresponding angles]

$\Rightarrow$ $a = \dfrac{120°}{6} \Rightarrow a = 20°$

Also, lines p, q are parallel and n is transversal.

Therefore, $4c = 120°$ [corresponding angles]

$\Rightarrow$ $c = \dfrac{120°}{4}$

$\Rightarrow$ $c = 30°$

Again, lines m, n are parallel and p is transversal.

Therefore, $4c = 3b$ [corresponding angles]

$\Rightarrow$ $b = \dfrac{4c}{3}$

$\Rightarrow$ $b = \dfrac{4 \times 30°}{3}$

$\Rightarrow$ $b = 40°$

Q. 109 In the given figure, state which pair of lines are parallel. Give reason.

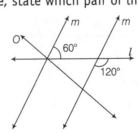

Sol.

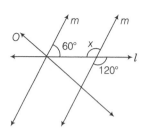

$$x = 120° \qquad \text{[vertically opposite angles]}$$

Now, $\qquad x + 60° = 120° + 60° = 180°$

Since, the sum of consecutive interior angles is 180°. Hence, *m* and *n* will be parallel.

Q. 110 In the given figure, examine whether the following pairs of lines are parallel or not.

      (i) *EF* and *GH*   (ii) *AB* and *CD*

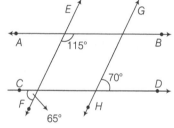

Sol. From the given figure, $x = 65°$ [vertically opposite angles]

and $\qquad\qquad y = 180° - 70° \qquad$ [linear pair]

$\Rightarrow \qquad\qquad y = 110°$

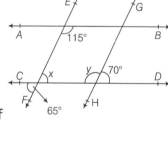

  (i) Now, $\qquad x + y = 65° + 110° = 175° \neq 180°$

      Hence, *EF* and *GH* are not parallel.

  (ii) Also, $\qquad x + 115° = 65° + 115° = 180°$

      Hence, *AB* and *CD* are parallel.

Q. 111 In the given figure, find out which pair of lines are parallel.

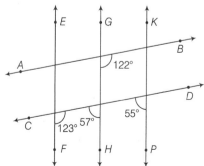

Sol.   From the given figure,

$$\angle 1 = 180° - 123°   \text{[linear pair]}$$

$$\Rightarrow \qquad \angle 1 = 57°$$

Also, $\angle 2 = 180° - 57°$ [linear pair]

$$\Rightarrow \qquad \angle 2 = 123°$$

Now, $\angle 1 + \angle 2 = 57° + 123° = 180°$

If sum of the consecutive angles are 180°, then the lines are parallel.

$$\therefore \qquad\qquad EF \| GH$$

Now, $\angle 3 = 180° - \angle 2$ [linear pair]

$$\Rightarrow \qquad \angle 3 = 180° - 123° = 57°$$

Also, $\angle 4 = 180° - 55°$

$$= 125°$$

$$\therefore \qquad \angle 3 + \angle 4 = 57° + 125° = 182° \ne 180°$$

[linear pair]

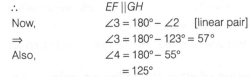

So, GH and KP are not parallel.

Also, $\angle 3 + 122° = 57° + 122° = 179° \ne 180°$

Hence, AB and CD are not parallel.

Q. 112 In the given figure, show that

(i) $AB \| CD$ 　　　　　　　　　　(ii) $EF \| GH$

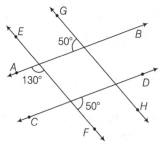

Sol.   (i) From the given figure,

$$\angle CIF + \angle FIJ = 180°   \text{[linear pair]}$$

$$\Rightarrow \qquad\qquad \angle CIF = 180° - \angle FIJ = 180° - 50° = 130°$$

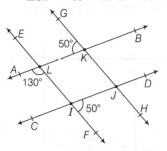

Now, 　　　　　　　　　　　$\angle ALI = \angle CIF = 130°$

$\therefore AB \| CD$ as their corresponding angles are equal.

(ii) From the given figure,

$$\angle GKL + \angle LKJ = 180°$$ [linear pair]

$\Rightarrow$ $\angle LKJ = 180° - \angle GKL = 180° - 50° = 130°$

Now, $\angle ALI = \angle LKJ = 130°$

$\therefore$ $EF \parallel GH$ as their corresponding angles are equal.

Q. 113 In the given figure, two parallel lines l and m are cut by two transversals p and q. Determine the values of x and y.

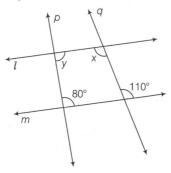

Sol. From the given figure, $x = 110°$ [alternate interior angles]

and $y + 80° = 180°$

[$\because$ sum of interior angles on the same side of transversal is 180°]

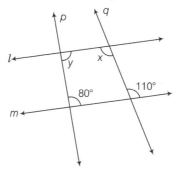

$\Rightarrow$ $y = 180° - 80°$

$\Rightarrow$ $y = 100°$

6

Triangles

Multiple Choice Questions (MCQs)

Q. 1 The sides of a triangle have lengths (in cm) 10, 6.5 and a, where a is a whole number. The minimum value that a can take is

  (a) 6   (b) 5   (c) 3   (d) 4

Sol. *(d)* As we know, sum of any two sides in a triangle is always greater than the third side.

So, only 4 is the minimum value that satisfies as a side in triangle.

$$\left.\begin{array}{l} 10 < 6.5 + 4 \\ 6.5 < 10 + 4 \\ 4 < 10 + 6.5 \end{array}\right]$$

Q. 2 ΔDEF of following figure is a right angled triangle with $\angle E = 90°$.

What type of angles are $\angle D$ and $\angle F$?

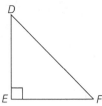

  (a) They are equal angles   (b) They form a pair of adjacent angles
  (c) They are complementary angles   (d) They are supplementary angles

Sol. *(c)* Since, $\angle D$ and $\angle F$ are complementary angles.

In ΔDEF,

$\angle D + \angle E + \angle F = 180°$ [angle sum property of a triangle]

$\Rightarrow \angle D + 90° + \angle F = 180°$ [$\because \angle E = 90°$, given]

$\Rightarrow \qquad \angle D + \angle F = 180° - 90°$

$\Rightarrow \qquad \angle D + \angle F = 90°$

Note Two angles whose measures add to 180° are known as **supplementary angles** and two angles whose measures add to 90° are known as **complementary angles**.

Q. 3 In the given figure, $PQ = PS$. The value of x is

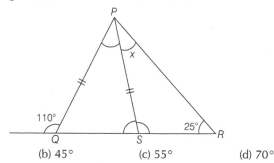

(a) 35°   (b) 45°   (c) 55°   (d) 70°

Sol. (b) In $\triangle PQS$,

$$110° + \angle 1 = 180° \qquad \text{[linear pair of angles]}$$
$$\Rightarrow \qquad \angle 1 = 180° - 110°$$
$$\Rightarrow \qquad \angle 1 = 70°$$

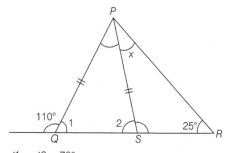

Also, $\angle 1 = \angle 2 = 70°$ $[\because PQ = PS]$

As we know, the measure of any exterior angle of a triangle is equal to the sum of the measures of its two interior opposite angles.

$$\therefore \qquad \angle 2 = x + 25°$$
$$\Rightarrow \qquad 70° = x + 25° \qquad [\because \angle 2 = 70°]$$
$$\Rightarrow \qquad x = 70° - 25°$$
$$\Rightarrow \qquad x = 45°$$

Q. 4 In a right angled triangle, the angles other than the right angle are

(a) obtuse   (b) right   (c) acute   (d) straight

Sol. (c) In right angled $\triangle ABC$, $\angle B = 90°$

$$\therefore \qquad \angle A + \angle B + \angle C = 180° \qquad \text{[angle sum property of a triangle]}$$

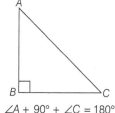

$$\Rightarrow \qquad \angle A + 90° + \angle C = 180°$$
$$\Rightarrow \qquad \angle A + \angle C = 180° - 90° = 90°$$

Hence, in a right angled triangle, the angles other than the right angle are acute.

Q. 5 In an isosceles triangle, one angle is 70°. The other two angles are of
   (i) 55° and 55°
   (ii) 70° and 40°
   (iii) any measure

In the given option(s) which of the above statement(s) are true?
   (a) (i) only   (b) (ii) only
   (c) (iii) only   (d) (i) and (ii)

Sol. *(d)* As we know, the sum of the interior angles of a triangle is 180°.
   (i) According to the question,
$$70° + 55° + 55° = 180°$$

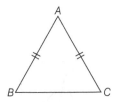

   (ii) According to the question,
$$70° + 70° + 40° = 180°$$
   (iii) Not possible, because two angles must be equal in an isosceles triangle.
       So, (i) and (ii) can be possible.

Q. 6 In a triangle, one angle is of 90°. Then,
   (i) the other two angles are of 45° each.
   (ii) in remaining two angles, one angle is 90° and other is 45°.
   (iii) remaining two angles are complementary.

In the given option(s) which is true?
   (a) (i) only   (b) (ii) only   (c) (iii) only   (d) (i) and (ii)

Sol. *(c)* In a right angled $\triangle ABC$,
$$\angle B = 90°$$

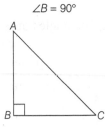

As we know,
$$\angle A + \angle B + \angle C = 180° \qquad \text{[angle sum property of a triangle]}$$
$$\Rightarrow \qquad \angle A + 90° + \angle C = 180°$$
$$\Rightarrow \qquad \angle A + \angle C = 180° - 90° = 90°$$
Hence, remaining two angles are complementary.

Q. 7 Lengths of sides of a triangle are 3 cm, 4 cm and 5 cm. The triangle is

      (a) obtuse angled triangle   (b) acute angled triangle

      (c) right angled triangle   (d) an isosceles right triangle

Sol. *(c)* Since, these sides satisfy the Pythagoras theorem, therefore it is right angled triangle.

Lengths of the sides of a triangle are 3 cm, 4 cm and 5 cm.

According to Pythagoras theorem,

$$3^2 + 4^2 = 5^2$$

$\Rightarrow$ $9 + 16 = 25$

$\Rightarrow$ $25 = 25$ (satisfied)

> **Note** *The area of the square built upon the hypotenuse of a right angled triangle is equal to the sum of the areas of the squares upon the remaining sides is known as Pythagoras theorem.*

Q. 8 In the given figure, $PB = PD$. The value of x is

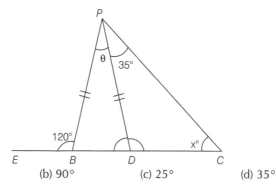

    (a) 85°   (b) 90°   (c) 25°   (d) 35°

Sol. *(c)* In ΔPBD, $\angle 1 + 120° = 180°$ [linear pair]

                       $\angle 1 = 180° - 120° = 60°$

Also, $\angle 1 = \angle 2 = 60°$ $[\because PB = PD]$

Also, $\angle 2 + \angle 3 = 180°$ [linear pair]

$\Rightarrow$ $60° + \angle 3 = 180°$ $\Rightarrow$ $\angle 3 = 180° - 60°$

$\Rightarrow$ $\angle 3 = 120°$

In ΔPDC, $35° + \angle 3 + x° = 180°$ [angle sum property of a triangle]

$\Rightarrow$ $35° + 120° + x° = 180°$

$\Rightarrow$ $155° + x° = 180°$ $\Rightarrow$ $x° = 180° - 155°$

$\Rightarrow$ $x = 25°$

Q. 9 In $\triangle PQR$,

    (a) $PQ - QR > PR$ (b) $PQ + QR < PR$

    (c) $PQ - QR < PR$ (d) $PQ + PR < QR$

Sol. *(c)* As we know, sum of the lengths of any two sides of a triangle is always greater than the length of the third side.

In $\triangle PQR$, $PR + QR > PQ$

$\Rightarrow$ $PR > PQ - QR$

$\Rightarrow$ $PQ - QR < PR$

Q. 10 In $\triangle ABC$,

    (a) $AB + BC > AC$ (b) $AB + BC < AC$

    (c) $AB + AC < BC$ (d) $AC + BC < AB$

Sol. *(a)* As we know, sum of any two sides in a triangle is always greater than the third side.

In $\triangle ABC$,

              $AB + BC > AC$

Q. 11 The top of a broken tree touches the ground at a distance of 12 m from its base. If the tree is broken at a height of 5 m from the ground, then the actual height of the tree is

    (a) 25 m   (b) 13 m   (c) 18 m   (d) 17 m

Sol. *(c)* Let AB be the given that tree of height h m, which is broken at D which is 12 m away from its base and the height of remaining part, i.e. CB is 5 m.

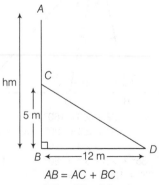

Now, $AB = AC + BC$

$\Rightarrow$ $AC = AB - BC = h - 5$

$\Rightarrow$ $AC = CD = h - 5$ ...(i)

In right angled $\triangle BDC$, $\quad CD^2 = CB^2 + BD^2$ [by Pythagoras theorem]

$\Rightarrow \qquad (h-5)^2 = (5)^2 + (12)^2$ [from Eq. (i)]

$\Rightarrow \qquad (h-5)^2 = 25 + 144$

$\Rightarrow \qquad (h-5)^2 = 169$

$\Rightarrow \qquad h - 5 = \sqrt{169} = 13$

$\Rightarrow \qquad h = 13 + 5$

$\Rightarrow \qquad h = 18\,\text{m}$

Hence, the height of the tree is 18 m.

Q. 12 The $\triangle ABC$ formed by $AB = 5$ cm, $BC = 8$ cm and $AC = 4$ cm is

    (a) an isosceles triangle only   (b) a scalene triangle only

    (c) an isosceles right triangle   (d) scalene as well as a right triangle

Sol. *(b)*   (i) It's not isosceles triangle as all the sides are of different measure.

         (ii) It's not right triangle, since it does not follow Pythagoras theorem.

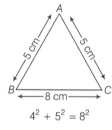

$$4^2 + 5^2 = 8^2$$

$\Rightarrow \qquad 16 + 25 = 64$

$\Rightarrow \qquad 41 \neq 64 \text{ (not satisfied)}$

Hence, it is a scalene triangle as all the sides are of different measure.

Q. 13 Two trees 7 m and 4 m high stand upright on a ground. If their bases (roots) are 4 m apart, then the distance between their tops is

    (a) 3 m   (b) 5 m   (c) 4 m   (d) 11 m

Sol. *(b)*   Let BE be the smaller tree and AD be the bigger tree. Now, we have to find AB (i.e. the distance between their tops).

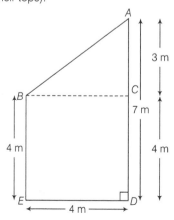

By observing,

$$ED = BC = 4\,\text{m and } BE = CD = 4\,\text{m}$$

In $\triangle ABC$, $BC = 4\,m$

and $AC = AD - CD = (7 - 4)\,m = 3\,m$

In right angled $\triangle ABC$,

$$AB^2 = AC^2 + BC^2 = 4^2 + 3^2 \text{ [by Pythagoras theorem]}$$

$$= 16 + 9$$

$\Rightarrow$ $AB^2 = 25$

$\Rightarrow$ $AB = \sqrt{25}$

$\Rightarrow$ $AB = 5\,m$

Therefore, the distance between their tops is 5 m.

Q. 14 If in an isosceles triangle, each of the base angle is 40°, then the triangle is

    (a) right angled triangle   (b) acute angled triangle

    (c) obtuse angled triangle   (d) isosceles right angled triangle

Sol. *(c)* As we know, the sum of the interior angles of a triangle is 180°.

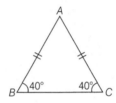

In $\triangle ABC$,

$$\angle A + \angle B + \angle C = 180° \qquad \text{[angle sum property of a triangle]}$$

$\Rightarrow$ $\angle A + 40° + 40° = 180°$

$\Rightarrow$ $\angle A = 180° - 80°$

$\Rightarrow$ $\angle A = 100° \qquad \text{[obtuse angle]}$

Therefore, it is an obtuse angled triangle. Since, it has one angle which is greater than 90°.

Q. 15 If two angles of a triangle are 60° each, then the triangle is

    (a) isosceles but not equilateral   (b) scalene

    (c) equilateral   (d) right angled

Sol. *(c)* In $\triangle ABC$,

$$\angle A + \angle B + \angle C = 180° \qquad \text{[angle sum property of a triangle]}$$

$\Rightarrow$ $\angle A + 60° + 60° = 180° \qquad [\because \angle B = \angle C = 60°, \text{ given}]$

$\Rightarrow$ $\angle A + 120° = 180°$

$\Rightarrow$ $\angle A = 60°$

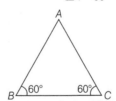

Since, all the angles are of 60°. So, it is an equilateral triangle.

Q. 16 The perimeter of the rectangle whose length is 60 cm and a diagonal is 61 cm is

    (a) 120 cm   (b) 122 cm   (c) 71 cm   (d) 142 cm

Sol. (*d*) Given, length of rectangle = 60 cm and its diagonal = 61 cm.

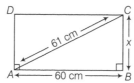

Let the breadth of a rectangle be x cm.

In right angled $\triangle ABC$,

$\Rightarrow$ $(AC)^2 = (AB)^2 + (BC)^2$

$\Rightarrow$ $(BC)^2 = (AC)^2 + (AB)^2$ [by Pythagoras theorem]

$\Rightarrow$ $x^2 = (61)^2 - (60)^2 = 3721 - 3600 = 121$

$\Rightarrow$ $x = \sqrt{121} = 11$ cm

$\therefore$ Breadth of rectangle = 11 cm and length of rectangle = 60 cm

Now, perimeter of rectangle = $2(l + b)$

                     $= 2(60 + 11) = 2 \times 71$

                     $= 142$ cm

Q. 17 In $\triangle PQR$, if $PQ = QR$ and $\angle Q = 100°$, then $\angle R$ is equal to

    (a) 40°   (b) 80°   (c) 120°   (d) 50°

Sol. (*a*) In $\triangle PQR$, $PQ = QR$ [given]

       Let $\angle P = \angle R = x$

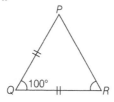

As we know,

$\therefore$ $\angle P + \angle Q + \angle R = 180°$ [angle sum property of a triangle]

$\Rightarrow$ $x + 100° + x = 180°$ [$\because \angle Q = 100°$, given]

$\Rightarrow$ $2x + 100° = 180°$

$\Rightarrow$ $2x = 80°$

$\Rightarrow$ $x = 40°$

Hence, $\angle P = \angle R = 40°$

Q. 18 Which of the following statements is not correct?

    (a) The sum of any two sides of a triangle is greater than the third side

    (b) A triangle can have all its angles acute

    (c) A right angled triangle cannot be equilateral

    (d) Difference of any two sides of a triangle is greater than the third side

Sol. (*d*) The difference of the length of any two sides of a triangle is always smaller than the length of the third side.

Q. 19 In the given figure, $BC = CA$ and $\angle A = 40°$. Then, $\angle ACD$ is equal to

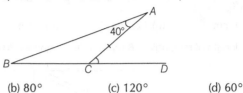

  (a) 40°   (b) 80°   (c) 120°   (d) 60°

Sol. *(b)* Given, $BC = CA$,

  $\therefore$ $\angle B = \angle A = 40°$ [$\because$ opposite angles of two equal sides are equal]

  As we know, the measure of any exterior angle of a triangle is equal to the sum of the measure of its two interior opposite angles.

  So, $\angle ACD = \angle A + \angle B = 40° + 40°$

  $\Rightarrow$ $\angle ACD = 80°$

Q. 20 The length of two sides of a triangle are 7 cm and 9 cm. The length of the third side may lie between

  (a) 1 cm and 10 cm   (b) 2 cm and 8 cm

  (c) 2 cm and 16 cm   (d) 1 cm and 16 cm

Sol. *(c)* The third side must be greater than the difference between two sides and less than the sum of two sides.

  Sum of two sides = $7 + 9 = 16\,cm$

  Difference of two sides = $9 - 7 = 2\,cm$

  So, length of the third side must lie between 2 cm and 16 cm.

Q. 21 From the following figure, the value of x is

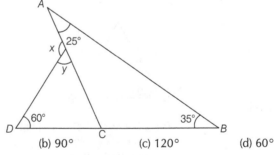

  (a) 75°   (b) 90°   (c) 120°   (d) 60°

Sol. *(c)* In $\triangle ABC$, $\angle CAB + \angle ABC + \angle BCA = 180°$ [angle sum property of a triangle]

  $\Rightarrow$ $25° + 35° + \angle BCA = 180°$

  $\Rightarrow$ $\angle BCA = 180° - 60°$

  $\Rightarrow$ $\angle BCA = 120°$

  Also, $\angle BCA$ is an exterior angle.

  $\therefore$ $\angle BCA = \angle D + y$

  $\Rightarrow$ $y = \angle BCA - \angle D = 120° - 60°$ [$\because \angle D = 60°$, given]

  $\Rightarrow$ $y = 60°$

  Now, $\angle x$ and $\angle y$ form a linear pair

  $\therefore$ $x + y = 180°$

  $\Rightarrow$ $x + 60° = 180°$

  $\Rightarrow$ $x = 180° - 60° = 120°$

Q. 22 In the given figure, the value of
$$\angle A + \angle B + \angle C + \angle D + \angle E + \angle F \text{ is}$$

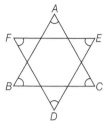

    (a) 190°   (b) 540°   (c) 360°   (d) 180°

Sol. *(c)* As we know, sum of all the interior angles of a triangle is 180°.

In $\triangle ABC$, $\angle A + \angle B + \angle C = 180°$ [interior angles of $\triangle ABC$] ...(i)

In $\triangle DEF$, $\angle D + \angle E + \angle F = 180°$ [interior angles of $\triangle DEF$] ...(ii)

On adding Eqs.(i) and (ii), we get
$$\angle A + \angle B + \angle C + \angle D + \angle E + \angle F = 180° + 180°$$
$$= 360°$$

Q. 23 In the given figure, $PQ = PR$, $RS = RQ$ and $ST \parallel QR$. If the exterior $\angle RPU$ is 140°, then the measure of $\angle TSR$ is

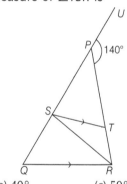

    (a) 55°   (b) 40°   (c) 50°   (d) 45°

Sol. *(b)* Here,

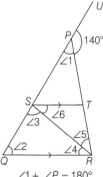

                 $\angle 1 + \angle P = 180°$ [linear pair]

$\Rightarrow$ $\angle 1 + 140° = 180°$

$\Rightarrow$ $\angle 1 = 180° - 140°$

$\Rightarrow$ $\angle 1 = 40°$

Since, $PQ = PR$

$\therefore$ $\angle Q = \angle R = x$ [say]

In $\triangle PQR$, $\angle P + \angle Q + \angle R = 180°$ [angle sum property of a triangle]

$\Rightarrow$ $40° + x + x = 180°$

$\Rightarrow$ $2x = 180° - 40° \Rightarrow 2x = 140°$

$\Rightarrow$ $x = 70°$

So, $\angle Q = \angle R = 70°$

Given that, $RS = RQ$

$\therefore$ $\angle 2 = \angle 3 = 70°$

In $\triangle SQR$, $\angle 2 + \angle 3 + \angle 4 = 180°$ [angle sum property of a triangle]

$\Rightarrow$ $70° + 70° + \angle 4 = 180°$

$\Rightarrow$ $\angle 4 = 180° - 140°$

$\Rightarrow$ $\angle 4 = 40°$

Also, $ST \parallel QR$ [given]

Now, $\angle 4 = \angle 6 = 40°$ [alternate interior angles]

$\therefore$ $\angle TSR = 40°$

Q. 24 In the given figure $\angle BAC = 90°$, $AD \perp BC$ and $\angle BAD = 50°$, then $\angle ACD$ is

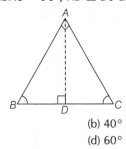

(a) 50°   (b) 40°

(c) 70°   (d) 60°

Sol. (a) Given, $\angle BAC = 90°$, $AD \perp BC$ and $\angle BAD = 50°$

In $\triangle ABD$, $\angle ABD + \angle DAB + \angle ADB = 180°$ [angle sum property of a triangle]

$\Rightarrow$ $\angle ABD + 50° + 90° = 180°$

$\Rightarrow$ $\angle ABD + 40° = 180° \Rightarrow \angle ABD = 180° - 40°$

$\Rightarrow$ $\angle ABD = 40°$

Now, in $\triangle ABC$, $\angle A + \angle B + \angle C = 180°$ [angle sum property of a triangle]

$\Rightarrow$ $90° + 40° + \angle C = 180°$

$\Rightarrow$ $\angle C = 180° - 130°$

$\Rightarrow$ $\angle C = 50°$

$\therefore$ $\angle ACD = 50°$

Q. 25 If one angle of a triangle is equal to the sum of the other two angles, the triangle is

(a) obtuse   (b) acute   (c) right   (d) equilateral

Sol. (c) Let A, B and C be the angles of the triangle. Then, one angle of a triangle is equal to the sum of the other two angles,

i.e. $\angle A = \angle B + \angle C$ ...(i)

As we know, $\quad\angle A + \angle B + \angle C = 180°$ [angle sum property of a triangle]

$\Rightarrow \quad\quad\quad\quad\quad \angle A + \angle A = 180°$ [from Eq. (i)]

$\Rightarrow \quad\quad\quad\quad\quad 2\angle A = 180° \Rightarrow \angle A = \dfrac{180°}{2}$

$\Rightarrow \quad\quad\quad\quad\quad \angle A = 90°$

Hence, the triangle is right angled.

Q. 26 If the exterior angle of a triangle is 130° and its interior opposite angles are equal, then measure of each interior opposite angle is

   (a) 55°   (b) 65°   (c) 50°   (d) 60°

Sol. *(b)* As we know, the measure of any exterior angle is equal to the sum of two opposite interior angles.

Let the interior angle be x.

Given that, interior opposite angles are equal.

$\therefore \quad\quad\quad\quad\quad\quad 130° = x + x$

$\Rightarrow \quad\quad\quad\quad\quad\quad 130° = 2x \Rightarrow x = \dfrac{130°}{2}$

$\Rightarrow \quad\quad\quad\quad\quad\quad x = 65°$

Hence, the interior angle is = 65°.

Q. 27 If one of the angle of a triangle is 110°, then the angle between the bisectors of the other two angles is

   (a) 70°   (b) 110°   (c) 35°   (d) 145°

Sol. *(d)* In $\triangle ABC$, $\quad\quad \angle A = 110°$ [given]

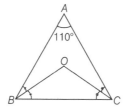

We know, that $\quad\angle A + \angle B + \angle C = 180°$ [angle sum property of a triangle]

$\Rightarrow \quad\quad\quad\quad\quad \angle B + \angle C = 180° - \angle A$

$\Rightarrow \quad\quad\quad\quad\quad \angle B + \angle C = 180° - 110°$

$\Rightarrow \quad\quad\quad\quad\quad \angle B + \angle C = 70°$ ...(i)

$\Rightarrow \quad\quad\quad \dfrac{1}{2}\angle B + \dfrac{1}{2}\angle C = \dfrac{70}{2} = 35°$ [∵Eq. (i) is divided by 2]

$\Rightarrow \quad\quad\quad\quad \dfrac{1}{2}(\angle B + \angle C) = 35°$

Now, in $\triangle BOC$,

$\quad\quad\quad\quad \angle BOC + \angle OBC + \angle OCB = 180°$ [angle sum property of a triangle] ...(ii)

$\Rightarrow \quad\quad\quad\quad \angle BOC + \dfrac{1}{2}(\angle B + \angle C) = 180°$

$\left[\because\right.$ OB and OC are the bisectors of $\angle B$ and $\angle C$, then $\angle OBC = \dfrac{1}{2}\angle B$ and $\angle OCB = \dfrac{1}{2}\angle C\left.\right]$

$\Rightarrow \quad\quad\quad \angle BOC + 35° = 180°$

$\Rightarrow \quad\quad\quad\quad \angle BOC = 180° - 35°$

$\Rightarrow \quad\quad\quad\quad \angle BOC = 145°$

Q. 28 In $\triangle ABC$, AD is the bisector of $\angle A$ meeting BC at D, $CF \perp AB$ and E is the mid-point of AC. Then, median of the triangle is
(a) AD (b) BE (c) FC (d) DE

Sol. *(b)* As we know, median of a triangle bisects the opposite sides.

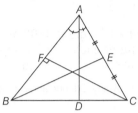

Hence, the median is BE as $AE = EC$.

Q. 29 In $\triangle PQR$, if $\angle P = 60°$ and $\angle Q = 40°$, then the exterior angle formed by producing QR is equal to
(a) $60°$ (b) $120°$
(c) $100°$ (d) $80°$

Sol. *(c)* As we know, the measure of exterior angle is equal to the sum of opposite two interior angles.

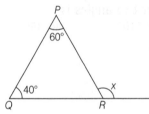

In $\triangle PQR$, $\angle x$ is the exterior angle.
So, $\angle x = \angle P + \angle Q$
                  $= 60° + 40° = 100°$

Q. 30 Which of the following triplets cannot be the angles of a triangle?
(a) $67°, 51°, 62°$
(b) $70°, 83°, 27°$
(c) $90°, 70°, 20°$
(d) $40°, 132°, 18°$

Sol. *(d)* We know that, the sum of the interior angles of a triangle is $180°$.
Now, we will verify the given triplets :
(a) $67° + 51° + 62° = 180°$
(b) $70° + 83° + 27° = 180°$
(c) $90° + 70° + 20° = 180°$
(d) $40° + 132° + 18° = 190°$
Clearly, triplets in option (d) cannot be the angles of a triangle.

Q. 31 Which of the following can be the length of the third side of a triangle whose two sides measure 18 cm and 14 cm?

(a) 4 cm   (b) 3 cm   (c) 5 cm   (d) 32 m

Sol. *(c)* As we know, sum of any two sides of a triangle is always greater than the third side. Hence, option (c) satisfies the given condition.

Verification
$$18 + 14 > 5$$
$$18 + 5 > 14$$
$$5 + 14 > 18$$

Q. 32 How many altitudes does a triangle have?

(a) 1   (b) 3   (c) 6   (d) 9

Sol. *(b)* A triangle has 3 altitudes.

Q. 33 If we join a vertex to a point on opposite side which divides that side in the ratio $1:1$, then what is the special name of that line segment?

(a) Median   (b) Angle bisector   (c) Altitude   (d) Hypotenuse

Sol. *(a)* Consider $\triangle ABC$ in which AD divides BC in the ratio $1:1$.

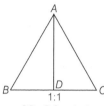

Now, $$BD : DC = 1:1$$
$$\Rightarrow \qquad \frac{BD}{DC} = \frac{1}{1}$$
$$\therefore \qquad BD = DC$$

Since, AD divides BC into two equal parts. Hence, AD is the median.

Note *The line segment joining a vertex of a triangle to the mid-point of its opposite side is called a **median**.*

Q. 34 The measures of $\angle x$ and $\angle y$ in the given figure are respectively

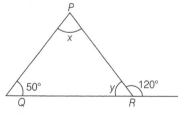

(a) $30°, 60°$ (b) $40°, 40°$ (c) $70°, 70°$ (d) $70°, 60°$

Sol. *(d)* As we know,

Measure of exterior angle = Sum of the opposite interior angles
$$\Rightarrow \qquad \angle R = \angle P + \angle Q$$
$$\Rightarrow \qquad 120° = x + 50° \qquad [\because \angle R = 120°]$$
$$\Rightarrow \qquad x = 120° - 50°$$
$$\Rightarrow \qquad x = 70°$$

Now, the sum of the interior angles of a triangle is 180°.

$$\therefore \qquad x + y + 50° = 180°$$
$$\Rightarrow \qquad 70° + y + 50° = 180°$$
$$\Rightarrow \qquad 120° + y = 180°$$
$$\Rightarrow \qquad y = 180° - 120°$$
$$\Rightarrow \qquad y = 60°$$

Q. 35 If two sides of a triangle are 6 cm and 10 cm, then the length of the third side can be

(a) 3 cm   (b) 4 cm

(c) 2 cm   (d) 6 cm

Sol. *(d)* As we know, sum of any two sides of a triangle is always greater than the third side.

So, option (d) satisfy this rule.

Verification $6 + 6 > 10$

$$6 + 10 > 6$$
$$10 + 6 > 6$$

Q. 36 In a right angled $\triangle ABC$, if $\angle B = 90°$, $BC = 3$ cm and $AC = 5$ cm, then the length of side AB is

(a) 3 cm   (b) 4 cm

(c) 5 cm   (d) 6 cm

Sol. *(b)* Since, $\triangle ABC$ is a right angled triangle.

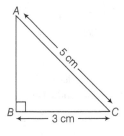

In right angled $\triangle ABC$,

$$AC^2 = AB^2 + BC^2 \qquad \text{[by Pythagoras theorem]}$$
$$\Rightarrow \qquad 5^2 = AB^2 + 3^2 \qquad [\because AC = 5 \text{ cm and } BC = 3 \text{ cm, given]}$$
$$\Rightarrow \qquad AB^2 = 25 - 9$$
$$\Rightarrow \qquad AB^2 = 16 \quad \Rightarrow \quad AB = \sqrt{16}$$
$$\Rightarrow \qquad AB = 4 \text{ cm}$$

Q. 37 In a right angled $\triangle ABC$, if $\angle B = 90°$, then which of the following is true?

(a) $AB^2 = BC^2 + AC^2$

(b) $AC^2 = AB^2 + BC^2$

(c) $AB = BC + AC$

(d) $AC = AB + BC$

Sol. *(b)* According to Pythagoras theorem,

(Hypotenuse)^2 = (Perpendicular)^2 + (Base)^2

$\Rightarrow \qquad AC^2 = AB^2 + BC^2$

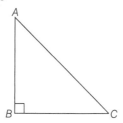

Q. 38 Which of the following figures will have it's altitude outside triangle?

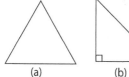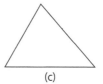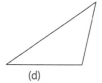

     (a)   (b)   (c)   (d)

Sol. *(d)* As we know, the perpendicular line segment from a vertex of a triangle to its opposite side is called an altitude of the triangle.

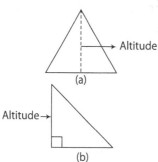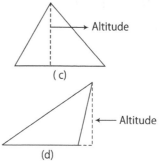

Hence, only option (d) has its altitude outside the triangle.

Q. 39 In the given figure, if $AB \parallel CD$, then

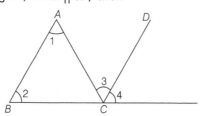

(a) $\angle 2 = \angle 3$ (b) $\angle 1 = \angle 4$

(c) $\angle 4 = \angle 1 + \angle 2$ (d) $\angle 1 + \angle 2 = \angle 3 + \angle 4$

Sol. *(d)* Given, $AB \parallel CD$ and AC is the transversal.

So, $\angle 1 = \angle 3$ [alternate interior angles]

Also, in $\triangle ABC$, $\angle 3 + \angle 4 = \angle 1 + \angle 2$

                           [∵ exterior angle = sum of two opposite interior angles]

Q. 40 In $\triangle ABC$, $\angle A = 100°$, AD bisects $\angle A$ and $AD \perp BC$. Then, $\angle B$ is equal to

    (a) 80°   (b) 20°

    (c) 40°   (d) 30°

Sol. *(c)*   Given, $\angle BAD = \angle DAC = 50°$ [∵ AD bisects $\angle A$ and $\angle A = 100°$]

          and $\angle BDA = \angle ADC = 90°$ [∵ $AD \perp BC$]

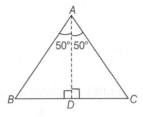

    Now, in $\triangle ABD$,

                 $\angle ABD + \angle BAD + \angle BDA = 180°$ [angle sum property of a triangle]

    $\Rightarrow$ $\angle ABD + 50° + 90° = 180°$

    $\Rightarrow$ $\angle ABD + 140° = 180°$

    $\Rightarrow$ $\angle ABD = 180° - 140°$

    $\Rightarrow$ $\angle ABD = 40°$

Q. 41 In $\triangle ABC$, $\angle A = 50°$, $\angle B = 70°$ and bisector of $\angle C$ meets AB in D as shown in the given figure. Measure of $\angle ADC$ is

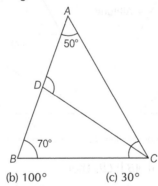

    (a) 50°   (b) 100°   (c) 30°   (d) 70°

Sol. *(b)*   In $\triangle ADC$,

                $\angle ADC + \angle DAC + \angle ACD = 180°$ [angle sum property of a triangle]

    $\Rightarrow$ $\angle ADC + 50° + \angle ACD = 180°$ [∵ $\angle DAC = 50°$]

    $\Rightarrow$ $\angle ACD = 130° - \angle ADC$ ... (i)

    In $\triangle DBC$, $\angle ADC = \angle DBC + \angle BCD$

                    [∵ exterior angle is equal to sum of opposite interior angles]

    $\Rightarrow$ $\angle ADC = 70° + \angle ACD$ [∵ $\angle ACD = \angle BCD$]

    $\Rightarrow$ $\angle ADC = 70° + 130° - \angle ADC$ [from Eq. (i)]

    $\Rightarrow$ $\angle ADC = 200° - \angle ADC$

    $\Rightarrow$ $2\angle ADC = 200°$

    $\Rightarrow$ $\angle ADC = \dfrac{200°}{2}$

    $\Rightarrow$ $\angle ADC = 100°$

Q. 42 If for $\triangle ABC$ and $\triangle DEF$, the correspondence $CAB \leftrightarrow EDF$ gives a congruence, then which of the following is not true?

    (a) $AC = DE$
    (b) $AB = EF$
    (c) $\angle A = \angle D$
    (d) $\angle C = \angle E$

Sol. *(b)* Two figures are said to be congruent, if the trace copy of figure 1 fits exactly on that of figure 2.

Now, if $\triangle ABC$ and $\triangle DEF$ are congruent, then

$$AB = DF, \quad BC = EF$$
$$AC = DE, \quad \angle A = \angle D$$
$$\angle B = \angle F, \quad \angle C = \angle E$$

Hence, option (b) is not true.

Q. 43 In the given figure, M is the mid-point of both AC and BD. Then,

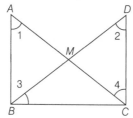

    (a) $\angle 1 = \angle 2$
    (b) $\angle 1 = \angle 4$
    (c) $\angle 2 = \angle 4$
    (d) $\angle 1 = \angle 3$

Sol. *(b)* In $\triangle AMB$ and $\triangle CMD$,

$AM = CM$	[M is the mid-point]
$BM = DM$	[M is the mid-point]
$\angle AMB = \angle CMD$	[vertically opposite angles]

By SAS congruence criterion,

$$\triangle AMB \cong \triangle CMD$$
$$\therefore \qquad \angle 1 = \angle 4 \qquad \text{[by CPCT]}$$

Q. 44 If D is the mid-point of side BC in $\triangle ABC$, where $AB = AC$, then $\angle ADC$ is

    (a) $60°$
    (b) $45°$
    (c) $120°$
    (d) $90°$

Sol. *(d)* In $\triangle ADB$ and $\triangle ADC$,

$BD = DC$	[D is the mid-point]
$AB = AC$	[given]
$AD = AD$	[common side]

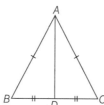

By SSS congruence criterion, $\triangle ABD \cong \triangle ACD$

$\therefore$ $\angle ADB = \angle ADC$ [by CPCT]

We know that, $\angle ADB + \angle ADC = 180°$ [linear pair]

$\Rightarrow$ $2\angle ADC = 180°$ $[\because \angle ADB = \angle ADC]$

$\Rightarrow$ $\angle ADC = 90°$

Q. 45 Two triangles are congruent, if two angles and the side included between them in one of the triangles are equal to the two angles and the side included between them of the other triangle. This is known as the

(a) RHS congruence criterion   (b) ASA congruence criterion

(c) SAS congruence criterion   (d) AAA congruence criterion

Sol. *(b)* Under ASA congruence criterion, two triangles are congruent, if two angles and the side included between them in one of the triangles are equal to the two angles and the side included between them of the other triangle.

Q. 46 By which congruency criterion, the two triangles in the given figure are congruent?

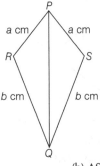

(a) RHS   (b) ASA

(c) SSS   (d) SAS

Sol. *(c)* In $\triangle PQR$ and $\triangle PQS$,

$$PR = PS = a\,cm$$
$$RQ = SQ = b\,cm$$
$$PQ = PQ = \text{Common line segment}$$

By SSS congruence criterion,

$$\triangle PQR \cong \triangle PQS$$

Q. 47 By which of the following criterion two triangles cannot be proved congruent?

(a) AAA   (b) SSS

(c) SAS   (d) ASA

Sol. *(a)* AAA is not a congruency criterion, because if all the three angles of two triangles are equal; this does not imply that both the triangles fit exactly on each other.

Q. 48 If $\triangle PQR$ is congruent to $\triangle STU$ as shown in the given figure, then what is the length of TU?

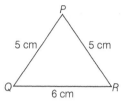 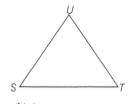

(a) 5 cm
(b) 6 cm
(c) 7 cm
(d) Cannot be determined

Sol. (*b*) Given that, $\triangle PQR \cong \triangle STU$

$\Rightarrow$ $\qquad\qquad PQ = ST$

$\Rightarrow$ $\qquad\qquad QR = TU$

$\Rightarrow$ $\qquad\qquad PR = SU$

Hence, $\qquad\qquad TU = QR = 6\,cm$

Q. 49 If $\triangle ABC$ and $\triangle DBC$ are on the same base BC, $AB = DC$ and $AC = DB$ as shown in the given figure, then which of the following gives a congruence relationship?

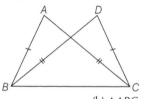

(a) $\triangle ABC \cong \triangle DBC$
(b) $\triangle ABC \cong \triangle CBD$
(c) $\triangle ABC \cong \triangle DCB$
(d) $\triangle ABC \cong \triangle BCD$

Sol. (*c*) Since, $\qquad\qquad AB = DC$ $\qquad\qquad$ [given]

and $\qquad\qquad AC = DB$

$\qquad\qquad BC = BC$ $\qquad\qquad$ [common base]

By SSS congruence criterion,

$\qquad\qquad \triangle ABC \cong \triangle DCB$

Fill in the Blanks

In questions 50 to 69, fill in the blanks to make the statements true.

Q. 50 The ____ triangle always has altitude outside itself.

Sol. The **obtuse** angled triangle always has altitude outside itself.

Q. 51 The sum of an exterior angle of a triangle and its adjacent angle is always _____.

Sol. The sum of an exterior angle of a triangle and its adjacent angle is always, **180°**, because they form a linear pair.

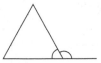

Q. 52 The longest side of a right angled triangle is called its _____ .

Sol. **Hypotenuse** is the longest side of a right angled triangle.

Q. 53 Median is also called _____ in an equilateral triangle.

Sol. Median is also called **an altitude** in an equilateral triangle.

Q. 54 Measures of each of the angles of an equilateral triangle is _____ .

Sol. Measures of each of the angles of an equilateral triangle is **60°** as all the angles in an equilateral triangle are equal.

Let x be the angle of equilateral triangle.

According to the angle sum property of a triangle,

$$x + x + x = 180°$$ [∵ measure of each angle = x (say)]

$\Rightarrow \qquad 3x = 180°$

$\Rightarrow \qquad x = \dfrac{180°}{3}$

$\Rightarrow \qquad x = 60°$

Q. 55 In an isosceles triangle, two angles are always _____ .

Sol. In an isosceles triangle, two angles are always **equal**. Since, if two sides are equal, then the angles opposite them are equal.

Q. 56 In an isosceles triangle, angles opposite to equal sides are _____ .

Sol. In an isosceles triangle, angles opposite to equal sides are **equal**. Since, if two angles are equal then the sides opposite to them are also equal.

Q. 57 If one angle of a triangle is equal to the sum of other two, then the measure of that angle is _____ .

Sol. Let the angles of a triangle be a, b and c. It is given that,

$$a = b + c$$

We also know that, $a + b + c = 180°$ [angle sum property of a triangle]

$\Rightarrow \qquad a + a = 180°$ [∵ $b + c = a$]

$\Rightarrow \qquad 2a = 180°$

$\Rightarrow \qquad a = \dfrac{180°}{2}$

$\Rightarrow \qquad a = 90°$

Hence, the measure of that angle is **90°**.

Q. 58 Every triangle has atleast _____ acute angle (s).

Sol. Every triangle has atleast **two** acute angles.

Q. 59 Two line segments are congruent, if they are of _____ lengths.

Sol. Two line segments are congruent, if they are of **equal** lengths.

Q. 60 Two angles are said to be _____, if they have equal measures.

Sol. Two angles are said to be **congruent**, if they have equal measures.

Q. 61 Two rectangles are congruent, if they have same _____ and _____ .

Sol. Two rectangles are congruent, if they have same **length** and **breadth**.

Q. 62 Two squares are congruent, if they have same ....

Sol. Two squares are congruent, if they have same **side**.

Q. 63 If $\triangle PQR$ and $\triangle XYZ$ are congruent under the correspondence $QPR \leftrightarrow XYZ$, then

   (i) $\angle R = $_____   (ii) $QR = $_____
   (iii) $\angle P = $_____   (iv) $QP = $_____
   (v) $\angle Q = $_____   (vi) $RP = $_____

Sol.

Given, $\triangle QPR \cong \triangle XYZ$

   (i) $\angle R = \angle Z$ (ii) $QR = XZ$
   (iii) $\angle P = \angle Y$ (iv) $QP = XY$
   (v) $\angle Q = \angle X$ (vi) $RP = ZY$

Q. 64 In the given figure, $\triangle PQR \cong \triangle$ ....

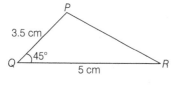 

Sol. In $\triangle PQR$ and $\triangle XZY$,

$$PQ = XZ = 3.5\,cm$$
$$QR = ZY = 5\,cm$$
$$\angle PQR = \angle XZY = 45°$$

By SAS congruence criterion,
$$\triangle PQR \cong \triangle XZY$$

Q. 65 In the given figure, $\triangle PQR \cong \triangle$ _____ .

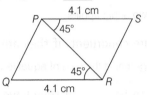

Sol. In $\triangle PQR$ and $\triangle RSP$, $QR = SP = 4.1\,cm$

$PR = PR$ [common side]

$\angle SPR = \angle QRP = 45°$

By SAS congruence criterion,

$\triangle PQR \cong \triangle RSP$

Q. 66 In the given figure, $\triangle$ _____ $\cong \triangle PQR$.

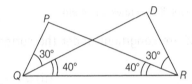

Sol. From the given figure, in $\triangle DRQ$ and $\triangle PQR$,

$QR = QR$ [common side]

$\angle DRQ = \angle PQR = 70°$

$\angle DQR = \angle PRQ = 40°$

By ASA congruence criterion, $\triangle DRQ \cong \triangle PQR$

Q. 67 In the given figure, $\triangle ARO \cong \triangle$ _____ .

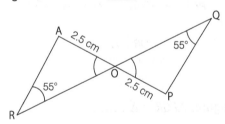

Sol. In $\triangle ARO$ and $\triangle PQO$, $\angle AOR = \angle POQ$ [vertically opposite angles]

$\angle ARO = \angle PQO = 55°$ [given]

$\Rightarrow$ $\angle RAO = \angle QPO$

Now, in $\triangle ARO$ and $\triangle PQO$, $\angle AOR = \angle POQ$ [vertically opposite angles]

$AO = PO = 2.5\,cm$

$\angle RAO = \angle QPO$ [proved above]

By ASS congruence criterion, $\triangle ARO \cong \triangle PQO$

Q. 68 In the given figure, $AB = AD$ and $\angle BAC = \angle DAC$. Then,

    (i) $\triangle$ ____ $\cong \triangle ABC$.

    (ii) $BC =$ ____ .

    (iii) $\angle BCA =$ ____ .

    (iv) Line segment AC bisects ____ and ____ .

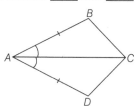

Sol. (i) In $\triangle ABC$ and $\triangle ADC$,

$$AB = AD \qquad \text{[given]}$$
$$AC = AC \qquad \text{[common side]}$$
$$\angle BAC = \angle DAC \qquad \text{[given]}$$

    By SAS congruence criterion,

$$\triangle ADC \cong \triangle ABC$$

(ii) Now, $BC = DC$ [by CPCT]

(iii) Also, $\angle BCA = \angle DCA$ [by CPCT]

(iv) Line segment AC bisects $\angle BAD$ and $\angle BCD$.

    Since, $\angle BAC = \angle DAC$

    and $\angle BCA = \angle DCA$

Q. 69 In the given figure,

    (i) $\angle TPQ = \angle$ ____ $+ \angle$ ____

    (ii) $\angle UQR = \angle$ ____ $+ \angle$ ____

    (iii) $\angle PRS = \angle$ ____ $+ \angle$ ____

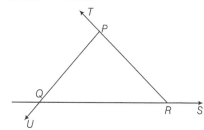

Sol. **Exterior angle property**

The measure of an exterior angle is equal to the sum of the two opposite interior angles.

(i) $\angle TPQ = \angle PQR + \angle PRQ$

(ii) $\angle UQR = \angle QRP + \angle QPR$

(iii) $\angle PRS = \angle RPQ + \angle RQP$

True/False

In questions 70 to 106, state whether the statements are True or False.

Q. 70 In a triangle, sum of squares of two sides is equal to the square of the third side.

Sol. *False*

Only in a right angled triangle, the sum of two shorter sides is equal to the square of the third side.

Q. 71 Sum of two sides of a triangle is greater than or equal to the third side.

Sol. *False*

Sum of two sides of a triangle is greater than the third side.

Q. 72 The difference between the lengths of any two sides of a triangle is smaller than the length of third side.

Sol. *True*

The difference between the lengths of any two sides of a triangle is smaller than the length of third side.

e.g. $AB - BC < AC$

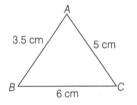

Q. 73 In $\triangle ABC$, $AB = 3.5$ cm, $AC = 5$ cm, $BC = 6$ cm and in $\triangle PQR$, $PR = 3.5$ cm, $PQ = 5$ cm, $RQ = 6$ cm. Then, $\triangle ABC \cong \triangle PQR$.

Sol. *False*

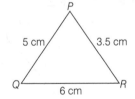

In $\triangle ABC$ and $\triangle PRQ$, $AB = PR = 3.5$ cm, $BC = RQ = 6$ cm and $AC = PQ = 5$ cm

By SSS congruence criterion, $\triangle ABC \cong \triangle PRQ$

Q. 74 Sum of any two angles of a triangle is always greater than the third angle.

Sol. *False*

It is not necessary that sum of any two angles of a triangle is always greater than the third angle. e.g. Let the angles of a triangle be 20°, 50° and 110°, respectively. Hence, 20° + 50° = 70°, which is less than 110°.

Q. 75 The sum of the measures of three angles of a triangle is greater than 180°.

Sol. *False*

The sum of the measures of three angles of a triangle is always equal to 180°.

Q. 76 It is possible to have a right angled equilateral triangle.

Sol. *False*

In a right angled triangle, one angle is equal to 90° and in equilateral triangle, all angles are equal to 60°.

Q. 77 If *M* is the mid-point of a line segment *AB*, then we can say that *AM* and *MB* are congruent.

Sol. *True*

Given that, *m* is mid-point of a line segment *AB*,

i.e.   *AM = MB*

We know that, two line segments are congruent that's why they are of same lengths.

Q. 78 It is possible to have a triangle in which two of the angles are right angles.

Sol. *False*

If in a triangle two angles are right angles, then third angle = 180° − (90° + 90°) = 0°, which is not possible.

Q. 79 It is possible to have a triangle in which two of the angles are obtuse.

Sol. *False*

Obtuse angles are those angles which are greater than 90°. So, sum of two obtuse angles will be greater than 180°, which is not possible as the sum of all the angles of a triangle is 180°.

Q. 80 It is possible to have a triangle in which two angles are acute.

Sol. *True*

In a triangle, atleast two angles must be acute angle.

Q. 81 It is possible to have a triangle in which each angle is less than 60°.

Sol. *False*

The sum of all angles in a triangle is equal to 180°. So, all three angles can never be less than 60°.

Q. 82 It is possible to have a triangle in which each angle is greater than 60°.

Sol. *False*

If all the angles are greater than 60° in a triangle, then the sum of all the three angles with exceed 180°, which cannot be possible in case of triangle

Q. 83 It is possible to have a triangle in which each angle is equal to 60°.

Sol. *True*

The triangle in which each angle is equal to 60° is called an equilateral triangle.

Q. 84 A right angled triangle may have all sides equal.

Sol. *False*

Hypotenuse is always the greater than the other two sides of the right angled triangle.

Q. 85 If two angles of a triangle are equal, the third angle is also equal to each of the other two angles.

Sol. *False*

In an isosceles triangle, always two angles are equal and not the third one.

Q. 86 In the given figures, two triangles are congruent by RHS.

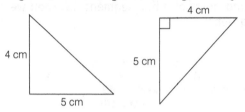

Sol. *True*

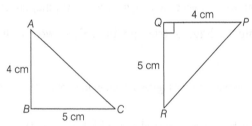

In $\triangle ABC$, $AC = \sqrt{AB^2 + BC^2} = \sqrt{4^2 + 5^2} = \sqrt{41}$ cm   [by Pythagoras theorem]

In $\triangle PQR$, $PR = \sqrt{PQ^2 + QR^2} = \sqrt{4^2 + 5^2} = \sqrt{41}$ cm   [by Pythagoras theorem]

Now, in $\triangle ABC$ and $\triangle PQR$,

$$AB = PQ = 4 \, cm$$
$$AC = PR = \sqrt{41} \, cm$$
$$\angle ABC = \angle PQR = 90°$$

By RHS congruence criterian, $\triangle ABC \cong \triangle PQR$

Q. 87 The congruent figures superimpose to each other completely.

Sol. *True*

Because congruent figures have same shape and same size.

Q. 88 A one rupee coin is congruent to a five rupees coin.

Sol. *False*

Because they don't have same shape and same size.

Q. 89 The top and bottom faces of a kaleidoscope are congruent.

Sol. *True*

Because they superimpose to each other.

Q. 90 Two acute angles are congruent.

Sol. *False*

Because the measure of two acute angles may be different.

Q. 91 Two right angles are congruent.

Sol. *True*

Since, the measure of right angles is always same.

Q. 92 Two figures are congruent, if they have the same shape.

Sol. *False*

Two figures are congruent, if they have the same shape and same size.

Q. 93 If the areas of two squares is same, they are congruent.

Sol. *True*

Because two squares will have same areas only if their sides are equal and squares with same sides will superimpose to each other.

Q. 94 If the areas of two rectangles are same, they are congruent.

Sol. *False*

Because rectangles with the different length and breadth may have equal areas. But, they will not superimpose to each other.

Q. 95 If the areas of two circles are the same, they are congruent.

Sol. *True*

Because areas of two circles will be equal only if their radii are equal and circle with same radii will superimpose to each other.

Q. 96 Two squares having same perimeter are congruent.

Sol. *True*

If two squares have same perimeter, then their sides will be equal. Hence, the squares will superimpose to each other.

Q. 97 Two circles having same circumference are congruent.

Sol. *True*

If two circles have same circumference, then their radii will be equal. Hence, the circles will superimpose to each other.

Q. 98 If three angles of two triangles are equal, triangles are congruent.

Sol. *False*

Consider two equilateral triangles with different sides.

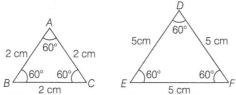

Both $\triangle ABC$ and $\triangle DEF$ have same angles but their size is different. So, they are not congruent.

Q. 99 If two legs of a right angled triangle are equal to two legs of another right angled triangle, then the right triangles are congruent.

Sol. *True*

If two legs of a right angled triangle are equal to two legs of another right angled triangle, then their third leg will also be equal. Hence, they will have same shape and same size.

Q. 100 If two sides and one angle of a triangle are equal to the two sides and angle of another triangle, then the two triangles are congruent.

Sol. *False*

Because if two sides and the angle included between them of the other triangle, then the two triangles will be congruent.

Q. 101 If two triangles are congruent, then the corresponding angles are equal.

Sol. *True*

Because if two triangles are congruent, then their sides and angles are equal.

Q. 102 If two angles and a side of a triangle are equal to two angles and a side of another triangle, then the triangles are congruent.

Sol. *False*

If two angles and the side included between them of a triangle are equal to two angles and included a side between them of the other triangle, then triangles are congruent.

Q. 103 If the hypotenuse of one right triangle is equal to the hypotenuse of another right triangle, then the triangles are congruent.

Sol. *False*

Two right angled triangles are congruent, if the hypotenuse and a side of one of the triangle are equal to the hypotenuse and one of the side of the other triangle.

Q. 104 If hypotenuse and an acute angle of one right angled triangle are equal to the hypotenuse and an acute angle of another right angled triangle, then the triangles are congruent.

Sol. *True*

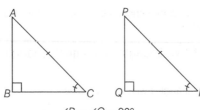

In $\triangle ABC$ and $\triangle PQR$,　　　$\angle B = \angle Q = 90°$

　　　　　　　　　　　　　　$\angle C = \angle R$　　　　　　　　　　[given]

$\Rightarrow$　　　　　　　　　　　　$\angle A = \angle P$

Now, in $\triangle ABC$ and $\triangle PQR$,　　$\angle A = \angle P$

　　　　　　　　　　　　　　$AC = PR$

　　　　　　　　　　　　　　$\angle C = \angle R$

By ASA congruence criterian, $\triangle ABC \cong \triangle PQR$

Q. 105 AAS congruence criterion is same as ASA congruence criterion.

Sol. *False*

In ASA congruence criterion, the side 'S' included between the two angles of the triangle.
In AAS congruence criterion, side 'S' is not included between two angles.

Q. 106 In the given figure, $AD \perp BC$ and AD is the bisector of angle BAC. Then, $\triangle ABD \cong \triangle ACD$ by RHS.

Sol. *False*

In $\triangle ABD$ and $\triangle ACD$,

$$AD = AD \qquad \text{[common side]}$$
$$\angle BAD = \angle CAD \qquad [\because AD \text{ is the bisector of } \angle BAC]$$
$$\angle ADB = \angle ADC = 90°$$

By ASA congruence criterion,

$$\triangle ABD \cong \triangle ACD$$

Q. 107 The measure of three angles of a triangle are in the ratio $5:3:1$. Find the measures of these angles.

Sol. Let measures of the given angles of a triangle be $5x$, $3x$ and x.

$\because$ Sum of all the angles in a triangle $= 180°$

$$\therefore \qquad 5x + 3x + x = 180°$$
$$\Rightarrow \qquad 9x = 180°$$
$$\Rightarrow \qquad x = \frac{180°}{9}$$
$$\Rightarrow \qquad x = 20°$$

So, the angles are $5x = 5 \times 20° = 100°$, $3x = 3 \times 20° = 60°$ and $x = 20°$ i.e. $100°$, $60°$ and $20°$.

Q. 108 In the given figure, find the value of x.

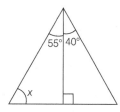

Sol. We know that, the sum of all three angles in a triangle is equal to $180°$.

So,
$$x + 55° + 90° = 180°$$
$$\Rightarrow \qquad x + 145° = 180°$$
$$\Rightarrow \qquad x = 180° - 145°$$
$$\Rightarrow \qquad x = 35°$$

Q. 109 In the given figures (i) and (ii), find the values of a, b and c.

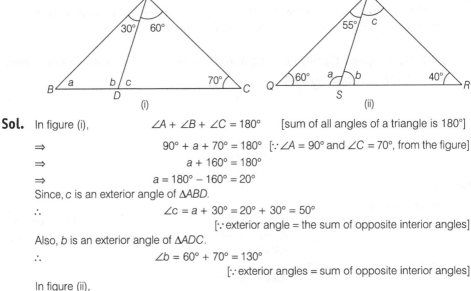

(i)   (ii)

Sol. In figure (i), $\angle A + \angle B + \angle C = 180°$ [sum of all angles of a triangle is 180°]

$\Rightarrow$ $90° + a + 70° = 180°$ [$\because \angle A = 90°$ and $\angle C = 70°$, from the figure]

$\Rightarrow$ $a + 160° = 180°$

$\Rightarrow$ $a = 180° - 160° = 20°$

Since, c is an exterior angle of $\triangle ABD$.

$\therefore$ $\angle c = a + 30° = 20° + 30° = 50°$

                                 [$\because$ exterior angle = the sum of opposite interior angles]

Also, b is an exterior angle of $\triangle ADC$.

$\therefore$ $\angle b = 60° + 70° = 130°$

                                 [$\because$ exterior angles = sum of opposite interior angles]

In figure (ii),

In $\triangle PQS$, $\angle QPS + \angle PQS + \angle PSQ = 180°$ [sum of all the angles of a triangle is 180°]

$\Rightarrow$ $55° + 60° + a = 180°$

$\Rightarrow$ $115° + a = 180°$

$\Rightarrow$ $a = 180° - 115° = 65°$

Now, $a + b = 180°$ [linear pair has sum of 180°]

$\Rightarrow$ $65° + b = 180°$

$\Rightarrow$ $b = 180° - 65° = 115°$

In $\triangle PSR$, $\angle PSR + \angle SPR + \angle PRS = 180°$

                                 [sum of all angles of a triangle is 180°]

$\Rightarrow$ $115° + c + 40° = 180°$

$\Rightarrow$ $155° + c = 180°$

$\Rightarrow$ $c = 180° - 155° = 25°$

Q. 110 In $\triangle XYZ$, the measure of $\angle X$ is 30° greater than the measure of $\angle Y$ and $\angle Z$ is a right angle. Find measure of $\angle Y$.

Sol. According to the question,

Measure of $\angle X = \angle Y + 30°$

Measure of $\angle Z = 90°$

We know that, the sum of all three angles in a triangle is equal to 180°.

i.e. $\angle X + \angle Y + \angle Z = 180°$

$\Rightarrow$ $\angle Y + (\angle Y + 30°) + 90° = 180°$

$\Rightarrow$ $2\angle Y + 120° = 180°$

$\Rightarrow$ $2\angle Y = 180° - 120° = 60°$

$\therefore$ $\angle Y = \dfrac{60°}{2} = 30°$

Q. 111 In a $\triangle ABC$, the measure of an $\angle A$ is 40° less than the measure of other $\angle B$ is 50° less than that of $\angle C$. Find the measure of $\angle A$.

Sol. According to the question,

Measure of $\qquad \angle A = \angle B - 40°$

Measure of $\qquad \angle C = \angle B - 40° + 50°$

We know that, the sum of all three angles in a triangle is equal to 180°.

i.e. $\qquad \angle A + \angle B + \angle C = 180°$

$\Rightarrow \qquad (\angle B - 40°) + \angle B + (\angle B - 40° + 50°) = 180°$

$\Rightarrow \qquad 3\angle B - 30° = 180° \quad \Rightarrow \quad 3\angle B = 210°$

$\therefore \qquad \angle B = \dfrac{210°}{3} = 70°$

So, the measure of $\angle A = 70° - 40° = 30°$.

Q. 112 I have three sides. One of my angle measures 15°. Another has a measure of 60°. What kind of a polygon am I? If I am a triangle, then what kind of triangle am I?

Sol. The polygon with three sides is called triangle.

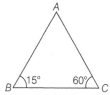

According to the angle sum property of a triangle,

$\Rightarrow \qquad \angle A + \angle B + \angle C = 180°$

$\Rightarrow \qquad \angle A + 15° + 60° = 180° \quad \Rightarrow \quad \angle A = 180° - 75°$

$\qquad \angle A = 105°$

As one angle in this triangle is greater than 90°, so it is an obtuse angled triangle.

Q. 113 Jiya walks 6 km due east and then 8 km due north. How far is she from her starting place?

Sol. As per the given information, we can draw the following figure, which is a right angled triangle at B.

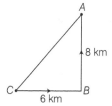

Distance from starting point to the final position is the hypotenuse of right angled $\triangle ABC$,

i.e. $\qquad AC^2 = AB^2 + BC^2 \qquad$ [by Pythagoras theorem]

$\Rightarrow \qquad (6)^2 + (8)^2 = (\text{Distance})^2 \qquad$ [$\because AC = \text{distance}$]

$\Rightarrow \qquad 36 + 64 = (\text{Distance})^2$

$\therefore \qquad \text{Distance} = \sqrt{100} = 10\,\text{km}$

Q. 114 Jayanti takes shortest route to her home by walking diagonally across a rectangular park. The park measures 60 m × 80 m. How much shorter is the route across park than the route around its edges?

Sol. As the park is rectangular, all the angles are of 90°.

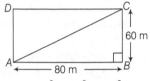

In right angled $\triangle ABC$, $AC^2 = AB^2 + BC^2$ [by Pythagoras theorem]

$\Rightarrow$ $AC^2 = (60)^2 + (80)^2 = 3600 + 6400$

$\Rightarrow$ $AC^2 = 10000$

$\Rightarrow$ $AC = \sqrt{10000}$

$\Rightarrow$ $AC = 100\,m$

If she goes through AB and AC, then total distance covered $= (60 + 80)\,m = 140\,m$

$\therefore$ Difference between two paths $= (140 - 100)\,m = 40\,m$

Q. 115 In $\triangle PQR$ of the given figure, $PQ = PR$. Find measures of $\angle Q$ and $\angle R$.

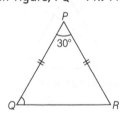

Sol. Since, $PQ = PR$ [given]

$\therefore$ $\angle Q = \angle R = x$ [say]

As we know, $\angle P + \angle Q + \angle R = 180°$ [angle sum property of a triangle]

$\Rightarrow$ $30° + x + x = 180°$

$\Rightarrow$ $2x = 150°$

$\Rightarrow$ $x = 75°$

Hence, $\angle Q = \angle R = 75°$

Q. 116 In the given figure, find the measures of $\angle x$ and $\angle y$.

Sol. Since, $\angle y$ and 45° form a linear pair.

So, $\angle y + 45° = 180°$ [∵ linear pair has sum of 180°]

$\Rightarrow$ $\angle y = 180° - 45°$

$\Rightarrow$ $\angle y = 135°$

∵ The sum of all angles in a triangle is equal to 180°.

So, $45° + 60° + \angle x = 180°$

$\Rightarrow$ $105° + \angle x = 180°$

$\Rightarrow$ $\angle x = 180° - 105° = 75°$

Q. 117 In the given figure, find the measures of $\angle PON$ and $\angle NPO$.

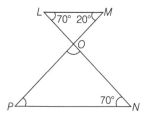

Sol. In ΔLOM,

$\angle OLM + \angle OML + \angle LOM = 180°$ [angle sum property of a triangle]

$\Rightarrow$ $70° + 20° + \angle LOM = 180°$

$\Rightarrow$ $90° + \angle LOM = 180°$

$\Rightarrow$ $\angle LOM = 180° - 90° = 90°$

Also $\angle PON = 90°$

                    [since, vertically opposite angles are equal]

In ΔPON, $\angle PON + \angle NPO + \angle ONP = 180°$ [angle sum property of a triangle]

$\Rightarrow$ $90° + \angle NPO + 70° = 180°$

$\Rightarrow$ $\angle NPO = 180° - 160° = 20°$

Q. 118 In the given figure, $QP \parallel RT$. Find the values of x and y.

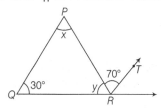

Sol. In the given figure, $QP \parallel RT$, where PR is a transversal line.

So, $\angle x$ and $\angle TRP$ are alternate interior angles,

∴ $\angle x = 70°$

We know that, the sum of all angles in a triangle is equal to 180°.

∴ $\angle x + 30° + \angle y = 180°$

$\Rightarrow$ $70° + 30° + \angle y = 180°$

$\Rightarrow$ $\angle y = 180° - 100°$

$\Rightarrow$ $\angle y = 80°$

Q. 119 Find the measure of $\angle A$ in the given figure.

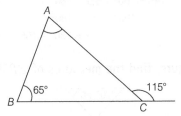

Sol. As we know, the measure of exterior angle is equal to the sum of opposite interior angles.

$\therefore$ $\qquad\qquad\qquad 115° = 65° + \angle A$

$\Rightarrow$ $\qquad\qquad\qquad \angle A = 115° - 65° = 50°$

Q. 120 In a right angled triangle, if an angle measures 35°, then find the measure of the third angle.

Sol. In a right angled $\triangle ABC$,

$\qquad\qquad\qquad \angle A + \angle B + \angle C = 180°$ $\qquad$ [angle sum property of a triangle]

$\Rightarrow$ $\qquad\qquad\qquad \angle A + 90° + 35° = 180°$ $\qquad$ [$\because \angle B = 90°$ and $\angle C = 35°$, given]

$\Rightarrow$ $\qquad\qquad\qquad \angle A + 125° = 180°$

$\Rightarrow$ $\qquad\qquad\qquad \angle A = 180° - 125° = 55°$

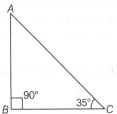

Q. 121 Each of the two equal angles of an isosceles triangle is four times the third angle. Find the angles of the triangle.

Sol. Let the third angle be x. Then, the other two angles are $4x$ and $4x$, respectively.

We know that, the sum of all three angles in a triangle is 180°.

i.e. $\qquad\qquad\qquad \angle A + \angle B + \angle C = 180°$

$\Rightarrow$ $\qquad\qquad\qquad x + 4x + 4x = 180°$

$\Rightarrow$ $\qquad\qquad\qquad 9x = 180°$

$\Rightarrow$ $\qquad\qquad\qquad x = \dfrac{180°}{9} = 20°$

Hence, the three angles are $4x = 4 \times 20° = 80°$, $4x = 4 \times 20° = 80°$ and $x = 20°$.

Q. 122 The angles of a triangle are in the ratio $2:3:5$. Find the angles.

Sol. Let measures of the given angles of a triangle be $2x$, $3x$ and $5x$.

∵ Sum of all the angles in a triangle $= 180°$

∴

$$2x + 3x + 5x = 180° \Rightarrow 10x = 180°$$

⇒

$$x = \frac{180°}{10} = 18°$$

So, the angles are $2x = 2 \times 18° = 36°$, $3x = 3 \times 18° = 54°$ and $5x = 5 \times 18° = 90°$.

Q. 123 If the sides of a triangle are produced in an order, show that the sum of the exterior angles so formed is 360°.

Sol. In $\triangle ABC$, by exterior angle property,

Exterior $\angle 1 =$ Interior $\angle A +$ Interior $\angle B$ ... (i)

Exterior $\angle 2 =$ Interior $\angle B +$ Interior $\angle C$ ... (ii)

Exterior $\angle 3 =$ Interior $\angle A +$ Interior $\angle C$ ... (iii)

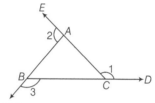

On adding Eqs. (i), (ii) and (iii), we get

$$\angle 1 + \angle 2 + \angle 3 = 2\,(\angle A + \angle B + \angle C)$$

[by angle sum property of a triangle, $\angle A + \angle B + \angle C = 180°$]

⇒

$$\angle 1 + \angle 2 + \angle 3 = 2 \times 180°$$

⇒

$$\angle 1 + \angle 2 + \angle 3 = 360°$$

Hence, the sum of exterior angles is 360°.

Q. 124 In $\triangle ABC$, if $\angle A = \angle C$ and exterior $\angle ABX = 140°$, then find the angles of the triangle.

Sol. Given, $\angle A = \angle C$ and exterior $\angle ABX = 140°$

Let $\angle A = \angle C = x$

According to the exterior angle property,

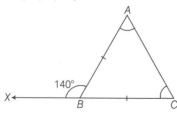

Exterior $\angle B =$ Interior $\angle A +$ Interior $\angle C$

⇒

$$140° = x + x \Rightarrow 140° = 2x$$

⇒

$$x = \frac{140°}{2} = 70°$$

So,

$$\angle A = \angle C = 70°$$

Now,　　　　　　　　$\angle A + \angle B + \angle C = 180°$　　[angle sum property of a triangle]

$\Rightarrow$　　　　　　　　$70° + \angle B + 70° = 180°$

$\Rightarrow$　　　　　　　　$\angle B + 140° = 180°$　$\Rightarrow$　$\angle B = 180° - 140°$

$\Rightarrow$　　　　　　　　$\angle B = 40°$

Hence, all the angles of the triangle are 70°, 40° and 70°.

Q. 125 Find the values of x and y in the given figure.

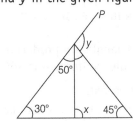

Sol.

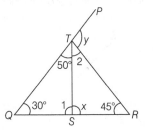

In ΔTQS,　　　　$\angle T + \angle Q + \angle S = 180°$　　[angle sum property of a triangle]

$\Rightarrow$　　　　　　　$50° + 30° + \angle 1 = 180°$

$\Rightarrow$　　　　　　　$80° + \angle 1 = 180°$

$\Rightarrow$　　　　　　　$\angle 1 = 180° - 80° = 100°$

Now,　　　　　　　$\angle 1 + x = 180°$　　　　　　　　[linear pair]

$\Rightarrow$　　　　　　　$100° + x = 180° = 180° - 100°$

$\Rightarrow$　　　　　　　$x = 80°$

In ΔTSR,　　　　$x + 45° + \angle 2 = 180°$　　[angle sum property of a triangle]

$\Rightarrow$　　　　　　　$\angle 2 = 180° - 80° - 45° = 55°$

Now,　　　　　　　$50° + \angle 2 + y = 180°$　　　　　[linear pair]

$\Rightarrow$　　　　　　　$y = 180° - 50° - 55° = 75°$

Q. 126 Find the value of x in the given figure.

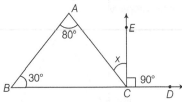

Sol.　In the given figure, $\angle BAC = 80°$, $\angle ABC = 30°$, $\angle ACE = x$ and $\angle ECD = 90°$.

In ΔABC, we know that, exterior angle is equal to the sum of interior opposite angles.

$\therefore$　　　　　　　$\angle ACD = \angle CAB + \angle ABC$

$\Rightarrow$　　　　$\angle ACE + \angle ECD = 80° + 30°$　　　$[\because \angle ACD = \angle ACE + \angle ECD]$

$\Rightarrow$　　　　$\angle ACE + 90° = 110°$　　　　　　　$[\because \angle ECD = 90°]$

$\Rightarrow$　　　　$\angle ACE = 110° - 90° = 20°$

Q. 127 The angles of a triangle are arranged in descending order of their magnitudes. If the difference between two consecutive angles is 10°, find the three angles.

Sol. Let one of the angles of a triangle be x. If angles are arranged in descending order. Then, angles will be x, $(x - 10°)$ and $(x - 20°)$.

We know that, the sum of all angles in a triangle is equal to 180°.

So, $x + (x - 10°) + (x - 20°) = 180°$
$\Rightarrow$ $x + x + x - 30° = 180°$
$\Rightarrow$ $3x = 180° + 30°$
$\Rightarrow$ $3x = 210°$
$\Rightarrow$ $x = \dfrac{210°}{3} = 70°$

Hence, angles will be 70°, 70° − 10° and 70° − 20° i.e. 70°, 60° and 50°

Q. 128 In $\triangle ABC$, $DE \parallel BC$ (see the figure). Find the values of x, y and z.

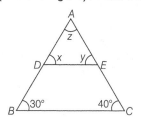

Sol. In $\triangle ABC$, $\angle A + \angle B + \angle C = 180°$ [sum of all angles of a triangle is 180°]
$\Rightarrow$ $z + 30° + 40° = 180°$
$\Rightarrow$ $z + 70° = 180°$
$\Rightarrow$ $z = 180° - 70° = 110°$
$\because$ $DE \parallel BC$
Now, $\angle ADE = \angle ABC$ [$\because$ corresponding angles are equal]
$\Rightarrow$ $\angle x = 30°$ and $\angle AED = \angle ACB$
                                        [$\because$ corresponding angles are equal]
$\Rightarrow$ $\angle y = 40°$

Q. 129 In the given figure, find the values of x, y and z.

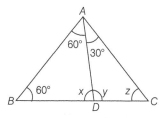

Sol. In the given figure, $\angle BAD = 60°$, $\angle ABD = 60°$, $\angle ADB = x$, $\angle DAC = 30°$, $\angle ADC = y$ and $\angle ACD = z$

We know that, the sum of all angles in a triangle is equal to 180°.
In $\triangle ABD$, $\angle BAD + \angle ABD + \angle ADB = 180°$

$\Rightarrow$ $\qquad$ $60° + 60° + x = 180°$

$\Rightarrow$ $\qquad$ $120° + x = 180°$

$\Rightarrow$ $\qquad$ $x = 180° - 120°$

$\Rightarrow$ $\qquad$ $x = 60°$

Now, $\qquad$ $y = \angle BAD + \angle ABD$

$\qquad$ [∵ exterior angle is equal to the sum of interior opposite angles]

$\Rightarrow$ $\qquad$ $y = 60° + 60°$

∴ $\qquad$ $y = 120°$

In $\triangle ADC$, $\qquad$ $\angle DAC + \angle ADC + \angle ACD = 180°$ $\qquad$ [angle sum property of a triangle]

$\Rightarrow$ $\qquad$ $30° + 120° + z = 180°$

$\Rightarrow$ $\qquad$ $150° + z = 180°$

$\Rightarrow$ $\qquad$ $z = 180° - 150°$

$\Rightarrow$ $\qquad$ $z = 30°$

Hence, $x = 60°$, $y = 120°$ and $z = 30°$.

Q. 130 If one angle of a triangle is 60° and the other two angles are in the ratio 1 : 2, find the angles.

Sol. Given, one angle of a triangle is 60°.

Let the other two angles be x and $2x$.

We know that, the sum of all angles in a triangle is equal to 180°.

So, $\qquad$ $x + 2x + 60° = 180°$

$\Rightarrow$ $\qquad$ $3x = 180° - 60°$

$\Rightarrow$ $\qquad$ $3x = 120°$

$\Rightarrow$ $\qquad$ $x = 40°$

So, the other two angles will be $x = 40°$ and $2x = 2 \times 40° = 80°$.

Q. 131 In $\triangle PQR$, if $3\angle P = 4\angle Q = 6\angle R$, calculate the angles of the triangle.

Sol. Given, $\qquad$ $3 \angle P = 4 \angle Q = 6 \angle R$

Then, $\qquad$ $\angle P = \dfrac{6}{3} \angle R = 2 \angle R$

$\qquad$ $\angle Q = \dfrac{6}{4} \angle R = \dfrac{3}{2} \angle R$

In $\triangle PQR$,

$\qquad$ $\angle P + \angle Q + \angle R = 180°$ $\qquad$ [angle sum property of a triangle]

$\Rightarrow$ $\qquad$ $2 \angle R + \dfrac{3}{2} \angle R + \angle R = 180°$

$\Rightarrow$ $\qquad$ $3 \angle R + \dfrac{3}{2} \angle R = 180°$

$\Rightarrow$ $\qquad$ $6 \angle R + 3 \angle R = 180° \times 2$ $\qquad$ [on taking LCM in LHS]

$\Rightarrow$ $\qquad$ $9 \angle R = 360°$

$\Rightarrow$ $\qquad$ $\angle R = \dfrac{360°}{9} = 40°$

$$\therefore \qquad \angle P = 2 \ \angle R = 2 \times 40° = 80°$$

and
$$\angle Q = \frac{3}{2} \ \angle R = \frac{3}{2} \times 40° = 60°$$

Hence, all the angles of the triangle are 80°, 60° and 40°.

Q. 132 In $\triangle DEF$, $\angle D = 60°$, $\angle E = 70°$ and the bisectors of $\angle E$ and $\angle F$ meet at O. Find (i) $\angle F$ (ii) $\angle EOF$.

Sol.

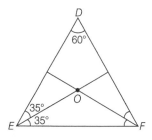

(i) As we know,

$$\angle D + \angle E + \angle F = 180° \qquad \text{[angle sum property of a triangle]}$$
$$\Rightarrow \qquad 60° + 70° + \angle F = 180° \qquad [\because \angle D = 60° \text{ and } \angle E = 70°]$$
$$\Rightarrow \qquad \angle F = 180° - 130°$$
$$\Rightarrow \qquad \angle F = 50°$$

(ii) Now, as FO is the bisector of $\angle F$.

So,
$$\angle EFO = \frac{\angle F}{2} = \frac{50°}{2} = 25°$$

and
$$\angle OEF = \frac{\angle E}{2} = \frac{70°}{2} = 35° \qquad [\because \angle D = 60° \text{ and } \angle E = 70°]$$

In $\triangle EOF$,
$$\angle EOF + \angle OEF + \angle OFE = 180° \qquad \text{[angle sum property of a triangle]}$$
$$\Rightarrow \qquad \angle EOF + 35° + 25° = 180°$$
$$\Rightarrow \qquad \angle EOF = 180° - 60°$$
$$\Rightarrow \qquad \angle EOF = 120°$$

Q. 133 In the given figure, $\triangle PQR$ is right angled at P. U and T are the points on line QRF. If $QP \parallel ST$ and $US \parallel RP$, find $\angle S$.

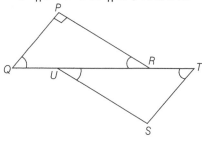

Sol. If $QP \parallel ST$ and QT is a transversal, then $\angle PQR = \angle STU$ \qquad [alternate interior angles]

and if $US \parallel RP$ and QT is a transversal, then $\angle PRQ = \angle SUT$ \qquad [alternate interior angles]

Hence, $\angle S$ must be equal to $\angle P$ i.e. 90°.

Q. 134 In each of the given pairs of triangles in given figures, applying only ASA congruence criterion, determine which triangles are congruent. Also, write the congruent triangles in symbolic form.

(a)

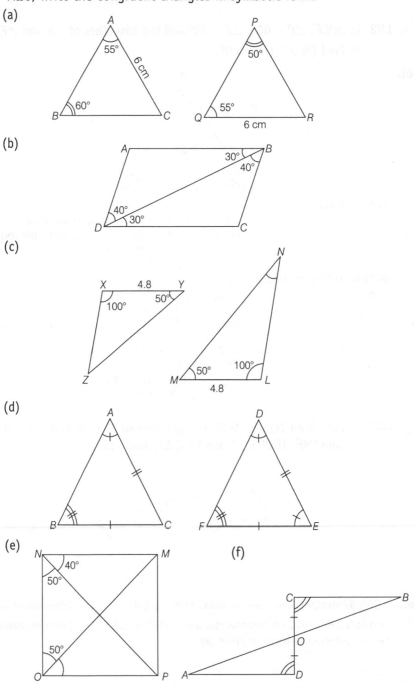

Sol. (a) Not possible, because the side is not included between two angles.

(b) $\triangle ABD \cong \triangle CDB$

(c) $\triangle XYZ \cong \triangle LMN$

(d) Not possible, because there is not any included side equal.

(e) $\triangle MNO \cong \triangle PON$

(f) $\triangle AOD \cong \triangle BOC$

Q. 135 In each of the given pairs of triangles in given figures, using only RHS congruence criterion, determine which pairs of triangles are congruent. In case of congruence, write the result in symbolic form.

(a)

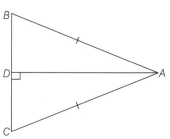

(b)

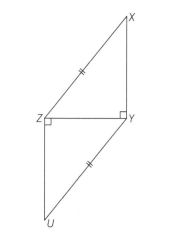

(c)

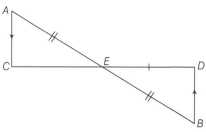

(d)

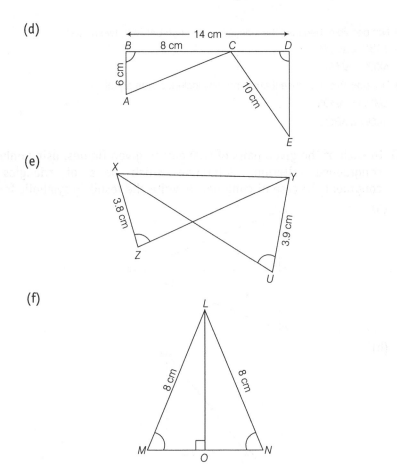

(e)

(f)

Sol. (a) In $\triangle ABD$ and $\triangle ACD$, $AB = AC$ [given]
                                                      $AD = AD$ [common side]
                                         $\angle ADB = \angle ADC = 90°$
            By RHS congruence criterion, $\triangle ABD \cong \triangle ACD$
     (b) In $\triangle XYZ$ and $\triangle UZY$, $\angle XYZ = \angle UZY = 90°$
                                                      $XZ = YU$ [given]
                                                      $ZY = ZY$ [common side]
            By RHS congruence criterion, $\triangle XYZ \cong \triangle UZY$
     (c) In $\triangle AEC$ and $\triangle BED$, $CE = DE$ [given]
                                                      $AE = BE$ [given]
                                         $\angle ACE = \angle BDE = 90°$
            By RHS congruence criterion, $\triangle AEC \cong \triangle BED$

(d) Here, $CD = BD - BC = 14 - 8 = 6$ cm

In right angled $\triangle ABC$,

$AC = \sqrt{AB^2 + BC^2} = \sqrt{6^2 + 8^2} = \sqrt{36 + 64}$ [by Pythagoras theorem]

$= \sqrt{100} = 10$ cm

In right angled $\triangle CDE$,

$$DE = \sqrt{CE^2 - CD^2} = \sqrt{10^2 - 6^2} = \sqrt{100 - 36} = \sqrt{64} = 8 \text{ cm}$$

In $\triangle ABC$ and $\triangle CDE$, $AC = CE = 10$ cm

$BC = DE = 8$ cm

$\angle ABC = \angle CDE = 90°$

By RHS congruence criterion, $\triangle ABC \cong \triangle CDE$

(e) Not possible, because there is not any right angle.

(f) In $\triangle LOM$ and $\triangle LON$, $LM = LN = 8$ cm

$LO = LO$ [common side]

$\angle LOM = \angle LON = 90°$

By RHS congruence criterion, $\triangle LOM \cong \triangle LON$

Q. 136 In the given figure, if $RP = RQ$, find the value of x.

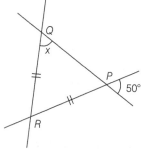

Sol. Given, $RP = RQ$

Since, $\angle 1 = 50°$ [vertically opposite angles]

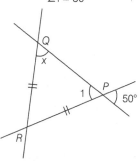

Also, $\angle 1 = x$ $[\because RP = RQ]$

So, $x = 50°$

Q. 137 In the given figure, if $ST = SU$, then find the values of x and y.

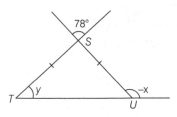

Sol. Given, $ST = SU$

∴ $\angle SUT = \angle STU = y$ [∵ angles opposite to equal sides are equal]

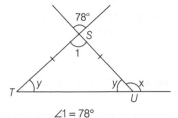

Also, $\angle 1 = 78°$ [vertically opposite angles]
In $\triangle SUT$, $78° + y + y = 180°$ [angle sum property of a triangle]
⇒ $78° + 2y = 180°$
⇒ $2y = 180° - 78° = 102°$
⇒ $y = \dfrac{102°}{2} = 51°$
Also, $x + y = 180°$ [linear pair]
⇒ $x + 51° = 180°$
⇒ $x = 180° - 51°$
⇒ $x = 129°$

Q. 138 Check whether the following measures (in cm) can be the sides of a right angled triangle or not.

     1.5, 3.6, 3.9

Sol. For a right angled triangle, the sum of square of two shorter sides must be equal to the square of the third side.
Now, $1.5^2 + 3.6^2 = 2.25 + 12.96$
                    $= 15.21$
Also, $(3.9)^2 = 15.21$
⇒ $(1.5)^2 + (3.6)^2 = (3.9)^2$
Hence, the given sides form right angled triangle.

Q. 139 Height of a pole is 8 m. Find the length of rope tied with its top from a point on the ground at a distance of 6 m from its bottom.

Sol. Given, height of a pole is 8 m.
Distance between the bottom of the pole and a point on the ground is 6 m.

On the basis of given information, we can draw the following figure:

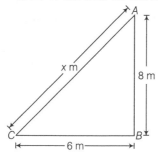

Let the length of the rope be x m.

$\because AB =$ Height of the pole

$BC =$ Distance between the bottom of the pole and a point on ground, where rope was tied

To find the length of the rope, we will use Pythagoras theorem, in right angled $\triangle ABC$.

$\therefore \qquad (AC)^2 = (AB)^2 + (BC)^2$

$\Rightarrow \qquad (x)^2 = (8)^2 + (6)^2 \quad \Rightarrow \quad x^2 = 64 + 36$

$\Rightarrow \qquad x^2 = 100 \quad \Rightarrow \quad x = \sqrt{100} = 10\, m$

Hence, the length of the rope is 10 m.

Q. 140 In the given figure, if y is five times x, find the value of z.

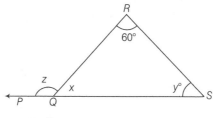

Sol. Given, $\qquad\qquad\qquad\qquad y = 5x$

According to the angle sum property of a triangle,

$\qquad\qquad 60° + x + y = 180°$

$\Rightarrow \qquad 60° + x + 5x = 180°$ $\qquad\qquad\qquad\qquad [\because y = 5x]$

$\Rightarrow \qquad 60° + 6x = 180° \quad \Rightarrow \quad 6x = 180° - 60° = 120°$

$\Rightarrow \qquad x = \dfrac{120°}{6} = 20°$

$\therefore \qquad y = 5x = 5 \times 20 = 100°$

According to the exterior angle property,

$\qquad\qquad z = 60° + y$

$\qquad\qquad = 60° + 100°$ $\qquad\qquad\qquad\qquad\qquad [\because y = 100°]$

$\qquad\qquad = 160°$

Q. 141 The lengths of two sides of an isosceles triangle are 9 cm and 20 cm. What is the perimeter of the triangle? Give reason.

Sol. Third side must be 20 cm, because sum of two sides should be greater than the third side.

$\therefore$ Perimeter of the triangle = Sum of all sides = $(9 + 20 + 20)$ cm

$\qquad\qquad\qquad = 49\, cm$

Q. 142 Without drawing the triangles write all six pairs of equal measures in each of the following pairs of congruent triangles.

(a) $\triangle STU \cong \triangle DEF$ (b) $\triangle ABC \cong \triangle LMN$

(c) $\triangle YZX \cong \triangle PQR$ (d) $\triangle XYZ \cong \triangle MLN$

Sol. We know that, corresponding parts of congruent triangles are equal.

(a) $\triangle STU \cong \triangle DEF$

$\angle S = \angle D, \angle T = \angle E$ and $\angle U = \angle F$

$ST = DE, TU = EF$ and $SU = DF$

(b) $\triangle ABC \cong \triangle LMN$

$\angle A = \angle L, \angle B = \angle M$ and $\angle C = \angle N$

$AB = LM, BC = MN$ and $AC = LN$

(c) $\triangle YZX \cong \triangle PQR$

$\angle Y = \angle P, \angle Z = \angle Q$ and $\angle X = \angle R$

$YZ = PQ, ZX = QR$ and $YX = PR$

(d) $\triangle XYZ \cong \triangle MLN$

$\angle X = \angle M, \angle Y = \angle L$ and $\angle Z = \angle N$

$XY = ML, YZ = LN$ and $XZ = MN$

Q. 143 In the following pairs of triangles in below figures, the lengths of the sides are indicated along the sides. By applying SSS congruence criterion, determine which triangles are congruent. If congruent, write the results in symbolic form.

(a)

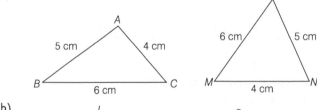

(b)

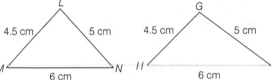

(c)

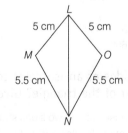

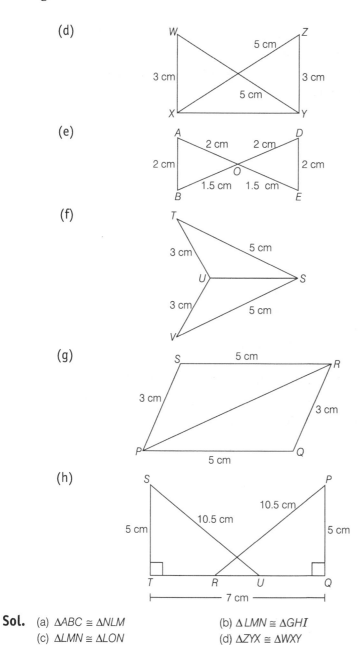

(d)

W   5 cm   Z
3 cm   3 cm
      5 cm
X   Y

(e)

A   2 cm   2 cm   D
2 cm   2 cm
        O
B   1.5 cm 1.5 cm E

(f)

T
3 cm   5 cm
     U   S
3 cm   5 cm
V

(g)

S   5 cm   R
3 cm   3 cm
P   Q
     5 cm

(h)

S   P
        10.5 cm
   10.5 cm
5 cm   5 cm
T   R   U   Q
       7 cm

Sol. (a) $\triangle ABC \cong \triangle NLM$ (b) $\triangle LMN \cong \triangle GHI$
(c) $\triangle LMN \cong \triangle LON$ (d) $\triangle ZYX \cong \triangle WXY$
(e) $\triangle AOB \cong \triangle DOE$ (f) $\triangle STU \cong \triangle SVU$
(g) $\triangle PSR \cong \triangle RQP$ (h) $\triangle STU \cong \triangle PQR$

Q. 144 *ABC* is an isosceles triangle with *AB = AC* and *D* is the mid-point of base *BC* (see the figure).
(a) State three pairs of equal parts in the △*ABD* and △*ACD*.
(b) Is △*ABD* ≅ △*ACD*? If so why?

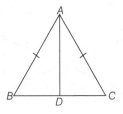

Sol. Given, $AB = AC$
and $BD = CD$
(a) In △*ABD* and △*ACD*,

$AB = AC$ [given]
$BD = CD$ [given]
$AD = AD$ [common side]

(b) Yes, by SSS congruence criterion,

$$\triangle ABD \cong \triangle ACD$$

Q. 145 In the given figure, it is given that *LM = ON* and *NL = MO*.
(a) State the three pairs of equal parts in the △*NOM* and △*MLN*.
(b) Is △*NOM* ≅ △*MLN*? Give reason.

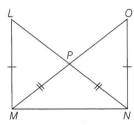

Sol. (a) In △*NOM* and △*MLN*, $LM = ON$ [given]
$MN = MN$ [common side]
$LN = OM$ [given]

(b) Yes, by SSS congruence criterion,
$$\triangle NOM \cong \triangle MLN$$

Q. 146 $\triangle DEF$ and $\triangle LMN$ are both isosceles with $DE = DF$ and $LM = LN$, respectively. If $DE = LM$ and $EF = MN$, then are the two triangles congruent? Which condition do you use?
If $\angle E = 40°$, what is the measure of $\angle N$?

Sol. Here,
$$DE = DF \qquad \qquad \ldots(i)$$
$$LM = LN \qquad \qquad \ldots(ii)$$
and
$$DE = LM \qquad \qquad \ldots(iii)$$

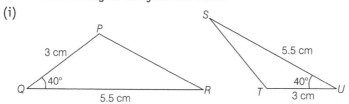

From Eqs. (i), (ii) and (iii), we get $DE = DF = LM = LN$
In $\triangle DEF$ and $\triangle LMN$,

	$DE = LM$	[given]
	$EF = MN$	[given]
	$DF = LN$	[proved above]

By SSS congruence criterion, $\triangle DEF \cong \triangle LMN$

$\therefore$ $\qquad \qquad \angle E = \angle M$ [by CPCT]
$\qquad \qquad \angle M = 40°$

Also, $\qquad \qquad \angle M = \angle N$
$\qquad [\because \angle M = \angle N$ and angles opposite to equal sides are equal]
$\Rightarrow \qquad \qquad \angle N = 40°$

Q. 147 If $\triangle PQR$ and $\triangle SQR$ are both isosceles triangle on a common base QR such that P and S lie on the same side of QR. Are $\triangle PSQ$ and $\triangle PSR$ congruent? Which condition do you use?

Sol. In $\triangle PSQ$ and $\triangle PSR$,
$\qquad \qquad \qquad PQ = PR$ [given]
$\qquad \qquad \qquad SQ = SR$ [given]
$\qquad \qquad \qquad PS = PS$ [common side]

By SSS congruence criterion, $\qquad \triangle PSQ \cong \triangle PSR$

Q. 148 In the given figures, which pairs of triangles are congruent by SAS congruence criterion (condition)? If congruent, write the congruence of the two triangles in symbolic form.

(i)

(ii)

(iii)

(iv)

(v)

(vi)

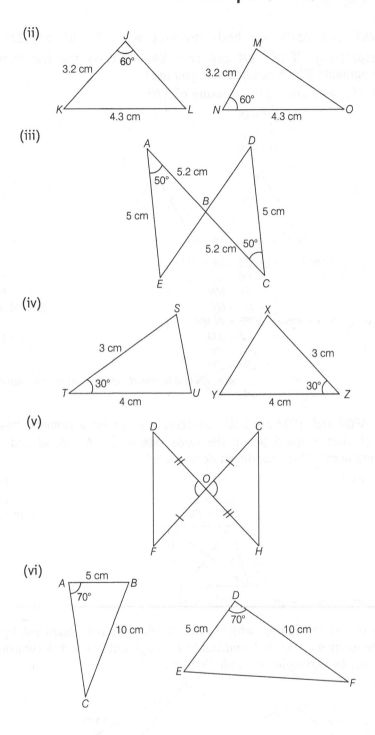

(vii)

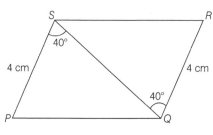

(viii)

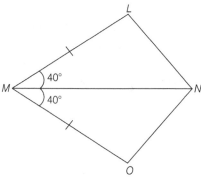

Sol.   (i) In ΔPQR and ΔTUS, $PQ = TU = 3\,$cm
$QR = US = 5.5\,$cm
$\angle PQR = \angle TUS = 40°$
By SAS congruence criterion, $\Delta PQR \cong \Delta TUS$

(ii) Not congruent, because angle in not included between two sides.

(iii) In ΔBCD and ΔBAE, $AB = CB = 5.2\,$cm
$DC = EA = 5\,$cm
$\angle EAB = \angle DCB = 50°$
By SAS congruence criterion, $\Delta BCD \cong \Delta BAE$

(iv) In ΔSTU and ΔXZY, $TU = ZY = 4\,$cm
$TS = ZX = 3\,$cm
$\angle STU = \angle XZY = 30°$
By SAS congruence criterion, $\Delta STU \cong \Delta XZY$

(v) In ΔDOF and ΔHOC, $DO = HO$ [given]
$CO = FO$ [given]
$\angle DOF = \angle HOC$ [vertically opposite angles]
By SAS congruence criterion, $\Delta DOF \cong \Delta HOC$

(vi) Not congruent, because angle is not included between two sides.

(vii) In ΔPSQ and ΔRQS, $PS = RQ = 4\,$cm
$SQ = SQ$ [common side]
$\angle PSQ = \angle RQS = 40°$
By SAS congruence criterion,
$\Delta PSQ \cong \Delta RQS$

(viii) In ΔLMN and ΔOMN,

$$LM = OM \qquad \text{[given]}$$
$$MN = MN \qquad \text{[common side]}$$
$$\angle LMN = \angle OMN = 40°$$

By SAS congruence criterion,

$$\Delta LMN \cong \Delta OMN$$

Q. 149 State which of the following pairs of triangles are congruent. If yes, write them in symbolic form (you may draw a rough figure).

(a) ΔPQR : PQ = 3.5 cm, QR   4.0 cm, ∠Q   60°
    ΔSTU : ST = 3.5 cm, TU = 4 cm, ∠T = 60°

(b) ΔABC : AB = 4.8 cm, ∠A = 90°, AC = 6.8 cm
    ΔXYZ : YZ = 6.8 cm, ∠X = 90°, ZX = 4.8 cm

Sol. (a)

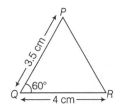 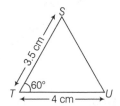

Both the triangles are congruent.

∴   ΔPQR ≅ ΔSTU   [by SAS congruence criterion]

(b)

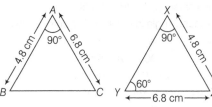

Both the triangles are not congruent.

Q. 150 In the given figure, PQ = PS and ∠1 = ∠2.

(i) Is ΔPQR ≅ ΔPSR? Give reason.
(ii) Is QR = SR? Give reason.

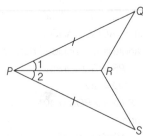

Sol. Yes,

(i) In $\triangle PQR$ and $\triangle PSR$, $\qquad$ $PQ = PS$ $\qquad$ [given]

$\angle 1 = \angle 2$ $\qquad$ [given]

$PR = PR$ $\qquad$ [common side]

By SAS congruence criterion, $\triangle PQR \cong \triangle PSR$

(ii) Yes, $QR = SR$ $\qquad$ [by CPCT]

Q. 151 In the given figure, $DE = IH$, $EG = FI$ and $\angle E = \angle I$. Is $\triangle DEF \cong \triangle HIG$? If yes, by which congruence criterion?

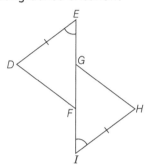

Sol. Given, $\qquad$ $EG = FI$

$EG + GF = FI + GF$ $\qquad$ [adding GF on both sides]

$EF = IG$

In $\triangle DEF$ and $\triangle HIG$, $\qquad$ $DE = IH$ $\qquad$ [given]

$EF = IG$ $\qquad$ [proved above]

$\angle E = \angle I$ $\qquad$ [given]

By SAS congruence criterion, $\qquad$ $\triangle DEF \cong \triangle HIG$

Q. 152 In the given figure, $\angle 1 = \angle 2$ and $\angle 3 = \angle 4$.

(i) Is $\triangle ADC \cong \triangle ABC$? Why?

(ii) Show that $AD = AB$ and $CD = CB$.

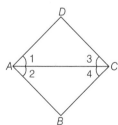

Sol. (i) In $\triangle ADC$ and $\triangle ABC$, $\qquad$ $\angle 1 = \angle 2$ $\qquad$ [given]

$AC = AC$ $\qquad$ [common side]

$\angle 3 = \angle 4$ $\qquad$ [given]

By ASA congruence criterion, $\triangle ADC \cong \triangle ABC$

(ii) $AD = AB$ $\qquad$ [by CPCT]

$CD = CB$ $\qquad$ [by CPCT]

Q. 153 Observe the following figure and state the three pairs of equal parts in $\triangle ABC$ and $\triangle DBC$.

    (i) Is $\triangle ABC \cong \triangle DCB$? Why?

    (ii) Is $AB = DC$? Why?

    (iii) Is $AC = DB$? Why?

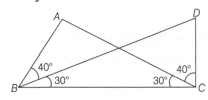

Sol.   (i) In $\triangle ABC$ and DCB,

$$BC = BC \qquad \text{[common side]}$$
$$\angle ABC = \angle DCB = 70°$$
$$\angle ACB = \angle DBC = 30°$$

By ASA congruence criterion,

$$\triangle ABC \cong \triangle DCB$$

   (ii) $AB = DC$ [by CPCT]

   (iii) $AC = DB$ [by CPCT]

Q. 154 In the given figure, $QS \perp PR$, $RT \perp PQ$ and $QS = RT$.

    (i) Is $\triangle QSR \cong \triangle RTQ$? Give reason.

    (ii) Is $\angle PQR = \angle PRQ$? Give reason.

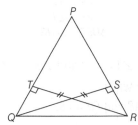

Sol.

   (i) In $\triangle QSR$ and $\triangle RTQ$ $QS = RT$ [given]

$$\angle QSR = \angle QTR = 90°$$
$$QR = QR \qquad \text{[common side]}$$

By RHS congruence criterion,

$$\triangle QSR \cong \triangle RTQ$$

   (ii) Yes, $\angle PQR = \angle PRQ$ [by CPCT]

Q. 155 Points A and B are on the opposite edges of a pond as shown in the given figure. To find the distance between the two points, the surveyor makes a rightangled triangle as shown. Find the distance AB.

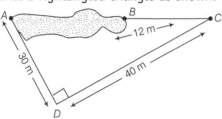

Sol.   Since, $\triangle ACD$ is a right angled triangle.
In right angled $\triangle ADC$, by Pythagoras theorem,
$$(AC)^2 = (AD)^2 + (CD)^2$$
$\Rightarrow \qquad (AC)^2 = (30)^2 + (40)^2 \qquad$ [$\because AD = 30\,cm$ and $CD = 40\,cm$, given]
$\Rightarrow \qquad (AC)^2 = 900 + 1600$
$\Rightarrow \qquad (AC)^2 = 2500$
$\Rightarrow \qquad \quad AC = \sqrt{2500}$
$\therefore \qquad \qquad AC = 50\,m$
Now, $AB = AC - BC = 50 - 12 = 38\,m$
Hence, the distance AB is 38 m.

Q. 156 Two poles of 10 m and 15 m stand upright on a plane ground. If the distance between the tops is 13 m, find distance between their feet.

Sol.

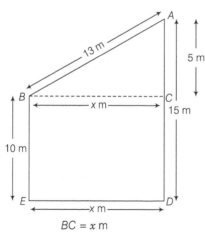

Let $\qquad\qquad\qquad\qquad\qquad\qquad BC = x\,m$
In right angled $\triangle ACB$,
$$AB^2 = AC^2 + BC^2 \qquad \text{[by Pythagoras theorem]}$$
$\Rightarrow \qquad\qquad (13)^2 = (5)^2 + x^2$
$\Rightarrow \qquad\qquad 169 - 25 = x^2$
$\Rightarrow \qquad\qquad\quad 144 = x^2$
$\Rightarrow \qquad\qquad\qquad x = \sqrt{144}$
$\Rightarrow \qquad\qquad\qquad x = 12\,m$
Hence, the distance between the feet of two poles is 12 m.

Q. 157 The foot of a ladder is 6 m away from its wall and its top reaches a window 8 m above the ground, (a) Find the length of the ladder. (b) If the ladder is shifted in such a way that its foot is 8 m away from the wall, to what height does its top reach?

Sol. (a) Let the length of the ladder be x m.

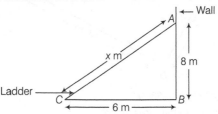

In right angled $\triangle ABC$,

$$AC^2 = AB^2 + BC^2 \qquad \text{[by Pythagoras theorem]}$$
$$\Rightarrow \qquad (x)^2 = (8)^2 + (6)^2$$
$$\Rightarrow \qquad = \sqrt{(8)^2 + (6)^2} = \sqrt{64 + 36} = \sqrt{100}$$
$$\Rightarrow \qquad x = 10\,\text{m}$$

Hence, the length of the ladder is 10 m.

(b) Let the height of the top be x m.

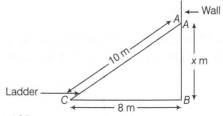

In right angled $\triangle ACB$,

$$AC^2 = AB^2 + BC^2 \qquad \text{[by Pythagoras theorem]}$$
$$\Rightarrow \qquad AB^2 = AC^2 - BC^2$$
$$\Rightarrow \qquad x^2 = (10)^2 - (8)^2 = 100 - 64$$
$$\Rightarrow \qquad x = \sqrt{36}$$
$$\Rightarrow \qquad x = 6\,\text{m}$$

Hence, the height of the top is 6 m.

Q. 158 In the given figure, state the three pairs of equal parts in $\triangle ABC$ and $\triangle EOD$. Is $\triangle ABC \cong \triangle EOD$? Why?

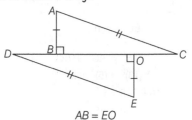

Sol. In $\triangle ABC$ and $\triangle EOD$, $\qquad\qquad AB = EO \qquad\qquad\qquad$ [given]

$$AC = ED \qquad\qquad\qquad \text{[given]}$$
$$\angle ABC = \angle EOD = 90°$$

By RHS congruence criterion, $\qquad \triangle ABC \cong \triangle EOD$

7

Comparing Quantities

Multiple Choice Questions (MCQs)

Q. 1 20% of 700 m is

    (a) 560 m   (b) 70 m   (c) 210 m   (d) 140 m

Sol. *(d)*   We have, 20% of 700 m $= \dfrac{20}{100} \times 700 = 20 \times 7 = 140 \, m$

        Hence, 20% of 700 m is 140 m.

Q. 2 Gayatri's income is ₹ 160000 per year. She pays 15% of this as house rent and 10% of the remainder on her child's education. The money left with her is

    (a) ₹ 136000   (b) ₹ 120000   (c) ₹ 122400   (d) ₹ 14000

Sol. *(c)*   Income of Gayatri = ₹ 160000   [given]

        Money paid as house rent = 15% of 160000 $= \dfrac{15}{100} \times 160000 =$ ₹ 24000

        Remaining amount = 160000 − 24000 = ₹ 136000

        Money spent on child's education = 10% of 136000 $= \dfrac{10}{100} \times 136000 =$ ₹ 13600

        Money left with her = 136000 − 13600 = ₹ 122400

Q. 3 The ratio of Fatima's income to her savings is 4 : 1. The percentage of money saved by her is

    (a) 20%   (b) 25%   (c) 40%   (d) 80%

Sol. *(a)*   Given, ratio of income to savings = 4 : 1

        Let income = $4x$ and savings = x.

        ∴ Percentage of money saved by her $= \dfrac{\text{Savings}}{(\text{Income} + \text{Savings})} \times 100\%$

$$= \dfrac{x}{4x + x} \times 100 = \dfrac{x}{5x} \times 100\% = \dfrac{1}{5} \times 100\% = 20\%$$

Q. 4 0.07 is equal to

    (a) 70%   (b) 7%

    (c) 0.7%   (d) 0.07%

Sol. *(b)* We have, 0.07

In percentage, $0.07 = \dfrac{7}{100} \times \dfrac{100}{100} = \dfrac{7}{100} \times 100\% = 7\%$

Note *To convert any number into per cent, we multiply that number by 100 alongwith the symbol '%.'*

Q. 5 In a scout camp, 40% of the scouts were from Gujarat state and 20% of these were from Ahmedabad. The percentage of scouts in the camp from Ahmedabad is

    (a) 25%   (b) 32.5%

    (c) 8%   (d) 50%

Sol. *(c)* Let the scouts in scout camp = 100

Then, scouts from Gujarat = 40% of $100 = \dfrac{40}{100} \times 100 = 40$

and scouts from Ahmedabad = 20% of $40 = \dfrac{20}{100} \times 40 = 8$

∴ Percentage of scouts from Ahmedabad = $\dfrac{\text{Scouts from Ahmedabad}}{\text{Total scouts}} \times 100\%$

$= \dfrac{8}{100} \times 100\% = 8\%$

Q. 6 What per cent of ₹ 4500 is ₹ 9000?

    (a) 200%   (b) $\dfrac{1}{2}\%$

    (c) 2%   (d) 50%

Sol. *(a)* Let $x\%$ of ₹ 4500 = ₹ 9000

Then, $\dfrac{x}{100} \times 4500 = 9000$

∴ $x \times 45 = 9000$

⇒ $x = \dfrac{9000}{45}$ ⇒ $x = 200\%$

Hence, 200% of ₹ 4500 is ₹ 9000.

Q. 7 5.2 is equal to

    (a) 52%   (b) 5.2%

    (c) 520%   (d) 0.52%

Sol. *(c)* We have, 5.2

In percentage, $\dfrac{52}{10} \times 100\% = 520\%$

Q. 8 The ratio 3 : 8 is equal to

    (a) 3.75%   (b) 37.5%   (c) 0.375%   (d) 267%

Sol. *(b)*   Given, ratio = 3 : 8

      In percentage, $\dfrac{3}{8} \times 100\% = 37.5\%$

Q. 9 225% is equal to

    (a) 9 : 4   (b) 4 : 9   (c) 3 : 2   (d) 2 : 3

Sol. *(a)*   We have, 225%

      For fraction, $225 \times \dfrac{1}{100} = \dfrac{225}{100} = \dfrac{9}{4}$

      $\therefore$ Required ratio = 9 : 4

      Note *The sign of percentage (%) is removed dividing the number by 100.*

Q. 10 A bicycle is purchased for ₹ 1800 and is sold at a profit of 12%. Its selling price is

    (a) ₹ 1584   (b) ₹ 2016   (c) ₹ 1788   (d) ₹ 1812

Sol. *(b)*   Given, cost price of bicycle = ₹ 1800

      and profit = 12%

      As we know,

      $\text{Profit}\% = \dfrac{\text{Profit}}{\text{CP}} \times 100$

      $\Rightarrow \quad 12 = \dfrac{\text{Profit}}{1800} \times 100$

      $\Rightarrow$ Profit = 12 × 18 = ₹ 216

      $\therefore$ SP = CP + Profit = 1800 + 216 = ₹ 2016

      Hence, the selling price for bicycle is ₹ 2016.

Q. 11 A cricket bat was purchased for ₹ 800 and was sold for ₹ 1600. Then, profit earned is

    (a) 100%   (b) 64%   (c) 50%   (d) 60%

Sol. *(a)*   Given, cost price of cricket bat = ₹ 800

      and selling price of cricket bat = ₹ 1600

      $\therefore$ Profit = SP − CP = ₹ (1600 − 800) = ₹ 800

      We know that,

      $\text{Profit}\% = \dfrac{\text{Profit}}{\text{CP}} \times 100\% = \dfrac{800}{800} \times 100\% = 100\%$

      Hence, profit earned is 100%.

Q. 12 A farmer bought a buffalo for ₹ 44000 and a cow for ₹ 18000. He sold the buffalo at a loss of 5% but made a profit of 10% on the cow. The net result of the transaction is

    (a) loss of ₹ 200   (b) profit of ₹ 400

    (c) loss of ₹ 400   (d) profit of ₹ 200

Sol. *(c)*   For buffalo, CP = ₹ 44000

Loss% = 5%

$\therefore$ $\text{Loss\%} = \dfrac{\text{Loss}}{\text{CP}} \times 100\%$

$\Rightarrow$ $5 = \dfrac{\text{Loss}}{44000} \times 100$

$\Rightarrow$ Loss = 5×440 = ₹ 2200

So,   SP = CP – Loss = 44000 – 2200 = ₹ 41800

For cow,   CP = ₹ 18000

Profit % = 10%

$\therefore$ $\text{Profit \%} = \dfrac{\text{Profit}}{\text{CP}} \times 100\% \Rightarrow 10 = \dfrac{\text{Profit}}{18000} \times 100$

Profit = ₹ 1800

So,   SP = CP + Profit = 18000 + 1800 = ₹ 19800

Total CP of buffalo and cow = 44000 + 18000 = ₹ 62000

Total SP of buffalo and cow = 41800 + 19800 = ₹ 61600

Net loss = CP – SP = 62000 – 61600 = ₹ 400

Q. 13 If Mohan's income is 25% more than Raman's income, then Raman's income is less than Mohan's income by

(a) 25%   (b) 80%

(c) 20%   (d) 75%

Sol. *(c)*   Let the Raman's income be x. It is given that Mohan's income is 25% more than Raman's income.

Then, Mohan's income $= x + 25\%$ of $x = x + \dfrac{25}{100} x = x\left(1 + \dfrac{25}{100}\right)$

$$= x\left(\dfrac{100 + 25}{100}\right) = \dfrac{125}{100} x$$

$\therefore$ Raman's income as compared to Mohan's income

$$= \dfrac{\text{Mohan's income} - \text{Raman's income}}{\text{Mohan's income}} \times 100\%$$

$$= \dfrac{\dfrac{125}{100} x - x}{\dfrac{125}{100} x} \times 100\% = \dfrac{\dfrac{125x - 100x}{100}}{\dfrac{125}{100} x} \times 100\%$$

$$= \dfrac{25x}{125x} \times 100\% = 20\%$$

Q. 14 The interest on ₹ 30000 for 3 yr at the rate of 15% per annum is

(a) ₹ 4500   (b) ₹ 9000   (c) ₹ 18000   (d) ₹ 13500

Sol. *(d)*   Given, P = ₹ 30000, T = 3 yr, R = 15%

We know that, $I = \dfrac{P \times R \times T}{100} = \dfrac{30000 \times 15 \times 3}{100} = ₹ 13500$

Q. 15 Amount received on ₹ 3000 for 2 yr at the rate of 11% per annum is

(a) ₹ 2340 (b) ₹ 3660 (c) ₹ 4320 (d) ₹ 3330

Sol. *(b)* Given, $P = ₹ 3000,$

$$T = 2 \text{ yr}$$

and $R = 11\%$

$\therefore \quad I = \dfrac{P \times R \times T}{100} = \dfrac{3000 \times 11 \times 2}{100} = ₹ 660$

Now, amount $(A) = P + I$

$$= 3000 + 660$$

$$= ₹ 3660$$

Q. 16 Interest on ₹ 12000 for 1 month at the rate of 10% per annum is

(a) ₹ 1200 (b) ₹ 600 (c) ₹ 100 (d) ₹ 12100

Sol. *(c)* Given, $P = ₹ 12000,$

$$R = 10\%,$$

$$T = 1 \text{ month} = \dfrac{1}{12} \text{ yr}$$

$\therefore \quad I = \dfrac{P \times R \times T}{100} = \dfrac{12000 \times 10 \times 1}{100 \times 12} = ₹100$

Q. 17 Rajni and Mohini deposited ₹ 3000 and ₹ 4000 in a company at the rate of 10% per annum for 3 yr and $2\dfrac{1}{2}$ yr, respectively. The difference of the amounts received by them will be

(a) ₹ 100 (b) ₹ 1000 (c) ₹ 900 (d) ₹ 1100

Sol. *(d)* For Rajni, $P = ₹ 3000,$

$$R = 10\% \text{ per annum}$$

$$T = 3 \text{ yr}$$

$$\therefore \quad I = \dfrac{P \times R \times T}{100}$$

$$= \dfrac{3000 \times 10 \times 3}{100} = ₹ 900$$

and $A = P + I = 3000 + 900 = ₹ 3900$

For Mohini, $P = ₹ 4000,$

$$R = 10\% \text{ per annum}$$

and $T = 2\dfrac{1}{2} \text{ yr} = \dfrac{5}{2} \text{ yr}$

$$\therefore \quad I = \dfrac{P \times R \times T}{100}$$

$$= \dfrac{4000 \times 10 \times 5}{100 \times 2} = ₹ 1000$$

and $A = P + I = 4000 + 1000 = ₹ 5000$

Difference in amounts $= 5000 - 3900 = ₹ 1100$

Q. 18 If 90% of x is 315 km, then the value of x is

    (a) 325 km   (b) 350 km   (c) 405 km   (d) 340 km

Sol. *(b)* Given, 90% of $x = 315$ km

$$\Rightarrow \quad \frac{90}{100} \times x = 315 \quad \Rightarrow \quad x = \frac{315 \times 100}{90}$$

$$\therefore \qquad\qquad x = 350 \text{ km}$$

Q. 19 On selling an article for ₹ 329, a dealer lost 6%. The cost price of the article is

    (a) ₹ 310.37   (b) ₹ 348.74   (c) ₹ 335   (d) ₹ 350

Sol. *(d)* Given, SP = ₹ 329 and loss% = 6%

We know that,

$$\text{Loss\%} = \frac{\text{Loss}}{\text{CP}} \times 100$$

$$\Rightarrow \qquad 6 = \frac{\text{CP} - \text{SP}}{\text{CP}} \times 100 \qquad [\because \text{loss} = \text{CP} - \text{SP}]$$

$$\Rightarrow \qquad 6\,\text{CP} = 100\,(\text{CP} - \text{SP})$$

$$\Rightarrow \qquad \frac{6}{100}\text{CP} = \text{CP} - \text{SP}$$

$$\Rightarrow \qquad \text{CP} - \frac{6}{100}\text{CP} = 329 \qquad [\because \text{SP} = ₹\,329, \text{given}]$$

$$\Rightarrow \qquad \frac{94}{100}\text{CP} = 329$$

$$\Rightarrow \qquad \text{CP} = \frac{329 \times 100}{94}$$

$$\therefore \qquad \text{CP} = ₹\,350$$

Q. 20 $\dfrac{25\% \text{ of } 50\% \text{ of } 100\%}{25 \times 50}$ is equal to

    (a) 1.1%   (b) 0.1%   (c) 0.01%   (d) 1%

Sol. *(c)* We have, $\dfrac{25\% \text{ of } 50\% \text{ of } 100\%}{25 \times 50} = \dfrac{25}{100} \times \dfrac{50}{100} \times \dfrac{100}{100} \times \dfrac{1}{25 \times 50}$

$$= \frac{125000}{1250 \times 100 \times 100 \times 100} = \frac{1}{10000} = 0.0001$$

In percentage, $0.0001 \times 100 \% = 0.01\%$

Q. 21 The sum which will earn a simple interest of ₹ 126 in 2 yr at 14% per annum, is

    (a) ₹ 394   (b) ₹ 395   (c) ₹ 450   (d) ₹ 540

Sol. *(c)* Given, $I = ₹\,126$, $R = 14\%$ and $T = 2$ yr

$$\therefore \qquad I = \frac{P \times R \times T}{100} \quad \Rightarrow \quad 126 = \frac{P \times 14 \times 2}{100}$$

$$\Rightarrow \quad 126 \times 100 = P \times 14 \times 2$$

$$\Rightarrow \qquad P = \frac{12600}{14 \times 2} \quad \Rightarrow \quad P = ₹\,450$$

Q. 22 The per cent that represents the unshaded region in the figure, is

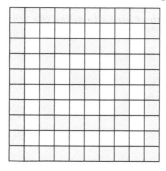

(a) 75%   (b) 50%   (c) 40%   (d) 60%

Sol. *(c)*   Given, total parts = 10 × 10 = 100

∵ Shaded parts = 60

∴ Per cent of shaded parts = $\dfrac{60}{100} \times 100\% = 60\%$

Then, per cent of unshaded parts = 100 − 60 = 40%

Hence, the unshaded region is 40%.

Q. 23 The per cent that represents the shaded region in the figure, is

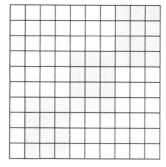

(a) 36%   (b) 64%   (c) 27%   (d) 48%

Sol. *(a)*   Given, total parts = 10 × 10 = 100

∵ Shaded parts = 36

∴ Per cent of shaded parts = $\dfrac{36}{100} \times 100\% = 36\%$

Hence, the shaded region is 36%.

Fill in the Blanks

In questions 24 to 59, fill in the blanks to make the statements true.

Q. 24 $2 : 3 =$ ____%

Sol. Given, ratio $= 2 : 3$

In percentage, $\frac{2}{3} \times 100\% = \mathbf{66\frac{2}{3}\%}$

Q. 25 $18\frac{3}{4}\% =$ ____ : ____

Sol. Given, percentage $= 18\frac{3}{4}\% = \frac{75}{4}\%$

$$\left[\because \text{ mixed fraction} = \text{improper fraction} = \frac{\text{whole number} \times \text{denominator} + \text{numerator}}{\text{denominator}}\right]$$

In fraction, $\frac{75}{4} \times \frac{1}{100} = \frac{3}{16}$

$\therefore$ Ratio $= \mathbf{3 : 16}$ $\left[\because a : b = \frac{a}{b}\right]$

Q. 26 30% of ₹ 360 = ____

Sol. We have, 30% of ₹ 360 $= \frac{30}{100} \times 360 = \mathbf{₹\ 108}$

Q. 27 120% of 50 km = ____

Sol. We have, 120% of 50 km $= \frac{120}{100} \times 50\,\text{km} = \mathbf{60\ km}$

Q. 28 $2.5 =$ ____%

Sol. We have, 2.5

In percentage, $2.5 \times 100\% = \mathbf{250\%}$

Q. 29 $\frac{8}{5} =$ ____%

Sol. We have, $\frac{8}{5}$

In percentage, $\frac{8}{5} \times 100\% = \mathbf{160\%}$

Q. 30 A ____ with its denominator 100 is called a per cent.

Sol. A **fraction** with its denominator 100 is called a per cent.

Q. 31 15 kg is ___ % of 50 kg.

Sol. Let $x\%$ of 50 kg be 15 kg.

Then, $\frac{x}{100} \times 50 = 15$

$\Rightarrow \qquad \frac{x}{2} = 15 \Rightarrow x = 15 \times 2$

$\therefore \qquad x = 30\%$

Hence, 15 kg is **30%** of 50 kg.

Q. 32 Weight of Nikhil increased from 60 kg to 66 kg. Then, the increase in weight is___%

Sol. We have, initial weight of Nikhil = 60 kg

After increase in weight, weight became = 66 kg

Increase in weight = 66 − 60 = 6 kg

$\therefore$ Increase percentage of weight $= \dfrac{\text{Increase}}{\text{Initial weight}} \times 100\% = \dfrac{6}{60} \times 100\% = \dfrac{60}{6}\% = 10\%$

So, increase in weight is **10%**.

Q. 33 In a class of 50 students 8% were absent on one day. The number of students present on that day, was____.

Sol. We have, total number of students = 50

Absent on one day = 8%

Percentage of present students on that day = 100 − 8 = 92%

$\therefore$ Number of students present on that day = 92% of 50 $= \dfrac{92}{100} \times 50 = \dfrac{92}{2} = 46$

So, the number of students present on that day, was **46**.

Q. 34 Savitri obtained 440 marks out of 500 in an examination. She secured ___% marks in the examination.

Sol. Marks obtained by Savitri out of 500 = 440

Percentage of marks obtained $= \dfrac{440}{500} \times 100\% = 88\%$

Hence, Savitri secured **88%** marks in the examination.

Q. 35 Out of a total deposit of ₹ 1500 in her bank account, Abida withdrew 40% of the deposit. Now, the balance in her account is___.

Sol. Total deposit = ₹ 1500

Amount withdrawn = 40% of ₹ 1500 $= \dfrac{40}{100} \times 1500 = ₹ 600$

$\therefore$ Balance in the account = 1500 − 600 = **₹ 900**

Q. 36 ___is 50% more than 60.

Sol. Let number be x. It is given that x is 50% more than 60.

Therefore, $x = 60 + 50\%$ of $60 = 60 + \dfrac{50}{100} \times 60 = 60 + 30 = \mathbf{90}$

Q. 37 John sells a bat for ₹ 75 and suffers a loss of ₹ 8. The cost price of the bat is___.

Sol. Given, SP of bat = ₹ 75 and loss = ₹ 8

We know that, CP = SP + Loss = 75 + 8 = ₹ 83

Hence, cost price of the bat is ₹ **83**.

Q. 38 If the price of sugar is decreased by 20%, then the new price of 3kg sugar originally costing ₹ 120, will be___.

Sol. Original price of 3 kg sugar = ₹ 120

Given that, price of sugar is decreased by 20%.

So, new price of sugar = Original price – 20% of original price = 120 – 20% of 120

$$= 120 - \dfrac{20}{100} \times 120 = 120 - 24 = ₹\ \mathbf{96}$$

Q. 39 Mohini bought a cow for ₹ 9000 and Sold it at a loss of ₹ 900. The selling price of the cow is___.

Sol. Given, CP of cow = ₹ 9000 and loss = ₹ 900

We know that, SP = CP – Loss = 9000 – 900 = ₹ 8100

Hence, the selling price of the cow is ₹ **8100**.

Q. 40 Devangi buys a chair for ₹ 700 and sells it for ₹ 750. She earns a profit of ___% in the transaction.

Sol. Given, CP of chair = ₹ 700

and SP of chair = ₹ 750

We know that, Profit = SP – CP = 750 – 700 = ₹ 50

Also, profit % $= \dfrac{\text{Profit}}{\text{CP}} \times 100\% = \dfrac{50}{700} \times 100\,\% = 7\dfrac{1}{7}\%$

Hence, profit earned by Devangi is $7\dfrac{1}{7}\%$.

Q. 41 Sonal bought a bed sheet for ₹ 400 and sold it for ₹ 440. Her___% is___ %.

Sol. Given, CP of a bed sheet = ₹ 400 and SP of a bed sheet = ₹ 440

Since, SP > CP,

∴ Profit = SP – CP = 440 – 400 = ₹ 40

Now, profit % $= \dfrac{\text{Profit}}{\text{CP}} \times 100 = \dfrac{40}{400} \times 100 = 10\%$

Hence, Sonal's **profit**% is 10%.

Q. 42 Nasim bought a pen for ₹ 60 and sold it for ₹ 54. His___% is ___.

Sol.   Given, CP of a pen = ₹ 60

and   SP of a pen = ₹ 54

Since, CP > SP

∴ Loss = CP − SP = 60 − 54 = ₹ 6

Now, loss% = $\dfrac{\text{Loss}}{\text{CP}}$ × 100% = $\dfrac{6}{60}$ × 100 % = 10 %

Hence, Nasim's **loss**% is **10%**.

Q. 43 Aahuti purchased a house for ₹ 5059700 and spent ₹ 40300 on its repairing. To make a profit of 5%, she should sell the house for ₹ ___.

Sol.   Given, CP of house = ₹ 5059700

and amount spent on repairing = ₹ 40300

So, total CP of house = 5059700 + 40300 = ₹ 5100000

We know that, profit % = $\dfrac{\text{Profit}}{\text{CP}}$ × 100 %

⇒ $\qquad\qquad 5 = \dfrac{\text{SP} - \text{CP}}{\text{CP}} \times 100$ $\qquad$ [∵ profit = SP − CP and profit % = 5, given]

⇒ $\qquad\qquad 5 = \dfrac{\text{SP} - 5100000}{5100000} \times 100$

⇒ $\qquad\qquad \dfrac{5 \times 5100000}{100} = \text{SP} - 5100000$

⇒ $\qquad\qquad 255000 = \text{SP} - 5100000$

⇒ $\qquad\qquad \text{SP} = 5100000 + 255000$

∴ $\qquad\qquad \text{SP} = ₹\ 5355000$

Q. 44 If 20 lemons are bought for ₹ 10 and sold at 5 for three rupees, then ___in the transaction is___%.

Sol.   CP of 20 lemons = ₹ 10

By unitary method,

If SP of 5 lemons = ₹ 3

Then, SP of 1 lemon = ₹ $\dfrac{3}{5}$

∴ SP of 20 lemons = $\dfrac{3}{5}$ × 20 = ₹ 12

Now, CP = ₹ 10 and SP = ₹ 12

Since, SP > CP

∴ Profit = SP − CP = 12 − 10 = ₹ 2

We know that, Profit % = $\dfrac{\text{Profit}}{\text{CP}}$ × 100 % = $\dfrac{2}{10}$ × 100% = 20%

Hence, **profit** in the transaction is **20%**.

Q. 45 Narain bought 120 oranges at ₹ 4 each. He sold 60% of the oranges at ₹ 5 each and the remaining at ₹ 3.50 each. His____is ____%.

Sol. Given, CP of 1 orange = ₹ 4

CP of 120 oranges = 4×120 = ₹ 480

Now, 60% of 120 oranges = $\dfrac{60}{100} \times 120 = 72$

∴ SP of 72 oranges = 72×5 = ₹ 360

and SP of remaining oranges = $(120 - 72) \times 3.50 = 48 \times 3.50$ = ₹ 168

∴ Total SP of 120 oranges = $360 + 168$ = ₹ 528

Since, SP > CP

Profit = SP − CP = $528 - 480$ = ₹ 48

We know that, Profit % = $\dfrac{\text{Profit}}{\text{CP}} \times 100\% = \dfrac{48}{480} \times 100\% = 10\%$

Hence, his **profit** is **10%**.

Q. 46 A fruit seller purchased 20 kg of apples at ₹ 50 per kg. Out of these, 5% of the apples were found to be rotten. If he sells the remaining apples at ₹ 60 per kg, then his____is____% .

Sol. We have, price for per kg apples = ₹ 50

Total purchased apples = 20 kg

Since, 5% were rotten, so good apples = 20 kg − 5% of 20 kg (rotten)

$$= 20 - \dfrac{5}{100} \times 20 = 20 - 1 = 19 \, \text{kg}$$

Also, he sells 19 kg apples at ₹ 60 per kg.

∴ Total selling price = 19×60 = ₹ 1140

∵ Cost price was 20 kg apples = 20×50 = ₹ 1000

∴ Profit = SP − CP = $1140 - 1000$ = ₹ 140

Now, profit % = $\dfrac{\text{Profit}}{\text{CP}} \times 100\% = \dfrac{140}{1000} \times 100\% = \dfrac{140}{10} = 14\%$

So, his **profit** is **14%**.

Q. 47 Interest on ₹ 3000 at 10% per annum for a period of 3 yr is____.

Sol. Given, P = ₹ 3000, R = 10% and T = 3 yr

We know that, $I = \dfrac{P \times R \times T}{100}$

$$= \dfrac{3000 \times 10 \times 3}{100} = ₹ \, 900$$

Hence, interest is ₹ **900**.

Q. 48 Amount obtained by depositing ₹ 20000 at 8% per annum for six months, is____ .

Sol. Deposited amount = ₹ 20000

Rate of interest = 8%

Time period = 6 months = $\dfrac{6}{12}$ yr = $\dfrac{1}{2}$ yr

$I = \dfrac{P \times R \times T}{100} = \dfrac{20000 \times 8 \times \dfrac{1}{2}}{100} = \dfrac{20000 \times 8}{200} = 100 \times 8 = ₹\ 800$

∴ Amount received = Principal + Interest = 20000 + 800 = ₹ **20800**

Q. 49 Interest on ₹ 12500 at 18% per annum for a period of 2 yr and 4 months is ____ .

Sol. Given, P = ₹ 12500 and R = 18%

$T = 2$ yr 4 months $= \left(2 + \dfrac{4}{12}\right)$ yr $= \left(2 + \dfrac{1}{3}\right)$ yr $= \dfrac{7}{3}$ yr

We know that, $I = \dfrac{P \times R \times T}{100} = \dfrac{12500 \times 18 \times 7}{3 \times 100} = ₹\ \mathbf{5250}$

Q. 50 25 mL is ____% of 5 L.

Sol. Let 25 mL be x% of 5 L.

Then, $\qquad\qquad$ 25 mL = x% of 5L

⇒ $\qquad\qquad 25 = \dfrac{x}{100} \times 5 \times 1000$ $\qquad$ [∵ 1L = 1000 mL]

⇒ $\qquad\qquad \dfrac{25 \times 100}{5 \times 1000} = x$

⇒ $\qquad\qquad x = 0.5$

Hence, 25 mL is **0.5**% of 5 L.

Q. 51 If A is increased by 20%, it equals B. If B is decreased by 50%, it equals C. Then, ____ % of A is equal to C.

Sol. Given, if A is increased by 20%, then it is equal to B.

∴ $\qquad\qquad A + 20\%$ of $A = B$

⇒ $\qquad\qquad A\left(1 + \dfrac{20}{100}\right) = B$

⇒ $\qquad\qquad \dfrac{120}{100}A = B$

⇒ $\qquad\qquad B = \dfrac{6}{5}A$ $\qquad\qquad$ ...(i)

If B is decreased by 50%, then it is equal to C.

∴ $\qquad\qquad B - 50\%$ of $B = C$

⇒ $\qquad\qquad B\left(1 - \dfrac{50}{100}\right) = C$

$$\Rightarrow \qquad B \times \frac{50}{100} = C$$

$$\Rightarrow \qquad \frac{1}{2}B = C$$

$$\Rightarrow \qquad B = 2C \qquad \qquad \text{...(ii)}$$

On comparing Eqs. (i) and (ii), we get

$$\frac{6}{5}A = 2C$$

$$\Rightarrow \qquad \frac{A}{C} = \frac{10}{6}$$

$$\Rightarrow \qquad C = \frac{6}{10}A$$

$$\Rightarrow \qquad C = \frac{3}{5}A$$

$$\therefore \text{In percentage,} \ \frac{C}{A} \times 100 = \frac{\frac{3}{5}A}{A} \times 100\%$$

$$= \frac{3}{5} \times 100\%$$

$$= 60\%$$

Hence, **60%** of A is equal to C.

Q. 52 Interest $= \dfrac{P \times R \times T}{100}$, where T is ____, $R\%$ is____ and P is____.

Sol. Here, T is **time period**, $R\%$ is **rate of interest** and P is **principal**.

Q. 53 The difference of interests for 2 yr and 3 yr on a sum of ₹ 2100 at 8% per annum is____.

Sol. Given, P = ₹ 2100 and R = 8%

For $T = 2$ yr,

$$I = \frac{P \times R \times T}{100} = \frac{2100 \times 8 \times 2}{100} = ₹\ 336$$

For 3 yr,

$$I = \frac{P \times R \times T}{100} = \frac{2100 \times 8 \times 3}{100} = ₹\ 504$$

$\therefore$ Difference between both interests $= 504 - 336 = ₹\ 168$

Q. 54 To convert a fraction into a per cent, we____ it by 100.

Sol. To convert a fraction into a per cent, we **multiply** it by 100.

Q. 55 To convert a decimal into a per cent, we shift the decimal point two places to the____.

Sol. To convert a decimal into a per cent, we shift the decimal point into places to the **right**.

Q. 56 The___of interests on a sum of ₹ 2000 at the rate of 6% per annum for $1\frac{1}{2}$ yr and 2 yr is ₹ 420.

Sol. Given, P = ₹ 2000 and R = 6%

For $1\frac{1}{2}$ yr, $\qquad I = \dfrac{P \times R \times T}{100}$

$\qquad\qquad\qquad = \dfrac{2000 \times 6 \times 3}{100 \times 2}$

$\qquad\qquad\qquad = ₹\ 180$

For 2 yr, $\qquad I = \dfrac{P \times R \times T}{100}$

$\qquad\qquad\qquad = \dfrac{2000 \times 6 \times 2}{100}$

$\qquad\qquad\qquad = ₹\ 240$

∴ The **sum** of both interests is ₹ (180 + 240), i.e. ₹420.

Q. 57 When converted into percentage, the value of 6.5 is___than 100%.

Sol. We have, 6.5

In percentage, 6.5 × 100% = 650%

Hence, when converted into percentage, the value of 6.5 is **more** than 100%.

In questions 58 and 59, copy each number line. Fill in the blanks, so that each mark on the number line is labelled with a per cent, a fraction and a decimal. Write all fractions in lowest terms.

Q. 58

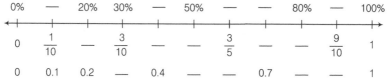

Sol. We know,

Percentage = Fraction ×100

$\qquad$ Fraction $= \dfrac{\text{Percentage}}{100}$

$\qquad$ Decimal $= \dfrac{\text{Percentage}}{100}$

Now, according to these formulae, we have

Percentage	Fraction	Decimal
0%	0	0
10%	$\dfrac{1}{10}$	0.1
20%	$\dfrac{1}{5}$	0.2
30%	$\dfrac{3}{10}$	**0.3**

Percentage	Fraction	Decimal
40%	$\dfrac{2}{5}$	0.4
50%	$\dfrac{1}{2}$	**0.5**
60%	$\dfrac{3}{5}$	**0.6**
70%	$\dfrac{7}{10}$	0.7
80%	$\dfrac{4}{5}$	**0.8**
90%	$\dfrac{9}{10}$	**0.9**
100%	1	1

Q. 59

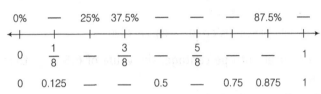

Sol. We know,

Percentage = Fraction ×100

$\text{Fraction} = \dfrac{\text{Percentage}}{100}$

$\text{Decimal} = \dfrac{\text{Percentage}}{100}$

Now, according to these formulae, we have

Percentage	Fraction	Decimal
0%	0	0
12.5%	$\dfrac{1}{8}$	0.125
25%	$\dfrac{1}{4}$	**0.25**
37.5%	$\dfrac{3}{8}$	**0.375**
50%	$\dfrac{1}{2}$	0.5
62.5%	$\dfrac{5}{8}$	**0.625**
75%	$\dfrac{3}{4}$	0.75
87.5%	$\dfrac{7}{8}$	0.875
100%	1	1

True/ False

In questions 60 to 79, state whether the statements are True or False.

Q. 60 $\frac{2}{3} = 66\frac{2}{3}\%$

Sol. *True*

Given, fraction $= \frac{2}{3}$

In percentage, $\frac{2}{3} \times 100\% = \frac{200}{3}\% = 66\frac{2}{3}\%$

Q. 61 When an improper fraction is converted into percentage, then the answer can also be less than 100.

Sol. *False*

Consider, an improper fraction $= \frac{12}{5}$ $(N > D)$

In percentage, $\frac{12}{5} \times 100\% = 240\%$

Hence, when an improper fraction is converted into percentage, then the answer is always greater than 100.

Q. 62 8 h is 50% of 4 days.

Sol. *False*

Let 8 h be $x\%$ of 4 days.

Then,   8 h $= x\%$ of 4 days

$\Rightarrow$ $8 = \frac{x}{100} \times 4 \times 24$ $[\because 1 \text{ day} = 24 \text{ h} \Rightarrow 4 \text{ days} = 4 \times 24 \text{ h}]$

$\Rightarrow$ $\frac{8 \times 100}{4 \times 24} = x$

$\Rightarrow$ $x = \frac{25}{3} = 8\frac{1}{3}$

Hence, 8 h is $8\frac{1}{3}\%$ of 4 days.

Q. 63 The interest on ₹ 350 at 5% per annum for 73 days is ₹ 35.

Sol. *False*

Given, $P = ₹\ 350, R = 5\%$

and $T = 73 \text{ days} = \frac{73}{365}$ yr

$\therefore$ $I = \frac{P \times R \times T}{100}$

$I = \frac{350 \times 5 \times 73}{100 \times 365} = \frac{127750}{36500}$

$I = ₹\ 3.5$

Q. 64 The simple interest on a sum of ₹ P for T yr at R% per annum is given by the formula

$$\text{Simple Interest} = \frac{T \times P \times R}{100}$$

Sol. *True*

$$SI = \frac{P \times R \times T}{100}$$

We can also write it as, $SI = \frac{T \times P \times R}{100}$ [since, multiplication is commutative]

Q. 65 $75\% = \frac{4}{3}$

Sol. *False*

We have, 75%

In fraction, $\frac{75}{100} = \frac{3}{4}$

∴ $75\% = \frac{3}{4}$

Q. 66 12% of 120 is 100.

Sol. *False*

Since, 12% of $120 = \frac{12}{100} \times 120 = \frac{1440}{100} = 14.4$

Therefore, 12% of 120 is 14.4.

Q. 67 If Ankita obtains 336 marks out of 600, then percentage of marks obtained by her is 33.6%.

Sol. *False*

Marks obtained by Ankita out of 600 = 336

Percentage, marks $= \frac{336}{600} \times 100\% = 56\%$

Hence, Ankita got 56% marks.

Q. 68 0.018 is equivalent to 8%.

Sol. *False*

Given, decimal = 0.018

In percentage, $0.018 \times 100 = 1.8\%$

Hence, 0.018 is equivalent to 1.8%.

Q. 69 50% of ₹ 50 is ₹ 25.

Sol. *True*

Since, 50% of ₹ 50 $= \dfrac{50}{100} \times 50 = ₹\,25$

Hence, 50% of ₹ 50 is ₹ 25.

Q. 70 250 cm is 4% of 1 km.

Sol. *False*

$\because \quad 250\,\text{cm} = \dfrac{250}{100} = 2.5\,\text{m}$ $\qquad$ [∵ 1 m = 100 cm]

Now, 4% of 1 km $= \dfrac{4}{100} \times 1000\,\text{m}$ $\qquad$ [∵ 1 km = 1000 m]

$= 40\,\text{m}$

Hence, 250 cm ≠ 4% of 1 km.

Q. 71 Out of 600 students of a school, 126 go for a picnic. The percentage of students that did not go for the picnic, is 75.

Sol. *False*

Total students = 600

Students went for picnic = 126

∴ Students did not go for picnic = 600 − 126 = 474

In percentage, $\dfrac{474}{600} \times 100\% = 79\%$

Hence, 79% of students did not go for picnic.

Q. 72 By selling a book for ₹ 50, a shopkeeper suffers a loss of 10%. The cost price of the book is ₹ 60.

Sol. *False*

Given, SP = ₹ 50 and loss per cent = 10%

We know that,

$$\text{Loss}\% = \dfrac{\text{Loss}}{\text{CP}} \times 100\%$$

$\Rightarrow \qquad \text{Loss}\% = \dfrac{\text{CP} - \text{SP}}{\text{CP}} \times 100$ $\qquad$ [∵ Loss = CP − SP]

$\Rightarrow \qquad 10 = \dfrac{(\text{CP} - 50)}{\text{CP}} \times 100$

$\Rightarrow \qquad 10\,\text{CP} = 100\,\text{CP} - 5000$

$\Rightarrow \qquad 90\,\text{CP} = 5000$

$\Rightarrow \qquad \text{CP} = \dfrac{5000}{90}$

$\therefore \qquad \text{CP} = ₹\,55.55$

Hence, the cost price of the book is ₹ 55.55.

Q. 73 If a chair is bought for ₹ 2000 and is sold at a gain of 10%, then selling price of the chair is ₹ 2010.

Sol. *False*

Given, CP = ₹ 2000 and profit % = 10%

We know that,

$$\text{Profit \%} = \frac{\text{Profit}}{\text{CP}} \times 100\%$$

$$\Rightarrow \quad \text{Profit \%} = \frac{\text{SP} - \text{CP}}{\text{CP}} \times 100\% \qquad [\because \text{Profit} = \text{SP} - \text{CP}]$$

$$\Rightarrow \quad 10 = \frac{\text{SP} - 2000}{2000} \times 100$$

$$\Rightarrow \quad \frac{10 \times 2000}{100} = \text{SP} - 2000$$

$$\Rightarrow \quad 200 = \text{SP} - 2000$$

$$\therefore \quad \text{SP} = ₹ 2200$$

Hence, the SP of chair is ₹ 2200.

Q. 74 If a bicycle was bought for ₹ 650 and sold for ₹ 585, then the percentage of profit is 10%.

Sol. *False*

Given, CP = ₹ 650 and SP = ₹ 585

Since, CP > SP

$$\text{Loss} = \text{CP} - \text{SP} = 650 - 585 = ₹ 65$$

Now, $\quad \text{Loss\%} = \dfrac{\text{Loss}}{\text{CP}} \times 100 = \dfrac{65}{650} \times 100 = 10\%$

Hence, the percentage of loss is 10%.

Q. 75 Sushma sold her watch for ₹ 3320 at a gain of ₹ 320. For earning a gain of 10%, she should have sold the watch for ₹ 3300.

Sol. *True*

Given that, SP = ₹ 3320 and profit = ₹ 320

CP = SP − Profit = 3320 − 320 = ₹ 3000

Now, for earning profit 10%, we have to find new SP.

$$\therefore \quad \text{Profit \%} = \frac{\text{Profit}}{\text{CP}} \times 100\% = \frac{\text{SP} - \text{CP}}{\text{CP}} \times 100\% \qquad [\because \text{Profit} = \text{SP} - \text{CP}]$$

$$10 = \frac{\text{SP} - 3000}{3000} \times 100$$

$$300 = \text{SP} - 3000$$

$$\text{SP} = ₹ 3300$$

Q. 76 Interest on ₹ 1200 for $1\frac{1}{2}$ yr at the rate of 15% per annum is ₹ 180.

Sol. *False*

Given, $P = ₹ 1200$, $T = 1\frac{1}{2}$ yr $= \frac{3}{2}$ yr and $R = 15\%$

$$\therefore \quad I = \frac{P \times R \times T}{100} = \frac{1200 \times 15 \times 3}{2 \times 100} = ₹ 270$$

So, the interest is ₹ 270.

Q. 77 Amount received after depositing ₹ 800 a period of 3 yr at the rate of 12% per annum is ₹ 896.

Sol. *False*

Given, P = ₹ 800, T = 3 yr and R = 12%

$$\therefore \quad I = \frac{P \times R \times T}{100} = \frac{800 \times 12 \times 3}{100} = ₹ 288$$

Also, amount, $(A) = P + I = 800 + 288 = ₹ 1088$

Hence, the amount received is ₹1088.

Q. 78 ₹ 6400 were lent to Feroz and Rashmi at 15% per annum for $3\frac{1}{2}$ and 5 yr, respectively. The difference in the interests paid by them is ₹ 150.

Sol. *False*

Given, Feroz borrowed ₹ 6400 for $3\frac{1}{2}$ yr at 15%.

Here, P_1 = ₹ 6400, $T_1 = 3\frac{1}{2} = \frac{7}{2}$ yr and R_1 = 15%

$$\therefore \quad I_1 = \frac{P_1 \times R_1 \times T_1}{100}$$

$$= \frac{6400 \times 15 \times 7}{100 \times 2} = ₹ 3360$$

Rashmi borrowed ₹ 6400 for 5 yr at 15%.

Here, P_2 = ₹ 6400, R_2 = 15% and T_2 = 5 yr

$$\therefore \quad I_2 = \frac{P_2 \times R_2 \times T_2}{100} = \frac{6400 \times 15 \times 5}{100} = ₹ 4800$$

$\therefore$ Difference between interests = $4800 - 3360 = ₹ 1440$

Hence, the difference in interest, paid by them is ₹ 1440.

Q. 79 A vendor purchased 720 lemons at ₹ 120 per hundred. 10% of the lemons were found rotten, which he sold at ₹ 50 per hundred. If he sells the remaining lemons at ₹ 125 per hundred, then his profit will be 16%.

Sol. *False*

Given, cost price of 100 lemons = ₹ 120

Cost price of 1 lemon = ₹ $\frac{120}{100}$

and cost price of 720 lemons = $\frac{120}{100} \times 720 = ₹ 864$

According to the question, 10% of the lemons were rotten.

$\therefore$ 10% of 720 lemons = $\frac{10}{100} \times 720 = 72$ lemons

Also, given, selling price of 100 rotten lemons = ₹ 50

Selling price of 1 rotten lemon = ₹ $\frac{50}{100}$

and selling price of 72 rotten lemons $= \dfrac{50}{100} \times 72 = ₹\,36$

Also, selling price of 100 good lemons $= ₹\,125$

$\therefore$ Selling price of good lemon $= ₹\,\dfrac{125}{100}$

and selling price of $(720 - 72)$ good lemons $= \dfrac{125}{100} \times (720 - 72) = \dfrac{125}{100} \times 648 = ₹\,810$

Now, total selling price of 720 lemons $= 36 + 810 = ₹\,846$

Clearly, selling price $<$ cost price.

Therefore, vendor will bear loss.

Q. 80 Find the value of x, if

    (a) 8% of ₹ x is ₹ 100.

    (b) 32% of x kg is 400 kg.

    (c) 35% of ₹ x is ₹280.

    (d) 45% of marks x is 405.

Sol.   (a) Given, 8% of ₹ x is ₹ 100.

$$\therefore \quad \dfrac{8}{100} \times x = 100$$

$$\Rightarrow \quad x = \dfrac{100 \times 100}{8}$$

$$\Rightarrow \quad x = ₹\,1250$$

(b) Given, 32% of x kg is 400 kg.

$$\therefore \quad \dfrac{32}{100} \times x = 400$$

$$\Rightarrow \quad x = \dfrac{400 \times 100}{32}$$

$$\Rightarrow \quad x = 1250\,\text{kg}$$

(c) Given, 35% of ₹ x is ₹280.

$$\therefore \quad \dfrac{35}{100} \times x = 280$$

$$\Rightarrow \quad x = \dfrac{280 \times 100}{35}$$

$$\Rightarrow \quad x = ₹\,800$$

(d) Given, 45% of marks x is 405.

$$\therefore \quad \dfrac{45}{100} \times x = 405$$

$$\Rightarrow \quad x = \dfrac{405 \times 100}{45}$$

$$\Rightarrow \quad x = 900\,\text{marks}$$

Q. 81 Imagine that, a 10 × 10 grid has value 300 and that this value is divided evenly among the small squares. In other words, each small square is worth 3. Use a new grid for each part of this problem and label each grid "Value : 300".

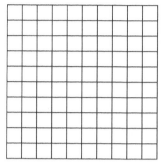

(a) Shade 25% of the grid. What is 25% of 300? Compare the two answers.

(b) What is the value of 25 squares?

(c) Shade 17% of the grid. What is 17% of 300? Compare the two answers.

(d) What is the value of $\dfrac{1}{10}$ of the grid?

Sol. (a) We have to shade 25% of the grid, i.e. $\left(\dfrac{1}{4}\right)$th part of grid.

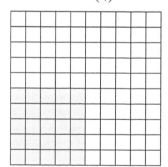

$\left(\dfrac{1}{4}\right)$th of grid covers 25 squares. Since, one square worth 3.

So, total value of 25 such squares = 25 × 3 = 75

Now, 25% of 300 = $\dfrac{25}{100}$ × 300 = 25 × 3 = 75

Hence, the above two values are equal.

(b) Value of 25 squares = 25 × 3 = 75

(c) 17% of grid means 17 squares. So, we will shade 17 squares.

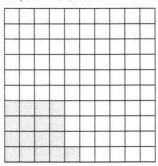

Total value of these 17 squares = 17 × 3 = 51

Now, 17% of 300 = $\dfrac{17}{100}$ × 300 = 17 × 3 = 51

Hence, the above two values are equal.

(d) Value of $\dfrac{1}{10}$ of the grid in percentage = $\dfrac{1}{10}$ × 100% = 10%

So, $\dfrac{1}{10}$ of the grid means 10% value of 300 = $\dfrac{10}{100}$ × 300 = 30

Q. 82 Express $\dfrac{1}{6}$ as a per cent.

Sol. We have, $\dfrac{1}{6}$

In percentage, $\dfrac{1}{6}$ × 100% = $\dfrac{50}{3}$ = 16.6%　　　　　[to convert in per cent, multiply by 100]

Q. 83 Express $\dfrac{9}{40}$ as a per cent.

Sol. We have, $\dfrac{9}{40}$

In percentage, $\dfrac{9}{40}$ × 100% = $22\dfrac{1}{2}$%

Q. 84 Express $\dfrac{1}{100}$ as a per cent.

Sol. We have, $\dfrac{1}{100}$

In percentage, $\dfrac{1}{100}$ × 100% = 1%

Q. 85 Express 80% as a fraction in its lowest form.

Sol. We have, 80%

For fraction, 80 × $\dfrac{1}{100}$ = $\dfrac{80}{100}$ = $\dfrac{4}{5}$　　　　　$\left[\text{to convert in fraction, multiply by } \dfrac{1}{100}\right]$

Q. 86 Express $33\frac{1}{3}\%$ as a ratio in the lowest form.

Sol. We have, $33\frac{1}{3}\%$

For ratio, $33\frac{1}{3}\% : 1 = \frac{100}{3} \times \frac{1}{100} : 1 = \frac{1}{3} : 1 = \frac{1}{3} \times 3 : 1 \times 3 = 1 : 3$

Q. 87 Express $16\frac{2}{3}\%$ as a ratio in the lowest form.

Sol. We have, $16\frac{2}{3}\% = \frac{50}{3}\%$

For ratio, $\frac{50}{3}\% : 1 = \frac{50}{3} \times \frac{1}{100} : 1 = \frac{1}{6} : 1 = \frac{1}{6} \times 6 : 1 \times 6 = 1 : 6$

Q. 88 Express 150% as a ratio in the lowest form.

Sol. We have, 150%

For ratio, $150\% : 1 = \frac{150}{100} : 1 = \frac{3}{2} : 1 = \frac{3}{2} \times 2 : 1 \times 2 = 3 : 2$

Q. 89 Sachin and Sanjana are calculating 23% of 800.

Now, calculate 52% of 700 using both the ways described above. Which way do you find easier?

Sol. **First way** 52% of 700 = (1% of 700) × 52

$$= \left(\frac{1}{100} \times 700\right) \times 52$$

$$= (0.01 \times 700) \times 52$$

$$= 7 \times 52$$

$$= 364$$

Second way

52% of 700 $= \frac{52}{100} \times 700 = 0.52 \times 700$

$$= 364$$

So, second way, we have to find easier.

Q. 90 Write 0.089 as a per cent.

Sol. We have, 0.089

In percentage, 0.089 × 100% = 8.9%   [to convert in per cent, multiply by 100]

Q. 91 Write 1.56 as a per cent.

Sol. We have, 1.56

In percentage, $1.56 \times 100\% = 156\%$

Q. 92 What is 15% of 20?

Sol. We have, 15% of 20

$$= \frac{15}{100} \times 20 = 3$$

Q. 93 What is 800% of 800?

Sol. We have, 800% of 800

$$= \frac{800}{100} \times 800 = 6400$$

Q. 94 What is 100% of 500?

Sol. We have, 100% of 500

$$= \frac{100}{100} \times 500 = 500$$

Q. 95 What per cent of 1 h is 30 min?

Sol. Let $x\%$ of 1 h be 30 min.

Then, $\frac{x}{100} \times 1\,h = 30\,min$

$\Rightarrow \quad \frac{x}{100} \times 60\,min = 30\,min$ $[\because 1\,h = 60\,min]$

$\Rightarrow \quad x = \frac{30 \times 100}{60}$

$\therefore \ x = 50\%$

Hence, 50% of 1 h is 30 min.

Q. 96 What per cent of 1 day is 1 min?

Sol. Let $x\%$ of 1 day be 1 min.

Then, $\frac{x}{100} \times 1\,day = 1\,min$ $[\because 1\,day = 24\,h\ and\ 1\,h = 60\,min]$

$\Rightarrow \quad \frac{x}{100} \times 24\,h = 1\,min$

$\Rightarrow \quad \frac{x}{100} \times 1440\,min = 1\,min$

$\Rightarrow \quad x = \frac{100}{1440} = \frac{10}{144}$

$\therefore \quad x = 0.069\%$

Hence, 0.069% of 1 day is 1 min.

Q. 97 What per cent of 1 km is 1000 m?

Sol. Let $x\%$ of 1 km be 1000 m.

Then, $\dfrac{x}{100} \times 1\,km = 1000\,m$

$\Rightarrow$ $\dfrac{x}{100} \times 1000\,m = 1000\,m$ $\quad[\because 1\,km = 1000\,m]$

$\Rightarrow$ $x \times 10 = 1000$

$\therefore$ $x = 100\%$

Hence, 100% of 1 km is 1000 m.

Q. 98 Find out 8% of 25 kg.

Sol. We have, 8% of 25 kg $= \dfrac{8}{100} \times 25 = 2\,kg$

Q. 99 What per cent of ₹ 80 is ₹ 100?

Sol. Let $x\%$ of ₹ 80 be ₹ 100.

Then, $\dfrac{x}{100} \times 80 = 100$

$\Rightarrow$ $x = \dfrac{100 \times 10}{8}$

$\therefore$ $x = 125\%$

Hence, 125% of ₹ 80 is ₹ 100.

Q. 100 45% of the population of a town are men and 40% are women. What is the percentage of children?

Sol. We have,

Percentage of men in town = 45%

Percentage of women in town = 40%

So, percentage of children in town = 100 − 45 − 40 = 100 − 85 = 15%

Hence, 15% of the population of a town are children.

Q. 101 The strength of a school is 2000. If 40% of the students are girls, then how many boys are there in the school?

Sol. As per the given information in the question,

The strength of school = 2000

Percentage of girls in school = 40%

Percentage of boys in school = 100 − 40 = 60%

Number of boys in school = 60% of 2000 $= \dfrac{60}{100} \times 2000 = 60 \times 20 = 1200$

Hence, number of boys in school is 1200.

Q. 102 Chalk contains 10% calcium, 3% carbon and 12% oxygen. Find the amount of carbon and calcium (in grams) in $2\frac{1}{2}$ kg of chalk.

Sol. We have,

Percentage of calcium in chalk = 10%

Percentage of carbon in chalk = 3%

Percentage of oxygen in chalk = 12%

$\because$ Weight of chalk $= 2\frac{1}{2}$ kg $= \frac{5}{2}$ kg $= 2.5$ kg $= 2.5 \times 1000$ g $= 2500$ gm   [$\because$ 1 kg = 1000 g]

$\therefore$ Amount of carbon in chalk = 3% of 2500 g $= \frac{3}{100} \times 2500 = 25 \times 3 = 75$ g

$\therefore$ Amount of calcium in chalk = 10% of 2500 g $= \frac{10}{100} \times 2500 = 10 \times 25 = 250$ g

Hence, amount of carbon and calcium are 75 g and 250 g, respectively.

Q. 103 800 kg of mortar consists of 55% sand, 33% cement and rest lime. What is the mass of lime in mortar?

Sol. We have,

Percentage of sand in mortar = 55%

Percentage of cement in mortar = 33%

So, percentage of lime in mortar = 100 – 55 – 33 = 100 – 88 = 12%

$\because$ Weight of mortar = 800 kg

$\therefore$ Mass of lime in mortar = 12% of 800 kg $= \frac{12}{100} \times 800 = 12 \times 8 = 96$ kg

Hence, weight of lime in mortar is 96 kg.

Q. 104 In a furniture shop, 24 tables were bought at the rate of ₹ 450 per table. The shopkeeper sold 16 of them at the rate of ₹ 600 per table and the remaining at the rate of 400 per table. Find her gain or loss per cent.

Sol. As per the given information in question,

Cost Price (CP) of per table = ₹ 450

Number of tables = 24

So, cost price of 24 tables = 24 × 450 = ₹ 10800

Since, 16 tables sold at the rate of ₹ 600.

$\therefore$ Selling price of 16 tables = 16 × 600 = ₹ 9600

$\therefore$ Remaining tables = 24 – 16 = 8

Since, 8 tables sold at the rate of ₹ 400.

Selling Price (SP) for 8 tables = 8 × 400 = ₹ 3200

Total selling price = 9600 + 3200 = ₹ 12800

$\therefore$ Profit or gain = SP – CP = 12800 – 10800 = ₹ 2000

Now, gain $= \frac{\text{Gain}}{\text{Cost price}} \times 100\% = \frac{2000}{10800} \times 100\% = \frac{2000}{108}\% = 18.51\%$

Hence, her gain is 18.51%.

Q. 105 Medha deposited 20% of her money in a bank. After spending 20% of the remainder, she has ₹ 4800 left with her. How much did she originally have?

Sol. Let medha has originally ₹ x.

Money deposited in bank = 20% of x = $\dfrac{20}{100} \times x = ₹\dfrac{1}{5}x$

Remaining money = $x - \dfrac{1}{5}x = ₹\dfrac{4}{5}x$

Money spent = 20% of remaining money = $\dfrac{20}{100} \times \dfrac{4}{5}x = \dfrac{1}{5} \times \dfrac{4}{5}x = ₹\dfrac{4}{25}x$

Now, money left = $\dfrac{4}{5}x - \dfrac{4}{25}x = ₹\dfrac{16}{25}x$

But given that, money = ₹ 4800

According to the question,

$$\dfrac{16}{25}x = 4800 \quad \Rightarrow \quad x = \dfrac{4800 \times 25}{16}$$

$\Rightarrow \qquad\qquad\qquad x = ₹\,7500$

Hence, Medha has ₹ 7500 in original.

Q. 106 The cost of a flower vase got increased by 12%. If the current cost is ₹ 896, what was its original cost?

Sol. Let the original cost be ₹ x.

Now, the cost of flower vase is increased by 12%.

So, $\qquad\qquad\qquad x + 12\%$ of x = ₹ 896

$\Rightarrow \qquad\qquad\qquad x + \dfrac{12}{100}x = 896$

$\Rightarrow \qquad\qquad\qquad \dfrac{112x}{100} = 896$

$\Rightarrow \qquad\qquad\qquad x = \dfrac{896 \times 100}{112}$

$\therefore \qquad\qquad\qquad x = ₹\,800$

Hence, original lost of flower vase is ₹ 800.

Q. 107 Radhika borrowed ₹ 12000 from her friends. Out of which ₹ 4000 were borrowed at 18% and the remaining at 15% rate of interest per annum. What is the total interest after 3 yr?

Sol. For first year interest, we have

$P_1 = ₹\,4000$, $R_1 = 18\%$ and $T_1 = 3$ yr

$\because \qquad\qquad\qquad I_1 = \dfrac{P_1 \times R_1 \times T_1}{100}$

$\therefore \qquad\qquad\qquad I_1 = \dfrac{4000 \times 18 \times 3}{100} = ₹\,2160$

For second year interest,

$$P_2 = 12000 - 4000 = ₹\,8000$$
$$R_2 = 15\% \text{ and } T_2 = 3\,\text{yr}$$

$\because$
$$I_2 = \frac{P_2 \times R_2 \times T_2}{100}$$

$\therefore$
$$I_2 = \frac{8000 \times 15 \times 3}{100} = ₹\,3600$$

Hence, after 3 yr, total interest $= I_1 + I_2 = 2160 + 3600 = ₹\,5760$

Q. 108 A man travelled 60 km by car and 240 km by train. Find what per cent of total journey did he travel by car and what per cent by train?

Sol. Distance covered by car $= 60\,\text{km}$

Distance covered by train $= 240\,\text{km}$

$\therefore$ Total journey $= 60 + 240 = 300\,\text{km}$

Let $x\%$ of total journey is travelled by car.

Then, $\qquad\qquad\qquad\qquad\qquad x\%$ of $300 = 60$

$\Rightarrow \qquad\qquad\qquad\qquad \dfrac{x}{100} \times 300 = 60 \quad\Rightarrow\quad x = \dfrac{60 \times 100}{300}$

$\Rightarrow \qquad\qquad\qquad\qquad\qquad\qquad x = 20\%$

Let $y\%$ of total journey is travelled by train.

Then, $\qquad\qquad\qquad\qquad\qquad y\%$ of $300 = 240$

$\Rightarrow \qquad\qquad\qquad\qquad \dfrac{y}{100} \times 300 = 240 \quad\Rightarrow\quad y = \dfrac{240 \times 100}{300}$

$\Rightarrow \qquad\qquad\qquad\qquad\qquad\qquad y = 80\%$

Hence, 20% distance is travelled by car and 80% distance is travelled by train.

Q. 109 By selling a chair for ₹ 1440, a shopkeeper loses 10%. At what price, did he buy it?

Sol. Given, SP $= ₹\,1440$ and loss $= 10\%$

We know that, $\qquad\qquad\qquad \text{Loss}\% = \dfrac{\text{Loss}}{\text{CP}} \times 100\%$

$\Rightarrow \qquad\qquad\qquad\qquad \text{Loss}\% = \dfrac{\text{CP} - \text{SP}}{\text{CP}} \times 100\% \qquad\qquad [\because \text{Lloss} = \text{CP} - \text{SP}]$

$\Rightarrow \qquad\qquad\qquad\qquad 10 = \dfrac{\text{CP} - 1440}{\text{CP}} \times 100$

$\Rightarrow \qquad\qquad\qquad\qquad \dfrac{10}{100}\text{CP} = \text{CP} - 1440$

$\Rightarrow \qquad\qquad\qquad \text{CP} - \dfrac{10}{100}\text{CP} = 1440$

$\Rightarrow \qquad\qquad\qquad\qquad \dfrac{9}{10}\text{CP} = 1440$

$\Rightarrow \qquad\qquad\qquad\qquad \text{CP} = \dfrac{1440 \times 10}{9}$

$\therefore \qquad\qquad\qquad\qquad \text{CP} = ₹\,1600$

Hence, the cost price of chair is ₹ 1600.

Q. 110 Dhruvika invested money for a period from May 2006 to April 2008 at the rate of 12% per annum. If interest received by her is ₹ 1620, then find the money invested.

Sol. Given, I = ₹ 1620 and R = 12%

Time = From May 2006 to April 2008 = 2 yr

$\because$
$$I = \frac{P \times R \times T}{100}$$

$\therefore$
$$P = \frac{I \times 100}{R \times T} = \frac{1620 \times 100}{12 \times 2}$$

$\Rightarrow$
$$P = ₹\, 6750$$

Hence, the invested money is ₹ 6750.

Q. 111 A person wanted to sell a scooter at a loss of 25%. But at the last moment, he changed his mind and sold the scooter at a loss of 20%. If the difference in the two SP's is ₹ 4000, then find the CP of the scooter.

Sol. Let cost price of the scooter be ₹ x.

If he sells the scooter at a loss of 25%, then

$$SP = x - 25\% \text{ of } x = x - \frac{25}{100}x = ₹\,\frac{75}{100}x$$

and if he sells the scooter at a loss of 20%, then

$$SP = x - 20\% \text{ of } x = x - \frac{20}{100}x = \frac{80}{100}x$$

It is given that the difference in the two SP's is ₹ 4000.

$\therefore$
$$\frac{80}{100}x - \frac{75}{100}x = 4000$$

$\Rightarrow$
$$\frac{80x - 75x}{100} = 4000$$

$\Rightarrow$
$$\frac{5x}{100} = 4000$$

$\Rightarrow$
$$x = \frac{4000 \times 100}{5} = ₹\, 80000$$

Hence, cost price of scooter is ₹ 80000.

Q. 112 The population of a village is 8000. Out of these, 80% are literate and of these literate people, 40% are women. Find the ratio of the number of literate women to the total population.

Sol. We have, total population = 8000

Literate people = 80% of total population = $\dfrac{80}{100} \times 8000 = 6400$

Literate women = 40% of literate people = $\dfrac{40}{100} \times 6400 = 2560$

Ratio of literate women to total population = $2560 : 8000 = \dfrac{2560}{320} : \dfrac{8000}{320} = 8 : 25$

Hence, the ratio of women to total population is 8 : 25.

Q. 113 In an entertainment programme, 250 tickets of ₹ 400 and 500 tickets of ₹ 100 were sold. If the entertainment tax is 40% on ticket of ₹ 400 and 20% on ticket of ₹ 100, then find how much entertainment tax was collected from the programme?

Sol. It is given that, 250 tickets of ₹ 400 were sold. Therefore, total amount received by selling these tickets $= 250 \times 400 = ₹ 100000$

Similarly, amount received by selling 500 tickets of ₹ 100 $= 500 \times 100 = ₹ 50000$

It is also given that, 40% and 20% of entertainment tax is on ₹ 400 and ₹ 100 tickets, respectively.

So, total entertainment tax collected

$$= 40\% \text{ of total amount received by selling tickets of } ₹ 400$$
$$+ 20\% \text{ of total amount received by selling tickets of } ₹ 100$$
$$= 40\% \text{ of } 100000 + 20\% \text{ of } 50000$$
$$= \frac{40}{100} \times 100000 + \frac{20}{100} \times 50000$$
$$= 40000 + 10000$$
$$= ₹ 50000$$

Hence, the total collected entertainment tax was ₹ 50000.

Q. 114 Bhavya earns ₹ 50000 per month and spends 80% of it. Due to pay revision, her monthly income increases by 20% but due to price rise, she has to spent 20% more. Find her new savings.

Sol. Given, Bhavya earns per month $= ₹ 50000$

She spends per month $= 80\% \text{ of } 50000 = \frac{80}{100} \times 50000 = ₹ 40000$

Then, her per month savings $= 50000 - 40000 = ₹ 10000$

$$[\because \text{saving} = \text{total income} - \text{expenditure}]$$

Also, given increment in monthly income $= 20\% \text{ of } 50000$

$$= \frac{20}{100} \times 50000 = ₹ 10000$$

$\therefore$ Bhavya's new income $= 50000 + 10000 = ₹ 60000$

Increase in expenditure $= 20\% \text{ of } 40000 = \frac{20}{100} \times 40000 = ₹ 8000$

So, new expenditure $= 40000 + 8000 = ₹ 48000$

Now, Bhavya's new savings $= 60000 - 48000 = ₹ 12000$

Q. 115 In an examination, there are three papers each of 100 marks. A candidate obtained 53 marks in the first paper and 75 marks in the second paper. How many marks must the candidate obtain in the third paper to get an overall of 70% marks?

Sol. Let x be the marks of candidate in third paper.

Then, total marks secured in all three papers $= 53 + 75 + x$

Total marks of three papers $= 100 + 100 + 100 = 300$

$$\therefore \text{Percentage of maks} = \left(\frac{\text{Total marks secured}}{\text{Total marks}}\right) \times 100\% = \frac{53 + 75 + x}{300} \times 100\%$$

But it is given that, he obtained overall of 70% marks.

$$\therefore \qquad \frac{53 + 75 + x}{300} \times 100 = 70$$

$$\Rightarrow \qquad \frac{128 + x}{3} = 70$$

$$\Rightarrow \qquad 128 + x = 210 \Rightarrow x = 210 - 128$$

$$\therefore \qquad x = 82$$

Hence, he must secure 82 marks in the third paper to get an overall of 70% marks.

Q. 116 Health Application

A doctor reports blood pressure in millimetres of mercury (mm Hg) as a ratio of systolic blood pressure to diastolic blood pressure (such as 140 over 80). Systolic pressure is measured when the heart beats and diastolic pressure is measured when it rests. Refer to the table of blood pressure ranges for adults.

Blood Pressure Ranges			
	Normal	Prehypertension	Hypertension (Very High)
Systolic	Under 120 mm Hg	120-139 mm Hg	140 mm Hg and above
Diastolic	Under 80 mm Hg	80-89 mm Hg	90 mm Hg and above

Manohar is a healthy 37 yr old man whose blood pressure is in the normal category.

(a) Calculate an approximate ratio of systolic to diastolic blood pressures in the normal range.

(b) If Manohar's systolic blood pressure is 102 mm Hg, then use the ratio from part (a) to predict his diastolic blood pressure.

(c) Calculate ratio of average systolic to average diastolic blood pressures in the prehypertension category.

Sol. (a) Systolic blood pressure in the normal range = 120 mm Hg

Diastolic blood pressure in the normal range = 80 mm Hg

Approximate ratio of systolic to diastolic blood pressure

$$= \frac{\text{Systolic blood pressure in normal range}}{\text{Diastolic blood pressure in normal range}} = \frac{120}{80} = \frac{3}{2}$$

[dividing numerator and denominator by 40]

Hence, approximate ratio is 3:2.

(b) Manohar's systolic blood pressure = 102 mm Hg

Let diastolic blood pressure = x mm Hg

According to the question,

$$\frac{\text{Systolic blood pressure}}{\text{Diastolic blood pressure}} = \frac{3}{2} \qquad \text{[from part (a)]}$$

$$\Rightarrow \qquad \frac{102}{x} = \frac{3}{2}$$

$$\Rightarrow \qquad x = \frac{102 \times 2}{3}$$

$\therefore \qquad\qquad x = 68 \text{mm Hg}$

Hence, Manohar's diastolic blood pressure is 68 mm Hg.

(c) Average systolic blood pressure in prehypertension category $= \dfrac{120 + 139}{2}$

$$= \frac{259}{2} \text{mm Hg}$$

Average diastolic blood pressure in prehypertension category $= \dfrac{80 + 89}{2}$

$$= \frac{169}{2} \text{mm Hg}$$

Hence, ratio of average systolic to average diastolic blood pressures

$$= \frac{\text{Average systolic blood pressure}}{\text{Average diastolic blood pressure}} = \frac{\dfrac{259}{2}}{\dfrac{169}{2}} = \frac{259}{2} \times \frac{2}{169} = \frac{259}{169}$$

Hence, required ratio is 259 : 169.

Q. 117 (a) **Science Application**

The king cobra can reach a length of 558 cm. This is only about 60% of the length of the largest reticulated python. Find the length of the largest reticulated python.

(b) **Physical Science Application**

Unequal masses will not balance on a fulcrum, if they are at equal distance from it, one side will go up and the other side will go down.

Unequal masses will balance when the following proportion is true.

$$\frac{\text{Mass 1}}{\text{Length 2}} = \frac{\text{Mass 2}}{\text{Length 1}}$$

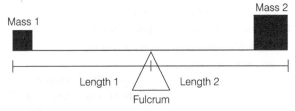

Two children can be balanced on a see saw, when

$$\frac{\text{mass 1}}{\text{length 2}} = \frac{\text{mass 2}}{\text{length 1}}.$$

The child on the left and child on the right are balanced. What is the mass of the child on the right?

24 kg

?

3 m   2 m

(c) **Life Science Application**

A DNA model was built using the scale 2 cm : 0.0000001 mm. If the model of the DNA chain is 17 cm long, what is the length of the actual chain?

Sol. (a) Length of the king cobra = 558 cm

According to the question,

60% of length of reticulated python = 558 cm

$\Rightarrow \dfrac{60}{100} \times$ Length of reticulated python = 558 cm

$\therefore$ Length of reticulated python = $558 \times \dfrac{100}{60}$ = 930 cm

(b) It is given that, for balancing, $\dfrac{\text{Mass 1}}{\text{Length 2}} = \dfrac{\text{Mass 2}}{\text{Length 1}}$

According to the question,

Mass 1 = 24 kg, length 1 = 3 m and length 2 = 2 m

$\therefore \qquad\qquad \dfrac{24}{2} = \dfrac{\text{Mass 2}}{3}$ \qquad [by cross-multiplication]

$\Rightarrow \qquad\qquad \text{Mass 2} = \dfrac{24 \times 3}{2} = 36\,\text{kg}$

(c) Let the length of the actual chain be x mm. Therefore,

$$\dfrac{2\ \text{cm}}{0.0000001\ \text{mm}} = \dfrac{17\ \text{cm}}{x\ \text{mm}}$$

$\Rightarrow \qquad\qquad x = \dfrac{17 \times 0.0000001}{2}$

$\qquad\qquad\qquad = 8.5 \times 0.0000001 = 0.00000085\,\text{mm}$

Q. 118 Language Application

Given below are few mathematical terms.

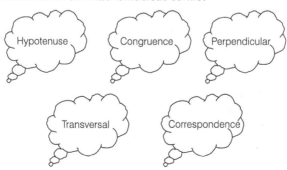

Hypotenuse   Congruence   Perpendicular

Transversal   Correspondence

Find

(a) The ratio of consonants to vowels in each of the terms.

(b) The percentage of consonants in each of the terms.

Sol.   (a) In mathematical term "Hypotenuse",

Number of consonants = 6, i.e. (h, y, p, t, n, s)

Number of vowels = 4, i.e. (o, e, u, e)

Ratio of consonants to vowels $= \dfrac{\text{Number of consonants}}{\text{Number of vowels}} = \dfrac{6}{4} = \dfrac{3}{2}$

Hence, ratio is 3 : 2.

In mathematical term "Congruence,"

Number of consonants = 6, i.e. (c, n, g, r, n, c)

Number of vowels = 4, i.e. (o, u, e, e)

Ratio of consonants to vowels $= \dfrac{\text{Number of consonants}}{\text{Number of vowels}} = \dfrac{6}{4} = \dfrac{3}{2}$

Hence, ratio is 3 : 2.

In mathematical term "Perpendicular",

Number of consonants = 8, i.e. (p, r, p, n, d, c, l, r)

Number of vowels = 5, i.e. (e, e, i, u, a)

Ratio of consonants to vowels $= \dfrac{\text{Number of consonants}}{\text{Number of vowels}} = \dfrac{8}{5}$

Hence ratio is 8 : 5.

In mathematical term "Transversal",

Number of consonants = 8, i.e. (t, r, n, s, v, r, s, l)

Number of vowels = 3, i.e. (a, e, a)

Ratio of consonants to vowels $= \dfrac{\text{Number of consonants}}{\text{Number of vowels}} = \dfrac{8}{3}$

Hence, ratio is 8 : 3.

In mathematical term "Correspondence",

Number of consonants = 9, i.e. (c, r, r, s, p, n, d, n, c)

Number of vowels = 5, i.e. (o, e, o, e, e)

Ratio of consonants to vowels $= \dfrac{\text{Number of consonants}}{\text{Number of vowels}} = \dfrac{9}{5}$

Hence, ratio is 9 : 5.

(b) In mathematical term "Hypotenuse",

Number of consonants = 6

Number of vowels = 4 (already calculated)

Total number of letters = Number of consonants + Number of vowels = 6 + 4 = 10

Percentage of consonants $= \dfrac{\text{Number of consonants}}{\text{Total number of letters}} \times 100\% = \dfrac{6}{10} \times 100\% = 60\%$

Hence, percentage of consonants is 60%.

In mathematical term "Congruence",

Number of consonants = 6

Number of vowels = 4 (already calculated)

Total number of letters = Number of consonants + Number of vowels = 6 + 4 = 10

Percentage of consonants $= \dfrac{\text{Number of consonants}}{\text{Total number of letters}} \times 100\% = \dfrac{6}{10} \times 100\%$

Hence, percentage of consonants is 60%.

In mathematical term "Perpendicular",

Number of consonants = 8

Number of vowels = 5 (already calculated)

Total number of letters = Number of consonants + Number of vowels = 8 + 5 = 13

Percentage of consonants = $\dfrac{\text{Number of consonants}}{\text{Total number of letters}} \times 100\% = \dfrac{8}{13} \times 100\% = 61.53\%$

Hence, percentage of consonants is 61.53%.

In mathematical term "Transversal",

Number of consonants = 8

Number of vowels = 3 (already calculated)

Total number of letters = Number of consonants + Number of vowels = 8 + 3 = 11

Percentage of consonants = $\dfrac{\text{Number of consonants}}{\text{Total number of letters}} \times 100\% = \dfrac{8}{11} \times 100\% = 72.72\%$

Hence, percentage of consonants is 72.72%.

In mathematical term "Correspondence",

Number of consonants = 9

Number of vowels = 5 (already calculated)

Total number of letters = Number of consonants + Number of vowels = 9 + 5 = 14

Percentage of consonants = $\dfrac{\text{Number of consonants}}{\text{Total number of letters}} \times 100\% = \dfrac{9}{14} \times 100\% = 64.28\%$

Hence, percentage of consonants is 64.28%.

Q. 119 What's the Error? An analysis showed that 0.06% of the T-shirts made by one company were defective. A student says this is 6 out of every 100. What is the student's error?

Sol. According to the analysis,

Defective T-shirts made by one company = 0.06%

$$= \frac{0.06}{100} = \frac{6}{10000}$$

But according to the student, defective T-shirts = 6 out of every 100 = $\dfrac{6}{100}$

Hence, student's error is that, the defective T-shirts are 6 out of every 10000 (not 100).

Q. 120 What's the Error? A student said that the ratios $\dfrac{3}{4}$ and $\dfrac{9}{16}$ were proportional. What error did the student make?

Sol. Two ratios $a : b$ and $c : d$ are said to be proportional, if $\dfrac{a}{b} = \dfrac{c}{d}$ or $ad = bc$.

But in the given ratios $\dfrac{3}{4}$ and $\dfrac{9}{16}$, $3 \times 16 \neq 4 \times 9$.

Hence, the ratios are not proportional. To make a ratio proportional to another ratio, we just simply multiply both numerator and denominator by same number.

In our given case, student had multiply numerator by 3 and denominator by 4, which is incorrect.

Q. 121 What's the Error? A clothing store charges ₹ 1024 for 4 T-shirts. A student says that the unit price is ₹ 25.6 per T-shirt. What is the error? What is the correct unit price?

Sol. By unitary method,

Cost of 4 T-shirts = ₹ 1024

Cost of 1 T-shirt = $\frac{1024}{4}$ = ₹ 256

Hence, the correct unit price is ₹ 256.

Q. 122 A tea merchant blends two varieties of tea in the ratio of 5 : 4. The cost of first variety is ₹ 200 per kg and that of second variety is ₹ 300 per kg. If he sells the blended tea at the rate of ₹ 275 per kg, then find out the percentage of his profit or loss.

Sol. Given, ratio of blended two varieties of tea (green tea : lemon tea) = 5 : 4

Cost of green tea = ₹ 200 per kg

Cost of lemon tea = ₹ 300 per kg

SP of blended tea = ₹ 275 per kg

According to the ratio,

Let green tea be $5x$ kg and lemon tea be $4x$ kg.

Then, cost of green tea = $5x \times 200$ = ₹ $1000x$

Cost of lemon tea = $4x \times 300$ = ₹ $1200x$

Total CP = $1000x + 1200x$ = ₹ $2200x$

Total quantity = $4x + 5x = 9x$ kg

So, for $9x$ kg,

∴ SP of blended tea = $275 \times 9x$ = ₹ $2475x$

∵　　　　　　　　　　　CP < SP

So, there is profit on blended tea.

Profit = SP – CP

= $2475x - 2200x$ = ₹ $275x$

Profit % = $\frac{\text{Profit}}{\text{CP}} \times 100\%$ = $\frac{275x}{2200x} \times 100\%$ = $\frac{275}{22}$ = 12.5%

Hence, there is 12.5% profit on blended tea (new variety).

Q. 123 A piece of cloth 5 m long shrinks 10% on washing. How long will the cloth be after washing?

Sol. Length of shrink cloth = 10% of 5 m = $\frac{10}{100} \times 5 = \frac{1}{2}$ m

∴ Length of cloth after wash = $5 - \frac{1}{2} = \frac{9}{2}$ = 4.5 m

Q. 124 Nancy obtained 426 marks out of 600 and the marks obtained by Rohit are 560 out of 800. Whose performance is better?

Sol. Nancy got marks = 426 out of 600.

Percentage marks = $\dfrac{426}{600} \times 100\% = 71\%$

Rohit got marks = 560 out of 800.

Percentage marks = $\dfrac{560}{800} \times 100\% = 70\%$

Hence, Nancy's performance is better, since she got 1% more than Rohit.

Q. 125 A memorial trust donates ₹ 500000 to a school, the interest on which is to be used for awarding 3 scholarships to students obtaining first three positions in the school examination every year. If the donation earns an interest of 12% per annum and the values of the second and third scholarships are ₹ 20000 and ₹ 15000 respectively, then find out the value of the first scholarship.

Sol. Donation amount = ₹ 500000

Rate of interest for each year = 12% per annum

Time period = 1 yr

Interest received after 1 yr = $\dfrac{500000 \times 12 \times 1}{100} = 5000 \times 12 = ₹\,60000$

Scholarship amount for second position = ₹ 20000

Scholarship amount for third position = ₹ 15000

∴ Remaining amount for first position student = 60000 − (20000 + 15000)

= 60000 − 35000 = ₹ 25000

Q. 126 Ambika got 99% marks in Mathematics, 76% marks in Hindi, 61% in English, 84% in Science and 95% in Social Science. If each subject carries 100 marks, then find the percentage of marks obtained by Ambika in the aggregate of all the subjects.

Sol. It is given that, each subject carries 100 marks.

∴ Ambika got marks in

Mathematics = 99

Hindi = 76

English = 61

Science = 84

Social Science = 95

Now, aggregate percentage of marks = $\dfrac{\text{Marks obtained by Ambika}}{\text{Total marks}} \times 100\%$

$= \dfrac{(99 + 76 + 61 + 84 + 95)}{500} \times 100\% = \dfrac{415}{5} = 83\%$

Q. 127 What sum of money lent out at 16% per annum simple interest, so that it would produce ₹ 9600 as interest in 2 yr?

Sol.   Here, $I = ₹\ 9600, T = 2$ yr and $R = 16\%$

$$\because \qquad I = \frac{P \times R \times T}{100}$$

$$\therefore \qquad P = \frac{I \times 100}{R \times T} = \frac{9600 \times 100}{16 \times 2}$$

$$\Rightarrow \qquad P = ₹\ 30000$$

Hence, the sum/principal is ₹ 30000.

Q. 128 Harish bought a gas-chullah for ₹ 900 and later sold it to Archana at a profit of 5%. Archana used it for a period of two years and later sold it to Babita at a loss of 20%. For how much did Babita get it?

Sol.   It is given that, Harish bought the chullah for ₹ 900 and sold it to Archana at a profit of 5%.

∴ Cost price of chullah for Archana = 900 + 5% of 900

$$= 900 + \frac{5}{100} \times 900 = 900 + 45 = 945$$

Now, Archana sold it to Babita at a loss of 20%.

∴ Cost price of chullah for Babita = 945 – 20% of ₹ 945

$$= 945 - \frac{20}{100} \times 945 = 945 - 189 = ₹\ 756$$

Hence, Babita got chullah at ₹ 756.

Q. 129 Match each of the entries in Column I with the appropriate entries in Column II.

	Column I		Column II
(i)	3 : 5	A.	₹ 54
(ii)	2.5	B.	₹ 47
(iii)	100%	C.	₹ 53
(iv)	$\dfrac{2}{3}$	D.	₹ 160
(v)	$6\dfrac{1}{4}\%$	E.	60%
(vi)	12.5%	F.	25%
(vii)	SP when CP = ₹ 50 and loss = 6%	G.	$\dfrac{1}{16}$
(viii)	SP when CP = ₹ 50 and profit = ₹ 4	H.	250%
(ix)	Profit % when CP = ₹ 40 and SP = ₹ 50	I.	₹ 159
(x)	Profit % when CP = ₹ 50 and SP = ₹ 60	J.	$66\dfrac{2}{3}\%$
(xi)	Interest when principal = ₹ 800, rate of interest = 10% per annum and period = 2 yr	K.	20%
(xii)	Amount when principal = ₹ 150, Rate of interest = 6% per annum and period = 1yr	L.	0.125
		M.	3 : 2
		N.	₹ 164
		O.	3 : 3

Sol. (i) → (E)

Given, ratio = 3 : 5

In percentage, $\dfrac{3}{5} \times 100\% = 60\%$

(ii) → (H)

We have, 2.5

In percentage, $2.5 \times 100\% = 250\%$

(iii) → (O)

We have, 100%

$$\text{Ratio} = 100\% : 1$$
$$= \dfrac{100}{100} : 1$$

∴ $\quad$ Ratio $= 1 : 1$
$$= 1 \times 3 : 1 \times 3 \qquad \text{[multiplying by 3 on both sides]}$$
$$= 3 : 3$$

(iv) → (J)

We have, $\dfrac{2}{3}$

In percentage, $\quad \dfrac{2}{3} \times 100\% = 66\dfrac{2}{3}\%$

(v) → (G)

We have, $\quad 6\dfrac{1}{4}\% = \dfrac{25}{4}\%$

For fraction, $\quad \dfrac{25}{4} \times \dfrac{1}{100} = \dfrac{1}{16}$

(vi) → (L)

We have, 12.5%

For fraction, $\quad \dfrac{125}{10} \times \dfrac{1}{100} = \dfrac{125}{1000}$

For decimal, $\quad \dfrac{125}{1000} = 0.125$

(vii) → (B)

Given, $\quad$ CP = ₹ 50, Loss% = 6%, SP = ?

We know that,

$$\text{Loss}\% = \dfrac{\text{Loss}}{\text{CP}} \times 100\%$$

⇒ $\quad \text{Loss}\% = \dfrac{\text{CP} - \text{SP}}{\text{CP}} \times 100\% \qquad [\because \text{Loss} = \text{CP} - \text{SP}]$

⇒ $\quad 6 = \dfrac{(50 - \text{SP})}{50} \times 100$

⇒ $\quad \dfrac{6 \times 50}{100} = 50 - \text{SP}$

∴ $\quad \text{SP} = ₹ 47$

(viii) → (A)

Given, CP = ₹ 50, Profit = ₹ 4, SP = ?

We know that,   Profit = SP − CP

⇒   SP = Profit + CP

∴   SP = 4 + 50 = ₹ 54

(ix) → (F)

Given, CP = ₹ 40, SP = ₹ 50, Profit% = ?

We know that,   Profit = SP − CP = 50 − 40 = ₹ 10

Now,   Profit % = $\dfrac{\text{Profit}}{\text{CP}} \times 100\% = \dfrac{10}{40} \times 100\%$

∴   Profit% = 25%

(x) → (K)

Given, CP = ₹ 50, SP = ₹ 60, Profit% = ?

We know that,

$$\text{Profit} = \text{SP} - \text{CP}$$

$$\text{Profit} = 60 - 50 = ₹\ 10$$

Now,   Profit % = $\dfrac{\text{Profit}}{\text{CP}} \times 100\% = \dfrac{10}{50} \times 100\%$

∴ Profit% = 20%

(xi) → (D)

Given, $P = ₹\ 800, R = 10\%, T = 2$ yr, $I = ?$

∴ $I = \dfrac{P \times R \times T}{100} = \dfrac{800 \times 10 \times 2}{100} = 160$

= ₹ 160

(xii) → (I)

Given, $P = ₹\ 150, R = 6\%, T = 1$yr, $A = ?$

∵ $I = \dfrac{P \times R \times T}{100}$

∴ $I = \dfrac{150 \times 6 \times 1}{100} = ₹\ 9$

Now, $A = P + I$

= 150 + 9

= ₹ 159

Q. 130 In a debate competition, the judges decide that 20% of the total marks would be given for accent and presentation. 60% of the rest are reserved for the subject matter and the rest are for rebuttal. If this means 8 marks for rebuttal, then find the total marks.

Sol.   Let x be the total marks.

Marks given for accent and presentation = 20% of $x = \dfrac{20}{100} \times x = \dfrac{x}{5}$

Remaining marks = $x - \dfrac{x}{5} = \dfrac{4x}{5}$

Marks reserved for subject matter = 60% of rest marks = $\dfrac{60}{100} \times \dfrac{4x}{5} = \dfrac{12x}{25}$

Now, remaining marks $= \dfrac{4x}{5} - \dfrac{12x}{25} = \dfrac{20x - 12x}{25} = \dfrac{8x}{25}$

According to the question,

$$\dfrac{8x}{25} = 8$$

$\Rightarrow \qquad x = \dfrac{8 \times 25}{8} = 25$

Hence, total marks are 25.

Q. 131 Divide ₹ 10000 in two parts, so that the simple interest on the first part for 4 yr at 12% per annum may be equal to the simple interest on the second part for 4.5 yr at 16% per annum.

Sol. Given, money = ₹ 10000

Now, we have divide ₹ 10000 in two parts such that SI on first part for 4 yr at 12% per annum may be equal to the SI on second part for 4.5 yr at 16%.

Let first part = ₹ x

Then, second part = ₹ $(10000 - x)$

For first part, we have $P_1 = ₹\, x, T_1 = 4\,\text{yr}$ and $R_1 = 12\%$

$\therefore \qquad \text{SI}_1 = \dfrac{P_1 \times R_1 \times T_1}{100} = \dfrac{x \times 12 \times 4}{100}$

For second part $(10000 - x)$, we have

$$P_2 = ₹(10000 - x), T_2 = 4.5\,\text{yr} \text{ and } R_2 = 16\%$$

$\therefore \qquad \text{SI}_2 = \dfrac{P_2 \times R_2 \times T_2}{100} = \dfrac{(10000 - x) \times 16 \times 4.5}{100}$

Since, SI_1 is equal to SI_2.

Then, according to the question,

$$\dfrac{x \times 12 \times 4}{100} = \dfrac{(10000 - x) \times 16 \times 4.5}{100}$$

$\Rightarrow \qquad 48x = (10000 - x) \times 16 \times 4.5$

$\Rightarrow \qquad \dfrac{48x}{4.5 \times 16} = (10000 - x)$

$\Rightarrow \qquad \dfrac{48x \times 10}{45 \times 16} = 10000 - x$

$\Rightarrow \qquad \dfrac{2}{3}x = 10000 - x \Rightarrow \dfrac{2}{3}x + x = 10000$

$\Rightarrow \qquad \dfrac{5x}{3} = 10000 \Rightarrow x = 10000 \times \dfrac{3}{5} = 6000$

First part = x = ₹ 6000

Second part = $10000 - x$ = $10000 - 6000$ = ₹ 4000

Hence, two parts of the sum are ₹ 6000 and ₹ 4000.

Q. 132 ₹ 9000 becomes ₹ 18000 at simple interest in 8 yr. Find the rate per cent per annum.

Sol. Given, $P = ₹\ 9000$, $A = ₹\ 18000$ and $T = 8\,yr$

As we know, $A = P + I$

$\Rightarrow \qquad\qquad I = A - P = 18000 - 9000$

$\Rightarrow \qquad\qquad I = ₹\ 9000$

Now, $\qquad\quad I = \dfrac{P \times R \times T}{100}$

$\Rightarrow \qquad\quad R = \dfrac{I \times 100}{P \times T} = \dfrac{9000 \times 100}{9000 \times 8}$

$\therefore \qquad\qquad R = 12.5\%$

Hence, the rate of interest per annum is 12.5%.

Q. 133 In how many years, will the simple interest on a certain sum be 4.05 times the principal at 13.5% per annum?

Sol. Let principal $= P$

$\qquad\qquad R = 13.5\%$

$\qquad\qquad I = 4.05$ times principal $= 4.05 \times P$

$\qquad\qquad T = ?$

We know that, $I = \dfrac{P \times R \times T}{100} \quad \Rightarrow \quad 4.05 \times P = \dfrac{P \times 13.5 \times T}{100}$

$\Rightarrow \qquad\qquad T = \dfrac{405P}{P \times 13.5} \quad \Rightarrow \quad \dfrac{405 \times 10}{135} = 30\,yr$

Q. 134 The simple interest on a certain sum for 8 yr at 12% per annum is ₹ 3120 more than the simple interest on the same sum for 5 yr at 14% per annum. Find the sum.

Sol. Given, $I_1 - I_2 = ₹\ 3120$,

$\qquad\qquad T_1 = 8\,yr,\ R_1 = 12\%$

$\qquad\qquad T_2 = 5\,yr,\ R_2 = 14\%$

and $\qquad\quad P_1 = P_2 = P$

According to the question,

$\qquad\qquad\qquad\qquad\qquad I_1 - I_2 = 3120$

$\Rightarrow \qquad\quad \dfrac{P_1 \times R_1 \times T_1}{100} - \dfrac{P_2 \times R_2 \times T_2}{100} = 3120$

$\Rightarrow \qquad\quad \dfrac{P \times 12 \times 8}{100} - \dfrac{P \times 14 \times 5}{100} = 3120$

$\Rightarrow \qquad\qquad \dfrac{P}{100}[12 \times 8 - 14 \times 5] = 3120$

$\Rightarrow \qquad\qquad\qquad P[96 - 70] = 3120 \times 100$

$\Rightarrow \qquad\qquad\qquad\qquad 26P = 312000$

$\Rightarrow \qquad\qquad\qquad\qquad\quad P = \dfrac{312000}{26}$

$\therefore \qquad\qquad\qquad\qquad\quad P = ₹\ 12000$

Hence, the sum is ₹ 12000.

Q. 135 The simple interest on a certain sum for 2.5 yr at 12% per annum is
₹ 300 less than the simple interest on the same sum for 4.5 yr at 8%
per annum. Find the sum.

Sol.   Let the sum be x.

Given that, $P_1 = x, R_1 = 12\%$ and $T_1 = 2.5\,\text{yr} = \dfrac{5}{2}\,\text{yr}$

and $P_2 = x, R_2 = 8\%$ and $T_2 = 4.5\,\text{yr} = \dfrac{9}{2}\,\text{yr}$

According to the question,

$$I_2 - I_1 = 300$$

$$\Rightarrow \qquad \frac{P_2 \times R_2 \times T_2}{100} - \frac{P_1 \times R_1 \times T_1}{100} = 300$$

$$\Rightarrow \qquad \frac{x \times 8 \times 9}{2 \times 100} - \frac{x \times 12 \times 5}{2 \times 100} = 300$$

$$\Rightarrow \qquad 72x - 60x = 300 \times 200$$

$$\Rightarrow \qquad 12x = 60000$$

$$\therefore \qquad x = ₹\,5000$$

Hence, the sum/principal is ₹ 5000.

Q. 136 Designing a Healthy Diet

When you design your healthy diet, you want to make sure that you
meet the dietary requirements to help you grow into a healthy adult.

As you plan your menu, follow the following guidelines.

1. Calculate your ideal weight as per your height from the table given
   at the end of this question.
2. An active child should eat around 55.11 calories for each kilogram
   desired weight.
3. 55% of calories should come from carbohydrates. There are
   4 calories in each gram of carbohydrates.
4. 15% of your calories should come from proteins. There are 4 calories
   in each gram of proteins.
5. 30% of your calories may come from fats. There are 9 calories in
   each gram of fats.

Following is an example to design your own healthy diet.

1. Ideal weight = 40 kg
2. The number of calories needed = $40 \times 55.11 = 2204.4$ calories
3. Calories that should come from carbohydrates = 2204.4×0.55

   $$= 1212.42 \text{ calories}$$

   Therefore, required quantity of carbohydrates = $\dfrac{1212.42}{4}$

   $$= 303.105\,\text{g} = 300\,\text{g (approx.)}$$

4. Calories that should come from proteins = 2204.4×0.15

   $$= 330.66 \text{ calories}$$

   Therefore, required quantity of proteins = $\dfrac{330.66}{4} = 82.66\,\text{g}$

5. Calories that may come from fats = 2204.4 × 0.3

= 661.3 calories

Therefore, required quantity of fats = $\dfrac{661.3}{9}$ = 73.48 g

Answer the given questions.

(i) Your ideal desired weight is ....kg.

(ii) The quantity of calories you need to at is ....

(iii) The quantity of proteins needed is .... g.

(iv) The quantity of fats required is .... g.

(v) The quantity of carbohydrates required is .... g.

Ideal Height and Weight Proportion

Men			Women		
Height		Weight	Height		Weight
Feet	Centimetres	Kilograms	Feet	Centimetres	Kilograms
5′	152	48	4′7″	140	34
5′1″	155	51	4′8″	142	36
5′2″	157	54	4′9″	145	39
5′3″	160	56	4′10″	147	41
5′4″	163	59	4′11″	150	43
5′5″	165	62	5′	152	45
5′6″	168	65	5′1″	155	48
5′7″	170	67	5′2″	157	50
5′8″	173	70	5′3″	160	52
5′9″	175	73	5′4″	163	55
5′10″	178	75	5′5″	165	57
5′11″	180	78	5′6″	168	59
6′	183	81	5′7″	170	61
6′1″	185	84	5′8″	173	64
6′2″	188	86	5′9″	175	66
6′3″	191	89	5′10″	178	68
6′4″	193	92	5′11″	180	70

Sol. (i) Let my height be 5 ft.

Then, according to the table, my ideal weight = 48 kg

(ii) The quantity of calories needed = 48 × 55.11 = 2645.28 calories

(iii) Calorie that should come from proteins = 2645.28 × 0.15 = 396.79 calories

Therefore, required quantity of protein = $\dfrac{396.79}{4}$ = 99.19 g

(iv) Calories that may come from fats = 2645.28 × 0.3 = 793.5 calories

Therefore, required quantity of fats = $\dfrac{793.5}{9}$ = 88.17 g

(v) Calorie that should come from carbohydrates = 2645.28 × 0.55 = 1454.90 calories

Therefore, required quantity of carbohydrates = $\dfrac{1454.90}{4}$ = 363.72 g = 360 g (approx.)

Q. 137 150 students are studying English, Maths or both. 62% of students study English and 68% are studying Maths. How many students are studying both?

Sol. Total students = 150

Students who study English = 62% of 150 = $\dfrac{62}{100} \times 150 = 93$

Students who study Maths = 68% of 150 = $\dfrac{68}{100} \times 150 = 102$

Total students studying English or Maths = 93 + 102 = 195

∴ Students who study English and Maths both = 195 − 150 = 45

Q. 138 Earth Science

The table lists the world's 10 largest deserts.

Largest Deserts in the World	
Desert	**Area** (in km^2)
Sahara (Africa)	8800000
Gobi (Asia)	1300000
Australian Desert (Australia)	1250000
Arabian Desert (Asia)	850000
Kalahari Desert (Africa)	580000
Chihuahuan Desert (North America)	370000
Takla Makan Desert (Asia)	320000
Kara Kum (Asia)	310000
Namib Desert (Africa)	310000
Thar Desert (Asia)	260000

(a) What are the mean, median and mode of the areas listed?

(b) How many times the size of the Gobi Desert is the Namib Desert?

(c) What percentage of the deserts listed are in Asia?

(d) What percentage of the total area of the deserts listed is in Asia?

Sol. (a) Mean = $\dfrac{\text{Total area of all deserts}}{\text{Number of deserts}}$

$$= \frac{\begin{bmatrix} 8800000 + 1300000 + 1250000 + 850000 + 580000 \\ + 370000 + 320000 + 310000 + 310000 + 260000 \end{bmatrix}}{10}$$

$$= \frac{14350000}{10} = 1435000 \text{ km}^2$$

Median = $\dfrac{\left(\dfrac{N}{2}\right)\text{th term} + \left(\dfrac{N}{2}+1\right)\text{th term}}{2} = \dfrac{\dfrac{10}{2}\text{th term} + \left(\dfrac{10}{2}+1\right)\text{th term}}{2}$

$= \dfrac{\text{5th term} + \text{6th term}}{2} = \dfrac{580000 + 370000}{2}$

$= \dfrac{950000}{2} = 475000 \text{ km}^2$ [here, $N = 10$]

Mode = Most frequent observation = 310000 km^2

(b) Let the size of Gobi desert is x times the Namib desert.

∴   Gobi desert = x × Namib desert

⇒ $1300000 = x \times 310000$

$$x = \frac{1300000}{310000} \Rightarrow x = 4.19$$

Hence, the size of Gobi desert is 4.19 times of Namib desert.

(c) Total number of deserts = 10

Number of deserts in Asia (Gobi, Arabian, Takla Makan, Kara Kum, Thar) = 5

Hence, percentage of deserts in Asia = $\dfrac{5}{10} \times 100\% = 50\%$

(d) Total area of all deserts = 14350000 km²   [as calculated in part (a)]

Total area of Asia's deserts = 1300000 + 850000 + 320000 + 310000 + 260000

= 3040000 km²

Hence, percentage of the total area of the deserts listed in Asia

$$= \frac{\text{Total area of Asia's deserts}}{\text{Total area of all deserts}}$$

$$= \frac{3040000}{14350000} \times 100\% = 21.1\%$$

Q. 139 Geography Application

Earth's total land is about 148428950 km². The land area of Asia is about 30% of this total. What is the approximate land area of Asia to the nearest square kilometre?

Sol.   Total land area of Earth = 148428950 km²

∴ Land area of Asia = 30% of land area of Earth   [given]

$$= \frac{30}{100} \times 148428950 = 3 \times 14842895$$

$$= 44528685 \text{ km}^2$$

Q. 140 The pieces of Tangrams have been rearranged to make the given shape.

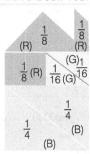

By observing the given shape, answer the following questions.

(a) What percentage of total has been coloured?

(i) Red (R) = _____

(ii) Blue (B) = _____

(iii) Green (G) = _____

(b) Check that the sum of all the percentages calculated above should be 100.

(c) If we rearrange the same pieces to form some other shape, will the percentage of colours change?

Sol. (a) Total coloured shape $= \dfrac{1}{8} + \dfrac{1}{8} + \dfrac{1}{8} + \dfrac{1}{16} + \dfrac{1}{16} + \dfrac{1}{4} + \dfrac{1}{4} = 1$

(i) Red coloured shape $= \dfrac{1}{8} + \dfrac{1}{8} + \dfrac{1}{8}$ [by observation]

$$= \dfrac{1+1+1}{8} = \dfrac{3}{8}$$

Hence, percentage of red coloured $= \dfrac{\text{Red coloured shape}}{\text{Total coloured shape}} \times 100\%$

$$= \dfrac{3/8}{1} \times 100\% = \dfrac{3}{8} \times 100\% = 37.5\%$$

(ii) Blue coloured shape $= \dfrac{1}{4} + \dfrac{1}{4} = \dfrac{1+1}{4}$ [by observation]

$$= \dfrac{2}{4} = \dfrac{1}{2}$$

Hence, percentage of blue coloured shape $= \dfrac{\text{Blue coloured shape}}{\text{Total coloured shape}} \times 100\%$

$$= \dfrac{1/2}{1} \times 100\% = \dfrac{1}{2} \times 100\% = 50\%$$

(iii) Green coloured shape $= \dfrac{1}{16} + \dfrac{1}{16} = \dfrac{1+1}{16} = \dfrac{2}{16} = \dfrac{1}{8}$ [by observation]

Hence, percentage of green coloured shape $= \dfrac{\text{Green coloured shape}}{\text{Total coloured shape}} \times 100\%$

$$= \dfrac{1/8}{1} \times 100\% = \dfrac{1}{8} \times 100\% = 12.5\%$$

(b) Sum of all percentages calculated

= Percentage of red coloured + Percentage of blue coloured
+ Percentage of green coloured

= 37.5 + 50 + 12.5   [already calculated]

= 100%

(c) If we rearrange the same pieces to form some other shape, the percentage of colours will not change, because we just rearrange the parts and not changing the percentage of colours.

8

Rational Numbers

Multiple Choice Questions (MCQs)

Q. 1 A rational number is defined as a number that can be expressed in the form $\dfrac{p}{q}$, where p and q are integers and

    (a) $q = 0$ (b) $q = 1$

    (c) $q \neq 1$ (d) $q \neq 0$

Sol. *(d)* By definition, a number that can be expressed in the form of $\dfrac{p}{q}$, where p and q are integers and $q \neq 0$, is called a rational number.

Q. 2 Which of the following rational numbers is positive?

    (a) $\dfrac{-8}{7}$ (b) $\dfrac{19}{-13}$

    (c) $\dfrac{-3}{-4}$ (d) $\dfrac{-21}{13}$

Sol. *(c)* We know that, when numerator and denominator of a rational number, both are negative, it is a positive rational number.

Hence, among the given rational numbers $\left(\dfrac{-3}{-4}\right)$ is positive.

Q. 3 Which of the following rational numbers is negative?

    (a) $-\left(\dfrac{-3}{7}\right)$ (b) $\dfrac{-5}{-8}$

    (c) $\dfrac{9}{8}$ (d) $\dfrac{3}{-7}$

Sol. *(d)*

    (a) $-\left(\dfrac{-3}{7}\right) = \dfrac{3}{7}$ (b) $\dfrac{-5}{-8} = \dfrac{5}{8}$ (c) $\dfrac{9}{8} = \dfrac{9}{8}$ (d) $\dfrac{3}{-7} = \dfrac{-3}{7}$

Q. 4 In the standard form of a rational number, the common factor of numerator and denominator is always

    (a) 0   (b) 1   c) – 2   (d) 2

Sol. *(b)* By definition, in the standard form of a rational number, the common factor of numerator and denominator is always 1.

    Note *Common factor means, a number which divides both the given two numbers.*

Q. 5 Which of the following rational numbers is equal to its reciprocal?

    (a) 1   (b) 2   (c) $\dfrac{1}{2}$ (d) 0

Sol. *(a)*

    (a) Reciprocal of $1 = \dfrac{1}{1} = 1$

    (b) Reciprocal of $2 = \dfrac{1}{2}$

    (c) Reciprocal of $\dfrac{1}{2} = \dfrac{1}{\frac{1}{2}} = 2$

    (d) Reciprocal of $0 = \dfrac{1}{0}$

    Note *1 is the only number, which is equal to its reciprocal.*

Q. 6 The reciprocal of $\dfrac{1}{2}$ is

    (a) 3   (b) 2   (c) – 1   (d) 0

Sol. *(b)* Reciprocal of $\dfrac{1}{2} = \dfrac{1}{\frac{1}{2}} = 2$

Q. 7 The standard form of $\dfrac{-48}{60}$ is

    (a) $\dfrac{48}{60}$ (b) $\dfrac{-60}{48}$ (c) $\dfrac{-4}{5}$ (d) $\dfrac{-4}{-5}$

Sol. *(c)* Given rational number is $\dfrac{-48}{60}$.

    For standard/simplest form, divide numerator and denominator by their HCF

    i.e. $\dfrac{-48 \div 12}{60 \div 12} = \dfrac{-4}{5}$ [∵ HCF of 48 and 60 = 12]

    Hence, the standard form of $\dfrac{-48}{60}$ is $\dfrac{-4}{5}$.

Q. 8 Which of the following is equivalent to $\dfrac{4}{5}$?

    (a) $\dfrac{5}{4}$ (b) $\dfrac{16}{25}$

    (c) $\dfrac{16}{20}$ (d) $\dfrac{15}{25}$

Sol. *(c)* Given rational number is $\dfrac{4}{5}$.

$$\text{So, equivalent rational number} = \dfrac{4 \times 4}{5 \times 4}$$

$$= \dfrac{16}{20} \qquad \text{[multiplying numerator and denominator by 4]}$$

> **Note** *If the numerator and denominator of a rational number is multiplied/divided by a non-zero integer, then the result we get, is equivalent rational number.*

Q. 9 How many rational numbers are there between two rational numbers?

(a) 1   (b) 0

(c) unlimited   (d) 100

Sol. *(c)* There are unlimited numbers between two rational numbers.

Q. 10 In the standard form of a rational number, the denominator is always a

(a) 0   (b) negative integer

(c) positive integer   (d) 1

Sol. *(c)* By definition, a rational number is said to be in the standard form, if its denominator is a positive integer.

Q. 11 To reduce a rational number to its standard form, we divide its numerator and denominator by their

(a) LCM   (b) HCF

(c) product   (d) multiple

Sol. *(b)* To reduce a rational number to its standard form, we divide its numerator and denominator by their HCF.

Q. 12 Which is greater number in the following?

(a) $-\dfrac{1}{2}$ (b) 0   (c) $\dfrac{1}{2}$ (d) -2

Sol. *(c)* Obviously, $\dfrac{1}{2}$ is greater, since this is the only number which is on the rightmost side of the number line among others.

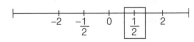

Fill in the Blanks

In questions 13 to 46, fill in the blanks to make the statements true.

Q. 13 $\dfrac{-3}{8}$ is a _____ rational number.

Sol. The given rational number $\dfrac{-3}{8}$ is a negative number, because its numerator is negative integer.

Hence, $\dfrac{-3}{8}$ is a **negative** rational number.

Q. 14 1 is a _____ rational number.

Sol. The given rational number 1 is positive number, because its numerator and denominator are positive integer.

Hence, 1 is a **positive** rational number.

Q. 15 The standard form of $\dfrac{-8}{-36}$ is _____ .

Sol. Given rational number is $\dfrac{-8}{-36}$.

For standard/simplest form, $\dfrac{-8 \div 4}{-36 \div 4} = \dfrac{-2}{-9} = \dfrac{2}{9}$ $[\because \text{HCF of 8 and 36} = 4]$

Hence, the standard form of $\dfrac{-8}{-36}$ is $\dfrac{2}{9}$.

Q. 16 The standard form of $\dfrac{18}{-24}$ is _____ .

Sol. Given rational number is $\dfrac{18}{-24}$.

For standard/simplest form, $\dfrac{18 \div 6}{-24 \div 6} = \dfrac{3}{-4}$ $[\because \text{HCF of 18 and 24} = 6]$

Hence, the standard form of $\dfrac{18}{-24}$ is $\dfrac{-3}{4}$.

Q. 17 On a number line, $\dfrac{-1}{2}$ is to the _____ of zero (0).

Sol. On a number line, $\dfrac{-1}{2}$ is to the **left** of zero (0).

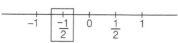

Note All the negative numbers lie on the left side of zero on the number line.

Q. 18 On a number line, $\dfrac{4}{3}$ is to the _____ of zero (0).

Sol. On a number line, $\dfrac{4}{3}$ is to the **right** of zero (0).

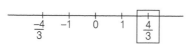

Note All the positive numbers lie on the right side of zero on the number line.

Q. 19 $\dfrac{-1}{2}$ is _____ than $\dfrac{1}{5}$.

Sol. Given rational numbers are $\dfrac{-1}{2}$ and $\dfrac{1}{5}$.

LCM of their denominators, i.e. 2 and 5 = 10

∴ $\dfrac{-1 \times 5}{2 \times 5} = \dfrac{-5}{10}$ and $\dfrac{1 \times 2}{5 \times 2} = \dfrac{2}{10}$

∵ $2 > -5$

So, $\dfrac{1}{5} > \dfrac{-1}{2}$

Hence, $\dfrac{-1}{2}$ is **smaller** than $\dfrac{1}{5}$.

Q. 20 $\dfrac{-3}{5}$ is _____ than 0.

Sol. Since, $\dfrac{-3}{5}$ lies on the left side of zero (0). On the number line, $\dfrac{-3}{5}$ is **smaller** than 0

i.e. $\dfrac{-3}{5} < 0$.

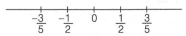

Q. 21 $\dfrac{-16}{24}$ and $\dfrac{20}{-16}$ represent _____ rational numbers.

Sol. Given numbers are $\dfrac{-16}{24} = \dfrac{-4}{6} = \dfrac{-2}{3}$ [lowest form]

and $\dfrac{20}{-16} = \dfrac{-5}{4}$ [lowest form]

∵ $\dfrac{-16}{24} \neq \dfrac{20}{-16}$

Hence, $\dfrac{-16}{24}$ and $\dfrac{20}{-16}$ represent **different** rational numbers.

Q. 22 $\dfrac{-27}{45}$ and $\dfrac{-3}{5}$ represent _____ rational numbers.

Sol. Given numbers are $\dfrac{-27}{45} = \dfrac{-9}{15} = \dfrac{-3}{5}$ [lowest form]

and $\dfrac{-3}{5}$ [already lowest form]

Hence, $\dfrac{-27}{45}$ and $\dfrac{-3}{5}$ represent **same** rational numbers.

Q. 23 Additive inverse of $\frac{2}{3}$ is _____ .

Sol. Since, additive inverse is the negative of a number.

Hence, additive inverse of $\frac{2}{3}$ is $\frac{-2}{3}$.

> **Note** Additive inverse is a number, which when added to a given number, we get result as zero.

Q. 24 $\frac{-3}{5} + \frac{2}{5} =$ _____

Sol. Given, $\frac{-3}{5} + \frac{2}{5} = \frac{-3+2}{5}$ [taking LCM]

$$= \frac{-1}{5}$$

Hence, $\frac{-3}{5} + \frac{2}{5} = \frac{-1}{5}$.

Q. 25 $\frac{-5}{6} + \frac{-1}{6} =$ _____

Sol. Given, $\frac{-5}{6} + \frac{-1}{6} = \frac{-5}{6} - \frac{1}{6} = \frac{-5-1}{6}$ [taking LCM]

$$= \frac{-6}{6}$$

$$= -1$$

Hence, $\frac{-5}{6} + \frac{-1}{6} = -1$.

Q. 26 $\frac{3}{4} \times \left(\frac{-2}{3}\right) =$ _____

Sol. Given, $\frac{3}{4} \times \left(\frac{-2}{3}\right)$

Product of rational numbers $= \dfrac{\text{Product of numerators}}{\text{Product of denominators}} = \dfrac{3 \times (-2)}{4 \times 3} = \dfrac{-6}{12}$

$$= \frac{-6 \div 6}{12 \div 6}$$ [dividing numerator and denominator by 6]

$$= \frac{-1}{2}$$

Hence, $\frac{3}{4} \times \left(\frac{-2}{3}\right) = \frac{-1}{2}$.

Q. 27 $\frac{-5}{3} \times \left(\frac{-3}{5}\right) =$ _____

Sol. Given, $\frac{-5}{3} \times \left(\frac{-3}{5}\right)$

$\because$ Product of rational numbers $= \dfrac{\text{Product of numerators}}{\text{Product of denominators}} = \dfrac{(-5) \times (-3)}{3 \times 5} = \dfrac{15}{15} = 1$

Hence, $\frac{-5}{3} \times \left(\frac{-3}{5}\right) = 1$.

Q. 28 Given, $\dfrac{-6}{7} = \dfrac{}{42}$

Sol. Let given expression is written as $\dfrac{-6}{7} = \dfrac{x}{42}$

$\Rightarrow \qquad x = \dfrac{42 \times (-6)}{7} = 6 \times (-6)$ \hfill [by cross-multiplication]

$\Rightarrow \qquad x = -36$

Hence, $\dfrac{-6}{7} = \dfrac{-36}{42}$.

Q. 29 $\dfrac{1}{2} = \dfrac{6}{}$

Sol. Let $\dfrac{1}{2} = \dfrac{6}{x}$

$\Rightarrow \qquad x = 12$ \hfill [by cross-multiplication]

Hence, $\dfrac{1}{2} = \dfrac{6}{12}$.

Q. 30 $\dfrac{-2}{9} - \dfrac{7}{9} = $ ____

Sol. Given, $\dfrac{-2}{9} - \dfrac{7}{9} = \dfrac{-2-7}{9}$ \hfill [taking LCM]

$= \dfrac{-9}{9} = -1$

Hence, $\dfrac{-2}{9} - \dfrac{7}{9} = -1$.

In questions 31 to 35, fill in the boxes with the correct symbol '>', '<' or '='.

Q. 31 $\dfrac{7}{-8} \;\square\; \dfrac{8}{9}$

Sol. Given rational numbers are $\dfrac{7}{-8}$ and $\dfrac{8}{9}$.

Since, $\dfrac{7}{-8} = \dfrac{-7}{8}$ is a negative rational number and $\dfrac{8}{9}$ is a positive rational number. Also, every positive rational number is greater than negative rational number.

Hence, $\dfrac{7}{-8} < \dfrac{8}{9}$.

Q. 32 $\dfrac{3}{7} \;\square\; \dfrac{-5}{6}$

Sol. Given rational numbers are $\dfrac{3}{7}$ and $\dfrac{-5}{6}$.

Since, $\dfrac{-5}{6}$ is a negative rational number and $\dfrac{3}{7}$ is a positive rational number.

Also, every positive rational number is greater than negative rational number.

Hence, $\dfrac{3}{7} > \dfrac{-5}{6}$.

Q. 33 $\frac{5}{6} \square \frac{8}{4}$

Sol. Given rational numbers are $\frac{5}{6}$ and $\frac{8}{4}$.

We convert the rational numbers with the same denominators.

$\therefore$ $\quad \frac{5 \times 2}{6 \times 2} = \frac{10}{12}$ and $\frac{8 \times 3}{4 \times 3} = \frac{24}{12}$ $\qquad$ [$\because$ LCM of 6 and 4 = 12]

i.e. $\quad 24 > 10 \Rightarrow \frac{24}{12} > \frac{10}{12}$

Hence, $\quad \frac{5}{6} < \frac{8}{4}$.

Q. 34 $\frac{-9}{7} \square \frac{4}{-7}$

Sol. Given rational numbers are $\frac{-9}{7}$ and $\frac{4}{-7}$. Since, both fractions have same denominator, the fraction which have greater numerator is greater. But in a negative number, the numerator which is smaller is the greater number.

Hence, $\quad \frac{-9}{7} < \frac{4}{-7}$.

Q. 35 $\frac{8}{8} \square \frac{2}{2}$

Sol. Given, $\frac{8}{8} = 1$ and $\frac{2}{2} = 1$

Hence, $\quad \frac{8}{8} = \frac{2}{2}$

Q. 36 The reciprocal of _____ does not exist.

Sol. The reciprocal of **zero** does not exist, as reciprocal of 0 is $\frac{1}{0}$, which is not defined.

Q. 37 The reciprocal of 1 is _____

Sol. The reciprocal of $1 = \frac{1}{1}$

Hence, the reciprocal of 1 is **1**.

Q. 38 $\frac{-3}{7} \div \left(\frac{-7}{3} \right) =$ _____

Sol. $\because$ Reciprocal of $\frac{-7}{3}$ is $\frac{3}{-7}$.

$\therefore \quad \frac{-3}{7} \times \left(\frac{3}{-7} \right)$

Product of rational numbers $= \frac{\text{Product of numerators}}{\text{Product of denominators}} = \frac{(-3 \times 3)}{7 \times (-7)} = \frac{-9}{-49} = \frac{9}{49}$

Hence, $\frac{-3}{7} \div \left(\frac{-7}{3} \right) = \frac{9}{49}$.

Q. 39 $0 \div \left(\dfrac{-5}{6} \right) = $ _____

Sol. Here, $0 \div \left(\dfrac{-5}{6} \right) = 0$

Because, 0 divided by any number is zero.

Q. 40 $0 \times \left(\dfrac{-5}{6} \right) = $ _____

Sol. Here, $0 \times \left(\dfrac{-5}{6} \right) = 0$

Because, zero multiplies by any number result is zero.

Q. 41 _____ $\times \left(\dfrac{-2}{5} \right) = 1$

Sol. Let $\qquad x \times \left(\dfrac{-2}{5} \right) = 1$

$\Rightarrow \qquad \dfrac{-2x}{5} = 1$

$\Rightarrow \qquad -2x = 5 \qquad\qquad\qquad$ [by cross-multiplication]

$\Rightarrow \qquad x = \dfrac{-5}{2}$

Hence, $\dfrac{-5}{2} \times \left(\dfrac{-2}{5} \right) = 1$

Q. 42 The standard form of rational number -1 is _____ .

Sol. $\because$ HCF of given rational number -1 is 1.

For standard form $= -1 \div 1 = -1$

Hence, the standard form of rational number -1 is -1.

Q. 43 If m is a common divisor of a and b, then $\dfrac{a}{b} = \dfrac{a \div m}{-}$

Sol. If m is a common divisor of a and b, then

$$\dfrac{a}{b} = \dfrac{a \div m}{b \div m}$$

Q. 44 If p and q are positive integers, then $\dfrac{p}{q}$ is a _____ rational number and

$\dfrac{p}{-q}$ is a _____ rational number.

Sol. If p and q are positive integers, then $\dfrac{p}{q}$ is a **positive** rational number, because both

numerator and denominator are positive and $\dfrac{p}{-q}$ is a **negative** rational number, because

denominator is in negative.

Q. 45 Two rational numbers are said to be equivalent or equal, if they have the same _____ form.

Sol. Two rational numbers are said to be equivalent or equal, if they have the same **simplest** form.

Q. 46 If $\dfrac{p}{q}$ is a rational number, then q cannot be _____

Sol. By definition, if $\dfrac{p}{q}$ is a rational number, then q *cannot be* **zero**.

True / False

In questions 47 to 65, state whether the following statements are True or False.

Q. 47 Every natural number is a rational number, but every rational number need not be a natural number.

Sol. *True*

e.g. $\dfrac{1}{2}$ is a rational number, but not a natural number.

Q. 48 Zero is a rational number.

Sol. *True*

e.g. Zero can be written as $0 = \dfrac{0}{1}$. We know that, a number of the form $\dfrac{p}{q}$, where p, q are integers and $q \neq 0$ is a rational number. So, zero is a rational number.

Q. 49 Every integer is a rational number but every rational number need not be an integer.

Sol. *True*

Integers ....,$- 3, -2, - 1, 0, 1, 2, 3,$ ...
Rational numbers:
...., $- 1, \dfrac{-1}{2}, 0, \dfrac{1}{2}, 1, \dfrac{3}{2},$ ....
Hence, every integer is rational number, but every rational number is not an integer.

Q. 50 Every negative integer is not a negative rational number.

Sol. *False*

Because all the integers are rational numbers, whether it is negative/positive but *vice-versa* is not true.

Q. 51 If $\dfrac{p}{q}$ is a rational number and m is a non-zero integer, then

$$\frac{p}{q} = \frac{p \times m}{q \times m}$$

Sol. *True*

e.g. Let $m = 1, 2, 3,$ ...

When $m = 1$, then $\quad \dfrac{p}{q} = \dfrac{p \times 1}{1 \times q} = \dfrac{p}{q}$

When $m = 2$, then $\quad \dfrac{p}{q} = \dfrac{p \times 2}{q \times 2} = \dfrac{p}{q}$

Hence, $\qquad \dfrac{p}{q} = \dfrac{p \times m}{q \times m}$

Note When both numerator and denominator of a rational number are multiplied/divide by a same non-zero number, then we get the same rational number.

Q. 52 If $\dfrac{p}{q}$ is a rational number and m is a non-zero common divisor of p and q,

then $\dfrac{p}{q} = \dfrac{p \div m}{q \div m}$.

Sol. *True*

e.g. Let $m = 1, 2, 3, \ldots$

When $m = 1$, then $\quad \dfrac{p}{q} = \dfrac{p \div 1}{q \div 1} = \dfrac{p}{1} \div \dfrac{q}{1} = \dfrac{p}{1} \times \dfrac{1}{q} = \dfrac{p}{q}$

When $m = 2$, then $\quad \dfrac{p}{q} = \dfrac{p \div 2}{q \div 2} = \dfrac{p}{2} \div \dfrac{q}{2} = \dfrac{p}{2} \times \dfrac{2}{q} = \dfrac{p}{q}$

Hence, $\qquad \dfrac{p}{q} = \dfrac{p \div m}{q \div m}$

Q. 53 In a rational number, denominator always has to be a non-zero integer.

Sol. *True*

Basic definition of the rational number is that, it is in the form of $\dfrac{p}{q}$, where $q \neq 0$. It is because any number divided by zero is not defined.

Q. 54 If $\dfrac{p}{q}$ is a rational number and m is a non-zero integer, then $\dfrac{p \times m}{q \times m}$ is a rational number not equivalent to $\dfrac{p}{q}$.

Sol. *False*

Let $\quad m = 1, 2, 3, \ldots$

When $m = 1$, then $\quad \dfrac{p \times m}{q \times m} = \dfrac{p \times 1}{q \times 1} = \dfrac{p}{q}$

when $m = 2$, then $\quad \dfrac{p \times m}{q \times m} = \dfrac{p \times 2}{q \times 2} = \dfrac{p}{q}$

For any non-zero value of m, $\dfrac{p \times m}{q \times m}$ is always equivalent to $\dfrac{p}{q}$.

Q. 55 Sum of two rational numbers is always a rational number.

Sol. *True*

Sum of two rational numbers is always a rational number, it is true.

e.g. $\dfrac{1}{2} + \dfrac{2}{3} = \dfrac{3+4}{6} = \dfrac{7}{6}$

Q. 56 All decimal numbers are also rational numbers.

Sol. *True*

All decimal numbers are also rational numbers, it is true.

e.g. $0.6 = \dfrac{6}{10} = \dfrac{3}{5}$

Q. 57 The quotient of two rationals is always a rational number.

Sol. *False*

The quotient of two rationals is not always a rational number.

e.g. $\dfrac{1}{0}$

Q. 58 Every fraction is a rational number.

Sol. *True*

Every fraction is a rational number but *vice-versa* is not true.

Q. 59 Two rationals with different numerators can never be equal.

Sol. *False*

Let $\dfrac{2}{3}$ and $\dfrac{4}{6}$ be two rational numbers, then $\dfrac{4}{6}$ can be written as $\dfrac{2}{3}$ in its lowest form.

$\because \dfrac{4}{6} = \dfrac{4 \div 2}{6 \div 2} = \dfrac{4}{2} \div \dfrac{6}{2} = \dfrac{2}{3}$

Hence, two rational numbers with different numerators can be equal.

Q. 60 8 can be written as a rational number with any integer as denominator.

Sol. 8 can be written as a rational number with any integer as denominator, it is false because 8 can be written as a rational number with 1 as denominator i.e. $\dfrac{8}{1}$.

Q. 61 $\dfrac{4}{6}$ is equivalent to $\dfrac{2}{3}$.

Sol. *True*

Given, $\dfrac{4}{6} = \dfrac{4 \div 2}{6 \div 2} = \dfrac{2}{3}$

Q. 62 The rational number $\dfrac{-3}{4}$ lies to the right of zero on the number line.

Sol. *False*

Because every negative rational number lies to the left of zero on the number line.

Q. 63 The rational number $\dfrac{-12}{-15}$ and $\dfrac{-7}{17}$ are on the opposite sides of zero on the number line.

Sol. Given rational numbers are $\dfrac{-12}{-15}$ i.e. $\dfrac{12}{15}$ and $\dfrac{-7}{17}$.

Hence, it is true, that rational numbers $\dfrac{12}{15}$ and $\dfrac{-7}{17}$ are on the opposite sides of zero on the number line as one is negative and one is positve.

$$\overset{\underset{\textstyle \frac{-7}{14}}{|}\quad\underset{\textstyle 0}{|}\quad\underset{\textstyle \frac{12}{15}}{|}}{\rule{9cm}{0.4pt}}$$

Q. 64 Every rational number is a whole number.

Sol. *False*

e.g. $\dfrac{-7}{8}$ is a rational number, but it is not a whole number, because whole numbers are 0, 1, 2 ... .

Q. 65 Zero is the smallest rational number.

Sol. *False*

Rational numbers can be negative and negative rational numbers are smaller than zero.

Q. 66 Match the following:

	Column I		Column II
(i)	$\dfrac{a}{b} \div \dfrac{a}{b}$	(a)	$\dfrac{-a}{b}$
(ii)	$\dfrac{a}{b} \div \dfrac{c}{d}$	(b)	-1
(iii)	$\dfrac{a}{b} \div (-1)$	(c)	1
(iv)	$\dfrac{a}{b} \div \dfrac{-a}{b}$	(d)	$\dfrac{bc}{ad}$
(v)	$\dfrac{b}{a} \div \left(\dfrac{d}{c}\right)$	(e)	$\dfrac{ad}{bc}$

Sol. (i) $\leftrightarrow$ (c)

Given, $\dfrac{a}{b} \div \dfrac{a}{b} = \dfrac{a}{b} \times \dfrac{b}{a}$ $\left[\because \text{Reciprocal of } \dfrac{a}{b} = \dfrac{b}{a}\right]$

$= 1$

(ii) $\leftrightarrow$ (e)

Given, $\dfrac{a}{b} \div \dfrac{c}{d} = \dfrac{a}{b} \times \dfrac{d}{c}$ $\left[\because \text{Reciprocal of } \dfrac{c}{d} = \dfrac{d}{c}\right]$

$= \dfrac{ad}{bc}$

(iii) $\leftrightarrow$ (a)

Given, $\dfrac{a}{b} \div (-1) = \dfrac{a}{b} \times (-1)$ $[\because \text{Reciprocal of } -1 = -1]$

$= \dfrac{-a}{b}$

(iv) ↔ (b)

Given, $\dfrac{a}{b} \div \dfrac{-a}{b} = \dfrac{a}{b} \times \left(\dfrac{-b}{a}\right)$ $\qquad \left[\because \text{ Reciprocal of } \dfrac{-a}{b} = \dfrac{-b}{a}\right]$

$= -1$

(v) ↔ (d)

Given, $\dfrac{b}{a} \div \left(\dfrac{d}{c}\right) = \dfrac{b}{a} \times \dfrac{c}{d}$ $\qquad \left[\because \text{ Reciprocal of } \dfrac{d}{c} = \dfrac{c}{d}\right]$

$= \dfrac{bc}{ad}$

Q. 67 Write each of the following rational numbers with positive denominators.

$$\dfrac{5}{-8}, \dfrac{15}{-28}, \dfrac{-17}{-13}$$

Sol. We can write, $\dfrac{5}{-8} = \dfrac{5 \times (-1)}{-8 \times (-1)} = \dfrac{-5}{8}$ [multiplying numerators and denominators by (-1)]

$\dfrac{15}{-28}$ can be written as $= \dfrac{15 \times (-1)}{-28 \times (-1)} = \dfrac{-15}{28}$

and $\dfrac{-17}{-13}$ can be written as $= \dfrac{-17 \times (-1)}{-13 \times (-1)} = \dfrac{17}{13}$, as both negative signs are cancelled.

Q. 68 Express $\dfrac{3}{4}$ as a rational number with denominator:

(a) 36 (b) −80

Sol. (a) To make the denominator 36, we have to multiply numerator and denominator by 9.

∴ $\dfrac{3 \times 9}{4 \times 9} = \dfrac{27}{36}$

(b) To make the denominator − 80, we have to multiply numerator and denominator by − 20.

∴ $\dfrac{3 \times (-20)}{4 \times (-20)} = \dfrac{-60}{-80}$

Q. 69 Reduce each of the following rational numbers in its lowest form.

(i) $\dfrac{-60}{72}$ (ii) $\dfrac{91}{-364}$

Sol. (i) $\dfrac{-60}{72}$ can be written as

$= \dfrac{-60 \div 12}{72 \div 12}$ [dividing numerator and denominator by HCF of 60 and 72 i.e. 12]

$= \dfrac{-60 \times \dfrac{1}{12}}{72 \times \dfrac{1}{12}}$ $\qquad \left[\because \text{Reciprocal of } 12 = \dfrac{1}{12}\right]$

$= \dfrac{-5}{6}$, which is the lowest form.

(ii) $\dfrac{91}{-364}$ can be written as

$$= \dfrac{91 \div 91}{-364 \div 91} \qquad \text{[dividing numerator and denominator by HCF of 91 and 364 i.e., 91]}$$

$$= \dfrac{91 \times \dfrac{1}{91}}{-364 \times \dfrac{1}{91}} \qquad \left[\because \text{ Reciprocal of } 91 = \dfrac{1}{91} \right]$$

$$= -\dfrac{1}{4}, \text{ which is the lowest form.}$$

Q. 70 Express each of the following rational numbers in its standard form

    (i) $\dfrac{-12}{-30}$ (ii) $\dfrac{14}{-49}$

    (iii) $\dfrac{-15}{35}$ (iv) $\dfrac{299}{-161}$

Sol.   (i) Given rational number is $\dfrac{-12}{-30}$.

        For standard form of given rational number $= \dfrac{-12 \div 6}{-30 \div 6}$ [$\because$ HCF of 12 and 30 = 6]

$$= \dfrac{-2}{-5} = \dfrac{2}{5}$$

        Hence, the standard form of $\dfrac{-12}{-30}$ is $\dfrac{2}{5}$.

  (ii) Given rational number is $\dfrac{14}{-49}$.

        For standard form of given rational number $= \dfrac{14 \div 7}{-49 \div 7}$ [$\because$ HCF of 14 and 49 = 7]

$$= \dfrac{2}{-7} = \dfrac{-2}{7}$$

        Hence, the standard form of $\dfrac{14}{-49}$ is $\dfrac{-2}{7}$.

  (iii) Given rational number is $\dfrac{-15}{35}$.

        For standard form of given rational number $= \dfrac{-15 \div 5}{35 \div 5}$ [$\because$ HCF of 15 and 35 = 5]

$$= \dfrac{-3}{7}$$

        Hence, the standard form of $\dfrac{-15}{35}$ is $\dfrac{-3}{7}$.

(iv) Given rational number is $\dfrac{299}{-161}$.

For standard form of given rational number $= \dfrac{299 \div 23}{-161 \div 23}$ $[\because \text{HCF of 299 and 61} = 23]$

$= \dfrac{13}{-7} = \dfrac{13 \div (-1)}{13 \div (-1)}$ [dividing by (-1) in both numerator and denominator]

$= \dfrac{-13}{7}$

Hence, the standard form of $\dfrac{299}{-161}$ is $\dfrac{-13}{7}$.

Q. 71 Are the rational numbers $\dfrac{-8}{28}$ and $\dfrac{32}{-112}$ equivalent? Give reason.

Sol. Given rational numbers are $\dfrac{-8}{28}$ and $\dfrac{32}{-112}$.

For standard form of $\dfrac{-8}{28} = \dfrac{-8 \div 4}{28 \div 4} = \dfrac{-2}{7}$ $[\because \text{HCF of 8 and 28} = 4]$

and standard form of $\dfrac{32}{-112} = \dfrac{32 \div 16}{-112 \div 16}$ $[\because \text{HCF of 32 and 112} = 16]$

$= \dfrac{2}{-7} = \dfrac{-2}{7}$

Yes

Since, the standard form of $\dfrac{-8}{28}$ and $\dfrac{32}{-112}$ are equal.

Hence, they are equivalent.

Q. 72 Arrange the rational numbers $\dfrac{-7}{10}, \dfrac{5}{-8}, \dfrac{2}{-3}, \dfrac{-1}{4}, \dfrac{-3}{5}$ in ascending order.

Sol. Given rational numbers are $\dfrac{-7}{10}, \dfrac{5}{-8}, \dfrac{2}{-3}, \dfrac{-1}{4}, \dfrac{-3}{5}$.

To arrange in any order, we make denominators of all rational numbers as same.

$\therefore$ LCM of 10, 8, 3, 4 and 5 is 120.

So, $\dfrac{-7 \times 12}{10 \times 12}, \dfrac{5 \times 15}{-8 \times 15}, \dfrac{2 \times 40}{-3 \times 40}, \dfrac{-1 \times 30}{4 \times 30}, \dfrac{-3 \times 24}{5 \times 24}$

$= \dfrac{-84}{120}, \dfrac{75}{-120}, \dfrac{80}{-120}, \dfrac{-30}{120}, \dfrac{-72}{120}$

$= \dfrac{-84}{120}, \dfrac{-75}{120}, \dfrac{-80}{120}, \dfrac{-30}{120}, \dfrac{-72}{120}$

Since, denominators are same, so ascending order of numerators are $-84, -80, -75, -72, -30$.

Hence, $\dfrac{-84}{120} < \dfrac{-80}{120} < \dfrac{-75}{120} < \dfrac{-72}{120} < \dfrac{-30}{120}$

i.e. $\dfrac{-7}{10} < \dfrac{2}{-3} < \dfrac{5}{-8} < \dfrac{-3}{5} < \dfrac{-1}{4}$

Q. 73 Represent the following rational numbers on a number line.

$$\frac{3}{8}, \frac{-7}{3}, \frac{22}{-6}$$

Sol.

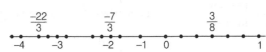

Q. 74 If $\frac{-5}{7} = \frac{x}{28}$, find the value of x.

Sol. Given,

$$\frac{-5}{7} = \frac{x}{28}$$

$\Rightarrow$ $\qquad\qquad 7 \times x = -5 \times 28$ $\qquad\qquad$ [by cross-multiplication]

$\Rightarrow$ $\qquad\qquad x = -\frac{5 \times 28}{7} = -5 \times 4$

$\Rightarrow$ $\qquad\qquad x = -20$

Hence, the value of x is -20.

Q. 75 Give three rational numbers equivalent to

(i) $\frac{-3}{4}$ $\qquad\qquad$ (ii) $\frac{7}{11}$

Sol. (i) Given rational number is $\frac{-3}{4}$.

So, the equivalent rational numbers are

$$\frac{-3 \times 2}{4 \times 2} = \frac{-6}{8}, \frac{-3 \times 3}{4 \times 3} = \frac{-9}{12} \text{ and } \frac{-3 \times 4}{4 \times 4} = \frac{-12}{16}$$

Hence, three equivalent rational numbers are $\frac{-6}{8}, \frac{-9}{12}$ and $\frac{-12}{16}$.

(ii) Given rational number is $\frac{7}{11}$.

So, the equivalent rational numbers are

$$\frac{7 \times 2}{11 \times 2} = \frac{14}{22}, \frac{7 \times 3}{11 \times 3} = \frac{21}{33} \text{ and } \frac{7 \times 4}{11 \times 4} = \frac{28}{44}$$

Hence, three equivalent rational numbers are $\frac{14}{22}, \frac{21}{23}$ and $\frac{28}{44}$.

Q. 76 Write the next three rational numbers to complete the pattern:

(i) $\frac{4}{-5}, \frac{8}{-10}, \frac{12}{-15}, \frac{16}{-20}, \underline{\quad}, \underline{\quad}, \underline{\quad}$

(ii) $\frac{-8}{7}, \frac{-16}{14}, \frac{-24}{21}, \frac{-32}{28}, \underline{\quad}, \underline{\quad}, \underline{\quad}$

Sol. (i) Given rational number is $\frac{4}{-5}$.

So, the next three equivalent rational numbers are

$$\frac{4 \times 5}{-5 \times 5} = \frac{20}{-25}, \frac{4 \times 6}{-5 \times 6} = \frac{24}{-30} \text{ and } \frac{4 \times 7}{-5 \times 7} = \frac{28}{-35}$$

Hence, the next equivalent numbers are $\frac{20}{-25}, \frac{24}{-30}, \frac{28}{-35}$.

(ii) Given rational number is $\dfrac{-8}{7}$.

So, the next three equivalent rational numbers are

$$\dfrac{-8\times 5}{7\times 5}=\dfrac{-40}{35},\ \dfrac{-8\times 6}{7\times 6}=\dfrac{-48}{42}\ \text{and}\ \dfrac{-8\times 7}{7\times 7}=\dfrac{-56}{49}$$

Hence, three next equivalent numbers are $\dfrac{-40}{35},\dfrac{-48}{42},\dfrac{-56}{49}.$

Q. 77 List four rational numbers between $\dfrac{5}{7}$ and $\dfrac{7}{8}$.

Sol. Given rational numbers are $\dfrac{5}{7}$ and $\dfrac{7}{8}$.

For making the same denominators: LCM of 7 and 8 = 56.

i.e. $\dfrac{5\times 8}{7\times 8}=\dfrac{40}{56}$ and $\dfrac{7\times 7}{8\times 7}=\dfrac{49}{56}$

So, the four rational numbers between $\dfrac{40}{56}$ and $\dfrac{49}{56}$ are

$$\dfrac{42}{56},\dfrac{44}{56},\dfrac{46}{56},\dfrac{48}{56}.$$

Q. 78 Find the sum of

(i) $\dfrac{8}{13}$ and $\dfrac{3}{11}$

(ii) $\dfrac{7}{3}$ and $\dfrac{-4}{3}$

Sol. (i) Given, $\dfrac{8}{13}$ and $\dfrac{3}{11}$

$$\text{Sum}=\dfrac{8}{13}+\dfrac{3}{11}=\dfrac{8\times 11}{13\times 11}+\dfrac{3\times 13}{11\times 13}=\dfrac{88}{143}+\dfrac{39}{143} \qquad [\because \text{LCM of 13 and 11}=143]$$

$$=\dfrac{88+39}{143}$$

$$=\dfrac{127}{143}$$

Hence, the sum of $\dfrac{8}{13}$ and $\dfrac{3}{11}$ is $\dfrac{127}{143}.$

(ii) Given, $\dfrac{7}{3}$ and $\dfrac{-4}{3}$

$$\text{Sum}=\dfrac{7}{3}+\left(-\dfrac{4}{3}\right)$$

$$=\dfrac{7}{3}-\dfrac{4}{3} \qquad [\because \text{LCM of 3 and 3}=3]$$

$$=\dfrac{7-4}{3}=\dfrac{3}{3}$$

$$=1$$

Hence, the sum of $\dfrac{7}{3}$ and $\dfrac{-4}{3}$ is 1.

Q. 79 Solve:

(i) $\dfrac{29}{4} - \dfrac{30}{7}$

(ii) $\dfrac{5}{13} - \dfrac{-8}{26}$

Sol. (i) Given, $\dfrac{29}{4} - \dfrac{30}{7} = \dfrac{29 \times 7}{4 \times 7} - \dfrac{30 \times 4}{7 \times 4}$

[∵ LCM of 4 and 7 is 28, so convert each of the given fractions to equivalent fractions with denominator 28]

$= \dfrac{203}{28} - \dfrac{120}{28}$

$= \dfrac{203 - 120}{28} = \dfrac{83}{28}$

(ii) Given, $\dfrac{5}{13} - \left(\dfrac{-8}{26}\right) = \dfrac{5}{13} + \dfrac{8}{26} = \dfrac{5 \times 2}{13 \times 2} + \dfrac{8 \times 1}{26 \times 1}$

[∵ LCM of 13 and 26 is 26, so convert each of the given fractions to equivalent fractions with denominator 26]

$= \dfrac{10}{26} + \dfrac{8}{26}$

$= \dfrac{10 + 8}{26} = \dfrac{18}{26}$

$= \dfrac{18 \div 2}{26 \div 2} = \dfrac{9}{13}$ [dividing numerator and denominator by 2]

Q. 80 Find the product of

(i) $\dfrac{-4}{5}$ and $\dfrac{-5}{12}$

(ii) $\dfrac{-22}{11}$ and $\dfrac{-21}{11}$

Sol. (i) Given, $\dfrac{-4}{5}$ and $\dfrac{-5}{12}$

∴ Product of rational numbers $= \dfrac{\text{Product of numerators}}{\text{Product of denominators}}$

$= \dfrac{(-4) \times (-5)}{5 \times 12} = \dfrac{20}{60}$

$= \dfrac{20 \div 20}{60 \div 20}$ [dividing numerator and denominator by 20]

$= \dfrac{1}{3}$

(ii) Given, $\dfrac{-22}{11}$ and $\dfrac{-21}{11}$

∴ Product of rational numbers $= \dfrac{\text{Product of numerators}}{\text{Product of denominators}} = \dfrac{(-22) \times (-21)}{11 \times 11} = \dfrac{462}{121}$

$= \dfrac{462 \div 11}{121 \div 11}$ [dividing numerator and denominator by 11]

$= \dfrac{42}{11}$

Q. 81 Simplify:

(i) $\dfrac{13}{11} \times \dfrac{-14}{5} + \dfrac{13}{11} \times \dfrac{-7}{5} + \dfrac{-13}{11} \times \dfrac{34}{5}$

(ii) $\dfrac{6}{5} \times \dfrac{3}{7} - \dfrac{1}{5} \times \dfrac{3}{7}$

Sol. (i) Given, $\dfrac{13}{11} \times \dfrac{-14}{5} + \dfrac{13}{11} \times \dfrac{-7}{5} + \dfrac{-13}{11} \times \dfrac{34}{5}$

$= \dfrac{13 \times (-14)}{11 \times 5} + \dfrac{13 \times (-7)}{11 \times 5} + \dfrac{(-13) \times 34}{11 \times 5}$

$= \dfrac{-182}{55} + \dfrac{(-91)}{55} + \dfrac{(-442)}{55}$

$= \dfrac{-182 - 91 - 442}{55}$ [taking LCM]

$= \dfrac{-715}{55} = -13$

(ii) Given, $\dfrac{6}{5} \times \dfrac{3}{7} - \dfrac{1}{5} \times \dfrac{3}{7}$

$= \dfrac{6 \times 3}{5 \times 7} - \dfrac{1 \times 3}{5 \times 7} = \dfrac{18}{35} - \dfrac{3}{35}$

$= \dfrac{18 - 3}{35} = \dfrac{15}{35} = \dfrac{15 \div 5}{35 \div 5}$ [dividing numerator and denominator by 5]

$= \dfrac{3}{7}$

Q. 82 Simplify:

(i) $\dfrac{3}{7} \div \left(\dfrac{21}{-55} \right)$

(ii) $1 \div \left(-\dfrac{1}{2} \right)$

Sol. (i) Given, $\dfrac{3}{7} \div \left(\dfrac{21}{-55} \right)$

The reciprocal of $\left(\dfrac{21}{-55} \right)$ is $\dfrac{-55}{21}$.

So, $\dfrac{3}{7} \div \left(\dfrac{21}{-55} \right) = \dfrac{3}{7} \times \dfrac{(-55)}{21} = \dfrac{(-55) \times 3}{7 \times 21} = \dfrac{-55}{49}$

(ii) Given, $1 \div \left(-\dfrac{1}{2} \right)$

The reciprocal of $\left(-\dfrac{1}{2} \right)$ is $\dfrac{2}{-1}$.

So, $1 \div \left(-\dfrac{1}{2} \right) = \dfrac{1}{1} \times \dfrac{2}{-1} = \dfrac{1 \times 2}{1 \times (-1)}$

$= \dfrac{2}{-1} = -2$

Q. 83 Which is greater in the following?

(i) $\dfrac{3}{4}, \dfrac{7}{8}$

(ii) $-3\dfrac{5}{7}, 3\dfrac{1}{9}$

Sol. (i) Given rational numbers are $\dfrac{3}{4}$ and $\dfrac{7}{8}$.

Here, $\dfrac{3}{4} = \dfrac{3 \times 2}{4 \times 2} = \dfrac{6}{8}$ and $\dfrac{7}{8} = \dfrac{7 \times 1}{8 \times 1} = \dfrac{7}{8}$ [∵ LCM of 4 and 8 = 8]

∵ $7 > 6$ [since, the denominators of both rational numbers are same]

So, $\dfrac{7}{8} > \dfrac{3}{4}$

Hence, the greater number is $\dfrac{7}{8}$.

(ii) Given rational numbers are $-3\dfrac{5}{7}$ and $3\dfrac{1}{9}$.

Here, $-3\dfrac{5}{7} = -\dfrac{[(3) \times 7 + 5]}{7} = \dfrac{-[(21) + 5]}{7} = \dfrac{-26}{7}$

Also, $3\dfrac{1}{9} = \dfrac{\{3 \times 9 + 1\}}{9} = \dfrac{\{27 + 1\}}{9} = \dfrac{28}{9}$

So, the rational numbers can be written as $\dfrac{-26}{7}$ and $\dfrac{28}{9}$.

$\dfrac{-26}{7} = \dfrac{-26 \times 9}{7 \times 9} = -\dfrac{234}{63}$ and $\dfrac{28}{9} = \dfrac{28 \times 7}{9 \times 7} = \dfrac{196}{63}$ [∵ LCM of 7 and 9 = 63]

∴ $196 > -234$ [since, the denominators of both rational numbers are same]

So, $3\dfrac{1}{9} > -3\dfrac{5}{7}$

Hence, the greater number is $3\dfrac{1}{9}$.

Q. 84 Write a rational number in which the numerator is less than '-7×11' and the denominator is greater than '$12 + 4$'.

Sol. Let, $-7 \times 11 = p = -77$

and $12 + 4 = q = 16$

Rational number $= \dfrac{p}{q} = \dfrac{-77}{16}$

Hence, it has more than one answer like $\dfrac{-78}{17}, \dfrac{-79}{18}, \dfrac{-80}{19}$.

Q. 85 If $x = \dfrac{1}{10}$ and $y = \dfrac{-3}{8}$, then evaluate $x + y$, $x - y$, $x \times y$ and $x \div y$.

Sol. Given, $x = \dfrac{1}{10}$ and $y = \dfrac{-3}{8}$

Now, $x + y = \dfrac{1}{10} + \dfrac{(-3)}{8} = \dfrac{1}{10} - \dfrac{3}{8}$

$= \dfrac{1 \times 4}{10 \times 4} - \dfrac{3 \times 5}{8 \times 5}$ [∵ LCM of 10 and 8 = 40]

$$= \frac{4}{40} - \frac{15}{40} = \frac{4-15}{40}$$

$$= -\frac{11}{40}$$

and

$$x - y = \frac{1}{10} - \left(-\frac{3}{8}\right) = \frac{1}{10} + \frac{3}{8}$$

$$= \frac{1 \times 4}{10 \times 4} + \frac{3 \times 5}{8 \times 5} \qquad [\because \text{LCM of 10 and 8} = 40]$$

$$= \frac{4}{40} + \frac{15}{40} = \frac{4 + 15}{40}$$

$$= \frac{19}{40}$$

$\therefore$ Product of rational numbers $= \dfrac{\text{Product of numerators}}{\text{Product of denominators}}$

$$\Rightarrow \qquad x \times y = \frac{1}{10} \times \frac{(-3)}{8} = \frac{1 \times (-3)}{10 \times 8} = \frac{-3}{80}$$

and

$$x \div y = \frac{1}{10} \div \left(\frac{-3}{8}\right)$$

The reciprocal of $\left(\dfrac{-3}{8}\right)$ is $\dfrac{8}{-3}$.

So,

$$x \div y = \frac{1}{10} \times \frac{8}{-3}$$

$$= \frac{1 \times 8}{10 \times -3} = \frac{-8}{30} = \frac{-8 \div 2}{30 \div 2} \qquad [\text{dividing numerator and denominator by 2}]$$

$$= \frac{-4}{15}$$

Q. 86 Find the reciprocal of the following:

(i) $\left(\dfrac{1}{2} \times \dfrac{1}{4}\right) + \left(\dfrac{1}{2} \times 6\right)$

(ii) $\dfrac{20}{51} \times \dfrac{4}{91}$

(iii) $\dfrac{3}{13} \div \dfrac{-4}{65}$

(iv) $\left(-5 \times \dfrac{12}{15}\right) - \left(-3 \times \dfrac{2}{9}\right)$

Sol. Reciprocal of any rational number of the form $\dfrac{p}{q}$ is equal to $\dfrac{q}{p}$.

(i) Given, $\left(\dfrac{1}{2} \times \dfrac{1}{4}\right) + \left(\dfrac{1}{2} \times 6\right)$

$$= \frac{1 \times 1}{2 \times 4} + \frac{1 \times 6}{2 \times 1} = \frac{1}{8} + \frac{6}{2} \qquad \left[\because \text{product of rational numbers} = \frac{\text{prodcut of numerators}}{\text{prodcut of denominators}}\right]$$

$$= \frac{1 \times 1}{8 \times 1} + \frac{6 \times 4}{2 \times 4} \qquad [\because \text{LCM of 8 and 2} = 8]$$

$$= \frac{1}{8} + \frac{24}{8} = \frac{1 + 24}{8}$$

$$= \frac{25}{8}$$

Hence, the reciprocal of $\dfrac{25}{8}$ is $\dfrac{8}{25}$.

(ii) Given, $\dfrac{20}{51} \times \dfrac{4}{91}$

$$= \dfrac{20 \times 4}{51 \times 91} \qquad \left[\because \text{product of rational numbers} = \dfrac{\text{product of numerators}}{\text{product of denominators}}\right]$$

$$= \dfrac{80}{4641}$$

Hence, the reciprocal of $\dfrac{80}{4641}$ is $\dfrac{4641}{80}$.

(iii) Given, $\dfrac{3}{13} \div \dfrac{-4}{65}$

The reciprocal of $\dfrac{-4}{65}$ is $\dfrac{65}{-4}$.

$$\therefore \quad \dfrac{3}{13} \div \dfrac{-4}{65} = \dfrac{3}{13} \times \dfrac{65}{-4} = \dfrac{65 \times 3}{13 \times (-4)} = \dfrac{15}{-4}$$

Hence, the reciprocal of $\dfrac{15}{-4}$ is $\dfrac{-4}{15}$.

(iv) Given, $\left(-5 \times \dfrac{12}{15}\right) - \left(-3 \times \dfrac{2}{9}\right) = \left(-\dfrac{12}{3}\right) - \left(-\dfrac{2}{3}\right)$

$$= -\dfrac{12}{3} + \dfrac{2}{3} = \dfrac{-12 + 2}{3} = -\dfrac{10}{3}$$

Hence, the reciprocal of $-\dfrac{10}{3}$ is $-\dfrac{3}{10}$.

Q. 87 Complete the following table by finding the sums.

+	$-\dfrac{1}{9}$	$\dfrac{4}{11}$	$\dfrac{-5}{6}$
$\dfrac{2}{3}$			
$-\dfrac{5}{4}$		$-\dfrac{39}{44}$	
$-\dfrac{1}{3}$			

Sol. Let

+	$-\dfrac{1}{9}$	$\dfrac{4}{11}$	$\dfrac{-5}{6}$
$\dfrac{2}{3}$	a	b	c
$-\dfrac{5}{4}$	d	$-\dfrac{39}{44}$	e
$-\dfrac{1}{3}$	f	g	h

Here, $a = \dfrac{2}{3} + \left(-\dfrac{1}{9}\right)$

$$= \dfrac{2}{3} - \dfrac{1}{9}$$

$$= \frac{2 \times 3}{3 \times 3} - \frac{1 \times 1}{9 \times 1}$$ [∵ LCM of 3 and 9 = 9]

$$= \frac{6}{9} - \frac{1}{9} = \frac{6-1}{9} = \frac{5}{9}$$

$$b = \frac{2}{3} + \frac{4}{11}$$

$$= \frac{2 \times 11}{3 \times 11} + \frac{4 \times 3}{11 \times 3}$$ [∵ LCM of 3 and 11 = 33]

$$= \frac{22}{33} + \frac{12}{33} = \frac{22+12}{33}$$

$$= \frac{34}{33}$$

$$c = \frac{2}{3} + \left(-\frac{5}{6} \right)$$

$$= \frac{2}{3} - \frac{5}{6} = \frac{2 \times 2}{3 \times 2} - \frac{5 \times 1}{6 \times 1}$$ [∵ LCM of 3 and 6 = 6]

$$= \frac{4}{6} - \frac{5}{6}$$

$$= \frac{4-5}{6} = -\frac{1}{6}$$

and $$d = -\frac{5}{4} + \left(-\frac{1}{9} \right) = \frac{-5}{4} - \frac{1}{9}$$

$$= \frac{-5 \times 9}{4 \times 9} - \frac{1 \times 4}{9 \times 4}$$ [∵ LCM of 4 and 9 = 36]

$$= \frac{-45}{36} - \frac{4}{36}$$

$$= \frac{-45-4}{36} = \frac{-49}{36}$$

$$e = -\frac{5}{4} + \left(-\frac{5}{6} \right) = -\frac{5}{4} - \frac{5}{6}$$

$$= \frac{-5 \times 3}{4 \times 3} - \frac{5 \times 2}{6 \times 2}$$ [∵ LCM of 4 and 6 = 12]

$$= \frac{-15}{12} - \frac{10}{12}$$

$$= \frac{-15-10}{12} = -\frac{25}{12}$$

and $$f = -\frac{1}{3} + \left(-\frac{1}{9} \right) = -\frac{1}{3} - \frac{1}{9}$$

$$= \frac{-1 \times 3}{3 \times 3} - \frac{1 \times 1}{9 \times 1}$$ [∵ LCM of 3 and 9 = 3]

$$= \frac{-3}{9} - \frac{1}{9} = \frac{-3-1}{9} = \frac{-4}{9}$$

$$g = -\frac{1}{3} + \frac{4}{11}$$

$$= \frac{-1 \times 11}{3 \times 11} + \frac{4 \times 3}{11 \times 3}$$ [∵ LCM of 3 and 11 = 33]

$$= \frac{-11}{33} + \frac{12}{33}$$

$$= \frac{-11+12}{33} = \frac{1}{33}$$

$$h = -\frac{1}{3} + \left(\frac{-5}{6}\right) = -\frac{1}{3} - \frac{5}{6}$$

$$= \frac{-1 \times 2}{3 \times 2} - \frac{5 \times 1}{6 \times 1} \quad [\because \text{LCM of 3 and } 6 = 6]$$

$$= \frac{-2}{6} - \frac{5}{6}$$

$$= \frac{-2-5}{6} = \frac{-7}{6}$$

Hence, the complete table is

+	$-\dfrac{1}{9}$	$\dfrac{4}{11}$	$\dfrac{-5}{6}$
$\dfrac{2}{3}$	$\dfrac{5}{9}$	$\dfrac{34}{33}$	$\dfrac{-1}{6}$
$-\dfrac{5}{4}$	$\dfrac{-49}{36}$	$-\dfrac{39}{44}$	$\dfrac{-25}{12}$
$-\dfrac{1}{3}$	$\dfrac{-4}{9}$	$\dfrac{1}{33}$	$\dfrac{-7}{6}$

Q. 88 Write each of the following numbers in the form $\dfrac{p}{q}$, where p and q are integers.

    (a) six-eighths   (b) three and half

    (c) opposite of 1   (d) one-fourth

    (e) zero   (f) opposite of three-fifths

Sol. (a) Six-eighths $= \dfrac{6}{8}$

    (b) Three and half $= 3\dfrac{1}{2} = \dfrac{3 \times 2 + 1}{2} = \dfrac{7}{2}$

    (c) Opposite of $1 = \dfrac{1}{1}$

    (d) One-fourth $= \dfrac{1}{4}$

    (e) $0 = \dfrac{0}{1}$

    (f) Here, three-fifths $= \dfrac{3}{5}$

       $\therefore$ Opposite of three-fifths $= \dfrac{5}{3}$

Q. 89 If $p = m \times t$ and $q = n \times t$, then $\dfrac{p}{q} = \dfrac{\Box}{\Box}$

Sol. Given, $p = m \times t$ and $q = n \times t$

    $\therefore \dfrac{p}{q} = \dfrac{m \times t}{n \times t} = \dfrac{\boxed{m}}{\boxed{n}}$

Q. 90 Given that, $\dfrac{p}{q}$ and $\dfrac{r}{s}$ are two rational numbers with different denominators and both of them are in standard form. To compare these rational numbers, we say that

(a) $\dfrac{\square}{\square} < \dfrac{\square}{\square}$, if $p \times s < r \times q$

(b) $\dfrac{p}{q} = \dfrac{r}{s}$, if $\dfrac{}{} = \dfrac{}{}$

(c) $\dfrac{\square}{\square} > \dfrac{\square}{\square}$, if $p \times s > r \times q$

Sol. (a) Given, $\qquad\qquad p \times s < r \times q$

$\Rightarrow \qquad\qquad\qquad \dfrac{p}{q} < \dfrac{r}{s}$ [by transferring sides]

(b) Given, $\qquad\qquad \dfrac{p}{q} = \dfrac{r}{s}$

$\Rightarrow \qquad\qquad p \times s = r \times q$ [by cross-multiplication]

(c) Given, $\qquad\qquad p \times s > r \times q$

$\Rightarrow \qquad\qquad\qquad \dfrac{p}{q} > \dfrac{r}{s}$ [by transferring sides]

Q. 91 In each of the following cases, write the rational number whose numerator and denominator are respectively as under:

(a) $5 - 39$ and $54 - 6$
(b) $(-4) \times 6$ and $8 \div 2$
(c) $35 \div (-7)$ and $35 - 18$
(d) $25 + 15$ and $81 \div 40$

Sol. (a) Given, $\qquad\qquad 5 - 39$ and $54 - 6$

Let numerator, $\qquad p = 5 - 39 = -34$

and denominator, $\qquad q = 54 - 6 = 48$

Hence, rational number $= \dfrac{p}{q} = \dfrac{-34}{48}$

(b) Given, $\qquad\qquad (-4) \times 6$ and $8 \div 2$

Let numerator, $\qquad p = (-4) \times 6 = -24$

and denominator $\qquad q = 8 \div 2 = \dfrac{8}{2} = 4$

Hence, rational number $= \dfrac{p}{q} = \dfrac{-24}{4}$

(c) Given, $35 \div (-7)$ and $35 - 18$

Let numerator, $\qquad p = 35 \div (-7) = \dfrac{35}{-7} = -5$

and denominator, $\qquad q = 35 - 18 = 17$

Hence, rational number $= \dfrac{p}{q} = \dfrac{-5}{17}$

(d) Given, $25 + 15$ and $81 \div 40$

Let numerator, $p = 25 + 15 = 40$

and denominator, $q = 81 \div 40 = \dfrac{81}{40}$

Hence, rational number $= \dfrac{p}{q} = 40 \div \dfrac{81}{40} = 40 \times \dfrac{40}{81}$ $\left[\because \text{reciprocal of } \dfrac{81}{40} = \dfrac{40}{81}\right]$

$= \dfrac{1600}{81}$

Q. 92 Write the following as rational numbers in their standard forms.

(a) 35%

(b) 1.2

(c) $-6\dfrac{3}{7}$

(d) $240 \div (-840)$

(e) $115 \div 207$

Sol. (a) Given, $35\% = \dfrac{35}{100}$

7	35
5	5
	1

2	100
2	50
5	25
5	5

By using prime factorisation, we get

$35 = 7 \times 5$ and $100 = 2 \times 2 \times 5 \times 5$

$\therefore$ HCF of 35 and 100 = 5

On dividing numerator and denominator by their HCF, we get

$\dfrac{35 \div 5}{100 \div 5} = \dfrac{7}{20}$

(b) Here, $1.2 = \dfrac{12}{10} = \dfrac{12 \div 2}{10 \div 2} = \dfrac{6}{5}$ $[\because \text{HCF of 12 and 10} = 2]$

(c) Here, $-6\dfrac{3}{7} = -\left(\dfrac{6 \times 7 + 3}{7}\right) = \dfrac{-45}{7}$

(d) Here, $240 \div (-840) = \dfrac{240}{-840}$

$\because$ HCF of 240 and 840 = 120

On dividing numerator and denominator by their HCF, we get

$\dfrac{240 \div 120}{-840 \div 120} = \dfrac{2}{-7}$

$= \dfrac{2 \times (-1)}{-7 \times (-1)}$ [multiplying numerator and denominator by (-1) for positive denominator]

$= \dfrac{-2}{7}$

(e) Given, $115 \div 207 = \dfrac{115}{207}$

5	115
23	23
	1

3	207
3	69
23	23
	1

By using prime factorisation, we get

$115 = 5 \times 23$ and $207 = 3 \times 23 \times 3$

$\therefore$ HCF of 115 and 207 = 23

On dividing numerator and denominator by their HCF, we get

$$\frac{115 \div 23}{207 \div 23} = \frac{5}{9}$$

Q. 93 Find a rational number exactly halfway between

(a) $\dfrac{-1}{3}$ and $\dfrac{1}{3}$

(b) $\dfrac{1}{6}$ and $\dfrac{1}{9}$

(c) $\dfrac{5}{-13}$ and $\dfrac{-7}{9}$

(d) $\dfrac{1}{15}$ and $\dfrac{1}{12}$

Sol. We know that, a rational number, which is halfway between two rational number i.e. a and b
$= \dfrac{a+b}{2}$.

(a) Given rational numbers are $\dfrac{-1}{3}$ and $\dfrac{1}{3}$.

Here, $a = -\dfrac{1}{3}$ and $b = \dfrac{1}{3}$

$\therefore \qquad \dfrac{a+b}{2} = \dfrac{-\dfrac{1}{3} + \dfrac{1}{3}}{2} = \dfrac{0}{2} = 0$

Hence, the exactly halfway between $-\dfrac{1}{3}$ and $\dfrac{1}{3}$ is 0 (zero).

(b) Given rational numbers are $\dfrac{1}{6}$ and $\dfrac{1}{9}$.

Here, $a = \dfrac{1}{6}$ and $b = \dfrac{1}{9}$

$\therefore \qquad \dfrac{a+b}{2} = \dfrac{\dfrac{1}{6} + \dfrac{1}{9}}{2} = \dfrac{\dfrac{1 \times 3}{6 \times 3} + \dfrac{1 \times 2}{9 \times 2}}{2}$ $\qquad$ [$\because$ LCM of 6 and 9 = 18]

$= \dfrac{\dfrac{3}{18} + \dfrac{2}{18}}{2}$

$= \dfrac{\dfrac{3+2}{18}}{2} = \dfrac{\dfrac{5}{18}}{2} = \dfrac{5}{18 \times 2} = \dfrac{5}{36}$

Hence, the exactly halfway between $\dfrac{1}{6}$ and $\dfrac{1}{9}$ is $\dfrac{5}{36}$.

(c) Given rational numbers are $\frac{5}{-13}$ and $\frac{-7}{9}$.

Here, $a = -\frac{5}{13}$ and $b = -\frac{7}{9}$

$\therefore$
$$\frac{a+b}{2} = \frac{\frac{-5}{13} + \left(-\frac{7}{9}\right)}{2} = \frac{\frac{-5}{13} - \frac{7}{9}}{2}$$

$$= \frac{\frac{-5 \times 9}{13 \times 9} - \frac{7 \times 13}{9 \times 13}}{2} \qquad [\because \text{LCM of 13 and } 9 = 117]$$

$$= \frac{\frac{-45}{117} - \frac{91}{117}}{2} = \frac{\frac{-45-91}{117}}{2}$$

$$= \frac{-136}{117 \times 2} = \frac{-136}{234}$$

Hence, the exactly of halfway between $\frac{5}{-13}$ and $\frac{-7}{9}$ is $-\frac{136}{234}$.

(d) Given rational numbers are $\frac{1}{15}$ and $\frac{1}{12}$.

Here, $a = \frac{1}{15}$ and $b = \frac{1}{12}$

$\therefore$
$$\frac{a+b}{2} = \frac{\frac{1}{15} + \frac{1}{12}}{2} = \frac{\frac{1 \times 4}{15 \times 4} + \frac{1 \times 5}{12 \times 5}}{2} \qquad [\because \text{LCM of 15 and } 12 = 60]$$

$$= \frac{\frac{4}{60} + \frac{5}{60}}{2} = \frac{\frac{4+5}{60}}{2} = \frac{9}{60 \times 2} = \frac{9}{120}$$

$$= \frac{3}{40}$$

Hence, the exactly halfway between $\frac{1}{15}$ and $\frac{1}{12}$ is $\frac{3}{40}$.

Q. 94 Taking $x = \frac{-4}{9}$, $y = \frac{5}{12}$ and $z = \frac{7}{18}$, find

    (a) The rational number which when added to x gives y.

    (b) The rational number which subtracted from y given z.

    (c) The rational number which when added to z gives us x.

    (d) The rational number which when multiplied by y to get x.

    (e) The reciprocal of $x + y$.

    (f) The sum of reciprocals of x and y.

    (g) $(x \div y) \times z$

    (h) $(x - y) + z$

    (i) $x + (y + z)$

    (j) $x \div (y \div z)$

    (k) $x - (y + z)$

Sol. Given, $x = \dfrac{-4}{9}, y = \dfrac{5}{12}$ and $z = \dfrac{7}{18}$

(a) Let we add A to x to get y.

$\therefore \qquad A + x = y$

$\Rightarrow A + \left(\dfrac{-4}{9}\right) = \dfrac{5}{12}$

$\Rightarrow A = \dfrac{5}{12} - \left(-\dfrac{4}{9}\right) = \dfrac{5}{12} + \dfrac{4}{9} = \dfrac{5 \times 3 + 4 \times 4}{36}$ [∵ LCM of 12 and 9 = 36]

$\qquad = \dfrac{15 + 16}{36} = \dfrac{31}{36}$

(b) Let we subtract A from y to get z.

$\therefore \qquad y - A = z$

$\Rightarrow \dfrac{5}{12} - A = \dfrac{7}{18}$

$\Rightarrow \qquad - A = \dfrac{7}{18} - \dfrac{5}{12} = \dfrac{7 \times 2 - 5 \times 3}{36}$ [∵ LCM of 18 and 12 = 36]

$\qquad = \dfrac{14 - 15}{36} = \dfrac{-1}{36}$

$\Rightarrow \qquad A = \dfrac{1}{36}$

(c) Let A be added to z to give x.

$\therefore \qquad\qquad A + z = x$

$\Rightarrow \qquad\qquad A + \dfrac{7}{18} = \dfrac{-4}{9}$

$\Rightarrow \qquad\qquad A = \dfrac{-4}{9} - \dfrac{7}{18} = \dfrac{-4 \times 2 - 7 \times 1}{18}$ [∵ LCM of 9 and 18 = 18]

$\qquad = \dfrac{-8 - 7}{18} = \dfrac{-15}{18} = \dfrac{-5}{6}$

(d) Suppose, if A is multiplied by y, then we get x.

i.e. $A \times y = x$

$\Rightarrow A \times \dfrac{5}{12} = \dfrac{-4}{9}$

$\Rightarrow \qquad A = \dfrac{-4}{9} \times \dfrac{12}{5} = \dfrac{-48}{45}$

(e) Here, $x + y = \dfrac{-4}{9} + \dfrac{5}{12} = \dfrac{-4 \times 4 + 5 \times 3}{36}$ [∵ LCM of 9 and 12 = 36]

$\Rightarrow \qquad\qquad x + y = \dfrac{-16 + 15}{36} = \dfrac{-1}{36}$

$\therefore$ Reciprocal of $x + y = \dfrac{1}{-1/36} = -36$

(f) Reciprocal of x and y is $\dfrac{1}{x}$ and $\dfrac{1}{y}$.

$\therefore$ Sum of reciprocals $= \dfrac{1}{x} + \dfrac{1}{y} = \dfrac{1}{-4/9} + \dfrac{1}{5/12}$

$\qquad\qquad = \dfrac{-9}{4} + \dfrac{12}{5} = \dfrac{-45 + 48}{20}$ [∵ LCM of 4 and 5 = 20]

$\qquad\qquad = \dfrac{3}{20}$

(g) We have, $(x \div y) \times z$

$$= \left(\frac{-4}{9} \div \frac{5}{12}\right) \times \frac{7}{18}$$

$$= \left(\frac{-4}{9} \times \frac{12}{5}\right) \times \frac{7}{18} \qquad \left[\because \text{reciprocal of } \frac{5}{12} = \frac{12}{5}\right]$$

$$= \frac{-4 \times 12 \times 7}{9 \times 5 \times 18} \qquad \left[\because \text{product of rational numbers} = \frac{\text{product of numerators}}{\text{product of denominators}}\right]$$

$$= \frac{-56}{135}$$

(h) We have,

$$(x - y) + z = \left(\frac{-4}{9} - \frac{5}{12}\right) + \frac{7}{18} = \frac{-4 \times 4 - 5 \times 3}{36} + \frac{7}{18} \qquad [\because \text{LCM of 9 and 12} = 36]$$

$$= \frac{-16 - 15}{36} + \frac{7}{18} = \left(\frac{-31}{36} + \frac{7}{18}\right)$$

$$= \frac{-31 + 7 \times 2}{36} = \frac{-31 + 14}{36}$$

$$= \frac{-17}{36}$$

(i) Here, $x + (y + z) = \frac{-4}{9} + \left(\frac{5}{12} + \frac{7}{18}\right) = \frac{-4}{9} + \left(\frac{5 \times 3 + 7 \times 2}{36}\right) [\because \text{LCM of 12 and 18} = 36]$

$$= \frac{-4}{9} + \left(\frac{15 + 14}{36}\right)$$

$$= \frac{-4}{9} + \frac{29}{36} = \frac{-4 \times 4 + 29}{36} = \frac{13}{36}$$

(j) Here, $x \div (y \div z) = \frac{-4}{9} \div \left(\frac{5}{12} \div \frac{7}{18}\right) = \frac{-4}{9} \div \left(\frac{5}{12} \times \frac{18}{7}\right) \qquad \left[\because \text{reciprocal of } \frac{7}{18} = \frac{18}{7}\right]$

$$= \frac{-4}{9} \div \frac{15}{14} = \frac{-4}{9} \times \frac{14}{15} = \frac{-56}{135} \qquad \left[\because \text{reciprocal of } \frac{15}{14} = \frac{14}{15}\right]$$

(k) Here, $x - (y + z) = \frac{-4}{9} - \left(\frac{5}{12} + \frac{7}{18}\right)$

$$= \frac{-4}{9} - \left(\frac{5 \times 3 + 7 \times 2}{36}\right) = \frac{-4}{9} - \left(\frac{15 + 14}{36}\right) [\because \text{LCM of 12 and 18} = 36]$$

$$= \frac{-4}{9} - \frac{29}{36} = \frac{-4 \times 4 - 29}{36} = \frac{-16 - 29}{36}$$

$$= \frac{-45}{36} = \frac{-5}{4}$$

Q. 95 What should be added to $\frac{-1}{2}$ to obtain the nearest natural number?

Sol. We know that, nearest number of $\frac{-1}{2}$ is 1.

Let x be added to $-\frac{1}{2}$ to obtain 1.

Then, $\qquad\qquad\qquad -\frac{1}{2} + x = 1$

$$\Rightarrow \qquad x = 1 + \frac{1}{2} = \frac{2+1}{2}$$

$$\Rightarrow \qquad x = \frac{3}{2}$$

Hence, $\frac{3}{2}$ should be added to $\frac{-1}{2}$ to obtain nearest natural number.

Q. 96 What should be subtracted from $\frac{-2}{3}$ to obtain the nearest integer?

Sol. Given rational number is $\frac{-2}{3}$.

We know that, nearest natural number of $\frac{-2}{3}$ is -1.

Let x be subtracted to $\frac{-2}{3}$ to obtain -1.

Then, $\qquad \frac{-2}{3} - x = -1$

$$\Rightarrow \qquad x = \frac{-2}{3} + 1 = \frac{1}{3}$$

So, we subtract $\frac{1}{3}$ from $\frac{-2}{3}$ to get the nearest integer.

Q. 97 What should be multiplied with $\frac{-5}{8}$ to obtain the nearest integer?

Sol. Let number be x.

We know that, nearest integer of $-\frac{5}{8}$ is -1

According to the question, $\qquad \frac{-5}{8} \times x = -1$

$$\Rightarrow \qquad x = -1 \times \frac{8}{-5} = \frac{8}{5}$$

Hence, the required number is $\frac{8}{5}$.

Q. 98 What should be divided by $\frac{1}{2}$ to obtain the greatest negative integer?

Sol. Let the number be x.

We know that, greatest negative integer is -1.

According to the question,

$$\frac{1}{2} \div x = -1$$

$$\Rightarrow \qquad \frac{1}{2} \times \frac{1}{x} = -1 \qquad \left[\because \text{reciprocal of } x = \frac{1}{x} \right]$$

$$\Rightarrow \qquad \frac{1}{x} = -1 \times \frac{2}{1}$$

$$\Rightarrow \qquad \frac{1}{x} = \frac{-2}{1}$$

$$\Rightarrow \qquad x = \frac{-1}{2}$$

Hence, the required number is $\frac{-1}{2}$.

Q. 99 From a rope 68 m long, pieces of equal size are cut. If length of one piece is $4\dfrac{1}{4}$ m, find the number of such pieces.

Sol. Given, length of the rope = 68 m

and length of small piece $= 4\dfrac{1}{4}\,\text{m} = \dfrac{(4 \times 4) + 1}{4}\,\text{m} = \dfrac{17}{4}\,\text{m}$

$\therefore$ Number of pieces $= \dfrac{\text{Total length of rope}}{\text{Length of small piece}} = \dfrac{68}{\dfrac{17}{4}}$

$= \dfrac{68}{1} \times \dfrac{4}{17}$ $\left[\because \text{reciprocal of } \dfrac{17}{4} = \dfrac{4}{17}\right]$

$= 4 \times 4 = 16$

Hence, the number of pieces is 16.

Q. 100 If 12 shirts of equal size can be prepared from 27 m cloth, what is length of cloth required for each shirt?

Sol. Given, total size of available cloth = 27 m

Since, 12 shirts can be made from 27 m long cloth.

$\therefore$ Length of cloth required for each shirt $= \dfrac{\text{Total available cloth}}{\text{Number of shirts}}$

$= \dfrac{27}{12} = \dfrac{9}{4}$

$= 2.25\,\text{m}$

Hence, 2.25 m cloth required for each shirt.

Q. 101 Insert 3 equivalent rational numbers between

(i) $\dfrac{-1}{2}$ and $\dfrac{1}{5}$ (ii) 0 and -10

Sol. (i) Given, rational numbers are $-\dfrac{1}{2}$ and $\dfrac{1}{5}$.

For common denominator, LCM of 2 and 5 = 10

$\therefore$ $\dfrac{-1 \times 5}{2 \times 5} = \dfrac{-5}{10}$ and $\dfrac{1 \times 2}{5 \times 2} = \dfrac{2}{10}$

Hence, three equivalent rational numbers between $\dfrac{-5}{10}$ and $\dfrac{2}{10}$ are $\dfrac{-3}{10}, \dfrac{-6}{20}, \dfrac{-9}{30}$.

(ii) Three equivalent rational numbers between 0 and -10 are $-2, \dfrac{-10}{5}, \dfrac{-20}{10}$.

Note *In this question, student should note that answer can vary.*

Q. 102 Put the (✓), wherever applicable

	Number	Natural number	Whole number	Integer	Fraction	Rational number
(a)	-114					
(b)	$\dfrac{19}{27}$					
(c)	$\dfrac{623}{1}$					
(d)	$-19\dfrac{3}{4}$					
(e)	$\dfrac{73}{71}$					
(f)	0					

Sol. We know that,

Natural numbers are 1, 2, 3, 4, ...

Whole numbers are 0, 1, 2, 3, ...

Integers are $-2, -1, 0, 1, 2, ...$

Fractions are $\dfrac{1}{2}, \dfrac{3}{5}, \dfrac{7}{2}, ...$

Rational numbers are $\dfrac{3}{2}, \dfrac{-1}{2}, \dfrac{-7}{8}, ...$

So, according to the number systems,

(a) $-114 \rightarrow$ Integer and rational number

(b) $\dfrac{19}{27} \rightarrow$ Fraction and rational number

(c) $\dfrac{623}{1} \rightarrow$ Natural number, whole number, integer, fraction and rational number

(d) $-19\dfrac{3}{4} = -\dfrac{79}{4} \rightarrow$ Rational number

(e) $\dfrac{73}{71} \rightarrow$ Fraction and rational number

(f) $0 \rightarrow$ Whole number, integer, fraction and rational number

Hence, the table is

Number	Natural number	Whole number	Integer	Fraction	Rational number
-114			✓		✓
$\dfrac{19}{27}$				✓	✓
$\dfrac{623}{1}$	✓	✓	✓	✓	✓
$-19\dfrac{3}{4}$					✓
$\dfrac{73}{71}$				✓	✓
0		✓	✓	✓	✓

Q. 103 'a' and 'b' are two different numbers taken from the numbers 1-50. What is the largest value that $\dfrac{a-b}{a+b}$ can have? What is the largest value that $\dfrac{a+b}{a-b}$ can have?

Sol. Given, a and b are two different numbers between 1 to 50.

Let a = 50 and b = 1

∴ $\dfrac{a-b}{a+b} = \dfrac{50-1}{50+1} = \dfrac{49}{51}$, which is the largest value.

Similarly,

Let a = 50 and b = 49

∴ $\dfrac{a+b}{a-b} = \dfrac{50+49}{50-49} = \dfrac{99}{1} = 99$, which is the largest value.

Q. 104 150 students are studying English, Maths or both. 62% of the students are studying English and 68% are studying Maths. How many students are studying both?

Sol. Given, total students in the class studying English, Maths or both = 150

Students studying English = 62% of 150 = $\dfrac{62}{100} \times 150 = 93$

Students studying Maths = 68% of 150 = $\dfrac{68}{100} \times 150 = 102$

Total students studying both = Students studying English + Students studying Maths
− Students studying English, Maths or both

= 93 + 102 − 150 = 45

Q. 105 A body floats $\dfrac{2}{9}$ of its volume above the surface. What is the ratio of the body submerged volume to its exposed volume? Rewrite it as a rational number.

Sol. Given, volume of body exposed = $\dfrac{2}{9}$

∴ Volume of body submerged = 1 − Volume of body exposed

$= 1 - \dfrac{2}{9} = \dfrac{9-2}{9} = \dfrac{7}{9}$

∴ Required ratio $= \dfrac{7}{9} : \dfrac{2}{9} = \dfrac{7}{9} \div \dfrac{2}{9} = \dfrac{7}{9} \times \dfrac{9}{2} = \dfrac{7}{2} = 7 : 2$

In rational number $= \dfrac{7}{2}$

In questions 106 to 109, find the odd one out of the following and give reason.

Q. 106 (a) $\dfrac{4}{3} \times \dfrac{3}{4}$ (b) $\dfrac{-3}{2} \times \dfrac{-2}{3}$

(c) $2 \times \dfrac{1}{2}$ (d) $\dfrac{-1}{3} \times \dfrac{3}{1}$

Sol. (a) Given, $\dfrac{4}{3} \times \dfrac{3}{4}$

$\therefore$ Product of rational numbers $= \dfrac{\text{Product of numerators}}{\text{Product of denominators}}$

$$= \dfrac{4 \times 3}{3 \times 4} = \dfrac{12}{12} = 1$$

(b) Similarly, $\dfrac{-3}{2} \times \dfrac{-2}{3} = \dfrac{(-3) \times (-2)}{2 \times 3} = \dfrac{6}{6} = 1$

(c) $\dfrac{2}{1} \times \dfrac{1}{2} = \dfrac{2 \times 1}{1 \times 2} = \dfrac{2}{2} = 1$

(d) $-\dfrac{1}{3} \times \dfrac{3}{1} = \dfrac{(-1) \times 3}{3 \times 1} = \dfrac{-3}{3} = -1$

Since, the value of options (a), (b), (c) are 1 and option (d) is -1.
Hence, option (d) is odd out.

Q. 107 (a) $\dfrac{4}{-9}$ (b) $\dfrac{-16}{36}$ (c) $\dfrac{-20}{-45}$ (d) $\dfrac{28}{-63}$

Sol. From the above given rational numbers, $\dfrac{-20}{-45}$ is odd among others, because $\dfrac{-20}{-45}$ can be written as $\dfrac{20}{45}$, which is only positive rational number among all.

Q. 108 (a) $\dfrac{-4}{3}$ (b) $\dfrac{-7}{6}$ (c) $\dfrac{-10}{3}$ (d) $\dfrac{-8}{7}$

Sol. From the above given rational numbers, $\dfrac{-7}{6}$ is odd among others, because all the three except $-\dfrac{7}{6}$ has even numerator and odd denominator.

Q. 109 (a) $\dfrac{-3}{7}$ (b) $\dfrac{-9}{15}$ (c) $\dfrac{24}{20}$ (d) $\dfrac{35}{25}$

Sol. From the above given rational numbers, we can see that $\dfrac{-3}{7}$ is in its lowest form while others have common factor in numerator and denominator.

Q. 110 What's the Error? Chhaya simplified a rational number is this manner $\dfrac{-25}{-30} = \dfrac{-5}{6}$. What error did the student make?

Sol. If a negative (–) sign comes in both numerator and denominator, then it will be cancelled. So, the resulting fraction will be positive.

$\therefore$ $\dfrac{-25}{-30} = \dfrac{25}{30} = \dfrac{5}{6}$

Here, Chhaya divided numerator by 5 but denominator by –5.

9

Perimeter and Area

Multiple Choice Questions (MCQs)

Q. 1 Observe the shapes 1, 2, 3 and 4 in the figures. Which of the following statements is not correct?

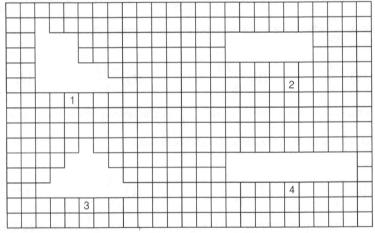

(a) Shapes 1, 3 and 4 have different areas and different perimeters
(b) Shapes 1 and 4 have the same areas as well as the same perimeters
(c) Shapes 1, 2 and 4 have the same areas
(d) Shapes 1, 3 and 4 have the same perimeters

Sol. *(a)*   **Shape 1**

Perimeter = 1+ 1+ 1+ 1+ 1+ 1+ 1+ 1+ 1+ 1+ 1+ 1+ 1+ 1+ 1+ 1+ 1+ 1+ 1+ 1+ 1+ 1
              = 22 units

     Area = 18 × 1
             = 18 sq units

Shape 2

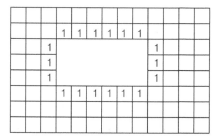

Perimeter = 1+ 1+ 1+ 1+ 1+ 1+ 1+ 1+ 1+ 1+ 1+ 1+ 1+ 1+ 1+ 1+ 1+ 1
              = 18 units

     Area = 18 × 1
             = 18 sq units

Shape 3

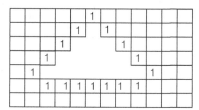

Perimeter = 1+ 1+ 1+ 1+ 1+ 1+ 1+ 1+ 1+ 1+ 1+ 1+ 1+ 1+ 1+ 1+ 1+ 1+ 1+ 1+ 1+ 1
              = 22 units

     Area = 16 × 1
             = 16 sq units

Shape 4

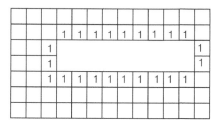

Perimeter = 1+ 1+ 1+ 1+ 1+ 1+ 1+ 1+ 1+ 1+ 1+ 1+ 1+ 1+ 1+ 1+ 1+ 1+ 1+ 1+ 1+ 1+ 1
              = 22 units

     Area = 18 × 1
             = 18 sq units

So, only option (a) is false.

Q. 2 A rectangular piece of dimensions 3 cm × 2 cm was cut from a rectangular sheet of paper of dimensions 6 cm × 5 cm (see the figure). Area of remaining sheet of paper is

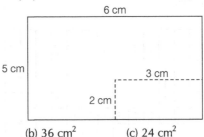

(a) 30 cm²   (b) 36 cm²   (c) 24 cm²   (d) 22 cm²

Sol. *(c)* Given dimensions of the bigger rectangle are 6 cm and 5 cm.

∴ Area of bigger rectangle = 6 cm × 5 cm   30 cm²

[∵ area of rectangle = length × breadth]

Also given, dimensions of the smaller rectangle are 3 cm and 2 cm.

∴ Area of smaller rectangle = 3 cm × 2 cm = 6 cm²

∴ Area of remaining sheet of paper = Area of bigger rectangle
− Area of smaller rectangle
= (30 − 6) cm² = 24 cm²

Q. 3 36 unit squares are joined to form a rectangle with the least perimeter. Perimeter of the rectangle is

(a) 12 units   (b) 26 units   (c) 24 units   (d) 36 units

Sol. *(b)* Area of rectangle formed = 36 units

We have, $36 = 6 \times 6$

$= 2 \times 3 \times 2 \times 3$

$= 2^2 \times 3^2$

$= 4 \times 9$

So, the sides of a rectangle are 4 cm and 9 cm.

∴ Perimeter

$= 2(l + b)$

$= 2(4 + 9)$

$= 2 \times 13$

$= 26$ units

Q. 4 A wire is bent to form a square of side 22 cm. If the wire is rebent to form a circle, its radius is

(a) 22 cm   (b) 14 cm   (c) 11 cm   (d) 7 cm

Sol. *(b)* Given, side of a square = 22 cm

Perimeter of square and circumference of circle are equal, because the wire has same length.

According to the question,

Perimeter of square = Circumference of circle

$\Rightarrow \qquad 4 \times (\text{Side}) = 2 \times \pi \times r$

$\Rightarrow \qquad 4 \times 22 = 2 \times \dfrac{22}{7} \times r \qquad\qquad \left[\because \pi = \dfrac{22}{7}\right]$

$\Rightarrow \qquad r = \dfrac{4 \times 22 \times 7}{2 \times 22}$

$\Rightarrow \qquad r = 14\,\text{cm}$

Hence, the radius is 14 cm.

Q. 5 Area of the circle obtained in Q.4 is

(a) 196 cm^2 (b) 212 cm^2 (c) 616 cm^2 (d) 644 cm^2

Sol. *(c)*   Area of the circle $= \pi r^2 = \dfrac{22}{7} \times 14 \times 14 = 616\,\text{cm}^2$ [$\because r = 14\,\text{cm}$, find above]

Q. 6 Area of a rectangle and the area of a circle are equal. If the dimensions of the rectangle are 14 cm × 11 cm, then radius of the circle is

(a) 21 cm   (b) 10.5 cm   (c) 14 cm   (d) 7 cm

Sol. *(d)*   Given, dimensions of rectangle, $l = 14\,\text{cm}$ and $b = 11\,\text{cm}$

According to the question,

Area of rectangle = Area of circle

$\Rightarrow \qquad l \times b = \pi r^2$

$\Rightarrow \qquad 14 \times 11 = \dfrac{22}{7} \times r^2 \quad \Rightarrow \quad r^2 = \dfrac{14 \times 11 \times 7}{22} \qquad\qquad \left[\because \pi = \dfrac{22}{7}\right]$

$\Rightarrow \qquad r^2 = 49 \quad \Rightarrow \quad r = \sqrt{49}$

$\Rightarrow \qquad r = 7\,\text{cm}$

Hence, the radius of circle is 7 cm.

Q. 7 Area of shaded portion in the figure given below is

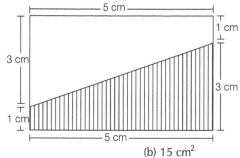

(a) 25 cm^2 (b) 15 cm^2

(c) 14 cm^2 (d) 10 cm^2

Sol. *(d)*   From the given figure,

Length of rectangle $(l) = 5\,\text{cm}$ and breadth of rectangle $(b) = 3 + 1 = 4\,\text{cm}$

$\therefore$ Area of shaded portion $= \dfrac{1}{2} \times$ Area of rectangle $= \dfrac{1}{2} \times (l \times b)$

$\qquad\qquad\qquad\qquad = \dfrac{1}{2} \times 5 \times 4 = 10\,\text{cm}^2$

Q. 8 Area of parallelogram *ABCD* (see the figure) is not equal to

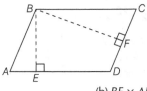

　　(a) $DE \times DC$　　　　　　　　　　　(b) $BE \times AD$
　　(c) $BF \times DC$　　　　　　　　　　　(d) $BE \times BC$

Sol. (a)　We know that,

Area of parallelogram = Base × Corresponding Height

So, area of parallelogram $ABCD = AD \times BE = BC \times BE$ 　　　　$[\because AD = BC]$

or area of parallelogram $ABCD = DC \times BF$

Q. 9 Area of △ *MNO* in the figure is

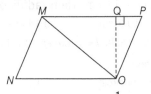

　　(a) $\dfrac{1}{2}MN \times NO$　　　　　　　　(b) $\dfrac{1}{2}NO \times MO$

　　(c) $\dfrac{1}{2}MN \times OQ$　　　　　　　　(d) $\dfrac{1}{2}NO \times OQ$

Sol (d)　We know that,

Area of triangle $= \dfrac{1}{2} \times$ Base × Height

$= \dfrac{1}{2} \times NO \times OQ$

Q. 10 Ratio of area of △*MNO* to the area of parallelogram *MNOP* in the same figure of Q.9 is

　　(a) 2 : 3　　　　　　　　　　　　　(b) 1 : 1
　　(c) 1 : 2　　　　　　　　　　　　　(d) 2 : 1

Sol. (c)　Area of △*MNO* : Area of parallelogram *MNOP*

$= \dfrac{1}{2} \times$ Base × Height : Base × Corresponding Height

$= \dfrac{1}{2} \times NO \times OQ : MP \times OQ = \dfrac{1}{2} \times NO : NO$　　　　$[\because NO = MP]$

$= 1 : 2$

Hence, the required ratio is $1 : 2$.

Q. 11 Ratio of areas of $\triangle MNO$, $\triangle MOP$ and $\triangle MPQ$ in the given figure is

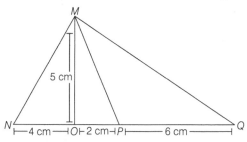

(a) 2 : 1 : 3   (b) 1 : 3 : 2

(c) 2 : 3 : 1   (d) 1 : 2 : 3

Sol *(a)*   From the given figure,

$$\text{Area of } \triangle MNO = \frac{1}{2} \times NO \times MO = \frac{1}{2} \times 4 \times 5 = 10\,\text{cm}^2$$

$$\left[\because \text{area of triangle} = \frac{1}{2} \times \text{base} \times \text{height} \right]$$

$$\text{Area of } \triangle MOP = \frac{1}{2} \times OP \times MO = \frac{1}{2} \times 2 \times 5 = 5\,\text{cm}^2$$

$$\text{Area of } \triangle MPQ = \frac{1}{2} \times PQ \times MO = \frac{1}{2} \times 6 \times 5 = 15\,\text{cm}^2$$

Hence, required ratio $= 10 : 5 : 15 = 2 : 1 : 3$

Q. 12 In the given figure, *EFGH* is a parallelogram, altitudes *FK* and *FI* are 8 cm and 4 cm, respectively. If *EF* = 10 cm, then the area of *EFGH* is

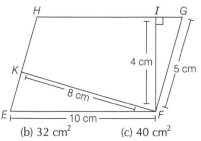

(a) 20 cm²   (b) 32 cm²   (c) 40 cm²   (d) 80 cm²

Sol. *(c)*   In parallelogram *EFGH*, $EF = HG = 10\,\text{cm}$ [given]

Area of parallelogram $EFGH = \text{Base} \times \text{Corresponding height} = 10 \times 4 = 40\,\text{cm}^2$

Q. 13 In reference to a circle the value of π is equal to

(a) $\dfrac{\text{Area}}{\text{Circumference}}$ (b) $\dfrac{\text{Area}}{\text{Diameter}}$ (c) $\dfrac{\text{Circumference}}{\text{Diameter}}$ (d) $\dfrac{\text{Circumference}}{\text{Radius}}$

Sol. *(c)*   We know that,

Circumference of a circle $= 2\pi r$

Circumference $= \pi \times \text{Diameter}$ [$\because$ diameter $= 2r$]

$$\Rightarrow \qquad \pi = \frac{\text{Circumference}}{\text{Diameter}}$$

Q. 14 Circumference of a circle is always

(a) more than three times of its diameter
(b) three times of its diameter
(c) less than three times of its diameter
(d) three times of its radius

Sol. *(a)*   We know that,

Circumference of a circle $= 2\pi r$

$\therefore$ Circumference $= 2 \times 3.14 \times r$ $\hspace{4cm}$ [$\because \pi = 3.14$]

$\Rightarrow$ Circumference $= 3.14 \times d$ $\hspace{4.5cm}$ [$\because d = 2r$]

So, circumference of circle is always more than three times of its diameter.

Q. 15 Area of $\triangle PQR$ is 100 cm^2 as shown in the below figure. If altitude QT is 10 cm, then its base PR is

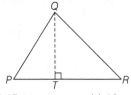

(a) 20 cm $\hspace{1.5cm}$ (b) 15 cm $\hspace{1.5cm}$ (c) 10 cm $\hspace{1.5cm}$ (d) 5 cm

Sol. *(a)*   Given, area of $\triangle PQR = 100$ cm^2

We know that,

Area of a triangle $= \dfrac{1}{2} \times$ Base $\times$ Height

$\therefore$ Area of $\triangle PQR = \dfrac{1}{2} \times PR \times QT$

$\Rightarrow \hspace{1.5cm} 100 = \dfrac{1}{2} \times PR \times 10$ $\hspace{2.5cm}$ [$\because QT = 10$ cm, given]

$\Rightarrow \hspace{1.5cm} PR = \dfrac{100 \times 2}{10}$

$\Rightarrow \hspace{1.5cm} PR = 20$ cm

Q. 16 In the given figure, if $PR = 12$ cm, $QR = 6$ cm and $PL = 8$ cm, then QM is

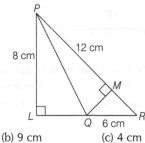

(a) 6 cm $\hspace{1.5cm}$ (b) 9 cm $\hspace{1.5cm}$ (c) 4 cm $\hspace{1.5cm}$ (d) 2 cm

Sol. *(c)*   Given that, $PR = 12$ cm, $QR = 6$ cm and $PL = 8$ cm

Now, in right angled $\triangle PLR$, using Pythagoras theorem,

(Hypotenuse)^2 = (Perpendicular)^2 + (Base)^2

$$\Rightarrow \qquad PR^2 = PL^2 + LR^2$$

$$\Rightarrow \qquad LR^2 = PR^2 - PL^2 = (12)^2 - (8)^2$$

$$\Rightarrow \qquad LR^2 = 144 - 64 = 80$$

$$\Rightarrow \qquad LR = \sqrt{80} = 4\sqrt{5} \text{ cm}$$

$$\because \qquad LR = LQ + QR \quad \Rightarrow \quad LQ = LR - QR = (4\sqrt{5} - 6)\text{ cm}$$

Now, area of $\triangle PLR$,

$$A_1 = \frac{1}{2} \times LR \times PL$$

$$= \frac{1}{2} \times (4\sqrt{5}) \times 8$$

$$= 16\sqrt{5} \text{ cm}^2$$

Again, area of $\triangle PLQ$,

$$A_2 = \frac{1}{2} \times LQ \times PL$$

$$= \frac{1}{2} \times (4\sqrt{5} - 6) \times 8$$

$$= (16\sqrt{5} - 24)\text{cm}^2$$

$\therefore$ Area of $\triangle PLR$ = Area of $\triangle PLQ$ + Area of $\triangle PQR$

$$\Rightarrow \qquad 16\sqrt{5} = (16\sqrt{5} - 24) + \text{Area of } \triangle PQR$$

$$\Rightarrow \qquad \text{Area of } \triangle PQR = 24 \text{ cm}^2$$

$$\Rightarrow \qquad \frac{1}{2} \times PR \times QM = 24$$

$$\Rightarrow \qquad \frac{1}{2} \times 12 \times QM = 24$$

$$\therefore \qquad QM = 4\text{cm}$$

Q. 17 In the given figure, $\triangle MNO$ is a right angled triangle. Its legs are 6 cm and 8 cm long. Length of perpendicular NP on the side MO is

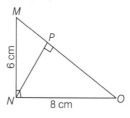

(a) 4.8 cm   (b) 3.6 cm   (c) 2.4 cm   (d) 1.2 cm

Sol. *(a)*   Given, $\triangle MNO$ is a right angled triangle.

So, according to Pythagoras theorem,

$$MO^2 = MN^2 + NO^2 = 6^2 + 8^2 = 36 + 64$$

$$\Rightarrow \qquad MO^2 = 100 \quad \Rightarrow \quad MO = \sqrt{100}$$

$$\Rightarrow \qquad MO = 10 \text{ cm}$$

$\therefore$ Area of $\triangle MNO = \dfrac{1}{2} \times$ Base $\times$ Height

$$\Rightarrow \qquad \frac{1}{2} \times MN \times NO = \frac{1}{2} \times MO \times NP$$

$$\Rightarrow \qquad \frac{1}{2} \times 6 \times 8 = \frac{1}{2} \times 10 \times NP$$

$$\Rightarrow \qquad NP = \frac{24}{5}$$

$$\Rightarrow \qquad NP = 4.8 \text{ cm}$$

Q. 18 Area of a right angled triangle is 30 cm². If its smallest side is 5 cm, then its hypotenuse is

(a) 14 cm   (b) 13 cm   (c) 12 cm   (d) 11 cm

Sol. (*b*)   Given, area of a right angled triangle = 30 cm²

and smallest side i.e. base = 5 cm

We know that,

Area of right angled triangle $= \dfrac{1}{2} \times$ Base $\times$ Height

∴ $\qquad\qquad 30 = \dfrac{1}{2} \times 5 \times$ Height

$\Rightarrow \qquad$ Height $= \dfrac{30 \times 2}{5}$

$\Rightarrow \qquad$ Height $= 12$ cm

Now, according to Pythagoras theorem,

$(\text{Hypotenuse})^2 = (\text{Perpendicular})^2 + (\text{Base})^2$

$\Rightarrow \qquad (\text{Hypotenuse})^2 = (12)^2 + (5)^2$ [∵ height = perpendicular]

$\Rightarrow \qquad (\text{Hypotenuse})^2 = 144 + 25$

$\Rightarrow \qquad (\text{Hypotenuse})^2 = 169$

$\Rightarrow \qquad$ Hypotenuse $= \sqrt{169}$

$\Rightarrow \qquad$ Hypotenuse $= 13$ cm

Q. 19 Circumference of a circle of diameter 5 cm is

(a) 3.14 cm   (b) 31.4 cm   (c) 15.7 cm   (d) 1.57 cm

Sol. (*c*)   Given, diameter of a circle = 5 cm

∴ Radius $= \dfrac{5}{2}$ cm $\left[∵ \text{radius} = \dfrac{\text{diameter}}{2} \right]$

Now, circumference $= 2\pi r = 2 \times \dfrac{22}{7} \times \dfrac{5}{2} = \dfrac{110}{7} = 15.7$ cm

Q. 20 Circumference of a circular disc is 88 cm. Its radius is

(a) 8 cm   (b) 11 cm   (c) 14 cm   (d) 44 cm

Sol. (*c*)   We know that, circumference $= 2\pi r$

$\Rightarrow \qquad 88 = 2 \times \dfrac{22}{7} \times r \quad \Rightarrow \quad r = \dfrac{88 \times 7}{2 \times 22}$ [∵ circumference = 88 cm, given]

$\Rightarrow \qquad r = 14$ cm

Hence, the radius is 14 cm.

Q. 21 Length of tape required to cover the edges of a semi-circular disc of radius 10 cm is

    (a) 62.8 cm   (b) 51.4 cm   (c) 31.4 cm   (d) 15.7 cm

Sol. *(b)*   In order to find the length of tape required to cover the edges of a semi-circular disc, we have to find the perimeter of semi-circle.

10 cm

From the above figure it is clear that,

Perimeter of semi-circle = Circumference of semi-circle + Diameter

∵ Circumference of semi-circle $= \dfrac{2\pi r}{2} = \pi \times r = \dfrac{22}{7} \times 10 = \dfrac{220}{7} = 31.4$ cm

∴ Total tape required $= 31.4 + 2 \times 10 = 51.4$ cm   [∵ diameter = 2 × radius]

Q. 22 Area of a circular garden with diameter 8 m is

    (a) 12.56 m²   (b) 25.12 m²   (c) 50.24 m²   (d) 200.96 m²

Sol. *(c)*   Given, diameter = 8 m

    So, radius $= \dfrac{8}{2}$ m = 4 m $\left[\because \text{radius} = \dfrac{\text{diameter}}{2} \right]$

    ∴ Area of circular garden $= \pi r^2 = \dfrac{22}{7} \times 4 \times 4 = 50.24$ m²

Q. 23 Area of a circle with diameter (*m*), radius (*n*) and circumference (*p*) is

    (a) $2\pi n$ (b) πm^2 (c) πp^2 (d) πn^2

Sol. *(d)*   Given, diameter = *m*, radius = *n* and circumference = *p*

    ∴ Area of circle $= \pi r^2 = \pi n^2$

Q. 24 A table top is semi-circular in shape with diameter 2.8 m. Area of this table top is

    (a) 3.08 m²   (b) 6.16 m²   (c) 12.32 m²   (d) 24.64 m²

Sol. *(a)*   Given, diameter = 2.8 m

    Now, radius $= \dfrac{2.8}{2}$ m = 1.4 m $\left[\because \text{radius} = \dfrac{\text{diameter}}{2} \right]$

    ∴ Area of table top = Area of semi-circle $= \dfrac{\pi r^2}{2} = \dfrac{22}{7} \times \dfrac{1.4}{2} \times 1.4 = 3.08$ m²

Q. 25 If 1 m² = *x* mm², then the value of *x* is

    (a) 1000   (b) 10000   (c) 100000   (d) 1000000

Sol. *(d)*   Given,   1 m² = *x* mm²

    ∴   (1000 mm)² = *x* mm²   [∵ 1 m = 1000 mm]

    ⇒   1000000 mm² = *x* mm²

    ⇒   *x* = 1000000

Q. 26 If p squares of each side 1mm makes a square of side 1 cm, then p is equal to

(a) 10   (b) 100

(c) 1000   (d) 10000

Sol. *(b)* $\because$ Area of 1 square of side 1 mm $= 1 \times 1$ mm$^2 = 1$ mm^2 [$\because$ area of square $=$ (side)^2]

Area of square of side 1 cm $= 1 \times 1$ cm$^2 = 1$ cm^2

According to the question,

Area of sqaures of side 1mm $=$ Area of square side 1cm

$\Rightarrow$ $p \times 1$ mm$^2 = 1$ cm^2 $\Rightarrow$ p mm$^2 = 1$ cm^2

$\Rightarrow$ p mm$^2 = (10$ mm$)^2$ [$\because 1$ cm $= 10$ mm]

$\Rightarrow$ p mm$^2 = 100$ mm^2

So, $p = 100$

Q. 27 12 m^2 is the area of

(a) a square with side 12 m   (b) 12 squares with side 1 m each

(c) 3 squares with side 4 m each   (d) 4 squares with side 3 m each

Sol. *(b)*   For option (a), Area of a square with side 12 cm $= 12 \times 12 = 144$ m^2

[$\because$ area of square $=$ (side)^2]

For option (b), Area of 12 squares with side 1 m each $= 12 \times 1 \times 1 = 12$ m^2

For option (c), Area of 3 squares with side 4 m each $= 3 \times$ Area of square of side 4 m

$= 3 \times 4 \times 4 = 48$ m^2

For option (d), Area of 4 squares with side 3 m $= 4 \times$ Area of square of side 3 m

$= 4 \times 3 \times 3 = 36$ m^2

Hence, option (b) is correct.

Q. 28 If each side of a rhombus is doubled, how much will its area increase?

(a) 1.5 times   (b) 2 times

(c) 3 times   (d) 4 times

Sol. *(b)*   Let b be the side and h be the height of a rhombus.

$\therefore$ Area of rhombus $= b \times h$ [$\because$ area of rhombus $=$ base $\times$ corresponding height]

If each side of rhombus is doubled, then side of rhombus $= 2b$

Now, area of rhombus $= 2b \times h = 2(b \times h) = 2$ times of original

Hence, the area of rhombus will be increased by 2 times.

Q. 29 If the sides of a parallelogram are increased to twice its original lengths, how much will the perimeter of the new parallelogram increase?

(a) 1.5 times   (b) 2 times

(c) 3 times   (d) 4 times

Sol. *(b)*   Let the length and breadth of the parallelogram be l and b, respectively.

Then, perimeter $= 2(l + b)$ [$\because$ perimeter of parallelogram $= 2 \times$ (length + breadth)]

If both sides are increased twice, then new length and breadth will be $2l$ and $2b$, respectively.

Now, new perimeter $= 2(2l + 2b) = 2 \times 2(l + b) = 2$ times of original perimeter.

Hence, the perimeter of parallelogram will be increased 2 times.

Q. 30 If radius of a circle is increased to twice its original length, how much will the area of the circle increase?

(a) 1.4 times (b) 2 times (c) 3 times (d) 4 times

Sol. *(d)* Let r be the radius of the circle.

∴ Area of circle $= \pi r^2$

If radius is increased to twice its original length, then radius will be $2r$.

Now, area of new circle $= \pi(2r)^2 = 4\pi r^2 = 4$ times of original area

Hence, the area of circle will be increased by 4 times.

Q. 31 What will be the area of the largest square that can be cut-out of a circle of radius 10 cm?

(a) 100 cm² (b) 200 cm² (c) 300 cm² (d) 400 cm²

Sol. *(b)* Given, radius of circle $= 10$ cm

The largest square that can be cut-out of a circle of radius 10 cm will have its diagonal equal to the diameter of the circle.

Let the side of a square be x.

Then, area of the square $= x \times x = x^2$ cm² [∵ area of square $= (\text{side})^2$]

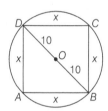

Now, in right angled $\triangle DAB$,

$$(BD)^2 = (AD)^2 + (AB)^2 \qquad \text{[by Pythagoras theorem]}$$

∵ $(20)^2 = x^2 + x^2$

[∵ diagonal = diameter and diameter $= 2 \times$ radius $= 2 \times 10 = 20$ cm]

⇒ $\qquad 2x^2 = 400$

⇒ $\qquad x^2 = 200$

∴ $\qquad (\text{Side})^2 = 200$

Hence, the area of the largest square is 200 cm².

Q. 32 What is the radius of the largest circle that can be cut-out of the rectangle measuring 10 cm in length and 8 cm in breadth?

(a) 4 cm (b) 5 cm (c) 8 cm (d) 10 cm

Sol. *(a)*

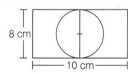

From the above figure, it is clear that largest circle will have diameter equals smaller side i.e. 8 cm.

So, diameter $= 8$ cm

∴ Radius $= \dfrac{\text{Diameter}}{2} = \dfrac{8}{2} = 4$ cm

Q. 33 The perimeter of the figure *ABCDEFGHIJ* is

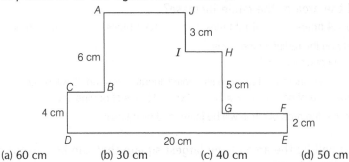

(a) 60 cm   (b) 30 cm   (c) 40 cm   (d) 50 cm

Sol. *(a)*   Perimeter = Sum of all sides

So, $AJ + JI + IH + HG + GF + FE + ED + CD + BC + AB$
$$= (AJ + IH + GF + BC) + 3 + 5 + 2 + 20 + 4 + 6$$
$$= DE + 40 \qquad\qquad [\because AJ + IH + GF + BC = DE]$$
$$= 20 + 40 = 60 \text{ cm}$$

Q. 34 The circumference of a circle whose area is $81\pi r^2$, is

(a) $9\pi r$ (b) $18\pi r$ (c) $3\pi r$ (d) $81\pi r$

Sol. *(b)*   Let the radius of circle be R.

$\therefore$ Area of circle $= \pi R^2$

$\Rightarrow \qquad 81\pi r^2 = \pi R^2 \qquad \Rightarrow \qquad R = \sqrt{81r^2}$

$\Rightarrow \qquad\qquad R = 9r$

Now, circumference of circle $= 2\pi R = 2\pi(9r) = 18\pi r$

Q. 35 The area of a square is 100 cm². The circumference (in cm) of the largest circle cut of it is

(a) 5π (b) 10π (c) 15π (d) 20π

Sol. *(b)* Let the side of square be a cm.

Given, area of square $= 100\text{ cm}^2$

$\therefore$ Area of square $= a^2$

$\Rightarrow \qquad\qquad a^2 = 100\text{ cm}^2 \qquad\qquad [\because \text{area of square} = (\text{side})^2]$

$\Rightarrow \qquad\qquad a = \sqrt{100}$

$\Rightarrow \qquad\qquad a = 10\text{ cm}$

Now, for the largest circle in the square, diameter of the circle must be equal to the side of square.

$\therefore$ Diameter = Side of a square = 10 cm

$\Rightarrow \qquad\qquad 2r = 10\text{ cm} \qquad\qquad [\because \text{diameter} = 2 \times \text{radius}]$

$\Rightarrow \qquad\qquad r = 5\text{ cm}$

$\therefore$ Circumference of the circle $= 2\pi r = 2 \times \pi \times 5 = 10\pi$ cm

Q. 36 If the radius of a circle is tripled, the area becomes

      (a) 9 times   (b) 3 times   (c) 6 times   (d) 30 times

Sol. *(a)* Let r be the radius of a circle.

        $\because$ Area of circle $= \pi r^2$

        If radius is tripled, then new radius will be $3r$.

        $\therefore$ Area of new circle $= \pi(3r)^2 = 9\pi r^2 = 9$ times of original

        Hence, the area of a cirlce becomes 9 times to the original area.

Q. 37 The area of a semi-circle of radius $4r$ is

      (a) $8\pi r^2$ (b) $4\pi r^2$ (c) $12\pi r^2$ (d) $2\pi r^2$

Sol. *(a)* Given, radius of semi-circle $= 4r$

        $\because$ Area of semi-circle $= \dfrac{1}{2} \times \pi r^2$

$$= \dfrac{1}{2} \times \pi \times (4r)^2 = \dfrac{16}{2}\pi r^2 = 8\pi r^2$$

Fill in the Blank

In questions 38 to 56, fill in the blanks to make the statements true.

Q. 38 Perimeter of a regular polygon = Length of one side × _____

Sol. Perimeter of regular polygon = Length of one side × **Number of sides.**

Q. 39 If a wire in the shape of a square is rebent into a rectangle, then the _____ of both shapes remain same, but _____ may vary.

Sol. When we change the shape, then the **perimeter** remains same as the length of wire is fixed, but **area** changes as shape changes.

Q. 40 Area of the square *MNOP* of the given figure is 144 cm². Area of each triangle is _____.

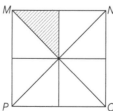

Sol. Given, area of square *MNOP* $= 144\ \text{cm}^2$

    Since, there are 8 identical triangles in the given square *MNOP*.

    Hence, area of each triangle $= \dfrac{1}{8} \times$ Area of square $MNOP = \dfrac{1}{8} \times 144 = \mathbf{18\ cm^2}$

Q. 41 In the given figure, area of parallelogram *BCEF* is _____ cm², where *ACDF* is a rectangle.

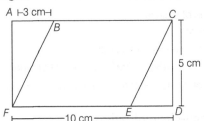

Sol. Area of parallelogram *BCEF* = Area of rectangle *ACDF* – Area of ΔABF – Area of ΔCDE

$$= 10 \times 5 - 2 \times \left(\frac{1}{2} \times 3 \times 5\right) \quad [\because \text{area of } \Delta ABF = \text{area of } \Delta CDE]$$

$$= 50 - 15 = \textbf{35} \, cm^2$$

$$[\because \text{area of trinagle} = \frac{1}{2} \times \text{base} \times \text{height and area of rectangle} = \text{length} \times \text{breadth}]$$

Q. 42 To find area, any side of a parallelogram can be chosen as _____ of the parallelogram.

Sol. While calculating the area of the parallelogram, we can choose any side as **base**.

Q. 43 Perpendicular dropped on the base of a parallelogram from the opposite vertex is known as the corresponding _____ of the base.

Sol. Perpendicular dropped on the base of a parallelogram from the opposite vertex is known as the corresponding **height/altitude** of the base.

Q. 44 The distance around a circle is its _____

Sol. The distance around a circle is its **circumference**.
In case of circle, perimeter is known as circumference.

Q. 45 Ratio of the circumference of a circle to its diameter is denoted by symbol _____.

Sol. $\because$ Circumference $= 2\pi r$

$\Rightarrow$ $\qquad\qquad\qquad\qquad C = \pi d \qquad\qquad\qquad\qquad\qquad [\because d = 2r]$

$\Rightarrow$ $\qquad\qquad\qquad\qquad \dfrac{C}{d} = \pi \Rightarrow \pi = C : d$

Hence, π is the answer.

Q. 46 If area of a triangular piece of cardboard is 90 cm², then the length of altitude corresponding to 20 cm long base is _____ cm.

Sol. Area of triangle $= \dfrac{1}{2} \times$ Base $\times$ Height

$\Rightarrow$ $\qquad\qquad 90 = \dfrac{1}{2} \times 20 \times h \Rightarrow h = 9 \, cm$

$\therefore$ Altitude or height = **9** cm.

Q. 47 Value of π is _____ approximately.

Sol. We know that, $\pi = \frac{22}{7} = 3.14$

Q. 48 Circumference C of a circle can be found by multiplying diameter d with _____ .

Sol. $\because$ Circumference $= 2\pi r$

Since, diameter $(d) = 2r$

So, $\qquad C = \pi \times d$

Hence, π is the answer.

Q. 49 Circumference 'C' of a circle is equal to $2\pi \times$ _____ .

Sol. $\because$ Circumference $= 2\pi \times r$

Hence, r is the answer.

Q. 50 $1\ m^2 =$ _____ cm^2

Sol. We know that, $1\ m = 100\ cm$

$\therefore \qquad 1\ m^2 = (100)^2\ cm^2$

$\Rightarrow \qquad 1\ m^2 = \mathbf{10000}\ cm^2$

Q. 51 $1\ cm^2 =$ _____ mm^2

Sol. We know that, $1\ cm = 10\ mm$

$\therefore 1\ cm^2 = (10)^2\ mm^2 = \mathbf{100}\ mm^2$

Q. 52 1 hectare $=$ _____ m^2

Sol. 1 hectare $= \mathbf{10000}\ m^2$

Q. 53 Area of triangle $= \frac{1}{2} \times$ base $\times$ _____ .

Sol. Area of triangle $= \frac{1}{2} \times$ Base $\times$ **Height**.

Q. 54 $1\ km^2 =$ _____ m^2

Sol. We know that, $1\ km = 1000\ m$

$\therefore 1\ km^2 = (1000)^2\ m^2 = \mathbf{1000000}\ m^2$

Q. 55 Area of a square of side 6 m is equal to the area of _____ squares of each side 1 cm.

Sol. Let number of squares having side $1\ cm = x$

According to the question,

Area of side 6 m square $=$ Area of side 1 cm square $\qquad [\because$ area of square $= (side)^2]$

$\therefore \qquad\qquad (6\ m)^2 = x \times (1\ cm)^2 \qquad\qquad [\because 1\ m = 100\ cm]$

$\Rightarrow$ $(600 \text{ cm})^2 = x \times (1 \text{ cm})^2$

$\Rightarrow$ $360000 \text{ cm}^2 = x \text{ cm}^2$

$\Rightarrow$ $x = 360000$

$\therefore$ Number of required squares = **360000**

Q. 56 $10 \text{ cm}^2 = $ _____ m^2.

Sol. $\because 10 \text{ cm}^2 = 10 \left(\dfrac{1}{100}\right)^2 \text{m}^2 = \dfrac{10}{10000} \text{m}^2$ $\left[\because 1 \text{ cm} = \dfrac{1}{100} \text{ m}\right]$

      $\Rightarrow 10 \text{ cm}^2 = \dfrac{1}{1000} \text{m}^2$

      $\therefore \; 10 \text{ cm}^2 = $ **0.001** m^2

True/False

In questions 57 to 72, state whether the statements are True or False.

Q. 57 In the given figure, perimeter of (ii) is greater than that of (i), but its area is smaller than that of (i).

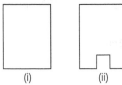

                 (i)   (ii)

Sol.   *True*

Perimeter is the sum of sides of any polygon and area is space that the polygon required. So, by observing the figures we can say that, perimeter of (ii) is greater than (i) and area is less than that of (i).

Q. 58 In the given figure,

     (a) Area of (i) is the same as the area of (ii).

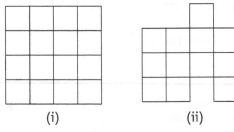

             (i)   (ii)

     (b) Perimeter of (ii) is the same as (i).

     (c) If (ii) is divided into squares of unit length, then its area is 13 unit squares.

     (d) Perimeter of (ii) is 18 units.

Sol.   (a) *True*

Area of both figures is same, because in both number of blocks are same.

(b) *False*

Because 2 new sides are added in (ii). So, the perimeter of (ii) is greater than (i).

(c) *False*

∴ Area of 1 square = 1 × 1 = 1 unit squares

∵ Number of squares = 12

So, total area = 12 × 1 = 12 unit squares

(d) *True*

∵ Perimeter is the sum of all sides. So, it is 18 units.

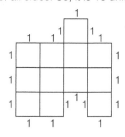

Q. 59 If perimeter of two parallelograms are equal, then their areas are also equal.

Sol. *False*

Their corresponding sides and height may be different. So, area cannot be equal.

Q. 60 All congruent triangles are equal in area.

Sol. *True*

Congruent triangles have equal shape and size. Hence, their areas are also equal.

Q. 61 All parallelograms having equal areas have same perimeters.

Sol. *False*

It is not necessary that all parallelograms having equal areas have same perimeters as their base and height may be different.

In questions 62 to 65, observe all the four triangles FAB, EAB, DAB and CAB as shown in the given figure.

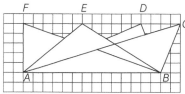

Q. 62 All triangles have the same base and the same altitude.

Sol. *True*

It is clear from the figure that all triangles have same base *AB* and all the vertices lie on the same line, so the distance between vertex and base of triangle (i.e. length of altitude) are equal.

Q. 63 All triangles are congruent.

Sol. *False*

It is clear from the figure that all triangles have only base line is equal and no such other lines are equal to each other.

Q. 64 All triangles are equal in area.

Sol. *True*

Because the triangles on same base and between same parallel lines have equal in area.

Q. 65 All triangles may not have the same perimeter.

Sol. *True*

It is clear from the figure that all triangles may not have the same perimeter.

Q. 66 In the given figure, ratio of the area of $\triangle ABC$ to the area of $\triangle ACD$ is the same as the ratio of base BC of $\triangle ABC$ to the base CD of $\triangle ACD$.

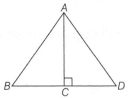

Sol. *True*

$\because$ Area of $\triangle ABC$: Area of $\triangle ACD = \dfrac{1}{2} \times BC \times AC : \dfrac{1}{2} \times CD \times AC$

[$\because$ area of triangle = base $\times$ height]

$= BC : CD$

Q. 67 Triangles having the same base have equal area.

Sol. *False*

$\because$ Area of triangle $= \dfrac{1}{2} \times$ Base $\times$ Height

So, area of triangle does not only depend on base, it also depends on height. Hence, if triangles have equal base and equal height, then only their areas are equal.

Q. 68 Ratio of circumference of a circle to its radius is always $2\pi : 1$.

Sol. *True*

$\because$ Circumference : Radius $= 2\pi r : r = 2\pi : 1$

Q. 69 5 hectare $= 500$ m^2

Sol. *False*

As we know that, 1 hectare $= 10000$ m^2

So, 5 hectare $= 5 \times 10000$ m$^2 = 50000$ m^2

Q. 70 An increase in perimeter of a figure always increases the area of the figure.

Sol. *False*

This is not necessary. See the Q. 57.

Q. 71 Two figures can have the same area but different perimeters.

Sol. *True*

See the Q. 58.

Q. 72 Out of two figures, if one has larger area, then its perimeter need not to be larger than the other figure.

Sol. *True*

Q. 73 A hedge boundary needs to be planted around a rectangular lawn of size 72 m × 18 m. If 3 shrubs can be planted in a metre of hedge, how many shrubs will be planted in all?

Sol. Here, length of rectangular lawn = 72 m and breadth of rectangular lawn = 18 m

∵ Perimeter of rectangle = 2 × (Length + Breadth)

∴ Perimeter of rectangular lawn = 2 (72 + 18) = 2 (90) = 180 m

If 3 shrubs can be planted in a metre of hedge.

Then, number of shrubs = 3 × Perimeter of rectangular lawn = 3 × 180 = 540

Q. 74 People of Khejadli village take good care of plants, trees and animals. They say that plants and animals can survive without us, but we cannot survive without them. Inspired by her elders Amrita marked some land for her pets (camel and ox) and plants. Find the ratio of the areas kept for animals and plants to the living area. What value depicted here?

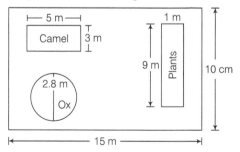

Sol. We know that,

Area of rectangle = $l \times b$ and area of circle = πr^2

From the given figure,

Area of total rectangular land = 15 m × 10 m = 150 m²

Area of land covered by plants = 9 m × 1 m = 9 m²

Area of land covered by camel = 5 m × 3 m = 15 m²

∴ Region of land covered by ox is circular area.

So, diameter, d = 2.8 m

$\therefore$ Radius $= \dfrac{d}{2} = \dfrac{2.8}{2} = 1.4\,m$ $\left[\because \text{radius} = \dfrac{\text{diameter}}{2}\right]$

$\therefore$ Area of land covered by ox $= \pi r^2 = \dfrac{22}{7} \times 1.4 \times 1.4 = 6.16\,m^2$

Total area covered by plants, camel and ox $= 9 + 15 + 6.16 = 30.16\,m^2$

Remaining land for living = Total area – Area covered by plants and animals
$$= (150 - 30.16)m^2 = 119.84\,m^2$$

$\therefore$ Ratio of areas kept for animals and plants to the living area
$$= 30.16 : 119.84 = 3016 : 11984 = 377 : 1498$$

The value depicted here is that, we should save our environment and balance the environment.

Q. 75 The perimeter of a rectangle is 40 m. Its length is four metres less than five times its breadth. Find the area of the rectangle.

Sol. Let breadth of the rectangle $= x$
Then, length of the rectangle $= 5x - 4$
We know that,
Perimeter of rectangle $= 2(l + b)$

$\Rightarrow$	$40 = 2(l + b)$	[$\because$ perimeter = 40 m, given]
$\Rightarrow$	$40 = 2(5x - 4 + x)$	
$\Rightarrow$	$40 = 2(6x - 4)$	
$\Rightarrow$	$12x - 8 = 40$	
$\Rightarrow$	$12x = 40 + 8$	
$\Rightarrow$	$12x = 48$	
$\Rightarrow$	$x = \dfrac{48}{12} = 4$	

So, breadth $= x = 4\,m$ and length $= 5x - 4 = 5 \times 4 - 4 = 16\,m$
$\because$ Area of rectangle $= l \times b = 4 \times 16 = 64\,m^2$

Hence, the area of rectangle is 64 m^2.

Q. 76 A wall of a room is of dimensions $5\,m \times 4\,m$. It has a window of dimensions $1.5\,m \times 1\,m$ and a door of dimensions $2.25\,m \times 1\,m$. Find the area of the wall, which is to be painted.

Sol. Given, a wall of a room is of dimensions $5\,m \times$ m.
$\therefore$ Length of the room = 5 m and breadth of the room = 4 m
$\therefore$ Area of the room $= l \times b = 5 \times 4 = 20\,m^2$

Also, length of the window = 1.5 m and breadth of the window = 1 m   [given]
$\therefore$ Area of the window $= l \times b = 1.5 \times 1 = 1.5\,m^2$

Now, length of the door = 2.25 m and breadth of the door = 1 m
$\therefore$ Area of the door $= l \times b = 2.25 \times 1 = 2.25\,m^2$

Now, area of the wall to be painted = Area of the room – (Area of the window + Area of the door) $= 20 - (1.5 + 2.25) = 20 - 3.75 = 16.25\,m^2$

Q. 77 Rectangle *MNOP* is made up of four congruent rectangles. If the area of one of the rectangles is 8m² and breadth is 2 m, then find the perimeter of *MNOP*.

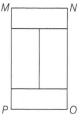

Sol. We have, area of one rectangle = 8 m²

and breadth = 2m

We know that,

Area of rectangle = $l \times b$

⇒ $l \times b = 8$

⇒ $l \times 2 = 8$

⇒ $l = 4$ m

Now, we have to find the perimeter of *MNOP*, which contains four congruent rectangles, it means they have same length and breadth.

∴ Perimeter of rectangle $MNOP = MN + NC + CD + DO + PO + PF + FA + MA$

= 4 + 2 + 4 + 2 + 4 + 2 + 4 + 2

= 24 m

Hence, the perimeter of *MNOP* is 24 m.

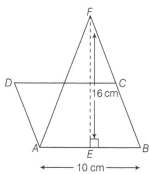

Q. 78 In the given figure, area of Δ*AFB* is equal to the area of parallelogram *ABCD*. If altitude *EF* is 16 cm long, find the altitude of the parallelogram to the base *AB* of length 10 cm. What is the area of Δ*DAO*, where 0 is the mid-point of *DC*?

Sol. Given,

Area of Δ*AFB* = Area of parallelogram *ABCD*

⇒ $\frac{1}{2} \times AB \times EF = CD \times$ (Corresponding height)

$$\left[\because \text{area of triangle} = \text{base} \times \text{height and area of} \right.$$

$$\left. \text{parallelogram} = \text{base} \times \text{corresponding height} \right]$$

$\Rightarrow \qquad \dfrac{1}{2} \times AB \times EF = CD \times EG$

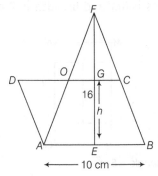

Let the corresponding height be h.

Then, $\qquad\qquad\qquad \dfrac{1}{2} \times 10 \times 16 = 10 \times h$

$\qquad\qquad\qquad$ [$\because$ altitude, $EF = 16$ cm and base, $AB = 10$ cm, given]   [$\because AB = CD$]

$\Rightarrow \qquad\qquad\qquad\qquad\qquad h = 8$ cm

In ΔDAO, $DO = 5$ cm $\qquad\qquad\qquad\qquad\qquad\qquad\qquad\qquad$ [$\because O$ is the mid-point of CD]

$\therefore$ Area of $\Delta DAO = \dfrac{1}{2} \times OD \times h$

$\qquad\qquad\qquad\quad = \dfrac{1}{2} \times 5 \times 8 = 20 \text{ cm}^2$

Q. 79 Ratio of the area of ΔWXY to the area of ΔWZY is $3 : 4$ in the given figure. If the area of ΔWXZ is 56 cm^2 and $WY = 8$ cm, find the lengths of XY and YZ.

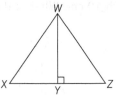

Sol.   Given, area of $\Delta WXZ = 56$ cm^2

$\Rightarrow \qquad \dfrac{1}{2} \times WY \times XZ = 56 \qquad\qquad \left[\because \text{ area of triangle} = \dfrac{1}{2} \times \text{base} \times \text{height}\right]$

$\Rightarrow \qquad \dfrac{1}{2} \times 8 \times XZ = 56 \quad \Rightarrow \quad XZ = 14$ cm $\qquad\qquad$ [$\because WY = 8$ cm, given]

$\therefore$ Area of ΔWXY : Area of $\Delta WZY = 3 : 4$

$\Rightarrow \qquad\qquad\qquad \dfrac{\text{Area of } \Delta WXY}{\text{Area of } \Delta WZY} = \dfrac{3}{4}$

$\Rightarrow \qquad\qquad\qquad \dfrac{\dfrac{1}{2} \times WY \times XY}{\dfrac{1}{2} \times YZ \times WY} = \dfrac{3}{4}$

$\Rightarrow \qquad\qquad\qquad\qquad \dfrac{XY}{YZ} = \dfrac{3}{4}$

$$\Rightarrow \qquad \frac{XY}{XZ - XY} = \frac{3}{4} \qquad [\because YZ = XZ - XY]$$

$$\Rightarrow \qquad \frac{XY}{14 - XY} = \frac{3}{4} \qquad \text{[by cross-multiplication]}$$

$$\Rightarrow \qquad 4XY = 42 - 3XY$$

$$7XY = 42 \quad \Rightarrow \quad XY = 6\,\text{cm}$$

So, $\qquad YZ = XZ - XY = 14 - 6$

$$YZ = 8\,\text{cm}$$

Hence, $XY = 6$ cm and $YZ = 8$ cm.

Q. 80 Rani bought a new field that is next to one she already owns in the given figure. This field is in the shape of a square of side 70 m. She makes a semi-circular lawn of maximum area in this field.

  (i) Find the perimeter of the lawn.
  (ii) Find the area of the square field excluding the lawn.

Sol. (i) Given, side of a square = 70 m

From the given figure, the diameter of semi-circle is same as the side of a square.

∴ Diameter of semi-circle = 70 m

∵ Dimeter of semi-circle = Side of square

∴ Radius = $\dfrac{70}{2}$ = 35 m $\qquad \left[\because \text{radius} = \dfrac{\text{diameter}}{2}\right]$

∴ Perimeter of lawn = $\pi r + 2r = \dfrac{22}{7} \times 35 + 2 \times 35 = 110 + 70 = 180$ m

(ii) Area of square = Side × Side = 70 × 70 = 4900 m^2

∴ Required area = Area of square − Area of semi-circle

$$= 4900 - \frac{1}{2} \times \pi \times (35)^2 \qquad \left[\because \text{area of semi-circle} = \frac{1}{2}\pi r^2\right]$$

$$= 4900 - \frac{1}{2} \times \frac{22}{7} \times 35 \times 35 = 4900 - 1925$$

$$= 2975\,\text{m}^2$$

Q. 81 In the given figure, find the area of parallelogram *ABCD*, if the area of shaded triangle is 9 cm².

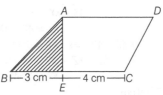

Sol.   Given, area of shaded triangle = 9 cm²

and base of the triangle   = 3 cm

∵ Area of a triangle = $\dfrac{1}{2}$ × Base × Height

⇒ $9 = \dfrac{1}{2} \times 3 \times h$ ⇒ $\dfrac{18}{3} = h$

⇒ $h = 6$ cm

∴ Area of parallelogram = Height × Base of parallelogram = 6 × (3 + 4) = 6 × 7 = 42 cm²

Q. 82 Pizza factory has comeout with two kinds of pizzas. A square pizza of side 45 cm costs ₹ 150 and a circular pizza of diameter 50 cm cost ₹ 160. Which pizza is a better deal?

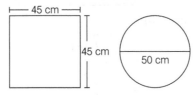

Sol.   Given, side of square pizza = 45 cm

∴ Area of a square pizza = (Side)² = (45)² = 2025 cm²

Diameter of circular pizza = 50 cm

∴ Radius = $\dfrac{50}{2}$ = 25 cm $\left[\because \text{radius} = \dfrac{\text{diameter}}{2}\right]$

Now, area of the circular pizza = $\dfrac{22}{7} \times 25 \times 25$

$= \dfrac{22}{7} \times 625$

$= \dfrac{13750}{7} = 1964.28$ cm²   [∵ area of circle − πr^2]

∴ Price of 1 cm square pizza = $\dfrac{2025}{150}$ = ₹13.5

and price of 1 cm circular pizza = $\dfrac{1964.28}{160}$

$= ₹12.27$

Hence, the circular pizza is a better deal.

Q. 83 Three squares are attached to each other as shown in the figure given below. Each square is attached at the mid-point of the side of the square to its right. Find the perimeter of the complete figure.

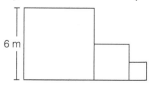

Sol.

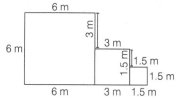

∴ Perimeter of the complete figure = 6 + 6 + 6 + 3 + 1.5 + 1.5 + 1.5 + 3 + 3 + 1.5 = 33 m

Q. 84 In the following figure, $ABCD$ is a square with $AB = 15$ cm. Find the area of the square $BDFE$.

Sol. Given, $ABCD$ is a square and $AB = 15$ cm
∴ Diagonal of square $ABCD = \sqrt{2}a = \sqrt{2} \times 15 = 15\sqrt{2}$ cm
From the figure, diagonal of square $ABCD$ is the side of square $BDEF$.
∴ Area of the square $BDFE = (Side)^2 = (15\sqrt{2})^2 = 15 \times 15 \times \sqrt{2} \times \sqrt{2}$
$$= 225 \times 2 = 450 \text{ cm}^2$$

Q. 85 In the given figures, perimeter of $\triangle ABC$ = perimeter of $\triangle PQR$. Find the area of $\triangle ABC$.

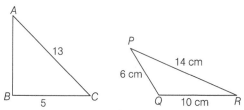

Sol. Given, perimeter of $\triangle ABC$ = perimeter of $\triangle PQR$
∴ Perimeter of $\triangle PQR = 14 + 6 + 10 = 30$ cm [∵ perimeter of triangle = sum of all sides]
Now, perimeter of $\triangle ABC = AB + BC + CA$

$$30 = AB + BC + AC$$
$\Rightarrow$ $$30 = AB + 5 + 13$$
$\Rightarrow$ $$30 = AB + 18$$
$\Rightarrow$ $$AB = 30 - 18 = 12 \text{ cm}$$
$\therefore$ Area of $\triangle ABC = \dfrac{1}{2} \times$ Base $\times$ Height

$$= \dfrac{1}{2} \times 5 \times 12 = 5 \times 6 = 30 \text{ cm}^2$$

Q. 86 Altitudes *MN* and *MO* of parallelogram *MGHK* are 8 cm and 4 cm long respectively in the below figure. One side *GH* is 6 cm long. Find the perimeter of *MGHK*.

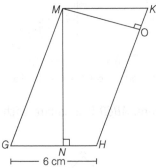

Sol.   Given, *MGHK* is a parallelogram, where $MN = 8$ cm, $MO = 4$ cm and $GH = 6$ cm.
∴Area of parallelogram *MGHK*, when base is *GH*   [∵ area of parallelogram = base × height]

$$= GH \times MN$$
$$= 6 \times 8 \text{ cm}^2 = 48 \text{ cm}^2 \qquad \qquad ...(i)$$

Area of parallelogram *MGHK*, when base is *HK*

$$= HK \times MO$$

$\Rightarrow$ $$48 = HK \times 4 \qquad \qquad \text{[from Eq. (i)]}$$
$\Rightarrow$ $$HK = \dfrac{48}{4}$$
$\Rightarrow$ $$HK = 12 \text{ cm}$$

In parallelogram, opposite sides are equal.
So, $GH = MK = 6$ cm and $MG = HK = 12$ cm
∴Perimeter of parallelogram $MGHK = (6 + 6 + 12 + 12)$ cm $= 36$ cm

Q. 87 In the given figure, area of $\triangle PQR$ is 20 cm^2 and area of $\triangle PQS$ is 44 cm^2. Find the length RS, if PQ is perpendicular to QS and QR is 5 cm.

Sol. Given, area of $\triangle PQR = 20$ cm^2 and area of $\triangle PQS = 44$ cm^2

We know that,

Area of triangle $= \dfrac{1}{2} \times$ Base $\times$ Height

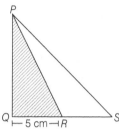

$\therefore$ Area of $\triangle PQR = \dfrac{1}{2} \times PQ \times QR$ $[\because PQ \perp QR]$

$\Rightarrow$ $20 = \dfrac{1}{2} \times PQ \times 5$ $\Rightarrow$ $\dfrac{20 \times 2}{5} = PQ$ $[\because QR = 5\,cm,\ given]$

$\Rightarrow$ $PQ = 8$ cm

$\therefore$ Area of $\triangle PQS = \dfrac{1}{2} \times PQ \times QS$

$\Rightarrow$ $44 = \dfrac{1}{2} \times 8 \times QS$ $\Rightarrow$ $QS = \dfrac{44 \times 2}{8}$ $[\because PQ = 8\,cm]$

$\Rightarrow$ $QS = 11$ cm

Now, $RS = QS - QR = 11 - 5 = 6$ cm

Q. 88 Area of an isosceles triangle is 48 cm^2. If the altitudes corresponding to the base of the triangle is 8 cm, find the perimeter of the triangle.

Sol Given, area of $\triangle ABC = 48$ cm^2 and altitude $= 8$ cm

$\because$ $\triangle ABC$ is an isosceles triangle, where $AB = AC$

$\therefore$ Area of $\triangle ABC = \dfrac{1}{2} \times BC \times AD = 48$

             $[\because$ area of triangle $=$ base $\times$ height$]$

$\Rightarrow$ $48 = \dfrac{1}{2} \times BC \times AD$

$\Rightarrow$ $\dfrac{1}{2} \times BC \times 8 = 48$ $\Rightarrow$ $BC = \dfrac{48 \times 2}{8}$

          $BC = 12$ cm

Now, in an isosceles triangle, $BD = DC = 6$ cm $[\because AD \perp BC]$

Applying Pythagoras theorem in right angled $\triangle ADB$,

         $AB^2 = BD^2 + AD^2$

$\Rightarrow$ $AB^2 = 6^2 + 8^2 = 36 + 64$

$\Rightarrow$ $AB^2 = 100$

$\Rightarrow$ $AB = 10$ cm

Now, perimeter of triangle $= AB + AC + BC = AB + AB + BC$ $[\because AB = AC]$

            $= 10 + 10 + 12$

            $= 32$ cm

Q. 89 Perimeter of a parallelogram shaped land is 96 m and its area is 270 m². If one of the sides of this parallelogram is 18 m, find the length of the other side. Also, find the lengths of altitudes l and m in the given figure.

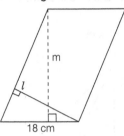

Sol. Given, perimeter of parallelogram = 96 m and area of parallelogram = 270 m².
In a parallelogram $ABCD$, $AB = CD = 18$ m and $AD = BC$

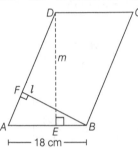

As we know, perimeter of a parallelogram $ABCD = AB + BC + CD + AD$

$\Rightarrow$ $\qquad\qquad 96 = 18 + AD + 18 + AD$ $\qquad\qquad\qquad$ [$\because AD = BC$]

$\Rightarrow$ $\qquad\qquad 96 = 36 + 2AD$

$\Rightarrow$ $\qquad\qquad 2AD = 60$

$\Rightarrow$ $\qquad\qquad AD = 30\,$cm

So, $\qquad AD = BC = 30\,$cm

Now, area of parallelogram $ABCD = $ Base $\times$ Corresponding height

$\Rightarrow$ $\qquad\qquad 270 = AB \times DE$ $\qquad\qquad\qquad$ [$\because$ base $= AB$]

$\Rightarrow$ $\qquad\qquad 270 = 18 \times DE$

$\Rightarrow$ $\qquad\qquad \dfrac{270}{18} = DE$

$\Rightarrow$ $\qquad\qquad DE = 15\,$m

Also, area of parallelogram $ABCD = AD \times BF$ $\qquad\qquad$ [$\because$ base $= AD$]

$\Rightarrow$ $\qquad\qquad 270 = 30 \times l$

$\Rightarrow$ $\qquad\qquad l = \dfrac{270}{30}$

$\Rightarrow$ $\qquad\qquad l = 9\,$m

Hence, altitudes $l = 9$ m and $m = 15$ m.

Q. 90 Area of a $\triangle PQR$ right angled at Q is 60 cm² in the figure. If the smallest side is 8 cm long, find the length of the other two sides.

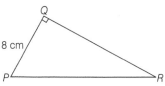

Sol. Given, area of $\triangle PQR = 60$ cm² and side $PQ = 8$ cm

$\therefore$ $\qquad$ Area of $\triangle PQR = \dfrac{1}{2} \times PQ \times QR$ $\qquad$ [$\because$ area of triangle = base × height]

$\Rightarrow$ $\qquad$ $60 = \dfrac{1}{2} \times 8 \times QR$ $\Rightarrow$ $QR = \dfrac{60 \times 2}{8}$

$\Rightarrow$ $\qquad$ $QR = 15$ cm

In right angled $\triangle PQR$, $\qquad$ $PR^2 = PQ^2 + QR^2$ $\qquad$ [by Pythagoras theorem]

$\Rightarrow$ $\qquad$ $PR^2 = 8^2 + 15^2 = 64 + 225$

$\Rightarrow$ $\qquad$ $PR^2 = 289$ $\Rightarrow$ $PR = \sqrt{289}$ $\quad = 17$ cm

Hence, the length of two sides are 15 cm and 17 cm.

Q. 91 In the given figure, a rectangle with perimeter 264 cm is divided into five congruent rectangles. Find the perimeter of one of the rectangles.

Sol. Let l and b be the length and breadth of each rectangle, respectively.

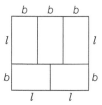

Given, perimeter of a rectangle = 264 cm

According to the figure, $\qquad$ $4l + 5b = 264$ $\qquad$ ... (i)

and $\qquad$ $2l = 3b$ $\qquad$ ... (ii)

Put the value of $3b$ from Eq. (ii) in Eq. (i), $2(2l) + 5b = 264$

$\Rightarrow$ $\qquad$ $2 \times 3b + 5b = 264$

$\Rightarrow$ $\qquad$ $6b + 5b = 264$

$\Rightarrow$ $\qquad$ $11b = 264$ $\Rightarrow$ $b = \dfrac{264}{11}$

$\Rightarrow$ $\qquad$ $b = 24$ cm

$\therefore$ $\qquad$ $l = \dfrac{3b}{2} = \dfrac{3 \times 24}{2} = 36$ cm

Hence, perimeter of the rectangle $= 2(l + b) = 2(36 + 24) = 120$ cm

Q. 92 Find the area of a square inscribed in a circle whose radius is 7 cm in the below figure.

[**Hint** Four right angled triangles joined at right angles to form a square]

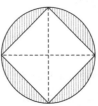

Sol.   Given that *ABCD* is a square.

According to the question,

Area of square *ABCD* = 4 × Area of a right angled triangle

∴ Area of square *ABCD* = 4 × Area of △*AOB*

$$= 4 \times \left(\frac{1}{2} \times AO \times BO \right)$$

$$\left[\because \text{area of a right angled triangle} = \frac{1}{2} \times \text{base} \times \text{height} \right]$$

$$= 2 \times 7 \times 7 = 98 \text{ cm}^2$$

[∵ *AO* = *BO* = radius of circle = 7cm, given]

Hence, the area of inscribed square is 98 cm².

Q. 93 Find the area of the shaded portion in question 92.

Sol.   Area of shaded portion = Area of circle − Area of square = πr^2 − 98

$$= \frac{22}{7} \times 7 \times 7 - 98 = 154 - 98 = 56 \text{ cm}^2$$

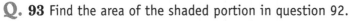

In questions 94 to 97, find the area enclosed by each of the following figures.

Q. 94

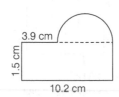

3.9 cm

1.5 cm

10.2 cm

Sol.   The given shape contains a rectangle and a semi-circle.

∴ Area of rectangle = *l* × *b* = (10.2 × 1.5) cm² = 15.3 cm²

Here, diameter of semi-circle = (10.2 − 3.9) cm = 6.3 cm

So, radius = $\frac{\text{diameter}}{2} = \frac{6.3}{2}$ = 3.15 cm

∴ Area of semi-circle = $\frac{1}{2} \pi r^2 = \frac{22}{7} \times \frac{1}{2} \times 3.15 \times 3.15 = 15.59 \text{ cm}^2$

∴ Total area = Area of rectangle + Area of semi-circle = 15.3 + 15.59 = 30.89 cm²

Q. 95

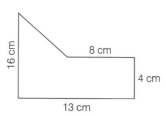

Sol. The given shape has a triangle and a rectangle.

For rectangle, $l = 13$ cm and $b = 4$ cm
∴ Area of rectangle $= l \times b = 13 \times 4 = 52$ cm²

For triangle, base $(b) = 5$ cm
and height $(h) = (16 - 4)$ cm $= 12$ cm

∴ Area of triangle $= \dfrac{1}{2} \times b \times h = \dfrac{1}{2} \times 5 \times 12 = 30$ cm²

∴ Total area enclosed by the shape
$$= (52 + 30)\,\text{cm}^2 = 82\,\text{cm}^2$$

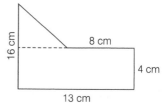

Q. 96

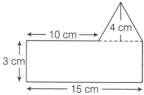

Sol. The given shape contains a rectangle and a triangle.
For rectangle, $l = 15$ cm and $b = 3$ cm

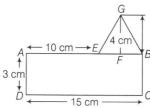

∴ Area of rectangle $= l \times b = 15 \times 3 = 45$ cm²

According to the figure,
$$BE = AB - AE = 15 - 10 = 5\,\text{cm}$$

For triangle, base $(b) = BE = 5$ cm and height $(h) = 4$ cm

∴ Area of $\triangle BEG = \dfrac{1}{2} \times b \times h = \dfrac{1}{2} \times 5 \times 4 = 10$ cm²

∴ Total area enclosed by the shape $= (45 + 10)\,\text{cm}^2 = 55\,\text{cm}^2$.

Q. 97

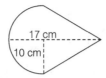

Sol. The given shape contains a semi-circle and a triangle.

$$\text{Area of semi-circle} = \frac{1}{2}\pi r^2 = \frac{1}{2} \times \frac{22}{7} \times 10 \times 10 = \frac{1100}{7} \text{ cm}^2$$

$$\text{Area of triangle} = \frac{1}{2} \times \text{Base} \times \text{Height} = \frac{1}{2} \times 20 \times 7 = 70 \text{ cm}^2$$

$$\text{Hence, total area enclosed by the shape} = \frac{1100}{7} + 70 = \frac{1100 + 490}{7}$$

$$= \frac{1590}{7} = 227 \text{ cm}^2 \text{ (approx.)}$$

In questions 98 and 99, find the areas of the shaded region.

Q. 98

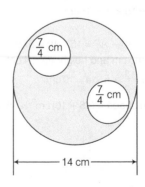

Sol. Let radius of smaller circle be r and bigger circle be R.

From the figure, $r = \dfrac{7}{2}$ cm and $R = \dfrac{7}{2} + 7 = \dfrac{21}{2}$ cm

∴ Area of shaded region = Area of bigger circle − Area of smaller circle

$$= \pi R^2 - \pi r^2$$

$$= \pi (R^2 - r^2) = \pi \left(\frac{21}{2} \times \frac{21}{2} - \frac{7}{2} \times \frac{7}{2} \right)$$

$$= \pi \left(\frac{441}{4} - \frac{49}{4} \right) = \frac{22}{7} \times \frac{392}{4} = 308 \text{ cm}^2$$

Hence, the area of shaded region is 308 cm².

Q. 99

Sol. ∵ Diameter of complete circle = 14 cm

$\therefore$ Radius = $\dfrac{14}{2}$ = 7 cm

$\left[\because \text{radius} = \dfrac{\text{diameter}}{2}\right]$

So, area of complete circle = $\pi r^2 = \dfrac{22}{7} \times 7 \times 7 = 154 \text{ cm}^2$

∵ Diameter of small circle = $\dfrac{7}{4}$ cm

$\therefore$ Radius = $\dfrac{7}{4 \times 2} = \dfrac{7}{8}$ cm

$\therefore$ Area of two small circles = $2 \times \pi r^2 = 2 \times \dfrac{22}{7} \times \dfrac{7}{8} \times \dfrac{7}{8} = \dfrac{77}{16} \text{ cm}^2$

$\therefore$ Area of shaded region = Area of complete circle − Area of two small circles

$$= 154 - \dfrac{77}{16} = \dfrac{154 \times 16 - 77}{16} \qquad \text{[taking LCM]}$$

$$= \dfrac{2464 - 77}{16} = \dfrac{2387}{16} = 149\dfrac{3}{16} \text{ cm}^2$$

Hence, the area of shaded region is $149\dfrac{3}{16} \text{ cm}^2$.

Q. 100 A circle with radius 16 cm is cut into four equal parts and rearranged to form another shaped as shown in the below figure.

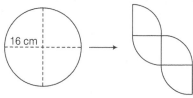

16 cm

Does the perimeter change? If it does change, by how much does it increase or decrease?

Sol. Yes, the perimeter changes. The perimeter is increased by $2r = 2 \times 16 = 32$ cm.

Q. 101 A large square is made by arranging a small square surrounded by four congruent rectangles as shown in the given figure. If the perimeter of each of the rectangle is 16 cm, find the area of the large square.

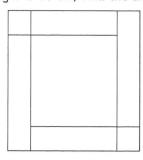

Sol.   Let the length and breadth of rectangle be l and b, respectively.

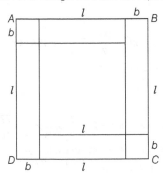

It is given that, perimeter of one rectangle = 16 cm^2

$\Rightarrow$ $2(l + b) = 16$ [$\because$ perimeter of rectangle = $2(l + b)$]

$\Rightarrow$ $l + b = 8$ cm

Since, the side of larger square is $(l + b)$.

Hence, area = (side)^2 = $(l + b)^2$ = $(8)^2$ = 64 cm^2

Q. 102 *ABCD is a parallelogram in which AE is perpendicular to CD as shown in the given figure. Also, AC = 5 cm, DE = 4 cm and area of $\triangle AED$ = 6 cm^2. Find the perimeter and area of parallelogram ABCD.*

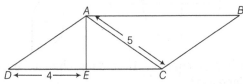

Sol.   Given, area of $\triangle AED$ = 6 cm^2 and AC = 5 cm and DE = 4 cm

$\therefore$ Area of $\triangle AED = \dfrac{1}{2} \times DE \times AE$ [$\because$ area of triangle = base $\times$ height]

$\Rightarrow$ $\dfrac{1}{2} \times 4 \times AE = 6$

$\Rightarrow$ $AE = \dfrac{6 \times 2}{4}$

$\Rightarrow$ $AE = 3$ cm

Now, in right angled $\triangle AEC$, AE = 3 cm and AC = 5 cm

So, $(EC)^2 = (AC)^2 - (AE)^2$ [by Pythagoras theorem]

$\Rightarrow$ $(EC)^2 = 5^2 - 3^2 = 25 - 9$

$\Rightarrow$ $EC = \sqrt{16}$

$\Rightarrow$ $EC = 4$ cm

$\because$ $DE + EC = DC$

$\Rightarrow$ $DC = 4 + 4 = 8$ cm

$\because ABCD$ is a parallelogram.

So, $AB = DC = 8$ cm

Now, in right angled $\triangle AED$, $AD^2 = AE^2 + ED^2$ [by Pythagoras theorem]

$\Rightarrow$ $AD^2 = 3^2 + 4^2 = 9 + 16$

$\Rightarrow$ $AD = \sqrt{25}$

$\Rightarrow$ $AD = 5\,cm$

So, $AD = BC = 5\,cm$ [$\because ABCD$ is a parallelogram]

$\therefore$ Perimeter of parallelogram $ABCD = 2(l + b) = 2(DC + AD) = 2(8 + 5) = 2 \times 13 = 26\,cm$

Area of parallelogram $ABCD$ = Base $\times$ Height = $DC \times AE = 8 \times 3 = 24\,cm^2$

Q. 103 Ishika has designed a small oval race track for her remote control car. Her design is shown in the given figure. What is the total distance around the track? Round your answer to the nearest whole centimetre.

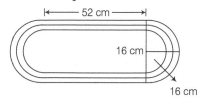

Sol.   Total distance around the track = Length of 2 parallel strips + Length of 2 semi-circles

                 $= 2 \times 52 + 2 \times \pi \times 16$ [$\because r = 16cm$]

                 $= 104 + 2 \times 3.14 \times 16$

                 $= 104 + 100.5009$

                 $= 205\,cm$ (approx.)

Q. 104 A table cover of dimensions 3 m 25 cm $\times$ 2 m 30 cm is spread on a table. If 30 cm of the table cover, is hanging all around the table, find the area of the table cover, which is hanging outside the top of the table. Also, find the cost of polishing the table top at ₹ 16 per square metre.

Sol.   To find the cost of polishing the table top, we have to find its area for which we require its length and breadth.

Given, length of cover = 3m 25cm = 3.25 m and breadth of cover = 2m 30cm = 2.30m

$\therefore$ Area of the table cover = $3.25 \times 2.30 = 7.475\,m^2$

Since, 30 cm width of cloth is outside the table an each side.

$\therefore$ Length of the table = $3.25 - 2 \times 0.30 = 2.65\,m$ $\left[\because 1\,cm = \dfrac{1}{100}\,m\right]$

and breadth of the table = $2.30 - 2 \times 0.30 = 1.70\,m$

$\therefore$ Area of the top of the table = $(2.65 \times 1.70)\,m^2$

                 $= 4.505\,m^2$

Area of the hanging table cover = Area of table cover – Area of the top of the table

                 $= (7.475 - 4.505)\,m^2$

                 $= 2.97\,m^2$

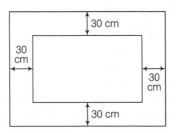

It is given that, the cost of polishing the table top is at the rate of ₹ 16 per square metre.
Therefore, cost of polishing the top = Area × Rate per square metre

$$= 4.505 \times 16$$
$$= ₹ 7.208$$

Q. 105 The dimensions of a plot are 200m × 150m. A builder builds 3 roads which are 3 m wide along the length on either side and one in the middle. On either side of the middle road he builds houses to sell. How much area did he get for building the houses?

Sol. Given that, dimersions of plot = 200 m × 150 m and width of road = 3 m

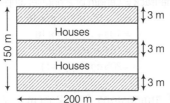

∴ Total area available for houses = Area of total plot − Area of 3 roads

$$= 200 \times 150 - 3 \times (3 \times 200) \qquad [\because \text{area of rectangle} = \text{length} \times \text{breadth}]$$
$$= 30000 - 1800 = 28200 \text{ m}^2$$

Q. 106 A room is 4.5 m long and 4 m wide. The floor of the room is to be covered with tiles of size 15 cm by 10 cm. Find the cost of covering the floor with tiles at the rate of ₹ 4.50 per tile.

Sol. Given, length of room = 4.5 m, width of room = 4 m and size of tiles = 15 cm × 10 cm

$\because$ Area of room = $l \times b$ = 4.5 × 4 = 18 m^2 = 18 × (100)^2 cm^2 = 180000 cm^2 [$\because$ 1 m = 100 cm]

∴ Area of 1 tile = 15 × 10 = 150 cm^2

So, number of tiles = $\dfrac{\text{Area of room}}{\text{Area of 1 tile}} = \dfrac{180000}{150} = 1200$

∴ Cost of covering the floor with tiles = ₹ 4.50 × 1200 = ₹ 5400

Q. 107 Find the total cost of wooden fencing around a circular garden of diameter 28 m, if 1 m of fencing costs ₹300.

Sol. Given, diameter of a circular garden = 28 m

Length of the fencing = Circumference of circle

$$= \pi d = \frac{22}{7} \times 28 = 88 \text{ m}$$

∴ Total cost of fencing = 88 × 300 = ₹ 26400

Q. 108 Priyanka took a wire and bent it to form a circle of radius 14 cm. She bent it into a rectangle with one side 24 cm long. What is the length of the wire? Which figure encloses more area, the circle or the rectangle?

Sol. Given that, radius of circle (r) = 14 cm and length of rectangle (l) = 24 cm

∴ Length of the wire = Circumference of the circle = $2\pi r = 2 \times \dfrac{22}{7} \times 14 = 88$ cm

Let b be the width of rectangle.
Since, the wire is rebent in the form of rectangle.
∴ Perimeter of rectangle = Circumference of circle

$\Rightarrow$ $\qquad$ $2(24 + b) = 88$
$\Rightarrow$ $\qquad$ $24 + b = 44$ $\Rightarrow$ $b = 44 - 24$
$\Rightarrow$ $\qquad$ $b = 20$ cm

$\qquad$ Area of circle = $\pi r^2 = \dfrac{22}{7} \times (14)^2 = 616$ cm²

∵ Area of rectangle = $l \times b = 24 \times 20 = 480$ cm²
Hence, the circle encloses more area than rectangle.

Q. 109 How much distance, in metres, a wheel of 25 cm radius will cover, if it rotates 350 times?

Sol. Given, radius of wheel (r) = 25 cm = $\dfrac{25}{100}$ m = $\dfrac{1}{4}$ m $\qquad\qquad$ $\left[\because 1\,\text{cm} = \dfrac{1}{100}\,\text{m}\right]$

∵ Distance travelled in one rotation = $2\pi r = 2 \times \dfrac{22}{7} \times \dfrac{1}{4} = \dfrac{11}{7}$ m

∴ Distance travelled in 350 rotation = $\dfrac{11}{7} \times 350 = 550$ m

Hence, the wheel coveres 550 m distance.

Q. 110 A circular pond is surrounded by a 2 m wide circular path. If outer circumference of circular path is 44 m, find the inner circumference of the circular path. Also, find area of the path.

Sol. Let R and r be the radius of outer circle and inner circle, respectively.

It is given that, circumference of outer circle is 44 m.

∴ $\qquad\qquad\qquad$ $2\pi R = 44$ $\qquad$ [∵ circumference of circle = $2\pi r$]

$\Rightarrow$ $\qquad\qquad\qquad$ $2 \times \dfrac{22}{7} \times R = 44$

$\Rightarrow$ $\qquad\qquad\qquad$ $R = \dfrac{44}{2 \times \dfrac{22}{7}} = \dfrac{7 \times 44}{2 \times 22} = 7$ m

Since, $\qquad\qquad\qquad$ $r = (R - 2)$m $= (7 - 2)$m $= 5$m

∴ Inner circumference of the circular path $= 2\pi r = 2 \times \dfrac{22}{7} \times 5 = 31.43$ m (approx.)

∵ Area of path = Area of outer circle − Area of inner circle $= \pi(R^2 - r^2)$

$= \dfrac{22}{7}(7^2 - 5^2) = \dfrac{22}{7} \times 24 = 75.43$ m² (approx.)

Q. 111 A carpet of size 5m × 2m has 25 cm wide red border. The inner part of the carpet is blue in colour (see the figure). Find the area of blue portion. What is the ratio of areas of red portion to blue portion?

Sol.　Given, size of carpet $= 5$ m$\times 2$ m and width of border $= 25$ cm $= \dfrac{25}{100} \times$ m $= 0.25$ m

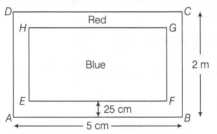

∴ Area of carpet $ABCD = AB \times BC = 5 \times 2 = 10$ m²　[∵ area of rectangle = length × breadth]

So, length of inner blue portion, $EF = AB - (2 \times 0.25$ cm$) = 5 - 0.50 = 4.5$ m

and breadth of inner blue portion $FG = BC - (2 \times 0.25) = 2 - 0.50 = 1.5$ m

Area of blue portion = Area of rectangle $EFGH = EF \times FG = 4.5 \times 1.5 = 6.75$ m²

Now, area of red portion = Area of $ABCD$ − Area of $EFGH = 10 - 6.75 = 3.25$ m²

∴ Ratio of areas of red portion to blue portion $= 3.25 : 6.75 = 13 : 27$

Q. 112 Use the following figure, showing the layout of a farm house.

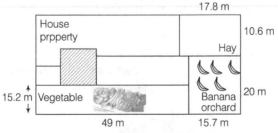

(a) What is the area of land used to grow hay?

(b) It costs ₹ 91 per m^2 to fertilise vegetable garden. What is total cost?

(c) A fence is to be enclosed around the house. The dimensions of house are 18.7 m × 12.6 m. Atleast how many metres of fencing are needed?

(d) Each banana tree required 1.25 m^2 of ground space. How many banana trees can there be in the orchard?

Sol. (a) Area of land used to grow hay = 17.8 m × 10.6 m = 188.68 m^2

[∵ area of rectangle = length × breadth]

(b) ∴ Area of vegetable garden = 49 m × 15.2 m = 744.80 m^2

∵ Cost to fertilise 1 m^2 vegetable garden = ₹ 91

∴ Cost to fertilise 744.80 m^2 vegetable garden = ₹ 91 × 744.80 = ₹ 67776.80

(c) Since, fence is to be enclosed around the house of dimensions 18.7 m × 12.6 m.

∵ Perimeter of the house = 2 × (l + b)

∴ Total length of fence = 2 × (18.7 + 12.6)m = 2 × 31.3 m = 62.6 m

(d) Area covered by banana orchard = 20 m × 15.7 m = 314 m^2

Since, 1.25 m^2 area is required by 1 banana tree.

∴ 314 m^2 area is required by number of banana trees = $\frac{314}{1.25}$ = 251.25 ≈ 251 trees

Q. 113 Study the layout given in the figure and answer the questions.

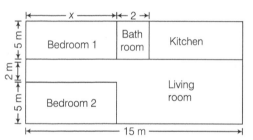

(a) Write an expression for the total area covered by both the bedrooms and the kitchen.

(b) Write an expression to calculate the perimeter of the living room.

(c) If the cost of carpeting is ₹ 50 per m^2, write an expression for calculating the total cost of carpeting both the bedrooms and the living room.

(d) If the cost of tiling is ₹ 30 per m^2, write an expression for calculating the total cost of floor tiles used for the bathroom and kitchen floors.

(e) If the floor area of each bedroom is 35 m^2, then find x.

Sol. (a) Area of both bedrooms and the kitchen = (Area of bedroom) × 2 + Area of kitchen

= (5 × x)2 + 15 − (x + 2) × 5

= 10x + (75 − 5x − 10) = 10x + 65 − 5x

= (65 + 5x) m^2

(b) Perimeter of the living room = 15 + 2 + 5 + (15 − x) + 5 + x + 2 = 44 m

(c) Total area of both the bedrooms and the living room = 5 × x + 7 × 15 = (5x + 105) m^2

∴ Total cost of carpeting = (5x + 105) × 50 = ₹ 250 (x + 21)

(d) Total area of bathroom and kitchen = $(15 - x) \times 5$ m^2

$\therefore$ Total cost of tiling = $(15 - x) \times 5 \times 30 = ₹\,150\,(15 - x)$

(e) Given, area of floor of each bedroom = 35 m^2

Area of one bedroom = $5x$ m^2

$\therefore 5x = 35 \implies x = 7$ m

Q. 114 A 10 m long and 4 m wide rectangular lawn is in front of a house. Along its three sides, a 50 cm wide flower bed is there is shown in the given figure. Find the area of the remaining portion.

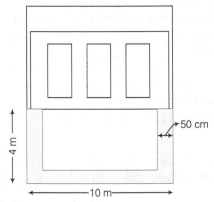

Sol. Given, dimensions of rectangular lawn = $10\,\text{m} \times 4\,\text{m}$ and width of flower bed = $50\,\text{cm}$

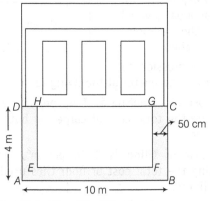

Length of remaining portion, $EF = AB - (50 \times 2\ \text{cm})$

$= 10\,\text{m} - 100\,\text{cm} = 10\,\text{m} - 1\,\text{m} = 9\,\text{m}$ $\qquad \left[\because 1\,\text{cm} = \dfrac{1}{100}\,\text{m} \right]$

Breadth of remaining portion, $EH = AD - 50\,\text{cm} = 4\,\text{m} - 0.5\,\text{m} = 3.5\,\text{m}$

$\therefore$ Required area = Area of portion $EFGH = EF \times EH = 9 \times 3.5 = 31.5$ m^2

Q. 115 A school playground is divided by a 2 m wide path, which is parallel to the width of the playground and a 3 m wide path which is parallel to the length of the ground in the given figure. If the length and width of the playground are 120 m and 80 m respectively, find the area of the remaining playground.

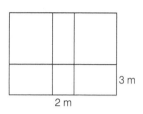

Sol. Given, dimensions of playground = 120 m × 80 m

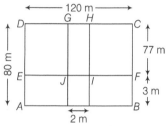

∵ Area of rectangle $ABCD = 120 \times 80 = 9600 \, m^2$

Area of rectangle $ABFE = AB \times BF$

$= 120 \times 3 = 360 \, m^2$ [∵ area of rectangle = length × breadth]

Area of rectangle $GHIJ = JI \times IH = 2 \times 77 = 154 \, m^2$

∴ Area of remaining ground rectangle $GHIJ$ = Area of rectangle $ABCD$

                   − Area of rectangle $ABFE$ − Area of $GHIJ$

                   $= 9600 - 360 - 154 = 9086 \, m^2$

Q. 116 In a park of dimensions 20 m × 15 m, there is a L shaped 1m wide flower bed as shown in the figure. Find the total cost of manuring for the flower bed at the rate of ₹ 45 per m^2.

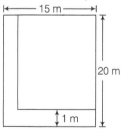

Sol. Given, dimensions of a park = 20 m × 15 m and with of a flower bed = 1 m

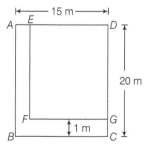

From the figure, $FG = BC - 1m = (15 - 1) = 14\,m$

$$EF = DC - 1m = (20 - 1) = 19\,m$$

$\therefore$ Area of flower bed = Area of $ABCD$ – Area of $EFGD$

$$= 20 \times 15 - 19 \times 14 = 300 - 266 = 34\,m^2$$

[$\because$ area of rectangle = length $\times$ breadth]

$\because$ Cost of manuring 1 m^2 of flower bed = ₹ 45

$\therefore$ Cost of manuring 34 m^2 the flower bed of = ₹34 $\times$ 45 = ₹1530

Q. 117 Dimensions of a painting are 60 cm $\times$ 38 cm. Find the area of the wooden frame of width 6 cm around painting as shown in given figure.

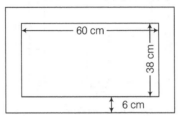

Sol. We have,

and length and breadth of inner rectangle is 60 cm and 38 cm, respectively.

$\therefore$ Area of inner rectangle = 60 $\times$ 38 = 2280 cm^2 [$\because$ area of rectangle = length $\times$ breadth]

$\therefore$ Breadth of outer rectangle = 38 + 6 + 6 = 50 cm

Length of outer rectangle = 60 + 6 + 6 = 72 cm   [$\because$ width of frame = 6 cm, given]

$\therefore$ Area of outer rectangle = 50 $\times$ 72 = 3600 cm^2

Now, area of wooden frame = 3600 – 2280 = 1320 cm^2

Q. 118 A design is made up of four congruent right triangles as shown in the given figure. Find the area of the shaded portion.

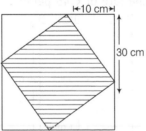

Sol.

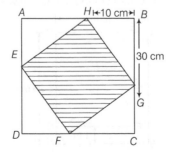

Area of one right angled triangle $= \frac{1}{2} \times BH \times BG = \frac{1}{2} \times 10 \times 30 = 150\,cm^2$

So, area of 4 right angled triangles $= 4 \times 150 = 600\,cm^2$

[∵ all the right angled triangles are congruent]

∵ Area of square $= (Side)^2$ [GC = 10 cm, because all the triangles are congruent]

Area of portion $ABCD = (30 + 10)^2 = 40^2 = 1600\,cm^2$

∴ Area of shaded portion $= 1600 - 600 = 1000\,cm^2$

Q. 119 A square tile of length 20 cm has four quarter circles at each corner as shown in the figure (i). Find the area of shaded portion. Another tile with same dimensions has a circle in the centre of the tile in the figure (ii). If the circle touches all the four sides of the square tile, find the area of the shaded portion. In which tile, area of shaded portion will be more? (Take, $\pi = 3.14$)

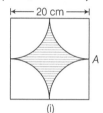

(i)

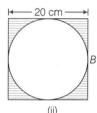

(ii)

Sol. (i) Area of shaded portion

= Area of square $-$ 4 × Area of quarter circle

$= 20 \times 20 - 4 \times \dfrac{\pi r^2}{4}$

[∵ area of square $= (side)^2$ and area of quarter circle $= \frac{1}{4}$ area of a circle]

$= 400 - 4 \times \dfrac{22}{7} \times \dfrac{1}{4} \times 10 \times 10$ [∵ radius of quarter circle $= \frac{1}{2}$ side of square = 10 cm]

$= 400 - \dfrac{2200}{7} = \dfrac{600}{7} = 85.71\,cm^2 \approx 86\,cm^2$

(ii) Area of shaded portion

= Area of square $-$ Area of circle

$= 20 \times 20 - \dfrac{22}{7} \times 10 \times 10$ [∵ radius of circle $= \frac{1}{2}$ side of square = 10 cm]

$= 400 - \dfrac{2200}{7} = \dfrac{600}{7} \approx 86\,cm^2$

Hence, area in both cases is equal i.e. $86\,cm^2$.

Q. 120 A rectangular field is 48 m long and 12 m wide. How many right triangular flower beds can be laid in this field, if sides including the right angle measure 2 m and 4 m, respectively?

Sol. Given, dimenstions of a rectangular field $= 48\,m \times 12\,m$

and dimensions of a right angled triangle $= 2\,m \times 4\,m$

$\therefore$ Number of right triangular flower beds $= \dfrac{\text{Area of field}}{\text{Area of right angled triangle}} = \dfrac{48 \times 12}{\dfrac{1}{2} \times 2 \times 4}$

$= 144$ $\left[\begin{array}{l} \because \text{ area of rectangle } = \text{length} \times \text{breadth and area} \\ \text{of a right angled triangle} = \dfrac{1}{2} \times \text{height} \times \text{breadth} \end{array} \right]$

Q. 121 Ramesh grew wheat in a rectangular field that measured 32 metres long and 26 metres wide. This year he increased the area for wheat by increasing the length but not the width. He increased the area of the wheat field by 650 square metres. What is the length of the expanded wheat field?

Sol. Given, dimenstions of a rectanglular field 32 m×26 m.

and area increased $= 650 \, m^2$

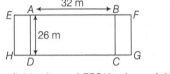

$\therefore$ Increased area of wheat field = Area of *EFGH* − Area of *ABCD* wheat field

$\Rightarrow$ $650 = EF \times EH - AB \times AD$

                     [$\because$ area of rectangle = length × breadth]

$\Rightarrow$ $650 = EF \times 26 - 32 \times 26$

$\Rightarrow$ $650 = 26EF - 832$

$\Rightarrow$ $1482 = 26EF \quad \Rightarrow \quad EF = 57m$

Hence, the length of the expanded wheat field is 57 m.

Q. 122 In the given figure, $\triangle AEC$ is right angled at *E*, *B* is a point on *EC*, *BD* is the altitude of $\triangle ABC$, *AC* = 25 cm, *BC* = 7 cm and *AE* = 15 cm. Find the area of $\triangle ABC$ and the length of *DB*.

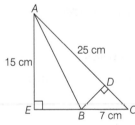

Sol. Given, *AC* = 25 cm, *BC* = 7 cm, and *AE* = 15 cm

In $\triangle AEC$, using Pythagoras theorem,

$$AC^2 = AE^2 + EC^2$$

$\Rightarrow$ $EC^2 = AC^2 - AE^2$

$\Rightarrow$ $EC^2 = (25)^2 - (15)^2 = 625 - 225$

$$= 400$$

$$EC = \sqrt{400} = 20 \, cm$$

and $EB = EC - BC = 20 - 7$

$$= 13 \, cm$$

$$\text{Area of } \triangle AEC = \frac{1}{2} \times AE \times EC$$

$$= \frac{1}{2} \times 15 \times 20 = 150 \text{ cm}^2$$

and
$$\text{Area of } \triangle AEB = \frac{1}{2} \times AE \times EB = \frac{1}{2} \times 15 \times 13 = 97.5 \text{ cm}^2$$

∴
$$\text{Area of } \triangle ABC = \text{Area of } \triangle AEC - \text{Area of } \triangle AEB$$
$$= 150 - 97.5$$
$$= 52.5 \text{ cm}^2$$

$$\text{Again, Area of } \triangle ABC = \frac{1}{2} \times BD \times AC$$

$$52.5 = \frac{1}{2} \times BD \times 25$$

⇒
$$BD = \frac{52.5 \times 2}{25} = 4.2 \text{ cm}$$

Hence, the area of $\triangle ABC$ is 52.5 cm^2 and the length of DB is 4.2 cm.

Q. 123

Sol. Number of pieces of chocolate
$$= \frac{\text{Area of sheet of chocolate}}{\text{Area of one chocolate}} = \frac{18 \times 18}{1.5 \times 2} = \frac{324}{3} = 108$$

Q. 124 Calculate the area of shaded region in the given figure, where all of the short line segments are at right angles to each other and 1 cm long.

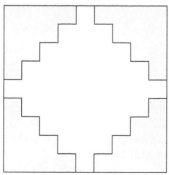

Sol.

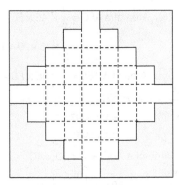

Length of the larger rectangle = 1 × 9 cm = 9 cm
Breadth of the larger rectangle = 1 × 9 cm = 9 cm
∴ Area of shaded region = Area of larger square – Area of 41 small identical square
= 9 × 9 – 41 × 1 × 1= 81 – 41= 40 cm^2

Q. 125 The plan and measurement for a house are given in the figure. The house is surrounded by a path 1 m wide.

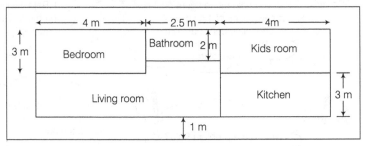

Find the following

    (i) Cost of paving the path with bricks at rate of ₹ 120 per m^2.

    (ii) Cost of wooden flooring inside the house except the bathroom at the cost of ₹ 1200 per m^2.

    (iii) Area of living room.

Sol.

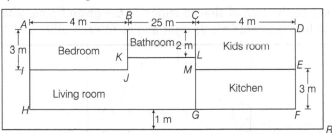

(i) Area of path = Area of rectangle PQRS – Area of rectangle ADFH
$$= PQ \times QR - AD \times DF$$
$$= (4 + 2.5 + 4 + 1 + 1) \times (3 + 3 + 1 + 1) - (4 + 2.5 + 4) \times (3 + 3)$$
$$= 12.5 \times 8 - 10.5 \times 6$$
$$= 37 m^2$$

∴ Cost of paving the path with bricks
    = Cost per unit m² × Total area of path
    = 120 × 37
    = ₹ 4440

(ii) Area of house except bathroom
        = Area of house – Area of bathroom
        = Area of rectangle ADFH – Area of rectangle BCLK
        = (4 + 2.5 + 4) × (3 + 3) − 2.5 × 2
        = 63 − 5 = 58 m²
    ∴ Cost of flouring = Cost per unit m² × Total area
            = 1200 × 58 = ₹ 69600

(iii) Area of living room = Area of rectangle ACGH – Area of rectangle ABJI
            − Area of rectangle BCLK
            = (4 + 2.5) × (3 + 3) − 4 × 3 − 2.5 × 2 = 39 − 12 − 5
            = 22 m²

Q. 126 Architects design many types of buildings. They draw plans for houses, such as the plant is shown in the following figure.

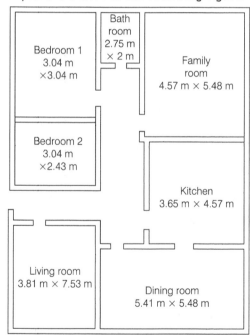

An architect wants to install a decorative moulding around the ceilings in the rooms. The decorative moulding costs ₹ 500 per m.

(a) Find how much moulding will be needed for each room.
    (i) family room   (ii) living room
    (iii) dining room   (iv) bedroom 1
    (v) bedroom 2

(b) The carpet costs ₹ 200 per m². Find the cost of carpeting each room.

(c) What is the total cost of moulding for all the five rooms?

Sol. (a) (i) Given, breadth of the family room = 5.48 m

and length of the family room = 4.57 m

∴ Perimeter of the family room = 2(Length + Breadth) = 2(5.48 + 4.57)

$$= 2 \times 10.05 = 20.10 \, m$$

(ii) Given, length of the living room = 3.81 m

and breadth of the living room = 7.53 m

∴ Perimeter of the living room = 2(Length + Breadth) = 2(3.81 + 7.53)

$$= 2 \times 11.34 = 22.68 \, m$$

(iii) Given, breadth of the dining room = 5.48 m

and length of the dining room = 5.41 m

∴ Perimeter of dinning room = 2 (Length + Breadth) = 2(5.41 + 5.48)

$$= 2 \times 10.89 = 21.78 \, m$$

(iv) Given, length of bedroom 1 = 3.04 m

and breadth of bedroom 1 = 3.04 m

∴ Perimeter of the bedroom 1 = 2(Length + Breadth) = 2(3.04 + 3.04)

$$= 2 \times 6.08 = 12.16 \, m$$

(v) Given, breadth of bedroom 2 = 2.43 m and length of bedroom 2 = 3.04 m

∴ Perimeter of the bedroom 2 = 2(Length + Breadth) = 2(3.04 + 2.43)

$$= 2 \times 5.47 = 10.94 \, m$$

(b) For bedroom 1,

Given, length of bedroom 1 = 3.04 m and breadth of bedroom 1 = 3.04 m

∴ Area of bedroom 1 = Length × Breadth

∴ Area of bedroom 1 = 3.04 × 3.04 = 9.2416 sq m

∵ Cost of carpeting 1 sq m = ₹ 200

∴ Cost of carpeting $9.2416 m^2$ = 9.2416 × 200 = ₹ 1848

For bedroom 2,

Given, length of bedroom 2 = 3.04 m

and breadth of bedroom 2 = 2.43 m

∴ Area of bedroom 2 = Length × Breadth = 3.04 × 2.43 = 7.3872 m^2

∴ Cost of carpeting 1 m^2 = ₹ 200

∴ Cost of carpeting 7.3872 m^2 = 7.3872 × 200 = ₹ 1477

For living room,

Given, length of living room = 3.81 m and breadth of living room = 7.53 m

∴ Area of living room = 3.81 × 7.53 = 28.6893 m^2

Cost of carpeting of living room 1 m^2 = ₹ 200

∵ Cost of carpeting 28.6893 m^2 = ₹ 200 × 28.6893 = ₹ 5737.86

For dining room,

Given, length of dining room = 5.41 m

and breadth of dining room = 5.48 m

∵ Area of dining room = 5.41 × 5.48 = 29.6468 m^2

∵ Cost of carpeting 1 m^2 = ₹ 200

∴ Cost of carpeting 29.6468 m^2 = 29.6468 × 200 = ₹ 5929.36

For family room,
Given, length of family room = 4.57 m
and breadth of family room = 5.48 m
∴ Area of family room = 5.48 × 4.57 = 25.0436 m²
So, cost of carpeting family room = 25.0436 × 200 = ₹ 5008.72

(c) Total perimeter of all the five rooms
       = 20.10 m + 22.68 m + 21.78 m + 12.16 m + 10.94 m = 87.66 m
∵ Given, cost of moulding each room = ₹ 500 per m
∴ Total cost of moulding all five rooms = 87.66 × 500 = ₹ 43830

Q. 127 *ABCD* is a given rectangle with length as 80 cm and breadth as 60 cm. *P, Q, R, S* are the mid-points of sides *AB, BC, CD, DA*, respectively. A circular rangoli of radius 10 cm is drawn at the centre as shown in the given figure. Find the area of shaded portion.

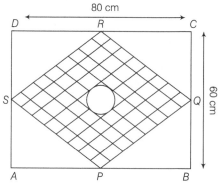

Sol.   Here, $AP = \dfrac{1}{2} AB = \dfrac{1}{2} \times 80 = 40$ cm

Also, $AS = \dfrac{1}{2} AD = \dfrac{1}{2} \times 60 = 30$ cm

Area of $\triangle APS = \dfrac{1}{2} \times AP \times AS = \dfrac{1}{2} \times 40 \times 30 = 600$ cm²

Area of portion $PQRS$ = Area of rectangle $ABCD$ − 4 × Area of $\triangle APS$ = 80 × 60 − 4 × 600
       = 4800 − 2400 = 2400 cm²

Area of circular rangoli = $\pi \times (10)^2 = \dfrac{22}{7} \times 100 = 314$ cm²   [∵ radius of circle = 10 cm]

∴ Area of shaded region = 2400 − 314 = 2086 cm²

Q. 128 4 squares each of the side 10 cm have been cut from each corner of a rectangular sheet of paper of size 100 cm × 80 cm. From the remaining piece of paper, an isosceles right triangle is removed whose equal sides are each of 10 cm length. Find the area of the remaining part of the paper.

Sol.   Area of each square = $(10)^2$ cm² = 100 cm²   [∵ area of square = (side)²]

Area of rectangular sheet = 100 × 80 cm²   [∵ area of rectangle = length × breadth]
       = 8000 cm²

Area of an isosceles right triangle $= \dfrac{1}{2} \times 10 \times 10 = 50 \, cm^2$

$$\left[\because \text{area of an isosceles right triangle} = \dfrac{1}{2} \times \text{base} \times \text{height} \right]$$

$\therefore$ Area of remaining part of paper $= 8000 - 4 \times 100 - 50$
$$= 7550 \, cm^2$$

Q. 129 A dinner plate is in the form of circle. A circular region encloses a beautiful design as shown in the given figure. The inner circumference is 352 mm and outer is 396 mm. Find the width of circular design.

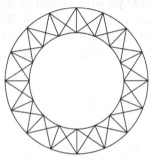

Sol.   Let the radius of inner and outer circle be r and R, respectively.
Given, inner circumference $= 352 \, mm$

$\Rightarrow$ $2 \pi r = 352$ [$\because$ circumference $= 2 \pi r$]

$\Rightarrow$ $2 \times \dfrac{22}{7} \times r = 352$

$\Rightarrow$ $r = \dfrac{352 \times 7}{2 \times 22} = \dfrac{2464}{44} = 56 \, mm$

and outer circumference $= 396 \, mm$ [given]

$\Rightarrow$ $2 \pi R = 396$

$\Rightarrow$ $2 \times \dfrac{22}{7} \times R = 396$

$\Rightarrow$ $R = \dfrac{396 \times 7}{2 \times 22} = 63 \, mm$

$\therefore$ Width of circular design $= R - r = 63 - 56 = 7 \, mm$

Q. 130 The moon is about 384000 km from earth and its path around the earth is nearly circular. Find the length of path described by moon in one complete revolution. (Take, $\pi = 3.14$)

Sol.   Length of path described by moon in one complete revolution $= 2 \pi r$
$$= 2 \times 3.14 \times 384000 \quad [\because \text{radius} = \text{distance of moon from the earth}]$$
$$= 2411520 \, km$$

Q. 131 A photograph of Billiard/Snooker table has dimensions as $\dfrac{1}{10}$ th of its actual size as shown in the given figure.

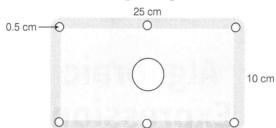

The portion excluding six holes each of diameter 0.5 cm needs to be polished at rate of ₹ 200 per m². Find the cost of polishing.

Sol. Actual length = 25 × 10 = 250 cm

Actual breadth = 10 × 10 = 100 cm

Area of table = 250 × 100 = 25000 cm²

Radius of 1 hole = $\dfrac{0.5}{2}$ = 0.25 cm

Area of 6 holes = 6 × πr^2 = 6 × $\dfrac{22}{7}$ × 0.25 × 0.25 = 1.18 cm²

Area of portion excluding holes = 25000 – 1.18 = 24998.8 cm²

∴ Cost of polishing = ₹ $\dfrac{24999}{10000}$ × 200 = ₹ 500 (approx.)

10

Algebraic Expression

Multiple Choice Questions (MCQs)

Q. 1 An algebraic expression containing three terms is called a

    (a) monomial   (b) binomial

    (c) trinomial   (d) All of these

Sol. *(c)* An algebraic expression containing one term is called monomial, two terms is called binomial and three terms is called trinomial.

Q. 2 Number of terms in the expression $3x^2y - 2y^2z - z^2x + 5$ is

    (a) 2   (b) 3

    (c) 4   (d) 5

Sol. *(c)* The terms in the expression are $3x^2y$, $-2y^2z$, $-z^2x$ and 5. Hence, total number of terms are 4.

Q. 3 The terms of expression $4x^2 - 3xy$ are

    (a) $4x^2$ and $-3xy$ (b) $4x^2$ and $3xy$

    (c) $4x^2$ and $-xy$ (d) x^2 and xy

Sol. *(a)* Terms in the expression $4x^2 - 3xy$ are $4x^2$ and $-3xy$.

Q. 4 Factors of $-5x^2y^2z$ are

    (a) $-5 \times x \times y \times z$

    (b) $-5 \times x^2 \times y \times z$

    (c) $-5 \times x \times x \times x \times y \times y \times z$

    (d) $-5 \times x \times y \times z^2$

Sol. *(c)* $-5x^2y^2z$ can be written as $-5 \times x \times x \times x \times y \times y \times z$

Q. 5 Coefficient of x in $-9xy^2z$ is

(a) $9yz$ (b) $-9yz$
(c) $9y^2z$ (d) $-9y^2z$

Sol. *(d)* Coefficient of x in $-9xy^2z = -9y^2z$

Q. 6 Which of the following is a pair of like terms?

(a) $-7xy^2z, -7x^2yz$ (b) $-10xyz^2, 3xyz^2$
(c) $3xyz, 3x^2y^2z^2$ (d) $4xyz^2, 4x^2yz$

Sol. *(b)* Like terms are those terms, having same algebraic factor.
Hence, $-10xyz^2$ and $3xyz^2$ are like terms as they contain xyz^2 same factor.

Q. 7 Identify the binomial out of the following

(a) $3xy^2 + 5y - x^2y$ (b) $x^2y - 5y - x^2y$
(c) $xy + yz + zx$ (d) $3xy^2 + 5y - xy^2$

Sol. *(d)* We know that, an algebraic expression containing two terms is called binomial.
So, taking option (d), $3xy^2 + 5y - xy^2 = 2xy^2 + 5y$
As it contains only two terms, hence it is known as binomial.

Q. 8 The sum of $x^4 - xy + 2y^2$ and $-x^4 + xy + 2y^2$ is

(a) monomial and polynomial in y (b) binomial and polynomial
(c) trinomial and polynomial   (d) monomial and polynomial in x

Sol. *(a)* Required sum $= (x^4 - xy + 2y^2) + (-x^4 + xy + 2y^2)$
$$= x^4 - xy + 2y^2 - x^4 + xy + 2y^2$$
$$= [(x^4 + (-x^4)] + (-xy + xy) + (2y^2 + 2y^2)$$
$$= 0 + 0 + 4y^2$$
$$= 4y^2$$

$4y^2$ is a monomial and polynomial in y.

Q. 9 The subtraction of 5 times of y from x is

(a) $5x - y$ (b) $y - 5x$ (c) $x - 5y$ (d) $5y - x$

Sol. *(c)* 5 times of $y = 5y$
Now, subtraction of 5 times of y from x is written as $x - 5y$.

Q. 10 $-b - 0$ is equal to

(a) $-1 \times b$ (b) $1 - b - 0$ (c) $0 - (-1) \times b$ (d) $-b - 0 - 1$

Sol. *(a)* We have, $-b - 0 = -b$

(a) $-1 \times b = -b$ (b) $1 - b - 0 = 1 - b$
(c) $0 - (-1) \times b = 0 + b = b$ (d) $-b - 0 - 1 = -b - 1$
Hence, option (a) is correct.

Q. 11 The side length of the top of square table is x. The expression for perimeter is

    (a) $4 + x$ (b) $2x$ (c) $4x$ (d) $8x$

Sol. *(c)*   Given, side length of a square table $= x$

        ∴ Perimeter of a square $= 4 \times$ Side

$$= 4 \times x$$
$$= 4x$$

Q. 12 The number of scarfs of length half metre that can be made from y metres of cloth is

    (a) $2y$ (b) $\dfrac{y}{2}$ (c) $y + 2$ (d) $y + \dfrac{1}{2}$

Sol. *(a)*   We have,

        Length of 1 scarf $= \dfrac{1}{2} m$

        So, number of scarfs which can be made from y metres $= \dfrac{y}{\frac{1}{2}} = 2y$

Q. 13 $123x^2 y - 138x^2 y$ is a like term of

    (a) $10xy$ (b) $-15xy$ (c) $-15xy^2$ (d) $10x^2 y$

Sol. *(d)*   We have, $123x^2 y - 138x^2 y = -15x^2 y$

        Hence, it is like term of $10x^2 y$ as both contain $x^2 y$.

Q. 14 The value of $3x^2 - 5x + 3$, when $x = 1$ is

    (a) 1   (b) 0   (c) -1 (d) 11

Sol. *(a)*   Putting $x = 1$ in given equation we get

        $3x^2 - 5x + 3 = 3(1)^2 - 5(1) + 3$

$$= 3 - 5 + 3$$
$$= 1$$

Q. 15 The expression for the number of diagonals that we can make from one vertex of a n-sided polygon is

    (a) $2n + 1$ (b) $n - 2$ (c) $5n + 2$ (d) $n - 3$

Sol. *(d)*   Since, vertex is formed by joining two sides. Diagonal is line segment joining the two opposite vertex. So, number of diagonal formed by one vertex $= n - 3$.

Q. 16 The length of a side of square is given as $2x + 3$. Which expression represents the perimeter of the square?

    (a) $2x + 16$ (b) $6x + 9$ (c) $8x + 3$ (d) $8x + 12$

Sol. *(d)*   Given, side of the square $= (2x + 3)$

        ∴ Perimeter of square $= 4 \times$ (Side)

$$= 4 \times (2x + 3)$$
$$= 8x + 12$$

Fill in the Blanks

In questions 17 to 32, fill in the blanks to make the statements true.

Q. 17 Sum or difference of two like terms is _____ .

Sol. Sum or difference of two like terms is a **like term**.

e.g. $138x^2y - 125x^2y = 13x^2y$

Q. 18 In the formula, area of circle $= \pi r^2$, the numerical constant of the expression πr^2 is _____.

Sol. In πr^2, the numerical constant is π as r^2 is variable.

Q. 19 $3a^2b$ and $-7ba^2$ are _____ terms.

Sol. $3a^2b$ and $-7ba^2$ are **like** terms as both have same algebraic factor a^2b.

Q. 20 $-5a^2b$ and $-5b^2a$ are _____ terms.

Sol. $-5a^2b$ and $-5b^2a$ are **unlike** terms as they do not have same algebraic factor.

Q. 21 In the expression $2\pi r$, the algebraic variable is _____.

Sol. In the expression $2\pi r$, 2π is constant while *r* is an algebraic variable.

Q. 22 Number of terms in a monomial is _____.

Sol. Number of terms in a monomial is **one**.

Q. 23 Like terms in the expression $n(n+1)+6(n-1)$ are _____ and _____.

Sol. We have, $n(n+1) + 6(n-1) = n^2 + n + 6n - 6$

Hence, like terms in the expression $n(n+1) + 6(n-1)$ are **n** and **6n**.

Q. 24 The expression $13+90$ is a _____.

Sol. $\because 13 + 90 = 103$

$\therefore 103$ is a **constant term**.

Q. 25 The speed of car is 55 km/h. The distance covered in *y* hours is _____.

Sol. Given, speed of car = 55 km/h.

$\because$ Distance = Speed $\times$ Time

$\therefore$ Distance covered in *y* hours $= 55 \times y = \mathbf{55y}$ km

Q. 26 $x + y + z$ is an expression which is neither monomial nor _____.

Sol. Since, $x + y + z$ has three terms, so it is trinomial. Hence, $x + y + z$ is an expression which is neither monomial nor **binomial**.

Q. 27 If $(x^2y + y^2 + 3)$ is subtracted from $(3x^2y + 2y^2 + 5)$, then coefficient of y in the result is _____.

Sol. We have, $(3x^2y + 2y^2 + 5) - (x^2y + y^2 + 3) = 3x^2y + 2y^2 + 5 - x^2y - y^2 - 3$

$$= 2x^2y + y^2 + 2$$

∴ Coefficient of $y = \mathbf{2x^2}$

Q. 28 $-a - b - c$ is same as $-a - ($_____$)$.

Sol. We have, $-a - b - c = -a - (b + c)$ [by taking common (−) minus sign]

So, $-a - b - c$ is same as $-a - (\mathbf{b + c})$.

Q. 29 The unlike terms in perimeters of following figures are _____ and _____ .

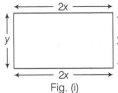
Fig. (i)

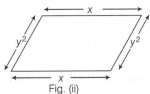
Fig. (ii)

Sol. In Fig. (i),

Perimeter = Sum of all sides

$$= 2x + y + 2x + y = 4x + 2y$$

In Fig. (ii),

Perimeter = Sum of all sides

$$= x + y^2 + x + y^2 = 2x + 2y^2$$

∴ Unlike terms in perimeters are $\mathbf{2y}$ and $\mathbf{2y^2}$.

Q. 30 On adding a monomial _____ to $-2x + 4y^2 + z$, the resulting expression becomes a binomial.

Sol. We can add $2x$, $-4y^2$ and $-z$ to the expression to make it binomial.

$$\Rightarrow \quad 2x + (-2x + 4y^2 + z) = 4y^2 + z$$

$$\Rightarrow \quad -4y^2 + (-2x + 4y^2 + z) = -2x + z$$

$$\Rightarrow \quad -z + (-2x + 4y^2 + z) = -2x + 4y^2$$

Hence, on adding a monomial $\mathbf{2x}$ or $\mathbf{-4y^2}$ or $\mathbf{-z}$ to $-2x + 4y^2 + z$, the resulting expression becomes a binomial.

Q. 31 $3x + 23x^2 + 6y^2 + 2x + y^2 + $_____$ = 5x + 7y^2$.

Sol. Let $(3x + 23x^2 + 6y^2 + 2x + y^2) + M = 5x + 7y^2$

$$\Rightarrow \quad M = (5x + 7y^2) - (3x + 23x^2 + 6y^2 + 2x + y^2)$$

$$\Rightarrow \quad M = 5x + 7y^2 - 3x - 23x^2 - 6y^2 - 2x - y^2$$

[with −ve sign, +ve sign in the bracket will change on opening it]

$$\Rightarrow \quad M = 5x - 3x - 2x + 7y^2 - 6y^2 - y^2 - 23x^2$$

$$M = 0 + 0 - 23x^2 = \mathbf{-23x^2}$$

Q. 32 If Rohit has 5xy toffees and Shantanu has 20yx toffees, then Shantanu has ____ more toffees.

Sol. We have, Rohit has toffees $= 5xy$

Shantanu has toffees $= 20yx$

$\therefore$ Difference $= 20xy - 5xy = 15xy$

Hence, Shantanu had $15xy$ more toffees.

True/False

In questions 33 to 52, state whether the statements given are True or False.

Q. 33 $1 + \dfrac{x}{2} + x^3$ is a polynomial.

Sol. *True*

Expression with one or more than one term is called a polynomial.

Q. 34 $(3a - b + 3) - (a + b)$ is a binomial.

Sol. *False*

We have , $(3a - b + 3) - (a + b) = 3a - b + 3 - a - b$

$= 3a - a - b - b + 3$

$= 2a - 2b + 3$

The expression has three terms, it is a trinomial.

Q. 35 A trinomial can be a polynomial.

Sol. *True*

Trinomial is a polynomial, because it has three terms.

Q. 36 A polynomial with more than two terms is a trinomial.

Sol. *False*

A polynomial with more than two terms can be trinomial or more. While a trinomial have exact three terms.

Q. 37 Sum of x and y is $x + y$.

Sol. *True*

Sum of x and y is $x + y$.

Q. 38 Sum of 2 and p is $2p$.

Sol. *False*

Sum of 2 and p is $2 + p$.

Q. 39 A binomial has more than two terms.

Sol. *False*

Binomial has exactly two unlike terms.

Q. 40 A trinomial has exactly three terms.

Sol. *True*

A trinomial has exactly three unlike terms.

Q. 41 In like terms, variables and their powers are the same.

Sol. *True*

In like terms, algebraic factors are same.

Q. 42 The expression $x + y + 5x$ is a trinomial.

Sol. *False*

∵ $x + y + 5x = 6x + y$

It is a binomial.

Q. 43 $4p$ is the numerical coefficient of q^2 in $-4pq^2$.

Sol. *False*

∵ Numerical coefficient of q^2 in $-4pq^2 = -4$.

Q. 44 $5a$ and $5b$ are unlike terms.

Sol. *True*

Because both the terms have different algebraic factors.

Q. 45 Sum of $x^2 + x$ and $y + y^2$ is $2x^2 + 2y^2$.

Sol. *False*

∵ Sum $= (x^2 + x) + (y + y^2) = x^2 + x + y + y^2$

$= x^2 + y^2 + x + y$

Q. 46 Subtracting a term from a given expression is the same as adding its additive inverse to given expression.

Sol. *True*

Because additive inverse is the negation of a number or expression.

Q. 47 The total number of planets of Sun can be denoted by the variable n.

Sol. *False*

As, Sun has infinite planets around it.

Q. 48 In like terms, the numerical coefficients should also be the same.

Sol. *False*

e.g. $-3x^2y$ and $4x^2y$ are like terms as they have same algebraic factor x^2y but have different numerical coefficients.

Q. 49 If we add a monomial and binomial, then answer can never be a monomial.

Sol. *False*

If we add a monomial and a binomial, then answer can be a monomial.

e.g. Add x^2 and $-x^2 + y^2$

$$= x^2 + (-x^2 + y^2)$$
$$= x^2 - x^2 + y^2 = y^2$$

Hence, the answer is monomial.

Q. 50 If we subtract a monomial from a binomial, then answer is atleast a binomial.

Sol. *False*

If we subtract a monomial from a binomial, then answer is atleast a monomial.

e.g. Subtract x and $x - y = x - (x - y) = x - x + y = y$, i.e. monomial.

Hence, the answer is monomial.

Q. 51 When we subtract a monomial from trinomial, then answer can be a polynomial.

Sol. *True*

When we subtract a monomial from a trinomial, then answer can be binomial or polynomial.

e.g. Subtract y^2 from $y^2 - x^2 - 2xy$.

$$= (y^2 - x^2 - 2xy) - y^2 = y^2 - y^2 - x^2 - 2xy = -x^2 - 2xy$$

Hence, answer is binomial.

Q. 52 When we add a monomial and a trinomial, then answer can be a monomial.

Sol. *False*

When we add a monomial and a trinomial, then it can be binomial or trinomial.

e.g. Add xy and $x^3 + 2xy - y^3$

$$= xy + (x^3 + 2xy - y^3)$$
$$= xy + 2xy + x^3 - y^3 = 3xy + x^3 - y^3$$

Hence, answer is trinomial.

Q. 53 Write the following statements in the form of algebraic expressions and write whether is monomial, binomial or trinomial.

(a) x is multiplied by itself and then added to the product of x and y.

(b) Three times of p and two times of q are multiplied and then subtracted from r.

(c) Product of p, twice of q and thrice of r.

(d) Sum of the products of a and b, b and c, c and a.

(e) Perimeter of an equilateral triangle of side x.

(f) Perimeter of a rectangle with length p and breadth q.

(g) Area of a triangle with base m and height n.

(h) Area of a square with side x.

(i) Cube of s subtracted from cube of t.

(j) Quotient of x and 15 multiplied by x.

(k) The sum of square of x and cube of z.

(l) Two times q subtracted from cube of q.

Sol. (a) $x^2 + xy$ [binomial]

(b) $r - (3p \times 2q) = r - 6pq$ [binomial]

(c) $p \times 2q \times 3r = 6pq$ [monomial]

(d) $ab + bc + ca$ [trinomial]

(e) $3x$ [monomial]   [∵ perimeter of an equilateral triangle] = 3 × side]

(f) $2(p + q) = 2p + 2q$ [binomial]   [∵ perimeter of a rectangle with length l and breadth $b = 2(l + b)$]

(g) $\frac{1}{2}mn$ [monomial]   [∵ area of a triangle $= \frac{1}{2} \times$ base × height]

(h) x^2 [monomial]   [∵ area of a square = (side)²]

(i) $t^3 - s^3$ [binomial]

(j) $(x \div 15)x$ or $\frac{x^2}{15}$ [monomial]

(k) $x^2 + z^3$ [binomial]

(l) $q^3 - 2q$ [binomial]

Q. 54 Write the coefficient of x^2 in the following:

(i) $x^2 - x + 4$ (ii) $x^3 - 2x^2 + 3x + 1$

(iii) $1 + 2x + 3x^2 + 4x^3$ (iv) $y + y^2x + y^3x^2 + y^4x^3$

Sol. (i) Coefficient of x^2 in $x^2 - x + 4 = 1$

(ii) Coefficient of x^2 in $x^3 - 2x^2 + 3x + 1 = -2$

(iii) Coefficient of x^2 in $1 + 2x + 3x^2 + 4x^3 = 3$

(iv) Coefficient of x^2 in $y + y^2x + y^3x^2 + y^4x^3 = y^3$

Q. 55 Find the numerical coefficient of each of the terms

(i) $x^3y^2z,\ xy^2z^3,\ -3xy^2z^3,\ 5x^3y^2z,\ -7x^2y^2z^2$

(ii) $10xyz,\ -7xy^2z,\ -9xyz,\ 2xy^2z,\ 2x^2y^2z^2$

Sol. (i) Numerical coefficient of, $x^3y^2z = 1$

$$xy^2z^3 = 1$$
$$-3xy^2z^3 = -3$$
$$5x^3y^2z = 5$$
$$-7x^2y^2z^2 = -7$$

(ii) Numerical coefficient of, $10xyz = 10$

$$-7xy^2z = -7$$
$$-9xyz = -9$$
$$2xy^2z = 2$$
$$2x^2y^2z^2 = 2$$

Q. 56 Simplify the following by combining the like terms and then write whether the expression is a monomial, a binomial or a trinomial.

(a) $3x^2yz^2 - 3xy^2z + x^2yz^2 + 7xy^2z$

(b) $x^4 + 3x^3y + 3x^2y^2 - 3x^3y - 3xy^3 + y^4 - 3x^2y^2$

(c) $p^3q^2r + pq^2r^3 + 3p^2qr^2 - 9p^2qr^2$

(d) $2a + 2b + 2c - 2a - 2b - 2c - 2b + 2c + 2a$

(e) $50x^3 - 21x + 107 + 41x^3 - x + 1 - 93 + 71x - 31x^3$

Sol. We have,

(a) $3x^2yz^2 - 3xy^2z + x^2yz^2 + 7xy^2z$

By combining the like terms,

$$= 3x^2yz^2 + x^2yz^2 - 3xy^2z + 7xy^2z$$
$$= 4x^2yz^2 + 4xy^2z$$

The expression contains two terms. So, it is binomial.

(b) $x^4 + 3x^3y + 3x^2y^2 - 3x^3y - 3xy^3 + y^4 - 3x^2y^2$

By combining the like terms,

$$= x^4 + 3x^3y - 3x^3y + 3x^2y^2 - 3x^2y^2 - 3x^3y + y^4$$
$$= x^4 + 0 + 0 - 3x^3y + y^4 = x^4 + y^4 - 3x^3y$$

The expression contains three terms. So, it is trinomial.

(c) $p^3q^2r + pq^2r^3 + 3p^2qr^2 - 9p^2qr^2$

By combining the like terms,

$$= p^3q^2r + pq^2r^3 + 3p^2qr^2 - 9p^2qr^2$$
$$= p^3q^2r + pq^2r^3 - 6p^2qr^2$$

The expression contains three terms. So, it is trinomial.

(d) $2a + 2b + 2c - 2a - 2b - 2c - 2b + 2c + 2a$

By combining the like terms,

$$= 2a - 2a + 2a + 2b - 2b - 2b + 2c - 2c + 2c$$
$$= 2a - 2b + 2c$$

The expression contains three terms. So, it is trinomial.

(e) $50x^3 - 21x + 107 + 41x^3 - x + 1 - 93 + 71x - 31x^3$

By combining the like terms,

$$= 50x^3 + 41x^3 - 31x^3 - 21x - x + 71x + 107 + 1 - 93$$
$$= 60x^3 + 49x + 15$$

The expression contains three terms. So, it is trinomial.

Note *We can add and subtract only like terms.*

Q. 57 Add the following expressions

(a) $p^2 - 7pq - q^2$ and $-3p^2 - 2pq + 7q^2$

(b) $x^3 - x^2y - xy^2 - y^3$ and $x^3 - 2x^2y + 3xy^2 + 4y$

(c) $ab + bc + ca$ and $-bc - ca - ab$

(d) $p^2 - q + r, q^2 - r + p$ and $r^2 - p + q$

(e) $x^3 y^2 + x^2 y^3 + 3y^4$ and $x^4 + 3x^2 y^3 + 4y^4$

(f) $p^2 qr + pq^2 r + pqr^2$ and $-3pq^2 r - 2pqr^2$

(g) $uv - vw, vw - wu$ and $wu - uv$

(h) $a^2 + 3ab - bc, b^2 + 3bc - ca$ and $c^2 + 3ca - ab$

(i) $\dfrac{5}{8} p^4 + 2p^2 + \dfrac{5}{8}, \dfrac{1}{8} - 17p + \dfrac{9}{8} p^2$ and $p^5 - p^3 + 7$

(j) $t - t^2 - t^3 - 14,\ 15\,t^3 + 13 + 9\,t - 8\,t^2;$

$\qquad 12t^2 - 19 - 24t$ and $4\,t - 9\,t^2 + 19\,t^3$

Sol.   (a) We have, $p^2 - 7pq - q^2 + (-3p^2 - 2pq + 7q^2)$

$\qquad\qquad\qquad = p^2 - 7pq - q^2 - 3p^2 - 2pq + 7q^2$

On combining the like terms,

$\qquad\qquad\qquad = p^2 - 3p^2 - 7pq - 2pq - q^2 + 7q^2 = -2p^2 - 9pq + 6q^2$

(b) We have, $x^3 - x^2 y - xy^2 - y^3 + x^3 - 2x^2 y + 3xy^2 + 4y$

On combining the like terms,

$\qquad\qquad = x^3 + x^3 - x^2 y - 2x^2 y - xy^2 + 3xy^2 - y^3 + 4y$

$\qquad\qquad = 2x^3 - 3x^2 y + 2xy^2 - y^3 + 4y$

(c) We have,

$ab + bc + ca + (-bc - ca - ab)$

$\qquad\qquad = ab + bc + ca - bc - ca - ab$

On combining the like terms,

$\qquad\qquad = ab - ab + bc - bc + ca - ca$

$\qquad\qquad = 0 + 0 + 0$

$\qquad\qquad = 0$

(d) We have,

$p^2 - q + r + (q^2 - r + p) + (r^2 - p + q)$

$\qquad\qquad = p^2 - q + r + q^2 - r + p + r^2 - p + q$

On combining the like terms,

$\qquad\qquad = p^2 + q^2 + r^2 - q + q + r - r + p - p$

$\qquad\qquad = p^2 + q^2 + r^2 + 0 + 0 + 0 = p^2 + q^2 + r^2$

(e) We have,

$(x^3 y^2 + x^2 y^3 + 3y^4) + (x^4 + 3x^2 y^3 + 4y^4)$

$\qquad\qquad = x^3 y^2 + x^2 y^3 + 3y^4 + x^4 + 3x^2 y^3 + 4y^4$

On combining the like terms,

$\qquad\qquad = x^3 y^2 + x^2 y^3 + 3x^2 y^3 + x^4 + 3y^4 + 4y^4$

$\qquad\qquad = x^4 + 7y^4 + x^3 y^2 + 4x^2 y^3$

(f) We have,

$p^2 qr + pq^2 r + pqr^2 + (-3pq^2 r - 2pqr^2)$

$\qquad\qquad = p^2 qr + pq^2 r + pqr^2 - 3pq^2 r - 2pqr^2$

Algebraic Expression

On combining the like terms,

$$= p^2qr + pq^2r - 3pq^2r + pqr^2 - 2pqr^2$$
$$= p^2qr - 2pq^2r - pqr^2$$

(g) We have,

$$uv - vw + (vw - wu) + (wu - uv)$$
$$= uv - vw + vw - wu + wu - uv$$

On combining like terms,

$$= uv - uv - vw + vw - wu + wu$$
$$= 0 + 0 + 0 = 0$$

(h) We have,

$$(a^2 + 3ab - bc) + (b^2 + 3bc - ca) + (c^2 + 3ca - ab)$$

On combining the like terms,

$$= a^2 + 3ab - bc + b^2 + 3bc - ca + c^2 + 3ca - ab$$
$$= a^2 + b^2 + c^2 + 3ab - ab - bc + 3bc - ca + 3ca$$
$$= a^2 + b^2 + c^2 + 2ab + 2bc + 2ca$$

(i) We have,

$$\left(\frac{5}{8}p^4 + 2p^2 + \frac{5}{8}\right) + \left(\frac{1}{8} - 17p + \frac{9}{8}p^2\right) + (p^5 - p^3 + 7)$$

$$= \frac{5}{8}p^4 + 2p^2 + \frac{5}{8} + \frac{1}{8} - 17p + \frac{9}{8}p^2 + p^5 - p^3 + 7$$

On combining the like terms,

$$= P^5 + \frac{5}{8}p^4 - p^3 + \left(2 + \frac{9}{8}\right)p^2 - 17p + \left(\frac{5}{8} + \frac{1}{8} + 7\right)$$

$$= p^5 + \frac{5}{8}p^4 - p^3 + \left(\frac{16+9}{8}\right)p^2 - 17p + \left(\frac{5+1+56}{8}\right)$$

$$= p^5 + \frac{5}{8}p^4 - p^3 + \frac{25}{8}p^2 - 17p + \frac{62}{8}$$

$$= p^5 + \frac{5}{8}p^4 - p^3 + \frac{25}{8}p^2 - 17p + \frac{31}{4}$$

(j) We have,

$$(t - t^2 - t^3 - 14) + (15t^3 + 13 + 9t - 8t^2) + (12t^2 - 19 - 24t) + (4t - 9t^2 + 19t^3)$$
$$= t - t^2 - t^3 - 14 + 15t^3 + 13 + 9t - 8t^2 + 12t^2 - 19 - 24t + 4t - 9t^2 + 19t^3$$

On combining the like terms,

$$= t + 9t - 24t + 4t - t^2 - 8t^2 + 12t^2 - 9t^2 - t^3 + 15t^3 + 19t^3 - 14 + 13 - 19$$
$$= -10t - 6t^2 + 33t^3 - 20$$
$$= 33t^3 - 6t^2 - 10t - 20$$

Q. 58 Subtract

(a) $-7p^2qr$ from $-3p^2qr$.

(b) $-a^2 - ab$ from $b^2 + ab$.

(c) $-4x^2y - y^3$ from $x^3 + 3xy^2 - x^2y$.

(d) $x^4 + 3x^3y^3 + 5y^4$ from $2x^4 - x^3y^3 + 7y^4$.

(e) $ab - bc - ca$ from $-ab + bc + ca$.

(f) $-2a^2 - 2b^2$ from $-a^2 - b^2 + 2ab$.

(g) $x^3 y^3 + 3x^2 y^2 - 7xy^3$ from $x^4 + y^4 + 3x^2 y^2 - xy^3$.

(h) $2(ab + bc + ca)$ from $-ab - bc - ca$.

(i) $4.5x^5 - 3.4x^2 + 5.7$ from $5x^4 - 3.2x^2 - 7.3x$.

(j) $11 - 15y^2$ from $y^3 - 15y^2 - y - 11$.

Sol. (a) We have,

$$-3p^2qr - (-7p^2qr) = -3p^2qr + 7p^2qr = p^2qr(-3 + 7) = 4p^2qr$$

[∵ with −ve sign, +ve sign will be change]

(b) We have, $b^2 + ab - (-a^2 - ab) = b^2 + ab + a^2 + ab$

On combining the like terms,

$$= b^2 + a^2 + ab + ab = a^2 + b^2 + 2ab$$

(c) We have,

$$x^3 + 3xy^2 - x^2y - (-4x^2y - y^3) = x^3 + 3xy^2 - x^2y + 4x^2y + y^3 = x^3 + y^3 + 3x^2y + 3xy^2$$

(d) We have,

$$2x^4 - x^3y^3 + 7y^4 - (x^4 + 3x^3y^3 + 5y^4) = 2x^4 - x^3y^3 + 7y^4 - x^4 - 3x^3y^3 - 5y^4$$

On combining the like terms,

$$= 2x^4 - x^4 - x^3y^3 - 3x^3y^3 + 7y^4 - 5y^4 = x^4 - 4x^3y^3 + 2y^4$$

(e) We have,

$$-ab + bc + ca - (ab - bc - ca) = -ab + bc + ca - ab + bc + ca$$

On combining the like terms,

$$= -ab - ab + bc + bc + ca + ca = -2ab + 2bc + 2ca$$

(f) We have,

$$(-a^2 - b^2 + 2ab) - (-2a^2 - 2b^2)$$
$$= -a^2 - b^2 + 2ab + 2a^2 + 2b^2$$

On combining the like terms,

$$= -a^2 + 2a^2 - b^2 + 2b^2 + 2ab$$
$$= a^2 + b^2 + 2ab$$

(g) We have,

$$x^4 + y^4 + 3x^2y^2 - xy^3 - (x^3y^3 + 3x^2y^2 - 7xy^3)$$
$$= x^4 + y^4 + 3x^2y^2 - xy^3 - x^3y^3 - 3x^2y^2 + 7xy^3$$

On combining the like terms,

$$= x^4 + y^4 + 3x^2y^2 - 3x^2y^2 - xy^3 + 7xy^3 - x^3y^3$$
$$= x^4 + y^4 + 6xy^3 - x^3y^3$$

(h) We have,

$$-ab - bc - ca - 2(ab + bc + ca)$$
$$= -ab - bc - ca - 2ab - 2bc - 2ca$$

On combining the like terms,

$$= -ab - 2ab - bc - 2bc - ca - 2ca$$
$$= -3ab - 3bc - 3ca$$

(i) We have,

$5x^4 - 3.2x^2 - 7.3x - (4.5x^5 - 3.4x^2 + 5.7)$

$= 5x^4 - 3.2x^2 - 7.3x - 4.5x^5 + 3.4x^2 - 5.7$

On combining the like terms,

$= -4.5x^5 + 5x^4 - 3.2x^2 + 3.4x^2 - 7.3x - 5.7$

$= -4.5x^5 + 5x^4 + 0.2x^2 - 7.3x - 5.7$

(j) We have,

$y^3 - 15y^2 - y - 11 - (11 - 15y^2)$

$= y^3 - 15y^2 - y - 11 - 11 + 15y^2$

On combining the like terms,

$= y^3 - 15y^2 + 15y^2 - y - 11 - 11$

$= y^3 - y - 22$

Q. 59   (a) What should be added to $x^3 + 3x^2y + 3xy^2 + y^3$ to get $x^3 + y^3$?

       (b) What should be added to $3pq + 5p^2q^2 + p^3$ to get $p^3 + 2p^2q^2 + 4pq$?

Sol.   (a) In order to find the solution subtract $x^3 + 3x^2y + 3xy^2 + y^3$ from $x^3 + y^3$.

Required expression is

$x^3 + y^3 - (x^3 + 3x^2y + 3xy^2 + y^3) = x^3 + y^3 - x^3 - 3x^2y - 3xy^2 - y^3$

On combining the like terms,

$= x^3 - x^3 + y^3 - y^3 - 3x^2y - 3xy^2$

$= -3x^2y - 3xy^2$

So, if we add $-3x^2y - 3xy^2$ in $x^3 + 3x^2y + 3xy^2 + y^3$, we get $x^3 + y^3$.

(b) In order to find the solution, subtract $3pq + 5p^2q^2 + p^3$ from $p^3 + 2p^2q^2 + 4pq$.

Required expression is

$p^3 + 2p^2q^2 + 4pq - (3pq + 5p^2q^2 + p^3)$

$= p^3 + 2p^2q^2 + 4pq - 3pq - 5p^2q^2 - p^3$

On combining the like terms,

$= p^3 - p^3 + 2p^2q^2 - 5p^2q^2 + 4pq - 3pq$

$= -3p^2q^2 + pq$

So, if we add $-3p^2q^2 + pq$ in $3pq^2 + 5p^2q^2 + p^3$, we get $p^3 + 2p^2q^2 + 4pq$

Q. 60   (a) What should be subtracted from $2x^3 - 3x^2y + 2xy^2 + 3y^3$ to get $x^3 - 2x^2y + 3xy^2 + 4y^3$?

       (b) What should be subtracted from $-7mn + 2m^2 + 3n^2$ to get $m^2 + 2mn + n^2$?

Sol. (a) In order to get the solution, we will subtract $x^3 - 2x^2y + 3xy^2 + 4y^3$ from $2x^3 - 3x^2y + 2xy^2 + 3y^3$.

Required expression is

$2x^3 - 3x^2y + 2xy^2 + 3y^3 - (x^3 - 2x^2y + 3xy^2 + 4y^3)$

$= 2x^3 - 3x^2y + 2xy^2 + 3y^3 - x^3 + 2x^2y - 3xy^2 - 4y^3$

On combining the like terms,

$= 2x^3 - x^3 - 3x^2y + 2x^2y + 2xy^2 - 3xy^2 + 3y^3 - 4y^3 = x^3 - x^2y - xy^2 - y^3$

So, if we subtract $x^3 - x^2y - xy^2 - y^3$ from $2x^3 - 3x^2y + 2xy^2 + 3y^3$, then we get $x^3 - 2x^2y + 3xy^2 + 4y^3$.

(b) In order to get solution, we will subtract $m^2 + 2mn + n^2$ from $-7mn + 2m^2 + 3n^2$.

Required expression is

$$-7mn + 2m^2 + 3n^2 - (m^2 + 2mn + n^2)$$
$$= -7mn + 2m^2 + 3n^2 - m^2 - 2mn - n^2$$

On combining the like terms,

$$= -7mn - 2mn + 2m^2 - m^2 + 3n^2 - n^2$$
$$= -9mn + m^2 + 2n^2$$

So, if we subtract $m^2 + 2n^2 - 9mn$ from $-7mn + 2m^2 + 3n^2$, then we get $m^2 + 2mn + n^2$.

Q. 61 How much is $21a^3 - 17a^2$ less than $89a^3 - 64a^2 + 6a + 16$?

Sol. Required expression is

$89a^3 - 64a^2 + 6a + 16 - (21a^3 - 17a^2)$

$= 89a^3 - 64a^2 + 6a + 16 - 21a^3 + 17a^2$

On combining the like terms,

$= 89a^3 - 21a^3 - 64a^2 + 17a^2 + 6a + 16$

$= 68a^3 - 47a^2 + 6a + 16$

So, $21a^3 - 17a^2$ is $68a^3 - 47a^2 + 6a + 16$ less than $89a^3 - 64a^2 + 6a + 16$.

Q. 62 How much is $y^4 - 12y^2 + y + 14$ greater than $17y^3 + 34y^2 - 51y + 68$?

Sol. Required expression is

$y^4 - 12y^2 + y + 14 - (17y^3 + 34y^2 - 51y + 68)$

$= y^4 - 12y^2 + y + 14 - 17y^3 - 34y^2 + 51y - 68$

On combining the like terms,

$= y^4 - 12y^2 - 34y^2 + y + 51y + 14 - 68 - 17y^3$

$= y^4 - 46y^2 + 52y - 17y^3 - 54$

$= y^4 - 17y^3 - 46y^2 + 52y - 54$

So, $y^4 - 12y^2 + y + 14$ is $y^4 - 17y^3 - 46y^2 + 52y - 54$ greater than $17y^3 + 34y^2 - 51y + 68$.

Q. 63 How much does $93p^2 - 55p + 4$ exceed $13p^3 - 5p^2 + 17p - 90$?

Sol. Required expression is

$93p^2 - 55p + 4 - (13p^3 - 5p^2 + 17p - 90)$

$\qquad = 93p^2 - 55p + 4 - 13p^3 + 5p^2 - 17p + 90$

On combining the like terms,

$\qquad = 93p^2 + 5p^2 - 55p - 17p + 4 + 90 - 13p^3$

$\qquad = 98p^2 - 72p + 94 - 13p^3$

$\qquad = -13p^3 + 98p^2 - 72p + 94$

So, $93p^2 - 55p + 4$ is $-13p^3 + 98p^2 - 72p + 94$ exceed from $13p^3 - 5p^2 + 17p - 90$.

Q. 64 To what expression must $99x^3 - 33x^2 - 13x - 41$ be added to make the sum zero?

Sol. In order to find the solution, we will subtract $99x^3 - 33x^2 - 13x - 41$ from 0.

Required expression is

$0 - (99x^3 - 33x^2 - 13x - 41) = 0 - 99x^3 + 33x^2 + 13x + 41$

$\qquad = -99x^3 + 33x^2 + 13x + 41$

So, if we add $-99x^3 + 33x^2 + 13x + 41$ to $99x^3 - 33x^2 - 13x - 41$, then the sum is zero.

Q. 65 Subtract $9a^2 - 15a + 3$ from unity.

Sol. In order to find solution, we will subtract $9a^2 - 15a + 3$ from unity, i.e. 1.

Required expression is

$1 - (9a^2 - 15a + 3) = 1 - 9a^2 + 15a - 3$

$\qquad = -9a^2 + 15a - 2$

Q. 66 Find the values of the following polynomials at $a = -2$ and $b = 3$.

(a) $a^2 + 2ab + b^2$

(b) $a^2 - 2ab + b^2$

(c) $a^3 + 3a^2b + 3ab^2 + b^3$

(d) $a^3 - 3a^2b + 3ab^2 - b^3$

(e) $\dfrac{a^2 + b^2}{3}$

(f) $\dfrac{a^2 - b^2}{3}$

(g) $\dfrac{a}{b} + \dfrac{b}{a}$

(h) $a^2 + b^2 - ab - b^2 - a^2$

Sol. Given, $a = -2$ and $b = 3$

So, putting $a = -2$ and $b = 3$ in the given expressions, we get

(a) $a^2 + 2ab + b^2 = (-2)^2 + 2(-2)(3) + (3)^2 = 4 - 12 + 9 = 1$

(b) $a^2 - 2ab + b^2 = (-2)^2 - 2(-2)(3) + (3)^2 = 4 + 12 + 9 = 25$

(c) $a^3 + 3a^2b + 3ab^2 + b^3 = (-2)^3 + 3(-2)^2(3) + 3(-2)(3)^2 + (3)^3 = -8 + 36 - 54 + 27 = 1$

(d) $a^3 - 3a^2b + 3ab^2 - b^3 = (-2)^3 - 3(-2)^2(3) + 3(-2)(3)^2 - (3)^3 = -8 - 36 - 54 - 27 = -125$

(e) $\dfrac{a^2 + b^2}{3} = \dfrac{(-2)^2 + (3)^2}{3} = \dfrac{4 + 9}{3} = \dfrac{13}{3}$

(f) $\dfrac{a^2-b^2}{3}=\dfrac{(-2)^2-(3)^2}{3}=\dfrac{4-9}{3}=\dfrac{-5}{3}$

(g) $\dfrac{a}{b}+\dfrac{b}{a}=\dfrac{(-2)}{3}+\dfrac{3}{(-2)}=\dfrac{-2}{3}-\dfrac{3}{2}=\dfrac{-4-9}{6}=\dfrac{-13}{6}$ [∵LCM of 2 and 3 is 6]

(h) $a^2+b^2-ab-b^2-a^2=(-2)^2+(3)^2-(-2)(3)-(3)^2-(-2)^2=4+9+6-9-4=6$

Q. 67 Find the values of following polynomials at $m=1, n=-1$ and $p=2$

(a) $m+n+p$ (b) $m^2+n^2+p^2$

(c) $m^3+n^3+p^3$ (d) $mn+np+pm$

(e) $m^3+n^3+p^3-3mnp$ (f) $m^2n^2+n^2p^2+p^2m^2$

Sol. Given, $m=1, n=-1$ and $p=2$

So, putting $m=1, n=-1$ and $p=2$ in the given expressions, we get

(a) $m+n+p=1-1+2=2$

(b) $m^2+n^2+p^2=(1)^2+(-1)^2+(2)^2=1+1+4=6$

(c) $m^3+n^3+p^3=(1)^3+(-1)^3+(2)^3=1-1+8=8$

(d) $mn+np+pm=(1)(-1)+(-1)(2)+(2)(1)=-1-2+2=-1$

(e) $m^3+n^3+p^3-3mnp=(1)^3+(-1)^3+(2)^3-3(1)(-1)(2)=1-1+8+6=14$

(f) $m^2n^2+n^2p^2+p^2m^2=(1)^2(-1)^2+(-1)^2(2)^2+(2)^2(1)^2=1+4+4=9$

Q. 68 If $A=3x^2-4x+1, B=5x^2+3x-8$ and $C=4x^2-7x+3$, then find

(i) $(A+B)-C$ (ii) $B+C-A$ (iii) $A+B+C$

Sol. Given, $A=3x^2-4x+1, B=5x^2+3x-8$ and $C=4x^2-7x+3$

(i) $(A+B)-C=(3x^2-4x+1+5x^2+3x-8)-(4x^2-7x+3)$

On combining the like terms,

$=(3x^2+5x^2-4x+3x+1-8)-(4x^2-7x+3)$
$=(8x^2-x-7)-(4x^2-7x+3)$
$=8x^2-x-7-4x^2+7x-3=8x^2-4x^2-x+7x-7-3$
$=4x^2+6x-10$

(ii) $B+C-A$
$=5x^2+3x-8+4x^2-7x+3-(3x^2-4x+1)$

On combining the like terms,

$=(5x^2+4x^2+3x-7x-8+3)-(3x^2-4x+1)$
$=(9x^2-4x-5)-(3x^2-4x+1)$
$=9x^2-4x-5-3x^2+4x-1$
$=9x^2-3x^2-4x+4x-5-1$
$=6x^2-6$

(iii) $A+B+C$
$=3x^2-4x+1+5x^2+3x-8+4x^2-7x+3$

On combining the like terms,

$=3x^2+5x^2+4x^2-4x+3x-7x+1-8+3$
$=12x^2-8x-4$

Q. 69 If $P = -(x-2)$, $Q = -2(y+1)$ and $R = -x+2y$, find a, when $P+Q+R=ax$.

Sol. Given, $P = -(x-2)$, $Q = -2(y+1)$ and $R = -x+2y$

Also given, $P+Q+R=ax$

On putting the values of P,Q and R on LHS, we get

$$-(x-2)+[-2(y+1)]+(-x+2y) = ax$$

$\Rightarrow \qquad -x+2+(-2y-2)-x+2y = ax$

$\Rightarrow \qquad -x+2-2y-2-x+2y = ax$

On combining the like terms,

$$-x-x-2y+2y+2-2 = ax$$

$\Rightarrow \qquad -2x = ax$

By comparing LHS and RHS, we get $\quad a = -2$

Q. 70 From the sum of x^2-y^2-1, y^2-x^2-1 and $1-x^2-y^2$, subtract $-(1+y^2)$.

Sol. Sum of x^2-y^2-1, y^2-x^2-1 and $1-x^2-y^2$

$$= x^2-y^2-1+y^2-x^2-1+1-x^2-y^2$$

On combining the like terms,

$$= x^2-x^2-x^2-y^2+y^2-y^2-1-1+1$$

$$= -x^2-y^2-1$$

Now, subtract $-(1+y^2)$ from $-x^2-y^2-1$

$$= -x^2-y^2-1-[-(1+y^2)]$$

$$= -x^2-y^2-1+1+y^2$$

$$= -x^2-y^2+y^2-1+1$$

$$= -x^2$$

Q. 71 Subtract the sum of $12ab-10b^2-18a^2$ and $9ab+12b^2+14a^2$ from the sum of $ab+2b^2$ and $3b^2-a^2$.

Sol. Sum of $12ab-10b^2-18a^2$ and $9ab+12b^2+14a^2$

$$= 12ab-10b^2-18a^2+9ab+12b^2+14a^2$$

On combining the like terms,

$$= 12ab+9ab-10b^2+12b^2-18a^2+14a^2$$

$$= 21ab+2b^2-4a^2$$

Sum of $ab+2b^2$ and $3b^2-a^2$

$$= ab+2b^2+3b^2-a^2$$

$$= ab+5b^2-a^2$$

Now, subtracting $21ab+2b^2-4a^2$ from $ab+5b^2-a^2$, we get

$$= (ab+5b^2-a^2)-(21ab+2b^2-4a^2)$$

$$= ab+5b^2-a^2-21ab-2b^2+4a^2$$

On combining the like terms,

$$= ab-21ab+5b^2-2b^2-a^2+4a^2$$

$$= -20ab+3b^2+3a^2 = 3a^2+3b^2-20ab$$

Q. 72 Each symbol given below represents an algebraic expression.

$$\triangle = 2x^2 + 3y, \quad \bigcirc = 5x^2 + 3x, \quad \square = 8y^2 - 3x^2 + 2x + 3y$$

The symbols are then represented in the expression

$$\triangle + \bigcirc - \square$$

Find the expression which is represented by the above symbols.

Sol. Given, $\triangle = 2x^2 + 3y, \bigcirc = 5x^2 + 3x$

and $\square = 8y^2 - 3x^2 + 2x + 3y$

∴ $\triangle + \bigcirc - \square$

$= (2x^2 + 3y) + (5x^2 + 3x) - (8y^2 - 3x^2 + 2x + 3y)$

$= 2x^2 + 3y + 5x^2 + 3x - 8y^2 + 3x^2 - 2x - 3y$

On combining the like terms,

$= 2x^2 + 5x^2 + 3x^2 + 3y - 3y + 3x - 2x - 8y^2$

$= 10x^2 - 8y^2 + x$

Q. 73 Observe the following nutritional chart carefully

Food Item (per unit =100 g)	Carbohydrates
Rajma	60 g
Cabbage	5 g
Potato	22 g
Carrot	11 g
Tomato	4 g
Apples	14 g

Write an algebraic expression for the amount of carbohydrates (in grams) for

(a) y units of potatoes and 2 units of rajma.

(b) $2x$ units tomatoes and y units apples.

Sol. (a) By unitary method,

∵ 1 unit of potatoes contain carbohydrates = 22 g

∴ y units of potatoes contain carbohydrates $= 22 \times y = 22y$ g

Similarly,

∵ 1 unit of rajma contain carbohydrates = 60 g

∴ 2 units of rajma contain carbohydrates $= (60 \times 2) = 120$ g

Hence, the required expression is $22y + 120$.

(b) By unitary method,

∵ 1 unit of tomatoes contain carbohydrates = 4 g

∴ $2x$ units of tomatoes contain carbohydrates $= 2x \times 4 = 8x$ g

Similarly,

∵ 1 unit apples contain carbohydrates = 14 g

∴ y units apples contain carbohydrates $= 14 \times y = 14y$ g

Hence, the required expression is $8x + 14y$.

Q. 74 Arjun bought a rectangular plot with length x and breadth y and then sold a triangular part of it whose base is y and height is z. Find the area of the remaining part of the plot.

Sol. Given,

Arjun bought a rectangular plot with length x and breadth y.

$\therefore$ Area of rectangular plot = Length × Breadth $= x \times y = xy$

Also, given triangular part with base y and height z is sold.

So, area of triangular part $= \dfrac{1}{2} \times y \times z = \dfrac{1}{2} yz$ $\qquad \left[\because \text{area of triangle} = \dfrac{1}{2} \times \text{height} \times \text{base} \right]$

$\therefore$ Area of remaining part of the plot

$= $ Area of rectangular plot − Area of triangular plot $= xy - \dfrac{1}{2} yz = y\left(x - \dfrac{1}{2} z \right)$

Q. 75 Amisha has a square plot of side m and another triangular plot with base and height each to m. What is the total area of both plots?

Sol. Given, side of square plot $= m$ and height and base of triangular plot $= m$

$\because$ Area of square plot $= m^2$ $\qquad [\because \text{area of square} = (\text{side})^2]$

$\therefore$ Area of triangular plot $= \dfrac{1}{2} \times m \times m = \dfrac{m^2}{2}$ $\qquad \left[\because \text{area of triangle} = \dfrac{1}{2} \times \text{height} \times \text{base} \right]$

$\therefore$ Total of both plots = Area of square plot + Area of triangular plot

$= m^2 + \dfrac{m^2}{2} = \dfrac{2m^2 + m^2}{2} = \dfrac{3m^2}{2}$ $\qquad [\text{taking LCM of 1 and 2 is 2}]$

Q. 76 A taxi service charges ₹ 8 per km levies a fixed charge of ₹ 50. Write an algebraic expression for the above situation, if the taxi is hired for x km.

Sol. As per the given information, taxi service charges ₹ 8 per km and fixed charge of ₹ 50.

If taxi is hired for x km.

Then, algebraic expression for the situation $= 8 \times x + 50 = 8x + 50$

Hence, the required expression is $8x + 50$.

Q. 77 Shiv works in a mall and gets paid ₹ 50 per hour. Last week he worked for 7 h and this week he will work for x hours. Write an algebraic expression for the money paid to him for both the weeks.

Sol. Given, money paid to shiv = ₹ 50 per h.

$\therefore$ Money paid last week $= ₹ 50 \times 7 = ₹ 350$

So, money paid this week $= ₹ 50 \times x = ₹ 50x$

$\therefore$ Total money paid to shiv $= ₹ (350 + 50x) = ₹ 50(x + 7)$

Q. 78 Sonu and Raj have to collect different kinds of leaves for science project. They go to a park where Sonu collects 12 leaves and Raj collects x leaves. After some time Sonu loses 3 leaves and Raj collects $2x$ leaves. Write an algebraic expression to find the total number of leaves collected by both of them.

Sol. According to the question,

Sonu collected leaves $= 12 - 3 = 9$

Raj collected leaves $= x + 2x = 3x$

$\because$ Total leaves collected $= 9 + 3x$

Hence, the required expression is $9 + 3x$.

Q. 79 A school has a rectangular playground with length x and breadth y and a square lawn with side x as shown in the figure given below. What is the total perimeter of both of them combined together?

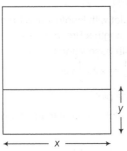

Sol. Given,

Length of rectangular playground, $AB = x$

and breadth of rectangular playground, $BC = y$

∵ $FCDE$ is a square, i.e. $FC = CD = EF = DE = x$ [∵ all sides of a square are equal]

∵ $ABCF$ is a rectangle, i.e. $AB = FC = x$ and $BC = AF = y$

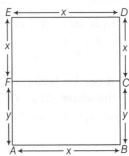

Now, perimeter of combined (playground + lawn) = Sum of all sides

$$= AB + BC + CD + DE + EF + FA$$
$$= x + y + x + x + x + y = 4x + 2y$$

Q. 80 The rate of planting the grass is ₹ x per square metre. Find the cost of planting the grass on a triangular lawn whose base is y metres and height is z metres.

Sol. Given, base of triangular lawn is y metres and height z metres.

∴ Area of triangular lawn $= \dfrac{1}{2} \times y \times z = \dfrac{1}{2} yz \, m^2$ $\left[\because \text{area of triangle} = \dfrac{1}{2} \times \text{height} \times \text{base} \right]$

∴ Cost of planting the grass on lawn $= \dfrac{1}{2} yz \times x = ₹ \dfrac{1}{2} xyz$

Q. 81 Find the perimeter of the figure given below.

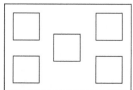

Sol. We know that, perimeter is the sum of all sides.

∴ Perimeter of the given figure $= AB + BC + CD + DA$

$$= (5x - y) + 2(x + y) + (5x - y) + 2(x + y)$$
$$= 5x - y + 2x + 2y + 5x - y + 2x + 2y$$

On combining the like terms,

$$= 5x + 2x + 5x + 2x - y + 2y - y + 2y$$
$$= 14x + 2y$$

Q. 82 In a rectangular plot, 5 square flower beds of side $(x+2)$ metres each have been laid (see the figure). Find the total cost of fencing the flower beds at the cost of ₹ 50 per 100 metres.

Sol. Given, side of one square flower bed $= (x + 2)$ m

∴ Perimeter of one square flower bed $= 4$ (Side) $= 4(x+2)$ m

Now, total perimeter of 5 such square flower beds $= 5 \times$ Perimeter of one square

$$= 5 \times 4(x+2)$$
$$= 20(x+2) \text{ m}$$

∵ Cost of fencing of 100 m $= ₹50$

∴   Cost of 1 m $= ₹\dfrac{50}{100}$

∴ Cost of $20(x+2)$ m $= \dfrac{50}{100} \times 20(x+2) = 10(x+2)$

$$= ₹(10x + 20)$$

Q. 83 A wire is $(7x - 3)$ metres long. A length of $(3x - 4)$ metres is cut for use, answer the following questions

(a) How much wire is left?

(b) If this left out wire is used for making an equilateral triangle. What is the length of each side of the triangle so formed?

Sol. Given, length of wire $= (7x - 3)$ m

and wire cut for use has length $= (3x - 4)$ m

(a) Left wire $= (7x - 3) - (3x - 4) = 7x - 3 - 3x + 4 = 7x - 3x - 3 + 4$

$$= (4x + 1) \text{ m}$$

(b) ∵ Left wire = $(4x+1)$ m

∴ Perimeter of equilateral triangle = Length of wire left

⇒ $\qquad 3 \times \text{Side} = (4x+1)$

⇒ $\qquad \text{Side} = \dfrac{4x+1}{3} = \dfrac{1}{3}(4x+1)$ m

Q. 84 Rohan's mother gave him ₹$3xy^2$ and his father gave him ₹$5(xy^2+2)$. Out of this money he spent ₹$(10-3xy^2)$ on his birthday party. How much money is left with him?

Sol.   Given, amount given to Rohan by his mother = ₹$3xy^2$

and amount given to Rohan by his father = ₹$5(xy^2+2)$

∴ Total amount Rohan have = $[(3xy^2)+(5xy^2+10)] = ₹\,[3xy^2+5xy^2+10]$

$\qquad\qquad\qquad = ₹\,(8xy^2+10)$

Total amount spent by Rohan = ₹$(10-3xy^2)$

∴ After spending, Rohan have left money

$\qquad = ₹\,[(8xy^2+10)-(10-3xy^2)]$

$\qquad = 8xy^2+10-10+3xy^2 = 8xy^2+3xy^2+10-10 = ₹\,11xy^2$

Q. 85   (i) A triangle is made up of 2 red sticks and 1 blue sticks.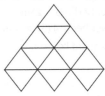

The length of a red stick is given by r and that of a blue stick is given by b. Using this information, write an expression for the total length of sticks in the pattern given below

(ii) In the given figure, the length of a green side is given by g and that of the red side is given by p.

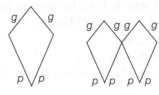

Write an expression for the following pattern. Also, write an expression if 100 such shapes are joined together.

Sol.   (i) Given, length of a red stick = 2r and length of a blue stick = b

From the given figure,

The total number of red sticks = 18

and the total number of blue sticks = 6

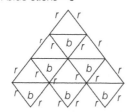

So, the total length of sticks = $18r + 6b = 6(3r + b)$

Hence, the required expression is $6(3r + b)$.

(ii) From the given figure,

Given, length of green side = g and length of red side = p

When we take three figures,

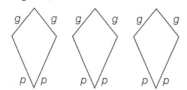

Total length of three figures = $3(2g + 2p) = 6g + 6p$

If 100 such shapes are joined together, then the expression becomes

$$= 100(2g + 2p)$$
$$= 200g + 200p$$
$$= 200(g + p)$$

Hence, the required expression is $200(g + p)$.

Q. 86 The sum of first n natural numbers is given by $\dfrac{1}{2}n^2 + \dfrac{1}{2}n$. Find

(i) The sum of first 5 natural numbers.

(ii) The sum of first 11 natural numbers.

(iii) The sum of natural numbers from 11 to 30.

Sol.   Given, sum of first n natural numbers = $\dfrac{1}{2}n^2 + \dfrac{1}{2}n$

(i) Sum of first 5 natural numbers = $\dfrac{1}{2}(5)^2 + \dfrac{1}{2}(5)$ [put n = 5]

$$= \dfrac{25}{2} + \dfrac{5}{2} = \dfrac{30}{2} = 15$$

(ii) Sum of first 11 natural numbers

$$= \dfrac{1}{2}(11)^2 + \dfrac{1}{2}(11) = \dfrac{1}{2} \times 121 + \dfrac{11}{2}$$ [put n = 11]

$$= \dfrac{121}{2} + \dfrac{11}{2} = \dfrac{132}{2} = 66$$

(iii) Sum of natural numbers from 11 to 30

= Sum of first 30 natural numbers − Sum of first 10 natural numbers

$$= \left[\frac{1}{2}(30)^2 + \frac{1}{2}(30)\right] - \left[\frac{1}{2}(10)^2 + \frac{1}{2}(10)\right]$$

$$= \frac{900}{2} + \frac{30}{2} - \frac{100}{2} - \frac{10}{2} \qquad \text{[divide each term by 2]}$$

$$= 450 + 15 - 50 - 5 = 410$$

Q. 87 The sum of squares of first n natural numbers is given by $\frac{1}{6}n(n+1)(2n+1)$

or $\frac{1}{6}(2n^3 + 3n^2 + n)$. Find the sum of squares of the first 10 natural numbers.

Sol. Given, the sum of squares of first n natural numbers $= \frac{1}{6}n(n+1)(2n+1)$

∴ The sum of squares of first 10 natural numbers

$$= \frac{1}{6}(10)(10+1)(2\times10+1) = \frac{1}{6}\times10\times11\times21 \qquad \text{[put } n = 10\text{]}$$

$$= 385$$

Q. 88 The sum of the multiplication table of natural number n is given by $55\times n$. Find the sum of

(a) Table of 7   (b) Table of 10   (c) Table of 19

Sol. Given, the sum of multiplication table of n natural numbers $= 55\times n$

(a) Sum of table of 7 = 55×7 = 385   [put $n = 7$]

(b) Sum of table of 10 = 55×10 = 550   [put $n = 10$]

(c) Sum of table of 19 = 55×19 = 1045   [put $n = 19$]

Q. 89 If $\triangle x = 2x+3$, $\boxed{x} = \frac{3}{2}x+7$ and $\textcircled{x} = x-3$

Then, find the value of

(i) $2 \triangle 6 + \boxed{3} - \textcircled{1}$ (ii) $\frac{1}{2}\boxed{2} + \textcircled{8} - 3\triangle 0$

Sol. Given,

$\triangle x = 2x+3$, $\boxed{x} = \frac{3}{2}x+7$ and $\textcircled{x} = x-3$

(i) $2\triangle 6 + \boxed{3} - \textcircled{1}$

$$= 2\times(2\times6+3) + \left(\frac{3}{2}\times3+7\right) - (1-3) = 2\times(12+3) + \left(\frac{9}{2}+7\right) - (-2)$$

$$= 2\times15 + \left(\frac{23}{2}\right) + 2 = 30 + 2 + \frac{23}{2}$$

$$= 32 + \frac{23}{2} = \frac{32\times2+23}{2} = \frac{64+23}{2}$$

$$= \frac{87}{2}$$

(ii) $\dfrac{1}{2}\boxed{2} + \bigcirc\!\!\!8 - 3\,\triangle\!\!\!0$

$$= \dfrac{1}{2}\left(\dfrac{3}{2}\times 2+7\right)+(8-3)-3(2\times 0+3)$$

$$= \dfrac{1}{2}(10)+5-3(3)$$

$$= 5+5-9=1$$

Q. 90 If $\triangle\!\!\!x = \dfrac{3}{4}x - 2$ and $\langle x\rangle = x+6$, then find the value of

    (i) $\triangle\!\!\!10 - \langle 4\rangle$ (ii) $2\,\langle 12\rangle - \dfrac{3}{2}\,\triangle\!\!\!1$

Sol.   Given, $\triangle\!\!\!x = \dfrac{3}{4}x - 2$ and $\langle x\rangle = x+6$

(i) $\triangle\!\!\!10 - \langle 4\rangle$

$$= \dfrac{3}{4}\times 10-2-4-6$$

$$= \dfrac{30}{4}-\dfrac{12}{1} \qquad\qquad\qquad [\because \text{LCM of 4 and 1 is 4}]$$

$$= \dfrac{30-48}{4}$$

$$= \dfrac{-18}{4}$$

$$= \dfrac{-9}{2}$$

(ii) $2\,\langle 12\rangle - \dfrac{3}{2}\,\triangle\!\!\!1$

$$=2\times(12+6)-\dfrac{3}{2}\left(\dfrac{3}{4}\times 1-2\right)= 36-\dfrac{3}{2}\left(\dfrac{3-2\times 4}{4}\right)$$

$$= 36-\dfrac{3}{2}\left(\dfrac{3-8}{4}\right)= 36-\dfrac{3}{2}\left(\dfrac{-5}{4}\right)$$

$$= 36+\dfrac{15}{8} = \dfrac{36\times 8+15}{8}$$

$$= \dfrac{288+15}{8} = \dfrac{303}{8}$$

Translate each of the following algebraic expressions questions 91 to 94 into words.

Q. 91 $4b-3$

Sol. Three subtracted from four times b.

Q. 92 $8\,(m+5)$

Sol.   Eight times the sum of m and 5.

Q. 93 $\dfrac{7}{8-x}$

Sol. Quotient on dividing seven by the difference of eight and $x\,(x<8)$.

Q. 94 $17\left(\dfrac{16}{w}\right)$

Sol. Seventeen times quotient of sixteen divided by w.

Q. 95　(i) **Critical Thinking** Write two different algebraic expressions for the word phrase $\left(\dfrac{1}{4}\right)$ of the sum of x and 7.

(ii) **What's the Error?** A student wrote an algebraic expression for "5 less than a number n divided by 3" as $\dfrac{n}{3}-5$. What error did the student make?

(iii) **Write About It** Shashi used addition to solve a word problem about the weekly cost of commuting by toll tax for ₹ 15 each day. Ravi solved the same problem by multiplying. They both got correct answer. How is this possible?

Sol.　(i) First expression $=\dfrac{1}{4}(x+7)$

As we know, the addition is commutative.

So, it can also be written as $=\dfrac{1}{4}(7+x)$

(ii) Since, the expression of 5 less than a number $n=n-5$

So, 5 less than a number n divided by 3 will be written $=\dfrac{n-5}{3}$.

So, student make an error of quotient.

(iii) By addition method,

Total weekly cost $=(15+15+15+15+15+15+15)$

$=$ ₹105

By multiplication method,

Total weekly cost $=$ Cost of one day $\times$ Seven days

$=15\times7$

$=$ ₹105

Q. 96 Challenge

Write an expression for the sum of 1 and twice a number n, if you let n be any odd number, will the result always be an odd number?

Sol. Let the number be n.

So, according to the statement, the expression can be written as $=2n+1$.

Yes, the result is always an odd number, because when a number becomes multiplied by 2, it becomes even and addition of 1 in that even number makes it an odd number.

Q. 97 Critical Thinking

Will the value of $11x$ for $x = -5$ be greater than 11 or less than 11? Explain.

Sol. Expression given is

$11x = 11 \times (-5) = -55$ [put $x = -5$]

Clearly, $-55 < 11$.

Hence, the value is greater than 11.

Q. 98 Match Column I with Column II in the following:

	Column I		Column II
1.	The difference of 3 and a number squared	(a)	$4 - 2x$
2.	5 less than twice a number squared	(b)	$n^2 - 3$
3.	Five minus twice the square of a number	(c)	$2n^2 - 5$
4.	Four minus a number multiplied by 2	(d)	$5 - 2n^2$
5.	Seven times the sum of a number and 1	(e)	$3 - n^2$
6.	A number squared plus 6	(f)	$2(n + 6)$
7.	2 times the sum of a number and 6	(g)	$7(n + 1)$
8.	Three less than the square of a number	(h)	$n^2 + 6$

Sol. $1 \rightarrow$ (e) Let the number be n.

So, according to the statements, we can write the equation $= 3 - n^2$

$2 \rightarrow$ (c) Let the number be n.

So, the equation is $2n^2 - 5$.

$3 \rightarrow$ (d) Let the number be n.

So, the equation is $5 - 2n^2$.

$4 \rightarrow$ (a) Let the number be x.

So, the equation is $4 - 2x$.

$5 \rightarrow$ (g) Let the number be n.

So, the equation is $7(n + 1)$.

$6 \rightarrow$ (h) Let the number be n.

So, the equation is $n^2 + 6$.

$7 \rightarrow$ (f) Let the number be n.

So, the equation is $2(n + 6)$.

$8 \rightarrow$ (b) Let the number be n.

So, the equation is $n^2 - 3$.

Q. 99 At age of 2 years, a cat or a dog is considered 24 "human" years old. Each year, after age 2 is equivalent to 4 "human" years. Fill in the expression $[24+[](a-2)]$, so that it represents the age of a cat or dog in human years. Also, you need to determine for what 'a' stands for. Copy the chart and use your expression to complete it.

Age	$[24+[](a-2)]$	Age (human years)
2		
3		
4		
5		
6		

Sol. The expression is $[24+4(a-2)]$.

Here, 'a' represents the present age of dog or cat.

Age	$[24+4(a-2)]$	Age (human years)
2	$[24+4(2-2)]$	24
3	$[24+4(3-2)]$	28
4	$[24+4(4-2)]$	32
5	$[24+4(5-2)]$	36
6	$[24+4(6-2)]$	40

Q. 100 Express the following properties with variables x, y and z.

(i) Commutative property of addition

(ii) Commutative property of multiplication

(iii) Associative property of addition

(iv) Associative property of multiplication

(v) Distributive property of multiplication over addition

Sol. (i) We know that,

Commutative property of addition, $a+b=b+c$

∴ Required expression is $x+y=y+x$

(ii) We know that,

Commutative property of multiplication, $a\times b=b\times a$

∴ Required expression is $x\times y=y\times x$

(iii) We know that,

Associative property of addition, $a+(b+c)=(a+b)+c$

∴ Required expression is $x+(y+z)=(x+y)+z$

(iv) We know that,

Associative property of multiplication, $a\times(b\times c)=(a\times b)\times c$

∴ Required expression is $x\times(y\times z)=(x\times y)\times z$

(v) We know that,

Distributive property of multiplication over addition,

$$a\times(b+c)=a\times b+a\times c$$

∴ Required expression is $x\times(y+z)=x\times y+x\times z$

11

Exponents and Powers

Multiple Choice Questions (MCQs)

Q. 1 $[(-3)^2]^3$ is equal to

    (a) $(-3)^8$ (b) $(-3)^6$

    (c) $(-3)^5$ (d) $(-3)^{23}$

Sol. *(b)*   We know that, if 'a' is a rational number, m and n are natural numbers, then

$$(a^m)^n = a^{m \times n}$$

So, $[(-3)^2]^3 = (-3)^{2 \times 3} = (-3)^6$

Q. 2 For a non-zero rational number x, $x^8 \div x^2$ is equal to

    (a) x^4 (b) x^6

    (c) x^{10} (d) x^{16}

Sol. *(b)*   We know that, if 'a' is a rational number, m and n are natural numbers such that $m > n$, then

$$a^m \div a^n = a^{m-n}$$

So, $x^8 \div x^2 = \dfrac{x^8}{x^2} = x^{8-2} = x^6$

Q. 3 x is a non-zero rational number. Product of the square of x with the cube of x is equal to the

    (a) second power of x (b) third power of x

    (c) fifth power of x (d) sixth power of x

Sol. *(c)*   Square of $x = x^2$

           Cube of $x = x^3$

           Product of square with the cube of $x = x^2 \times x^3 = x^{2+3}$ $[\because a^m \times a^n = a^{m+n}]$

                                      $= x^5$

           i.e. fifth power of x.

Q. 4 For any two non-zero rational numbers x and y, $x^5 \div y^5$ is equal to

(a) $(x \div y)^1$ (b) $(x \div y)^0$

(c) $(x \div y)^5$ (d) $(x \div y)^{10}$

Sol. *(c)*   Given, $x^5 \div y^5 = \dfrac{x^5}{y^5}$

As we know, $\dfrac{p^n}{q^n} = \left(\dfrac{p}{q}\right)^n$

Thus, $\dfrac{x^5}{y^5} = \left(\dfrac{x}{y}\right)^5 = (x \div y)^5$

Q. 5 $a^m \times a^n$ is equal to

(a) $(a^2)^{mn}$ (b) a^{m-n}

(c) a^{m+n} (d) a^{mn}

Sol. *(c)*   We know that, if 'a' is a rational number, m and n are natural numbers, then
$$a^m \times a^n = a^{m+n}$$

Q. 6 $(1^0 + 2^0 + 3^0)$ is equal to

(a) 0   (b) 1

(c) 3   (d) 6

Sol. *(c)*   As we know, $a^0 = 1$

$\therefore$ $1^0 + 2^0 + 3^0 = 1 + 1 + 1$

$= 3$

Q. 7 The value of $\dfrac{10^{22} + 10^{20}}{10^{20}}$ is

(a) 10   (b) 10^{42} (c) 101   (d) 10^{22}

Sol. *(c)*   We can write the given expression as

$$\dfrac{10^{22}}{10^{20}} + \dfrac{10^{20}}{10^{20}} = 10^{22-20} + 1 \qquad \left[\because \dfrac{a^m}{a^n} = a^{m-n}, m > n\right]$$

$$= 10^2 + 1 = 10 \times 10 + 1 = 100 + 1 = 101$$

Q. 8 The standard form of the number 12345 is

(a) 1234.5×10^1 (b) 123.45×10^2

(c) 12.345×10^3 (d) 1.2345×10^4

Sol. *(d)*   A number in standard form is written as $a \times 10^k$, where a is a terminating decimal such that $1 \le a \le 10$ and k is any integer.

So, $12345 = 1.2345 \times 10^4$

Q. 9 If $2^{1998} - 2^{1997} - 2^{1996} + 2^{1995} = k \cdot 2^{1995}$, then the value of k is

    (a) 1   (b) 2

    (c) 3   (d) 4

Sol. *(c)*   Given,

$$2^{1998} - 2^{1997} - 2^{1996} + 2^{1995} = k \cdot 2^{1995}$$

$$\Rightarrow \quad 2^{1995 + 3} - 2^{1995 + 2} - 2^{1995 + 1} + 2^{1995} \times 1 = k \cdot 2^{1995}$$

$$\Rightarrow \quad 2^{1995}[2^3 - 2^2 - 2^1 + 1] = k \cdot 2^{1995} \qquad [\because a^{m+n} = a^m \times a^n]$$

$$\Rightarrow \quad 2^{1995}[8 - 4 - 2 + 1] = k \cdot 2^{1995}$$

$$\Rightarrow \quad 3 = \frac{k \cdot 2^{1995}}{2^{1995}}$$

$$\Rightarrow \quad 3 = k \text{ or } k = 3$$

So, the value of k is 3.

Q. 10 Which of the following is equal to 1?

    (a) $2^0 + 3^0 + 4^0$ (b) $2^0 \times 3^0 \times 4^0$

    (c) $(3^0 - 2^0) \times 4^0$ (d) $(3^0 - 2^0) \times (3^0 + 2^0)$

Sol. *(b)*   Let us solve all the expressions.

For option (a),

$$2^0 + 3^0 + 4^0 = 1 + 1 + 1 \qquad [\because a^0 = 1]$$

$$= 3$$

For option (b),

$$2^0 \times 3^0 \times 4^0 = 1 \times 1 \times 1 \qquad [\because a^0 = 1]$$

$$= 1$$

Hence, option (b) is the answer.

Q. 11 In standard form, the number 72105.4 is written as 7.21054×10^n, where n is equal to

    (a) 2   (b) 3

    (c) 4   (d) 5

Sol. *(c)*   We know that, if the given number is greater than or equal to 10, then the power of 10 (i.e. n) is a positive integer equal to the number of places the decimal point has been shifted.

Hence, $72105.4 = 7.21054 \times 10^4$

Q. 12 Square of $\left(\dfrac{-2}{3}\right)$ is

    (a) $\dfrac{-2}{3}$ (b) $\dfrac{2}{3}$ (c) $\dfrac{-4}{9}$ (d) $\dfrac{4}{9}$

Sol. *(d)*   Square of $\dfrac{-2}{3}$ is $\left(\dfrac{-2}{3}\right)^2$.

So, $\left(\dfrac{-2}{3}\right)^2 = \left(\dfrac{-2}{3}\right) \times \left(\dfrac{-2}{3}\right) = \dfrac{4}{9}$

                [$\because$ multiplication of two rational numbers with same sign is always positive]

Q. 13 Cube of $\left(\dfrac{-1}{4}\right)$ is

(a) $\dfrac{-1}{12}$ (b) $\dfrac{1}{16}$ (c) $\dfrac{-1}{64}$ (d) $\dfrac{1}{64}$

Sol. *(c)* Cube of $\left(\dfrac{-1}{4}\right)$ is $\left(\dfrac{-1}{4}\right)^3$.

So, $\left(\dfrac{-1}{4}\right)^3 = \left(\dfrac{-1}{4}\right)\times\left(\dfrac{-1}{4}\right)\times\left(\dfrac{-1}{4}\right) = \dfrac{(-1)\times(-1)\times(-1)}{4\times4\times4} = \dfrac{-1}{64}$

Q. 14 Which of the following is not equal to $\left(\dfrac{-5}{4}\right)^4$?

(a) $\dfrac{(-5)^4}{4^4}$ (b) $\dfrac{5^4}{(-4)^4}$

(c) $-\dfrac{5^4}{4^4}$ (d) $\left(-\dfrac{5}{4}\right)\times\left(-\dfrac{5}{4}\right)\times\left(-\dfrac{5}{4}\right)\times\left(-\dfrac{5}{4}\right)$

Sol. *(c)* We know that, $\left(\dfrac{p}{q}\right)^m = \dfrac{p^m}{q^m}$

So, $\left(\dfrac{-5}{4}\right)^4 = \dfrac{(-5)^4}{(4)^4}$ or $\left(\dfrac{-5}{4}\right)^4 = \dfrac{(5)^4}{(-4)^4}$

or $\left(\dfrac{-5}{4}\right)^4 = \left(\dfrac{-5}{4}\right)\times\left(\dfrac{-5}{4}\right)\times\left(\dfrac{-5}{4}\right)\times\left(\dfrac{-5}{4}\right)$

Hence, option (c) is not equal to 1.

Q. 15 Which of the following is not equal to 1?

(a) $\dfrac{2^3\times3^2}{4\times18}$ (b) $[(-2)^3\times(-2)^4]\div(-2)^7$

(c) $\dfrac{3^0\times5^3}{5\times25}$ (d) $\dfrac{2^4}{(7^0+3^0)^3}$

Sol. *(d)* Let us solve the expressions.

For option (a), $\dfrac{2^3\times3^2}{4\times18} = \dfrac{2\times2\times2\times3\times3}{4\times18} = \dfrac{4\times18}{4\times18} = 1$

For option (b), $[(-2)^3\times(-2)^4]\div(-2)^7 = \dfrac{(-2)^3\times(-2)^4}{(-2)^7}$

$= \dfrac{(-2)^{3+4}}{(-2)^7}$ $[\because a^m\times a^n = a^{m+n}]$

$= \dfrac{(-2)^7}{(-2)^7} = 1$ $\left[\because \dfrac{a^m}{a^n} = a^{m-n}\right]$

For option (c), $\dfrac{3^0\times5^3}{5\times25} = \dfrac{1\times5\times5\times5}{5\times25}$

$= \dfrac{5\times25}{5\times25}$ $[\because a^0 = 1]$

$= 1$

Exponents and Powers

For option (d), $\dfrac{2^4}{(7^0 + 3^0)^3} = \dfrac{2^4}{(1 + 1)^3}$ $[\because a^0 = 1]$

$$= \dfrac{2^4}{2^3} = 2^{4-3}$$ $\left[\because \dfrac{a^m}{a^n} = a^{m-n}, m > n\right]$

$$= -2^1 = 2$$

Hence, option (d) is not equal to 1.

Q. 16 $\left(\dfrac{2}{3}\right)^3 \times \left(\dfrac{5}{7}\right)^3$ is equal to

(a) $\left(\dfrac{2}{3} \times \dfrac{5}{7}\right)^9$ (b) $\left(\dfrac{2}{3} \times \dfrac{5}{7}\right)^6$ (c) $\left(\dfrac{2}{3} \times \dfrac{5}{7}\right)^3$ (d) $\left(\dfrac{2}{3} \times \dfrac{5}{7}\right)^0$

Sol. (c) We know that, if a, b and m are rational numbers, then

$$a^m \times b^m = (ab)^m$$

So, $\left(\dfrac{2}{3}\right)^3 \times \left(\dfrac{5}{7}\right)^3 = \left(\dfrac{2}{3} \times \dfrac{5}{7}\right)^3$

Q. 17 In standard form, the number 829030000 is written as $K \times 10^8$, where K is equal to

(a) 82903   (b) 829.03   (c) 82.903   (d) 8.2903

Sol. (d) We have,

A number in a standard form is written as $K \times 10^8$, then K will be a terminating decimal such that $1 \le K \le 10$.

So, there is only one option, where $K = 8.2903 < 10$.

Q. 18 Which of the following has the largest value?

(a) 0.0001   (b) $\dfrac{1}{10000}$

(c) $\dfrac{1}{10^6}$ (d) $\dfrac{1}{10^6} \div 0.1$

Sol. (a,b) For option (a), $0.0001 = \dfrac{1}{10000}$

For option (b), $\dfrac{1}{10000}$

For option (c), $\dfrac{1}{10^6} = \dfrac{1}{10 \times 10 \times 10 \times 10 \times 10 \times 10} = \dfrac{1}{1000000}$

For option (d), $\dfrac{1}{10^6} \div 0.1 = \dfrac{1}{10^6} \times \dfrac{1}{0.1} = \dfrac{1}{10^6} \times \dfrac{10}{1} = \dfrac{10}{10^6} = \dfrac{1}{10^5}$

$$= \dfrac{1}{10 \times 10 \times 10 \times 10 \times 10} = \dfrac{1}{100000}$$

The fraction whose denominator is smallest will be largest.

Hence, (a) and (b) are the largest.

Q. 19 In standard form 72 crore is written as

(a) 72×10^7 (b) 72×10^8 (c) 7.2×10^8 (d) 7.2×10^7

Sol. *(c)*   We know that,

A number in standard form is written as $a \times 10^k$, where a is the terminating decimal such that $1 \le a \le 10$ and k is any integer.

So,   72 crore $= 720000000 = 7.2 \times 10^8$

Note Here, power of 10 (i.e. k) is a positive integer equal to the number of places the decimal point has been shifted.

Q. 20 For non-zero numbers a and b, $\left(\dfrac{a}{b}\right)^m \div \left(\dfrac{a}{b}\right)^n$, where $m > n$, is equal to

(a) $\left(\dfrac{a}{b}\right)^{mn}$ (b) $\left(\dfrac{a}{b}\right)^{m+n}$ (c) $\left(\dfrac{a}{b}\right)^{m-n}$ (d) $\left(\left(\dfrac{a}{b}\right)^m\right)^n$

Sol. *(c)*   We know that,

$$a^m \div a^n = a^{m-n}, (m > n)$$

So, $\left(\dfrac{a}{b}\right)^m \div \left(\dfrac{a}{b}\right)^n = \left(\dfrac{a}{b}\right)^{m-n}$

Q. 21 Which of the following is not true?

(a) $3^2 > 2^3$ (b) $4^3 = 2^6$ (c) $3^3 = 9$ (d) $2^5 > 5^2$

Sol. *(c)*   For option (a), $3^2 > 2^3$

$$3 \times 3 > 2 \times 2 \times 2$$
$$9 > 8 \text{ (true)}$$

For option (b), $4^3 = 2^6$

$$(2^2)^3 = 2^6$$
$$2^6 = 2^6 \text{ (true)} \qquad\qquad [\because (a^m)^n = a^{m \times n}]$$

For option (c), $3^3 = 9$

$$3 \times 3 \times 3 = 9$$
$$27 \ne 9 \text{ (not true)}$$

For option (d), $2^5 > 5^2$

$$2 \times 2 \times 2 \times 2 \times 2 > 5 \times 5$$
$$32 > 25 \text{ (true)}$$

Hence, option (c) is not true.

Q. 22 Which power of 8 is equal to 2^6?

(a) 3   (b) 2   (c) 1   (d) 4

Sol. *(b)*   Let power of 8 be x.

According to the question,

$$8^x = 2^6$$

$\Rightarrow$ $(2^3)^x = 2^6$ $[\because 8 = 2 \times 2 \times 2 = 2^3]$

$\Rightarrow$ $2^{3x} = 2^6$ $[\because (a^m)^n = a^{m \times n}]$

Since, base are equal, then by equating their exponents, we get

$$3x = 6$$
$$\Rightarrow \quad \frac{3x}{3} = \frac{6}{3} \quad \text{[dividing both sides by 3]}$$
$$\Rightarrow \quad x = 2$$

Hence, the power of 8 is 2, which is equal to 2^6.

Fill in the Blank

In questions 23 to 39, fill in the blanks to make the statements true.

Q. 23 $(-2)^{31} \times (-2)^{13} = (-2)^{-}$

Sol. Here, $(-2)^{31} \times (-2)^{13} = (-2)^{31+13}$ $\qquad [\because a^m \times a^n = a^{m+n}]$

$$= (-2)^{44}$$

$$\therefore \quad (-2)^{31} \times (-2)^{13} = (-2)^{44}$$

Q. 24 $(-3)^8 \div (-3)^5 = (-3)^{-}$

Sol. Here, $(-3)^8 \div (-3)^5 = (-3)^{8-5} = (-3)^3$ $\qquad [\because a^m \div a^n = a^{m-n}, m>n]$

$$\therefore \quad (-3)^8 \div (-3)^5 = (-3)^3$$

Q. 25 $\left(\frac{11}{15}\right)^4 \times (\underline{\quad})^5 = \left(\frac{11}{15}\right)^9$

Sol. Let $\left(\frac{11}{15}\right)^4 \times (x)^5 = \left(\frac{11}{15}\right)^9$

$$\Rightarrow \quad (x)^5 = \frac{\left(\frac{11}{15}\right)^9}{\left(\frac{11}{15}\right)^4}$$

$$\Rightarrow \quad (x)^5 = \left(\frac{11}{15}\right)^9 \left(\frac{11}{15}\right)^{-4}$$

$$\Rightarrow \quad (x)^5 = \left(\frac{11}{15}\right)^{9-4} \quad [\because a^m \times a^{-n} = a^{m+(-n)} = a^{m-n}]$$

$$\Rightarrow \quad (x)^5 = \left(\frac{11}{15}\right)^5$$

Since, the powers are same.

$$\therefore \quad x = \frac{11}{15}$$

Hence, $\left(\frac{11}{15}\right)^4 \times \left(\frac{11}{15}\right)^5 = \left(\frac{11}{15}\right)^9$

Q. 26 $\left(\dfrac{-1}{4}\right)^3 \times \left(\dfrac{-1}{4}\right)^- = \left(\dfrac{-1}{4}\right)^{11}$

Sol. Let $\left(\dfrac{-1}{4}\right)^3 \times \left(\dfrac{-1}{4}\right)^x = \left(\dfrac{-1}{4}\right)^{11}$

$\Rightarrow \quad \left(\dfrac{-1}{4}\right)^x = \dfrac{\left(\dfrac{-1}{4}\right)^{11}}{\left(\dfrac{-1}{4}\right)^3}$

$\Rightarrow \quad \left(\dfrac{-1}{4}\right)^x = \left(\dfrac{-1}{4}\right)^{11-3}$ $[\because a^m \div a^n = a^{m-n}, m>n]$

$\Rightarrow \quad \left(\dfrac{-1}{4}\right)^x = \left(\dfrac{-1}{4}\right)^8$

Since, base are equal. So, by equating the powers, we get

$x = 8$

$\therefore \quad \left(-\dfrac{1}{4}\right)^3 \times \left(-\dfrac{1}{4}\right)^8 = \left(-\dfrac{1}{4}\right)^{11}$

Q. 27 $\left[\left(\dfrac{7}{11}\right)^3\right]^4 = \left(\dfrac{7}{11}\right)^-$

Sol. Here, $\left[\left(\dfrac{7}{11}\right)^3\right]^4 = \left(\dfrac{7}{11}\right)^{3\times4} = \left(\dfrac{7}{11}\right)^{12}$ $[\because (a^m)^n = a^{mn}]$

$\therefore \quad \left[\left(\dfrac{7}{11}\right)^3\right]^4 = \left(\dfrac{7}{11}\right)^{12}$

Q. 28 $\left(\dfrac{6}{13}\right)^{10} \div \left[\left(\dfrac{6}{13}\right)^5\right]^2 = \left(\dfrac{6}{13}\right)^-$

Sol. Here, $\left(\dfrac{6}{13}\right)^{10} \div \left[\left(\dfrac{6}{13}\right)^5\right]^2 = \left(\dfrac{6}{13}\right)^{10} \div \left(\dfrac{6}{13}\right)^{5\times2}$ $[\because (a^m)^n = a^{mn}]$

$= \left(\dfrac{6}{13}\right)^{10} \div \left(\dfrac{6}{13}\right)^{10} = \left(\dfrac{6}{13}\right)^{10-10}$ $[\because a^m \div a^n = a^{m-n}, (m>n)]$

$= \left(\dfrac{6}{13}\right)^0$

$\therefore \quad \left(\dfrac{6}{13}\right)^{10} \div \left[\left(\dfrac{6}{13}\right)^5\right]^2 = \left(\dfrac{6}{13}\right)^0$

Q. 29 $\left[\left(\dfrac{-1}{4}\right)^{16}\right]^2 = \left(\dfrac{-1}{4}\right)^{-}$

Sol. Here, $\left[\left(\dfrac{-1}{4}\right)^{16}\right]^2 = \left(\dfrac{-1}{4}\right)^{16 \times 2}$

$\qquad\qquad\qquad [\because (a^m)^n = a^{mn}]$

$$= \left(\dfrac{-1}{4}\right)^{32}$$

$\therefore \quad \left[\left(-\dfrac{1}{4}\right)^{16}\right]^2 = \left(-\dfrac{1}{4}\right)^{\mathbf{32}}$

Q. 30 $\left(\dfrac{13}{14}\right)^5 \div (\underline{\quad})^2 = \left(\dfrac{13}{14}\right)^3$

Sol. Let $\left(\dfrac{13}{14}\right)^5 \div (x)^2 = \left(\dfrac{13}{14}\right)^3$

$\Rightarrow \qquad (x)^2 = \dfrac{\left(\dfrac{13}{14}\right)^5}{\left(\dfrac{13}{14}\right)^3}$

$\Rightarrow \qquad (x)^2 = \left(\dfrac{13}{14}\right)^{5-3}$

$\qquad\qquad\qquad \left[\because \dfrac{a^m}{a^n} = a^{m-n}\right]$

$\Rightarrow \qquad (x)^2 = \left(\dfrac{13}{14}\right)^2$

Since, powers are same.

$\therefore \qquad\qquad x = \dfrac{13}{14}$

Hence, $\qquad \left(\dfrac{13}{14}\right)^5 \div \left(\dfrac{\mathbf{13}}{\mathbf{14}}\right)^2 = \left(\dfrac{13}{14}\right)^3$

Q. 31 $a^6 \times a^5 \times a^0 = a^{-}$

Sol. Since, $a^6 \times a^5 \times a^0 = (a)^{6+5+0}$

$\qquad\qquad\qquad [\because a^m \times a^n = a^{m+n}]$

$$= a^{11}$$

$\therefore \qquad a^6 \times a^5 \times a^0 = a^{\mathbf{11}}$

Q. 32 1 lakh $= 10^{-}$

Sol. Here, 1 lakh $= 100000 = 10^5$

$\therefore \qquad$ 1 lakh $= 10^{\mathbf{5}}$

Q. 33 1 million $= 10^{-}$

Sol. Here, 1 million $= 1000000 = 10^6$

$\therefore \qquad$ 1 million $= 10^{\mathbf{6}}$

Q. 34 $729 = 3^{—}$

Sol. Here, firstly we findout the factors of given expression.

3	729
3	243
3	81
3	27
3	9
3	3
	1

So, $729 = 3 \times 3 \times 3 \times 3 \times 3 \times 3 = 3^6$

∴ $729 = 3^6$

Q. 35 $432 = 2^4 \times 3^{—}$

Sol. Firstly, we findout the factors of given expression.

2	432
2	216
2	108
2	54
3	27
3	9
3	3
	1

So, $432 = 2 \times 2 \times 2 \times 2 \times 3 \times 3 \times 3 = 2^4 \times 3^3$

∴ $432 = 2^4 \times 3^3$

Q. 36 $53700000 = \underline{\quad} \times 10^7$

Sol. Given, 53700000

For standard form, $53700000 = 537 \times 10^5$ $[\because 10^5 = 100000]$

Also, $537 = 5.37 \times 10^2$

So, $5.37 \times 10^2 \times 10^5 = 5.37 \times 10^7$ $[\because a^m \times a^n = a^{m+n}]$

∴ $53700000 = \mathbf{5.37} \times 10^7$

Q. 37 $88880000000 = \underline{\quad} \times 10^{10}$

Sol. Given, 88880000000

For standard form, $88880000000 = 8888 \times 10^7$

Also, $8888 = 8.888 \times 10^3$

So, $8.888 \times 10^3 \times 10^7 = 8.888 \times 10^{10}$ $[\because a^m \times a^n = a^{m+n}]$

∴ $88880000000 = \mathbf{8.888} \times 10^{10}$

Q. 38 $27500000 = 2.75 \times 10^{-}$

Sol. Given, 27500000

For standard form, $27500000 = 275 \times 10^5$

Also, $\qquad 275 = 2.75 \times 10^2$

So, $\qquad 2.75 \times 10^2 \times 10^5 = 2.75 \times 10^7 \qquad\qquad [\because a^m \times a^n = a^{m+n}]$

$\therefore \quad 27500000 = 2.75 \times 10^7$

Q. 39 $340900000 = 3.409 \times 10^{-}$

Sol. For standard form, $340900000 = 3409 \times 10^5$

Also, $\qquad 3409 = 3.409 \times 10^3$

So, $\qquad 3.409 \times 10^3 \times 10^5 = 3.409 \times 10^8 \qquad\qquad [\because a^m \times a^n = a^{m+n}]$

$\therefore \qquad\qquad 340900000 = 3.409 \times 10^8$

Q. 40 Fill in the blanks with <, > or = sign.

(a) 3^2 _____ 15   (b) 2^3 _____ 3^2

(c) 7^4 _____ 5^4 (d) 10000 _____ 10^5

(e) 6^3 _____ 4^4

Sol. (a) 3^2 _____ 15

$\because \qquad\qquad 3^2 = 3 \times 3 = 9$

So, $\qquad\qquad 9 < 15$

$\therefore \qquad\qquad 3^2 < 15$

(b) 2^3 _____ 3^2

$\because \qquad\qquad 2^3 = 2 \times 2 \times 2 = 8$

and $\qquad\qquad 3^2 = 3 \times 3 = 9$

So, $\qquad\qquad 8 < 9$

$\therefore \qquad\qquad 2^3 < 3^2$

(c) 7^4 _____ 5^4

Obviously, $7^4 > 5^4$ [$\because$ powers are same, so if base is greater, then the number is greater]

(d) 10000 _____ 10^5

$\because 10000 = 10^4$

So, $\quad 10^4 < 10^5$ [$\because$ base are same, so if power is greater, then the number is greater]

$\therefore \qquad 10000 < 10^5$

(e) 6^3 _____ 4^4

$\because \qquad 6^3 = 6 \times 6 \times 6 = 216$

and $\quad 4^4 = 4 \times 4 \times 4 \times 4 = 256$

So, $\qquad 216 < 256$

$\therefore \qquad\qquad 6^3 < 4^4$

True/ False

In questions 41 to 65, state whether the given statements are True or False.

Q. 41 One million = 10^7

Sol. *False*

∵ One million = 10 lakhs = 1000000 = 10^6

Hence, $10^6 \neq 10^7$

Q. 42 One hour = 60^2 seconds

Sol. *True*

∵ 1 h = 60 min = 60 × 60 s = 60^2 s

Q. 43 $1^0 \times 0^1 = 1$

Sol. *False*

∵ $1^0 \times 0^1 = 1 \times 0 = 0 \neq 1$ $[\because a^0 = 1]$

Q. 44 $(-3)^4 = -12$

Sol. *False*

∵ $(-3)^4 = (-3) \times (-3) \times (-3) \times (-3)$

$= 81 \neq -12$

Q. 45 $3^4 > 4^3$

Sol. *True*

∵ $3^4 = 3 \times 3 \times 3 \times 3 = 81$

and $4^3 = 4 \times 4 \times 4 = 64$

∴ $81 > 64$

Hence, $3^4 > 4^3$

Q. 46 $\left(\dfrac{-3}{5}\right)^{100} = \dfrac{-3^{100}}{-5^{100}}$

Sol. *True*

Taking LHS, we have

$$\left(\frac{-3}{5}\right)^{100} = \left(\frac{-1 \times 3}{5}\right)^{100} \qquad [\because -3 = -1 \times 3]$$

$$= \frac{(-1)^{100} \times 3^{100}}{5^{100}} \qquad [\because (a \times b)^m = a^m \times b^m]$$

$$= \frac{1 \times 3^{100}}{5^{100}} \qquad [\because (-1)^n = 1, \text{ if } n \text{ is even}]$$

$$= \frac{3^{100}}{5^{100}}$$

Now, taking RHS, we have $\dfrac{-3^{100}}{-5^{100}} = \dfrac{3^{100}}{5^{100}}$

[∵ if both numerator and denominator have negative sign, then it is cancelled out]

∴ LHS = RHS

Hence, $\dfrac{-3^{100}}{5} = \dfrac{-3^{100}}{-5^{100}}$

Q. 47 $(10 + 10)^{10} = 10^{10} + 10^{10}$

Sol. *False*

We know that, $(a \times b)^m = a^m \times b^m$

So, $(10 \times 10)^{10} = 10^{10} \times 10^{10}$

Q. 48 $x^0 \times x^0 = x^0 \div x^0$ is true for all non-zero values of x.

Sol. *True*

∵ $x^0 \times x^0 = 1 \times 1 = 1$ [∵ $a^0 = 1$]

and $x^0 \div x^0 = 1 \div 1 = 1$ [∵ $a^0 = 1$]

Hence, $x^0 \times x^0 = x^0 \div x^0$

Q. 49 In the standard form, a large number can be expressed as a decimal number between 0 and 1, multiplied by a power of 10.

Sol. *False*

A number in standard form is written as $a \times 10^k$, where $1 \le a \le 10$ and k is any integer.

Q. 50 4^2 is greater than 2^4.

Sol. *False*

∵ $4^2 = 4 \times 4 = 16$ [∵ $a^m = a \times a \times a \times ... \times a\ (m\ \text{times})$]

and $2^4 = 2 \times 2 \times 2 \times 2 = 16$

So, $4^2 = 2^4$

Q. 51 $x^m + x^m = x^{2m}$, where x is a non-zero rational number and m is a positive integer.

Sol. *False*

∵ $a^m \times a^n = a^{m+n}$

∴ $x^m \times x^m = x^{m+m} = x^{2m}$

Also, $a^k + a^k = 2a^k$

So, $x^m + x^m = 2x^m$

Q. 52 $x^m \times y^m = (x \times y)^{2m}$, where x and y are non-zero rational numbers and m is a positive integer.

Sol. *False*

If a and b are rational numbers, then

$a^m \times b^m = (ab)^m$

∴ $x^m \times y^m = (xy)^m = (x \times y)^m$

Hence, $x^m \times y^m \ne (x \times y)^{2m}$

Q. 53 $x^m \div y^m = (x \div y)^m$, where x and y are non-zero rational numbers and m is a positive integer.

Sol. *True*

If x and y are rational numbers, then

$$\frac{x^m}{y^m} = \left(\frac{x}{y}\right)^m \text{ or } x^m \div y^m = (x \div y)^m$$

Q. 54 $x^m \times x^n = x^{m+n}$, where x is a non-zero rational number and m, n are positive integers.

Sol. *True*

If x is a rational number and m and n are positive integers, then
$$x^m \times x^n = x^{m+n}$$

Q. 55 4^9 is greater than 16^3.

Sol. *True*

$\because \ 16^3 = (4^2)^3$ $[\because 16 = 4 \times 4 = 4^2]$

$\quad\ \ = 4^6$ $[\because (a^m)^n = a^{mn}]$

Now, in 4^9 and 4^6, $4^9 > 4^6$ as powers $9 > 6$

$\qquad\qquad$ [if base is same, then power is greater number is also greater]

Q. 56 $\left(\dfrac{2}{5}\right)^3 \div \left(\dfrac{5}{2}\right)^3 = 1$

Sol. *False*

Here, $\left(\dfrac{2}{5}\right)^3 \div \left(\dfrac{5}{2}\right)^3 = \left(\dfrac{2}{5}\right)^3 \times \left(\dfrac{2}{5}\right)^3$ $\left[\because \left(\dfrac{a}{b}\right) \div \left(\dfrac{c}{d}\right) = \dfrac{a}{b} \times \dfrac{d}{c}\right]$

$\qquad\qquad\qquad\qquad = \left(\dfrac{2}{5}\right)^{3+3} = \left(\dfrac{2}{5}\right)^6$ $[\because a^m \times a^n = a^{m+n}]$

Hence, $\left(\dfrac{2}{5}\right)^3 \div \left(\dfrac{5}{2}\right)^3 \neq 1$

Q. 57 $\left(\dfrac{4}{3}\right)^5 \times \left(\dfrac{5}{7}\right)^5 = \left(\dfrac{4}{3} \div \dfrac{5}{7}\right)^5$

Sol. *False*

Here, $\left(\dfrac{4}{3}\right)^5 \times \left(\dfrac{5}{7}\right)^5 = \left(\dfrac{4}{3} \times \dfrac{5}{7}\right)^5$ $[\because a^m \times b^m = (ab)^m]$

and $\left[\left(\dfrac{4}{3}\right) \div \left(\dfrac{5}{7}\right)\right]^5 = \left(\dfrac{4}{3} \times \dfrac{7}{5}\right)^5$ $\left[\because \left(\dfrac{a}{b}\right) \div \left(\dfrac{c}{d}\right) = \dfrac{a}{b} \times \dfrac{d}{c}\right]$

Hence, $\left(\dfrac{4}{3} \times \dfrac{5}{7}\right)^5 \neq \left(\dfrac{4}{3} \times \dfrac{7}{5}\right)^5$

Q. 58 $\left(\dfrac{5}{8}\right)^9 \div \left(\dfrac{5}{8}\right)^4 = \left(\dfrac{5}{8}\right)^4$

Sol. *False*

Here, $\left(\dfrac{5}{8}\right)^9 \div \left(\dfrac{5}{8}\right)^4 = \left(\dfrac{5}{8}\right)^{9-4} = \left(\dfrac{5}{8}\right)^5$ $\qquad [\because a^m \div a^n = a^{m-n}]$

Hence, $\left(\dfrac{5}{8}\right)^9 \div \left(\dfrac{5}{8}\right)^4 \neq \left(\dfrac{5}{8}\right)^4$

Q. 59 $\left(\dfrac{7}{3}\right)^2 \times \left(\dfrac{7}{3}\right)^5 = \left(\dfrac{7}{3}\right)^{10}$

Sol. *False*

Here, $\left(\dfrac{7}{3}\right)^2 \times \left(\dfrac{7}{3}\right)^5 = \left(\dfrac{7}{3}\right)^{2+5}$ $\qquad [\because a^m \times a^n = a^{m+n}]$

$= \left(\dfrac{7}{3}\right)^7$

Hence, $\left(\dfrac{7}{3}\right)^2 \times \left(\dfrac{7}{5}\right)^5 \neq \left(\dfrac{7}{3}\right)^{10}$

Q. 60 $5^0 \times 25^0 \times 125^0 = (5^0)^6$

Sol. *True*

Here, $5^0 \times 25^0 \times 125^0 = 5^0 \times (5 \times 5)^0 \times (5 \times 5 \times 5)^0$ $\qquad [\because 25 = 5 \times 5 \text{ and } 125 = 5 \times 5 \times 5]$

$= 5^0 \times 5^0 \times 5^0 \times 5^0 \times 5^0 \times 5^0$ $\qquad [\because (a \times b)^m = a^m b^m]$

$= (5^0)^6$

Hence, $5^0 \times 25^0 \times 125^0 = (5^0)^6$

Q. 61 $876543 = 8 \times 10^5 + 7 \times 10^4 + 6 \times 10^3 + 5 \times 10^2 + 4 \times 10^1 + 3 \times 10^0$

Sol. *True*

Take RHS $= 8 \times 10^5 + 7 \times 10^4 + 6 \times 10^3 + 5 \times 10^2 + 4 \times 10^1 + 3 \times 10^0$

$= 8 \times 100000 + 7 \times 10000 + 6 \times 1000 + 5 \times 100 + 4 \times 10 + 3 \times 1$ $\qquad [\because a^0 = 1]$

$= 800000 + 70000 + 6000 + 500 + 40 + 3$

$= 876543$

$= \text{LHS}$

Hence, RHS $=$ LHS

Q. 62 $600060 = 6 \times 10^5 + 6 \times 10^2$

Sol. *False*

Take RHS $= 6 \times 10^5 + 6 \times 10^2 = 6 \times 100000 + 6 \times 100 = 600000 + 600$

$= 600600 \neq \text{LHS}$

Hence, RHS $\neq$ LHS

Q. 63 $4 \times 10^5 + 3 \times 10^4 + 2 \times 10^3 + 1 \times 10^0 = 432010$

Sol. *False*

Take LHS

$$= 4 \times 10^5 + 3 \times 10^4 + 2 \times 10^3 + 1 \times 10^0$$
$$= 4 \times 100000 + 3 \times 10000 + 2 \times 1000 + 1 \times 1 \qquad [\because a^0 = 1]$$
$$= 400000 + 30000 + 2000 + 1$$
$$= 432001 \neq \text{RHS}$$

Hence, LHS $\neq$ RHS

Q. 64 $8 \times 10^6 + 2 \times 10^4 + 5 \times 10^2 + 9 \times 10^0 = 8020509$

Sol. *True*

Take LHS

$$= 8 \times 10^6 + 2 \times 10^4 + 5 \times 10^2 + 9 \times 10^0$$
$$= 8 \times 1000000 + 2 \times 10000 + 5 \times 100 + 9 \times 1 \qquad [\because a^0 = 1]$$
$$= 8000000 + 2000 + 500 + 9$$
$$= 8020509 = \text{RHS}$$

Hence, LHS $=$ RHS

Q. 65 $4^0 + 5^0 + 6^0 = (4 + 5 + 6)^0$

Sol. *False*

Here, $4^0 + 5^0 + 6^0 = 1 + 1 + 1 = 3$ $\qquad [\because a^0 = 1]$

and $\qquad (4 + 5 + 6)^0 = (15)^0 = 1$

Hence, $4^0 + 5^0 + 6^0 \neq (4 + 5 + 6)^0$

Q. 66 Arrange in ascending order.

$$2^5, 3^3, 2^3 \times 2, (3^3)^2, 3^5, 4^0, 2^3 \times 3^1$$

Sol. In ascending order, the numbers are arranged from smallest to largest.

We have, $2^5 = 2 \times 2 \times 2 \times 2 \times 2 = 32$

$$3^3 = 3 \times 3 \times 3 = 27$$
$$2^3 \times 2 = 2 \times 2 \times 2 \times 2 = 16$$
$$(3^3)^2 = 3^{3 \times 2} \qquad [\because (a^m)^n = a^{mn}]$$
$$= 3^6 = 3 \times 3 \times 3 \times 3 \times 3 \times 3 = 729$$
$$3^5 = 3 \times 3 \times 3 \times 3 \times 3 = 243$$
$$4^0 = 1 \qquad [\because a^0 = 1]$$

and $2^3 \times 3^1 = 2 \times 2 \times 2 \times 3 = 24$

Thus, the required ascending order will be

$$4^0 < 2^3 \times 2 < 2^3 \times 3^1 < 3^3 < 2^5 < 3^5 < (3^3)^2.$$

Q. 67 Arrange the following exponents in descending order.

$$2^{2+3}, (2^2)^3, 2 \times 2^2, \frac{3^5}{3^2}, 3^2 \times 3^0, 2^3 \times 5^2$$

Sol. In descending order, the numbers are arranged from largest to smallest.

We have, $2^{2+3} = 2^5 = 2 \times 2 \times 2 \times 2 \times 2 = 32$

$(2^2)^3 = 2^{2 \times 3}$ $[\because (a^m)^n = a^{mn}]$

$= 2^6 = 2 \times 2 \times 2 \times 2 \times 2 \times 2 = 64$

$2 \times 2^2 = 2^{1+2}$ $[\because a^m \times a^n = a^{m+n}]$

$= 2^3 = 2 \times 2 \times 2 = 8$

$\frac{3^5}{3^2} = 3^{5-2}$ $\left[\because \frac{a^m}{a^n} = a^{m-n}\right]$

$= 3^3 = 3 \times 3 \times 3 = 27$

$3^2 \times 3^0 = 3^{2+0}$ $[\because a^m \times a^n = a^{m+n}]$

$= 3^2 = 3 \times 3 = 9$

$2^3 \times 5^2 = 2 \times 2 \times 2 \times 5 \times 5 = 8 \times 25 = 200$

Thus, the required descending order will be

$$2^3 \times 5^2 > (2^2)^3 > 2^{2+3} > \frac{3^5}{3^2} > 3^2 \times 3^0 > 2 \times 2^2$$

Q. 68 By what number should $(-4)^5$ be divided so that the quotient may be equal to $(-4)^3$?

Sol. In order to find the number, which should divide $(-4)^5$ to get the quotient $(-4)^3$, we will divide $(-4)^5$ by $(-4)^3$.

Hence, required number $= \dfrac{(-4)^5}{(-4)^3} = (-4)^{5-3}$ $\left[\because \frac{a^m}{a^n} = a^{m-n}\right]$

$= (-4)^2$

Q. 69 Find m, so that $\left(\dfrac{2}{9}\right)^3 \times \left(\dfrac{2}{9}\right)^6 = \left(\dfrac{2}{9}\right)^{2m-1}$.

Sol. We have, $\left(\dfrac{2}{9}\right)^3 \times \left(\dfrac{2}{9}\right)^6 = \left(\dfrac{2}{9}\right)^{2m-1}$

$\Rightarrow \quad \left(\dfrac{2}{9}\right)^{3+6} = \left(\dfrac{2}{9}\right)^{2m-1}$ $[\because a^m \times a^n = a^{m+n}]$

$\Rightarrow \quad \left(\dfrac{2}{9}\right)^9 = \left(\dfrac{2}{9}\right)^{2m-1}$

$\Rightarrow \quad 9 = 2m - 1$ $[\because a^m = a^n \Rightarrow m = n]$

$\Rightarrow \quad 9 + 1 = 2m$ [transposing (-1) to LHS]

$\Rightarrow \quad 10 = 2m$

$\Rightarrow \quad \dfrac{10}{2} = \dfrac{2m}{2}$ [dividing both sides by 2]

$\Rightarrow \quad 5 = m$

Hence, $m = 5$.

Q. 70 If $\dfrac{p}{q} = \left(\dfrac{3}{2}\right)^2 \div \left(\dfrac{9}{4}\right)^0$, find the value of $\left(\dfrac{p}{q}\right)^3$.

Sol. We have, $\left(\dfrac{p}{q}\right) = \left(\dfrac{3}{2}\right)^2 \div \left(\dfrac{9}{4}\right)^0$

$\Rightarrow \quad \dfrac{p}{q} = \left(\dfrac{3}{2}\right)^2 \div \dfrac{1}{1}$ $[\because a^0 = 1]$

$\Rightarrow \quad \dfrac{p}{q} = \left(\dfrac{3}{2}\right)^2$ $\left[\because \dfrac{a}{b} \div \dfrac{c}{d} = \dfrac{a}{b} \times \dfrac{d}{c}\right]$

$\Rightarrow \quad \dfrac{p}{q} = \dfrac{3^2}{2^2}$ $\left[\because \left(\dfrac{a}{b}\right)^n = \dfrac{a^n}{b^n}\right]$

$\Rightarrow \quad \dfrac{p}{q} = \dfrac{9}{4}$

On taking cube both sides, we get

$$\left(\dfrac{p}{q}\right)^3 = \left(\dfrac{9}{4}\right)^3$$

$\therefore \qquad \left(\dfrac{p}{q}\right)^3 = \dfrac{9 \times 9 \times 9}{4 \times 4 \times 4} = \dfrac{729}{64}$

Q. 71 Find the reciprocal of the rational number $\left(\dfrac{1}{2}\right)^2 \div \left(\dfrac{2}{3}\right)^3$.

Sol. Given, $\left(\dfrac{1}{2}\right)^2 \div \left(\dfrac{2}{3}\right)^3 = \dfrac{\left(\dfrac{1}{2}\right)^2}{\left(\dfrac{2}{3}\right)^3}$ $\left[\because a \div b = \dfrac{a}{b}\right]$

$= \dfrac{\dfrac{(1)^2}{(2)^2}}{\dfrac{(2)^3}{(3)^3}} = \dfrac{\left(\dfrac{1}{4}\right)}{\left(\dfrac{8}{27}\right)}$ $\left[\because \left(\dfrac{a}{b}\right)^n = \dfrac{a^n}{b^n}\right]$

$[\because 1^2 = 1, 2^2 = 4, 2^3 = 8 \text{ and } 3^3 = 27]$

$= \dfrac{1}{4} \times \dfrac{27}{8} = \dfrac{27}{4 \times 8} = \dfrac{27}{32}$ $\left[\because \dfrac{a}{b} \div \dfrac{c}{d} = \dfrac{a}{b} \times \dfrac{d}{c}\right]$

We know that, reciprocal of a rational number is obtained by interchanging numerator and denominator.

$\therefore$ Reciprocal of given number $= \dfrac{32}{27}$

Q. 72 Find the value of

(a) 7^0

(b) $7^7 \div 7^7$

(c) $(-7)^{2 \times 7 - 6 - 8}$

(d) $(2^0 + 3^0 + 4^0)(4^0 - 3^0 - 2^0)$

(e) $2 \times 3 \times 4 \div 2^0 \times 3^0 \times 4^0$

(f) $(8^0 - 2^0) \times (8^0 + 2^0)$

Exponents and Powers

Sol.   (a) $7^0 = 1$ $[\because a^0 = 1]$

(b) $7^7 \div 7^7 = \dfrac{7^7}{7^7} = 7^{7-7}$ $\left[\because \dfrac{a^m}{a^n} = a^{m-n}\right]$

$= 7^0 = 1$ $[\because a^0 = 1]$

(c) $(-7)^{2 \times 7 - 6 - 8} = (-7)^{14-14} = (-7)^0 = 1$ $[\because a^0 = 1]$

(d) $(2^0 + 3^0 + 4^0)(4^0 - 3^0 - 2^0) = (1 + 1 + 1)(1 - 1 - 1)$ $[\because a^0 = 1]$

$= (3)(-1) = -3$

(e) $2 \times 3 \times 4 \div 2^0 \times 3^0 \times 4^0 = 2 \times 3 \times 4 \div 1 \times 1 \times 1$ $[\because a^0 = 1]$

$= \dfrac{2 \times 3 \times 4}{1 \times 1 \times 1} = 2 \times 3 \times 4 = 24$

(f) $(8^0 - 2^0) \times (8^0 + 2^0) = (1 - 1) \times (1 + 1) = 0 \times 2 = 0$ $[\because a^0 = 1]$

Q. 73 Find the value of n, where n is an integer and $2^{n-5} \times 6^{2n-4} = \dfrac{1}{12^4 \times 2}$.

Sol.   We have, $2^{n-5} \times 6^{2n-4} = \dfrac{1}{12^4 \times 2}$

$\Rightarrow$ $\dfrac{2^n}{2^5} \times \dfrac{6^{2n}}{6^4} = \dfrac{1}{12^4 \times 2}$ $\left[\because a^{m-n} = \dfrac{a^m}{a^n}\right]$

$\Rightarrow$ $\dfrac{2^n \times 6^{2n}}{2^5 \times 6^4} = \dfrac{1}{(2 \times 6)^4 \times 2}$ $[\because 12 = 6 \times 2]$

$\Rightarrow$ $2^n \times (6^2)^n = \dfrac{2^5 \times 6^4}{2^4 \times 6^4 \times 2}$ [by cross-multiplication]

$[\because a^{mn} = (a^m)^n$ and $(a \times b)^m = a^m \times b^m]$

$\Rightarrow$ $2^n \times 36^n = \dfrac{2^5 \times 6^4}{2^5 \times 6^4}$ $[\because a^m \times a^n = a^{m+n}]$

$\Rightarrow$ $2^n \times 36^n = 1$

$\Rightarrow$ $(2 \times 36)^n = 1$ $[\because a^m \times b^m = (ab)^m]$

$\Rightarrow$ $(72)^n = (72)^0$ $[\because a^0 = 1]$

$\therefore$ $n = 0$ $[\because \text{if } a^m = a^n \Rightarrow m = n]$

Q. 74 Express the following in usual form.

(a) 8.01×10^7 (b) 1.75×10^{-3}

Sol.   (a) Here, $8.01 \times 10^7 = \dfrac{801}{100} \times 10000000 = 80100000$

(b) Here, $1.75 \times 10^{-3} = \dfrac{175}{100} \times \dfrac{1}{10^3} = \dfrac{175}{100000} = 0.00175$ $\left[\because a^{-m} = \dfrac{1}{a^m}\right]$

Q. 75 Find the value of

(a) 2^5 (b) (-3^5) (c) $-(-4)^4$

Sol.   We know that, $a^n = a \times a \times a \times ... \times a$ (n times)

(a) $2^5 = 2 \times 2 \times 2 \times 2 \times 2 = 32$

(b) $(-3^5) = (-1)^5 \times 3^5 = -1 \times 3 \times 3 \times 3 \times 3 \times 3 = -243$ $[\because (-1)^n = -1, \text{ if } n \text{ is odd}]$

(c) $-(-4)^4 = -[(-4) \times (-4) \times (-4) \times (-4)] = -[(-1)^4(4 \times 4 \times 4 \times 4)] = -(256) = -256$

$[\because (-1)^n = 1, \text{ if } n \text{ is even}]$

Q. 76 Express the following in exponential form.

   (a) $3 \times 3 \times 3 \times a \times a \times a \times a$

   (b) $a \times a \times b \times b \times b \times c \times c \times c \times c$

   (c) $s \times s \times t \times t \times s \times s \times t$

Sol. We know that,

   $a \times a \times ... \times a\ (n\ \text{times}) = a^n$

   (a) $3 \times 3 \times 3 \times a \times a \times a \times a = 3^3 \times a^4 = 27a^4$

   (b) $a \times a \times b \times b \times b \times c \times c \times c \times c = a^2 \times b^3 \times c^4$

   (c) $s \times s \times t \times t \times s \times s \times t = s \times s \times s \times s \times t \times t \times t = s^4 \times t^3$

Q. 77 How many times of 30 must be added together to get a sum equal to 30^7.

Sol. Let n be the number of times that 30 must be added together to get a sum equal to 30^7. Therefore, we can write that

$$\underbrace{30 + 30 + ... + 30}_{n\ \text{times}} = 30^7$$

$\Rightarrow \qquad 30 \times n = 30^7 \qquad\qquad [\because \underbrace{a + a + ... + a}_{n\ \text{times}} = a \times n]$

$\Rightarrow \qquad \dfrac{30 \times n}{30} = \dfrac{30^7}{30} \qquad\qquad [\text{dividing both sides by 30}]$

$\Rightarrow \qquad n = 30^{7-1} \qquad\qquad \left[\because \dfrac{a^m}{a^n} = a^{m-n}\right]$

$\therefore \qquad n = 30^6$

Hence, if 30 is added 30^6 times, then we get 30^7.

Q. 78 Express each of the following numbers using exponential notations.

   (a) 1024   (b) 1029   (c) $\dfrac{144}{875}$

Sol. For solving these type of questions, we use here prime factorisation method.

   (a) Given, 1024

2	1024
2	512
2	256
2	128
2	64
2	32
2	16
2	8
2	4
2	2
	1

Using prime factorisation of 1024, we have

$1024 = 2 \times 2 \times 2 \times 2 \times 2 \times 2 \times 2 \times 2 \times 2 \times 2 = 2^{10}$

(b) Given, 1029

3	1029
7	343
7	49
7	7
	1

Using prime factorisation of 1029, we have
$$1029 = 3 \times 7 \times 7 \times 7 = 3 \times 7^3$$

(c) Given, $\dfrac{144}{875}$

2	144
2	72
2	36
2	18
3	9
3	3
	1

5	875
5	175
5	35
7	7
	1

Using prime factorisation of 144 and 875, we have
$$\frac{144}{875} = \frac{2 \times 2 \times 2 \times 2 \times 3 \times 3}{5 \times 5 \times 5 \times 7} = \frac{2^4 \times 3^2}{5^3 \times 7^1}$$

Q. 79 Identify the greater number, in each of the following.

      (a) 2^6 or 6^2 (b) 2^9 or 9^2 (c) 7.9×10^4 or 5.28×10^5

Sol. (a) We have, $2^6 = 2 \times 2 \times 2 \times 2 \times 2 \times 2 = 64$

      and $6^2 = 6 \times 6 = 36$

      So, $2^6 > 6^2$

(b) We have, $2^9 = 2 \times 2 \times 2 \times 2 \times 2 \times 2 \times 2 \times 2 \times 2 = 512$

      and $9^2 = 9 \times 9 = 81$

      So, $2^9 > 9^2$

(c) We have, $7.9 \times 10^4 = 7.9 \times 10000 = 79000$

      and $5.28 \times 10^5 = 5.28 \times 100000 = 528000$

      So, $5.28 \times 10^5 > 7.9 \times 10^4$

Q. 80 Express each of following as a product of powers of their prime factors.

      (a) 9000   (b) 2025   (c) 800

Sol. (a)

2	9000
2	4500
2	2250
3	1125
3	375
5	125
5	25
5	5
	1

Using prime factorisation of 9000, we have

$$9000 = 2 \times 2 \times 2 \times 3 \times 3 \times 5 \times 5 \times 5$$

∴ $$9000 = 2^2 \times 3^2 \times 5^3$$

(b)

3	2025
3	675
3	225
3	75
5	25
5	5
	1

Using prime factorisation of 2025, we have

$$2025 = 3 \times 3 \times 3 \times 3 \times 5 \times 5$$

∴ $$2025 = 3^4 \times 5^2$$

(c)

2	800
2	400
2	200
2	100
2	50
5	25
5	5
	1

Using prime factorisation of 800, we have

$$800 = 2 \times 2 \times 2 \times 2 \times 2 \times 5 \times 5$$

∴ $$800 = 2^5 \times 5^2$$

Q. 81 Express each of the following in single exponential form.

(a) $2^3 \times 3^3$ (b) $2^4 \times 4^2$

(c) $5^2 \times 7^2$ (d) $(-5)^5 \times (-5)$

(e) $(-3)^3 \times (-10)^3$ (f) $(-11)^2 \times (-2)^2$

Sol.   (a) We have, $2^3 \times 3^3 = (2 \times 3)^3$ $[\because a^m \times b^m = (a \times b)^m]$

$= 6^3$

(b) We have, $2^4 \times 4^2 = 2^4 \times (2^2)^2$ $[\because 4 = 2^2]$

$= 2^4 \times 2^4$ $[\because (a^m)^n = a^{mn}]$

$= 2^{4+4}$ $[\because a^m \times a^n = a^{m+n}]$

$= 2^8$

(c) We have, $5^2 \times 7^2 = (5 \times 7)^2$ $[\because a^m \times b^m = (a \times b)^m]$

$= 35^2$

(d) We have, $(-5)^5 \times (-5) = (-5)^{5+1} = (-5)^6$ $[\because a^m \times a^n = a^{m+n}]$

$= (-1 \times 5)^6 = (-1)^6 \times (5)^6$ $[\because (a \times b)^m = a^m \times b^m]$

$= 1 \times 5^6$ $[\because (-1)^n = 1, \text{ if } n \text{ is even}]$

$= 5^6$

(e) We have, $(-3)^3 \times (-10)^3 = [(-3) \times (-10)]^3$ $\qquad [\because a^m \times b^m = (a \times b)^m]$

$\qquad\qquad = (30)^3$ $\qquad\qquad\qquad\qquad\qquad [\because (-3) \times (-10) = 30]$

(f) We have, $(-11)^2 \times (-2)^2 = [(-11) \times (-2)]^2$ $\qquad [\because a^m \times b^m = (a \times b)^m]$

$\qquad\qquad = 22^2$ $\qquad\qquad\qquad\qquad\qquad\qquad [\because (-11) \times (-2) = 22]$

Q. 82 Express the following numbers in standard form.

(a) 76,47,000   (b) 8,19,00,000

(c) 5,83,00,00,00,000   (d) 24 billion

Sol. (a) We have, $76,47,000 = 7647000.00$

A number in standard form is written as $a \times 10^k$, where a is the terminating decimal such that $1 \le a \le 10$ and k is any integer.

So, $7647000 = 7647 \times 10^3$

$\qquad = 7.647 \times 10^3 \times 10^3$

$\qquad = 7.647 \times 10^6$

Similarly,

(b) $8,19,00,000 = 81900000.00 = 819 \times 10^5 = 8.19 \times 10^2 \times 10^5 = 8.19 \times 10^7$

(c) $5,83,00,00,00,000 = 583000000000.00 = 583 \times 10^9 = 5.83 \times 10^2 \times 10^9 = 5.83 \times 10^{11}$

(d) 24 billion $= 24,00,00,00,000 = 24 \times 10^9 = 2.4 \times 10^1 \times 10^9 = 2.4 \times 10^{10}$

Q. 83 The speed of light in vacuum is 3×10^8 m/s. Sunlight takes about 8 minutes to reach the Earth. Express distance of Sun from Earth in standard form.

Sol. It is given that,

Speed of light $= 3 \times 10^8$ m/s

Time taken by light to reach the Earth $= 8$ min $= 8 \times 60$ s $= 480$ s $\qquad [\because 1$ min $= 60$ s$]$

We know that,

Distance $=$ Speed $\times$ Time $= 3 \times 10^8 \times 480 = 1440 \times 10^8$

$\qquad = 1.440 \times 10^3 \times 10^8$

$\qquad = 1.44 \times 10^{11}$ $\qquad\qquad\qquad\qquad [\because 10^3 \times 10^8 = 10^{11}]$

Hence, the distance of Sun from the Earth is 1.44×10^{11} m.

Q. 84 Simplify and express each of the following in exponential form.

(a) $\left[\left(\frac{3}{7}\right)^4 \times \left(\frac{3}{7}\right)^5\right] \div \left(\frac{3}{7}\right)^7$

(b) $\left[\left(\frac{7}{11}\right)^5 \div \left(\frac{7}{11}\right)^2\right] \times \left(\frac{7}{11}\right)^2$

(c) $(3^7 \div 3^5)^4$

(d) $\left(\frac{a^6}{a^4}\right) \times a^5 \times a^0$

(e) $\left[\left(\frac{3}{5}\right)^3 \times \left(\frac{3}{5}\right)^8\right] \div \left[\left(\frac{3}{5}\right)^2 \times \left(\frac{3}{5}\right)^4\right]$

(f) $(5^{15} \div 5^{10}) \times 5^5$

Sol.   (a) We have, $\left[\left(\dfrac{3}{7}\right)^4 \times \left(\dfrac{3}{7}\right)^5\right] \div \left(\dfrac{3}{7}\right)^7$

$$= \left(\dfrac{3}{7}\right)^{4+5} \div \left(\dfrac{3}{7}\right)^7 \qquad [\because a^m \times a^n = a^{m+n}]$$

$$= \left(\dfrac{3}{7}\right)^9 \div \left(\dfrac{3}{7}\right)^7 = \dfrac{\left(\dfrac{3}{7}\right)^9}{\left(\dfrac{3}{7}\right)^7} = \left(\dfrac{3}{7}\right)^{9-7} \qquad \left[\because \dfrac{a^m}{a^n} = a^{m-n}\right]$$

$$= \left(\dfrac{3}{7}\right)^2$$

(b) We have, $\left[\left(\dfrac{7}{11}\right)^5 \div \left(\dfrac{7}{11}\right)^2\right] \times \left(\dfrac{7}{11}\right)^2$

$$= \left[\dfrac{\left(\dfrac{7}{11}\right)^5}{\left(\dfrac{7}{11}\right)^2}\right] \times \left(\dfrac{7}{11}\right)^2 = \left(\dfrac{7}{11}\right)^{5-2} \times \left(\dfrac{7}{11}\right)^2 \qquad \left[\because \dfrac{a^m}{a^n} = a^{m-n}\right]$$

$$= \left(\dfrac{7}{11}\right)^3 \times \left(\dfrac{7}{11}\right)^2 = \left(\dfrac{7}{11}\right)^{3+2} \qquad [\because a^m \times a^n = a^{m+n}]$$

$$= \left(\dfrac{7}{11}\right)^5$$

(c) We have, $(3^7 \div 3^5)^4 = \left(\dfrac{3^7}{3^5}\right)^4 = (3^{7-5})^4 \qquad \left[\because \dfrac{a^m}{a^n} = a^{m-n}\right]$

$$= (3^2)^4 = 3^{2 \times 4} \qquad [\because (a^m)^n = a^{mn}]$$

$$= 3^8$$

(d) We have, $\left(\dfrac{a^6}{a^4}\right) \times a^5 \times a^0 = (a^{6-4} \times a^5 \times 1) \qquad \left[\because \dfrac{a^m}{a^n} = a^{m-n} \text{ and } a^0 = 1\right]$

$$= a^2 \times a^5 = a^{2+5} \qquad [\because a^m \times a^n = a^{m+n}]$$

$$= a^7$$

(e) We have, $\left[\left(\dfrac{3}{5}\right)^3 \times \left(\dfrac{3}{5}\right)^8\right] \div \left[\left(\dfrac{3}{5}\right)^2 \times \left(\dfrac{3}{5}\right)^4\right]$

$$= \left(\dfrac{3}{5}\right)^{3+8} \div \left(\dfrac{3}{5}\right)^{2+4} \qquad [\because a^m \times a^n = a^{m+n}]$$

$$= \left(\dfrac{3}{5}\right)^{11} \div \left(\dfrac{3}{5}\right)^6 = \dfrac{\left(\dfrac{3}{5}\right)^{11}}{\left(\dfrac{3}{5}\right)^6} = \left(\dfrac{3}{5}\right)^{11-6} \qquad \left[\because \dfrac{a^m}{a^n} = a^{m-n}\right]$$

$$= \left(\dfrac{3}{5}\right)^5$$

(f) We have, $(5^{15} \div 5^{10}) \times 5^5 = \left(\dfrac{5^{15}}{5^{10}}\right) \times 5^5 = 5^{15-10} \times 5^5 \qquad \left[\because \dfrac{a^m}{a^n} = a^{m-n}\right]$

$$= 5^5 \times 5^5 = 5^{5+5} = 5^{10} \qquad [\because a^m \times a^n = a^{m+n}]$$

Q. 85 Evaluate

(a) $\dfrac{7^8 \times a^{10} b^7 c^{12}}{7^6 \times a^8 b^4 c^{12}}$

(b) $\dfrac{5^4 \times 7^4 \times 2^7}{8 \times 49 \times 5^3}$

(c) $\dfrac{125 \times 5^2 \times a^7}{10^3 \times a^4}$

(d) $\dfrac{3^4 \times 12^3 \times 36}{2^5 \times 6^3}$

(e) $\left(\dfrac{6 \times 10}{2^2 \times 5^3}\right)^2 \times \dfrac{25}{27}$

(f) $\dfrac{15^4 \times 18^3}{3^3 \times 5^2 \times 12^2}$

(g) $\dfrac{6^4 \times 9^2 \times 25^3}{3^2 \times 4^2 \times 15^6}$

Sol. (a) We have, $\dfrac{7^8 \times a^{10} b^7 c^{12}}{7^6 \times a^8 b^4 c^{12}} = \left(\dfrac{7^8}{7^6}\right) \times \left(\dfrac{a^{10}}{a^8}\right) \times \left(\dfrac{b^7}{b^4}\right) \times \left(\dfrac{c^{12}}{c^{12}}\right)$

$$= 7^{8-6} \times a^{10-8} \times b^{7-4} \times c^{12-12} \qquad \left[\because \dfrac{a^m}{a^n} = a^{m-n}\right]$$

$$= 7^2 \times a^2 \times b^3 \times c^0 = 49\, a^2 b^3 \qquad [\because c^0 = 1]$$

(b) We have, $\dfrac{5^4 \times 7^4 \times 2^7}{8 \times 49 \times 5^3} = \dfrac{5^4 \times 7^4 \times 2^7}{2^3 \times 7^2 \times 5^3} \qquad [\because 8 = 2^3 \text{ and } 49 = 7^2]$

$$= \left(\dfrac{5^4}{5^3}\right) \times \left(\dfrac{2^7}{2^3}\right) \times \left(\dfrac{7^4}{7^2}\right) = 5^{4-3} \times 2^{7-3} \times 7^{4-2} \quad \left[\because \dfrac{a^m}{a^n} = a^{m-n}\right]$$

$$= 5 \times 2^4 \times 7^2 = 5 \times 16 \times 49$$

$$= 3920$$

(c) We have, $\dfrac{125 \times 5^2 \times a^7}{10^3 \times a^4} = \dfrac{5^3 \times 5^2 \times a^7}{(2 \times 5)^3 \times a^4} \qquad [\because 125 = 5^3]$

$$= \dfrac{5^{3+2} \times a^7}{2^3 \times 5^3 \times a^4} \quad [\because a^m \times a^n = a^{m+n} \text{ and } (a \times b)^m = a^m \times b^m]$$

$$= \dfrac{5^5 \times a^7}{2^3 \times 5^3 \times a^4} = \left(\dfrac{5^5}{5^3}\right) \times \left(\dfrac{a^7}{a^4}\right) \times \left(\dfrac{1}{2^3}\right)$$

$$= \dfrac{5^{5-3} \times a^{7-4}}{2^3} \qquad \left[\because \dfrac{a^m}{a^n} = a^{m-n}\right]$$

$$= \dfrac{5^2 \times a^3}{2^3} = \dfrac{25 a^3}{8}$$

(d) We have, $\dfrac{3^4 \times 12^3 \times 36}{2^5 \times 6^3}$

$$= \dfrac{3^4 \times (2^2 \times 3)^3 \times (2^2 \times 3^2)}{2^5 \times (2 \times 3)^3}$$

$$[\because 12 = 2 \times 2 \times 3 \text{ and } 36 = 2 \times 2 \times 3 \times 3]$$

$$= \dfrac{3^4 \times 2^6 \times 3^3 \times 2^2 \times 3^2}{2^5 \times 2^3 \times 3^3} \qquad [\because (a \times b)^m = a^m \times b^m]$$

$$= \dfrac{(3^4 \times 3^2 \times 3^3) \times (2^6 \times 2^2)}{(2^5 \times 2^3) \times 3^3}$$

$$= \frac{3^{4+2+3} \times 2^{6+2}}{2^{5+3} \times 3^3}$$ $[\because a^m \times a^n = a^{m+n}]$

$$= \frac{3^9 \times 2^8}{3^3 \times 2^8} = 3^{9-3} \times 2^{8-8}$$ $\left[\because \frac{a^m}{a^n} = a^{m-n}\right]$

$$= 3^6 \times 2^0 = 3^6 \times 1 = 729$$ $[\because a^0 = 1]$

(e) We have, $\left(\frac{6 \times 10}{2^2 \times 5^3}\right)^2 \times \frac{25}{27} = \left(\frac{2 \times 3 \times 2 \times 5}{2^2 \times 5^3}\right)^2 \times \frac{5^2}{3^3}$ $[\because 6 = 2 \times 3 \text{ and } 10 = 2 \times 5]$

$$= \left(\frac{2^2 \times 3 \times 5}{2^2 \times 5^3}\right)^2 \times \frac{5^2}{3^3} = \left(\frac{3}{5^2}\right)^2 \times \frac{5^2}{3^3}$$ $[\because (a \times b)^m = a^m \times b^m]$

$$= \frac{3^2}{5^4} \times \frac{5^2}{3^3} = \frac{1}{5^2 \times 3} = \frac{1}{25 \times 3} = \frac{1}{75}$$ $[\because (a^m)^n = a^{mn}]$

(f) We have, $\frac{15^4 \times 18^3}{3^3 \times 5^2 \times 12^2} = \frac{(3 \times 5)^4 \times (2 \times 3^2)^3}{3^3 \times 5^2 \times (2^2 \times 3)^2}$ $[\because 18 = 2 \times 3 \times 3 \text{ and } 12 = 2 \times 2 \times 3]$

$$= \frac{3^4 \times 5^4 \times 2^3 \times 3^6}{3^3 \times 5^2 \times 2^4 \times 3^2}$$ $[\because (a \times b)^m = a^m \times b^m]$

$$= \frac{3^{4+6-3-2} \times 5^{4-2}}{2^{4-3}}$$ $\left[\because \frac{a^m}{a^n} = a^{m-n} \text{ and } a^m \times a^n = a^{m+n}\right]$

$$= \frac{3^5 \times 5^2}{2} = \frac{243 \times 25}{2} = \frac{6075}{2}$$

(g) We have, $\frac{6^4 \times 9^2 \times 25^3}{3^2 \times 4^2 \times 15^6} = \frac{(2 \times 3)^4 \times (3^2)^2 \times (5^2)^3}{3^2 \times (2^2)^2 \times (3 \times 5)^6}$

$$= \frac{2^4 \times 3^4 \times 3^4 \times 5^6}{3^2 \times 2^4 \times 3^6 \times 5^6}$$ $[\because (a \times b)^m = a^m \times b^m]$

$$= 2^{4-4} \times 3^{4+4-2-6} \times 5^{6-6}$$ $\left[\because \frac{a^m}{a^n} = a^{m-n}\right]$

$$= 2^0 \times 3^0 \times 5^0$$

$$= 1 \times 1 \times 1 = 1$$

Q. 86 Express the given information in Scientific notation (standard form) and then arrange them in ascending order of their size.

S. N.	Deserts of the World	Area (in sq km)
1.	Kalahari, South Africa	932,100
2.	Thar, India	199,430
3.	Gibson, Australia	155,400
4.	Great Victoria, Australia	647,500
5	Sahara, North Africa	8,598,800

Sol.   1. Area of Kalahari, South Africa $= 932,400 = 932400.00$ $[\because \text{standard form } a \times 10^k]$

$$= 9324 \times 10^2 = 9.324 \times 10^3 \times 10^2 = 9.324 \times 10^5$$

2. Area of Thar, India $= 199,430 = 199430.00 = 19943 \times 10^1 = 1.9943 \times 10^4 \times 10^1$

$$= 1.9943 \times 10^5$$

3. Area of Gibson, Australia $= 155,400 = 155400.00 = 1554 \times 10^2 = 1.554 \times 10^3 \times 10^2$

$$= 1.554 \times 10^5$$

4. Area of Great Victoria, Australia $= 647,500 = 647500.00$

$$= 6475 \times 10^2 = 6.475 \times 10^3 \times 10^5 = 6.475 \times 10^5$$

5. Area of Sahara, North-Africa $= 8,598,800 = 8598800.00$

$$= 85988 \times 10^2 = 8.5988 \times 10^4 \times 10^2 = 8.5988 \times 10^6$$

Two numbers written in scientific notation can be compared. The number with the larger power of 10 is greater than the number with the smaller power of 10. If the powers of ten are the same, then the number with larger factor is the larger number.

Hence, required ascending order of the size will be

Gibson, Australia $<$ Thar, India $<$ Great Victoria, Australia $<$ Kalahari, South-Africa

$< $ Sahara, North-Africa.

Q. 87 Express the given information in scientific notation and then arrange them in descending order of their size.

S. N.	Name of the planet	Mass (in kg)
1.	Mercury	330000000000000000000000
2.	Venus	4870000000000000000000000
3.	Earth	5980000000000000000000000
4.	Mars	642000000000000000000000
5.	Jupiter	1900000000000000000000000000
6.	Saturn	569000000000000000000000000
7.	Uranus	86900000000000000000000000
8.	Neptune	102000000000000000000000000
9.	Pluto	13100000000000000000000

Sol. A number is written in standard form as $a \times 10^k$, where a is terminating decimal and k is an integer.

S. N.	Name of the planet	Mass (in standard form)
1.	Mercury	3.3×10^{23}
2.	Venus	4.87×10^{24}
3.	Earth	5.98×10^{24}
4.	Mars	6.42×10^{23}
5.	Jupiter	1.9×10^{27}
6.	Saturn	5.69×10^{26}
7.	Uranus	8.69×10^{25}
8.	Neptune	1.02×10^{26}
9.	Pluto	1.31×10^{22}

Two numbers written in scientific notation can be compared. The number with the larger power of 10 is greater than the number with the smaller power of 10. If the powers of ten are the same, then the number with larger factor is the larger number.

Hence, the required descending order of the size will be

Jupiter $>$ Saturn $>$ Neptune $>$ Uranus $>$ Earth $>$ Venus $>$ Mars $>$ Mercury $>$ Pluto

Q. 88 Write the number of seconds in scientific notation.

S. N.	Unit	Value in seconds
1.	1 minute	60
2.	1 hour	3,600
3.	1 day	86,400
4.	1 month	2,600,000
5.	1 year	32,000,000
6.	10 years	3,20,000,000

Sol. 1. $1 \min = 60\,s = 6.0 \times 10^1\,s = 6 \times 10^1\,s$

2. $1h = 3{,}600\,s = 36 \times 10^2 s = 3.6 \times 10 \times 10^2\,s = 3.6 \times 10^3\,s$

3. $1\,day = 86{,}400\,s = 864 \times 10^2 s = 8.64 \times 10^2 \times 10^2 s = 8.64 \times 10^4 s = 8.6 \times 10^4\,s$

4. $1\,month = 2{,}600{,}000\,s = 26 \times 10^5 s = 2.6 \times 10 \times 10^5\,s = 2.6 \times 10^6\,s$

5. $1\,yr = 32{,}000{,}000\,s = 32 \times 10^6 s = 3.2 \times 10^6 s = 3.2 \times 10 \times 10^6\,s = 3.2 \times 10^7\,s$

6. $10\,yr = 3{,}20{,}000{,}000\,s = 32 \times 10^7 s = 3.2 \times 10 \times 10^7\,s = 3.2 \times 10^8\,s$

Q. 89 In our own planet Earth, 361,419,000 square kilometre of area is covered with water and 148,647,000 square kilometre of area is covered by land. Find the approximate ratio of area covered with water to area covered by land converting these numbers into scientific notation.

Sol. Given,

Area covered by water = $361419000\,km^2$

Area covered by land = $148647000\,km^2$

Convertion of area into scientific notation,
$$361419000 = 361419 \times 10^3$$

Also, $$361419 = 3.61419 \times 10^5$$

So, $$3.61419 \times 10^5 \times 10^3 = 3.61419 \times 10^8$$

∴ Area covered by water = $3.61419 \times 10^8\,km^2$

Similarly, $$148647000 = 148647 \times 10^3$$

Also, $$148647 = 1.48647 \times 10^5$$

So, $$1.48647 \times 10^5 \times 10^3 = 1.48647 \times 10^8$$

∴ Area covered by land = $1.48647 \times 10^8\,km^2$

Let $$3.61419 \times 10^8 \approx 3.6 \times 10^8$$

and $$1.48647 \times 10^8 \approx 1.5 \times 10^8$$

∴ Ratio of water to land $= \dfrac{3.6}{1.5} = 12:5$

Q. 90 If $2^{n+2} - 2^{n+1} + 2^n = c \times 2^n$, then find c.

Sol. We have, $2^{n+2} - 2^{n+1} + 2^n = c \times 2^n$

$\Rightarrow$ $\qquad 2^n \cdot 2^2 - 2^n \cdot 2^1 + 2^n = c \times 2^n \qquad\qquad [\because a^{m+n} = a^m \times a^n]$

$\Rightarrow$ $\qquad 2^n[2^2 - 2^1 + 1] = c \times 2^n \qquad\qquad$ [taking common 2^n in LHS]

$\Rightarrow$ $\qquad 2^n[4 - 2 + 1] = c \times 2^n$

$\Rightarrow$ $\qquad 3 \times 2^n = c \times 2^n$

$\qquad\qquad 3 \times 2^n \times 2^{-n} = c \times 2^n \times c^{-n}$ [multiplying both sides by 2^{-n}]

$$\Rightarrow \qquad 3 \times 2^{n-n} = c \times 2^{n-n} \qquad [\because a^m \times a^n = a^{m+n}]$$
$$\Rightarrow \qquad 3 \times 2^0 = c \times 2^0$$
$$\Rightarrow \qquad 3 \times 1 = c \times 1 \qquad [\because a^0 = 1]$$
$$\therefore \qquad 3 = c$$

Q. 91 A light year is the distance that light can travel in one year.
1 light year = 9,460,000,000,000 km.
  (a) Express one light year in scientific notation.
  (b) The average distance between Earth and Sun is 1.496×10^8 km. Is the distance between Earth and the Sun greater than, less than or equal to one light year?

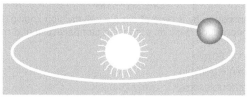

Sol. (a) Given, 1 light year = 9,460,000,000, 000 km
For standard form = 946×10^{10} km = $\dfrac{946}{100} \times 10^{10} \times 100$ km
$$= 9.46 \times 10^{12} \text{ km}$$

(b) The average distance between Earth and Sun = 1.496×10^8 km
$\therefore$ Distance between Earth and Sun = $\dfrac{1.496}{10000} \times 10^8 \times 10^4$ km = 0.0001496×10^{12} km

Since, $\qquad\qquad\qquad 9.46 > 0.0001496$
So, the distance between Earth and Sun less than one light year.

Q. 92 Geometry Application

The number of diagonals of an n-sided figure is $\dfrac{1}{2}(n^2 - 3n)$. Use the formula to find the number of diagonals for a 6-sided figure (hexagon).

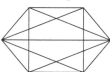

Sol. Given, a polygon has n sides, then number of diagonals is $\dfrac{1}{2}(n^2 - 3n)$.

In hexagon, there are six sides.
Therefore for calculating number of diagonals in hexagon, put $n = 6$ in the above formula.
$\therefore$ Number of diagonals = $\dfrac{1}{2}[n^2 - 3n] = \dfrac{1}{2}(6^2 - 3 \times 6)$
$$= \dfrac{1}{2}(6 \times 6 - 3 \times 6) = \dfrac{1}{2}(36 - 18) = \dfrac{1}{2}(18) = 9$$

Hence, a hexagon has 9 diagonals.

Q. 93 Life Science

Bacteria can divide in every 20 minutes. So, 1 bacterium can multiply to 2 in 20 minutes, 4 in 40 minutes, and so on. How many bacteria will there be in 6 hours? Write your answer using exponents, then evaluate.

Most Bacteria reproduce by a type of simple cell division known as binary fission. Each species reproduce best at a specific temperature and moisture level.

Sol.   We know that, 1 h = 60 min

∴   6 h = 60 × 6 min = 360 min

Given, a bacteria doubles itself in every 20 min.

∴ Number of times it will double itself $= \dfrac{360 \text{ min}}{20 \text{ min}} = 18$

∴ Bacteria will there in 6 h = 2 × 2 × 2 × ... × 2 (18 times) = 2^{18}

Q. 94 Blubber makes up 27 per cent of a blue whale's body weight. Deepak found the average weight of blue whales and used it to calculate the average weight of their blubber. He wrote the amount as $2^2 \times 3^2 \times 5 \times 17$ kg. Evaluate this amount.

Sol.   Weight calculated by Deepak = $2^2 \times 3^2 \times 5 \times 17$ kg

$= 2 \times 2 \times 3 \times 3 \times 5 \times 17$

$= 4 \times 9 \times 5 \times 17$

$= 36 \times 5 \times 17 = 180 \times 17 = 3060$ kg

Hence, weight calculated by Deepak was 3060 kg.

Q. 95 Life Science Application

The major components of human blood are red blood cells, white blood cells, platelets and plasma. A typical red blood cell has a diameter of approx 7×10^{-6} metre. A typical platelet has a diameter of approximately 2.33×10^{-6} metre.

Which has a greater diameter, a red blood cell or a platelet?

Sol. Given, diameter of red blood cell $= 7 \times 10^{-6}$ m

and diameter of platelet $= 2.33 \times 10^{-6}$ m

We know that, two numbers written in scientific notation can be compared. The number with the larger power of 10 is greater than the number with the smaller power of 10. If the powers of ten are the same, then the number with the larger factor is the larger number.

Therefore, red blood cell has a greater diameter than a platelet.

Q. 96 A googol is the number 1 followed by 100 zeroes.

(a) How is a googol written as a power?

(b) How is a googol times a googol written as a power?

Sol. (a) 1 googol $= \underbrace{1000\_\_\_0}_{100\,\text{times}} = 1 \times 10^{100}$ [as there are 100 zeroes after 1]

(b) Googol times googol means multiply googol by googol.

$\therefore$ Required number $=$ googol $\times$ googol $= 10^{100} \times 10^{100}$ $[\because 1 \text{ googol} = 10^{100}]$

$= 10^{100 + 100}$ $[\because a^m \times a^n = a^{m+n}]$

$= 100^{200}$

Q. 97 What's the Error?

A student said that $\dfrac{3^5}{9^5}$ is the same as $\dfrac{1}{3}$. What mistake has the student made?

Sol. We have, $\dfrac{3^5}{9^5} = \dfrac{3^5}{(3^2)^5}$ $[\because 9 = 3 \times 3 = 3^2]$

$= \dfrac{3^5}{3^{10}} = \dfrac{1}{3^{10-5}} = \dfrac{1}{3^5}$ $\left[\because \dfrac{a^m}{a^n} = a^{m-n}\right]$

So, $\dfrac{1}{3}$ is not same as $\dfrac{1}{3^5}$.

Student has multiplied the base by its exponent.
This is the error.

12

Practical Geometry Symmetry and Visualising Solid Shapes

Multiple Choice Questions (MCQs)

Q. 1 A triangle can be constructed by taking its sides as
   (a) 1.8 cm, 2.6 cm, 4.4 cm
   (b) 2 cm, 3 cm, 4 cm
   (c) 2.4 cm, 2.4 cm, 6.4 cm
   (d) 3.2 cm, 2.3 cm, 5.5 cm

Sol. *(b)* Triangle can be constructed only if they satisfy the given condition.
   Sum of two sides > Third side
   Clearly, only option (b) satisfies the given condition.
$$(2 + 3)\,cm > 4\ cm$$
   i.e. $$5\,cm > 4\ cm$$

Q. 2 A triangle can be constructed by taking two of its angles as
   (a) 110°, 40°   (b) 70°, 115°
   (c) 135°, 45°   (d) 90°, 90°

Sol. *(a)* We know that, the sum of all the angles of a triangle is equal to 180°.
   So, sum of any two angles of a triangle should be less than 180°.
   110° + 40° = 150° i.e. less than 180°.
   70° + 115° = 185° i.e. greater than 180°.
   135° + 45° = 180° i.e. equal to 180°.
   90° + 90° = 180° i.e. equal to 180°.
   Hence, (a) is the correct option.

Q. 3 The number of lines of symmetry in the figure given below is

     (a) 4   (b) 8   (c) 6   (d) infinitely many

Sol. *(c)* The given figure has 6 lines of symmetry.

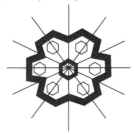

Q. 4 The number of lines of symmetry in the figure given below is

     (a) 1   (b) 3   (c) 6   (d) infinitely many

Sol. *(b)* The given figure has 3 lines of symmetry.

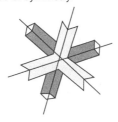

Q. 5 The order of rotational symmetry in the figure given below is

     (a) 4   (b) 8   (c) 6   (d) infinitely many

Sol. *(c)* Since, the number of times a figure fits onto itself in one full turn is called order of rotational symmetry.

Therefore, the given figure has rotational symmetry of order 6.

Q. 6 The order of rotational symmetry in the figure given below is

    (a) 4   (b) 2   (c) 1   (d) infinitely many

Sol. *(b)* Since, the number of times a figure fits onto itself in one full turn is called order of rotational symmetry.

So, the given figure has rotational symmetry of order 2.

Q. 7 The name of the given solid in the figure is

    (a) triangular pyramid   (b) rectangular pyramid
    (c) rectangular prism   (d) triangular prism

Sol. *(b)* It is a combination of rectangle and pyramid.

Hence, (b) is the correct option.

Q. 8 The name of the solid in figure is

    (a) triangular pyramid   (b) rectangular prism
    (c) triangular prism   (d) rectangular pyramid

Sol. *(c)* It is a combination of triangle and prism.

Hence, (c) is the correct option.

Q. 9 All faces of a pyramid are always

    (a) triangular   (b) rectangular   (c) congruent   (d) None of these

Sol. *(d)* The faces of a pyramid can be triangular and rectangular.

Hence, (d) is the correct option.

Q. 10 A solid that has only one vertex is

    (a) pyramid   (b) cube   (c) cone   (d) cylinder

Sol. *(c)* The cone is the shape, that has only one vertex.

Hence, (c) is the correct option.

Q. 11 Out of the following which is a 3-D figure?

    (a) Square   (b) Sphere   (c) Triangle   (d) Circle

Sol. *(b)* Square, triangle and circle are 2-D figures while sphere is the 3-D figure.

Hence, (b) is the correct option.

Q. 12 Total number of edges a cylinder has

(a) 0   (b) 1

(c) 2   (d) 3

Sol. *(c)* The cylinder has 2 edges.

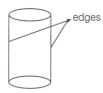

Hence, (c) is the correct option.

Q. 13 A solid that has two opposite identical faces and other faces as parallelograms is a

(a) prism   (b) pyramid

(c) cone   (d) sphere

Sol. *(a)* Prism has two opposite identical faces and other faces as parallelograms.

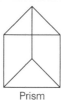

Prism

Q. 14 The solid with one circular face, one curved surface and one vertex is known as

(a) cone   (b) sphere

(c) cylinder   (d) prism

Sol. *(a)* Cone has one circular face, one curved surface and one vertex.

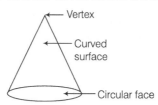

Q. 15 If three cubes each of edge 4cm are placed end to end, then the dimensions of resulting solid are

(a) 12 cm × 4 cm × 4 cm   (b) 4 cm × 8 cm × 4 cm

(c) 4 cm × 8 cm × 12 cm   (d) 4 cm × 6 cm × 8 cm

Sol. *(a)* If the three cubes are placed end to end that means length is increased. The new cuboid having dimensions

12 cm × 4 cm × 4 cm.

Hence, (a) is the correct option.

Q. 16 When we cut a corner of a cube as shown in the figure, we get the cutout piece as

(a) square pyramid

(b) trapezium prism

(c) triangular pyramid

(d) a triangle

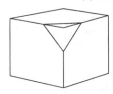

Sol. *(c)* If we cut a corner of a cube, then we get cut-out of a piece in the form of triangular pyramid.

Q. 17 If we rotate a right-angled triangle of height 5cm and base 3cm about its height a full turn, we get

(a) cone of height 5 cm, base 3 cm

(b) triangle of height 5 cm, base 3 cm

(c) cone of height 5 cm, base 6 cm

(d) triangle of height 5 cm, base 6 cm

Sol. *(a)* If we rotate a right-angled triangle of height 5 cm and base 3 cm about its height a full turn, then we get a cone of height 5 cm and base 3 cm.

Q. 18 If we rotate a right-angled triangle of height 5 cm and base 3 cm about its base, we get

(a) cone of height 3 cm and base 3 cm

(b) cone of height 5 cm and base 5 cm

(c) cone of height 5 cm and base 3 cm

(d) cone of height 3 cm and base 5 cm

Sol. *(d)* If we rotate a right-angled triangle of height 5 cm and base 3 cm about its base, we get a cone of height 3 cm and base 5 cm.

Q. 19 When a torch is pointed towards one of the vertical edges of a cube you get a shadow of cube in the shape of

(a) square

(b) rectangle but not a square

(c) circle

(d) triangle

Sol. *(b)* When a torch is pointed towards one of the vertical edges of a cube, you get a shadow of cube in the shape of rectangle but not a square.

Q. 20 Which of the following sets of triangles could be the lengths of the sides of a right-angled triangle?

(a) 3 cm, 4 cm, 6 cm

(b) 9 cm, 16 cm, 26cm

(c) 1.5 cm, 3.6 cm, 3.9 cm

(d) 7 cm, 24 cm, 26 cm

Sol. *(c)* The sides of right-angled triangle must satisfy Pythagoras theorem.

$(\text{Hypotenuse})^2 = (\text{Base})^2 + (\text{Perpendicular})^2$

Note *Hypotenuse is the largest side of all the sides. So, check all options by putting the values in above formula.*

Let us check all the options.

(a) $(6)^2 = (3)^2 + (4)^2$

$\quad 36 = 9 + 16$

$\quad 36 \neq 25$

(b) $(26)^2 = (16)^2 + (9)^2$

$\quad 676 = 256 + 81$

$\quad 676 \neq 337$

(c) $(3.9)^2 = (1.5)^2 + (3.6)^2$

$\quad 15.21 = 2.25 + 12.96$

$\quad 15.21 = 15.21 \;\; \text{(satisfied)}$

(d) $(26)^2 = (7)^2 + (24)^2$

$\quad 676 = 49 + 576$

$\quad 676 \neq 625$

Clearly, option (c) is correct.

Q. 21 In which of the following cases, a unique triangle can be drawn?

(a) $AB = 4$ cm, $BC = 8$ cm and $CA = 2$ cm

(b) $BC = 5.2$ cm, $\angle B = 90°$ and $\angle C = 110°$

(c) $XY = 5$ cm, $\angle X = 45°$ and $\angle Y = 60°$

(d) An isosceles triangle with the length of each equal side 6.2 cm

Sol. *(c)* Let us draw the triangle according to measurements given in respective options.

For (a) As we can see, triangle cannot be drawn.

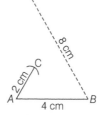

For (b) Triangle cannot be formed.

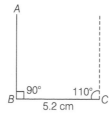

For (c) Unique triangle can be drawn by these measurements.

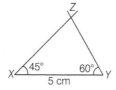

For (d) Using given data, we can form as many triangles as we want.

Hence, option (c) is correct.

Q. 22 Which of the following has a line of symmetry?

Sol. *(c)* The following figure has one line of symmetry.

Q. 23 Which of the following are reflections of each other?

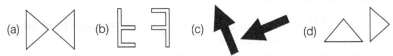

Sol. *(a)* Since, in the figure (a), the image of one side of the figure is exactly same as the figure on the other side of the line of symmetry.

Q. 24 Which of these nets is a net of a cube?

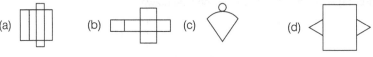

Sol. *(b)*

Q. 25 Which of the following nets is a net of a cylinder?

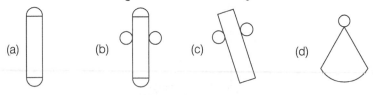

Sol. *(c)*

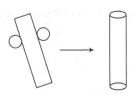

Q. 26 Which of the following letters of English alphabets have more than 2 lines of symmetry?

(a) Z   (b) O   (c) E   (d) H

Sol. *(c)* The letter *O* has more than two lines of symmetry.

Q. 27 Take a square piece of paper as shown in figure (1). Fold it along its diagonals as shown in figure (2). Again fold it as shown in figure (3). Imagine that you have cut off 3 pieces of the form of congruent isosceles right-angled triangles out of it as shown in figure 4.

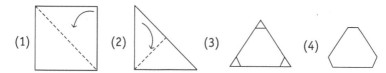

(1)   (2)   (3)   (4)

On opening the piece of paper which of the following shapes will you get?

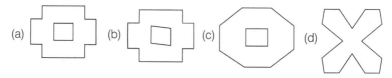

(a)   (b)   (c)   (d)

Sol. *(a)* As per the given condition, if we open the piece of paper, we will get the figure as shown in option (a).

Q. 28 Which of the following 3-dimensional figures has the top, side and front as triangles?

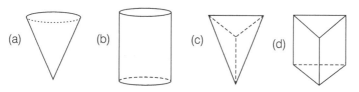

(a)   (b)   (c)   (d)

Sol. *(c)* Figure in option (c) will show all (top, side and front) views as triangle.

Fill in the Blanks

In questions 29 to 58, fill in the blanks to make the statements true.

Q. 29 In an isosceles right triangle, the number of lines of symmetry is ____.

Sol. Since, an isosceles triangle has **one** line of symmetry which is along the median through the vertex.

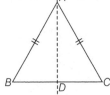

Q. 30 Rhombus is a figure that has ____ lines of symmetry and has a rotational symmetry of order ____.

Sol. two, two

A rhombus has two lines of symmetry along the diagonal and has a rotational symmetry of order two.

Q. 31 ____ triangle is a figure that has a line of symmetry but lacks rotational symmetry.

Sol. Isosceles

An isosceles triangle is a figure that has a line of symmetry but lacks rotational symmetry.

Q. 32 ____ is a figure that has neither a line of symmetry nor a rotational symmetry.

Sol. Quadrilateral

Quadrilateral is a figure that has neither a line of symmetry nor a rotational symmetry.

Q. 33 ____ and ____ are the capital letters of English alphabets that have one line of symmetry but they interchange to each other when rotated through 180°.

Sol. M, W

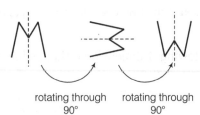

rotating through   rotating through
90°   90°

Q. 34 The common portion of two adjacent faces of a cuboid is called ____.

Sol. edge

edge

The common portion of two adjacent faces of a cuboid is called edge.

Q. 35 A plane surface of a solid enclosed by edges is called ____.

Sol. face

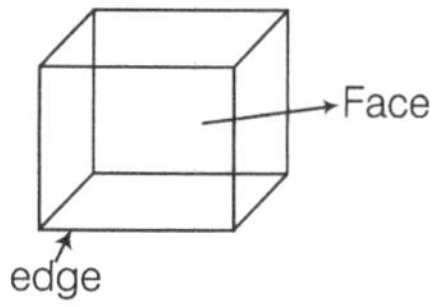

A plane surface of a solid enclosed by edges is called face.

Q. 36 The corners of solid shapes are called its ____.

Sol. vertices

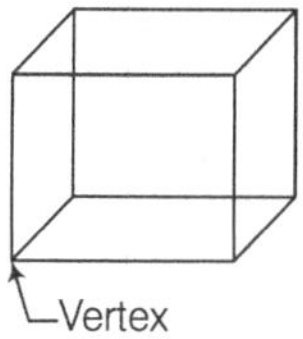

The corners of solid shapes are called its vertices.

Q. 37 A solid with no vertex is ____.

Sol. sphere

Since, a sphere is a solid with 0 vertex, 0 edge and 1 curved surface.

Q. 38 A triangular prism has ____ faces, ____ edges and ____ vertices.

Sol. 5,9,6

A triangular prism has 5 faces, 9 edges and 6 vertices.

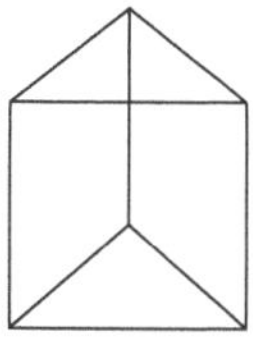

Q. 39 A triangular pyramid has ____ faces, ____ edges and ____ vertices,

Sol. 4,6,4

A triangular pyramid has 4 faces, 6 edges and 4 vertices.

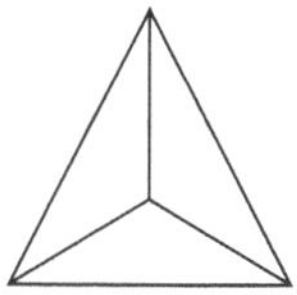

Q. 40 A square pyramid has ____ faces, ____ edges and ____ vertices.

Sol. 5,8,5

A square pyramid has 5 faces, 8 edges and 5 vertices.

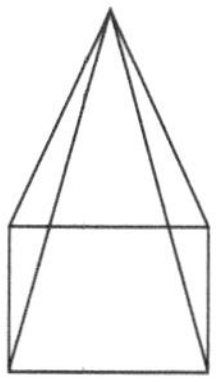

Q. 41 Out of _____ faces of a triangular prism, _____ are rectangles and _____ are triangles.

Sol. Out of **5** faces of a triangular prism, **3** are rectangles and **2** are triangles.

Q. 42 The base of a triangular pyramid is a _____.

Sol. The base of a triangular pyramid is a **triangle**.

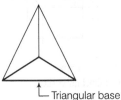

Triangular base

Q. 43 Out of _____ faces of a square pyramid, _____ are triangles and _____ is/are squares.

Sol. Out of **5** faces of a square pyramid, **4** are triangles and **1** is square.

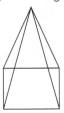

Q. 44 Out of _____ faces of a rectangular pyramid _____ are triangles and base is _____.

Sol. Out of **5** faces of a rectangular pyramid, **4** are triangles and base is **rectangle**.

Q. 45 Each of the letters H, N, S and Z has a rotational symmetry of order _____.

Sol. 2

Each of the letters H,N,S and Z has a rotational symmetry of order two.

Q. 46 Order of rotational symmetry of a rectangle is _____.

Sol. Order of rotational symmetry of a rectangle is **two**.

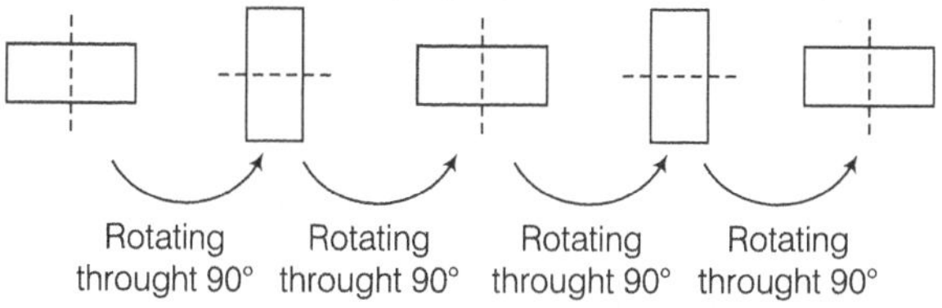

Rotating   Rotating   Rotating   Rotating
throught 90°   throught 90°   throught 90°   throught 90°

Q. 47 Order of rotational symmetry of a circle is _____.

Sol. Since, the number of times a figure fits onto itself in one complete rotation is called the order of rotational symmetry.
∴ Order of rotational symmetry of a circle is **2**.

Q. 48 Each face of a cuboid is a _____.

Sol. Since, a solid bounded by six rectangular faces is called a cuboid.
∴ Each face of a cuboid is a **rectangle**.

Q. 49 Line of symmetry for an angle is its _____.

Sol. Line of symmetry for an angle is its **bisector**.

Q. 50 A parallelogram has _____ line of symmetry.

Sol. A parallelogram has **no** line of symmetry.

Q. 51 Order of rotational symmetry of 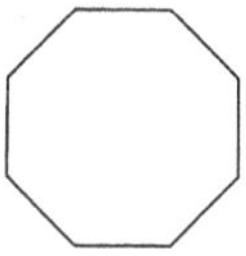 is _____.

Sol. **8**

Since, the order of rotational symmetry is the number of times a figure fits onto itself in one full turn.
∴ Order of rotational symmetry of a given figure is 8.

Q. 52 A _____ triangle has no lines of symmetry.

Sol. **scalene**

Since, all the angles and sides are unequal in scalene triangle.

Q. 53 Cuboid is a rectangular _____.

Sol. **prism**

Since, rectangular prism and cuboid refer to the same solid.

Q. 54 A sphere has _____ vertex, _____ edge and _____ curved surface.

Sol. A sphere has **0** vertex, **0** edge and **1** curved surface.

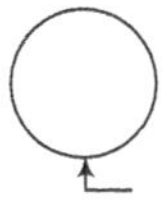

Q. 55 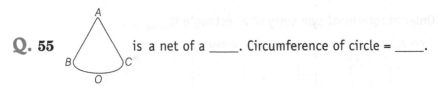 is a net of a ____. Circumference of circle = ____.

Sol. cone, $2\pi r$

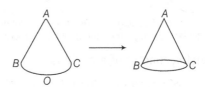

Q. 56 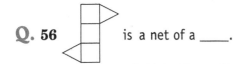 is a net of a ____.

Sol. triangular prism

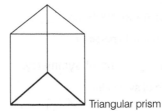

Triangular prism

Q. 57 Order of rotational symmetry of 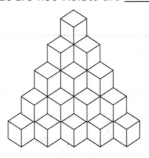 is ____.

Sol. 1

Since, isosceles triangle has rotational symmetry of order 1.

Q. 58 Identical cubes are stacked in the corner of a room as shown below. The number of cubes that are not visible are ____.

Sol. 20

The number of cubes that are not visible are 20.

True/False

In questions 59 to 92, state whether the given statements are True or False.

Q. 59 We can draw exactly one triangle whose angles are 70°, 30° and 80°.

Sol. *False*

Since, we can draw infinite triangles of angles 70°, 30° and 80° all having different sides.

Q. 60 The distance between the two parallel lines is the same everywhere.

Sol. *True*

Since, the distance between the two parallel lines is always same everywhere.

Q. 61 A circle has two lines of symmetry.

Sol. *False*

Since, a circle has infinite lines of symmetry.

Q. 62 An angle has two lines of symmetry.

Sol. *False*

Since, an angle has only one line of symmetry i.e. its bisector.

Q. 63 A regular hexagon has six lines of symmetry .

Sol. *True*

Since, a regular polygon has many lines of symmetry as the number of its sides.

Q. 64 An isosceles trapezium has one line of symmetry.

Sol. *True*

Isosceles trapezium has only one line of symmetry along the line segment joining the mid-points of two parallel sides which is shown in figure.

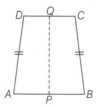

Q. 65 A parallelogram has two lines of symmetry.

Sol. *False*

Because in a parallelogram, there is no line of symmetry.

Q. 66 Order of rotational symmetry of a rhombus is four.

Sol. *False*

Order of rotational symmetry of a rhombus is two.

Q. 67 An equilateral triangle has six lines of symmetry.

Sol. *False*

Since, in an equilateral triangle, there are three lines of symmetry along the three medians of the triangle.

Q. 68 Order of rotational of a semi circle is two.

Sol. *False*

Order of rotational symmetry of a semi circle is one.

Q. 69 In oblique sketch of the solid, the measurements are kept proportional.

Sol. *False*

In oblique sketch of the solid, the measurements are not kept proportional.

Q. 70 An isometric sketch does not have proportional length.

Sol. *False*

An isometric sketch always have proportional length.

Q. 71 A cylinder has no vertex.

Sol. *True*

A cylinder has 3 faces, 2 edges but no vertex.

Q. 72 All the faces, except the base of a square pyramid are triangular.

Sol. *True*

A square pyramid has 4 triangular faces and one square base.

Q. 73 A pyramid has only one vertex.

Sol. *False*

A pyramid has atleast 4 vertices (in triangular pyramid).

Q. 74 A triangular prism has 5 faces, 9 edges and 6 vertices.

Sol. *True*

A triangular prism has 5 faces, 9 edges and 6 vertices.

Q. 75 If the base of a pyramid is a square, it is called a square pyramid.

Sol. *True*

The name of a pyramid is based on the base of pyramid. So, if the base of a pyramid is a square, then it is called a square pyramid.

Q. 76 A rectangular pyramid has 5 rectangular faces.

Sol. *False*

A rectangular pyramid has 1 rectangular face and 4 triangular faces.

Q. 77 Rectangular prism and cuboid refer to the same solid.

Sol. *True*

Rectangular prism and cuboid refer to the same solid.

Q. 78 A tetrahedron has 3 triangular faces and 1 rectangular face.

Sol. *False*

A tetrahedron has 4 triangular faces.

Q. 79 While rectangle is a 2-D figure, cuboid is a 3-D figure.

Sol. *True*

A rectangle is a 2-D figure and cuboid is a 3-D figure.

Q. 80 While sphere is a 2-D figure, circle is a 3-D figure.

Sol. *False*

Circle is a 2-D figure and sphere is a 3-D figure.

Q. 81 Two dimensional figures are also called plane figures.

Sol. *True*

2-D figures are also called plane figures.

Q. 82 A cone is a polyhedron.

Sol. *False*

A cone is not a polyhedron.

Q. 83 A prism has four bases.

Sol. *False*

A prism has only one base.

Q. 84 The number of lines of symmetry of a regular polygon is equal to the vertices of the polygon.

Sol. *True*

The number of lines of symmetry of a regular polygon is equal to the vertices of the polygon.

Q. 85 The order of rotational symmetry of a figure is 4 and the angle of rotation is 180° only.

Sol. *False*

If the order of rotational symmetry of a figure is 4, then the angle of rotation must be 90°.

Q. 86 After rotating a figure by 120° about its centre, the figure coincides with its original position. This will happen again, if the figure is rotated at an angle of 240°.

Sol. *True*

After rotating a figure by 120° about its centre, the figure coincides with its original position. This will happen again, if the figure is rotated at an angle of 240°.

Q. 87 Mirror reflection leads to symmetry always.

Sol. *False*

Mirror reflection not always lead to symmetry.

Q. 88 Rotation turns an object about a fixed point which is known as centre of rotation.

Sol. *True*

Centre of rotation turns an object about a fixed point.

Q. 89 Isometric sheet divides the paper into small isosceles triangles made up of dots or lines.

Sol. *False*

Isometric sheet divides the paper into small equilateral triangles made up of dots or lines.

Q. 90 The circle, the square, the rectangle and the triangle are examples of plane figures.

Sol. *True*

The circle, the square, the rectangle and the triangle are examples of plane figures.

Q. 91 The solid shapes are of 2-dimensional.

Sol. *False*

The solid shapes are of 3-dimensional.

Q. 92 Triangle with length of sides as 5cm, 6cm and 11cm can be constructed.

Sol. *False*

We know that,

in a triangle, sum of any two sides is always greater than or equal to the third side.

∴ $5 + 6 = 11$

                                  $6 + 11 \ngeqslant 5$

These measurements do not satisfy the basic condition of a triangle.

Hence, the triangle cannot be constructed.

Q. 93 Draw the top, side and front views of the solids given below in figures 12.21 and 12.22.

(i)

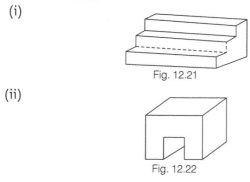

Fig. 12.21

(ii)

Fig. 12.22

Sol. For given figure (i),

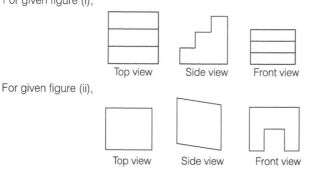

Top view   Side view   Front view

For given figure (ii),

Top view   Side view   Front view

Q. 94 Draw a solid using the top, side and front views as shown below. [Use Isometric Paper.]

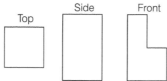

Sol. Do yourself.

Q. 95 Construct a right angled triangle whose hypotenuse measures 5 cm and one of the other sides measures 3.2 cm.

Sol. **Steps of construction**

Step I Draw a line $AB = 3.2$ cm.

Step II Construct a right angle (90°) at point B, i.e. $\angle ABY = 90°$

Step III Now, from point A, cut an arc 5 cm on BY at C.

Step IV Joint C to A.

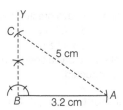

Hence, $\triangle ABC$ is the required triangle, having hypotenuse $AC = 5$ cm and $AB = 3.2$ cm.

Q. 96 Construct a right angled isosceles triangle with one side (other than hypotenuse) of length 4.5 cm.

Sol. **Steps of construction**

Step I Draw a line $AB = 4.5$ cm.

Step II Construct a right angle (90°) at point B, i.e. $\angle ABY = 90°$.

Step III From point B, cut an arc 4.5 cm on BY at C.

Step IV Join C to A.

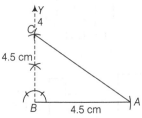

Hence, $\triangle ABC$ is the required triangle having $AB = AC = 4.5$ cm.

Q. 97 Draw two parallel lines at a distance of 2.2 cm apart.

Sol. **Steps of construction**

Step I Draw a line l and mark a point C outside it.

Step II Take a point B on line l and join BC.

Step III Draw line parallel to line l passing through C.

Step IV Mark a point D on line m, at a distance of 2.2 cm from C.

Step V Through D draw $AD \parallel BC$.

∴ Line l is parallel to line m

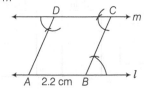

Also, $AD \parallel BC$, $AB = DC = 2.2$ cm

Q. 98 Draw an isosceles triangle with each of equal sides of length 3 cm and the angle between them as 45°.

Sol. Steps of construction

Step I Firstly, we draw a rough sketch of triangle with given measures marked on it.

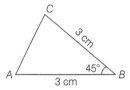

Step II Draw a line segment *AB* of length 3 cm.

Step III Draw an angle of 45° on point *B* and produce it to ray *Y*.

Step IV With *B* as centre, draw an arc of 3 cm which intersects ray *BY* at *C*.

Step V Join *AC*.

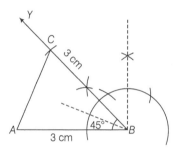

Thus, △*ABC* is the required isosceles triangle.

Q. 99 Draw a triangle whose sides are of lengths 4 cm, 5 cm and 7 cm.

Sol. Let us assume that given sides are *BC* = 7 cm, *AB* = 4 cm and *AC* = 5 cm

Steps of construction

Step I Draw a line *BC* = 7 cm

Step II With centre *B* and radius 4 cm draw an arc.

Step III With centre *C* and radius 5 cm, draw an arc which cuts the previous arc at *A*.

Step IV Join *AB* and *AC*.

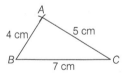

Hence, △*ABC* is the required triangle in which

$$AB = 4 \text{ cm}, BC = 7 \text{ cm and } AC = 5 \text{ cm}$$

Q. 100 Construct an obtuse angled triangle which has a base of 5.5 cm and base angles of 30° and 120°.

Sol. Steps of construction

Step I   Draw a line segment *BC* of length 5.5 cm.

Step II Draw an angle of 120° on point *B* and produce it to ray *Y*.

Step III Draw an angle of 30° on point *C* and produce it to ray *X*.

Step IV Extend $\overline{BY}$ and $\overline{CX}$ to intersect at point A.

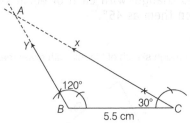

Hence, ΔABC is the required triangle with BC = 5.5, ∠ABC = 120° and ∠ACB = 30°.

Q. 101 Construct an equilateral triangle ABC of side 6 cm.

Sol. **Steps of construction**

Step I Draw a line segment AB = 6 cm.

Step II Draw an arc of radius 6 cm from point A.

Step III Now, draw another arc of radius 6 cm from point B to cut previous arc at C.

Step IV Join A to C and B to C.

Hence, ΔABC is the required triangle.

Q. 102 By what minimum angle does a regular hexagon rotate so as to coincide with its origional position for the first time?

Sol. A regular hexagon must be rotated through a minimum angle of 60°. So, that it can coincide with its original position for the first time. Because the angle of rotation of hexagon

$$= \frac{360°}{\text{Number of sides}} = \frac{360°}{6} = 60°$$

Q. 103 In each of the following figures, write the number of lines of symmetry and order of rotational symmetry.

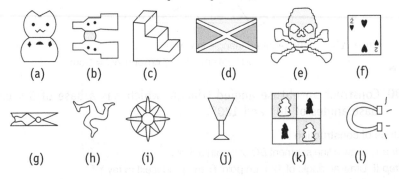

(a)   (b)   (c)   (d)   (e)   (f)

(g)   (h)   (i)   (j)   (k)   (l)

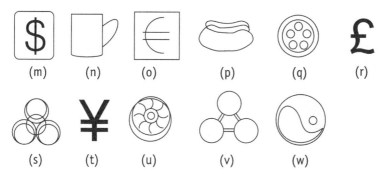

	(m)	(n)	(o)	(p)	(q)	(r)

	(s)	(t)	(u)	(v)	(w)

[**Hint** Consider these as 2-D figures not as 3-D objects.]

Sol.

Figure	Number of lines of symmetry	Order of rotational Symmetry
a	1	1
b	1	1
c	1	1
d	2	2
e	1	2
f	0	1
g	1	1
h	0	3
i	4	4
j	1	1
k	0	1
l	1	1
m	0	2
n	0	1
o	1	1
p	0	1
q	1	1
r	0	1
s	3	3
t	1	1
u	10	10
v	3	3
w	0	1

Q. 104 In the figure of a cube,

(i) which edge is the intersection of faces *EFGH* and *EFBA*?

(ii) which faces intersect at edge *FB*?

(iii) which three faces form the vertex *A*?

(iv) which vertex is formed by the faces *ABCD*, *ADHE* and *CDHG*?

(v) Give all the edges that are parallel to edge *AB*.

(vi) Give the edges that are neither parallel nor perpendicular to edge *BC*.

(vii) Give all the edges that are perpendicular to edge *AB*.

(viii) Give four vertices that do not all lie in one plane.

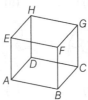

Sol. (i) From the given figure, we can observe that *EF* is the intersection of faces *EFGH* and *EFBA*.

(ii) From the given figure, we can observe that faces *EFBA* and *FBCG* intersect at edge *FB*.

(iii) Faces *ABFE*, *ADHE* and *ABCD* form the vertex *A*.

(iv) Vertex *D* is formed by the faces *ABCD*, *CDHG* and *ADHE*.

(v) The edges parallel to edge *AB* are *CD*, *EF* and *HG*.

(vi) From the given figure, we can observe that edges *AE*, *EF*, *GH* and *HD* are neither parallel nor perpendicular to edge *BC*.

(vii) From the given figure, we can observe that edges *AE*, *BF*, *AD* and *BC* are perpendicular to edge *AB*.

(viii) Vertices *A*, *B*, *G* and *H* do not lie in one plane.

Q. 105 Draw a net of a cuboid having same breadth and height, but length double the breadth.

Sol. Required net of a cuboid will be

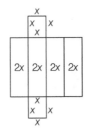

Q. 106 Draw the nets of the following

(i) Triangular prism

(ii) Tetrahedron

(iii) Cuboid

Sol. (i) Net for triangular prism,

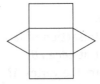

(ii) Net for tetrahedron,

(iii) Net for cuboid,

Q. 107 Draw a net of the solid given in the figure

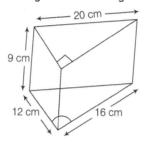

Sol. The net of the given solid figure will be

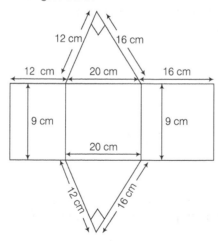

Q. 108 Draw an isometric view of a cuboid 6 cm× 4 cm× 2 cm.

Sol.

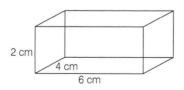

Isometric view of a cuboid = 6 cm× 4 cm× 2 cm= $l \times b \times h$

Q. 109 The net given below in the figure can be used to make a cube.

    (i) Which edge meets *AN*?   (ii) Which edge meets *DE*?

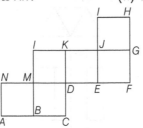

Sol.   (i) The given net of a cube shows that edge *GH* meets edge *AN*.

      (ii) The given net of a cube shows that edge *DC* meets edge *DE*.

Q. 110 Draw the net of triangular pyramid with base as equilateral triangle of side 3 cm and slant edges 5 cm.

Sol. The net of such triangular pyramid will be

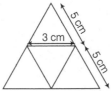

Q. 111 Draw the net of a square pyramid with base as square of side 4 cm and slant edges 6 cm.

Sol. The net of such square pyramid will be

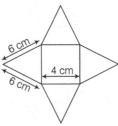

Q. 112 Draw the net of rectangular pyramid with slant edge 6 cm and base as rectangle with length 4 cm and breadth 3 cm.

Sol. The net of such rectangular pyramid will be

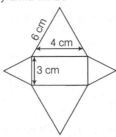

Q. 113 Find the number of cubes in each of the following figures and in each case give the top, front, left side and right side view (arrow indicating the front view).

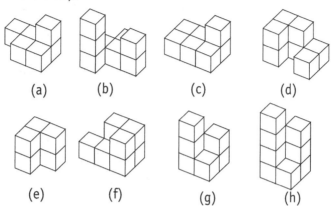

    (a)   (b)   (c)   (d)

    (e)   (f)   (g)   (h)

Sol. (a) The number of cubes in the given figure is 6.
For given figure,

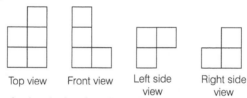

    Top view   Front view   Left side view   Right side view

(b) The number of cubes in the given figure is 8.
For given figure,

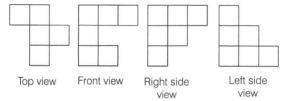

    Top view   Front view   Right side view   Left side view

(c) The number of cubes in the given figure is 7.
For given figure,

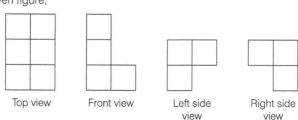

    Top view   Front view   Left side view   Right side view

(d) The number of cubes in the given figure is 8.
For given figure,

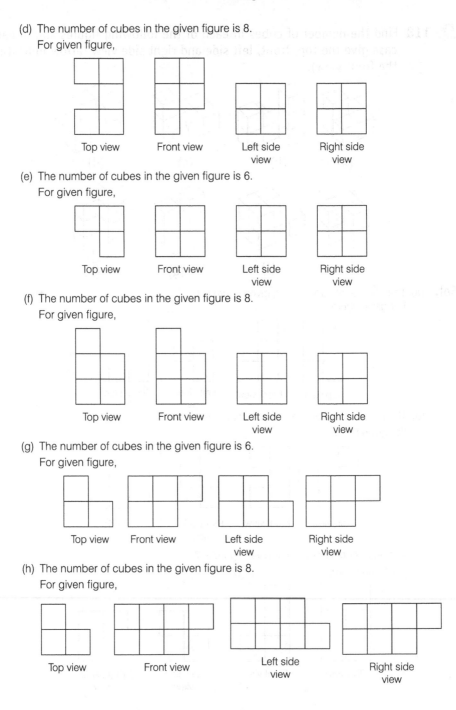

(e) The number of cubes in the given figure is 6.
For given figure,

(f) The number of cubes in the given figure is 8.
For given figure,

(g) The number of cubes in the given figure is 6.
For given figure,

(h) The number of cubes in the given figure is 8.
For given figure,

Q. 114 Draw all lines of symmetry for each of the following figures as given below.

(a)

(b)

(c)

Sol. (a)

1 line of symmetry

(b)

No line of symmetry

(c)

2 lines of symmetry

Q. 115 How many faces does figure have?

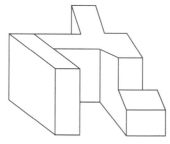

Sol. There are total 16 faces in the given figure.

Q. 116 Trace each figure. Then draw all lines of symmetry, if it has.

(a)

(b)

(c)

Sol. (a)

2 lines of symmetry

(b)

No line of symmetry

(c)

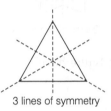

3 lines of symmetry

Q. 117 Tell whether each figure has rotational symmetry or not.

(a)   (b)

(c)   (d)

(e)   (f)

Sol. (a) Yes   (b) No
      (c) Yes   (d) Yes
      (e) Yes   (f) Yes

Q. 118 Draw all lines of symmetry for each of the following figures.

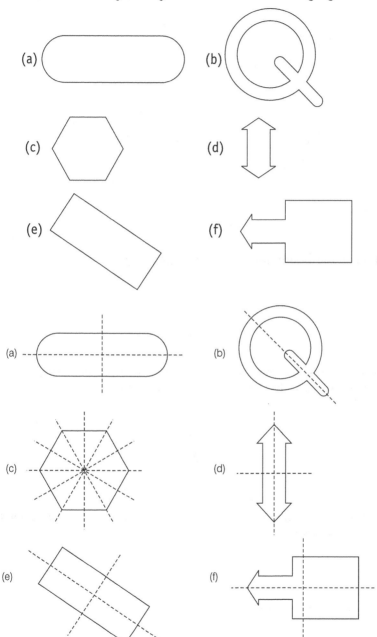

Sol.

Q. 119 Tell whether each figure has rotational symmetry. Write yes or no.

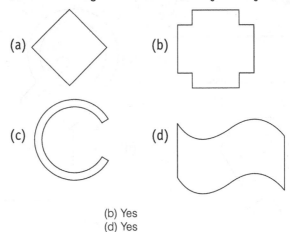

(a)   (b)

(c)   (d)

Sol. (a) Yes   (b) Yes
      (c) No   (d) Yes

Q. 120 Does the figure have rotational symmetry?

Sol. The given figure does not show rotational symmetry because one part of design is undarken, whereas other three part are darken. Hence, the design does not show symmetry.

Q. 121 The flag of Japan is shown below. How many lines of symmetry does the flag have?

Sol. The given flag has two lines of symmetry.

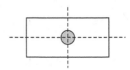

Q. 122 Which of the figures given below have both line and rotational symmetry?

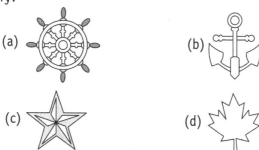

(a)   (b)

(c)   (d)

Sol. Only (a) and (c) have both line and rotational symmetry.
In the given figure, line of symmetry will be shown as

Also, rotational symmetry will be shown as

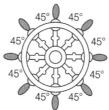

$\dfrac{360°}{8} = 45°$, i.e. rotational angle is equal to 45°.

In the given figure, line of symmetry will be shown as

Also, rotational symmetry will be shown as

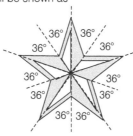

$\dfrac{360°}{10} = 36°$, i.e. rotational angle is equal to 36°.

Q. 123 Which of the following figures do not have line symmetry?

(a)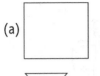

(b)

(c)

(d)

Sol. (a) We observe that the given figure has 2 lines of symmetry.

(b) The given figure has no line of symmetry.
(c) We observe that the given figure has 2 lines of symmetry.

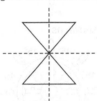

(d) The given figure has no line of symmetry.

Q. 124 Which capital letters of English alphabet have no line of symmetry?

Sol. The letters F, G, J, L, N, P, Q, R, S and Z have no line of symmetry.